Microsoft® WORD® 2010

INTRODUCTORY

Gary B. Shelly
Misty E. Vermaat

Australia • Brazil • Japan • Korea • Mexico • Singapore • Spain • United Kingdom • United States

Microsoft® Word® 2010: Introductory
Gary B. Shelly, Misty E. Vermaat

Vice President, Publisher: Nicole Pinard
Executive Editor: Kathleen McMahon
Senior Product Manager: Mali Jones
Associate Product Manager: Aimee Poirier
Editorial Assistant: Lauren Brody
Director of Marketing: Cheryl Costantini
Marketing Manager: Tristen Kendall
Marketing Coordinator: Stacey Leasca
Print Buyer: Julio Esperas
Director of Production: Patty Stephan
Senior Content Project Manager: Jill Braiewa
Development Editor: Lyn Markowicz
Copyeditor: Foxxe Editorial Services
Proofreader: Chris Clark
Indexer: Rich Carlson
QA Manuscript Reviewers: Chris Scriver, John Freitas, Serge Palladino, Susan Pedicini, Danielle Shaw
Art Director: Marissa Falco
Cover Designer: Lisa Kuhn, Curio Press, LLC
Cover Photo: Tom Kates Photography
Text Design: Joel Sadagursky
Compositor: PreMediaGlobal

Library of Congress Control Number: 2010929406
ISBN-13: 978-1-4390-7845-7
ISBN-10: 1-4390-7845-9

Course Technology
20 Channel Center Street
Boston, MA 02210
USA

We dedicate this book to the memory of James S. Quasney (1940 – 2009), who for 18 years co-authored numerous books with Tom Cashman and Gary Shelly and provided extraordinary leadership to the Shelly Cashman Series editorial team. As series editor, Jim skillfully coordinated, organized, and managed the many aspects of our editorial development processes and provided unending direction, guidance, inspiration, support, and advice to the Shelly Cashman Series authors and support team members. He was a trusted, dependable, loyal, and well-respected leader, mentor, and friend. We are forever grateful to Jim for his faithful devotion to our team and eternal contributions to our series.

The Shelly Cashman Series Team

Printed in the United States of America
4 5 6 7 16 15 14 13

Microsoft® WORD® 2010 INTRODUCTORY

Contents

Microsoft Word 2010

CHAPTER ONE
Creating, Formatting, and Editing a Word Document with Pictures

CHAPTER TWO
Creating a Research Paper with Citations and References

CHAPTER THREE
Creating a Business Letter with a Letterhead and Table

Appendices

APPENDIX A
Project Planning Guidelines

APPENDIX B
Publishing Office 2010 Web Pages Online

APPENDIX C
Saving to the Web Using Windows Live SkyDrive

APPENDIX D

APA Research Paper — Chapter 2 Supplement

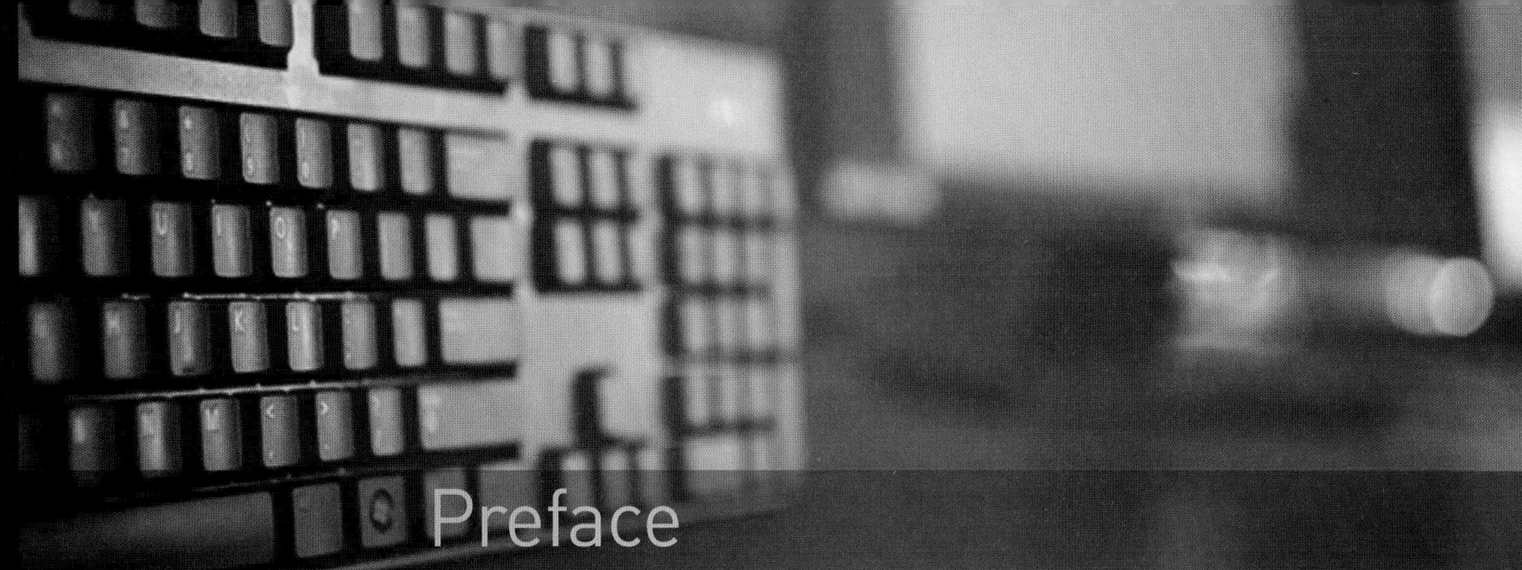

Preface

The Shelly Cashman Series® offers the finest textbooks in computer education. We are proud that since Mircosoft Office 4.3, our series of Microsoft Office textbooks have been the most widely used books in education. With each new edition of our Office books, we make significant improvements based on the software and comments made by instructors and students. For this Microsoft Word 2010 text, the Shelly Cashman Series development team carefully reviewed our pedagogy and analyzed its effectiveness in teaching today's Office student. Students today read less, but need to retain more. They need not only to be able to perform skills, but to retain those skills and know how to apply them to different settings. Today's students need to be continually engaged and challenged to retain what they're learning.

With this Microsoft Word 2010 text, we continue our commitment to focusing on the user and how they learn best.

Objectives of This Textbook

Microsoft Word 2010: Introductory is intended for a first course on Word 2010. No experience with a computer is assumed, and no mathematics beyond the high school freshman level is required. The objectives of this book are:

- To offer an introduction to Microsoft Word 2010
- To expose students to practical examples of the computer as a useful tool
- To acquaint students with the proper procedures to create documents suitable for coursework, professional purposes, and personal use
- To help students discover the underlying functionality of Word 2010 so they can become more productive
- To develop an exercise-oriented approach that allows learning by doing

New to This Edition

Microsoft Word 2010: Introductory offers a number of new features and approaches, which improve student understanding, retention, transference, and skill in using Word 2010. The following enhancements will enrich the learning experience:

- Office 2010 and Windows 7: Essential Concepts and Skills chapter presents basic Office 2010 and Windows 7 skills.
- Streamlined first chapter allow the ability to cover more advanced skills earlier.
- Chapter topic redistribution offers concise chapters that ensure complete skill coverage.
- New pedagogical elements enrich material creating an accessible and user-friendly approach.
- Break Points, a new boxed element, identify logical stopping points and give students instructions regarding what they should do before taking a break.
- Within step instructions, Tab | Group Identifiers, such as (Home tab | Bold button), help students more easily locate elements in the groups and on the tabs on the Ribbon.
- Modified step-by-step instructions tell the student what to do and provide the generic reason why they are completing a specific task, which helps students easily transfer given skills to different settings.

The Shelly Cashman Approach

A Proven Pedagogy with an Emphasis on Project Planning

Each chapter presents a practical problem to be solved, within a project planning framework. The project orientation is strengthened by the use of Plan Ahead boxes, which encourage critical thinking about how to proceed at various points in the project. Step-by-step instructions with supporting screens guide students through the steps. Instructional steps are supported by the Q&A, Experimental Step, and BTW features.

A Visually Engaging Book that Maintains Student Interest

The step-by-step tasks, with supporting figures, provide a rich visual experience for the student. Call-outs on the screens that present both explanatory and navigational information provide students with information they need when they need to know it.

Supporting Reference Materials (Appendices, Quick Reference)

The appendices provide additional information about the Application at hand and include such topics and project planning guidelines and certification. With the Quick Reference, students can quickly look up information about a single task, such as keyboard shortcuts, and find page references of where in the book the task is illustrated.

Integration of the World Wide Web

The World Wide Web is integrated into the Word 2010 learning experience by (1) BTW annotations; (2) BTW, Q&A, and Quick Reference Summary Web pages; and (3) the Learn It Online section for each chapter.

End-of-Chapter Student Activities

Extensive end-of-chapter activities provide a variety of reinforcement opportunities for students where they can apply and expand their skills.

Instructor Resources

The Instructor Resources include both teaching and testing aids and can be accessed via CD-ROM or at www.cengage.com/login.

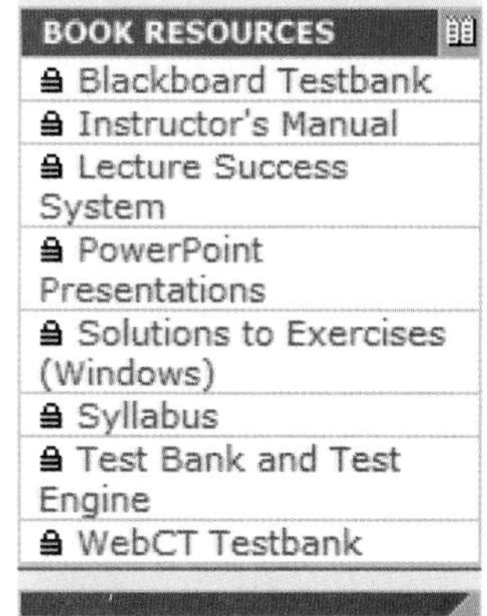

BOOK RESOURCES
Blackboard Testbank
Instructor's Manual
Lecture Success System
PowerPoint Presentations
Solutions to Exercises (Windows)
Syllabus
Test Bank and Test Engine
WebCT Testbank

Instructor's Manual Includes lecture notes summarizing the chapter sections, figures and boxed elements found in every chapter, teacher tips, classroom activities, lab activities, and quick quizzes in Microsoft Word files.

Syllabus Easily customizable sample syllabi that cover policies, assignments, exams, and other course information.

Figure Files Illustrations for every figure in the textbook in electronic form.

PowerPoint Presentations A multimedia lecture presentation system that provides slides for each chapter. Presentations are based on chapter objectives.

Solutions To Exercises Includes solutions for all end-of-chapter and chapter reinforcement exercises.

Test Bank & Test Engine Test Banks include 112 questions for every chapter, featuring objective-based and critical thinking question types, and including page number references and figure references, when appropriate. Also included is the test engine, ExamView, the ultimate tool for your objective-based testing needs.

Data Files for Students Includes all the files that are required by students to complete the exercises.

Additional Activities for Students Consists of Chapter Reinforcement Exercises, which are true/false, multiple-choice, and short answer questions that help students gain confidence in the material learned.

SAM: Skills Assessment Manager

SAM 2010 is designed to help bring students from the classroom to the real world. It allows students to train on and test important computer skills in an active, hands-on environment.

SAM's easy-to-use system includes powerful interactive exams, training, and projects on the most commonly used Microsoft Office applications. SAM simulates the Microsoft Office 2010 application environment, allowing students to demonstrate their knowledge and think through the skills by performing real-world tasks such as bolding word text or setting up slide transitions. Add in live-in-the-application projects, and students are on their way to truly learning and applying skills to business-centric documents.

Designed to be used with the Shelly Cashman Series, SAM includes handy page references so that students can print helpful study guides that match the Shelly Cashman textbooks used in class. For instructors, SAM also includes robust scheduling and reporting features.

Content for Online Learning

Course Technology has partnered with the leading distance learning solution providers and class-management platforms today. To access this material, instructors will visit our password-protected instructor resources available at www.cengage.com/coursetechnology. Instructor resources include the following: additional case projects, sample syllabi, PowerPoint presentations per chapter, and more. For additional information or for an instructor user name and password, please contact your sales representative. For students to access this material, they must have purchased a WebTutor PIN-code specific to this title and your campus platform. The resources for students may include (based on instructor preferences), but are not limited to: topic review, review questions, and practice tests.

CourseNotes

Course Technology's CourseNotes are six-panel quick reference cards that reinforce the most important and widely used features of a software application in a visual and user-friendly format. CourseNotes serve as a great reference tool during and after the student completes the course. CourseNotes are available for software applications such as Microsoft Office 2010, Word 2010, Excel 2010, Access 2010, PowerPoint 2010, and Windows 7. Topic-based CourseNotes are available for Best Practices in Social Networking, Hot Topics in Technology, and Web 2.0. Visit www.cengage.com/ct/coursenotes to learn more!

A Guided Tour

Add excitement and interactivity to your classroom with "*A Guided Tour*" product line. Play one of the brief mini-movies to spice up your lecture and spark classroom discussion. Or, assign a movie for homework and ask students to complete the correlated assignment that accompanies each topic. "*A Guided Tour*" product line takes the prep work out of providing your students with information about new technologies and applications and helps keep students engaged with content relevant to their lives; all in under an hour!

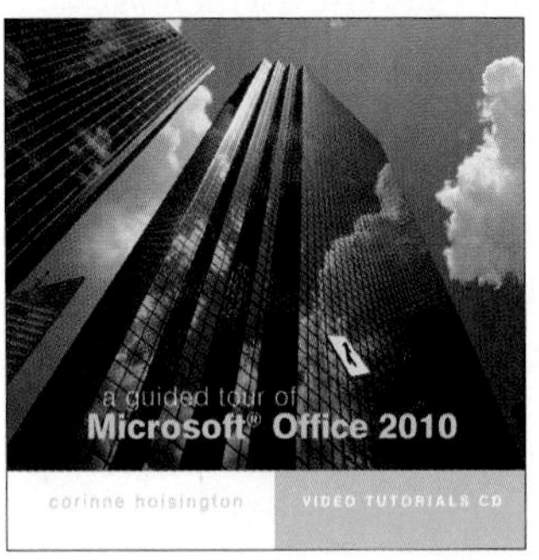

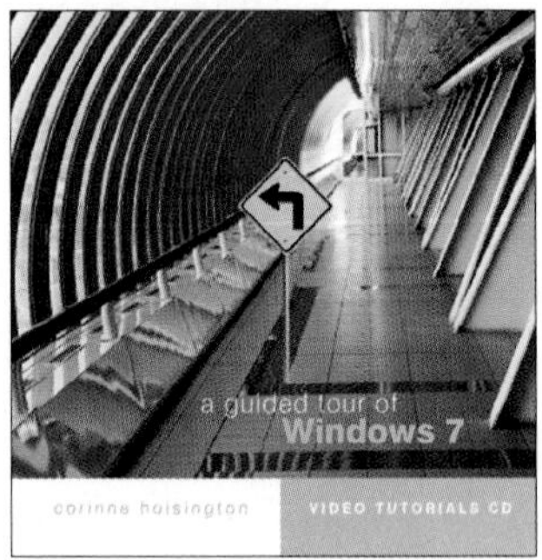

About Our Covers

The Shelly Cashman Series is continually updating our approach and content to reflect the way today's students learn and experience new technology. This focus on student success is reflected on our covers, which feature real students from Westfield State College using the Shelly Cashman Series in their courses, and reflect the varied ages and backgrounds of the students learning with our books. When you use the Shelly Cashman Series, you can be assured that you are learning computer skills using the most effective courseware available.

Textbook Walk-Through

The Shelly Cashman Series Pedagogy: Project-Based — Step-by-Step — Variety of Assessments

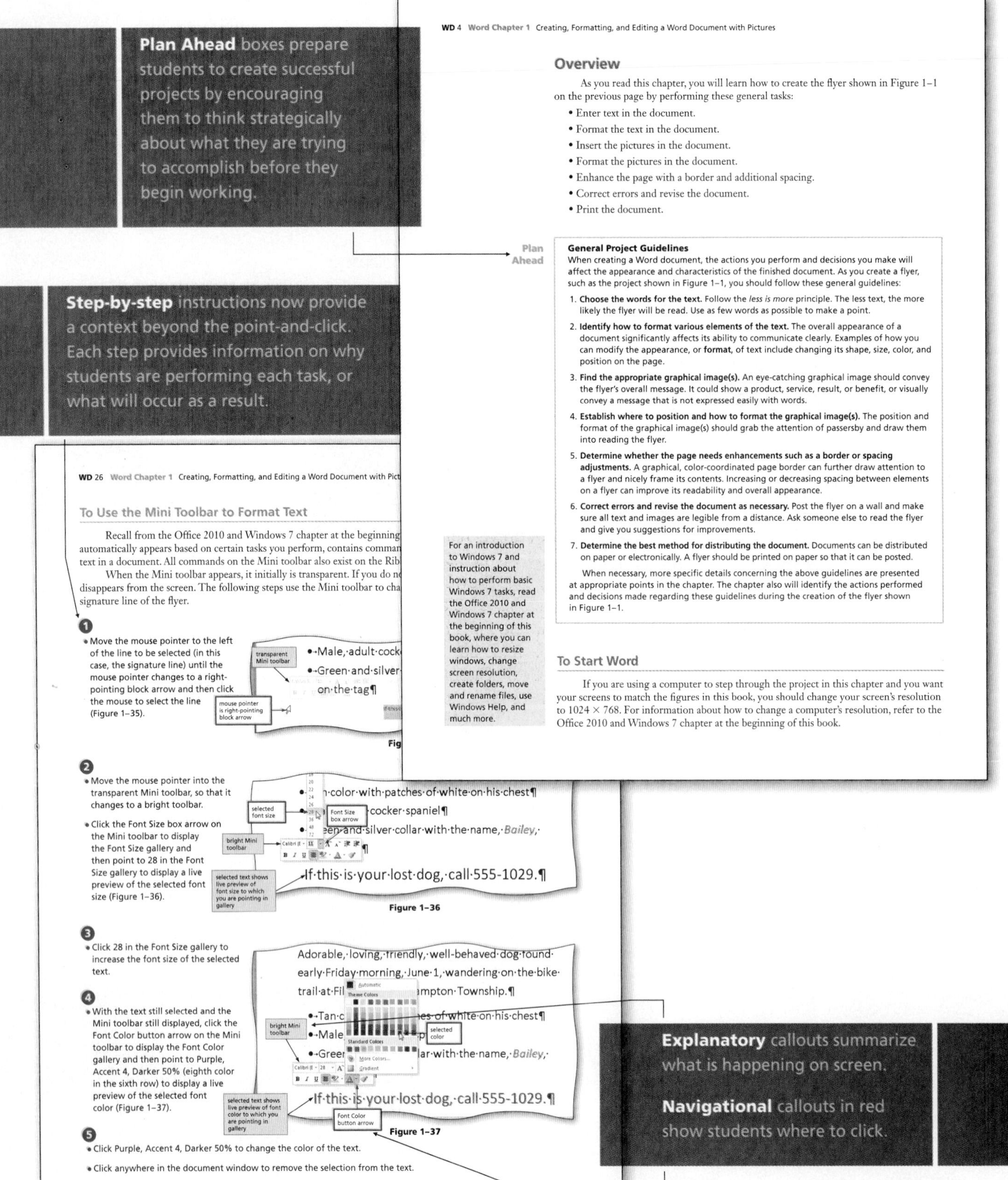

Plan Ahead boxes prepare students to create successful projects by encouraging them to think strategically about what they are trying to accomplish before they begin working.
Step-by-step instructions now provide a context beyond the point-and-click. Each step provides information on why students are performing each task, or what will occur as a result.
Explanatory callouts summarize what is happening on screen.
Navigational callouts in red show students where to click.

WD 4 Word Chapter 1 Creating, Formatting, and Editing a Word Document with Pictures

Overview

As you read this chapter, you will learn how to create the flyer shown in Figure 1–1 on the previous page by performing these general tasks:

- Enter text in the document.
- Format the text in the document.
- Insert the pictures in the document.
- Format the pictures in the document.
- Enhance the page with a border and additional spacing.
- Correct errors and revise the document.
- Print the document.

Plan Ahead

General Project Guidelines

When creating a Word document, the actions you perform and decisions you make will affect the appearance and characteristics of the finished document. As you create a flyer, such as the project shown in Figure 1–1, you should follow these general guidelines:

1. **Choose the words for the text.** Follow the *less is more* principle. The less text, the more likely the flyer will be read. Use as few words as possible to make a point.
2. **Identify how to format various elements of the text.** The overall appearance of a document significantly affects its ability to communicate clearly. Examples of how you can modify the appearance, or **format**, of text include changing its shape, size, color, and position on the page.
3. **Find the appropriate graphical image(s).** An eye-catching graphical image should convey the flyer's overall message. It could show a product, service, result, or benefit, or visually convey a message that is not expressed easily with words.
4. **Establish where to position and how to format the graphical image(s).** The position and format of the graphical image(s) should grab the attention of passersby and draw them into reading the flyer.
5. **Determine whether the page needs enhancements such as a border or spacing adjustments.** A graphical, color-coordinated page border can further draw attention to a flyer and nicely frame its contents. Increasing or decreasing spacing between elements on a flyer can improve its readability and overall appearance.
6. **Correct errors and revise the document as necessary.** Post the flyer on a wall and make sure all text and images are legible from a distance. Ask someone else to read the flyer and give you suggestions for improvements.
7. **Determine the best method for distributing the document.** Documents can be distributed on paper or electronically. A flyer should be printed on paper so that it can be posted.

When necessary, more specific details concerning the above guidelines are presented at appropriate points in the chapter. The chapter also will identify the actions performed and decisions made regarding these guidelines during the creation of the flyer shown in Figure 1–1.

For an introduction to Windows 7 and instruction about how to perform basic Windows 7 tasks, read the Office 2010 and Windows 7 chapter at the beginning of this book, where you can learn how to resize windows, change screen resolution, create folders, move and rename files, use Windows Help, and much more.

To Start Word

If you are using a computer to step through the project in this chapter and you want your screens to match the figures in this book, you should change your screen's resolution to 1024 × 768. For information about how to change a computer's resolution, refer to the Office 2010 and Windows 7 chapter at the beginning of this book.

WD 26 Word Chapter 1 Creating, Formatting, and Editing a Word Document with Pict

To Use the Mini Toolbar to Format Text

Recall from the Office 2010 and Windows 7 chapter at the beginning automatically appears based on certain tasks you perform, contains comman text in a document. All commands on the Mini toolbar also exist on the Rib

When the Mini toolbar appears, it initially is transparent. If you do n disappears from the screen. The following steps use the Mini toolbar to cha signature line of the flyer.

1
- Move the mouse pointer to the left of the line to be selected (in this case, the signature line) until the mouse pointer changes to a right-pointing block arrow and then click the mouse to select the line (Figure 1–35).

Fig

2
- Move the mouse pointer into the transparent Mini toolbar, so that it changes to a bright toolbar.
- Click the Font Size box arrow on the Mini toolbar to display the Font Size gallery and then point to 28 in the Font Size gallery to display a live preview of the selected font size (Figure 1–36).

Figure 1–36

3
- Click 28 in the Font Size gallery to increase the font size of the selected text.

4
- With the text still selected and the Mini toolbar still displayed, click the Font Color button arrow on the Mini toolbar to display the Font Color gallery and then point to Purple, Accent 4, Darker 50% (eighth color in the sixth row) to display a live preview of the selected font color (Figure 1–37).

Figure 1–37

5
- Click Purple, Accent 4, Darker 50% to change the color of the text.
- Click anywhere in the document window to remove the selection from the text.

Q&A boxes offer questions students may have when working through the steps and provide additional information about what they are doing right where they need it.

Experiment Steps within our step-by-step instructions, encourage students to explore, experiment, and take advantage of the features of the Word 2010 user interface. These steps are not necessary to complete the projects, but are designed to increase the confidence with the software and build problem-solving skills.

Word Chapter 3

1

- With the shape still selected, click the More button (shown in Figure 3–6) in the Shape Styles gallery (Drawing Tools Format tab | Shape Styles group) to expand the gallery.

Q&A What if my shape is no longer selected?

Click the shape to select it.

- Point to Intense Effect - Brown, Accent 4 in the Shape Styles gallery to display a live preview of that style applied to the shape in the document (Figure 3–7).

Experiment

- Point to various styles in the Shape Styles gallery and watch the style of the shape change in the document.

2

- Click Intense Effect - Brown, Accent 4 in the Shape Styles gallery to apply the selected style to the shape.

expanded gallery

style format changes to Intense Effect - Brown, Accent 4, showing live preview of style to which you are pointing in expanded gallery

mouse pointer on Intense Effect - Brown, Accent 4 style

Figure 3–7

Other Ways

1. Click Format Shape Dialog Box Launcher (Drawing Tools Format tab | Shape Styles group), click Picture Color in left pane (Format Shape dialog box), select desired colors, click Close button
2. Right-click shape, click Format Shape on shortcut menu, click Picture Color in left pane (Format Shape dialog box), select desired colors, click Close button

...on name to the shape. The following steps add text to a shape.

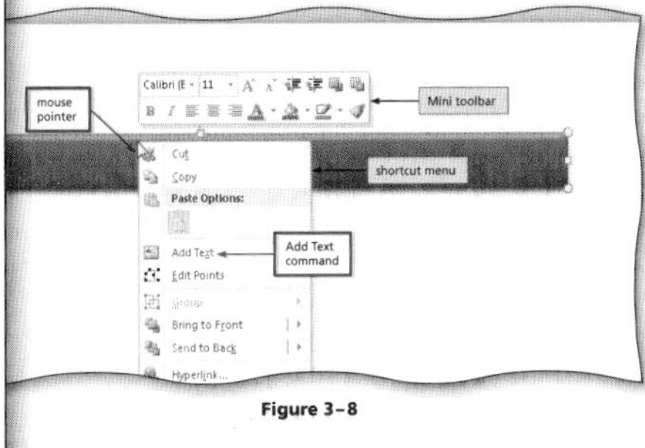

Figure 3–8

Selecting Text

In many of the previous steps, you have selected text. Table 1–3 summarizes the techniques used to select various items.

Table 1–3 Techniques for Selecting Text

Item to Select	Mouse	Keyboard (where applicable)
Block of text	Click at beginning of selection, scroll to end of selection, position mouse pointer at end of selection, hold down SHIFT key and then click; or drag through the text.	
Character(s)	Drag through character(s).	SHIFT+RIGHT ARROW or SHIFT+LEFT ARROW
Document	Move mouse to left of text until mouse pointer changes to a right-pointing block arrow and then triple-click.	CTRL+A
Graphic	Click the graphic.	
Line	Move mouse to left of line until mouse pointer changes to a right-pointing block arrow and then click.	HOME, then SHIFT+END or END, then SHIFT+HOME
Lines	Move mouse to left of first line until mouse pointer changes to a right-pointing block arrow and then drag up or down.	HOME, then SHIFT+DOWN ARROW or END, then SHIFT+UP ARROW
Paragraph	Triple-click paragraph; or move mouse to left of paragraph until mouse pointer changes to a right-pointing block arrow and then double-click.	CTRL+SHIFT+DOWN ARROW or CTRL+SHIFT+UP ARROW
Paragraphs	Move mouse to left of paragraph until mouse pointer changes to a right-pointing block arrow, double-click, and then drag up or down.	CTRL+SHIFT+DOWN ARROW or CTRL+SHIFT+UP ARROW repeatedly
Sentence	Press and hold down CTRL key and then click sentence.	
Word	Double-click the word.	CTRL+SHIFT+RIGHT ARROW or CTRL+SHIFT+LEFT ARROW
Words	Drag through words.	CTRL+SHIFT+RIGHT ARROW or CTRL+SHIFT+LEFT ARROW repeatedly

To Save an Existing Document with the Same File Name

You have made several modifications to the document since you last saved it. Thus, you should save it again. The following step saves the document again. For an example of the step listed below, refer to the Office 2010 and Windows 7 chapter at the beginning of this book.

1 Click the Save button on the Quick Access Toolbar to overwrite the previously saved file.

Break Point: If you wish to take a break, this is a good place to do so. You can quit Word now (refer to page WD 44 for instructions). To resume at a later time, start Word (refer to pages WD 4 and WD 5 for instructions), open the file called Found Dog Flyer (refer to page WD 45 for instructions), and continue following the steps from this location forward.

Break Points identify logical breaks in the chapter if students need to stop before completing the project.

Inserting and Formatting Pictures in a Word Document

With the text formatted in the flyer, the next step is to insert digital pictures in the flyer and format the pictures. Flyers usually contain graphical images, such as a picture, to attract the attention of passersby. In the following pages, you will perform these tasks:

1. Insert the first digital picture into the flyer and then reduce its size.
2. Insert the second digital picture into the flyer and then reduce its size.
3. Change the look of the first picture and then the second picture.

Textbook Walk-Through

Chapter Summary A concluding paragraph, followed by a listing of the tasks completed within a chapter together with the pages on which the step-by-step, screen-by-screen explanations appear.

To Quit Word

The project now is complete. Thus, the following steps quit Word. For an example of the step listed below, refer to the Office 2010 and Windows 7 chapter at the beginning of this book.

1. If you have one Word document open, click the Close button on the right side of the title bar to close the document and quit Word; or if you have multiple Word documents open, click File on the Ribbon to open the Backstage view and then click Exit in the Backstage view to close all open documents and quit Word.
2. If a Microsoft Word dialog box appears, click the Save button to save any changes made to the document since the last save.

BTW **Printed Borders** If one or more of your borders do not print, click the Page Borders button (Page Layout tab | Page Background group), click the Options button (Borders and Shading dialog box), click the Measure from box arrow and click Text, change the four text boxes to 15 pt, and then click the OK button in each dialog box. Try printing the document again. If the borders still do not print, adjust the text boxes in the dialog box to a number smaller than 15 point.

Word Chapter 1

Chapter Summary

In this chapter, you have learned how to enter text in a document, format text, insert a picture, format a picture, add a page border, and print a document. The items listed below include all the new Word skills you have learned in this chapter.

1. Start Word (WD 4)
2. Type Text (WD 6)
3. Display Formatting Marks (WD 7)
4. Insert a Blank Line (WD 7)
5. Wordwrap Text as You Type (WD 8)
6. Check Spelling and Grammar as You Type (WD 9)
7. Save a Document (WD 12)
8. Center a Paragraph (WD 14)
9. Select a Line (WD 15)
10. Change the Font Size of Selected Text (WD 16)
11. Change the Font of Selected Text (WD 17)

... 18)

... D 19)

... VD 26)

23. Bold Text (WD 28)
24. Change Theme Colors (WD 28)
25. Save an Existing Document with the Same File Name (WD 30)
26. Insert a Picture (WD 31)
27. Zoom the Document (WD 33)
28. Resize a Graphic (WD 34)
29. Resize a Graphic by Entering Exact Measurements (WD 36)
30. Apply a Picture Style (WD 37)
31. Apply Picture Effects (WD 38)
32. View One Page (WD 40)
33. Add a Page Border (WD 41)
34. Change Spacing before and after a Paragraph (WD 44)
35. Quit Word (WD 44)
36. Open a Document from Word (WD 45)
37. Insert Text in an Existing Document (WD 46)
38. Delete Text (WD 47)
39. Move Text (WD 47)
40. Change Document Properties (WD 49)
41. Print a Document (WD 51)

... profile, your instructor may have assigned an autogradable ... f so, log into the SAM 2010 Web site at www.cengage.com/sam2010 ... and start files.

BTW **Quick Reference** For a table that lists how to complete the tasks covered in this book using the mouse, Ribbon, shortcut menu, and keyboard, see the Quick Reference Summary at the back of this book, or visit the Word 2010 Quick Reference Web page (scsite.com/wd2010/qr).

STUDENT ASSIGNMENTS

Learn It Online

Test your knowledge of chapter content and key terms.

Instructions: To complete the Learn It Online exercises, start your browser, click the Address bar, and then enter the Web address **scsite.com/wd2010/learn**. When the Word 2010 Learn It Online page is displayed, click the link for the exercise you want to complete and then read the instructions.

Chapter Reinforcement TF, MC, and SA
A series of true/false, multiple choice, and short answer questions that test your knowledge of the chapter content.

Flash Cards
An interactive learning environment where you identify chapter key terms associated with displayed definitions.

Practice Test
A series of multiple choice questions that test your knowledge of chapter content and key terms.

Who Wants To Be a Computer Genius?
An interactive game that challenges your knowledge of chapter content in the style of a television quiz show.

Wheel of Terms
An interactive game that challenges your knowledge of chapter key terms in the style of the television show *Wheel of Fortune*.

Crossword Puzzle Challenge
A crossword puzzle that challenges your knowledge of key terms presented in the chapter.

Apply Your Knowledge

Reinforce the skills and apply the concepts you learned in this chapter.

Modifying Text and Formatting a Document

Note: To complete this assignment, you will be required to use the Data Files for Students. See the inside back cover of this book for instructions on downloading the Data Files for Students, or contact your instructor for information about accessing the required files.

Instructions: Start Word. Open the document, Apply 1-1 Buffalo Photo Shoot Flyer Unformatted, from the Data Files for Students. The document you open is an unformatted flyer. You are to modify text, format paragraphs and characters, and insert a picture in the flyer.

Perform the following tasks:

1. Delete the word, single, in the sentence of body copy below the headline.
2. Insert the word, Creeks, between the words, Twin Buffalo, in the sentence of body copy below the headline.
3. At the end of the signature line, change the period to an exclamation point.
4. Center the headline and the signature line.
5. Change the theme colors to the Aspect color scheme.
6. Change the font and font size of the headline to 48-point Impact, or a similar font. Change the case of the headline text to all capital letters. Apply the text effect called Gradient Fill – Orange, Accent 1, Outline – White to the headline.
7. Change the font size of body copy between the headline and the signature line to 20 point.
8. Use the Mini toolbar to change the font size of the signature line to 26 point.
9. Select the words, hundreds of buffalo, in the paragraph below the headline and underline them.

Learn It Online Every chapter features a Learn It Online section that is comprised of six exercises. These exercises include True/False, Multiple Choice, Short Answer, Flash Cards, Practice Test, and Learning Games.

Apply Your Knowledge This exercise usually requires students to open and manipulate a file from the Data Files that parallels the activities learned in the chapter. To obtain a copy of the Data Files for Students, follow the instructions on the inside back cover of this text.

WD 56 Word Chapter 1 Creating, Formatting, and Editing a Word Document with Pictures

STUDENT ASSIGNMENTS

Extend Your Knowledge

Extend the skills you learned in this chapter and experiment with new skills. You may need to use Help to complete the assignment.

Modifying Text and Picture Formats and Adding Page Borders

Note: To complete this assignment, you will be required to use the Data Files for Students. See the inside back cover of this book for instructions on downloading the Data Files for Students, or contact your instructor for information about accessing the required files.

Instructions: Start Word. Open the document, Extend 1-1 TVC Cruises Flyer, from the Data Files for Students. You will enhance the look of the flyer shown in Figure 1–76. *Hint:* Remember, if you make a mistake while formatting the picture, you can reset it by clicking the Reset Picture button or Reset Picture button arrow (Picture Tools Format tab | Adjust group).

Perform the following tasks:

1. Use Help to learn about the following formats: remove bullets, grow font, shrink font, art page borders, decorative underline(s), picture bullets, picture border shading, shadow picture effects, and color saturation and tone.
2. Remove the bullet from the paragraph below the picture.
3. Select the text, 10 percent, and use the Grow Font button to increase its font size.
4. Add an art page border to the flyer. If the border is not in color, add color to it.
5. Change the solid underline below the word, cruises, to a decorative underline. Change

add art page border

NEED AN ESCAPE?

change border color and add shadow effect; change color saturation and color tone

remove bullet

• Tango Vacation Club members receiv
a 10 percent discount for cruises
booked during May. Select from a
variety of destinations.

use Grow Font button to increase font size

An experience of a lifetime awaits yo

change to picture bullets

• Ultimate relaxation
• Endless fun and entertainment
• Breathtaking scenery
• Friendly, attentive staff
• Clean facilities

Interested? Call TVC at 555-1029

Figure 1–76

Extend Your Knowledge projects at the end of each chapter allow students to extend and expand on the skills learned within the chapter. Students use critical thinking to experiment with new skills to complete each project.

Creating, Formatting, and Editing a Word Document with Pictures Word Chapter 1 WD 57

Word Chapter 1

STUDENT ASSIGNMENTS

Make It Right

Analyze a document and correct all errors and/or improve the design.

Correcting Spelling and Grammar Errors

Note: To complete this assignment, you will be required to use the Data Files for Students. See the inside back cover of this book for instructions on downloading the Data Files for Students, or contact your instructor for information about accessing the required files.

Instructions: Start Word. Open the document, Make It Right 1-1 Karate Academy Flyer Unchecked, from the Data Files for Students. The document is a flyer that contains spelling and grammar errors, as shown in Figure 1–77. You are to correct each spelling (red wavy underline) and grammar error (green and blue wavy underlines) by right-clicking the flagged text and then clicking the appropriate correction on the shortcut menu.

If your screen does not display the wavy underlines, click File on the Ribbon and then click Options in the Backstage view. When the Word Options dialog box is displayed, click Proofing in the left pane, be sure the 'Hide spelling errors in this document only' and 'Hide grammar errors in this document only' check boxes do not contain check marks, and then click the OK button. If your screen still does not display the wavy underlines, redisplay the Word Options dialog box, click Proofing, and then click the Recheck Document button.

Change the document properties, including keywords, as specified by your instructor. Save the revised document with the name, Make It Right 1-1 Karate Academy Flyer, and then submit it in the format specified by your instructor.

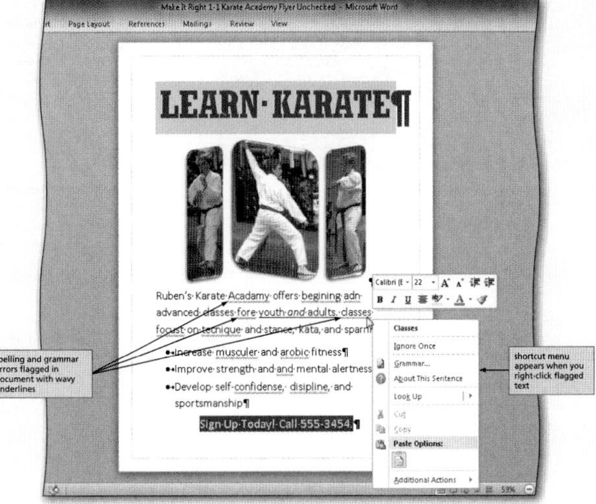

Figure 1–77

Make It Right projects call on students to analyze a fi le, discover errors in it, and fix them using the skills they learned in the chapter.

Textbook Walk-Through

WD 58 Word Chapter 1 Creating, Formatting, and Editing a Word Document with Pictures

STUDENT ASSIGNMENTS

In the Lab

Design and/or create a document using the guidelines, concepts, and skills presented in this chapter. Labs are listed in order of increasing difficulty.

Lab 1: Creating a Flyer with a Picture

Problem: As a part-time employee in the Student Services Center at school, you have been asked to prepare a flyer that advertises study habits classes. First, you prepare the unformatted flyer shown in Figure 1–78a, and then you format it so that it looks like Figure 1–78b. *Hint:* Remember, if you make a mistake while formatting the flyer, you can click the Undo button on the Quick Access Toolbar to undo your last action.

Note: To complete this assignment, you will be required to use the Data Files for Students. See the inside back cover of this book for instructions on downloading the Data Files for Students, or contact your instructor for information about accessing the required files.

Instructions: Perform the following tasks:

1. Start Word. Display formatting marks on the screen.
2. Type the flyer text, unformatted, as shown in Figure 1–78a, inserting a blank line between the headline and the body copy. If Word flags any misspelled words as you type, check their spelling and correct them.
3. Save the document using the file name, Lab 1-1 Study Habits Flyer.
4. Center the headline and the signature line.
5. Change the theme colors to Concourse.
6. Change the font size of the headline to 36 point and the font to Ravie, or a similar font. Apply the text effect called Gradient Fill – Dark Red, Accent 6, Inner Shadow.
7. Change the font size of body copy between the headline and the signature line to 20 point.
8. Change the font size of the signature line to 22 point. Bold the text in the signature line.

Studying All Night?

blank line

Let us help you! Our expert instructors teach effective stu
energy-building techniques.

Classes are $15.00 per session

Sessions last four weeks

Classes meet in the Student Services Center twice a week

Call 555-2838 or stop by to sign up today!

Figure 1–78 (a) Unform

In the Lab Three all new in-depth assignments per chapter require students to utilize the chapter concepts and techniques to solve problems on a computer.

Creating a Business Letter with a Letterhead and Table Word Chapter 3 WD 199

Word Chapter 3

STUDENT ASSIGNMENTS

create a building block for Fair Grove Elementary School and insert the building block whenever you have to enter the school name. Resize table columns to fit contents. Check the spelling of the letter. Change the document properties, as specified by your instructor. Save the letter with Lab 3-3 Education Board Letter as the file name.

Cases and Places

Apply your creative thinking and problem solving skills to design and implement a solution.

Note: To complete these assignments, you may be required to use the Data Files for Students. See the inside back cover of this book for instructions on downloading the Data Files for Students, or contact your instructor for information about accessing the required files.

1: Create a Letter to a Potential Employer

Academic

As a student about to graduate, you are actively seeking employment in your field and have located an advertisement for a job in which you are interested. You decide to write a letter to the potential employer: Ms. Janice Tremont at Home Health Associates, 554 Mountain View Lane, Blue Dust, MO 64319.

The draft wording for the letter is as follows: I am responding to your advertisement for the nursing position in the *Blue Dust Press*. I have tailored my activities and education for a career in geriatric medicine. This month, I will graduate with concentrations in Geriatric Medicine (24 hours), Osteopathic Medicine (12 hours), and Holistic Nursing (9 hours). In addition to receiving my bachelor degree in nursing, I have enhanced my education by participating in the following activities: volunteered at Blue Dust's free health care clinic; attended several continuing education and career-specific seminars, including An Aging Populace, Care of the Homebound, and Special Needs of the Elderly; completed one-semester internship at Blue Dust Community Hospital in spring semester of 2012; completed Certified Nursing Assistant (CNA) program at Blue Dust Community College; and worked as nurse's aide for two years during college. I look forward to an interview so that we can discuss the position you offer and my qualifications. With my background and education, I am confident that I will make a positive contribution to Home Health Associates.

The letter should contain a letterhead that uses a shape and clip art, a table (use a table to present the areas of concentration), and a bulleted list (use a bulleted list to present the activities). Insert nonbreaking spaces in the newspaper name. Use the concepts and techniques presented in this chapter to create and format a letter according to the modified block style, creating appropriate paragraph breaks and rewording the draft as necessary. Use your personal information for contact information in the letter. Be sure to check the spelling and grammar of the finished letter. Submit your assignment in the format specified by your instructor.

2: Create a Letter Requesting Donations

Personal

As an alumnus of your historic high school, you are concerned that the building is being considered for demolition. You decide to write a letter to another graduate: Mr. Jim Lemon, 87 Travis Parkway, Vigil, CT 06802.

The draft wording for the letter is as follows: As a member of the class of 1988, you, like many others, probably have many fond memories of our alma mater, Vigil East High School. I recently learned that the building is being considered for demolition because of its age and structural integrity.

Continued >

Cases & Places exercises call on students to create open-ended projects that reflect academic, personal, and business settings.

Office 2010 and Windows 7: Essential Concepts and Skills

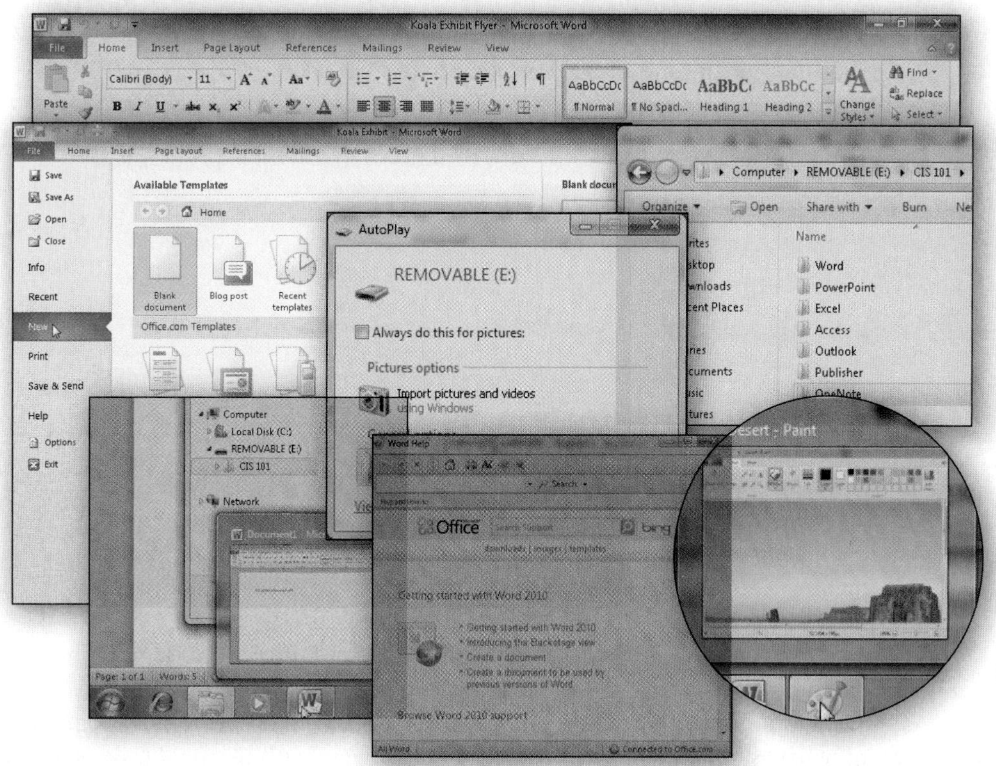

Objectives

You will have mastered the material in this chapter when you can:

- Perform basic mouse operations
- Start Windows and log on to the computer
- Identify the objects on the Windows 7 desktop
- Identify the programs in and versions of Microsoft Office
- Start a program
- Identify the components of the Microsoft Office Ribbon
- Create folders
- Save files
- Change screen resolution
- Perform basic tasks in Microsoft Office programs
- Manage files
- Use Microsoft Office Help and Windows Help

Office 2010 and Windows 7: Essential Concepts and Skills

Office 2010 and Windows 7

This introductory chapter uses Word 2010 to cover features and functions common to Office 2010 programs, as well as the basics of Windows 7.

Overview

As you read this chapter, you will learn how to perform basic tasks in Windows and Word by performing these general activities:

- Start programs using Windows.
- Use features in Word that are common across Office programs.
- Organize files and folders.
- Change screen resolution.
- Quit programs.

Introduction to the Windows 7 Operating System

Windows 7 is the newest version of Microsoft Windows, which is the most popular and widely used operating system. An **operating system** is a computer program (set of computer instructions) that coordinates all the activities of computer hardware such as memory, storage devices, and printers, and provides the capability for you to communicate with the computer.

The Windows 7 operating system simplifies the process of working with documents and programs by organizing the manner in which you interact with the computer. Windows 7 is used to run **application software**, which consists of programs designed to make users more productive and/or assist them with personal tasks, such as word processing.

Windows 7 has two interface variations, Windows 7 Basic and Windows 7 Aero. Computers with up to 1 GB of RAM display the Windows 7 Basic interface (Figure 1a). Computers with more than 1 GB of RAM also can display the Windows Aero interface (Figure 1b), which provides an enhanced visual appearance. The Windows 7 Professional, Windows 7 Enterprise, Windows 7 Home Premium, and Windows 7 Ultimate editions have the capability to use Windows Aero.

Using a Mouse

Windows users work with a mouse that has at least two buttons. For a right-handed user, the left button usually is the primary mouse button, and the right mouse button is the secondary mouse button. Left-handed people, however, can reverse the function of these buttons.

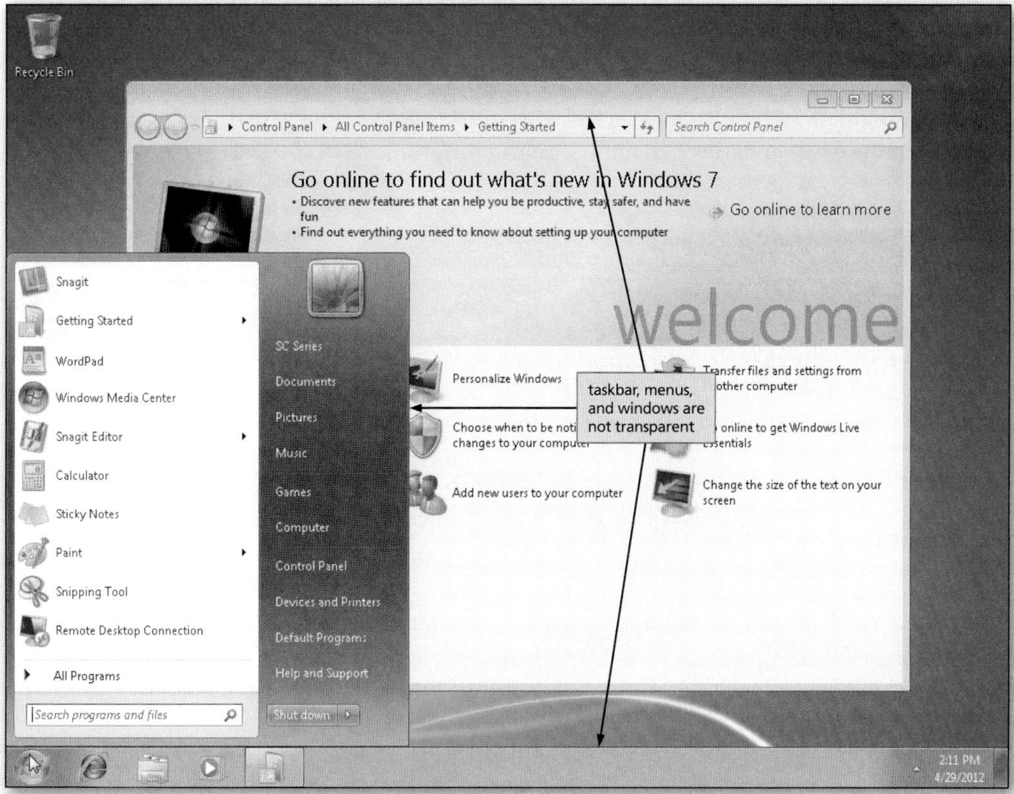

Figure 1 (a) Windows 7 Basic interface

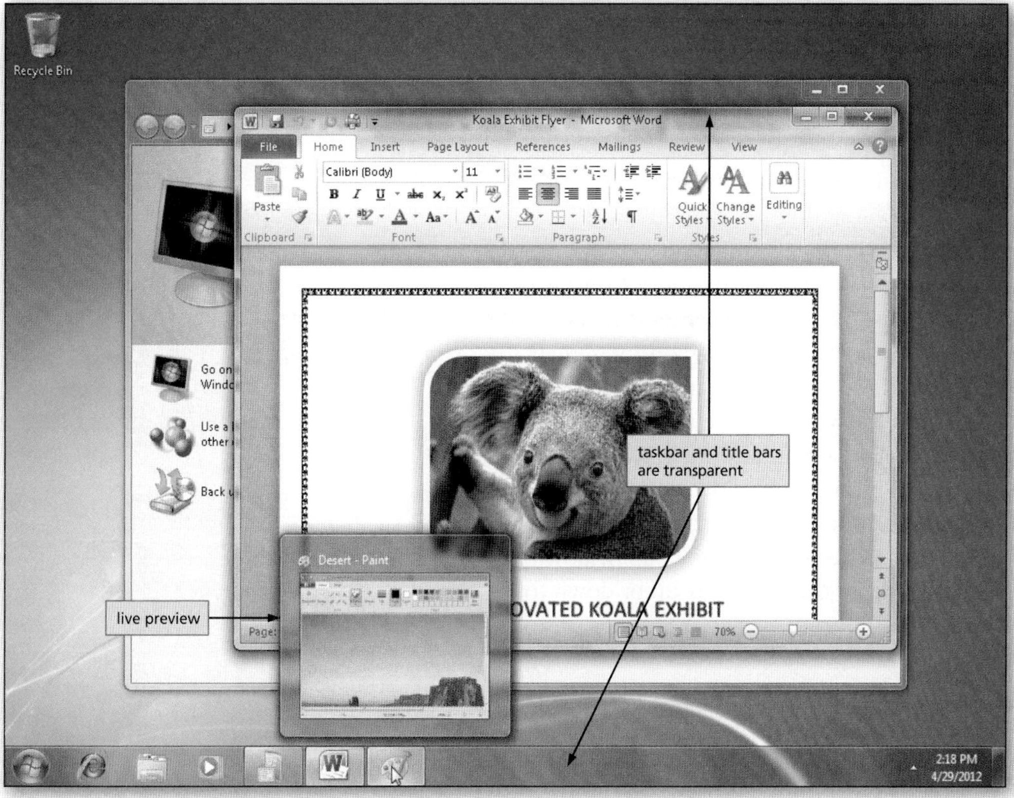

Figure 1 (b) Windows 7 Aero interface

Table 1 explains how to perform a variety of mouse operations. Some programs also use keys in combination with the mouse to perform certain actions. For example, when you hold down the CTRL key while rolling the mouse wheel, text on the screen becomes larger or smaller based on the direction you roll the wheel. The function of the mouse buttons and the wheel varies depending on the program.

Table 1 Mouse Operations

Operation	Mouse Action	Example*
Point	Move the mouse until the pointer on the desktop is positioned on the item of choice.	Position the pointer on the screen.
Click	Press and release the primary mouse button, which usually is the left mouse button.	Select or deselect items on the screen or start a program or program feature.
Right-click	Press and release the secondary mouse button, which usually is the right mouse button.	Display a shortcut menu.
Double-click	Quickly press and release the left mouse button twice without moving the mouse.	Start a program or program feature.
Triple-click	Quickly press and release the left mouse button three times without moving the mouse.	Select a paragraph.
Drag	Point to an item, hold down the left mouse button, move the item to the desired location on the screen, and then release the left mouse button.	Move an object from one location to another or draw pictures.
Right-drag	Point to an item, hold down the right mouse button, move the item to the desired location on the screen, and then release the right mouse button.	Display a shortcut menu after moving an object from one location to another.
Rotate wheel	Roll the wheel forward or backward.	Scroll vertically (up and down).
Free-spin wheel	Whirl the wheel forward or backward so that it spins freely on its own.	Scroll through many pages in seconds.
Press wheel	Press the wheel button while moving the mouse.	Scroll continuously.
Tilt wheel	Press the wheel toward the right or left.	Scroll horizontally (left and right).
Press thumb button	Press the button on the side of the mouse with your thumb.	Move forward or backward through Web pages and/or control media, games, etc.

*Note: The examples presented in this column are discussed as they are demonstrated in this chapter.

BTW

Minimize Wrist Injury
Computer users frequently switch between the keyboard and the mouse during a word processing session; such switching strains the wrist. To help prevent wrist injury, minimize switching. For instance, if your fingers already are on the keyboard, use keyboard keys to scroll. If your hand already is on the mouse, use the mouse to scroll.

Scrolling

A **scroll bar** is a horizontal or vertical bar that appears when the contents of an area may not be visible completely on the screen (Figure 2). A scroll bar contains **scroll arrows** and a **scroll box** that enable you to view areas that currently cannot be seen. Clicking the up and down scroll arrows moves the screen content up or down one line. You also can click above or below the scroll box to move up or down a section, or drag the scroll box up or down to move up or down to a specific location.

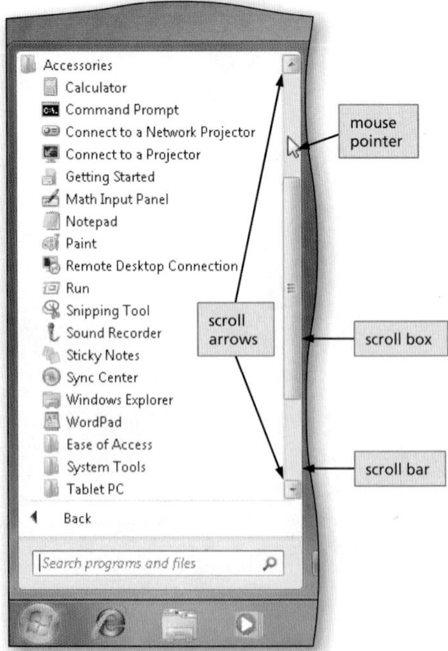

Figure 2

Shortcut Keys

In many cases, you can use the keyboard instead of the mouse to accomplish a task. To perform tasks using the keyboard, you press one or more keyboard keys, sometimes identified as a **shortcut key** or **keyboard shortcut**. Some shortcut keys consist of a single key, such as the F1 key. For example, to obtain help about Windows 7, you can press the F1 key. Other shortcut keys consist of multiple keys, in which case a plus sign separates the key names, such as CTRL+ESC. This notation means to press and hold down the first key listed, press one or more additional keys, and then release all keys. For example, to display the Start menu, press CTRL+ESC, that is, hold down the CTRL key, press the ESC key, and then release both keys.

Starting Windows 7

It is not unusual for multiple people to use the same computer in a work, educational, recreational, or home setting. Windows 7 enables each user to establish a **user account**, which identifies to Windows 7 the resources, such as programs and storage locations, a user can access when working with a computer.

Each user account has a user name and may have a password and an icon, as well. A **user name** is a unique combination of letters or numbers that identifies a specific user to Windows 7. A **password** is a private combination of letters, numbers, and special characters associated with the user name that allows access to a user's account resources. A **user icon** is a picture associated with a user name.

When you turn on a computer, an introductory screen consisting of the Windows logo and copyright messages is displayed. The Windows logo is animated and glows as the Windows 7 operating system is loaded. After the Windows logo appears, depending on your computer's settings, you may or may not be required to log on to the computer. **Logging on** to a computer opens your user account and makes the computer available for use. If you are required to log on to the computer, the **Welcome screen** is displayed, which shows the user names of users on the computer (Figure 3). Clicking the user name or picture begins the process of logging on to the computer.

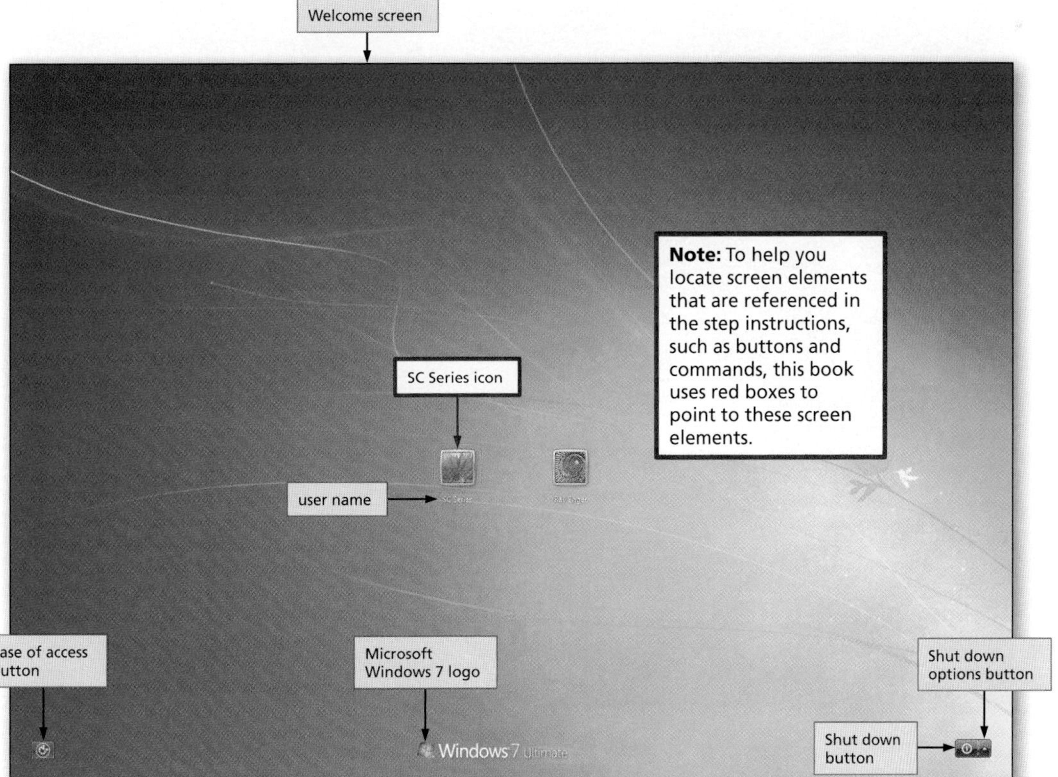

Figure 3

At the bottom of the Welcome screen is the 'Ease of access' button, Windows 7 logo, a Shut down button, and a 'Shut down options' button. The following list identifies the functions of the buttons and commands that typically appear on the Welcome screen:

- Clicking the 'Ease of access' button displays the Ease of Access Center, which provides tools to optimize your computer to accommodate the needs of the mobility-, hearing-, and vision-impaired users.
- Clicking the Shut down button shuts down Windows 7 and the computer.
- Clicking the 'Shut down options' button, located to the right of the Shut down button, displays a menu containing commands that perform actions such as restarting the computer, placing the computer in a low-powered state, and shutting down the computer. The commands available on your computer may differ.
    - The **Restart command** closes open programs, shuts down Windows 7, and then restarts Windows 7 and displays the Welcome screen.
    - The **Sleep command** waits for Windows 7 to save your work and then turns off the computer fans and hard disk. To wake the computer from the Sleep state, press the power button or lift a notebook computer's cover, and log on to the computer.
    - The **Shut down command** shuts down and turns off the computer.

To Log On to the Computer

After starting Windows 7, you might need to log on to the computer. The following steps log on to the computer based on a typical installation. You may need to ask your instructor how to log on to your computer. This set of steps uses SC Series as the user name. The list of user names on your computer will be different.

- Click the user icon (SC Series, in this case) on the Welcome screen (shown in Figure 3 on the previous page); depending on settings, this either will display a password text box (Figure 4) or will log on to the computer and display the Windows 7 desktop.

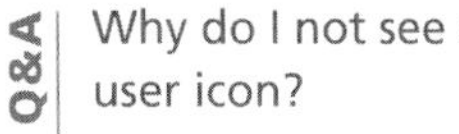

Q&A Why do I not see a user icon?
Your computer may require you to type a user name instead of clicking an icon.

Q&A What is a text box?
A text box is a rectangular box in which you type text.

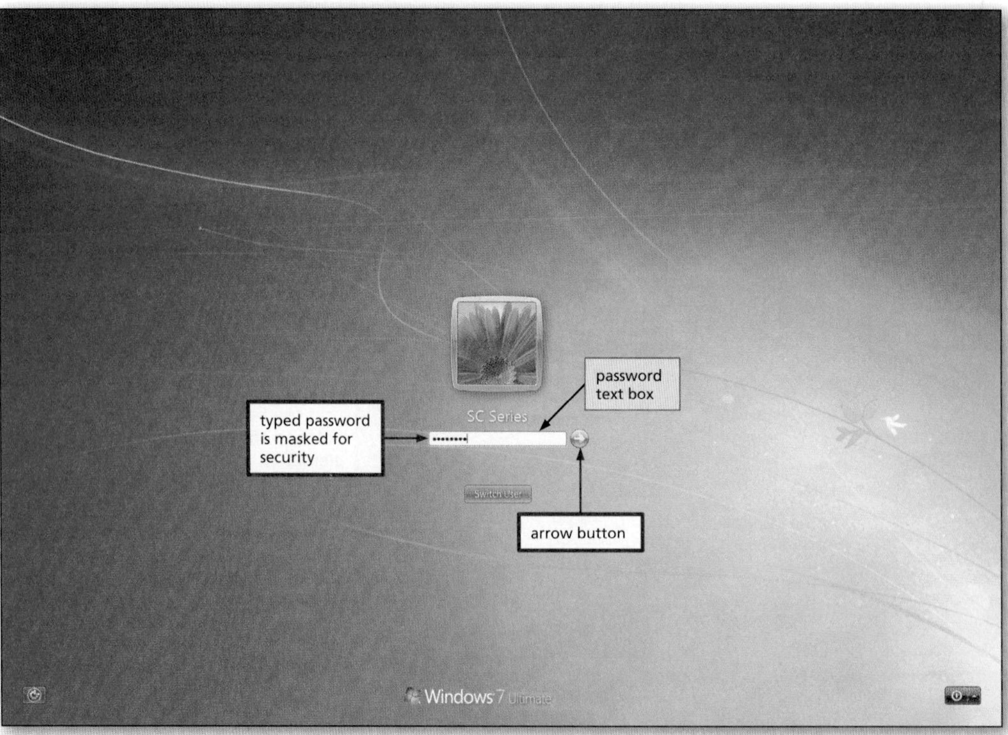

Figure 4

Q&A Why does my screen not show a password text box?
Your account does not require a password.

2

- If Windows 7 displays a password text box, type your password in the text box and then click the arrow button to log on to the computer and display the Windows 7 desktop (Figure 5).

Q&A Why does my desktop look different from the one in Figure 5?

The Windows 7 desktop is customizable, and your school or employer may have modified the desktop to meet its needs. Also, your screen resolution, which affects the size of the elements on the screen, may differ from the screen resolution used in this book. Later in this chapter, you learn how to change screen resolution.

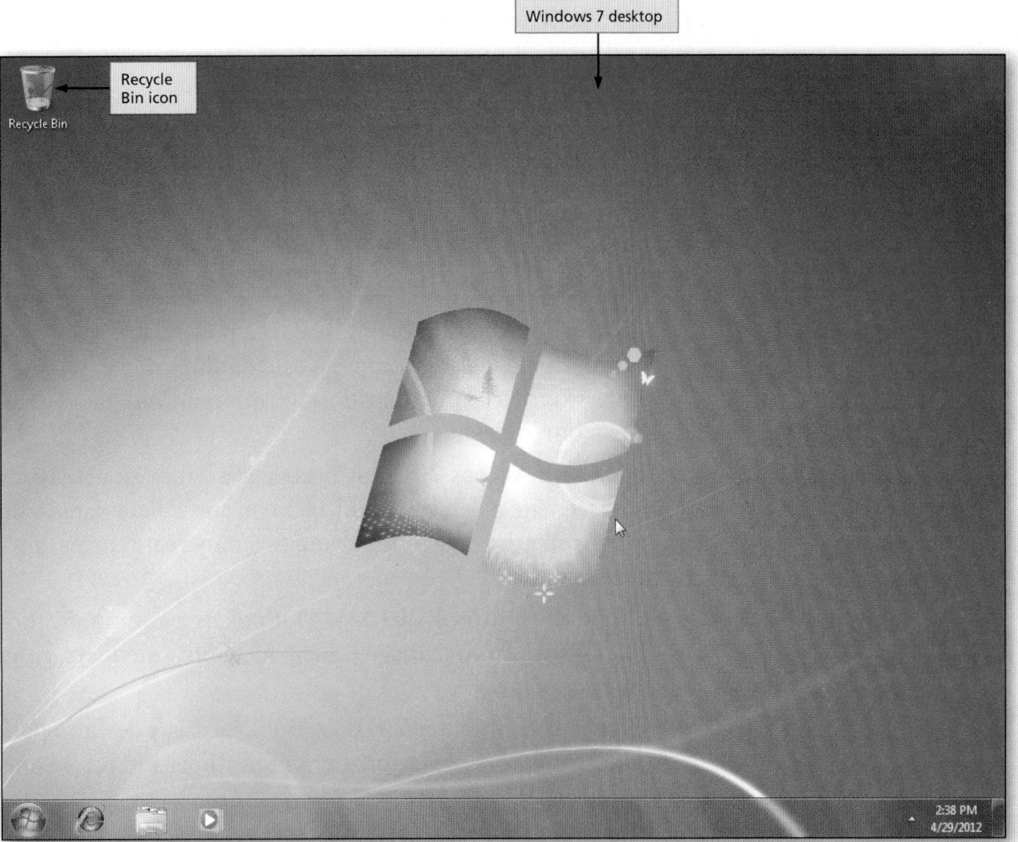

Figure 5

The Windows 7 Desktop

The Windows 7 desktop (Figure 5) and the objects on the desktop emulate a work area in an office. Think of the Windows desktop as an electronic version of the top of your desk. You can perform tasks such as placing objects on the desktop, moving the objects around the desktop, and removing items from the desktop.

When you start a program in Windows 7, it appears on the desktop. Some icons also may be displayed on the desktop. For instance, the icon for the **Recycle Bin**, the location of files that have been deleted, appears on the desktop by default. A **file** is a named unit of storage. Files can contain text, images, audio, and video. You can customize your desktop so that icons representing programs and files you use often appear on your desktop.

Introduction to Microsoft Office 2010

Microsoft Office 2010 is the newest version of Microsoft Office, offering features that provide users with better functionality and easier ways to work with the various files they create. These features include enhanced design tools, such as improved picture formatting tools and new themes, shared notebooks for working in groups, mobile versions of Office programs, broadcast presentation for the Web, and a digital notebook for managing and sharing multimedia information.

Microsoft Office 2010 Programs

Microsoft Office 2010 includes a wide variety of programs such as Word, PowerPoint, Excel, Access, Outlook, Publisher, OneNote, InfoPath, SharePoint Workspace, Communicator, and Web Apps:

- **Microsoft Word 2010**, or Word, is a full-featured word processing program that allows you to create professional-looking documents and revise them easily.
- **Microsoft PowerPoint 2010**, or PowerPoint, is a complete presentation program that allows you to produce professional-looking presentations.
- **Microsoft Excel 2010**, or Excel, is a powerful spreadsheet program that allows you to organize data, complete calculations, make decisions, graph data, develop professional-looking reports, publish organized data to the Web, and access real-time data from Web sites.
- **Microsoft Access 2010**, or Access, is a database management system that allows you to create a database; add, change, and delete data in the database; ask questions concerning the data in the database; and create forms and reports using the data in the database.
- **Microsoft Outlook 2010**, or Outlook, is a communications and scheduling program that allows you to manage e-mail accounts, calendars, contacts, and access to other Internet content.
- **Microsoft Publisher 2010**, or Publisher, is a desktop publishing program that helps you create professional-quality publications and marketing materials that can be shared easily.
- **Microsoft OneNote 2010**, or OneNote, is a note taking program that allows you to store and share information in notebooks with other people.
- **Microsoft InfoPath 2010**, or InfoPath, is a form development program that helps you create forms for use on the Web and gather data from these forms.
- **Microsoft SharePoint Workspace 2010**, or SharePoint, is collaboration software that allows you to access and revise files stored on your computer from other locations.
- **Microsoft Communicator** is communications software that allows you to use different modes of communications such as instant messaging, video conferencing, and sharing files and programs.
- **Microsoft Web Apps** is a Web application that allows you to edit and share files on the Web using the familiar Office interface.

Microsoft Office 2010 Suites

A **suite** is a collection of individual programs available together as a unit. Microsoft offers a variety of Office suites. Table 2 lists the Office 2010 suites and their components.

Programs in a suite, such as Microsoft Office, typically use a similar interface and share features. In addition, Microsoft Office programs use **common dialog boxes** for performing actions such as opening and saving files. Once you are comfortable working with these elements and this interface and performing tasks in one program, the similarity can help you apply the knowledge and skills you have learned to another Office program(s). For example, the process for saving a file in Word is the same in PowerPoint, Excel, and the other Office programs. While briefly showing how to use Word, this chapter illustrates some of the common functions across the Office programs and also identifies the characteristics unique to Word.

Table 2 Microsoft Office 2010 Suites

	Microsoft Office Professional Plus 2010	Microsoft Office Professional 2010	Microsoft Office Home and Business 2010	Microsoft Office Standard 2010	Microsoft Office Home and Student 2010
Microsoft Word 2010	✔	✔	✔	✔	✔
Microsoft PowerPoint 2010	✔	✔	✔	✔	✔
Microsoft Excel 2010	✔	✔	✔	✔	✔
Microsoft Access 2010	✔	✔	✗	✗	✗
Microsoft Outlook 2010	✔	✔	✔	✔	✗
Microsoft Publisher 2010	✔	✔	✗	✔	✗
Microsoft OneNote 2010	✔	✔	✔	✔	✔
Microsoft InfoPath 2010	✔	✗	✗	✗	✗
Microsoft SharePoint Workspace 2010	✔	✗	✗	✗	✗
Microsoft Communicator	✔	✗	✗	✗	✗

Starting and Using a Program

To use a program, such as Word, you must instruct the operating system to start the program. Windows 7 provides many different ways to start a program, one of which is presented in this section (other ways to start a program are presented throughout this chapter). After starting a program, you can use it to perform a variety of tasks. The following pages use Word to discuss some elements of the Office interface and to perform tasks that are common to other Office programs.

Word

Word is a full-featured word processing program that allows you to create professional-looking documents and revise them easily. A document is a printed or electronic medium that people use to communicate with others. With Word, you can develop many types of personal and business documents, including flyers, letters, memos, resumes, reports, fax cover sheets, mailing labels, and newsletters. Word also provides tools that enable you to create Web pages and save these Web pages directly on a Web server.

Word has many features designed to simplify the production of documents and add visual appeal. Using Word, you easily can change the shape, size, and color of text. You also can include borders, shading, tables, images, pictures, charts, and Web addresses in documents.

While you are typing, Word performs many tasks automatically. For example, Word detects and corrects spelling and grammar errors in several languages. Word's thesaurus allows you to add variety and precision to your writing. Word also can format text, such as headings, lists, fractions, borders, and Web addresses, as you type.

To Start a Program Using the Start Menu

Across the bottom of the Windows 7 desktop is the **taskbar**. The taskbar contains the **Start button**, which you use to access programs, files, folders, and settings on a computer. A **folder** is a named location on a storage medium that usually contains related documents. The taskbar also displays a button for each program currently running on a computer.

Clicking the Start button displays the Start menu. The **Start menu** allows you to access programs, folders, and files on the computer and contains commands that allow you to start programs, store and search for documents, customize the computer, and obtain help about thousands of topics. A **menu** is a list of related items, including folders, programs, and commands. Each **command** on a menu performs a specific action, such as saving a file or obtaining help.

The following steps, which assume Windows 7 is running, use the Start menu to start the Microsoft Word 2010 program based on a typical installation. You may need to ask your instructor how to start Word for your computer. Although the steps illustrate starting the Word program, the steps to start any program are similar.

1

- Click the Start button on the Windows 7 taskbar to display the Start menu (Figure 6).

Q&A Why does my Start menu look different?

It may look different depending on your computer's configuration. The Start menu may be customized for several reasons, such as usage requirements or security restrictions.

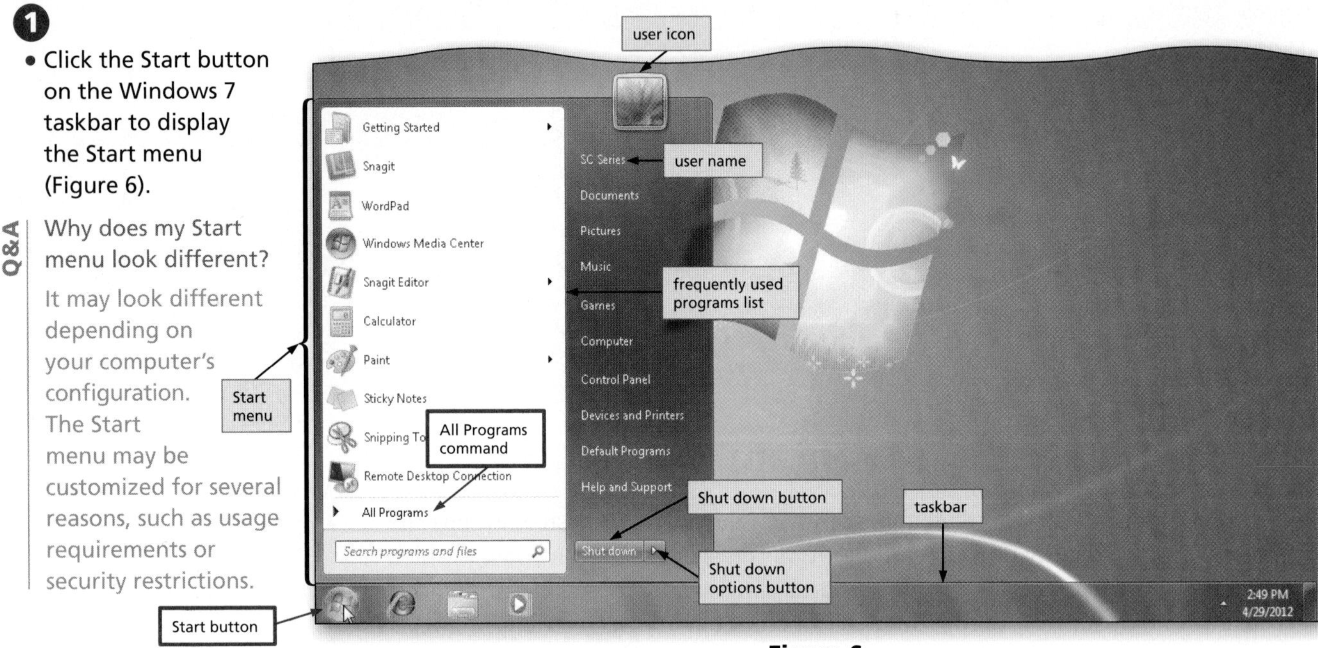

Figure 6

2

- Click All Programs at the bottom of the left pane on the Start menu to display the All Programs list (Figure 7).

Q&A What is a pane?

A **pane** is an area of a window that displays related content. For example, the left pane on the Start menu contains a list of frequently used programs, as well as the All Programs command.

Q&A Why might my All Programs list look different?

Most likely, the programs installed on your computer will differ from those shown in Figure 7. Your All Programs list will show the programs that are installed on your computer.

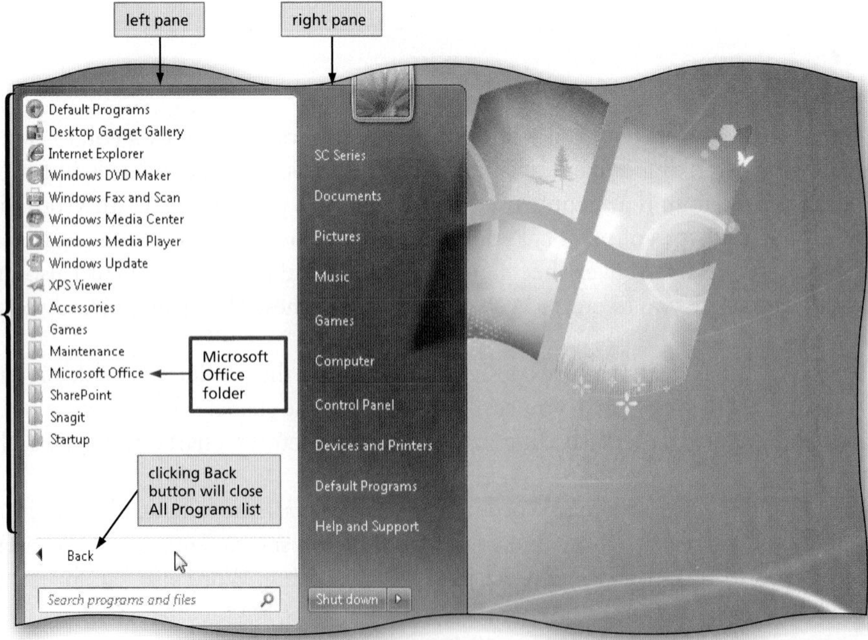

Figure 7

- If the program you wish to start is located in a folder, click or scroll to and then click the folder (Microsoft Office, in this case) in the All Programs list to display a list of the folder's contents (Figure 8).

Microsoft Office list

Q&A

Why is the Microsoft Office folder on my computer?

During installation of Microsoft Office 2010, the Microsoft Office folder was added to the All Programs list.

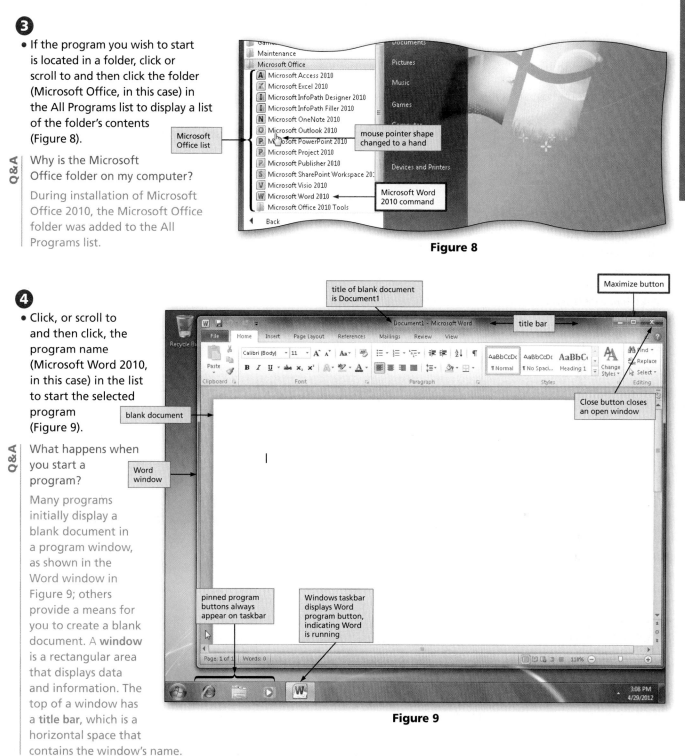

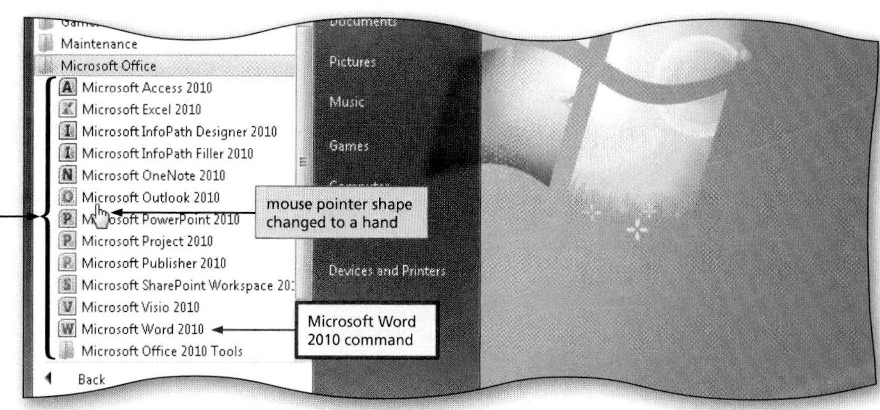

Figure 8

4

- Click, or scroll to and then click, the program name (Microsoft Word 2010, in this case) in the list to start the selected program (Figure 9).

Q&A

What happens when you start a program?

Many programs initially display a blank document in a program window, as shown in the Word window in Figure 9; others provide a means for you to create a blank document. A **window** is a rectangular area that displays data and information. The top of a window has a **title bar**, which is a horizontal space that contains the window's name.

title of blank document is Document1

Maximize button

title bar

Close button closes an open window

blank document

Word window

pinned program buttons always appear on taskbar

Windows taskbar displays Word program button, indicating Word is running

Figure 9

Q&A

Why is my program window a different size?

The Word window shown in Figure 9 is not maximized. Your Word window already may be maximized. The steps on the next page maximize a window.

Other Ways

1. Double-click program icon on desktop, if one is present
2. Click program name in left pane of Start menu, if present
3. Display Start menu, type program name in search box, click program name
4. Double-click file created using program you want to start

To Maximize a Window

Sometimes content is not visible completely in a window. One method of displaying the entire contents of a window is to **maximize** it, or enlarge the window so that it fills the entire screen. The following step maximizes the Word window; however, any Office program's window can be maximized using this step.

1

- If the program window is not maximized already, click the Maximize button (shown in Figure 9 on the previous page) next to the Close button on the window's title bar (the Word window title bar, in this case) to maximize the window (Figure 10).

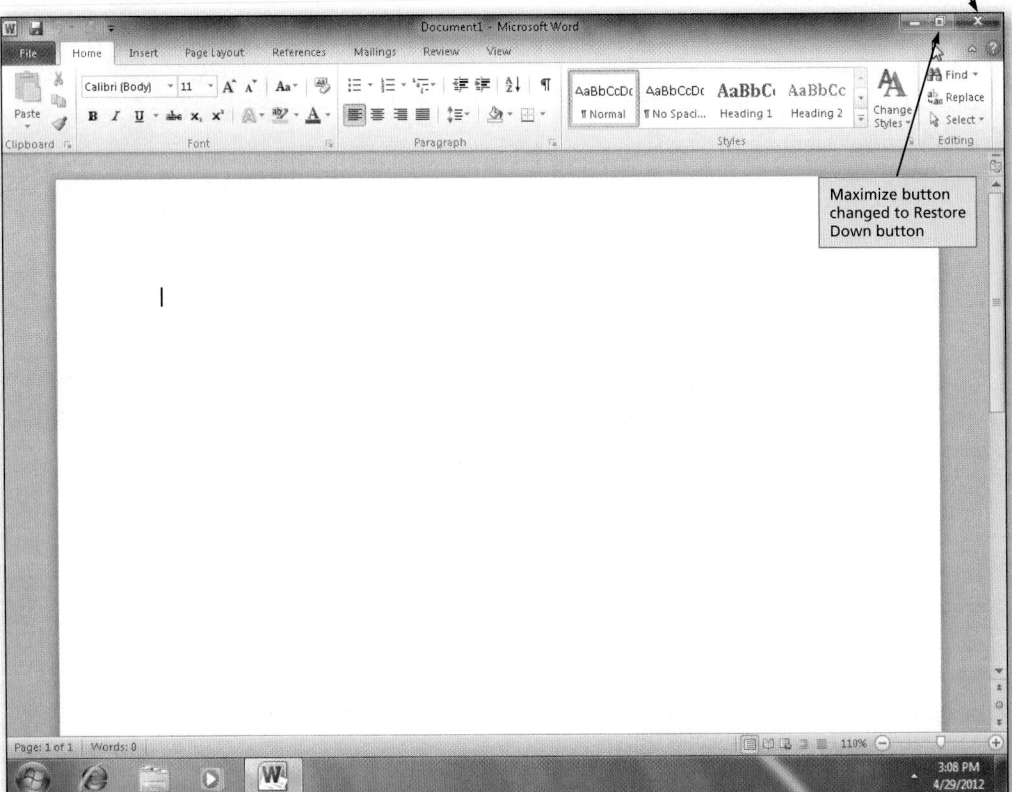

Figure 10

Q&A What happened to the Maximize button?

It changed to a Restore Down button, which you can use to return a window to its size and location before you maximized it.

Q&A How do I know whether a window is maximized?

A window is maximized if it fills the entire display area and the Restore Down button is displayed on the title bar.

Other Ways

1. Double-click title bar
2. Drag title bar to top of screen

The Word Document Window, Ribbon, and Elements Common to Office Programs

The Word window consists of a variety of components to make your work more efficient and documents more professional. These include the document window, Ribbon, Mini toolbar, shortcut menus, and Quick Access Toolbar. Most of these components are common to other Microsoft Office 2010 programs; others are unique to Word.

You view a portion of a document on the screen through a **document window** (Figure 11). The default (preset) view is **Print Layout view**, which shows the document on a mock sheet of paper in the document window.

Scroll Bars You use a scroll bar to display different portions of a document in the document window. At the right edge of the document window is a vertical scroll bar. If a document is too wide to fit in the document window, a horizontal scroll bar also appears at the bottom of the document window. On a scroll bar, the position of the scroll box reflects the location of the portion of the document that is displayed in the document window.

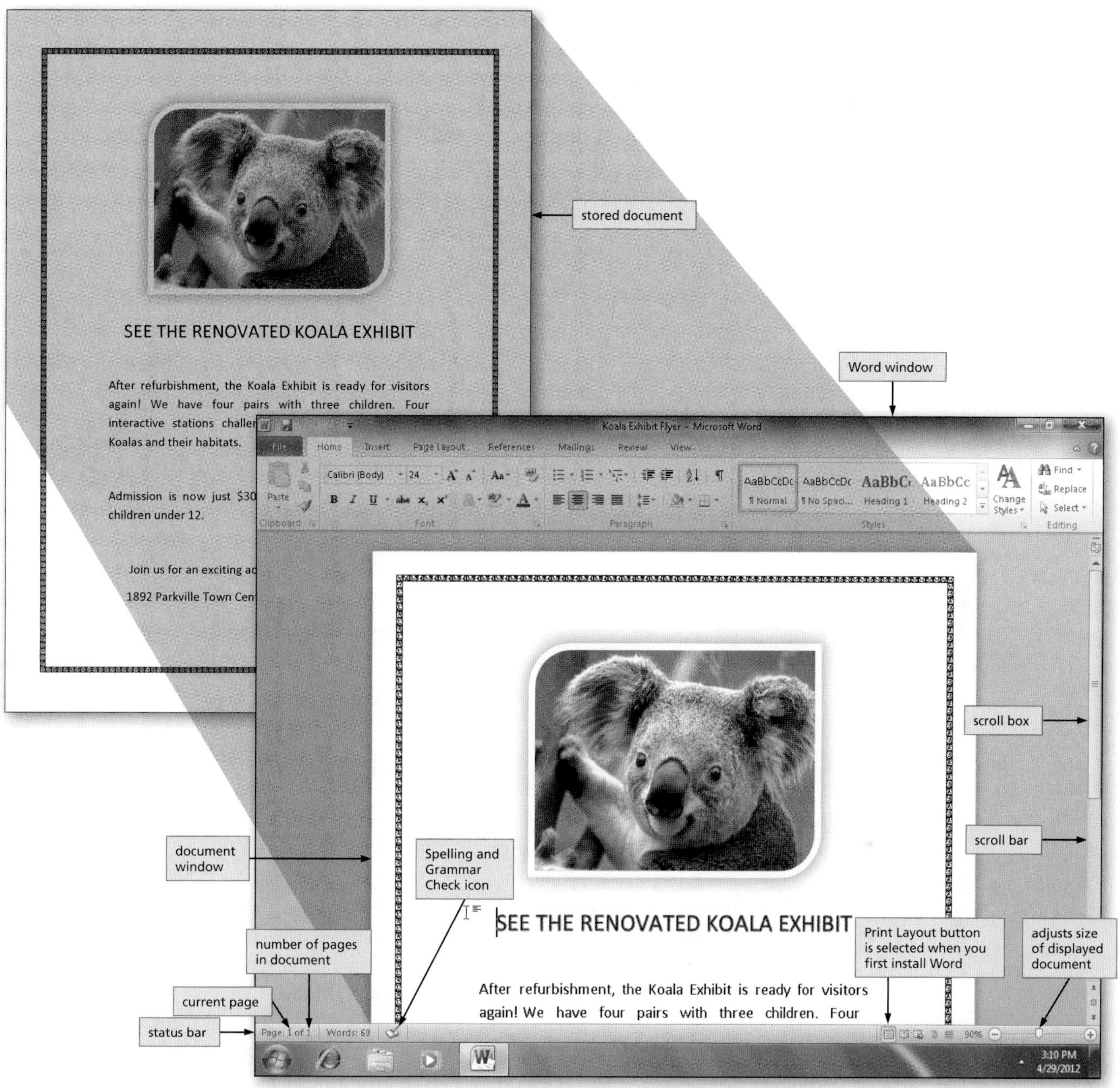

Figure 11

Status Bar The **status bar**, located at the bottom of the document window above the Windows 7 taskbar, presents information about the document, the progress of current tasks, and the status of certain commands and keys; it also provides controls for viewing the document. As you type text or perform certain tasks, various indicators and buttons may appear on the status bar.

The left side of the status bar in Figure 11 shows the current page followed by the total number of pages in the document, the number of words in the document, and an icon to check spelling and grammar. The right side of the status bar includes buttons and controls you can use to change the view of a document and adjust the size of the displayed document.

Ribbon The Ribbon, located near the top of the window below the title bar, is the control center in Word and other Office programs (Figure 12). The Ribbon provides easy, central access to the tasks you perform while creating a document. The Ribbon consists of tabs, groups, and commands. Each **tab** contains a collection of groups, and each **group** contains related functions. When you start an Office program, such as Word, it initially displays several main tabs, also called default tabs. All Office programs have a **Home tab**, which contains the more frequently used commands.

In addition to the main tabs, Office programs display **tool tabs**, also called contextual tabs (Figure 13), when you perform certain tasks or work with objects such as pictures or tables. If you insert a picture in a Word document, for example, the Picture Tools tab and its related subordinate Format tab appear, collectively referred to as the Picture Tools Format tab. When you are finished working with the picture, the Picture Tools Format tab disappears from the Ribbon. Word and other Office programs determine when tool tabs should appear and disappear based on tasks you perform. Some tool tabs, such as the Table Tools tab, have more than one related subordinate tab.

Items on the Ribbon include buttons, boxes (text boxes, check boxes, etc.), and galleries (Figure 12). A **gallery** is a set of choices, often graphical, arranged in a grid or in a list. You can scroll through choices in an in-Ribbon gallery by clicking the gallery's scroll arrows. Or, you can click a gallery's More button to view more gallery options on the screen at a time.

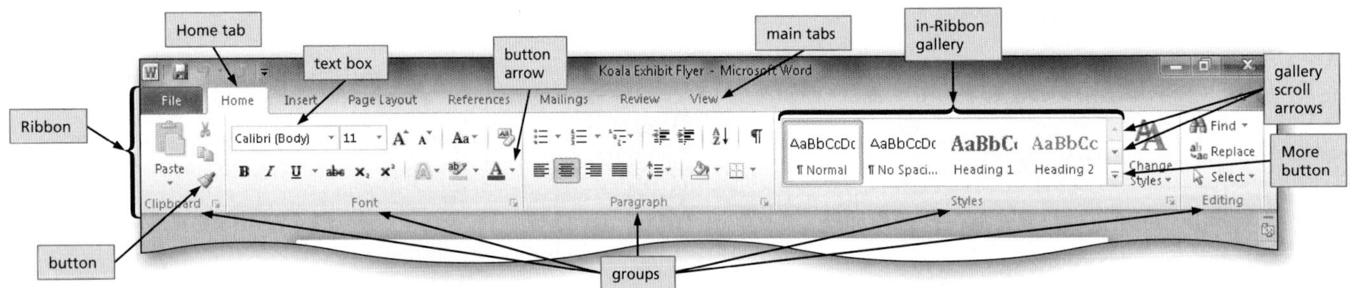

Figure 12

Some buttons and boxes have arrows that, when clicked, also display a gallery; others always cause a gallery to be displayed when clicked. Most galleries support **live preview**, which is a feature that allows you to point to a gallery choice and see its effect in the document — without actually selecting the choice (Figure 13).

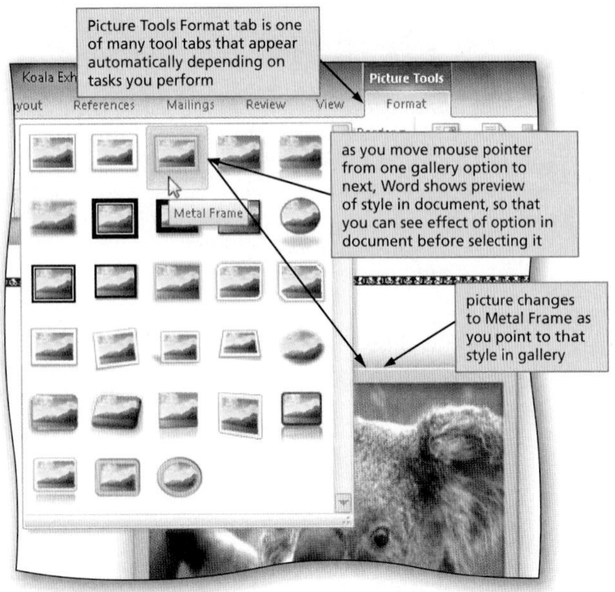

Figure 13

Some commands on the Ribbon display an image to help you remember their function. When you point to a command on the Ribbon, all or part of the command glows in shades of yellow and orange, and an Enhanced ScreenTip appears on the screen. An **Enhanced ScreenTip** is an on-screen note that provides the name of the command, available keyboard shortcut(s), a description of the command, and sometimes instructions for how to obtain help about the command (Figure 14). Enhanced ScreenTips are more detailed than a typical ScreenTip, which usually displays only the name of the command.

Some groups on the Ribbon have a small arrow in the lower-right corner, called a **Dialog Box Launcher**, that when clicked, displays a dialog box or a task pane with additional options for the group (Figure 15). When presented with a dialog box, you make selections and must close the dialog box before returning to the document. A **task pane**, in contrast to a dialog box, is a window that can remain open and visible while you work in the document.

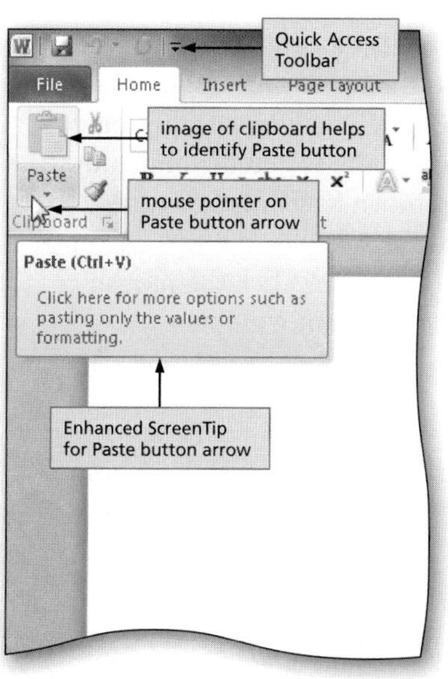

Figure 14

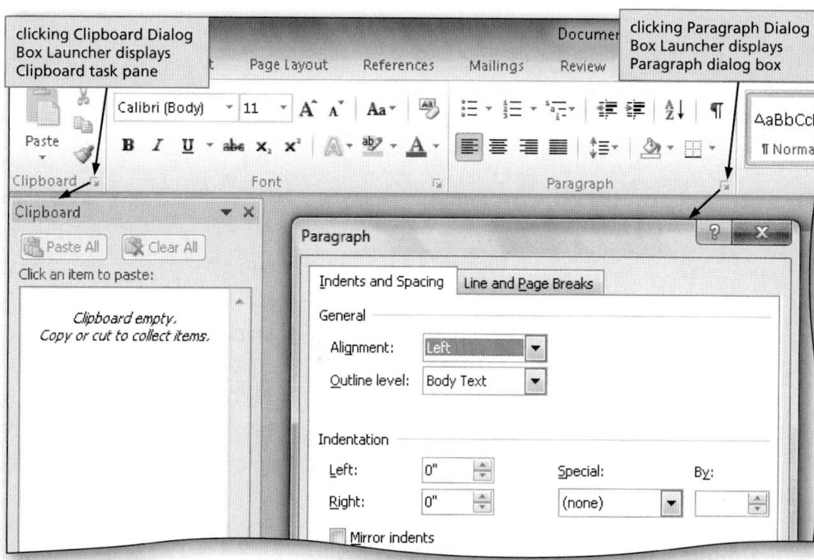

Figure 15

Mini Toolbar The **Mini toolbar**, which appears automatically based on tasks you perform, contains commands related to changing the appearance of text in a document. All commands on the Mini toolbar also exist on the Ribbon. The purpose of the Mini toolbar is to minimize mouse movement.

When the Mini toolbar appears, it initially is transparent (Figure 16a). If you do not use the transparent Mini toolbar, it disappears from the screen. To use the Mini toolbar, move the mouse pointer into the toolbar, which causes the Mini toolbar to change from a transparent to bright appearance (Figure 16b). If you right-click an item in the document window, Word displays both the Mini toolbar and a shortcut menu, which is discussed in a later section in this chapter.

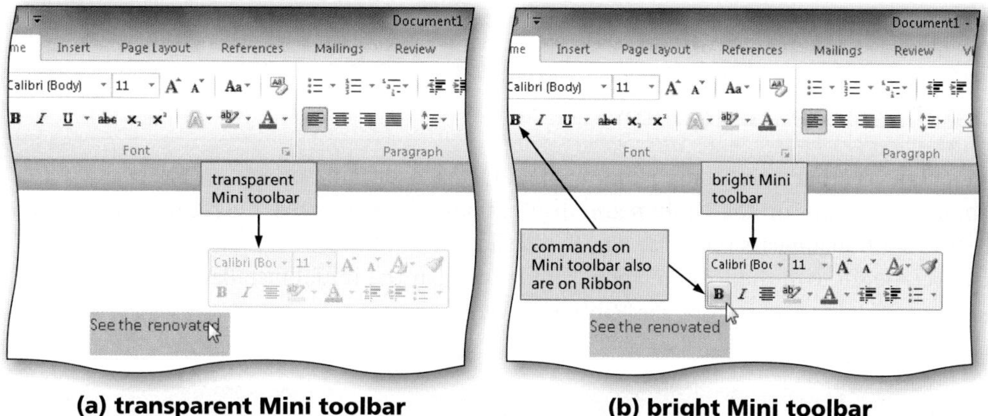

(a) transparent Mini toolbar **(b) bright Mini toolbar**

Figure 16

BTW

Turning Off the Mini Toolbar

If you do not want the Mini toolbar to appear, click File on the Ribbon to open the Backstage view, click Options in the Backstage view, click General (Options dialog box), remove the check mark from the Show Mini Toolbar on selection check box, and then click the OK button.

Quick Access Toolbar The **Quick Access Toolbar**, located initially (by default) above the Ribbon at the left edge of the title bar, provides convenient, one-click access to frequently used commands (Figure 14). The commands on the Quick Access Toolbar always are available, regardless of the task you are performing. The Quick Access Toolbar is discussed in more depth later in the chapter.

KeyTips If you prefer using the keyboard instead of the mouse, you can press the ALT key on the keyboard to display **KeyTips**, or keyboard code icons, for certain commands

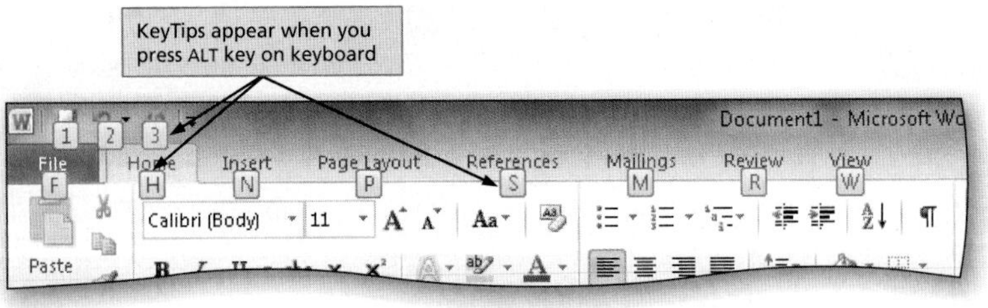

KeyTips appear when you press ALT key on keyboard

Figure 17

(Figure 17). To select a command using the keyboard, press the letter or number displayed in the KeyTip, which may cause additional KeyTips related to the selected command to appear. To remove KeyTips from the screen, press the ALT key or the ESC key until all KeyTips disappear, or click the mouse anywhere in the program window.

To Display a Different Tab on the Ribbon

When you start Word, the Ribbon displays eight main tabs: File, Home, Insert, Page Layout, References, Mailings, Review, and View. The tab currently displayed is called the **active tab.**

The following step displays the Insert tab, that is, makes it the active tab.

- Click Insert on the Ribbon to display the Insert tab (Figure 18).

Experiment

- Click the other tabs on the Ribbon to view their contents. When you are finished, click the Insert tab to redisplay the Insert tab.

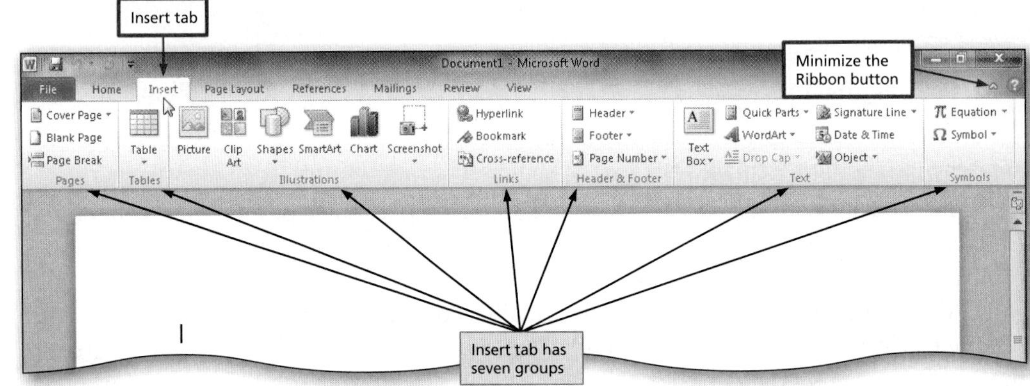

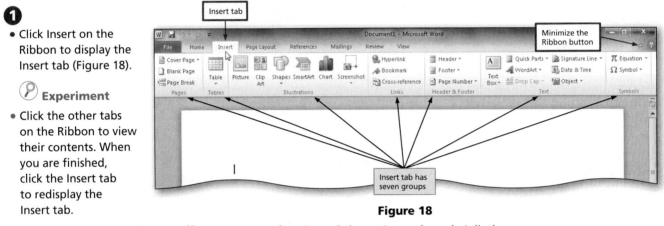

Figure 18

Q&A If I am working in a different Office program, such as PowerPoint or Access, how do I display a different tab on the Ribbon?

Follow this same procedure; that is, click the desired tab on the Ribbon.

To Minimize, Display, and Restore the Ribbon

To display more of a document or other item in the window of an Office program, some users prefer to minimize the Ribbon, which hides the groups on the Ribbon and displays only the main tabs. Each time you start an Office program, such as Word, the Ribbon appears the same way it did the last time you used that Office program. The chapters in this book, however, begin with the Ribbon appearing as it did at the initial installation of Word.

The following steps minimize, display, and restore the Ribbon in Word.

- Click the Minimize the Ribbon button on the Ribbon (shown in Figure 18) to minimize the Ribbon (Figure 19).

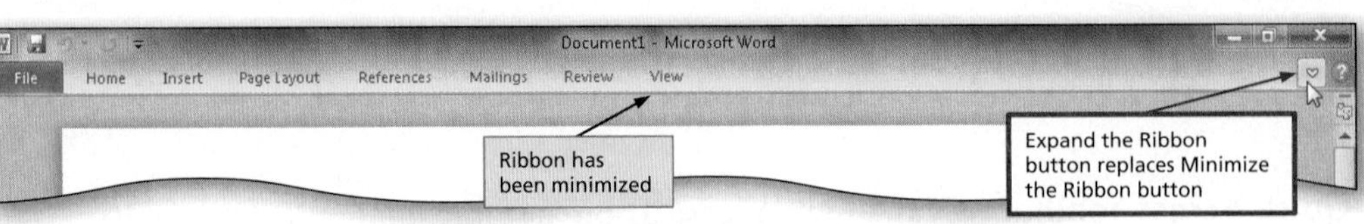

Figure 19

Q&A What happened to the groups on the Ribbon?

When you minimize the Ribbon, the groups disappear so that the Ribbon does not take up as much space on the screen.

Q&A What happened to the Minimize the Ribbon button?

The Expand the Ribbon button replaces the Minimize the Ribbon button when the Ribbon is minimized.

2

- Click Home on the Ribbon to display the Home tab (Figure 20).

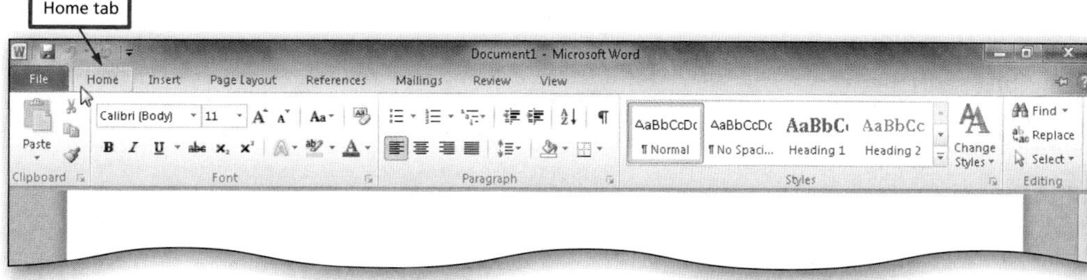

Figure 20

Q&A Why would I click the Home tab?

If you want to use a command on a minimized Ribbon, click the main tab to display the groups for that tab. After you select a command on the Ribbon, the groups will be hidden once again. If you decide not to use a command on the Ribbon, you can hide the groups by clicking the same main tab or clicking in the program window.

3

- Click Home on the Ribbon to hide the groups again (shown in Figure 19).
- Click the Expand the Ribbon button on the Ribbon (shown in Figure 19) to restore the Ribbon.

Other Ways

1. Double-click Home on the Ribbon
2. Press CTRL+F1

To Display and Use a Shortcut Menu

When you right-click certain areas of the Word and other program windows, a shortcut menu will appear. A **shortcut menu** is a list of frequently used commands that relate to the right-clicked object. When you right-click a scroll bar, for example, a shortcut menu appears with commands related to the scroll bar. When you right-click the Quick Access Toolbar, a shortcut menu appears with commands related to the Quick Access Toolbar. You can use shortcut menus to access common commands quickly. The following steps use a shortcut menu to move the Quick Access Toolbar, which by default is located on the title bar.

1

- Right-click the Quick Access Toolbar to display a shortcut menu that presents a list of commands related to the Quick Access Toolbar (Figure 21).

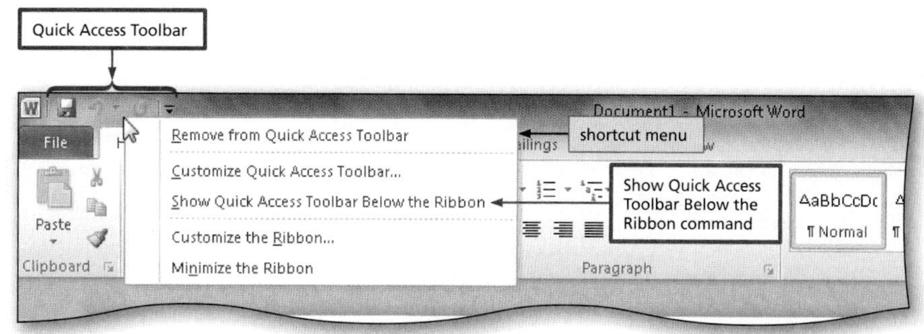

Figure 21

2

- Click Show Quick Access Toolbar Below the Ribbon on the shortcut menu to display the Quick Access Toolbar below the Ribbon (Figure 22).

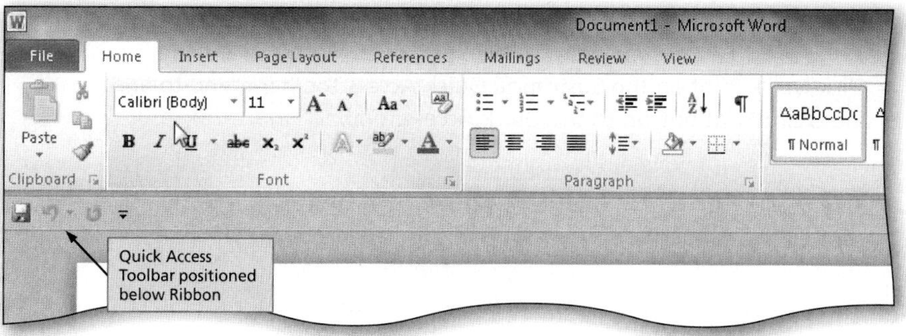

Figure 22

3

- Right-click the Quick Access Toolbar to display a shortcut menu (Figure 23).

4

- Click Show Quick Access Toolbar Above the Ribbon on the shortcut menu to return the Quick Access Toolbar to its original position (shown in Figure 21 on the previous page).

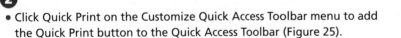

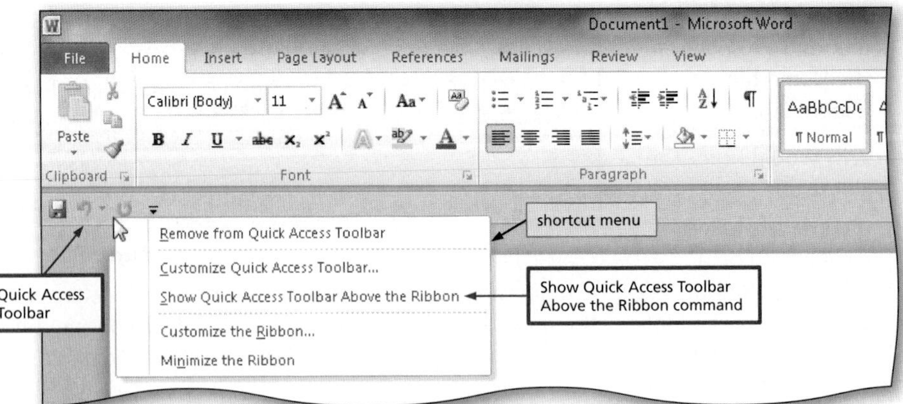

Figure 23

To Customize the Quick Access Toolbar

The Quick Access Toolbar provides easy access to some of the more frequently used commands in Office programs. By default, the Quick Access Toolbar contains buttons for the Save, Undo, and Redo commands. You can customize the Quick Access Toolbar by changing its location in the window, as shown in the previous steps, and by adding more buttons to reflect commands you would like to access easily. The following steps add the Quick Print button to the Quick Access Toolbar in the Word window.

1

- Click the Customize Quick Access Toolbar button to display the Customize Quick Access Toolbar menu (Figure 24).

Q&A Which commands are listed on the Customize Quick Access Toolbar menu?

It lists commands that commonly are added to the Quick Access Toolbar.

Q&A What do the check marks next to some commands signify?

Check marks appear next to commands that already are on the Quick Access Toolbar. When you add a button to the Quick Access Toolbar, a check mark will be displayed next to its command name.

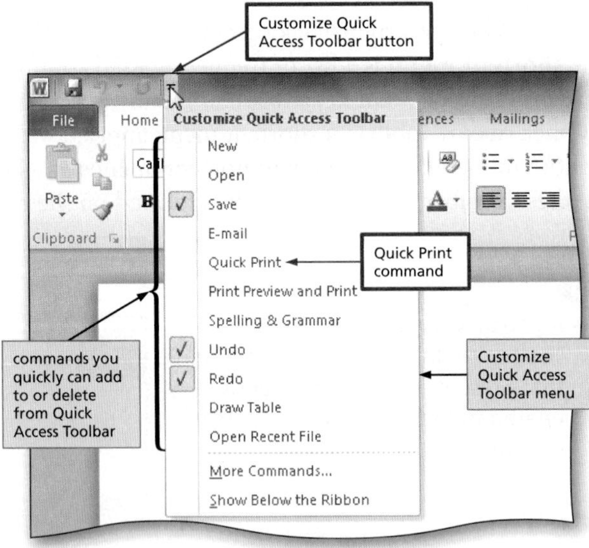

Figure 24

2

- Click Quick Print on the Customize Quick Access Toolbar menu to add the Quick Print button to the Quick Access Toolbar (Figure 25).

Q&A How would I remove a button from the Quick Access Toolbar?

You would right-click the button you wish to remove and then click Remove from Quick Access Toolbar on the shortcut menu. If you want your screens to match the screens in the remaining chapters in this book, you would remove the Quick Print button from the Quick Access Toolbar.

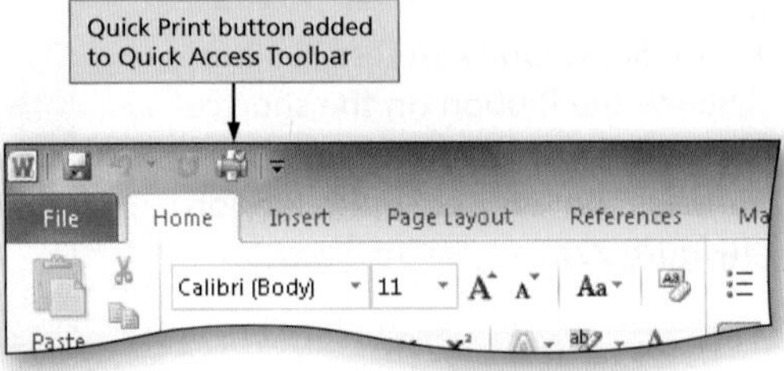

Figure 25

To Enter Text in a Document

The first step in creating a document is to enter its text by typing on the keyboard. By default, Word positions text at the left margin as you type. To begin creating a flyer, for example, you type the headline in the document window. The following steps type this first line of text, a headline, in a document.

- Type **SEE THE RENOVATED KOALA EXHIBIT** as the text (Figure 26).

Q&A What is the blinking vertical bar to the right of the text?

The insertion point. It indicates where text, graphics, and other items will be inserted in the document. As you type, the insertion point moves to the right, and when you reach the end of a line, it moves downward to the beginning of the next line.

Q&A What if I make an error while typing?

You can press the BACKSPACE key until you have deleted the text in error and then retype the text correctly.

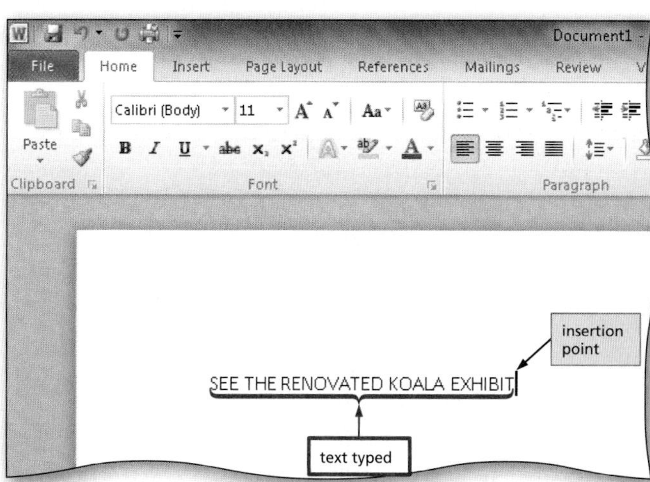

Figure 26

- Press the ENTER key to move the insertion point to the beginning of the next line (Figure 27).

Q&A Why did blank space appear between the entered text and the insertion point?

Each time you press the ENTER key, Word creates a new paragraph and inserts blank space between the two paragraphs.

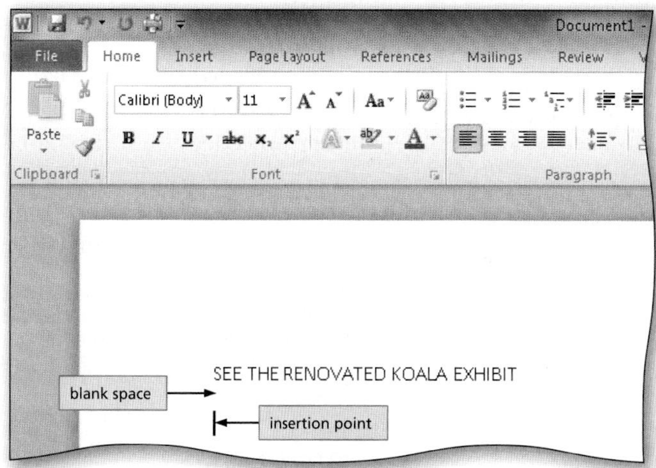

Figure 27

Saving and Organizing Files

While you are creating a document, the computer stores it in memory. When you save a document, the computer places it on a storage medium such as a hard disk, USB flash drive, or optical disc. A saved document is referred to as a file. A **file name** is the name assigned to a file when it is saved. It is important to save a document frequently for the following reasons:

- The document in memory might be lost if the computer is turned off or you lose electrical power while a program is running.
- If you run out of time before completing a project, you may finish it at a future time without starting over.

When saving files, you should organize them so that you easily can find them later. Windows 7 provides tools to help you organize files.

Organizing Files and Folders

A file contains data. This data can range from a research paper to an accounting spreadsheet to an electronic math quiz. You should organize and store these files in folders to avoid misplacing a file and to help you find a file quickly.

If you are a freshman taking an introductory computer class (CIS 101, for example), you may want to design a series of folders for the different subjects covered in the class. To accomplish this, you can arrange the folders in a hierarchy for the class, as shown in Figure 28.

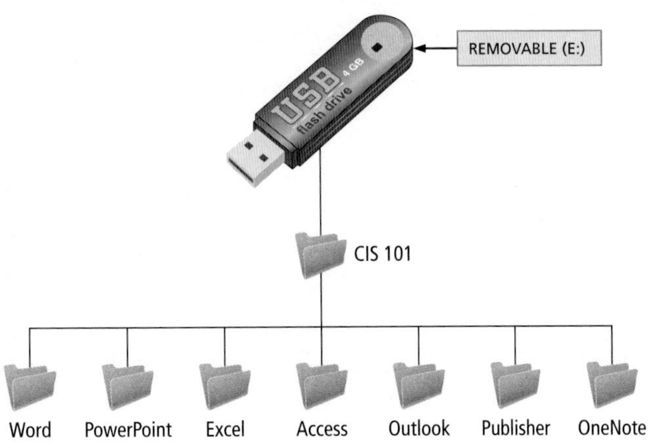

Figure 28

The hierarchy contains three levels. The first level contains the storage device, in this case a USB flash drive. Windows 7 identifies the storage device with a letter, and, in some cases, a name. In Figure 28, the USB flash drive is identified as REMOVABLE (E:). The second level contains the class folder (CIS 101, in this case), and the third level contains seven folders, one each for a different Office program that will be covered in the class (Word, PowerPoint, Excel, Access, Outlook, Publisher, and OneNote).

When the hierarchy in Figure 28 is created, the USB flash drive is said to contain the CIS 101 folder, and the CIS 101 folder is said to contain the separate Office folders (i.e., Word, PowerPoint, Excel, etc.). In addition, this hierarchy easily can be expanded to include folders from other classes taken during additional semesters.

The vertical and horizontal lines in Figure 28 form a pathway that allows you to navigate to a drive or folder on a computer or network. A **path** consists of a drive letter (preceded by a drive name when necessary) and colon, to identify the storage device, and one or more folder names. Each drive or folder in the hierarchy has a corresponding path.

Table 3 shows examples of paths and their corresponding drives and folders.

Table 3 Paths and Corresponding Drives and Folders

Path	Drive and Folder
Computer ▶ REMOVABLE (E:)	Drive E (REMOVABLE (E:))
Computer ▶ REMOVABLE (E:) ▶ CIS 101	CIS 101 folder on drive E
Computer ▶ REMOVABLE (E:) ▶ CIS 101 ▶ Word	Word folder in CIS 101 folder on drive E

BTW

Saving Online
Instead of saving files on a USB flash drive, some people prefer to save them online so that they can access the files from any computer with an Internet connection. For more information, read Appendix C.

The following pages illustrate the steps to organize folders for a class and save a file in a folder:

1. Create a folder identifying your class.
2. Create a Word folder in the folder identifying your class.
3. Save a file in the Word folder.
4. Verify the location of the saved file.

To Create a Folder

When you create a folder, such as the CIS 101 folder shown in Figure 28, you must name the folder. A folder name should describe the folder and its contents. A folder name can contain spaces and any uppercase or lowercase characters, except a backslash (\), slash (/), colon (:), asterisk (*), question mark (?), quotation marks ("), less than symbol (<), greater than symbol (>), or vertical bar (|). Folder names cannot be CON, AUX, COM1, COM2, COM3, COM4, LPT1, LPT2, LPT3, PRN, or NUL. The same rules for naming folders also apply to naming files.

To store files and folders on a USB flash drive, you must connect the USB flash drive to an available USB port on a computer. The following steps create your class folder (CIS 101, in this case) on a USB flash drive.

1

- Connect the USB flash drive to an available USB port on the computer to open the AutoPlay window (Figure 29). (You may need to click the Windows Explorer program button on the taskbar to make the AutoPlay window visible.)

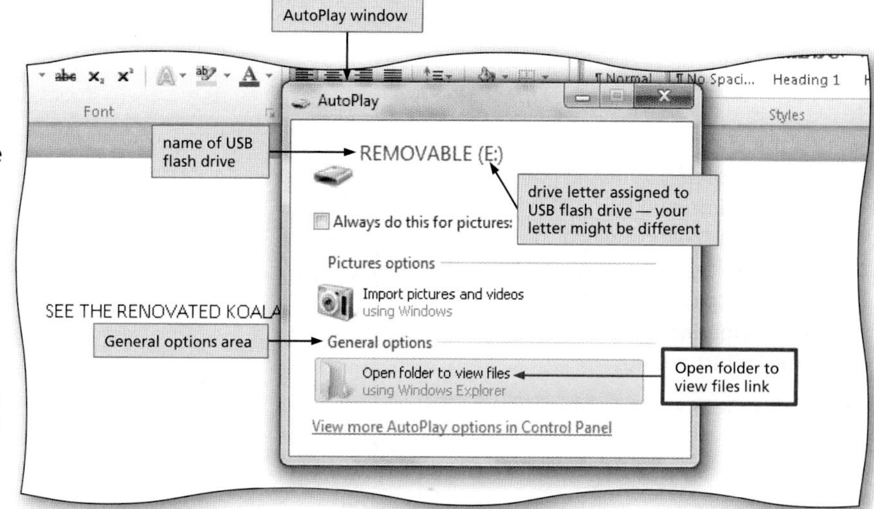

Figure 29

Q&A Why does the AutoPlay window not open?

Some computers are not configured to open an AutoPlay window. Instead, they might display the contents of the USB flash drive automatically, or you might need to access contents of the USB flash drive using the Computer window. To use the Computer window to display the USB flash drive's contents, click the Start button, click Computer on the Start menu, and then click the icon representing the USB flash drive and then proceed to Step 3 on the next page.

Q&A Why does the AutoPlay window look different from the one in Figure 29?

The AutoPlay window that opens on your computer might display different options. The type of USB flash drive, its contents, and the next available drive letter on your computer all will determine which options are displayed in the AutoPlay window.

2

- Click the 'Open folder to view files' link in the AutoPlay window to open the USB flash drive window (Figure 30).

Q&A Why does Figure 30 show REMOVABLE (E:) for the USB flash drive?

REMOVABLE is the name of the USB flash drive used to illustrate these steps. The (E:) refers to the drive letter assigned by Windows 7 to the USB flash drive. The name and drive letter of your USB flash drive probably will be different.

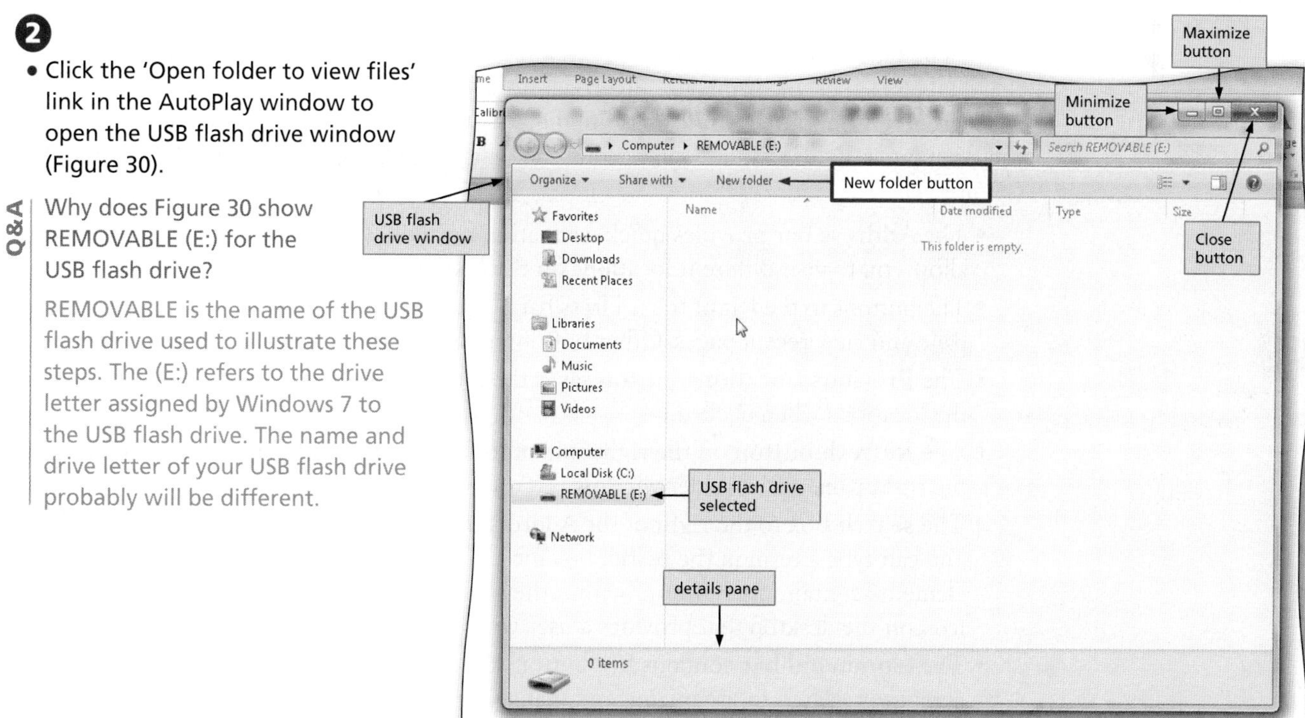

Figure 30

3

- Click the New folder button on the toolbar to display a new folder icon with the name, New folder, selected in a text box.
- Type `CIS 101` (or your class code) in the text box to name the folder.
- Press the ENTER key to create a folder identifying your class on the selected drive (Figure 31). If the CIS 101 folder does not appear in the navigation pane, double-click REMOVABLE (E:) in the navigation pane to display the folder just added.

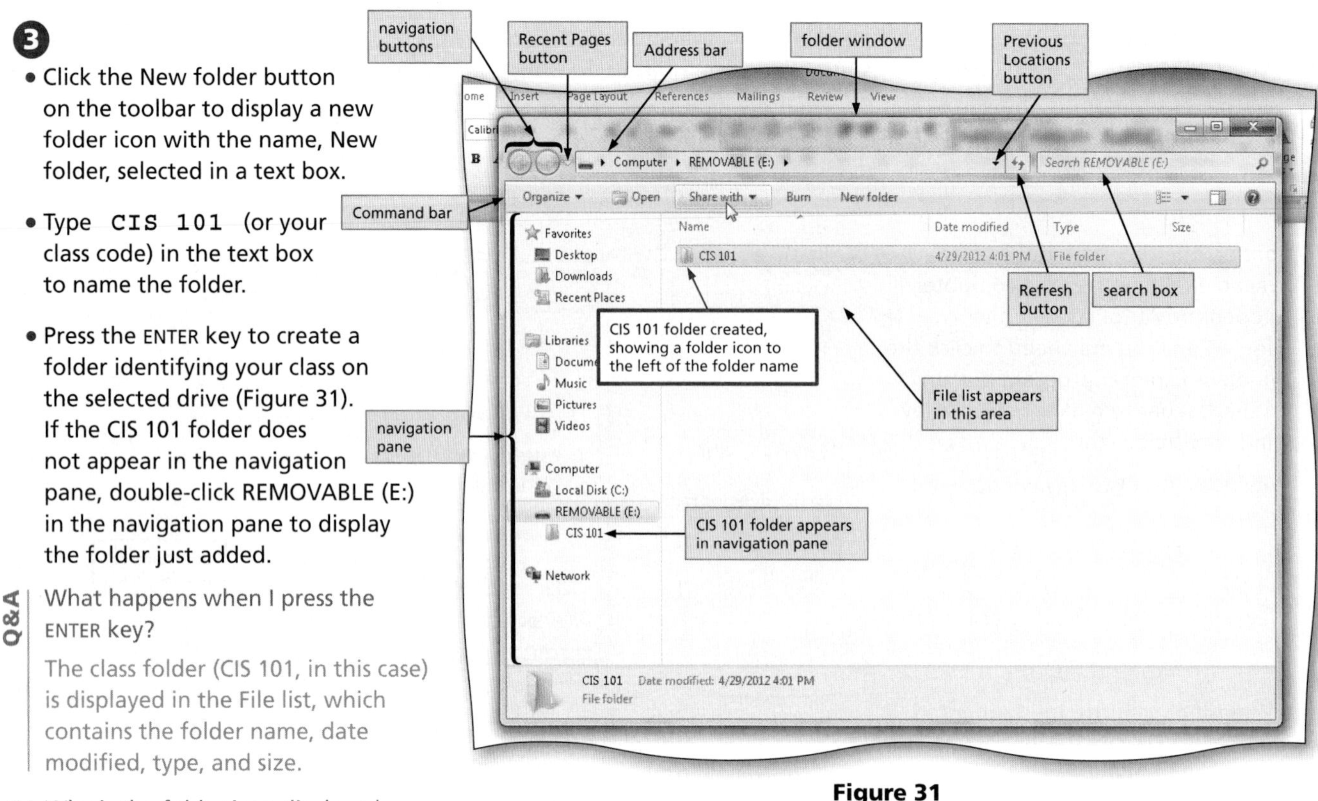

Figure 31

Q&A What happens when I press the ENTER key?

The class folder (CIS 101, in this case) is displayed in the File list, which contains the folder name, date modified, type, and size.

Q&A Why is the folder icon displayed differently on my computer?

Windows might be configured to display contents differently on your computer.

Folder Windows

The USB flash drive window (shown in Figure 31) is called a folder window. Recall that a folder is a specific named location on a storage medium that contains related files. Most users rely on **folder windows** for finding, viewing, and managing information on their computer. Folder windows have common design elements, including the following (Figure 31).

- The **Address bar** provides quick navigation options. The arrows on the Address bar allow you to visit different locations on the computer.
- The buttons to the left of the Address bar allow you to navigate the contents of the left pane and view recent pages. Other buttons allow you to specify the size of the window.
- The **Previous Locations button** saves the locations you have visited and displays the locations when clicked.
- The **Refresh button** on the right side of the Address bar refreshes the contents of the right pane of the folder window.
- The **search box** to the right of the Address bar contains the dimmed word, Search. You can type a term in the search box for a list of files, folders, shortcuts, and elements containing that term within the location you are searching. A **shortcut** is an icon on the desktop that provides a user with immediate access to a program or file.
- The **Command bar** contains five buttons used to accomplish various tasks on the computer related to organizing and managing the contents of the open window.
- The **navigation pane** on the left contains the Favorites area, Libraries area, Computer area, and Network area.

- The **Favorites area** contains links to your favorite locations. By default, this list contains only links to your Desktop, Downloads, and Recent Places.
- The **Libraries area** shows links to files and folders that have been included in a library.

A **library** helps you manage multiple folders and files stored in various locations on a computer. It does not store the files and folders; rather, it displays links to them so that you can access them quickly. For example, you can save pictures from a digital camera in any folder on any storage location on a computer. Normally, this would make organizing the different folders difficult; however, if you add the folders to a library, you can access all the pictures from one location regardless of where they are stored.

To Create a Folder within a Folder

With the class folder created, you can create folders that will store the files you create using Word. The following steps create a Word folder in the CIS 101 folder (or the folder identifying your class).

1

- Double-click the icon or folder name for the CIS 101 folder (or the folder identifying your class) in the File list to open the folder (Figure 32).

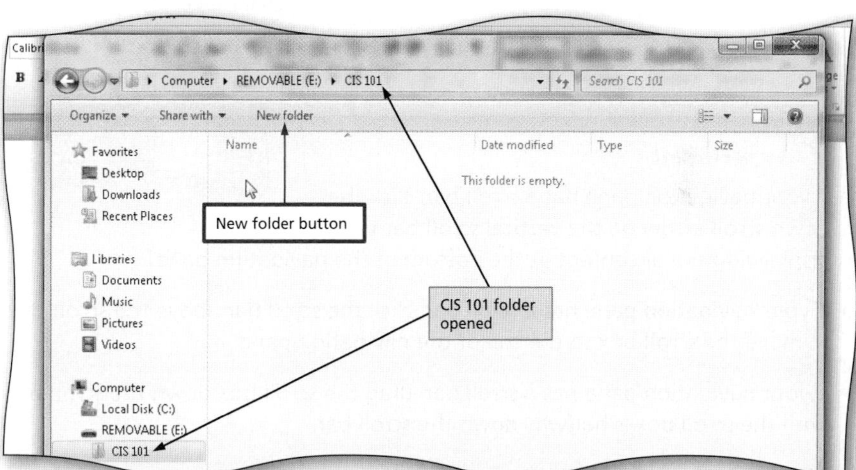

Figure 32

- Click the New folder button on the toolbar to display a new folder icon and text box for the folder.
- Type `Word` in the text box to name the folder.
- Press the ENTER key to create the folder (Figure 33).

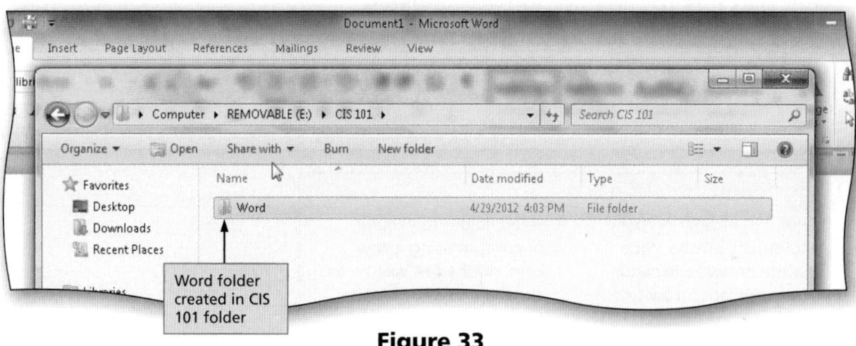

Figure 33

To Expand a Folder, Scroll through Folder Contents, and Collapse a Folder

Folder windows display the hierarchy of items and the contents of drives and folders in the right pane. You might want to expand a drive in the navigation pane to view its contents, scroll through its contents, and collapse it when you are finished viewing its contents. When a folder is expanded, it lists all the folders it contains. By contrast, a collapsed folder does not list the folders it contains. The steps on the next page expand, scroll through, and then collapse the folder identifying your class (CIS 101, in this case).

1

- Double-click the folder identifying your class (CIS 101, in this case) in the navigation pane, which expands the folder to display its contents and displays a black arrow to the left of the folder icon (Figure 34).

Q&A Why is the Word folder indented below the CIS 101 folder in the navigation pane?

It shows that the folder is contained within the CIS 101 folder.

Q&A Why did a scroll bar appear in the navigation pane?

When all contents cannot fit in a window or pane, a scroll bar appears. As described earlier, you can view areas currently not visible by (1) clicking the scroll arrows, (2) clicking above or below the scroll bar, and (3) dragging the scroll box.

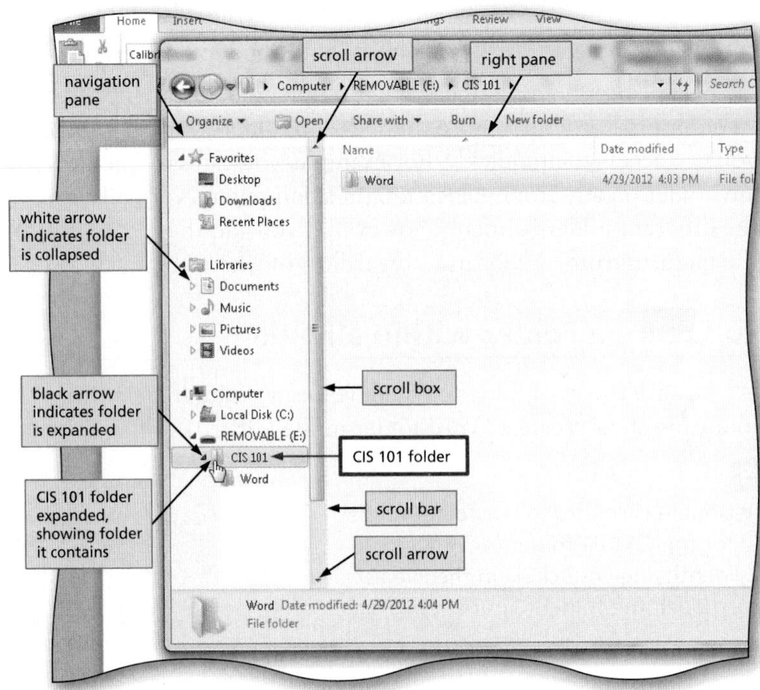

Figure 34

Experiment

- If your navigation pane has a scroll bar, click the down scroll arrow on the vertical scroll bar to display additional content at the bottom of the navigation pane.
- If your navigation pane has a scroll bar, click the scroll bar above the scroll box to move the scroll box to the top of the navigation pane.
- If your navigation pane has a scroll bar, drag the scroll box down the scroll bar until the scroll box is halfway down the scroll bar.

2

- Double-click the folder identifying your class (CIS 101, in this case) in the navigation pane to collapse the folder (Figure 35).

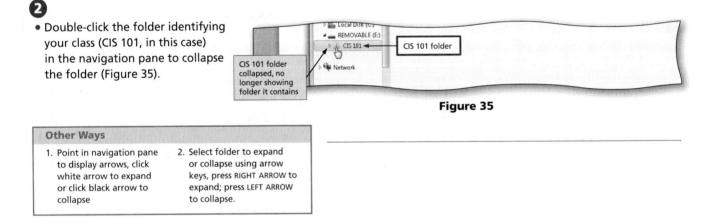

Figure 35

Other Ways	
1. Point in navigation pane to display arrows, click white arrow to expand or click black arrow to collapse	2. Select folder to expand or collapse using arrow keys, press RIGHT ARROW to expand; press LEFT ARROW to collapse.

To Switch from One Program to Another

The next step is to save the Word file containing the headline you typed earlier. Word, however, currently is not the active window. You can use the program button on the taskbar and live preview to switch to Word and then save the document in the Word document window.

If Windows Aero is active on your computer, Windows displays a live preview window whenever you move your mouse on a button or click a button on the taskbar. If Aero is not supported or enabled on your computer, you will see a window title instead of a live preview. These steps use the Word program; however, the steps are the same for any active Office program currently displayed as a program button on the taskbar.

The next steps switch to the Word window.

- Point to the Word program button on the taskbar to see a live preview of the open document(s) or the window title(s) of the open document(s), depending on your computer's configuration (Figure 36).

2

- Click the program button or the live preview to make the program associated with the program button the active window (shown in Figure 27 on page OFF 19).

Q&A What if multiple documents are open in a program?

If Aero is enabled on your computer, click the desired live preview. If Aero is not supported or not enabled, click the window title.

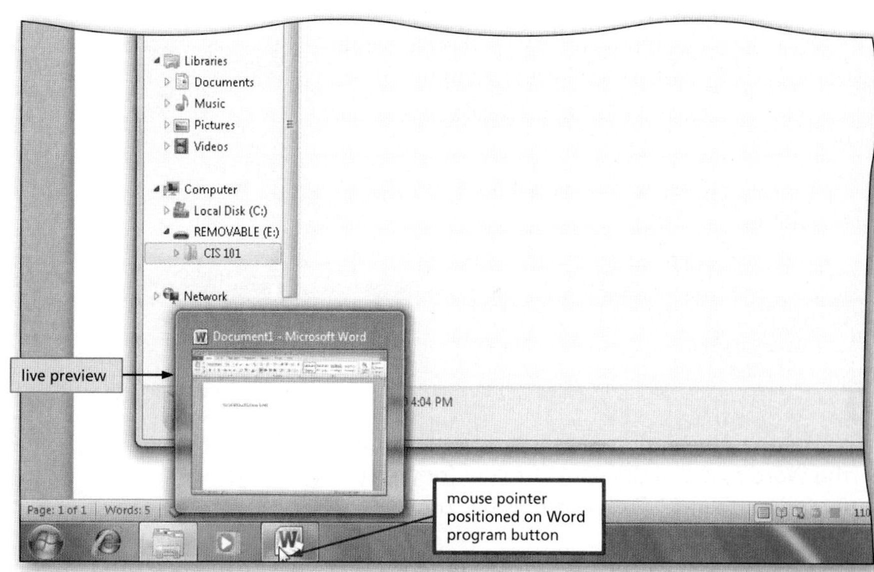

Figure 36

To Save a File in a Folder

Now that you have created the Word folder for storing files, you can save the Word document in that folder. The following steps save a file on a USB flash drive in the Word folder contained in your class folder (CIS 101, in this case) using the file name, Koala Exhibit.

1

- With a USB flash drive connected to one of the computer's USB ports, click the Save button on the Quick Access Toolbar to display the Save As dialog box (Figure 37).

Q&A Why does a file name already appear in the File name text box?

Word automatically suggests a file name the first time you save a document. The file name normally consists of the first few words contained in the document. Because the suggested file name is selected, you do not need to delete it; as soon as you begin typing, the new file name replaces the selected text.

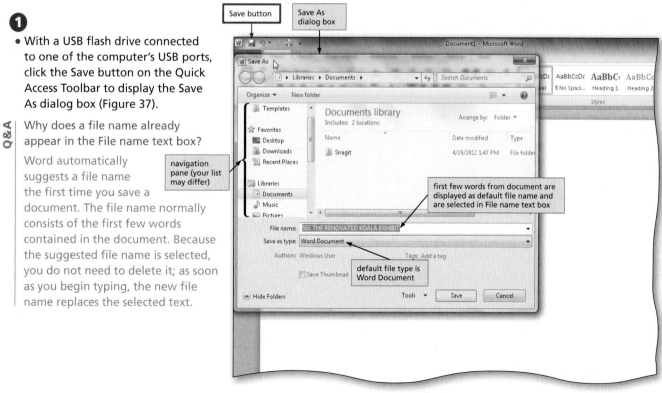

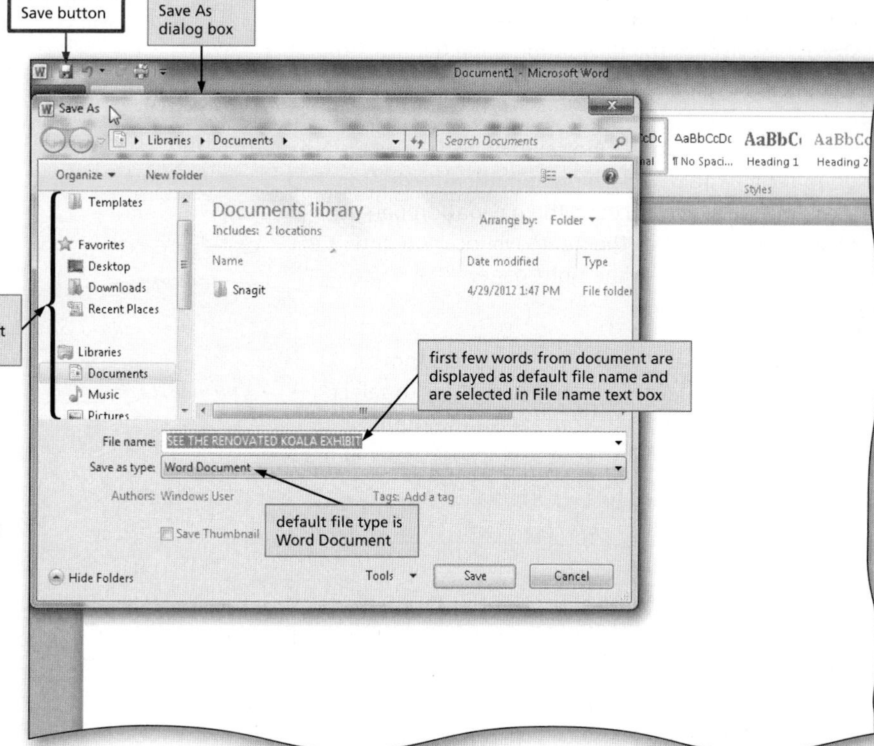

Figure 37

- Type **Koala Exhibit** in the File name text box (Save As dialog box) to change the file name. Do not press the ENTER key after typing the file name because you do not want to close the dialog box at this time (Figure 38).

Q&A What characters can I use in a file name?

The only invalid characters are the backslash (\), slash (/), colon (:), asterisk (*), question mark (?), quotation mark ("), less than symbol (<), greater than symbol (>), and vertical bar (|).

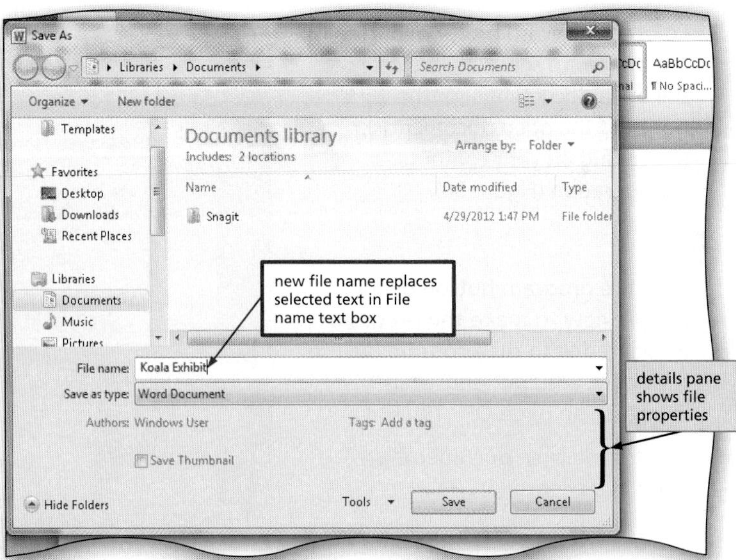

Figure 38

- Navigate to the desired save location (in this case, the Word folder in the CIS 101 folder [or your class folder] on the USB flash drive) by performing the tasks in Steps 3a – 3c.

- If the navigation pane is not displayed in the dialog box, click the Browse Folders button to expand the dialog box.
- If Computer is not displayed in the navigation pane, drag the navigation pane scroll bar until Computer appears.
- If Computer is not expanded in the navigation pane, double-click Computer to display a list of available storage devices in the navigation pane.
- If necessary, scroll through the dialog box until your USB flash drive appears in the list of available storage devices in the navigation pane (Figure 39).

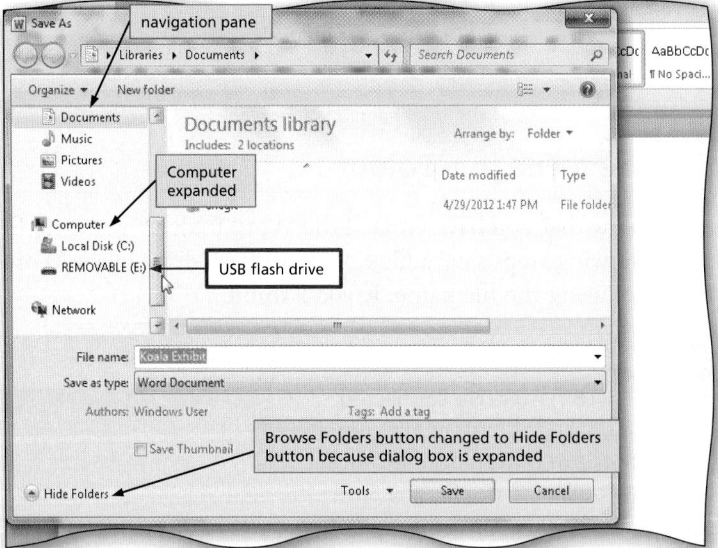

Figure 39

- If your USB flash drive is not expanded, double-click the USB flash drive in the list of available storage devices in the navigation pane to select that drive as the new save location and display its contents in the right pane.

- If your class folder (CIS 101, in this case) is not expanded, double-click the CIS 101 folder to select the folder and display its contents in the right pane.

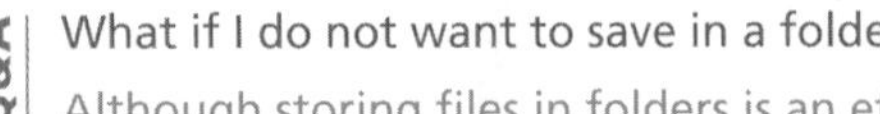

Q&A What if I do not want to save in a folder?

Although storing files in folders is an effective technique for organizing files, some users prefer not to store files in folders. If you prefer not to save this file in a folder, skip all instructions in Step 3c and proceed to Step 4.

- Click the Word folder to select the folder and display its contents in the right pane (Figure 40).

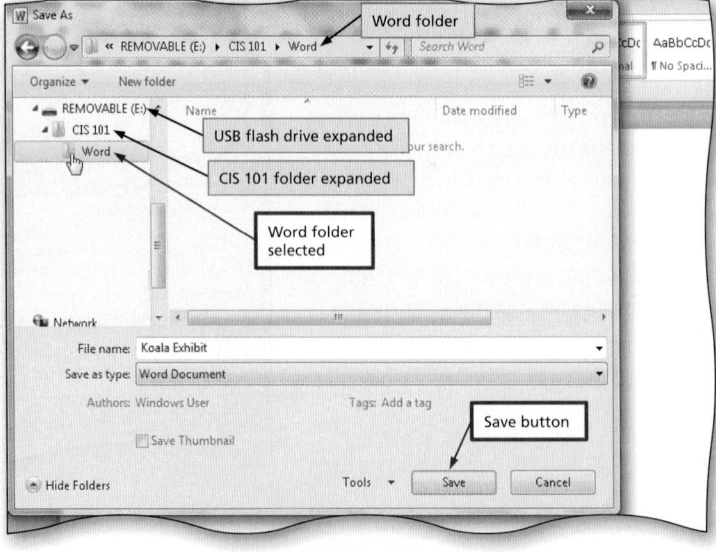

Figure 40

- Click the Save button (Save As dialog box) to save the document in the selected folder on the selected drive with the entered file name (Figure 41).

Q&A How do I know that the file is saved?

While an Office program such as Word is saving a file, it briefly displays a message on the status bar indicating the amount of the file saved. In addition, the USB flash drive may have a light that flashes during the save process.

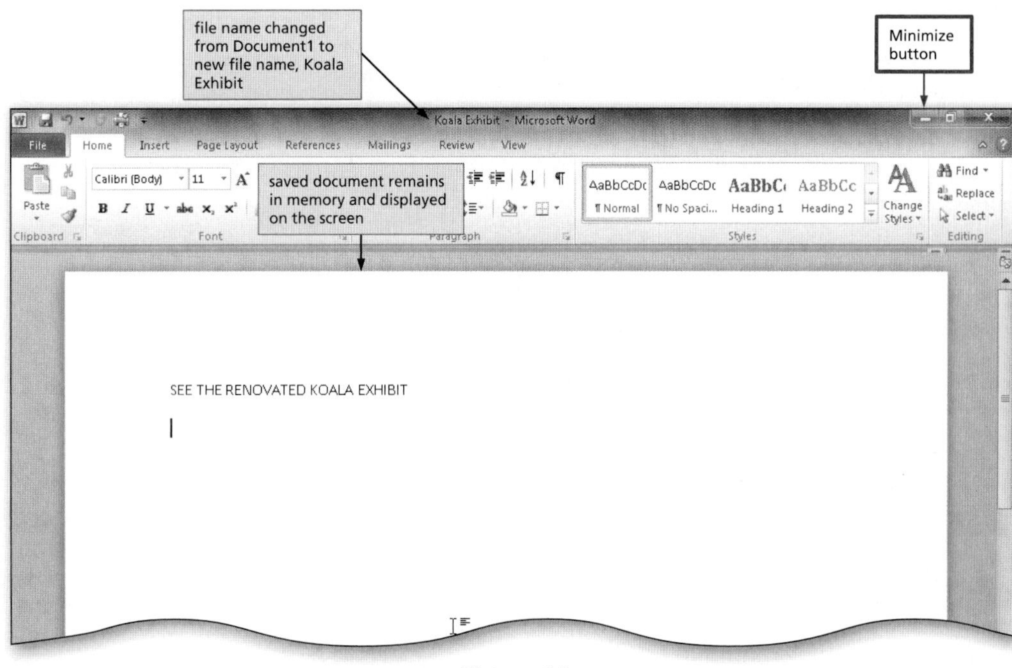

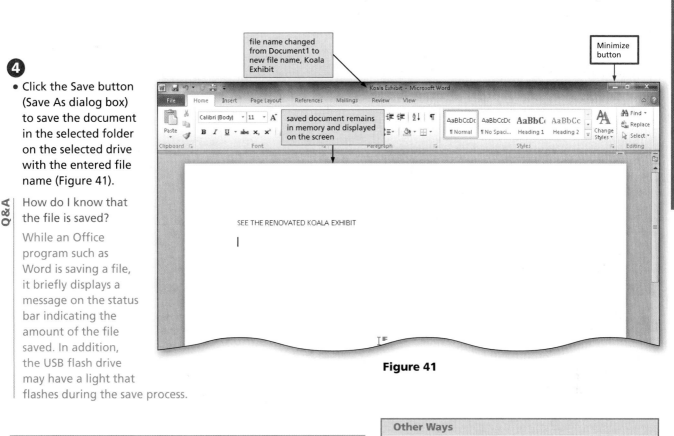

Figure 41

Other Ways	
1. Click File on Ribbon, click Save, type file name, navigate to desired save location, click Save button	2. Press CTRL+S or press SHIFT+F12, type file name, navigate to desired save location, click Save button

Navigating in Dialog Boxes

Navigating is the process of finding a location on a storage device. While saving the Koala Exhibit file, for example, Steps 3a – 3c in the previous set of steps navigated to the Word folder located in the CIS 101 folder. When performing certain functions in Windows programs, such as saving a file, opening a file, or inserting a picture in an existing document, you most likely will have to navigate to the location where you want to save the file or to the folder containing the file you want to open or insert. Most dialog boxes in Windows programs requiring navigation follow a similar procedure; that is, the way you navigate to a folder in one dialog box, such as the Save As dialog box, is similar to how you might navigate in another dialog box, such as the Open dialog box. If you chose to navigate to a specific location in a dialog box, you would follow the instructions in Steps 3a – 3c on page OFF 26.

File Type
Depending on your Windows 7 settings, the file type .docx may be displayed immediately to the right of the file name after you save the file. The file type .docx is a Word 2010 document.

To Minimize and Restore a Window

Before continuing, you can verify that the Word file was saved properly. To do this, you will minimize the Word window and then open the USB flash drive window so that you can verify the file is stored on the USB flash drive. A **minimized window** is an open window hidden from view but that can be displayed quickly by clicking the window's program button on the taskbar.

In the following example, Word is used to illustrate minimizing and restoring windows; however, you would follow the same steps regardless of the Office program you are using.

The steps on the next page minimize the Word window, verify that the file is saved, and then restore the minimized window.

1

- Click the Minimize button on the program's title bar (shown in Figure 41 on the previous page) to minimize the window (Figure 42).

Q&A Is the minimized window still available?

The minimized window, Word in this case, remains available but no longer is the active window. It is minimized as a program button on the taskbar.

- If necessary, click the Windows Explorer program button on the taskbar to open the USB flash drive window.

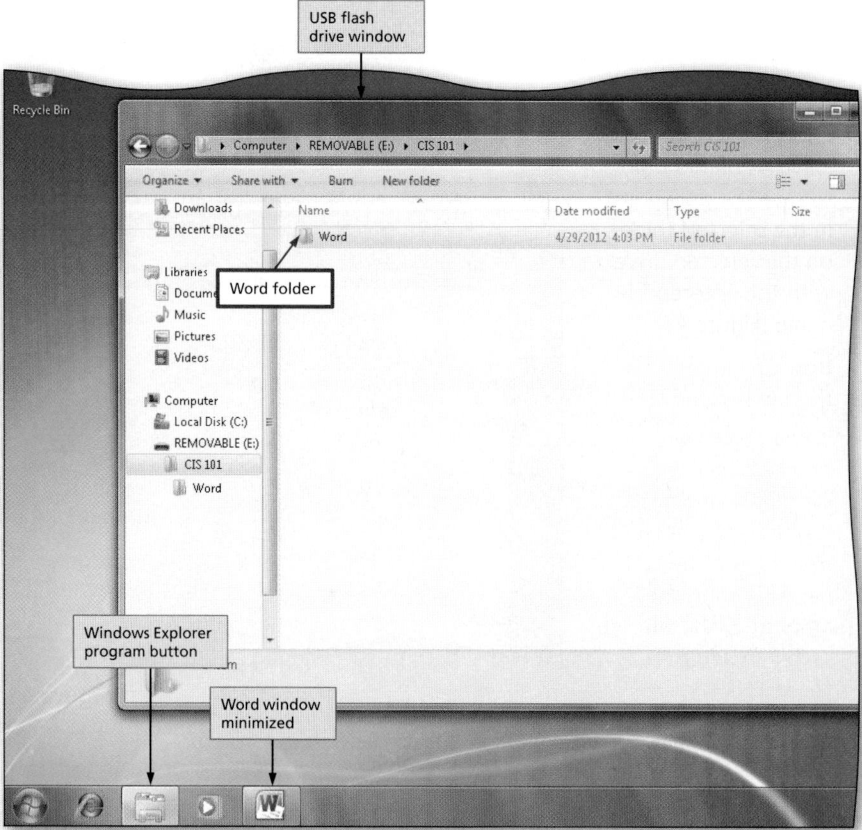

Figure 42

2

- Double-click the Word folder to select the folder and display its contents (Figure 43).

Q&A Why does the Windows Explorer button on the taskbar change?

The button changes to reflect the status of the folder window (in this case, the USB flash drive window). A selected button indicates that the folder window is active on the screen. When the button is not selected, the window is open but not active.

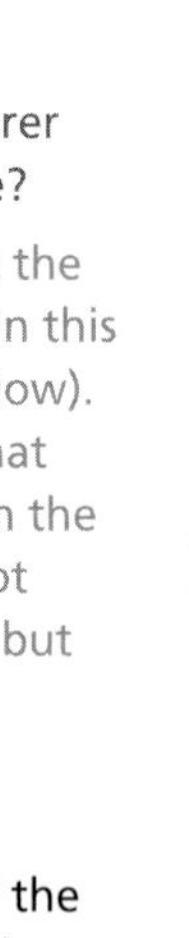

3

- After viewing the contents of the selected folder, click the Word program button on the taskbar to restore the minimized window (as shown in Figure 41 on the previous page).

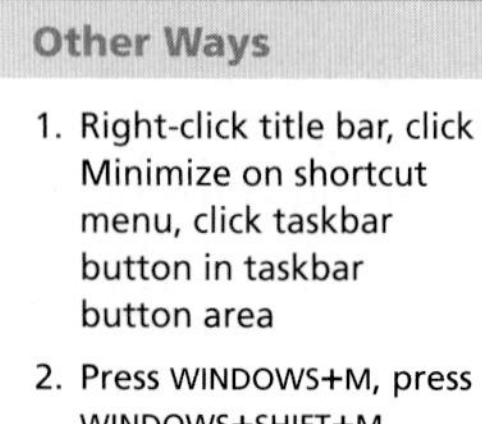

Other Ways

1. Right-click title bar, click Minimize on shortcut menu, click taskbar button in taskbar button area
2. Press WINDOWS+M, press WINDOWS+SHIFT+M

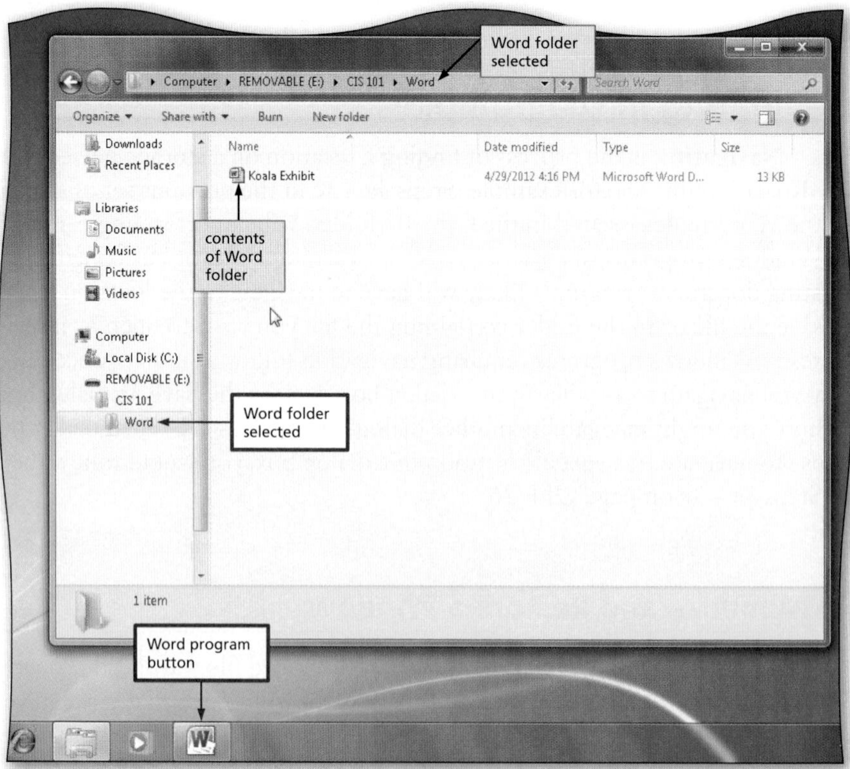

Figure 43

Screen Resolution

Screen resolution indicates the number of pixels (dots) that the computer uses to display the letters, numbers, graphics, and background you see on the screen. When you increase the screen resolution, Windows displays more information on the screen, but the information decreases in size. The reverse also is true: as you decrease the screen resolution, Windows displays less information on the screen, but the information increases in size.

Screen resolution usually is stated as the product of two numbers, such as 1024 × 768 (pronounced "ten twenty-four by seven sixty-eight"). A 1024 × 768 screen resolution results in a display of 1,024 distinct pixels on each of 768 lines, or about 786,432 pixels. Changing the screen resolution affects how the Ribbon appears in Office programs. Figure 44, for example, shows the Word Ribbon at screen resolutions of 1024 × 768 and 1280 × 800. All of the same commands are available regardless of screen resolution. Word, however, makes changes to the groups and the buttons within the groups to accommodate the various screen resolutions. The result is that certain commands may need to be accessed differently depending on the resolution chosen. A command that is visible on the Ribbon and available by clicking a button at one resolution may not be visible and may need to be accessed using its Dialog Box Launcher at a different resolution.

Comparing the two Ribbons in Figure 44, notice the changes in content and layout of the groups and galleries. In some cases, the content of a group is the same in each resolution, but the layout of the group differs. For example, the same gallery and buttons appear in the Styles groups in the two resolutions, but the layouts differ. In other cases, the content and layout are the same across the resolution, but the level of detail differs with the resolution. In the Clipboard group, when the resolution increases to 1280 × 800, the names of all the buttons in the group appear in addition to the buttons themselves. At the lower resolution, only the buttons appear.

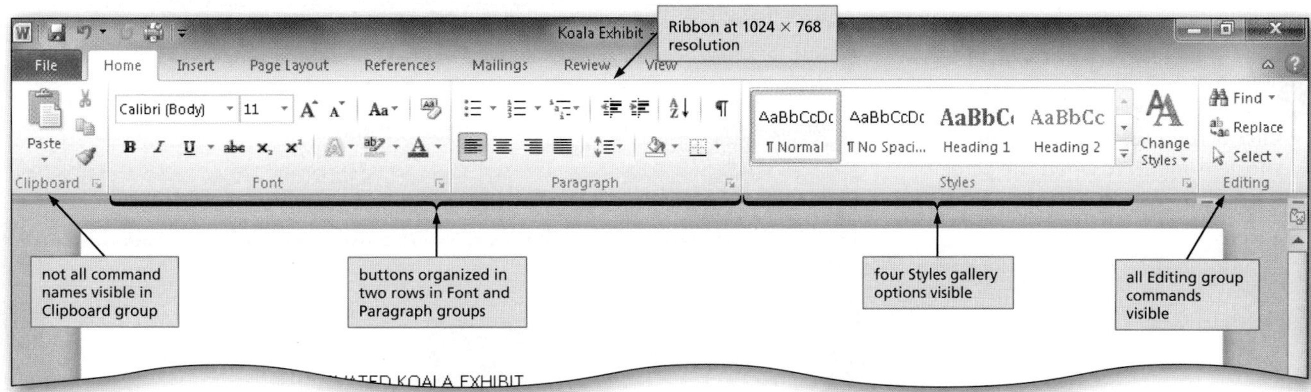

Figure 44 (a) Ribbon at Resolution of 1024 x 768

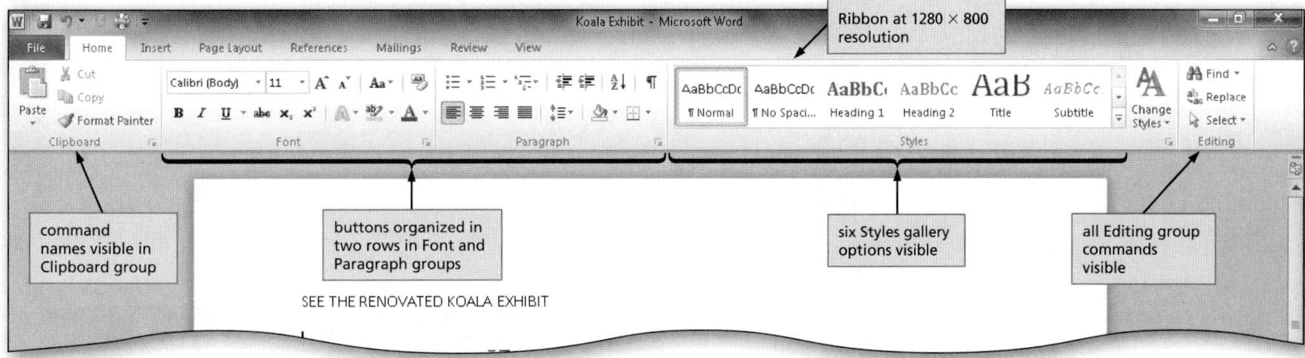

Figure 44 (b) Ribbon at Resolution of 1280 x 800

To Change the Screen Resolution

If you are using a computer to step through the chapters in this book and you want your screen to match the figures, you may need to change your screen's resolution. The figures in this book use a screen resolution of 1024 × 768. The following steps change the screen resolution to 1024 × 768. Your computer already may be set to 1024 × 768 or some other resolution. Keep in mind that many computer labs prevent users from changing the screen resolution; in that case, read the following steps for illustration purposes.

- Click the Show desktop button on the taskbar to display the Windows 7 desktop.
- Right-click an empty area on the Windows 7 desktop to display a shortcut menu that displays a list of commands related to the desktop (Figure 45).

Q&A Why does my shortcut menu display different commands?

Depending on your computer's hardware and configuration, different commands might appear on the shortcut menu.

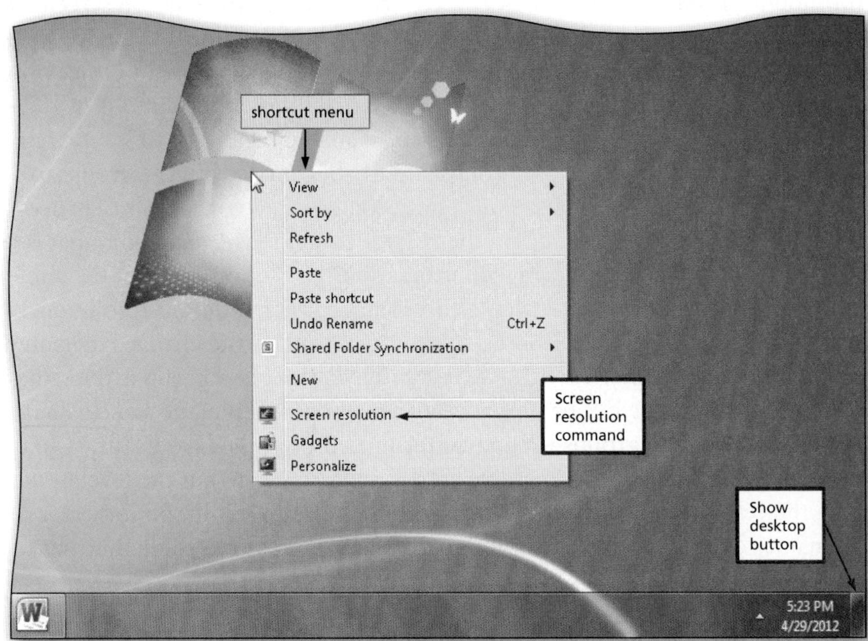

Figure 45

- Click Screen resolution on the shortcut menu to open the Screen Resolution window (Figure 46).

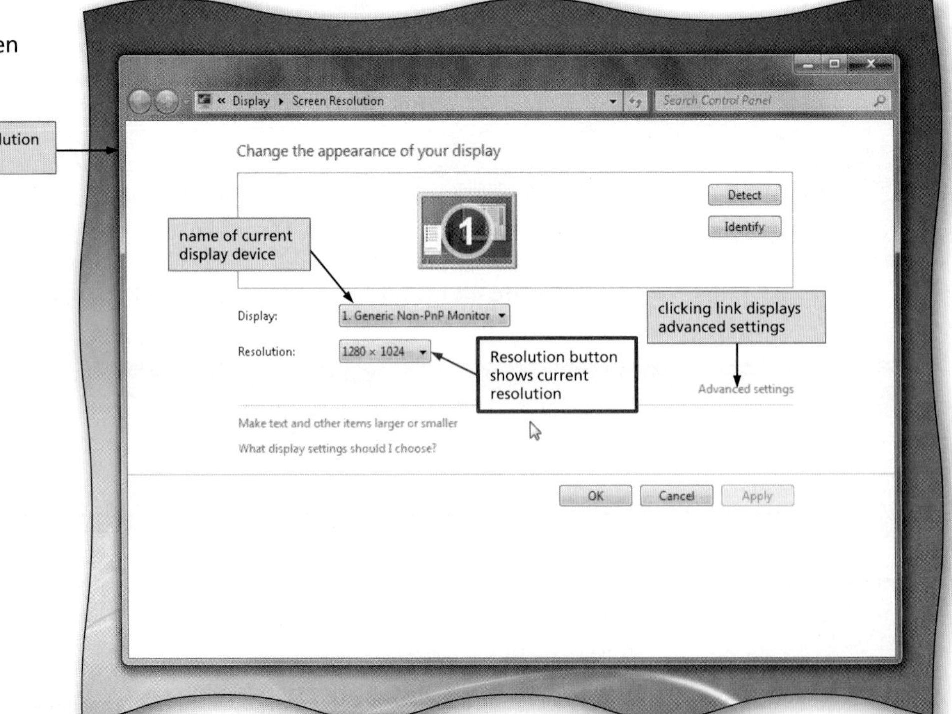

Figure 46

3

- Click the Resolution button in the Screen Resolution window to display the resolution slider.

Q&A What is a slider?

A **slider** is an object that allows users to choose from multiple predetermined options. In most cases, these options represent some type of numeric value. In most cases, one end of the slider (usually the left or bottom) represents the lowest of available values, and the opposite end (usually the right or top) represents the highest available value.

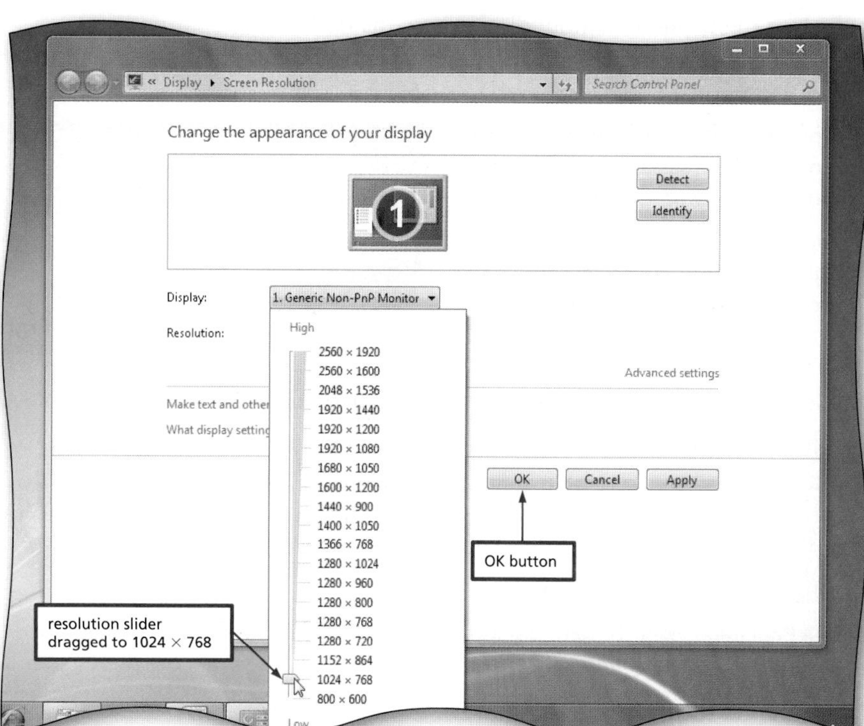

Figure 47

4

- If necessary, drag the resolution slider until the desired screen resolution (in this case, 1024 × 768) is selected (Figure 47).

Q&A What if my computer does not support the 1024 × 768 resolution?

Some computers do not support the 1024 × 768 resolution. In this case, select a resolution that is close to the 1024 × 768 resolution.

5

- Click an empty area of the Screen Resolution window to close the resolution slider.
- Click the OK button to change the screen resolution and display the Display Settings dialog box (Figure 48).
- Click the Keep changes button (Display Settings dialog box) to accept the new screen resolution.

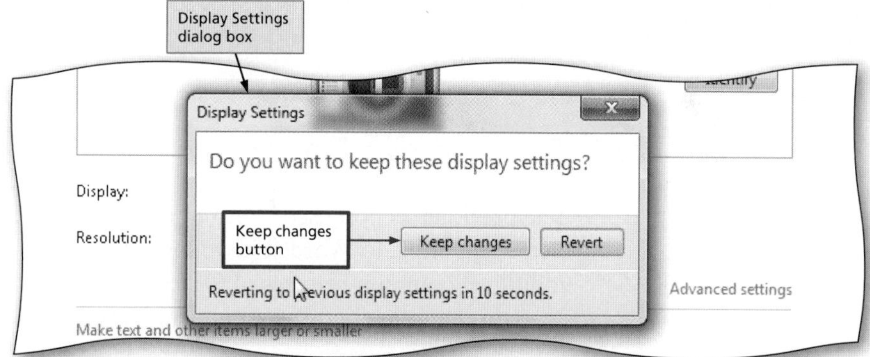

Figure 48

Q&A Why does a message display stating that the image quality can be improved?

Some computer monitors are designed to display contents better at a certain screen resolution, sometimes referred to as an optimal resolution.

To Quit a Program with One Document Open

When you quit an Office program, such as Word, if you have made changes to a file since the last time the file was saved, the Office program displays a dialog box asking if you want to save the changes you made to the file before it closes the program window. The dialog box contains three buttons with these resulting actions: the Save button saves the changes and then quits the Office program, the Don't Save button quits the Office program without saving changes, and the Cancel button closes the dialog box and redisplays the file without saving the changes.

If no changes have been made to an open document since the last time the file was saved, the Office program will close the window without displaying a dialog box.

The following steps quit Word. You would follow similar steps in other Office programs.

- If necessary, click the Word program button on the taskbar to display the Word window on the desktop.
- Point to the Close button on the right side of the program's title bar, Word in this case (Figure 49).

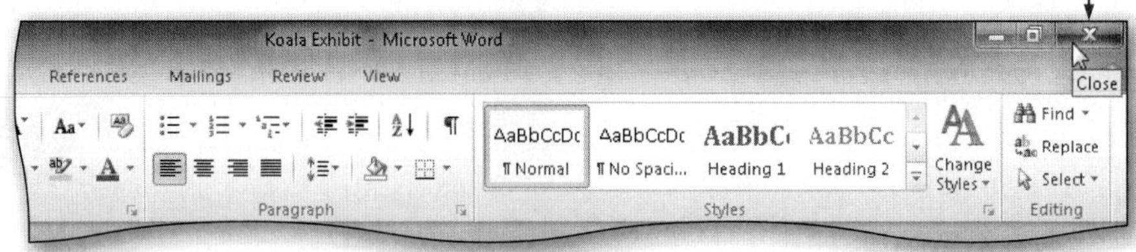

Figure 49

- Click the Close button to close the document and quit Word.

Q&A What if I have more than one document open in Word?

You would click the Close button for each open document. When you click the last open document's Close button, Word also quits. As an alternative, you could click File on the Ribbon to open the Backstage view and then click Exit in the Backstage view to close all open documents and quit Word.

Q&A What is the Backstage view?

The **Backstage view** contains a set of commands that enable you to manage documents and data about the documents. The Backstage view is discussed in more depth later in this chapter.

- If a Microsoft Word dialog box appears, click the Save button to save any changes made to the document since the last save.

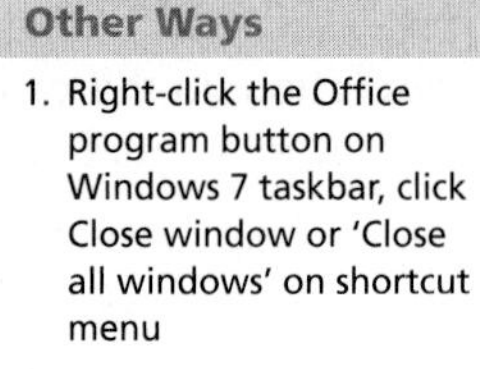

Other Ways

1. Right-click the Office program button on Windows 7 taskbar, click Close window or 'Close all windows' on shortcut menu
2. Press ALT+F4

Break Point: If you wish to take a break, this is a good place to do so. To resume at a later time, continue to follow the steps from this location forward.

Additional Common Features of Office Programs

The previous section used Word to illustrate common features of Office and some basic elements unique to Word. The following sections continue to use Word to present additional common features of Office.

In the following pages, you will learn how to do the following:

1. Start an Office program (Word) using the search box.
2. Open a document in an Office program (Word).
3. Close the document.
4. Reopen the document just closed.
5. Create a blank Office document from Windows Explorer and then open the file.
6. Save a document with a new file name.

To Start a Program Using the Search Box

The next steps, which assume Windows 7 is running, use the search box to start Word based on a typical installation; however, you would follow similar steps to start any program. You may need to ask your instructor how to start programs for your computer.

1

- Click the Start button on the Windows 7 taskbar to display the Start menu.

2

- Type **Microsoft Word** as the search text in the 'Search programs and files' text box and watch the search results appear on the Start menu (Figure 50).

Q&A Do I need to type the complete program name or correct capitalization?

No, just enough of it for the program name to appear on the Start menu. For example, you may be able to type Word or word, instead of Microsoft Word.

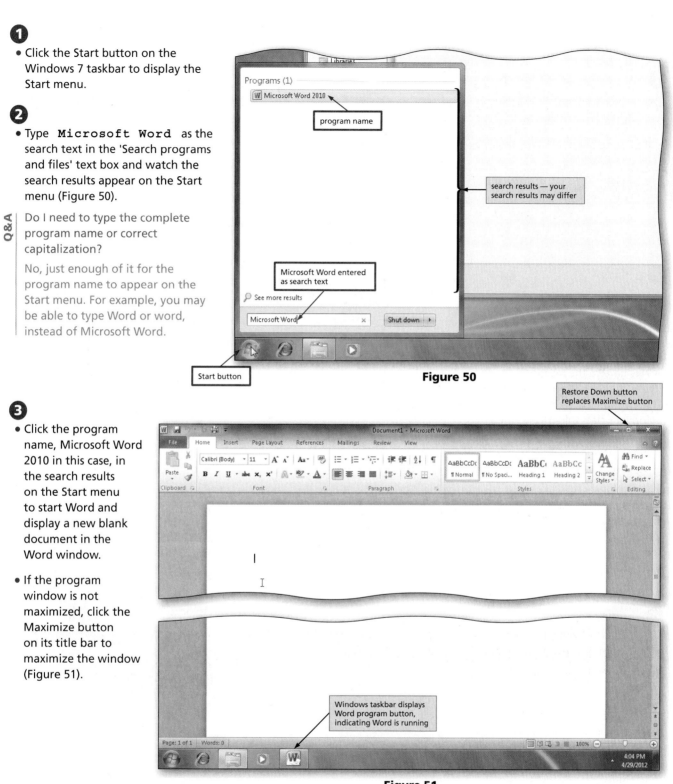

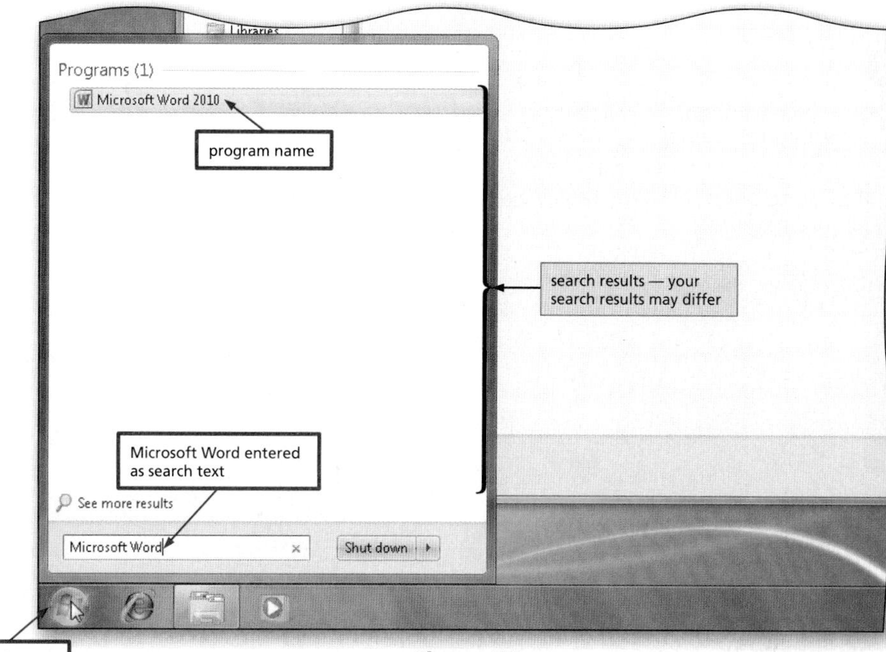

Figure 50

3

- Click the program name, Microsoft Word 2010 in this case, in the search results on the Start menu to start Word and display a new blank document in the Word window.
- If the program window is not maximized, click the Maximize button on its title bar to maximize the window (Figure 51).

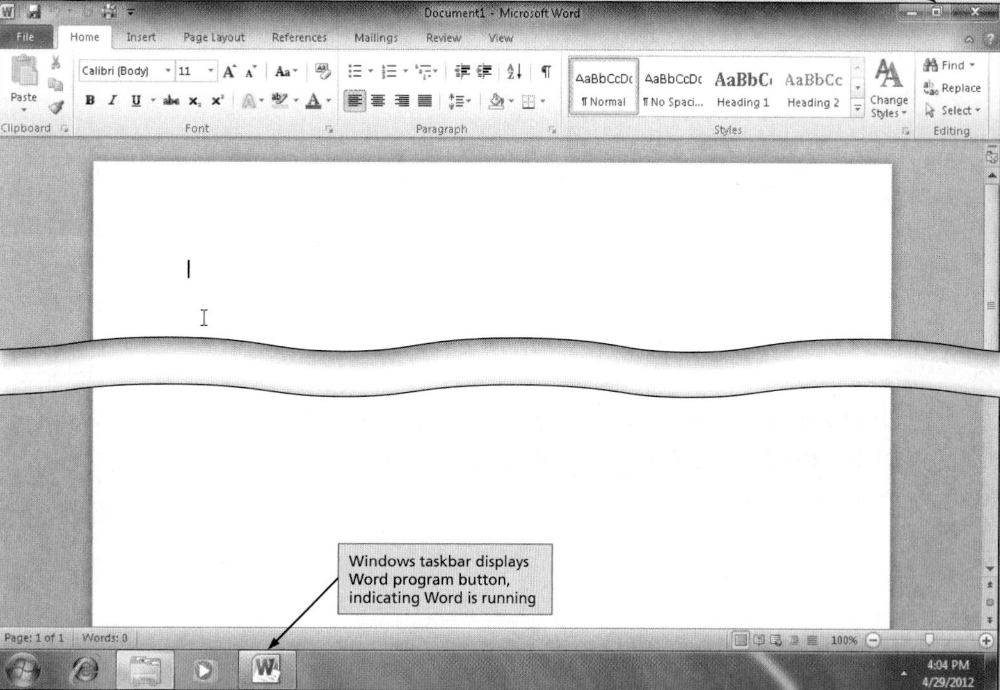

Figure 51

To Open an Existing File from the Backstage View

As discussed earlier, the Backstage view provides data about documents and contains a set of commands that assist you with managing documents. From the Backstage view in Word, for example, you can create, open, print, and save documents. You also can share documents, manage versions, set permissions, and modify document properties.

Assume you wish to continue working on an existing file, that is, a file you previously saved. The following steps use the Backstage view to open a saved file, specifically the Koala Exhibit file, from the USB flash drive.

1

- With your USB flash drive connected to one of the computer's USB ports, if necessary, click File on the Ribbon to open the Backstage view (Figure 52).

Q&A What is the purpose of the File tab?

The File tab is used to display the Backstage view for each Office program.

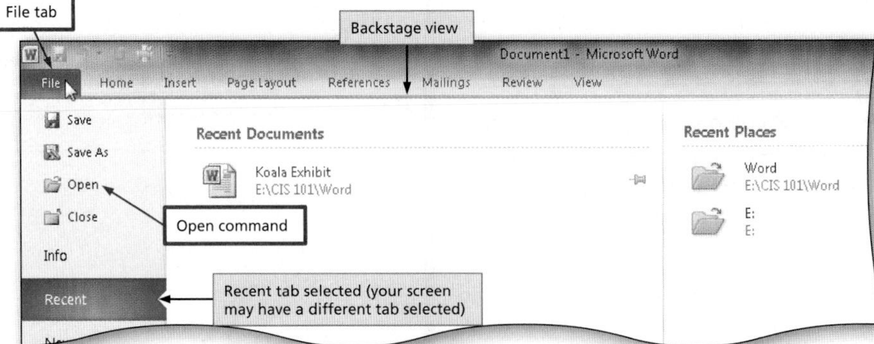

Figure 52

- Click Open in the Backstage view to display the Open dialog box (Figure 53).

- Navigate to the location of the file to be opened (in this case, the USB flash drive, then to the CIS 101 folder [or your class folder], and then to the Word folder). For detailed steps about navigating, see Steps 3a – 3c on page OFF 26.

Q&A What if I did not save my file in a folder?

If you did not save your file in a folder, the file you wish to open should be displayed in the Open dialog box before navigating to any folders.

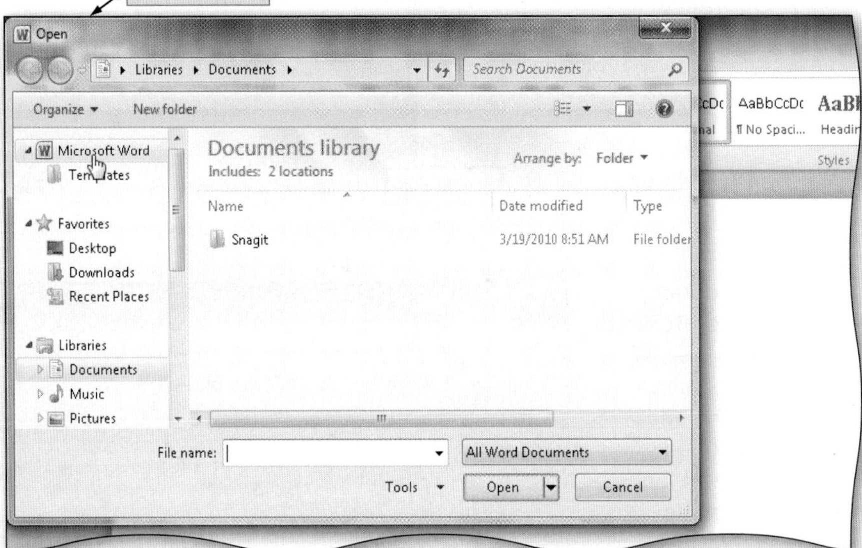

Figure 53

- Click the file to be opened, Koala Exhibit in this case, to select the file (Figure 54).

- Click the Open button (Open dialog box) to open the selected file and display the opened file in the current program window (shown in Figure 41 on page OFF 27).

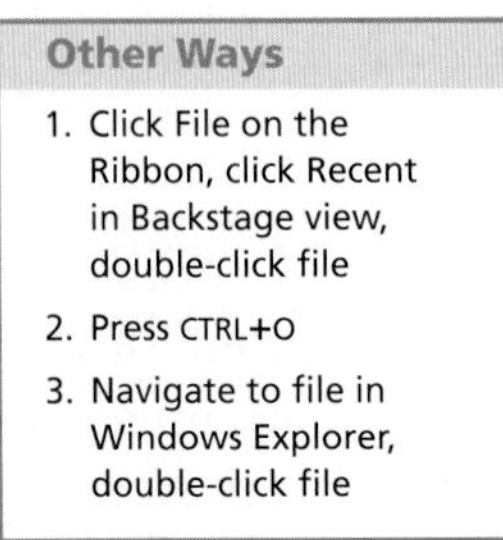

Other Ways

1. Click File on the Ribbon, click Recent in Backstage view, double-click file
2. Press CTRL+O
3. Navigate to file in Windows Explorer, double-click file

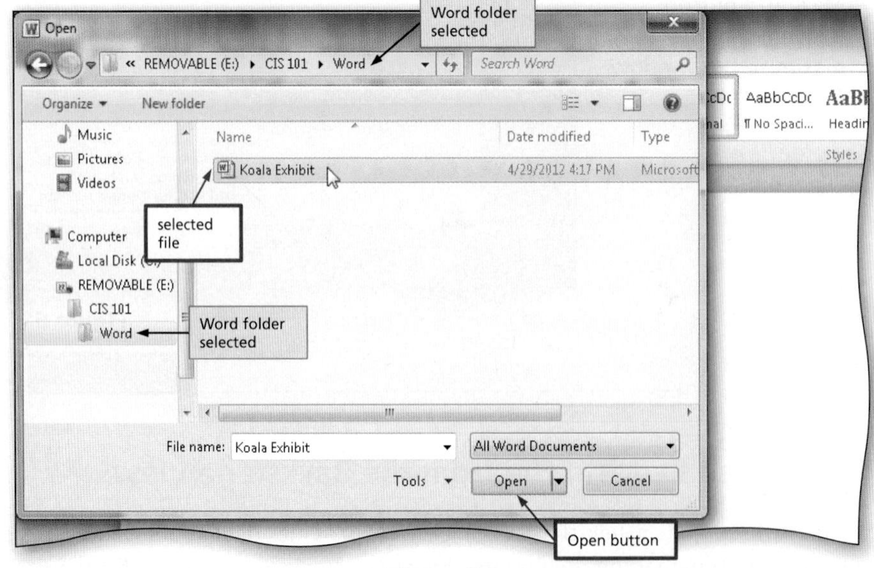

Figure 54

To Create a New Document from the Backstage View

You can create multiple documents at the same time in an Office program, such as Word. The following steps create a file, a blank document in this case, from the Backstage view.

1

- Click File on the Ribbon to open the Backstage view.
- Click the New tab in the Backstage view to display the New gallery (Figure 55).

Q&A Can I create documents through the Backstage view in other Office programs?

Yes. If the Office program has a New tab in the Backstage view, the New gallery displays various options for creating a new file.

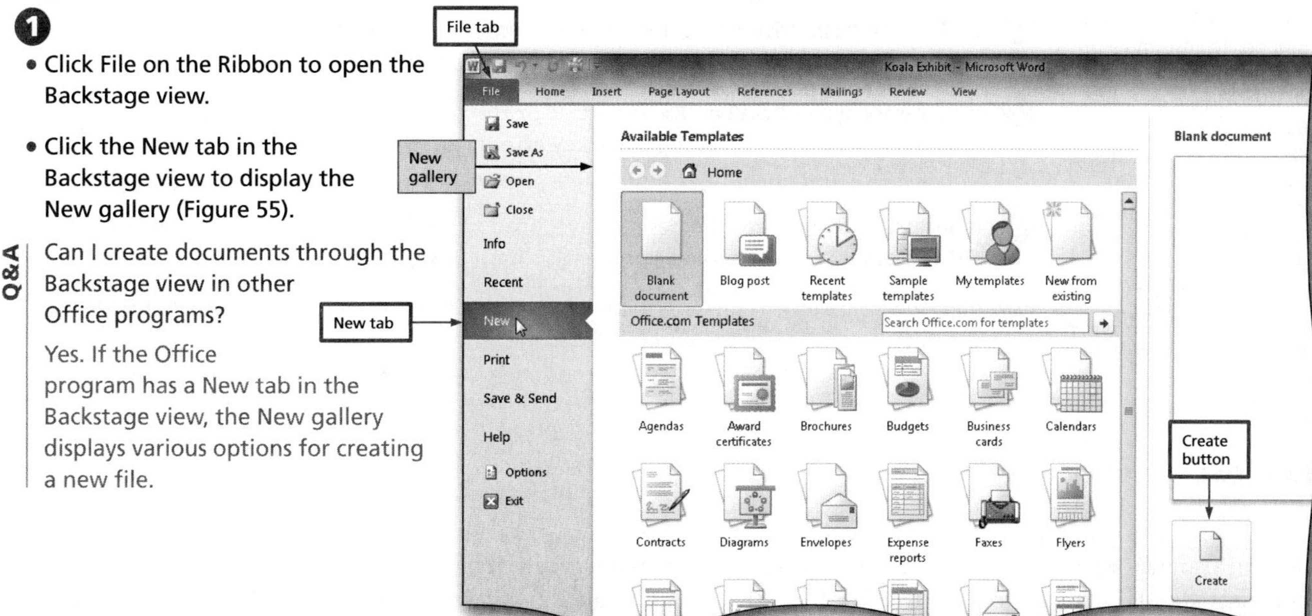

Figure 55

2

- Click the Create button in the New gallery to create a new document (Figure 56).

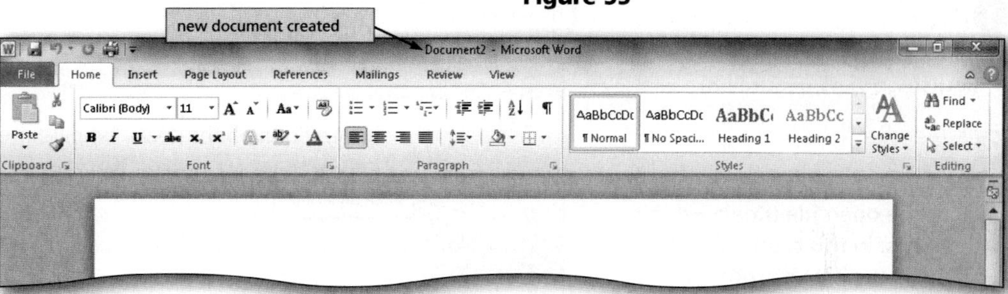

Figure 56

Other Ways

1. Press CTRL+N

To Enter Text in a Document

The next Word document identifies the names of the Koala Exhibit sponsors. The following step enters text in a document.

1 Type `List of Current Sponsors for the Koala Exhibit` and then press the ENTER key to move the insertion point to the beginning of the next line (Figure 57).

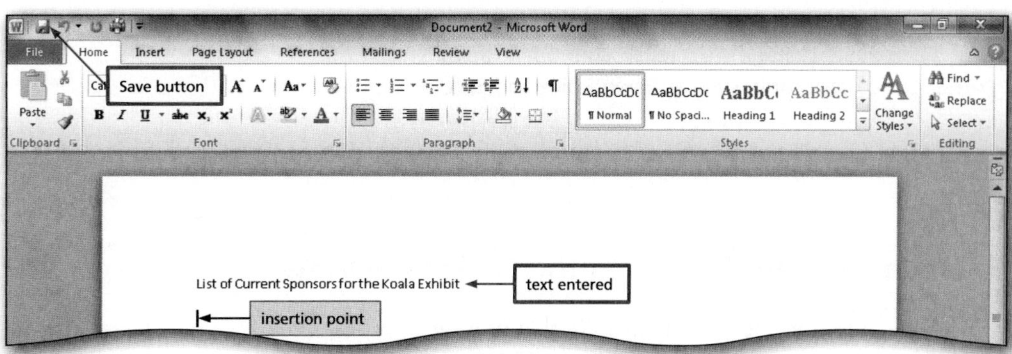

Figure 57

BTW

Customizing the Ribbon
In addition to customizing the Quick Access Toolbar, you can add items to and remove items from the Ribbon. To customize the Ribbon, click File on the Ribbon to open the Backstage view, click Options in the Backstage view, and then click Customize Ribbon in the left pane of the Options dialog box. More information about customizing the Ribbon is presented in a later chapter.

To Save a File in a Folder

The following steps save the second document in the Word folder in the class folder (CIS 101, in this case) on a USB flash drive using the file name, Koala Exhibit Sponsors.

1. With a USB flash drive connected to one of the computer's USB ports, click the Save button on the Quick Access Toolbar to display the Save As dialog box.
2. If necessary, type `Koala Exhibit Sponsors` in the File name text box to change the file name. Do not press the ENTER key after typing the file name because you do not want to close the dialog box at this time.
3. If necessary, navigate to the desired save location (in this case, the Word folder in the CIS 101 folder [or your class folder] on the USB flash drive).
4. Click the Save button (Save As dialog box) to save the document in the selected folder on the selected drive with the entered file name.

To Close a File Using the Backstage View

Sometimes, you may want to close an Office file, such as a Word document, entirely and start over with a new file. You also may want to close a file when you are finished working with it so that you can begin a new file. The following steps close the current active Word file (that is, the Koala Exhibit Sponsors document) without quitting the active program (Word in this case).

1

- Click File on the Ribbon to open the Backstage view (Figure 58).

2

- Click Close in the Backstage view to close the open file (Koala Exhibit Sponsors, in this case) without quitting the active program.

Q&A What if Word displays a dialog box about saving?

Click the Save button if you want to save the changes, click the Don't Save button if you want to ignore the changes since the last time you saved, and click the Cancel button if you do not want to close the document.

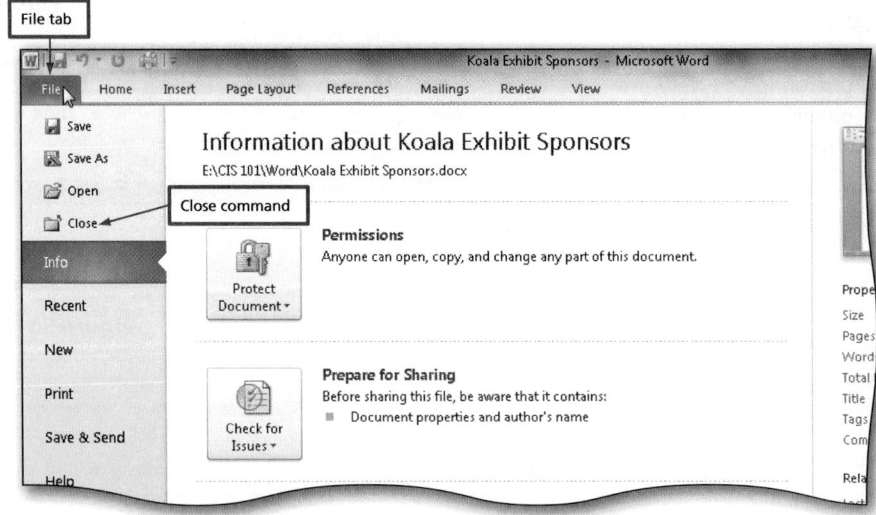

Figure 58

Q&A Can I use the Backstage view to close an open file in other Office programs, such as PowerPoint and Excel?

Yes.

To Open a Recent File Using the Backstage View

You sometimes need to open a file that you recently modified. You may have more changes to make such as adding more content or correcting errors. The Backstage view allows you to access recent files easily. The next steps reopen the Koala Exhibit Sponsors file just closed.

1

- Click File on the Ribbon to open the Backstage view.
- Click the Recent tab in the Backstage view to display the Recent gallery (Figure 59).

2

- Click the desired file name in the Recent gallery, Koala Exhibit Sponsors in this case, to open the file (shown in Figure 57 on page OFF 35).

Q&A Can I use the Backstage view to open a recent file in other Office programs, such as PowerPoint and Excel?

Yes, as long as the file name appears in the list of recent files in the Recent gallery.

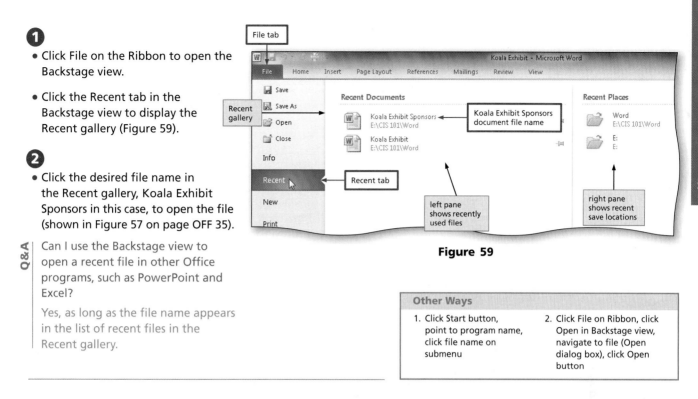

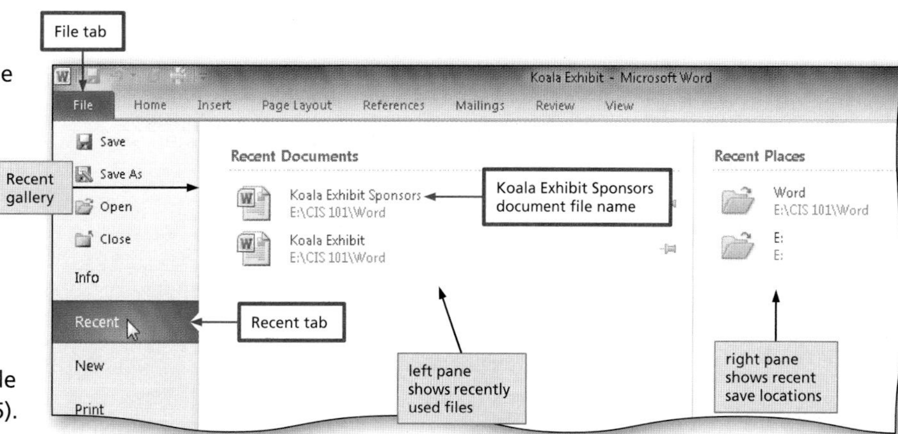

Figure 59

Other Ways

1. Click Start button, point to program name, click file name on submenu
2. Click File on Ribbon, click Open in Backstage view, navigate to file (Open dialog box), click Open button

To Create a New Blank Document from Windows Explorer

Windows Explorer provides a means to create a blank Office document without ever starting an Office program. The following steps use Windows Explorer to create a blank Word document.

1

- Click the Windows Explorer program button on the taskbar to make the folder window the active window in Windows Explorer.
- If necessary, navigate to the desired location for the new file (in this case, the Word folder in the CIS 101 folder [or your class folder] on the USB flash drive).
- With the Word folder selected, right-click an open area in the right pane to display a shortcut menu.
- Point to New on the shortcut menu to display the New submenu (Figure 60).

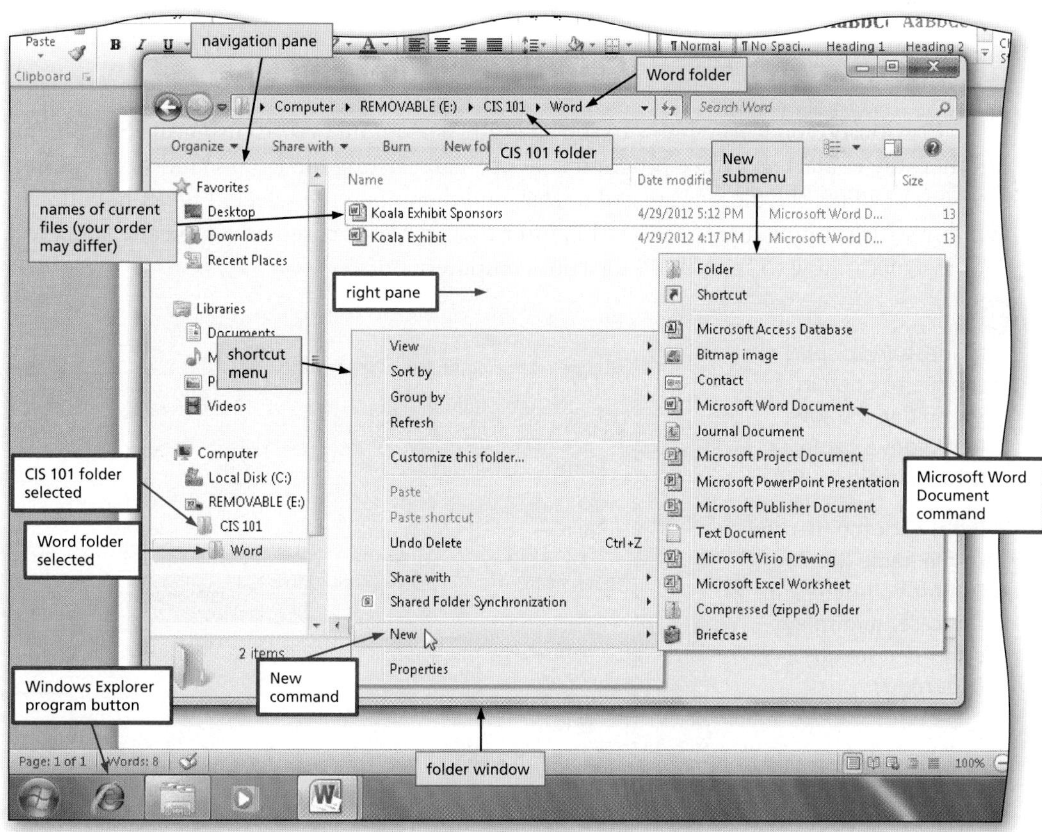

Figure 60

- Click Microsoft Word Document on the New submenu to display an icon and text box for a new file in the current folder window (Figure 61).

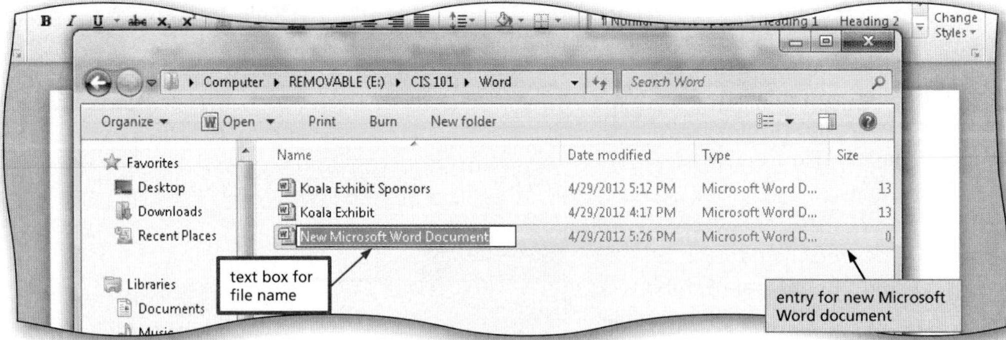

Figure 61

- Type **Koala Exhibit Volunteers** in the text box and then press the ENTER key to assign a name to the new file in the current folder (Figure 62).

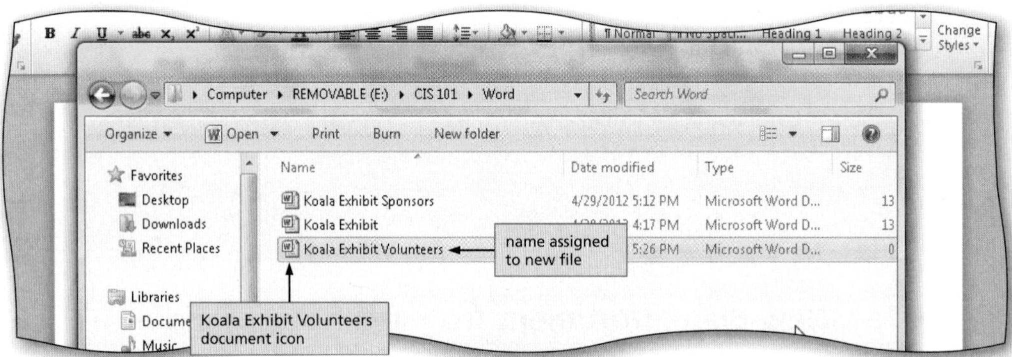

Figure 62

To Start a Program from Windows Explorer and Open a File

Previously, you learned how to start an Office program (Word) using the Start menu and the search box. Another way to start an Office program is to open an existing file from Windows Explorer, which causes the program in which the file was created to start and then open the selected file. The following steps, which assume Windows 7 is running, use Windows Explorer to start Word based on a typical installation. You may need to ask your instructor how to start Word for your computer.

- If necessary, display the file to open in the folder window in Windows Explorer (shown in Figure 62).
- Right-click the file icon or file name (Koala Exhibit Volunteers, in this case) to display a shortcut menu (Figure 63).

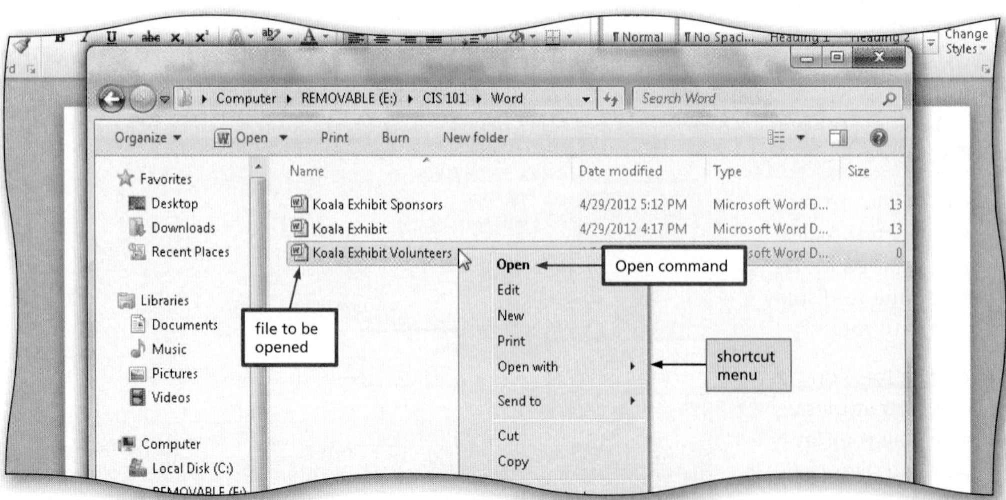

Figure 63

2

- Click Open on the shortcut menu to open the selected file in the program used to create the file, Microsoft Word in this case (Figure 64).
- If the program window is not maximized, click the Maximize button on the title bar to maximize the window.

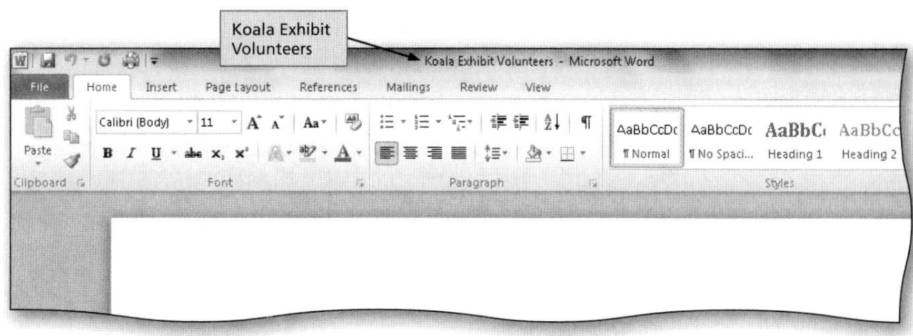

Figure 64

To Enter Text in a Document

The next step is to enter text in this blank Word document. The following step enters a line of text.

1 Type **`Koala Exhibit Staff and Volunteers`** and then press the ENTER key to move the insertion point to the beginning of the next line (shown in Figure 65).

To Save an Existing Document with the Same File Name

Saving frequently cannot be overemphasized. You have made modifications to the file (document) since you created it. Thus, you should save again. Similarly, you should continue saving files frequently so that you do not lose your changes since the time you last saved the file. You can use the same file name, such as Koala Exhibit Volunteers, to save the changes made to the document. The following step saves a file again.

1

- Click the Save button on the Quick Access Toolbar to overwrite the previously saved file (Koala Exhibit Volunteers, in this case) on the USB flash drive (Figure 65).

Q&A Why did the Save As dialog box not appear?

Office programs, including Word, overwrite the document using the setting specified the first time you saved the document.

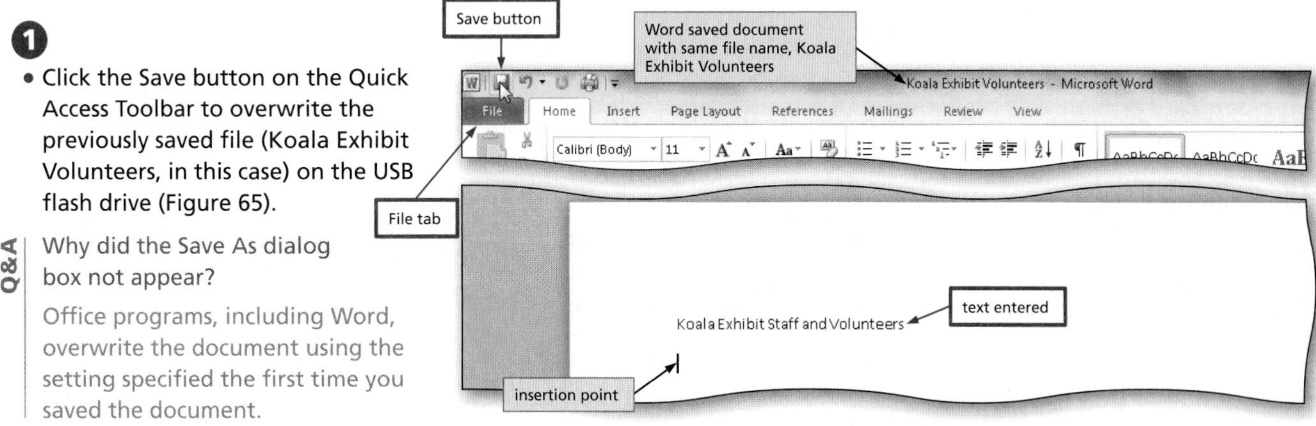

Figure 65

Other Ways

1. Press CTRL+S or press SHIFT+F12

To Use Save As to Change the Name of a File

You might want to save a file with a different name and even to a different location. For example, you might start a homework assignment with a data file and then save it with a final file name for submitting to your instructor, saving it to a location designated by your instructor. The following steps save a file with a different file name.

1 With your USB flash drive connected to one of the computer's USB ports, click File on the Ribbon to open the Backstage view.

2. Click Save As in the Backstage view to display the Save As dialog box.
3. Type **Koala Exhibit Staff and Volunteers** in the File name text box (Save As dialog box) to change the file name. Do not press the ENTER key after typing the file name because you do not want to close the dialog box at this time.
4. If necessary, navigate to the desired save location (the Word folder in the CIS 101 folder [or your class folder] on the USB flash drive, in this case).
5. Click the Save button (Save As dialog box) to save the file in the selected folder on the selected drive with the new file name.

BTW

Multiple Open Files
If the program button on the taskbar displays as a tiered stack, you have multiple files open in the program.

To Quit an Office Program

You are finished using Word. The following steps quit Word. You would use similar steps to quit other office programs.

1. Because you have multiple Word documents open, click File on the Ribbon to open the Backstage view and then click Exit in the Backstage view to close all open documents and quit Word.
2. If a dialog box appears, click the Save button to save any changes made to the file since the last save.

Moving, Renaming, and Deleting Files

Earlier in this chapter, you learned how to organize files in folders, which is part of a process known as **file management**. The following sections cover additional file management topics including renaming, moving, and deleting files.

To Rename a File

In some circumstances, you may want to change the name of, or rename, a file or a folder. For example, you may want to distinguish a file in one folder or drive from a copy of a similar file, or you may decide to rename a file to better identify its contents. The Word folder shown in Figure 66 contains the Word document, Koala Exhibit. The following steps change the name of the Koala Exhibit file in the Word folder to Koala Exhibit Flyer.

1

- If necessary, click the Windows Explorer program button on the taskbar to display the folder window in Windows Explorer.
- If necessary, navigate to the location of the file to be renamed (in this case, the Word folder in the CIS 101 [or your class folder] folder on the USB flash drive) to display the file(s) it contains in the right pane.
- Right-click the Koala Exhibit icon or file name in the right pane to select the Koala Exhibit file and display a shortcut menu that presents a list of commands related to files (Figure 66).

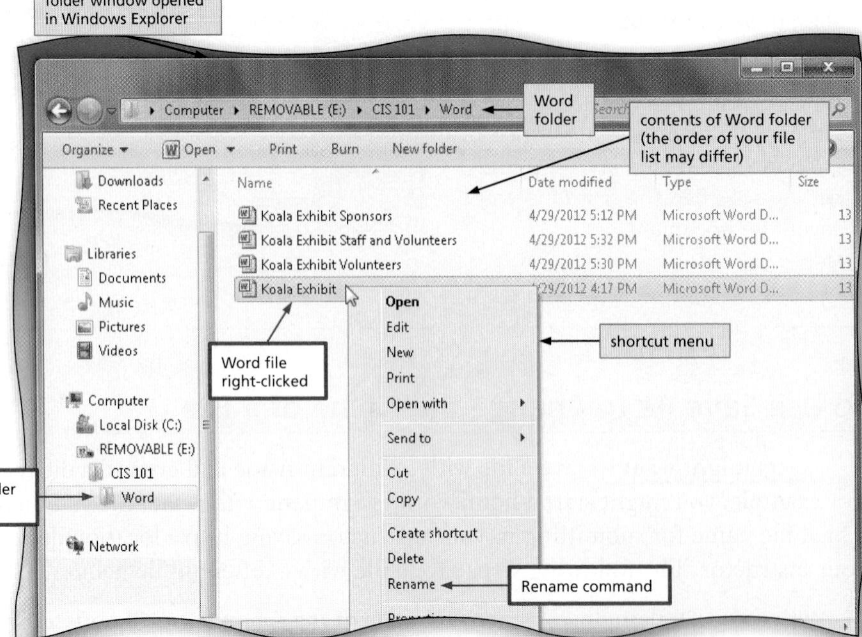

Figure 66

2

- Click Rename on the shortcut menu to place the current file name in a text box.
- Type `Koala Exhibit Flyer` in the text box and then press the ENTER key (Figure 67).

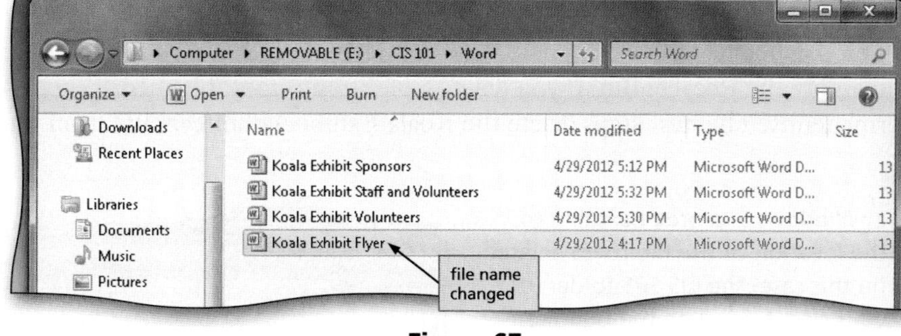

Figure 67

Q&A Are any risks involved in renaming files that are located on a hard disk?

If you inadvertently rename a file that is associated with certain programs, the programs may not be able to find the file and, therefore, may not execute properly. Always use caution when renaming files.

Q&A Can I rename a file when it is open?

No, a file must be closed to change the file name.

Other Ways

1. Select file, press F2, type new file name, press ENTER

To Move a File

At some time, you may want to move a file from one folder, called the source folder, to another, called the destination. When you move a file, it no longer appears in the original folder. If the destination and the source folders are on the same disk drive, you can move a file by dragging it. If the folders are on different disk drives, then you will need to right-drag the file. The following step moves the Koala Exhibit Volunteers file from the Word folder to the CIS 101 folder.

1

- In Windows Explorer, if necessary, navigate to the location of the file to be moved (in this case, the Word folder in the CIS 101 folder [or your class folder] on the USB flash drive).
- If necessary, click the Word folder in the navigation pane to display the files it contains in the right pane.
- Drag the Koala Exhibit Volunteers file in the right pane to the CIS 101 folder in the navigation pane and notice the ScreenTip as you drag the mouse (Figure 68).

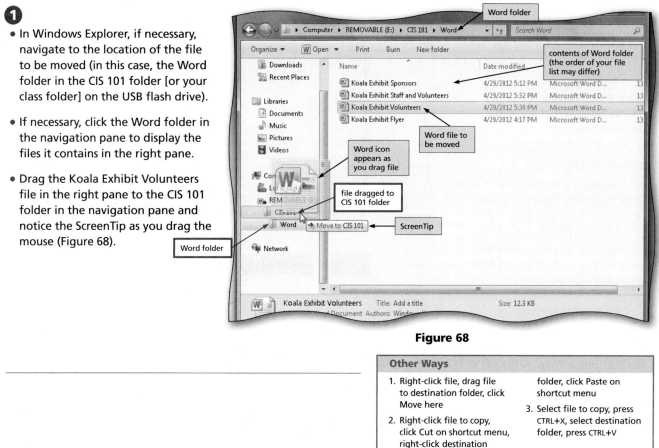

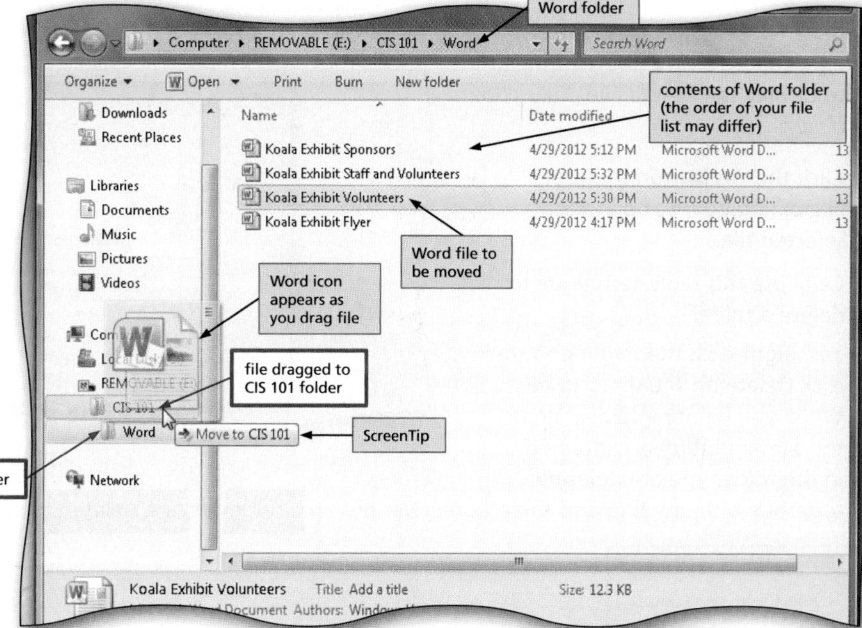

Figure 68

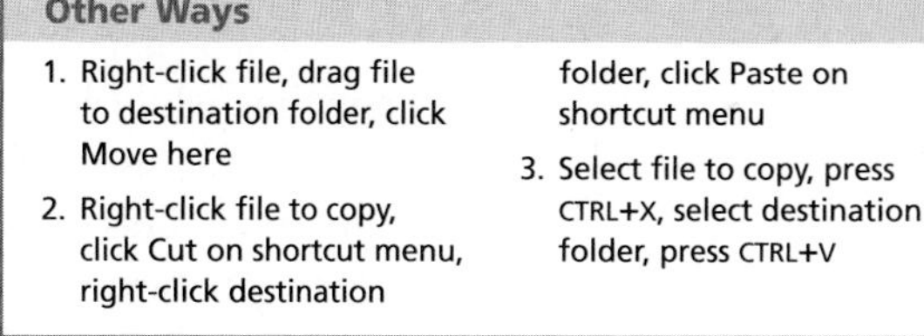

Other Ways

1. Right-click file, drag file to destination folder, click Move here
2. Right-click file to copy, click Cut on shortcut menu, right-click destination folder, click Paste on shortcut menu
3. Select file to copy, press CTRL+X, select destination folder, press CTRL+V

To Delete a File

A final task you may want to perform is to delete a file. Exercise extreme caution when deleting a file or files. When you delete a file from a hard disk, the deleted file is stored in the Recycle Bin where you can recover it until you empty the Recycle Bin. If you delete a file from removable media, such as a USB flash drive, the file is deleted permanently. The next steps delete the Koala Exhibit Volunteers file from the CIS 101 folder.

- In Windows Explorer, navigate to the location of the file to be deleted (in this case, the CIS 101 folder [or your class folder] on the USB flash drive).
- If necessary, click the CIS 101 folder in the navigation pane to display the files it contains in the right pane.
- Right-click the Koala Exhibit Volunteers icon or file name in the right pane to select the file and display a shortcut menu (Figure 69).

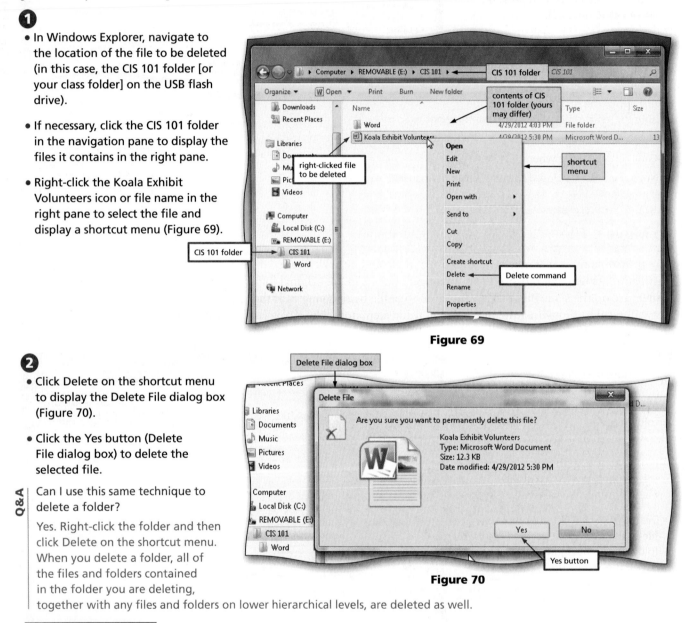

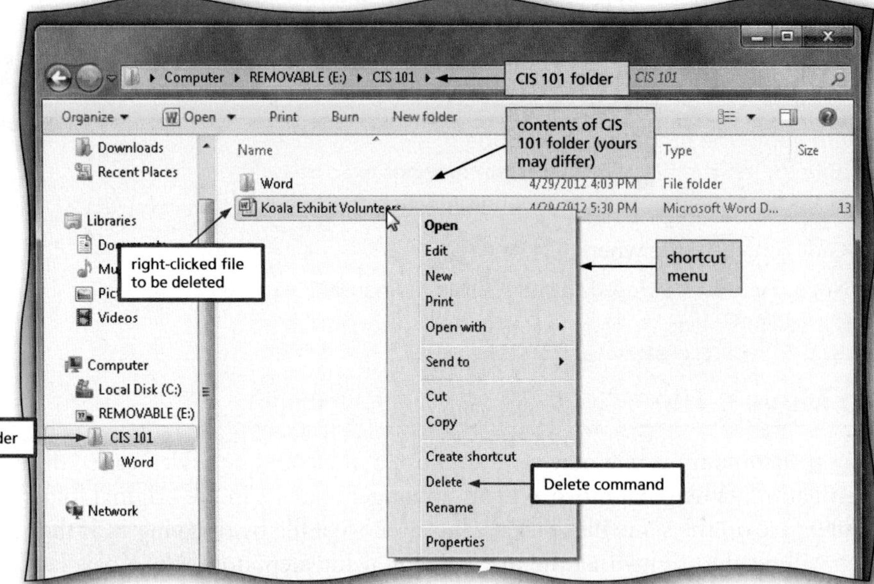

Figure 69

- Click Delete on the shortcut menu to display the Delete File dialog box (Figure 70).
- Click the Yes button (Delete File dialog box) to delete the selected file.

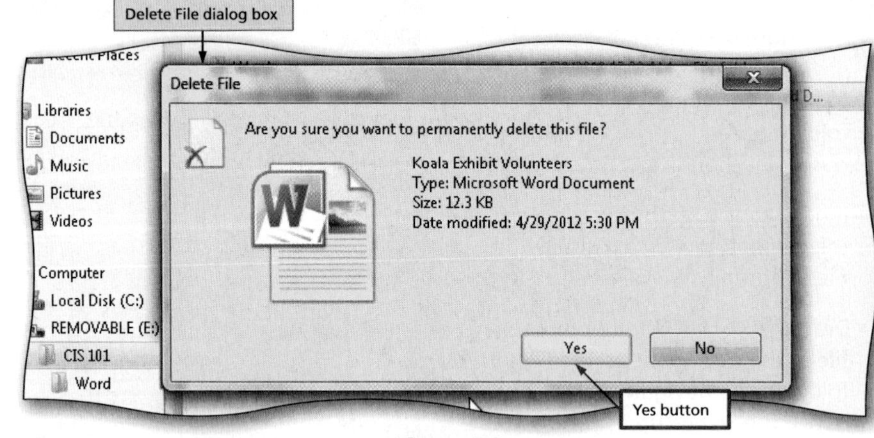

Figure 70

Q&A Can I use this same technique to delete a folder?

Yes. Right-click the folder and then click Delete on the shortcut menu. When you delete a folder, all of the files and folders contained in the folder you are deleting, together with any files and folders on lower hierarchical levels, are deleted as well.

Other Ways

1. Select icon, press DELETE

Microsoft Office and Windows Help

At any time while you are using one of the Microsoft Office 2010 programs, such as Word, you can use Office Help to display information about all topics associated with the program. This section illustrates the use of Word Help. Help in other Office 2010 programs operates in a similar fashion.

In Office 2010, Help is presented in a window that has Web-browser-style navigation buttons. Each Office 2010 program has its own Help home page, which is the starting Help page that is displayed in the Help window. If your computer is connected to the Internet, the contents of the Help page reflect both the local help files installed on the computer and material from Microsoft's Web site.

To Open the Help Window in an Office Program

The following step opens the Word Help window. The step to open a Help window in other Office programs is similar.

- Start Word.
- Click the Microsoft Word Help button near the upper-right corner of the program window to open the Word Help window (Figure 71).

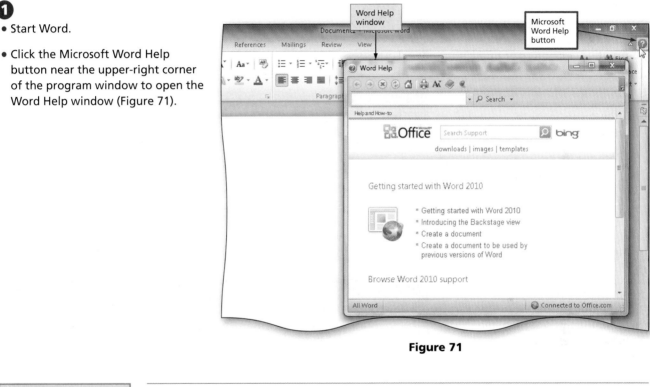

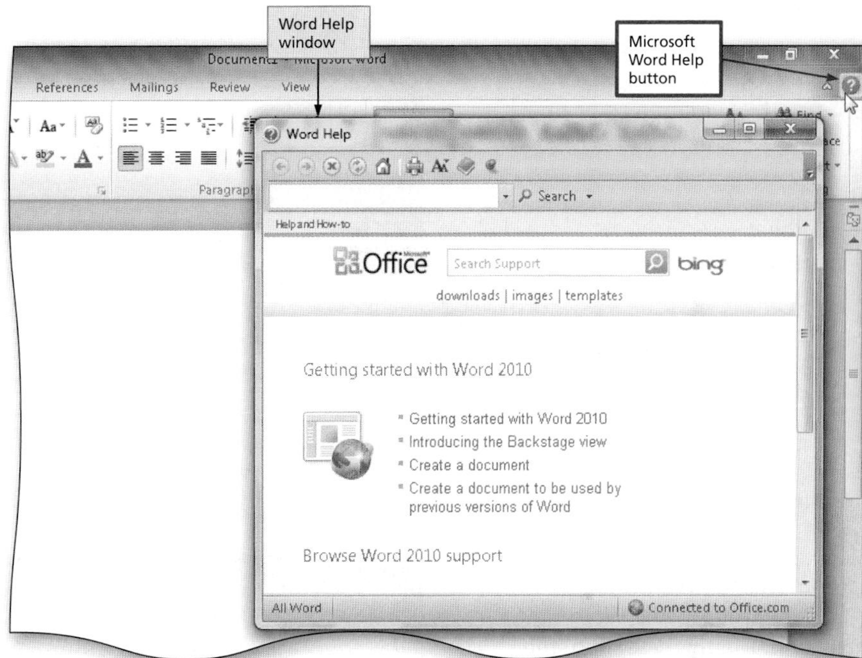

Figure 71

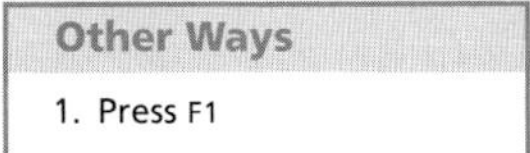
Other Ways

1. Press F1

Moving and Resizing Windows

Up to this point, this chapter has used minimized and maximized windows. At times, however, it is useful, or even necessary, to have more than one window open and visible on the screen at the same time. You can resize and move these open windows so that you can view different areas of and elements in the window. In the case of the Help window, for example, it could be covering document text in the Word window that you need to see.

To Move a Window by Dragging

You can move any open window that is not maximized to another location on the desktop by dragging the title bar of the window. The step on the next page drags the Word Help window to the top left of the desktop.

- Drag the window title bar (the Word Help window title bar, in this case) so that the window moves to the top left of the desktop, as shown in Figure 72.

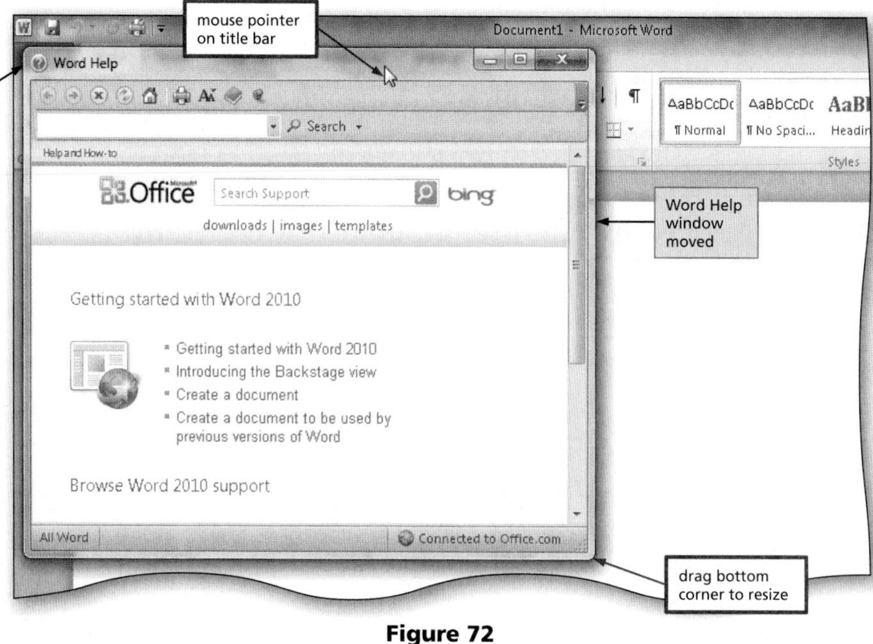

Figure 72

Other Ways

1. Right-click title bar, click Move on shortcut menu, drag window

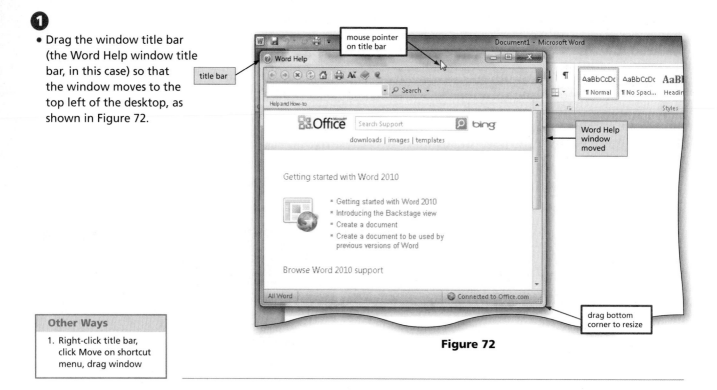

To Resize a Window by Dragging

Sometimes, information is not visible completely in a window. A method used to change the size of the window is to drag the window borders. The following step changes the size of the Word Help window by dragging its borders.

- Point to the lower-right corner of the window (the Word Help window, in this case) until the mouse pointer changes to a two-headed arrow.
- Drag the bottom border downward to display more of the active window (Figure 73).

Q&A Can I drag other borders on the window to enlarge or shrink the window?

Yes, you can drag the left, right, and top borders and any window corner to resize a window.

Q&A Will Windows 7 remember the new size of the window after I close it?

Yes. When you reopen the window, Windows 7 will display it at the same size it was when you closed it.

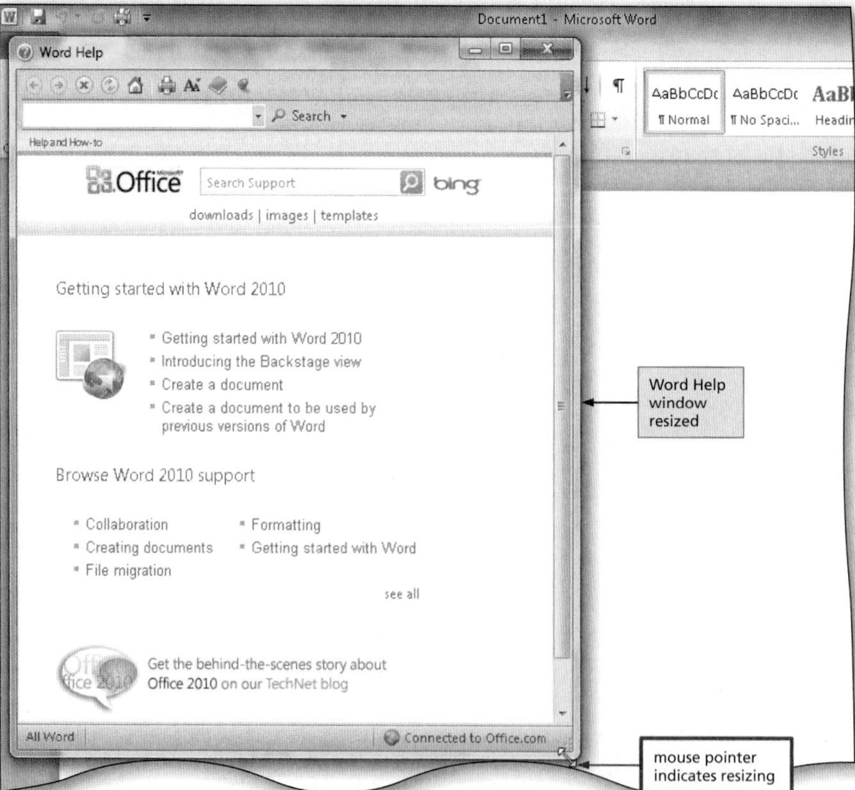

Figure 73

Using Office Help

Once an Office program's Help window is open, several methods exist for navigating Help. You can search for help by using any of the three following methods from the Help window:

1. Enter search text in the 'Type words to search for' text box.
2. Click the links in the Help window.
3. Use the Table of Contents.

To Obtain Help Using the 'Type words to search for' Text Box

Assume for the following example that you want to know more about the Backstage view. The following steps use the 'Type words to search for' text box to obtain useful information about the Backstage view by entering the word, Backstage, as search text.

1

- Type `Backstage` in the 'Type words to search for' text box at the top of the Word Help window to enter the search text.
- Click the Search button arrow to display the Search menu (Figure 74).
- If it is not selected already, click All Word on the Search menu, so that Help performs the most complete search of the current program (Word, in this case). If All Word already is selected, click the Search button arrow again to close the Search menu.

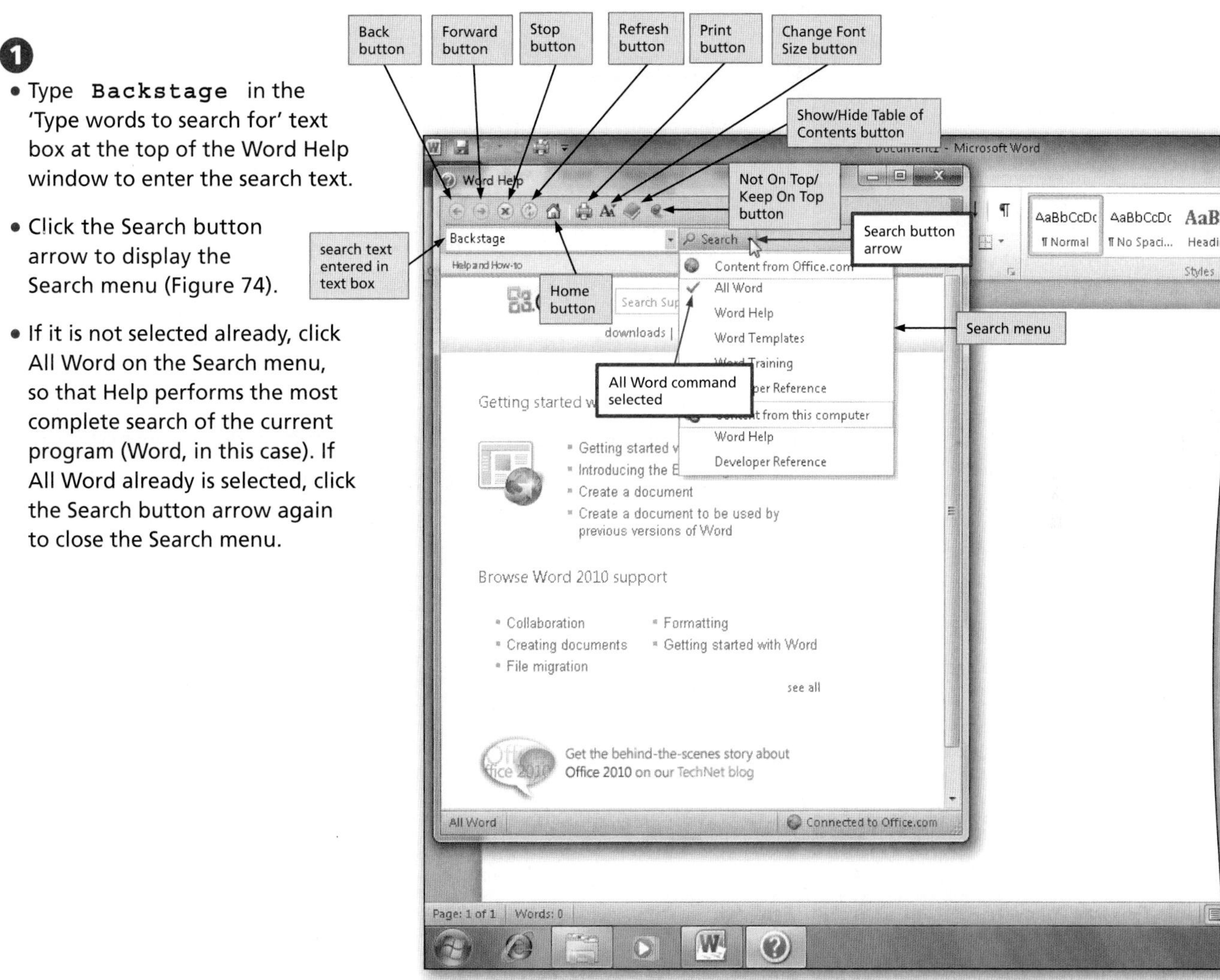

Figure 74

Q&A

Why select All Word on the Search menu?

Selecting All Word on the Search menu ensures that Word Help will search all possible sources for information about your search term. It will produce the most complete search results.

2

- Click the Search button to display the search results (Figure 75).

Q&A Why do my search results differ?

If you do not have an Internet connection, your results will reflect only the content of the Help files on your computer. When searching for help online, results also can change as material is added, deleted, and updated on the online Help Web pages maintained by Microsoft.

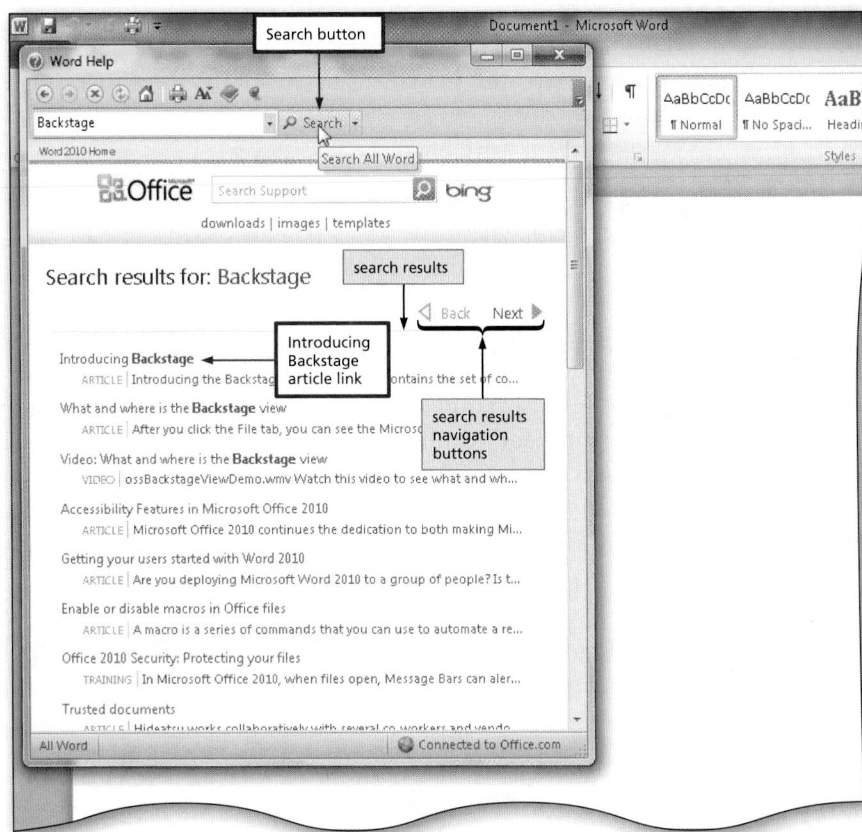

Figure 75

Q&A Why were my search results not very helpful?

When initiating a search, be sure to check the spelling of the search text; also, keep your search specific, with fewer than seven words, to return the most accurate results.

3

- Click the Introducing Backstage link to open the Help document associated with the selected topic (Figure 76).

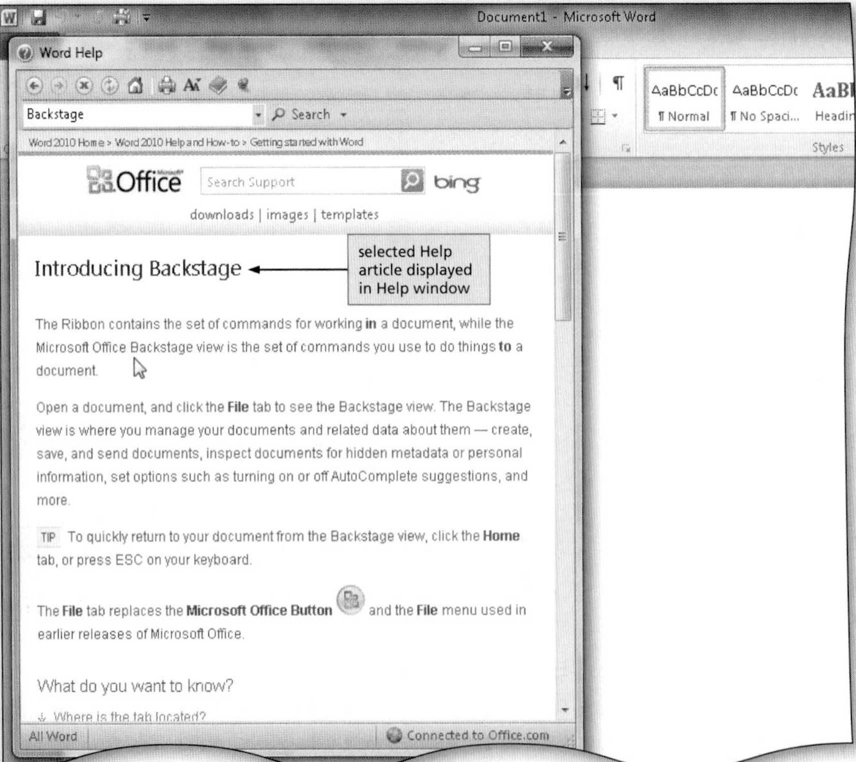

Figure 76

- Click the Home button on the toolbar to clear the search results and redisplay the Help home page (Figure 77).

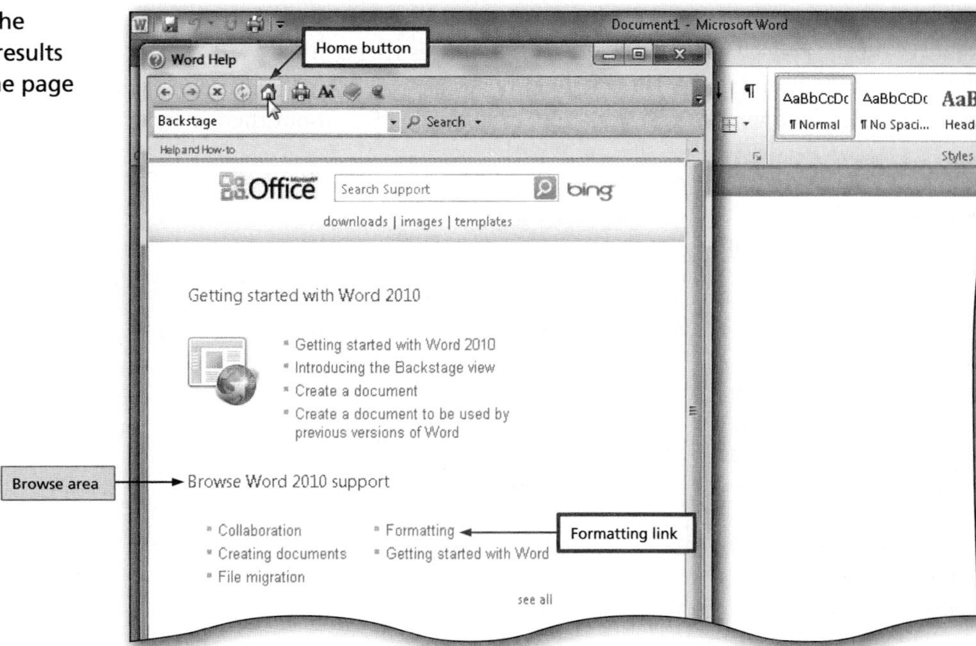

Figure 77

To Obtain Help Using the Help Links

If your topic of interest is listed in the Browse area of the Help window, you can click the link to begin browsing the Help categories instead of entering search text. You browse Help just as you would browse a Web site. If you know which category contains your Help information, you may wish to use these links. The following step finds the Formatting Help information using the category links from the Word Help home page.

- Click the Formatting link on the Help home page (shown in Figure 77) to display the Formatting page (Figure 78).

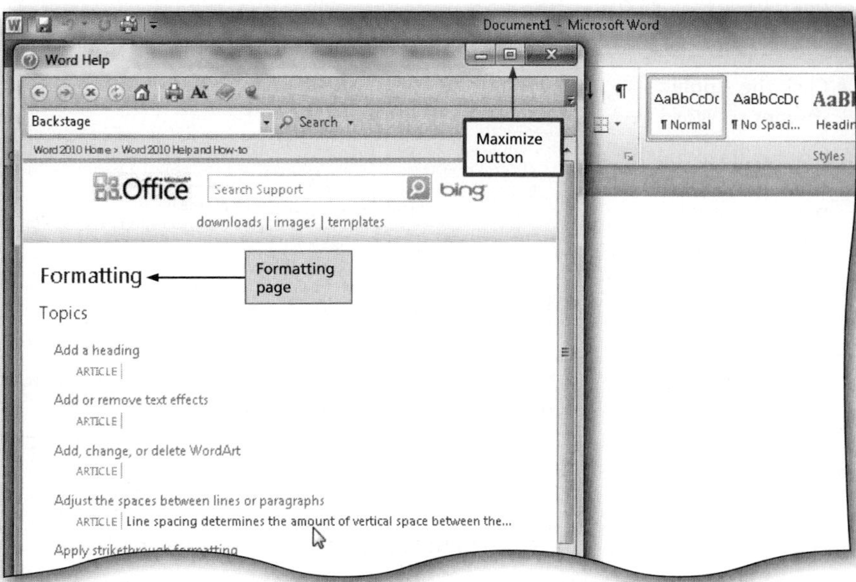

Figure 78

To Obtain Help Using the Help Table of Contents

A third way to find Help in Office programs is through the Help Table of Contents. You can browse through the Table of Contents to display information about a particular topic or to familiarize yourself with an Office program. The following steps access the Help information about themes by browsing through the Table of Contents.

1

- Click the Home button on the toolbar to display the Help home page.
- Click the Show Table of Contents button on the toolbar to display the Table of Contents pane on the left side of the Help window. If necessary, click the Maximize button on the Help title bar to maximize the window (Figure 79).

Figure 79

Q&A Why does the appearance of the Show Table of Contents button change?

When the Table of Contents is displayed in the Help window, the Hide Table of Contents button replaces the Show Table of Contents button.

2

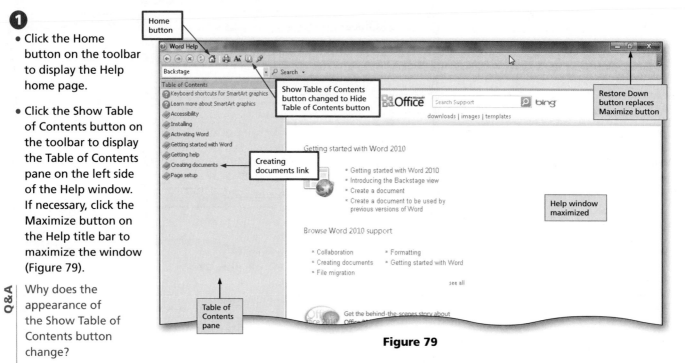

- Click the Creating documents link in the Table of Contents pane to view a list of Help subtopics.
- Click the Apply themes to Word documents link in the Table of Contents pane to view the selected Help document in the right pane (Figure 80).
- After reviewing the page, click the Close button to quit Help.
- Click Word's Close button to quit Word.

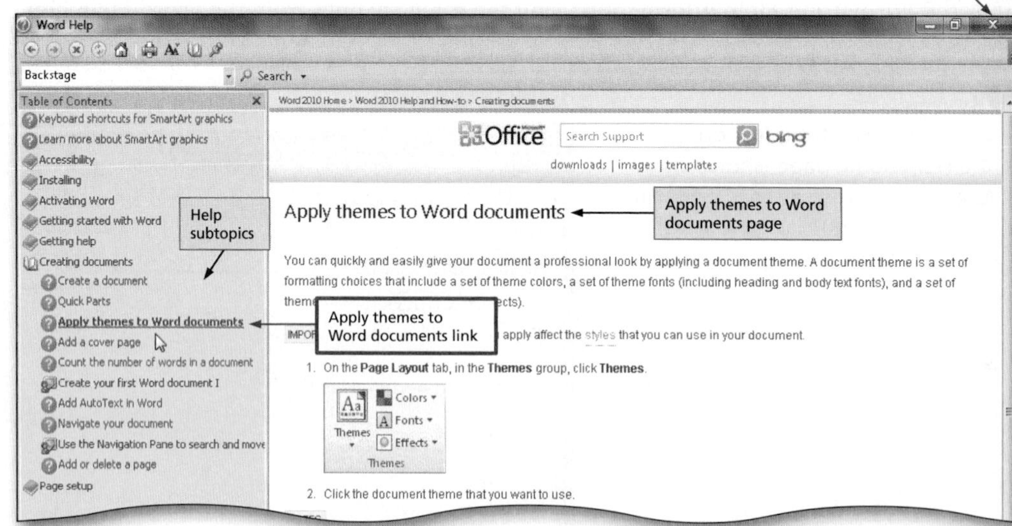

Figure 80

Q&A How do I remove the Table of Contents pane when I am finished with it?

The Show Table of Contents button acts as a toggle. When the Table of Contents pane is visible, the button changes to Hide Table of Contents. Clicking it hides the Table of Contents pane and changes the button to Show Table of Contents.

Obtaining Help while Working in an Office Program

Help in Office programs, such as Word, provides you with the ability to obtain help directly, without the need to open the Help window and initiate a search. For example, you may be unsure about how a particular command works, or you may be presented with a dialog box that you are not sure how to use.

Figure 81 shows one option for obtaining help while working in Word. If you want to learn more about a command, point to the command button and wait for the Enhanced ScreenTip to appear. If the Help icon appears in the Enhanced ScreenTip, press the F1 key while pointing to the command to open the Help window associated with that command.

Figure 82 shows a dialog box that contains a Help button. Pressing the F1 key while the dialog box is displayed opens a Help window. The Help window contains help about that dialog box, if available. If no help file is available for that particular dialog box, then the main Help window opens.

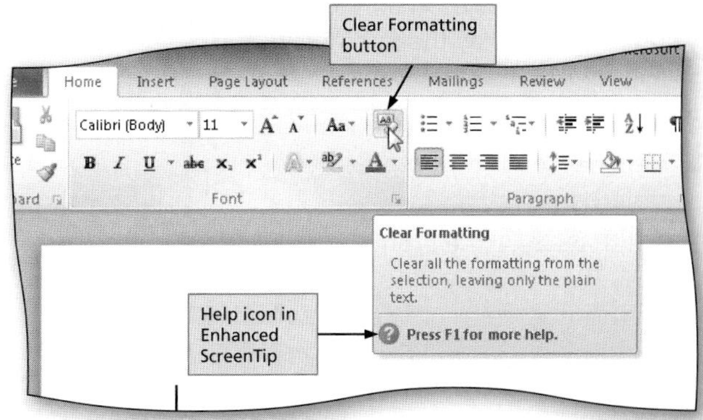

Figure 81

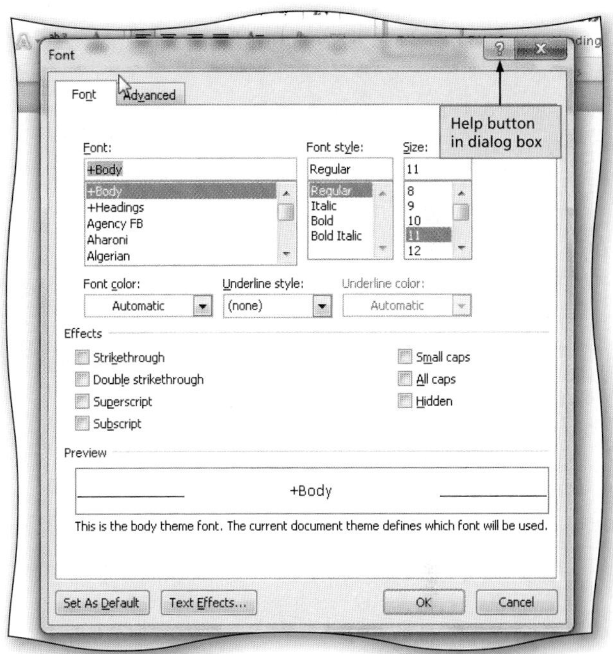

Figure 82

Using Windows Help and Support

One of the more powerful Windows 7 features is Windows Help and Support. **Windows Help and Support** is available when using Windows 7 or when using any Microsoft program running under Windows 7. This feature is designed to assist you in using Windows 7 or the various programs. Table 4 describes the content found in the Help and Support Center. The same methods used for searching Microsoft Office Help can be used in Windows Help and Support. The difference is that Windows Help and Support displays help for Windows 7, instead of for Microsoft Office.

Table 4 Windows Help and Support Center Content Areas

Area	Function
Find an answer quickly	This area contains instructions about how to do a quick search using the search box.
Not sure where to start?	This area displays three topics to help guide a user: How to get started with your computer, Learn about Windows Basics, and Browse Help topics. Clicking one of the options navigates to corresponding Help and Support pages.
More on the Windows Website	This area contains links to online content from the Windows Web site. Clicking the links navigates to the corresponding Web pages on the Web site.

To Start Windows Help and Support

The steps on the next page start Windows Help and Support and display the Windows Help and Support window, containing links to more information about Windows 7.

- Click the Start button on the taskbar to display the Start menu (Figure 83).

Q&A Why are the programs that are displayed on the Start menu different?

Windows adds the programs you have used recently to the left pane on the Start menu. You have started Word while performing the steps in this chapter, so that program now is displayed on the Start menu.

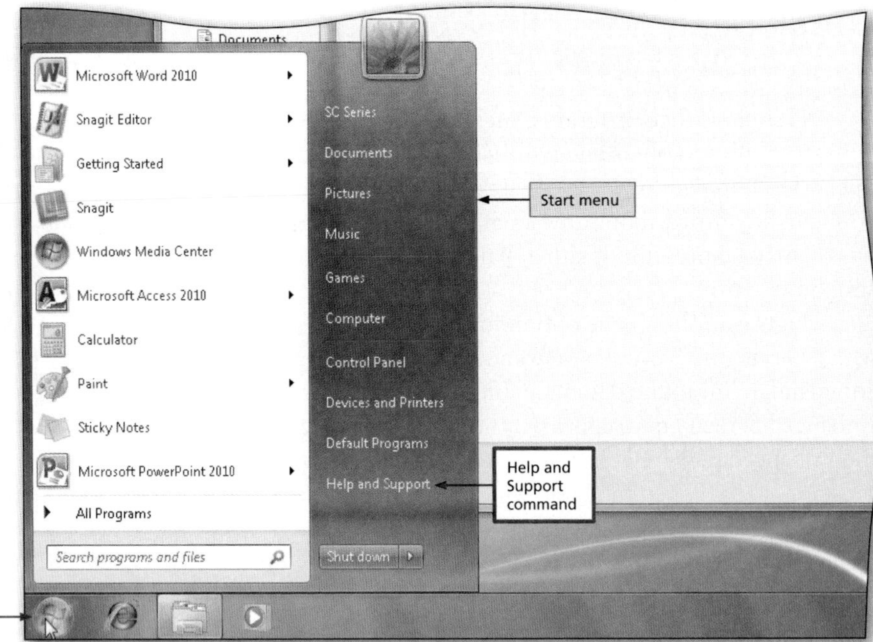

Figure 83

- Click Help and Support on the Start menu to open the Windows Help and Support window (Figure 84).
- After reviewing the Windows Help and Support window, click the Close button to quit Windows Help and Support.

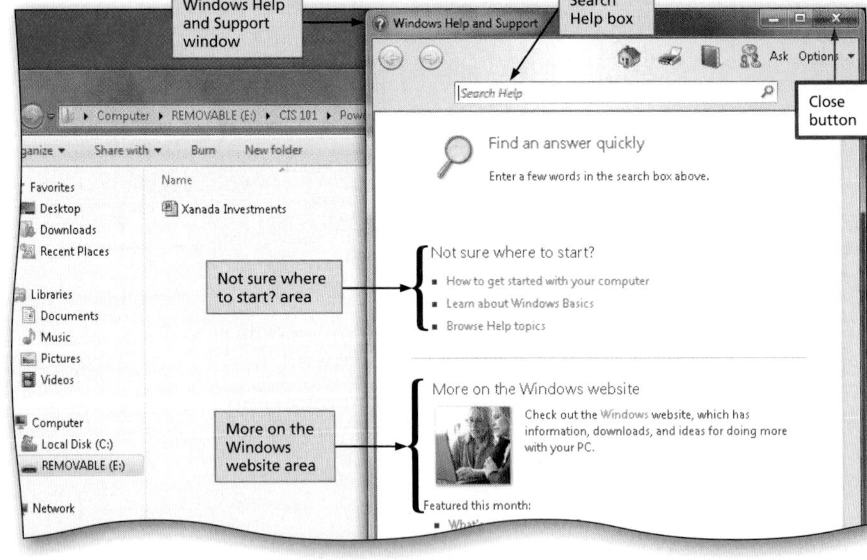

Figure 84

Other Ways

1. Press CTRL+ESC, press RIGHT ARROW, press UP ARROW, press ENTER
2. Press WINDOWS+F1

Chapter Summary

In this chapter, you learned about the Windows 7 interface. You started Windows 7, were introduced to the components of the desktop, and learned several mouse operations. You opened, closed, moved, resized, minimized, maximized, and scrolled a window. You used folder windows to expand and collapse drives and folders, display drive and folder contents, create folders, and rename and then delete a file.

You also learned some basic features of Microsoft Word 2010. As part of this learning process, you discovered the common elements that exist among Microsoft Office programs.

Microsoft Office Help was demonstrated using Word, and you learned how to use the Word Help window. You were introduced to the Windows 7 Help and Support Center and learned how to use it to obtain more information about Windows 7.

The items listed below include all of the new Windows 7 and Word 2010 skills you have learned in this chapter.

1. Log On to the Computer (OFF 6)
2. Start a Program Using the Start Menu (OFF 10)
3. Maximize a Window (OFF 12)
4. Display a Different Tab on the Ribbon (OFF 16)
5. Minimize, Display, and Restore the Ribbon (OFF 16)
6. Display and Use a Shortcut Menu (OFF 17)
7. Customize the Quick Access Toolbar (OFF 18)
8. Enter Text in a Document (OFF 19)
9. Create a Folder (OFF 20)
10. Create a Folder within a Folder (OFF 23)
11. Expand a Folder, Scroll through Folder Contents, and Collapse a Folder (OFF 23)
12. Switch from One Program to Another (OFF 24)
13. Save a File in a Folder (OFF 25)
14. Minimize and Restore a Window (OFF 27)
15. Change the Screen Resolution (OFF 30)
16. Quit a Program with One Document Open (OFF 31)
17. Start a Program Using the Search Box (OFF 32)
18. Open an Existing file from the Backstage View (OFF 33)
19. Create a New Document from the Backstage View (OFF 35)
20. Close a File Using the Backstage View (OFF 36)
21. Open a Recent File Using the Backstage View (OFF 36)
22. Create a New Blank Document from Windows Explorer (OFF 37)
23. Start a Program from Windows Explorer and Open a File (OFF 38)
24. Save an Existing Document with the Same File Name (OFF 39)
25. Rename a File (OFF 40)
26. Move a File (OFF 40)
27. Delete a File (OFF 42)
28. Open the Help Window in an Office Program (OFF 43)
29. Move a Window by Dragging (OFF 43)
30. Resize a Window by Dragging (OFF 44)
31. Obtain Help Using the 'Type words to search for' Text Box (OFF 45)
32. Obtain Help Using the Help Links (OFF 47)
33. Obtain Help Using the Help Table of Contents (OFF 48)
34. Start Windows Help and Support (OFF 49)

If you have a SAM 2010 user profile, your instructor may have assigned an autogradable version of this assignment. If so, log into the SAM 2010 Web site at www.cengage.com/sam2010 to download the instruction and start files.

Learn It Online

Test your knowledge of chapter content and key terms.

Instructions: To complete the Learn It Online exercises, start your browser, click the Address bar, and then enter the Web address **`scsite.com/office2010/learn`**. When the Office 2010 Learn It Online page is displayed, click the link for the exercise you want to complete and then read the instructions.

Chapter Reinforcement TF, MC, and SA

A series of true/false, multiple choice, and short answer questions that test your knowledge of the chapter content.

Flash Cards

An interactive learning environment where you identify chapter key terms associated with displayed definitions.

Practice Test

A series of multiple choice questions that test your knowledge of chapter content and key terms.

Who Wants To Be a Computer Genius?

An interactive game that challenges your knowledge of chapter content in the style of a television quiz show.

Wheel of Terms

An interactive game that challenges your knowledge of chapter key terms in the style of the television show *Wheel of Fortune*.

Crossword Puzzle Challenge

A crossword puzzle that challenges your knowledge of key terms presented in the chapter.

STUDENT ASSIGNMENTS

Apply Your Knowledge

Reinforce the skills and apply the concepts you learned in this chapter.

Creating a Folder and a Document

Instructions: You will create a Word folder and then create a Word document and save it in the folder.

Perform the following tasks:

1. Connect a USB flash drive to an available USB port and then open the USB flash drive window.
2. Click the New folder button on the toolbar to display a new folder icon and text box for the folder name.
3. Type `Word` in the text box to name the folder. Press the ENTER key to create the folder on the USB flash drive.
4. Start Word.
5. Enter the text shown in Figure 85.
6. Click the Save button on the Quick Access Toolbar. Navigate to the Word folder on the USB flash drive and then save the document using the file name, Apply 1 Class List.
7. If your Quick Access Toolbar does not show the Quick Print button, add the Quick Print button to the Quick Access Toolbar. Print the document using the Quick Print button on the Quick Access Toolbar. When you are finished printing, remove the Quick Print button from the Quick Access Toolbar.
8. Submit the printout to your instructor.
9. Quit Word.

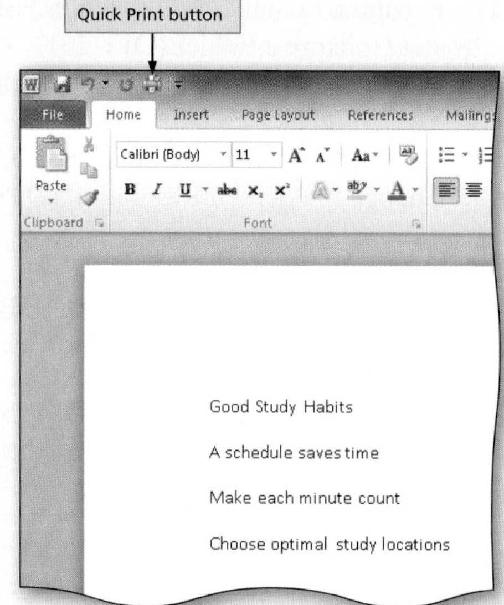

Figure 85

Extend Your Knowledge

Extend the skills you learned in this chapter and experiment with new skills. You will use Help to complete the assignment.

Using Help

Instructions: Use Word Help to perform the following tasks.

Perform the following tasks:

1. Start Word.
2. Click the Microsoft Word Help button to open the Word Help window (Figure 86).

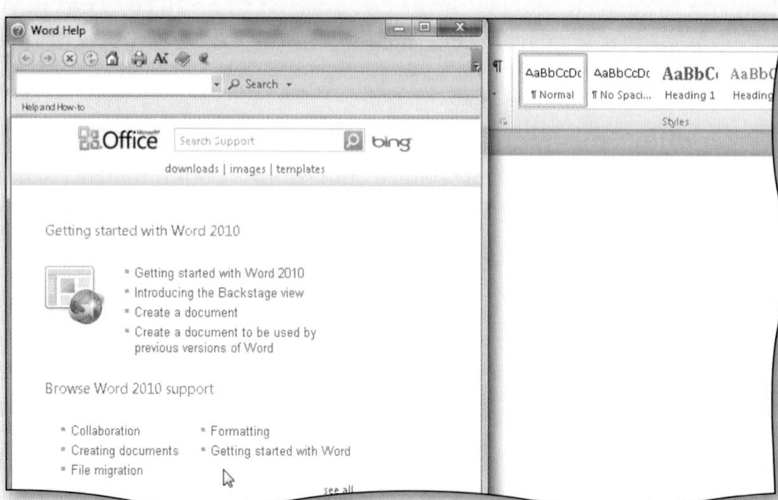

Figure 86

3. Search Word Help to answer the following questions.
   a. What are three features new to Word 2010?
   b. What type of training courses are available through Help?
   c. What are the steps to add a new group to the Ribbon?
   d. What are Quick Parts?
   e. What are document properties?
   f. What is a template?
   g. How do you print a document?
   h. What type of graphics can you insert in a document?
   i. What is cropping?
   j. What is the purpose of the Navigation Pane?
4. Submit the answers from your searches in the format specified by your instructor.
5. Quit Word.

Make It Right

Analyze a file structure and correct all errors and/or improve the design.

Organizing Vacation Photos

Note: To complete this assignment, you will be required to use the Data Files for Students. See the inside back cover of this book for instructions on downloading the Data Files for Students, or contact your instructor for information about accessing the required files.

Instructions: Traditionally, you have stored photos from past vacations together in one folder. The photos are becoming difficult to manage, and you now want to store them in appropriate folders. You will create the folder structure shown in Figure 87. You then will move the photos to the folders so that they will be organized properly.

1. Connect a USB flash drive to an available USB port to open the USB flash drive window.
2. Create the hierarchical folder structure shown in Figure 87.
3. Move one photo to each folder in the folder structure you created in Step 2. The five photos are available on the Data Files for Students.
4. Submit your work in the format specified by your instructor.

Figure 87

In the Lab

Use the guidelines, concepts, and skills presented in this chapter to increase your knowledge of Windows 7 and Word 2010. Labs are listed in order of increasing difficulty.

Lab 1: Using Windows Help and Support

Problem: You have a few questions about using Windows 7 and would like to answer these questions using Windows Help and Support.

Instructions: Use Windows Help and Support to perform the following tasks:

1. Display the Start menu and then click Help and Support to start Windows Help and Support.
2. Use the Help and Support Content page to answer the following questions.
   a. How do you reduce computer screen flicker?
   b. Which dialog box do you use to change the appearance of the mouse pointer?
   c. How do you minimize all windows?
   d. What is a VPN?
3. Use the Search Help text box in Windows Help and Support to answer the following questions.
   a. How can you minimize all open windows on the desktop?
   b. How do you start a program using the Run command?
   c. What are the steps to add a toolbar to the taskbar?
   d. What wizard do you use to remove unwanted desktop icons?
4. The tools to solve a problem while using Windows 7 are called **troubleshooters.** Use Windows Help and Support to find the list of troubleshooters (Figure 88), and answer the following questions.
   a. What problems does the HomeGroup troubleshooter allow you to resolve?
   b. List five Windows 7 troubleshooters that are not listed in Figure 88.
5. Use Windows Help and Support to obtain information about software licensing and product activation, and answer the following questions.
   a. What is genuine Windows?
   b. What is activation?
   c. What steps are required to activate Windows?
   d. What steps are required to read the Microsoft Software License Terms?
   e. Can you legally make a second copy of Windows 7 for use at home, work, or on a mobile computer or device?
   f. What is registration?
6. Close the Windows Help and Support window.

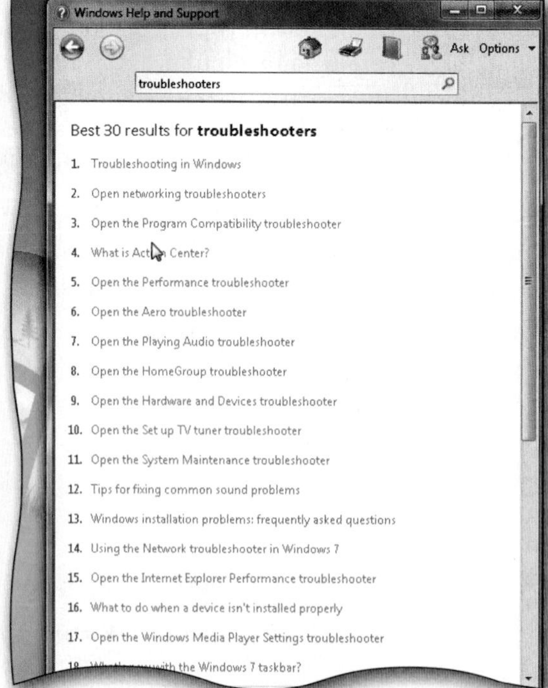

Figure 88

In the Lab

Lab 2: Creating Folders for a Pet Supply Store

Problem: Your friend works for Pete's Pet Supplies. He would like to organize his files in relation to the types of pets available in the store. He has five main categories: dogs, cats, fish, birds, and exotic. You are to create a folder structure similar to Figure 89.

Instructions: Perform the following tasks:

1. Connect a USB flash drive to an available USB port and then open the USB flash drive window.
2. Create the main folder for Pete's Pet Supplies.
3. Navigate to the Pete's Pet Supplies folder.
4. Within the Pete's Pet Supplies folder, create a folder for each of the following: Dogs, Cats, Fish, Birds, and Exotic.
5. Within the Exotic folder, create two additional folders, one for Primates and the second for Reptiles.
6. Submit the assignment in the format specified by your instructor.

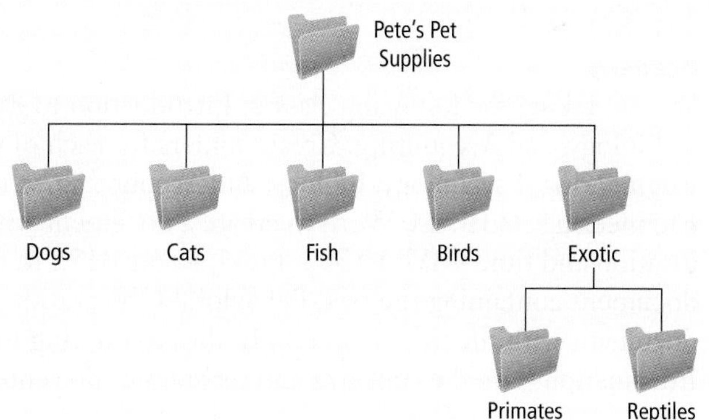

Figure 89

In the Lab

Lab 3: Creating Word Documents and Saving Them in Appropriate Folders

Problem: You are taking a class that requires you to complete three Word chapters. You will save the work completed in each chapter in a different folder (Figure 90).

Instructions: Create the folders shown in Figure 90. Then, using Word, create three small files to save in each folder.

1. Connect a USB flash drive to an available USB port and then open the USB flash drive window.
2. Create the folder structure shown in Figure 90.
3. Navigate to the Chapter 1 folder.
4. Create a Word document containing the text, My Chapter 1 Word Document, and then save it in the Chapter 1 folder using the file name, Word Chapter 1 Document.
5. Navigate to the Chapter 2 folder.
6. Create another Word document containing the text, My Chapter 2 Word Document, and then save it in the Chapter 2 folder using the file name, Word Chapter 2 Document.
7. Navigate to the Chapter 3 folder.
8. Create another Word document containing the text, My Chapter 3 Word Document, and then save it in the Chapter 3 folder using the file name, Word Chapter 3 Document.
9. Quit Word.
10. Submit the assignment in the format specified by your instructor.

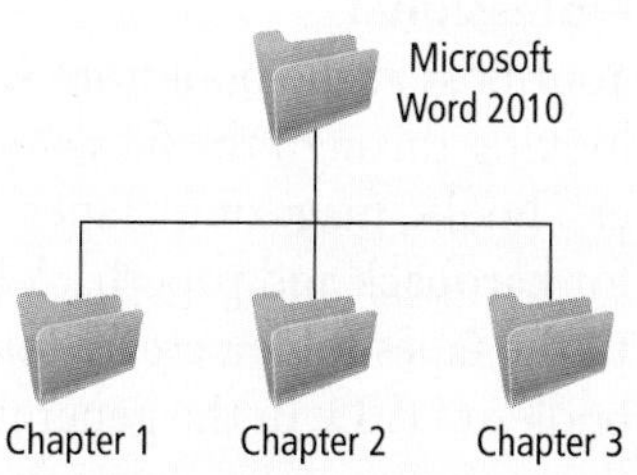

Figure 90

Cases and Places

Apply your creative thinking and problem solving skills to design and implement a solution.

Note: To complete these assignments, you may be required to use the Data Files for Students. See the inside back cover of this book for instructions on downloading the Data Files for Students, or contact your instructor for information about accessing the required files.

1: Creating Beginning Files for Classes

Academic

You are taking the following classes: Introduction to Engineering, Beginning Psychology, Introduction to Biology, and Accounting. Create folders for each of the classes. Use the following folder names: Engineering, Psychology, Biology, and Accounting, when creating the folder structure. In the Engineering folder, use Word to create a document with the name of the class and the class meeting location and time (MW 10:30 – 11:45, Room 317). In the Psychology folder, use Word to create a document containing the text, Behavioral Observations. In the Biology folder, use Word to create a document with the title Research. In the Accounting folder, create a Word document with the text, Tax Information. Use the concepts and techniques presented in this chapter to create the folders and files.

2: Using Help

Personal

Your parents enjoy working and playing games on their home computers. Your mother uses a notebook computer downstairs, and your father uses a desktop computer upstairs. They expressed interest in sharing files between their computers and sharing a single printer, so you offered to research various home networking options. Start Windows Help and Support, and search Help using the keywords, home networking. Use the link for installing a printer on a home network. Start Word and then type the main steps for installing a printer. Use the link for setting up a HomeGroup and then type the main steps for creating a HomeGroup in the Word document. Use the concepts and techniques presented in this chapter to use Help and create the Word document.

3: Creating Folders

Professional

Your boss at the bookstore where you work part-time has asked for help with organizing her files. After looking through the files, you decided upon a file structure for her to use, including the following folders: books, magazines, tapes, DVDs, and general merchandise. Within the books folder, create folders for hardback and paperback books. Within magazines, create folders for special issues and periodicals. In the tapes folder, create folders for celebrity and major release. In the DVDs folder, create a folder for book to DVD. In the general merchandise folder, create folders for novelties, posters, and games. Use the concepts and techniques presented in this chapter to create the folders.

1 Creating, Formatting, and Editing a Word Document with Pictures

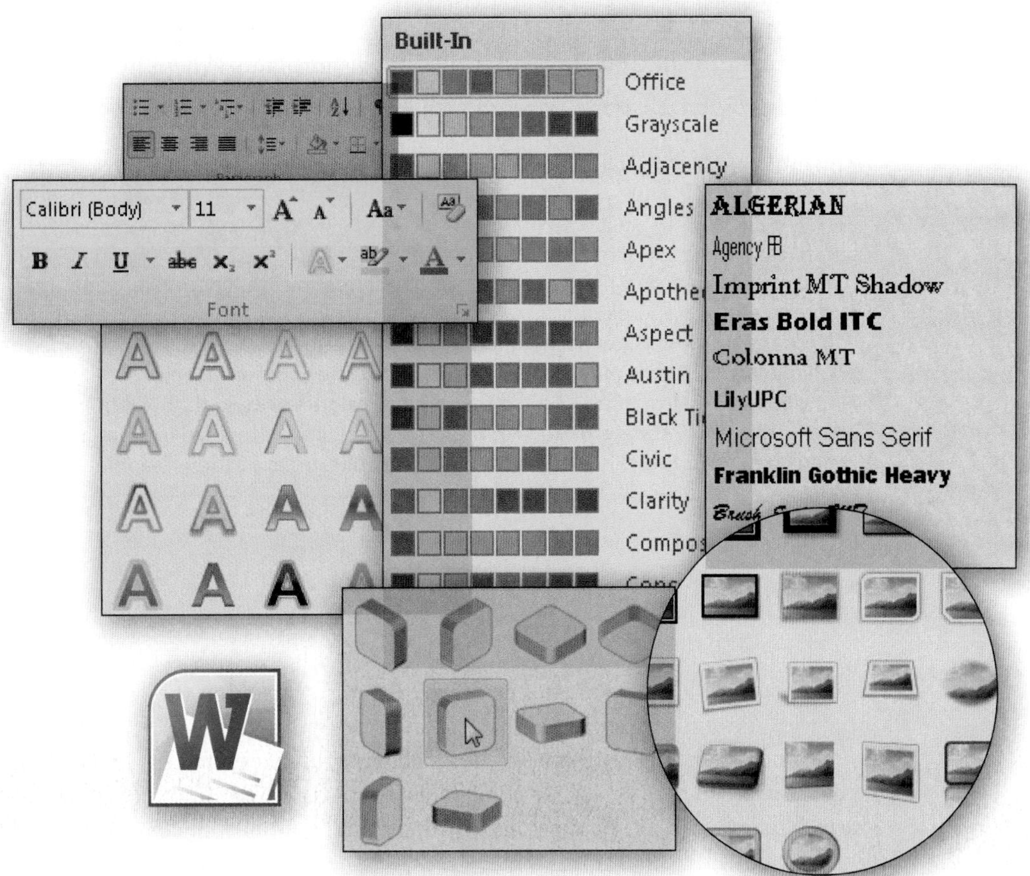

Objectives

You will have mastered the material in this chapter when you can:

- Enter text in a Word document
- Check spelling as you type
- Format paragraphs
- Format text
- Undo and redo commands or actions
- Change theme colors
- Insert digital pictures in a Word document
- Format pictures
- Add a page border
- Correct errors and revise a document
- Change document properties
- Print a document

1 Creating, Formatting, and Editing a Word Document with Pictures

Introduction

To advertise a sale, promote a business, publicize an event, or convey a message to the community, you may want to create a flyer and hand it out in person or post it in a public location. Libraries, schools, religious organizations, grocery stores, coffee shops, and other places often provide bulletin boards or windows for flyers. These flyers announce personal items for sale or rent (car, boat, apartment); garage or block sales; services being offered (animal care, housecleaning, lessons); membership, sponsorship, or donation requests (club, religious organization, charity); and other messages such as a lost or found pet.

Project Planning Guidelines

The process of developing a document that communicates specific information requires careful analysis and planning. As a starting point, establish why the document is needed. Once the purpose is determined, analyze the intended readers of the document and their unique needs. Then, gather information about the topic and decide what to include in the document. Finally, determine the document design and style that will be most successful at delivering the message. Details of these guidelines are provided in Appendix A. In addition, each project in this book provides practical applications of these planning considerations.

Project — Flyer with Pictures

Individuals and businesses create flyers to gain public attention. Flyers, which usually are a single page in length, are an inexpensive means of reaching the community. Many flyers, however, go unnoticed because they are designed poorly.

The project in this chapter follows general guidelines and uses Word to create the flyer shown in Figure 1–1. This colorful, eye-catching flyer announces that a dog has been found. The pictures of the dog, taken with a camera phone, entice passersby to stop and look at the flyer. The headline on the flyer is large and colorful to draw attention into the text. The body copy below the pictures briefly describes where and when the dog was found, along with a bulleted list that concisely highlights important identifying information. The signature line of the flyer calls attention to the contact phone number. The dog's name, Bailey, and signature line are in a different color so that they stand apart from the rest of the text on the flyer. Finally, the graphical page border nicely frames and complements the contents of the flyer.

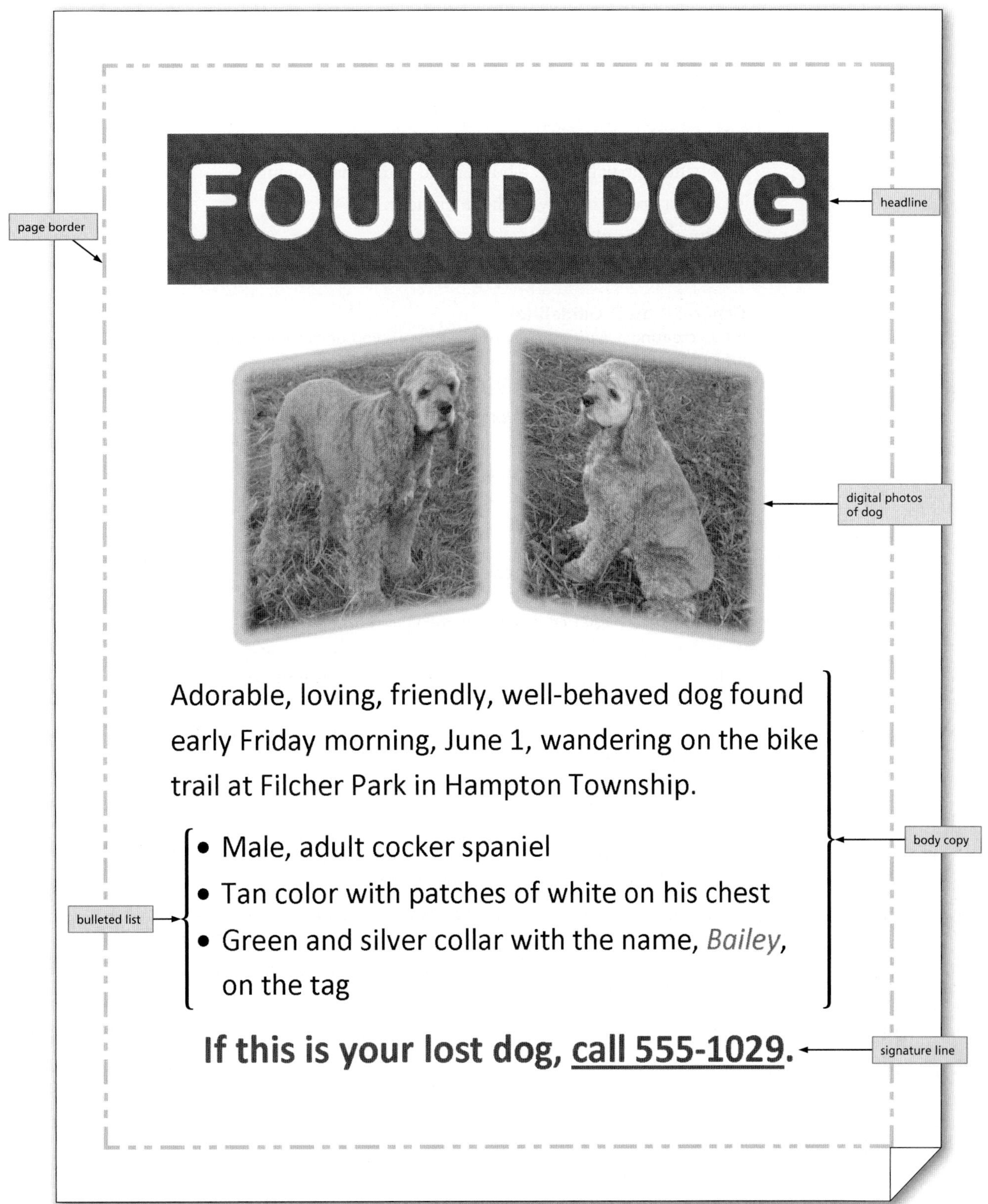
FOUND DOG
headline
page border
digital photos of dog
Adorable, loving, friendly, well-behaved dog found early Friday morning, June 1, wandering on the bike trail at Filcher Park in Hampton Township.
• Male, adult cocker spaniel
• Tan color with patches of white on his chest
• Green and silver collar with the name, *Bailey*, on the tag
body copy
bulleted list
If this is your lost dog, call 555-1029.
signature line

Figure 1–1

Overview

As you read this chapter, you will learn how to create the flyer shown in Figure 1–1 on the previous page by performing these general tasks:

- Enter text in the document.
- Format the text in the document.
- Insert the pictures in the document.
- Format the pictures in the document.
- Enhance the page with a border and additional spacing.
- Correct errors and revise the document.
- Print the document.

Plan Ahead

General Project Guidelines
When creating a Word document, the actions you perform and decisions you make will affect the appearance and characteristics of the finished document. As you create a flyer, such as the project shown in Figure 1–1, you should follow these general guidelines:

1. **Choose the words for the text.** Follow the *less is more* principle. The less text, the more likely the flyer will be read. Use as few words as possible to make a point.
2. **Identify how to format various elements of the text.** The overall appearance of a document significantly affects its ability to communicate clearly. Examples of how you can modify the appearance, or **format**, of text include changing its shape, size, color, and position on the page.
3. **Find the appropriate graphical image(s).** An eye-catching graphical image should convey the flyer's overall message. It could show a product, service, result, or benefit, or visually convey a message that is not expressed easily with words.
4. **Establish where to position and how to format the graphical image(s).** The position and format of the graphical image(s) should grab the attention of passersby and draw them into reading the flyer.
5. **Determine whether the page needs enhancements such as a border or spacing adjustments.** A graphical, color-coordinated page border can further draw attention to a flyer and nicely frame its contents. Increasing or decreasing spacing between elements on a flyer can improve its readability and overall appearance.
6. **Correct errors and revise the document as necessary.** Post the flyer on a wall and make sure all text and images are legible from a distance. Ask someone else to read the flyer and give you suggestions for improvements.
7. **Determine the best method for distributing the document.** Documents can be distributed on paper or electronically. A flyer should be printed on paper so that it can be posted.

When necessary, more specific details concerning the above guidelines are presented at appropriate points in the chapter. The chapter also will identify the actions performed and decisions made regarding these guidelines during the creation of the flyer shown in Figure 1–1.

For an introduction to Windows 7 and instruction about how to perform basic Windows 7 tasks, read the Office 2010 and Windows 7 chapter at the beginning of this book, where you can learn how to resize windows, change screen resolution, create folders, move and rename files, use Windows Help, and much more.

To Start Word

If you are using a computer to step through the project in this chapter and you want your screens to match the figures in this book, you should change your screen's resolution to 1024 × 768. For information about how to change a computer's resolution, refer to the Office 2010 and Windows 7 chapter at the beginning of this book.

The following steps, which assume Windows 7 is running, start Word based on a typical installation. You may need to ask your instructor how to start Word for your computer. For a detailed example of the procedure summarized below, refer to the Office 2010 and Windows 7 chapter.

For an introduction to Office 2010 and instruction about how to perform basic tasks in Office 2010 programs, read the Office 2010 and Windows 7 chapter at the beginning of this book, where you can learn how to start a program, use the Ribbon, save a file, open a file, quit a program, use Help, and much more.

1. Click the Start button on the Windows 7 taskbar to display the Start menu.
2. Type `Microsoft Word` as the search text in the 'Search programs and files' text box and watch the search results appear on the Start menu.
3. Click Microsoft Word 2010 in the search results on the Start menu to start Word and display a new blank document in the Word window.
4. If the Word window is not maximized, click the Maximize button next to the Close button on its title bar to maximize the window.
5. If the Print Layout button on the status bar is not selected (shown in Figure 1–2 on the next page), click it so that your screen is in Print Layout view.

Q&A What is Print Layout view?

The default (preset) view in Word is **Print Layout view**, which shows the document on a mock sheet of paper in the document window.

6. If Normal (Home tab | Styles group) is not selected in the Quick Style gallery (shown in Figure 1–2), click it so that your document uses the Normal style.

Q&A What is the Normal style?

When you create a document, Word formats the text using a particular style. The default style in Word is called the **Normal style**, which is discussed later in this book.

Q&A What if rulers appear on my screen?

Click the View Ruler button above the vertical scroll bar to hide the rulers, or click View on the Ribbon to display the View tab and then place a check mark in the Ruler check box.

BTW **The Word Window**
The chapters in this book begin with the Word window appearing as it did at the initial installation of the software. Your Word window may look different depending on your screen resolution and other Word settings.

Entering Text

The first step in creating a document is to enter its text. With the projects in this book, you enter text by typing on the keyboard. By default, Word positions text you type at the left margin. In a later section of this chapter, you will learn how to format, or change the appearance of, the entered text.

Plan Ahead

Choose the words for the text.
The text in a flyer is organized into three areas: headline, body copy, and signature line.

- The **headline** is the first line of text on the flyer. It conveys the product or service being offered, such as a car for sale or personal lessons, or the benefit that will be gained, such as a convenience, better performance, greater security, higher earnings, or more comfort; or it can contain a message such as a lost or found pet.
- The **body copy** consists of all text between the headline and the signature line. This text highlights the key points of the message in as few words as possible. It should be easy to read and follow. While emphasizing the positive, the body copy must be realistic, truthful, and believable.
- The **signature line**, which is the last line of text on the flyer, contains contact information or identifies a call to action.

BTW **Zooming**
If text is too small for you to read on the screen, you can zoom the document by dragging the Zoom slider on the status bar or clicking the Zoom Out or Zoom In buttons on the status bar. Changing the zoom has no effect on the printed document.

To Type Text

To begin creating the flyer in this chapter, type the headline in the document window. The following steps type this first line of text in the document.

1

- Type **Found Dog** as the headline (Figure 1–2).

Q&A What if I make an error while typing?

You can press the BACKSPACE key until you have deleted the text in error and then retype the text correctly.

Q&A Why did the Spelling and Grammar Check icon appear on the status bar?

When you begin typing text, the **Spelling and Grammar Check icon** appears on the status bar with an animated pencil writing on paper to indicate that Word is checking for spelling and grammar errors. When you stop typing, the pencil changes to a blue check mark (no errors) or a red X (potential errors found). Word flags potential errors in the document with a red, green, or blue wavy underline. Later in this chapter, you will learn how to fix flagged errors.

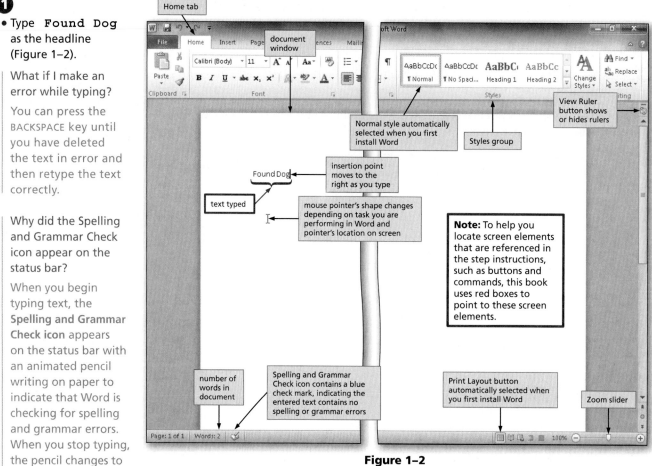

Note: To help you locate screen elements that are referenced in the step instructions, such as buttons and commands, this book uses red boxes to point to these screen elements.

Figure 1–2

2

- Press the ENTER key to move the insertion point to the beginning of the next line (Figure 1–3).

Q&A Why did blank space appear between the headline and the insertion point?

Each time you press the ENTER key, Word creates a new paragraph and inserts blank space between the two paragraphs. Later in this chapter, you will learn how to adjust the spacing between paragraphs.

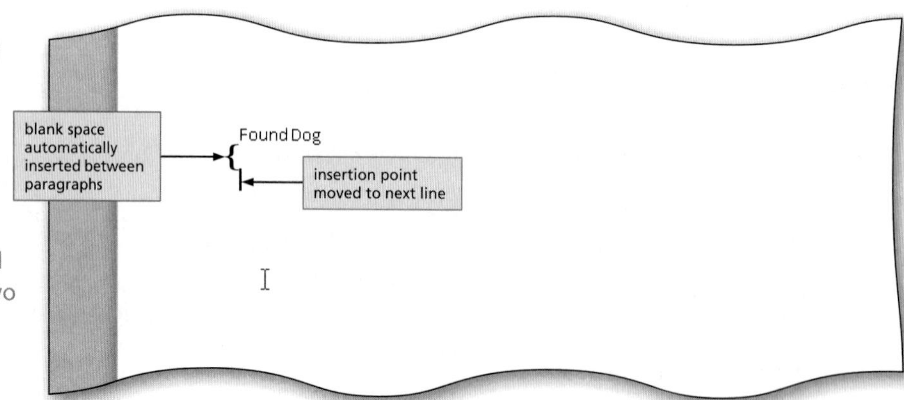

Figure 1–3

To Display Formatting Marks

To indicate where in a document you press the ENTER key or SPACEBAR, you may find it helpful to display formatting marks. A **formatting mark**, sometimes called a **nonprinting character**, is a character that Word displays on the screen but is not visible on a printed document. For example, the paragraph mark (¶) is a formatting mark that indicates where you press the ENTER key. A raised dot (·) shows where you press the SPACEBAR. Other formatting marks are discussed as they appear on the screen.

Depending on settings made during previous Word sessions, your Word screen already may display formatting marks (Figure 1–4). The following step displays formatting marks, if they do not show already on the screen.

- If the Home tab is not the active tab, click Home on the Ribbon to display the Home tab.
- If it is not selected already, click the Show/Hide ¶ button (Home tab | Paragraph group) to display formatting marks on the screen (Figure 1–4).

Q&A What if I do not want formatting marks to show on the screen?

You can hide them by clicking the Show/Hide ¶ button (Home tab | Paragraph group) again. It is recommended that you display formatting marks so that you visually can identify when you press the ENTER key, SPACEBAR, and other keys associated with nonprinting characters; therefore, most of the document windows presented in this book show formatting marks.

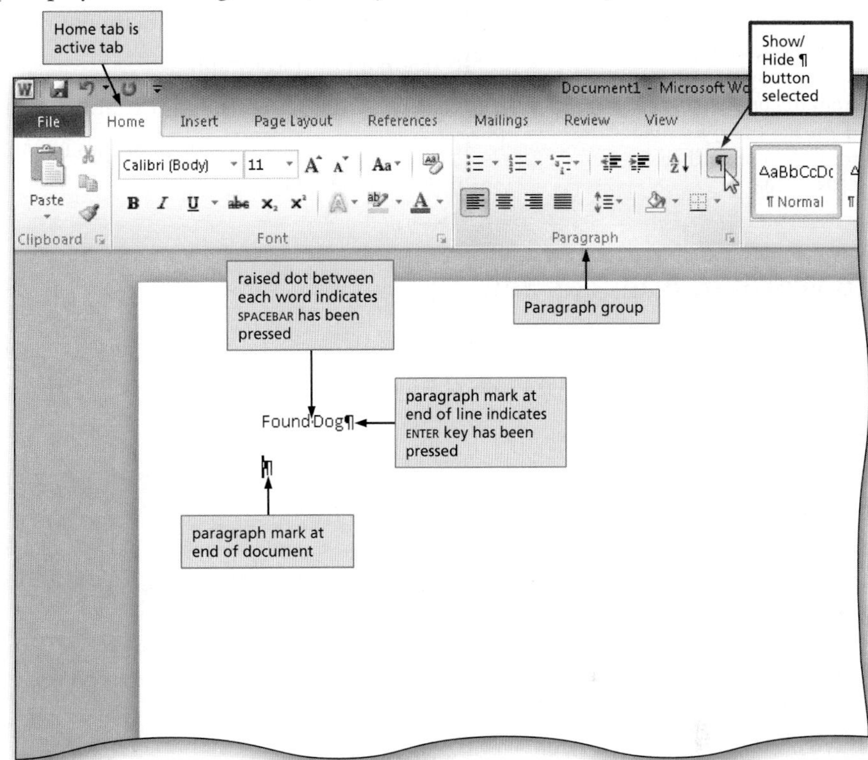

Figure 1–4

Other Ways

1. Press CTRL+SHIFT+*

To Insert a Blank Line

In the flyer, the digital pictures of the dog appear between the headline and body copy. You will not insert these pictures, however, until after you enter and format all text. Thus, you leave a blank line in the document as a placeholder for the pictures. To enter a blank line in a document, press the ENTER key without typing any text on the line. The following step inserts one blank line below the headline.

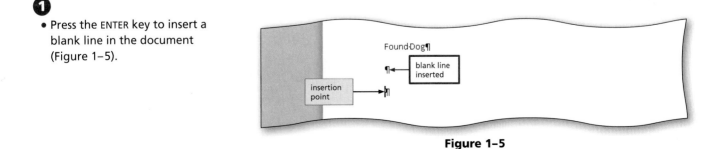

- Press the ENTER key to insert a blank line in the document (Figure 1–5).

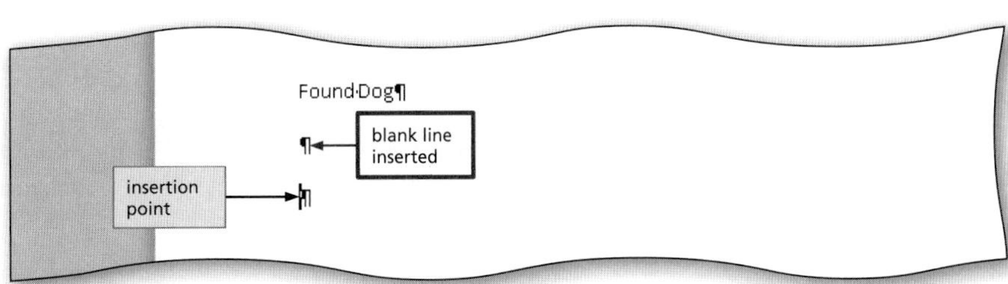

Figure 1–5

Wordwrap

Wordwrap allows you to type words in a paragraph continually without pressing the ENTER key at the end of each line. As you type, if a word extends beyond the right margin, Word also automatically positions that word on the next line along with the insertion point.

Word creates a new paragraph each time you press the ENTER key. Thus, as you type text in the document window, do not press the ENTER key when the insertion point reaches the right margin. Instead, press the ENTER key only in these circumstances:

1. To insert a blank line(s) in a document (as shown in the steps on the previous page)
2. To begin a new paragraph
3. To terminate a short line of text and advance to the next line
4. To respond to questions or prompts in Word dialog boxes, task panes, and other on-screen objects

BTW

The Ribbon and Screen Resolution
Word may change how the groups and buttons within the groups appear on the Ribbon, depending on the computer's screen resolution. Thus, your Ribbon may look different from the ones in this book if you are using a screen resolution other than 1024 × 768.

To Wordwrap Text as You Type

The next step in creating the flyer is to type the body copy. The following step illustrates how the body copy text wordwraps as you enter it in the document.

1

- Type the first sentence of the body copy: **`Adorable, loving, friendly, well-behaved dog found early Friday morning, June 1, wandering on the bike trail at Filcher Park in Hampton Township.`**

Q&A

Why does my document wrap on different words?

The printer connected to a computer is one factor that can control where wordwrap occurs for each line in a document. Thus, it is possible that the same document could wordwrap differently if printed on different printers.

- Press the ENTER key to position the insertion point on the next line in the document (Figure 1–6).

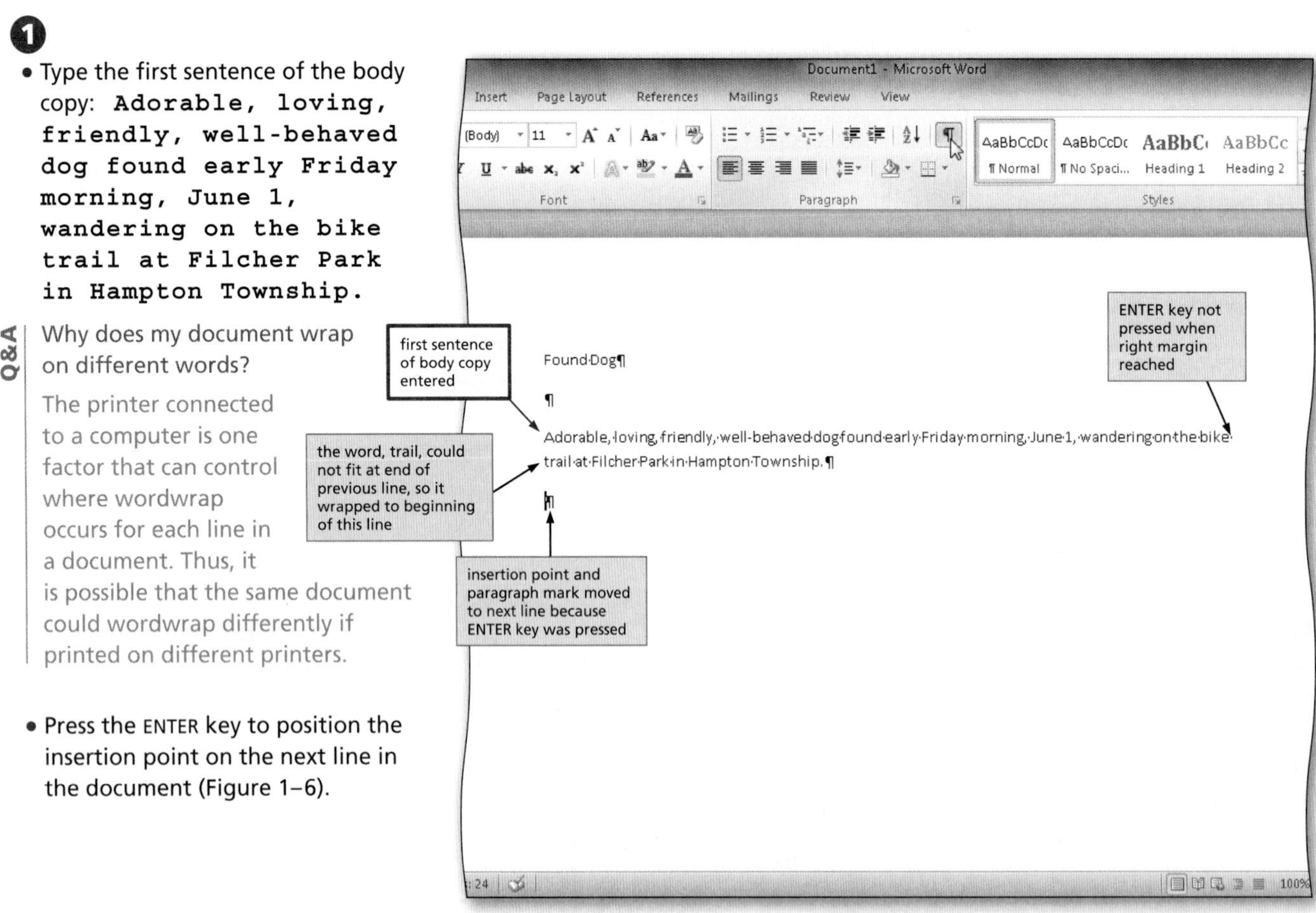

Figure 1–6

Spelling and Grammar Check

As you type text in a document, Word checks your typing for possible spelling and grammar errors. If all of the words you have typed are in Word's dictionary and your grammar is correct, as mentioned earlier, the Spelling and Grammar Check icon on the status bar displays a blue check mark. Otherwise, the icon shows a red X. In this case, Word flags the potential error in the document window with a red, green, or blue wavy underline. A red wavy underline means the flagged text is not in Word's dictionary (because it is a proper name or misspelled). A green wavy underline indicates the text may be incorrect grammatically. A blue wavy underline indicates the text may contain a contextual spelling error such as the misuse of homophones (words that are pronounced the same but that have different spellings or meanings, such as one and won). Although you can check the entire document for spelling and grammar errors at once, you also can check flagged errors as they appear on the screen.

A flagged word is not necessarily misspelled. For example, many names, abbreviations, and specialized terms are not in Word's main dictionary. In these cases, you can instruct Word to ignore the flagged word. As you type, Word also detects duplicate words while checking for spelling errors. For example, if your document contains the phrase, to the the store, Word places a red wavy underline below the second occurrence of the word, the.

BTW

Automatic Spelling Correction
As you type, Word automatically corrects some misspelled words. For example, if you type recieve, Word automatically corrects the misspelling and displays the word, receive, when you press the SPACEBAR or type a punctuation mark. To see a complete list of automatically corrected words, click File on the Ribbon to open the Backstage view, click Options in the Backstage view, click Proofing in the left pane (Word Options dialog box), click the AutoCorrect Options button, and then scroll through the list near the bottom of the dialog box.

To Check Spelling and Grammar as You Type

In the following steps, the word, patches, has been misspelled intentionally as paches to illustrate Word's check spelling as you type feature. If you are doing this project on a computer, your flyer may contain different misspelled words, depending on the accuracy of your typing.

1

- Type `Tan color with paches` and then press the SPACEBAR so that a red wavy line appears below the misspelled word (Figure 1–7).

Q&A

What if Word does not flag my spelling and grammar errors with wavy underlines?

To verify that the check spelling and grammar as you type features are enabled, click File on the Ribbon to open the Backstage view and then click Options in the Backstage view. When the Word Options dialog box is displayed, click Proofing in the left pane, and then ensure the 'Check spelling as you type' and 'Mark grammar errors as you type' check boxes contain check marks. Also ensure the 'Hide spelling errors in this document only' and 'Hide grammar errors in this document only' check boxes do not have check marks. Click the OK button.

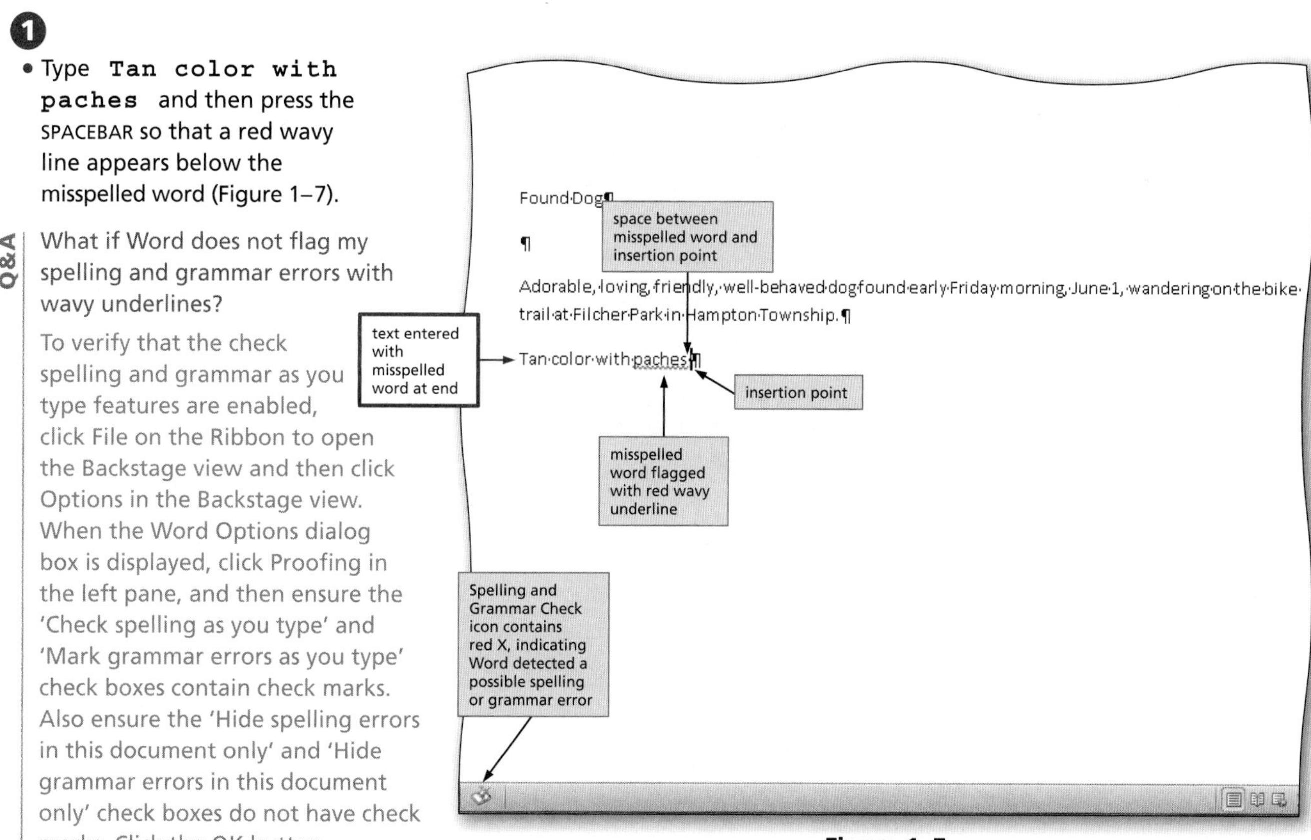

Figure 1–7

2

- Right-click the flagged word (paches, in this case) to display a shortcut menu that presents a list of suggested spelling corrections for the flagged word (Figure 1–8).

Q&A What if, when I right-click the misspelled word, my desired correction is not in the list on the shortcut menu?

You can click outside the shortcut menu to close the shortcut menu and then retype the correct word, or you can click Spelling on the shortcut menu to display the Spelling dialog box. Chapter 2 discusses the Spelling dialog box.

Q&A What if a flagged word actually is, for example, a proper name and spelled correctly?

Right-click it and then click Ignore All on the shortcut menu to instruct Word not to flag future occurrences of the same word in this document.

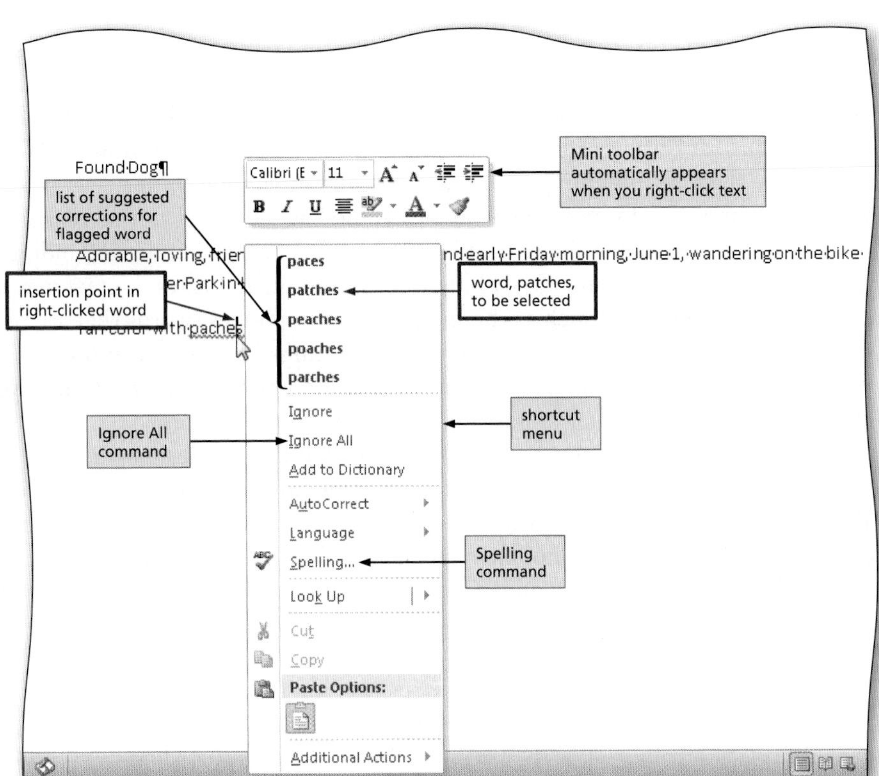

Figure 1–8

3

- Click patches on the shortcut menu to replace the misspelled word in the document with a correctly spelled word (Figure 1–9).

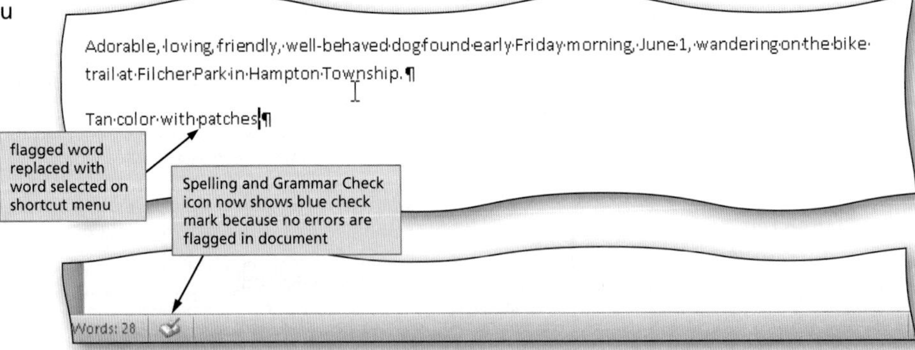

Figure 1–9

Other Ways

1. Click Spelling and Grammar Check icon on status bar, click desired word on shortcut menu

BTW **Character Widths**

Many word processing documents use variable character fonts, where some characters are wider than others; for example, the letter w is wider than the letter i.

To Enter More Text

In the flyer, the text yet to be entered includes the remainder of the body copy, which will be formatted as a bulleted list, and the signature line. The next steps enter the remainder of text in the flyer.

1. Press the END key to move the insertion point to the end of the current line.
2. Type `of white on his chest` and then press the ENTER key.
3. Type `Male, adult cocker spaniel` and then press the ENTER key.
4. Type `Green and silver collar with the name, Bailey, on the tag` and then press the ENTER key.
5. Type the signature line in the flyer (Figure 1–10): `If this is your lost dog, call 555-1029.`

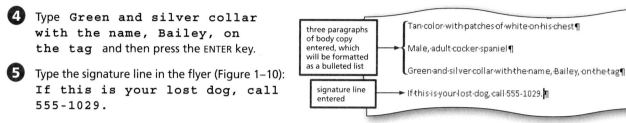

three paragraphs of body copy entered, which will be formatted as a bulleted list
Tan·color·with·patches·of·white·on·his·chest¶
Male,·adult·cocker·spaniel¶
Green·and·silver·collar·with·the·name,·Bailey,·on·the·tag¶
signature line entered
If·this·is·your·lost·dog,·call·555-1029.¶

Figure 1–10

Navigating a Document

You view only a portion of a document on the screen through the document window. At some point when you type text or insert graphics, Word probably will **scroll** the top or bottom portion of the document off the screen. Although you cannot see the text and graphics once they scroll off the screen, they remain in the document.

You can use either the keyboard or the mouse to scroll to a different location in a document and/or move the insertion point around a document. When you use the keyboard, the insertion point automatically moves when you press the desired keys. For example, the previous steps used the END key to move the insertion point to the end of the current line. Table 1–1 outlines various techniques to navigate a document using the keyboard.

With the mouse, you can use the scroll arrows or the scroll box on the scroll bar to display a different portion of the document in the document window and then click the mouse to move the insertion point to that location. Table 1–2 explains various techniques for using the scroll bar to scroll vertically with the mouse.

BTW

Minimize Wrist Injury
Computer users frequently switch between the keyboard and the mouse during a word processing session; such switching strains the wrist. To help prevent wrist injury, minimize switching. For instance, if your fingers already are on the keyboard, use keyboard keys to scroll. If your hand already is on the mouse, use the mouse to scroll.

Table 1–1 Moving the Insertion Point with the Keyboard

Insertion Point Direction	Key(s) to Press	Insertion Point Direction	Key(s) to Press
Left one character	LEFT ARROW	Up one paragraph	CTRL+UP ARROW
Right one character	RIGHT ARROW	Down one paragraph	CTRL+DOWN ARROW
Left one word	CTRL+LEFT ARROW	Up one screen	PAGE UP
Right one word	CTRL+RIGHT ARROW	Down one screen	PAGE DOWN
Up one line	UP ARROW	To top of document window	ALT+CTRL+PAGE UP
Down one line	DOWN ARROW	To bottom of document window	ALT+CTRL+PAGE DOWN
To end of line	END	To beginning of document	CTRL+HOME
To beginning of line	HOME	To end of document	CTRL+END

Table 1–2 Using the Scroll Bar to Scroll Vertically with the Mouse

Scroll Direction	Mouse Action	Scroll Direction	Mouse Action
Up	Drag the scroll box upward.	Down one screen	Click anywhere below the scroll box on the vertical scroll bar.
Down	Drag the scroll box downward.	Up one line	Click the scroll arrow at the top of the vertical scroll bar.
Up one screen	Click anywhere above the scroll box on the vertical scroll bar.	Down one line	Click the scroll arrow at the bottom of the vertical scroll bar.

BTW

Organizing Files and Folders
You should organize and store files in folders so that you easily can find the files later. For example, if you are taking an introductory computer class called CIS 101, a good practice would be to save all Word files in a Word folder in a CIS 101 folder. For a discussion of folders and detailed examples of creating folders, refer to the Office 2010 and Windows 7 chapter at the beginning of this book.

To Save a Document

You have performed many tasks while creating this flyer and do not want to risk losing work completed thus far. Accordingly, you should save the document.

The following steps assume you already have created folders for storing your files, for example, a CIS 101 folder (for your class) that contains a Word folder (for your assignments). Thus, these steps save the document in the Word folder in the CIS 101 folder on a USB flash drive using the file name, Found Dog Flyer. For a detailed example of the procedure summarized below, refer to the Office 2010 and Windows 7 chapter at the beginning of this book.

1. With a USB flash drive connected to one of the computer's USB ports, click the Save button on the Quick Access Toolbar to display the Save As dialog box.
2. Type **`Found Dog Flyer`** in the File name text box to change the file name. Do not press the ENTER key after typing the file name because you do not want to close the dialog box at this time.
3. Navigate to the desired save location (in this case, the Word folder in the CIS 101 folder [or your class folder] on the USB flash drive).
4. Click the Save button (Save As dialog box) to save the document in the selected folder on the selected drive with the entered file name.

Formatting Paragraphs and Characters

With the text for the flyer entered, the next step is to **format**, or change the appearance of, its text. A paragraph encompasses the text from the first character in the paragraph up to and including its paragraph mark (¶). **Paragraph formatting** is the process of changing the appearance of a paragraph. For example, you can center or add bullets to a paragraph. Characters include letters, numbers, punctuation marks, and symbols. **Character formatting** is the process of changing the way characters appear on the screen and in print. You use character formatting to emphasize certain words and improve readability of a document. For example, you can color or underline characters. Often, you apply both paragraph and character formatting to the same text. For example, you may center a paragraph (paragraph formatting) and underline some of the characters in the same paragraph (character formatting).

Although you can format paragraphs and characters before you type, many Word users enter text first and then format the existing text. Figure 1–11a shows the flyer in this chapter before formatting its paragraphs and characters. Figure 1–11b shows the flyer after formatting. As you can see from the two figures, a document that is formatted is easier to read and looks more professional. The following pages discuss how to format the flyer so that it looks like Figure 1–11b.

Characters that appear on the screen are a specific shape and size. The **font**, or typeface, defines the appearance and shape of the letters, numbers, and special characters. In Word, the default font usually is Calibri (shown in Figure 1–12 on page WD 14). You can leave characters in the default font or change them to a different font. **Font size** specifies the size of the characters and is determined by a measurement system called points. A single **point** is about 1/72 of one inch in height. The default font size in Word typically is 11 (Figure 1–12). Thus, a character with a font size of 11 is about 11/72 or a little less than 1/6 of one inch in height. You can increase or decrease the font size of characters in a document.

A document **theme** is a set of unified formats for fonts, colors, and graphics. Word includes a variety of document themes to assist you with coordinating these visual elements in a document. The default theme fonts are Cambria for headings and Calibri for body text. By changing the document theme, you quickly can give your document a new look. You also can define your own document themes.

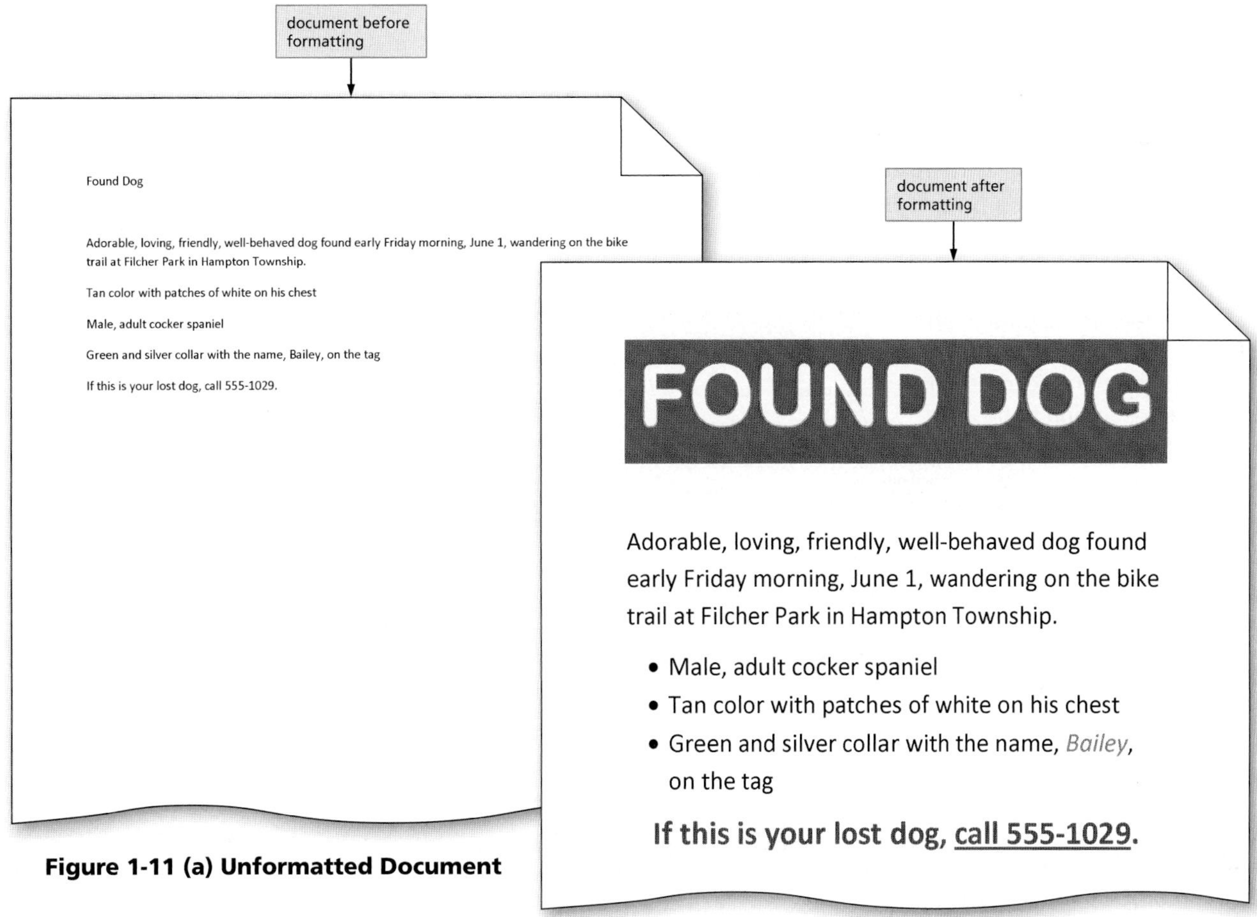
document before formatting
Found Dog
Adorable, loving, friendly, well-behaved dog found early Friday morning, June 1, wandering on the bike trail at Filcher Park in Hampton Township.
Tan color with patches of white on his chest
Male, adult cocker spaniel
Green and silver collar with the name, Bailey, on the tag
If this is your lost dog, call 555-1029.
document after formatting
FOUND DOG
Adorable, loving, friendly, well-behaved dog found early Friday morning, June 1, wandering on the bike trail at Filcher Park in Hampton Township.
• Male, adult cocker spaniel
• Tan color with patches of white on his chest
• Green and silver collar with the name, Bailey, on the tag
If this is your lost dog, call 555-1029.

Figure 1-11 (a) Unformatted Document

Figure 1-11 (b) Formatted Document

Plan Ahead

Identify how to format various elements of the text.
By formatting the characters and paragraphs in a document, you can improve its overall appearance. In a flyer, consider the following formatting suggestions.

- **Increase the font size of characters.** Flyers usually are posted on a bulletin board or in a window. Thus, the font size should be as large as possible so that passersby easily can read the flyer. To give the headline more impact, its font size should be larger than the font size of the text in the body copy. If possible, make the font size of the signature line larger than the body copy but smaller than the headline.
- **Change the font of characters.** Use fonts that are easy to read. Try to use only two different fonts in a flyer, for example, one for the headline and the other for all other text. Too many fonts can make the flyer visually confusing.
- **Change paragraph alignment.** The default alignment for paragraphs in a document is **left-aligned**, that is, flush at the left margin of the document with uneven right edges. Consider changing the alignment of some of the paragraphs to add interest and variety to the flyer.
- **Highlight key paragraphs with bullets.** A bulleted paragraph is a paragraph that begins with a dot or other symbol. Use bulleted paragraphs to highlight important points in a flyer.
- **Emphasize important words.** To call attention to certain words or lines, you can underline them, italicize them, or bold them. Use these formats sparingly, however, because overuse will minimize their effect and make the flyer look too busy.
- **Use color.** Use colors that complement each other and convey the meaning of the flyer. Vary colors in terms of hue and brightness. Headline colors, for example, can be bold and bright. Signature lines should stand out more than body copy but less than headlines. Keep in mind that too many colors can detract from the flyer and make it difficult to read.

To Center a Paragraph

The headline in the flyer currently is left-aligned (Figure 1–12). You want the headline to be **centered**, that is, positioned horizontally between the left and right margins on the page. Recall that Word considers a single short line of text, such as the two-word headline, a paragraph. Thus, you will center the paragraph containing the headline. The following steps center a paragraph.

1

- Click somewhere in the paragraph to be centered (in this case, the headline) to position the insertion point in the paragraph to be formatted (Figure 1–12).

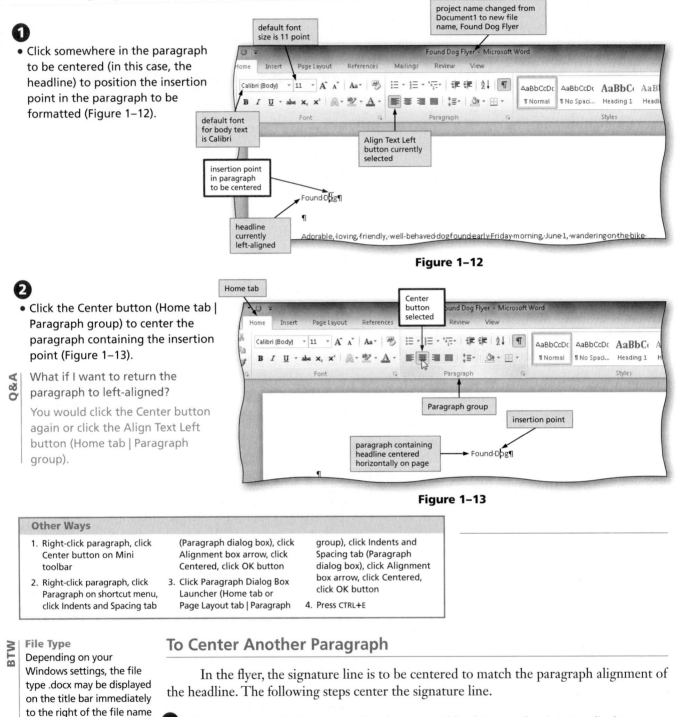

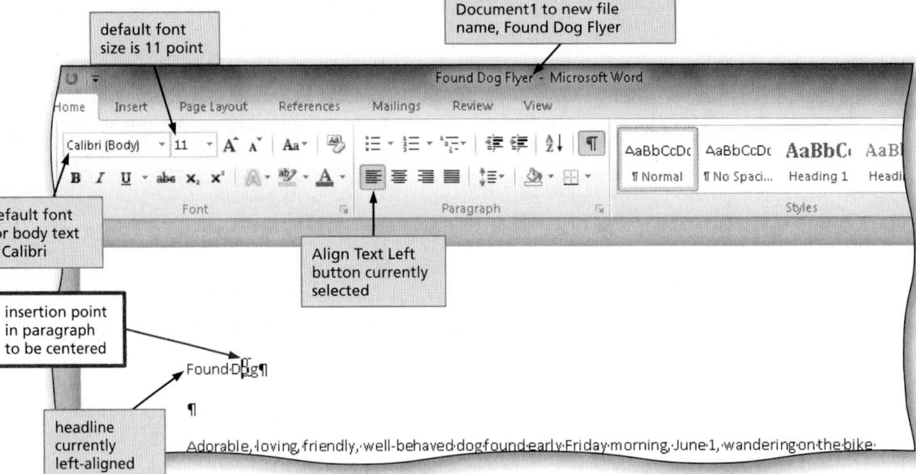

Figure 1–12

2

- Click the Center button (Home tab | Paragraph group) to center the paragraph containing the insertion point (Figure 1–13).

Q&A What if I want to return the paragraph to left-aligned?

You would click the Center button again or click the Align Text Left button (Home tab | Paragraph group).

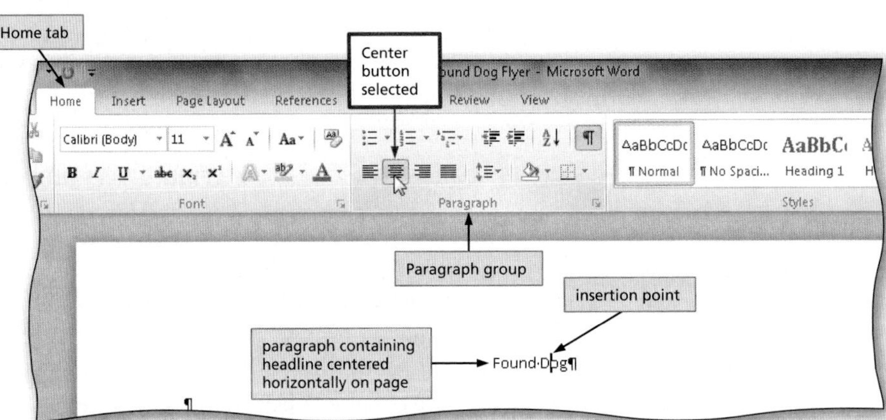

Figure 1–13

Other Ways

1. Right-click paragraph, click Center button on Mini toolbar
2. Right-click paragraph, click Paragraph on shortcut menu, click Indents and Spacing tab (Paragraph dialog box), click Alignment box arrow, click Centered, click OK button
3. Click Paragraph Dialog Box Launcher (Home tab or Page Layout tab | Paragraph group), click Indents and Spacing tab (Paragraph dialog box), click Alignment box arrow, click Centered, click OK button
4. Press CTRL+E

BTW **File Type**
Depending on your Windows settings, the file type .docx may be displayed on the title bar immediately to the right of the file name after you save the file. The file type .docx is a Word 2010 document.

To Center Another Paragraph

In the flyer, the signature line is to be centered to match the paragraph alignment of the headline. The following steps center the signature line.

1. Click somewhere in the paragraph to be centered (in this case, the signature line) to position the insertion point in the paragraph to be formatted.

2. Click the Center button (Home tab | Paragraph group) to center the paragraph containing the insertion point (shown in Figure 1–14).

Formatting Single versus Multiple Paragraphs and Characters

As shown on the previous pages, to format a single paragraph, simply move the insertion point in the paragraph, to make it the current paragraph, and then format the paragraph. Similarly, to format a single word, position the insertion point in the word, to make it the current word, and then format the word.

To format multiple paragraphs or words, however, you first must select the paragraphs or words you want to format and then format the selection. If your screen normally displays dark letters on a light background, which is the default setting in Word, then selected text displays light letters on a dark background.

BTW

Selecting Nonadjacent Items

In Word, you can select nonadjacent items, that is, items not next to each other. This is helpful when you are applying the same formatting to multiple items. To select nonadjacent items (text or graphics), select the first item, such as a word or paragraph, as usual; then, press and hold down the CTRL key. While holding down the CTRL key, select additional items.

To Select a Line

The default font size of 11 point is too small for a headline in a flyer. To increase the font size of the characters in the headline, you first must select the line of text containing the headline. The following steps select a line.

- Move the mouse pointer to the left of the line to be selected (in this case, the headline) until the mouse pointer changes to a right-pointing block arrow (Figure 1–14).

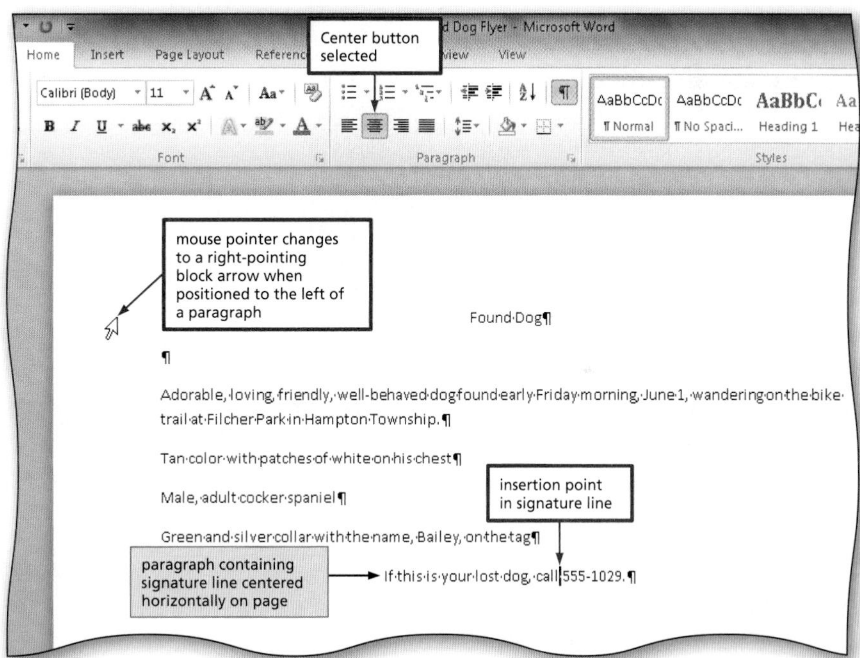
Center button selected
mouse pointer changes to a right-pointing block arrow when positioned to the left of a paragraph
Found·Dog¶
Adorable,·loving,·friendly,·well-behaved·dog·found·early·Friday·morning,·June·1,·wandering·on·the·bike·trail·at·Filcher·Park·in·Hampton·Township.¶
Tan·color·with·patches·of·white·on·his·chest¶
Male,·adult·cocker·spaniel¶
insertion point in signature line
Green·and·silver·collar·with·the·name,·Bailey,·on·the·tag¶
paragraph containing signature line centered horizontally on page
If·this·is·your·lost·dog,·call·555-1029.¶

Figure 1–14

2

- While the mouse pointer is a right-pointing block arrow, click the mouse to select the entire line to the right of the mouse pointer (Figure 1–15).

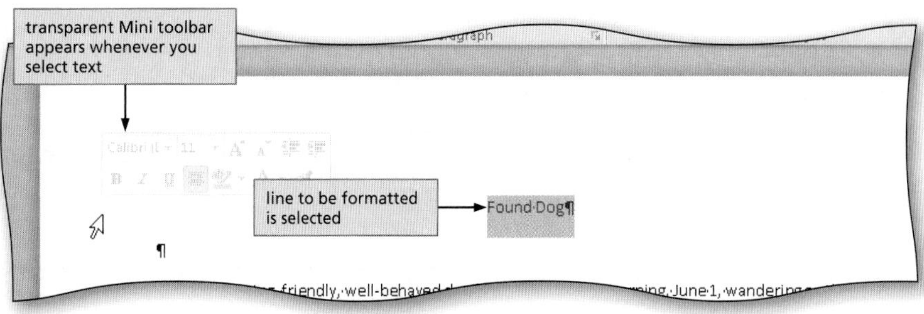
transparent Mini toolbar appears whenever you select text
line to be formatted is selected
Found·Dog¶

Figure 1–15

Other Ways

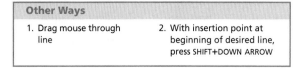

1. Drag mouse through line
2. With insertion point at beginning of desired line, press SHIFT+DOWN ARROW

To Change the Font Size of Selected Text

The next step is to increase the font size of the characters in the selected headline. You would like the headline to be as large as possible and still fit on a single line, which in this case is 72 point. The following steps increase the font size of the headline from 11 to 72 point.

- With the text selected, click the Font Size box arrow (Home tab | Font group) to display the Font Size gallery (Figure 1–16).

Q&A Why are the font sizes in my Font Size gallery different from those in Figure 1–16?

Font sizes may vary depending on the current font and your printer driver.

Q&A What happened to the Mini toolbar?

The Mini toolbar disappears if you do not use it. These steps use the Font Size box arrow on the Home tab instead of the Font Size box arrow on the Mini toolbar.

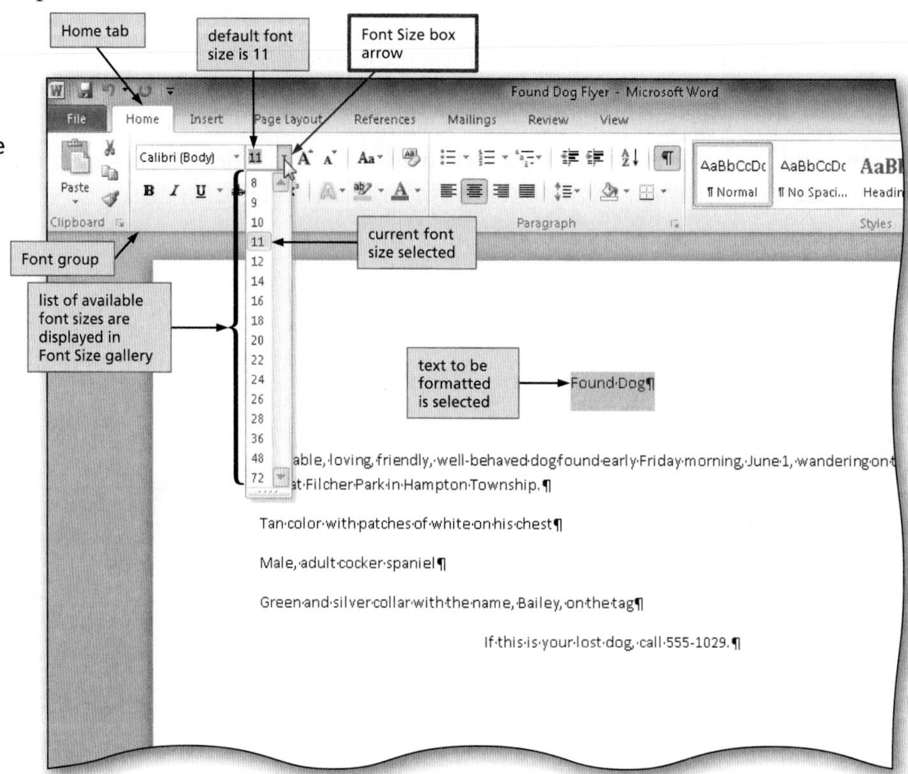

Figure 1–16

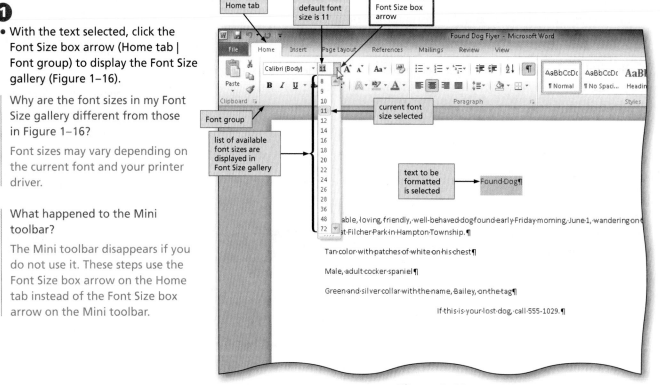

- Point to 72 in the Font Size gallery to display a live preview of the selected text at the selected point size (Figure 1–17).

Experiment

- Point to various font sizes in the Font Size gallery and watch the font size of the selected text change in the document window.

- Click 72 in the Font Size gallery to increase the font size of the selected text.

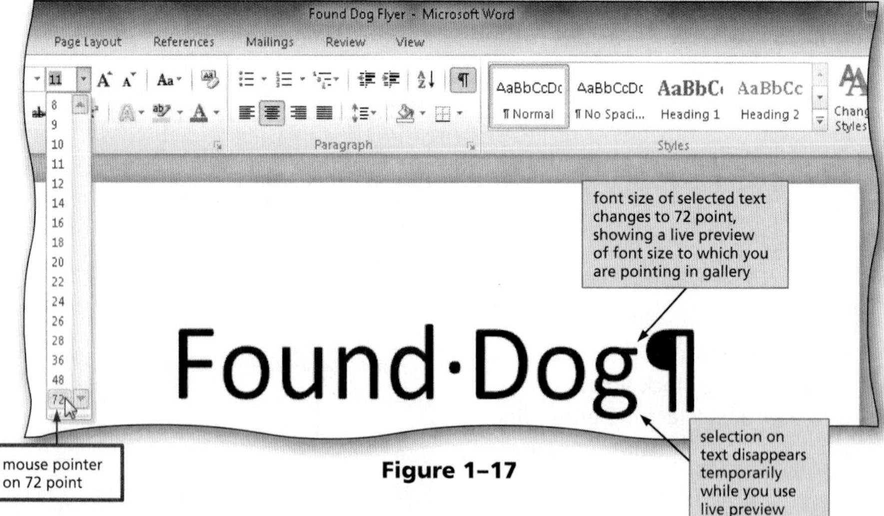

Figure 1–17

Other Ways

1. Click Font Size box arrow on Mini toolbar, click desired font size in Font Size gallery
2. Right-click selected text, click Font on shortcut menu, click Font tab (Font dialog box), select desired font size in Size list, click OK button
3. Click Font Dialog Box Launcher, click Font tab (Font dialog box), select desired font size in Size list, click OK button
4. Press CTRL+D, click Font tab (Font dialog box), select desired font size in Size list, click OK button

To Change the Font of Selected Text

The default theme font for headings is Cambria and for all other text, called body text in Word, is Calibri. Many other fonts are available, however, so that you can add variety to documents.

To draw more attention to the headline, you change its font so that it differs from the font of other text in the flyer. The following steps change the font of the headline from Calibri to Arial Rounded MT Bold.

1

- With the text selected, click the Font box arrow (Home tab | Font group) to display the Font gallery (Figure 1–18).

Q&A Will the fonts in my Font gallery be the same as those in Figure 1–18?

Your list of available fonts may differ, depending on the type of printer you are using and other settings.

Q&A What if the text is no longer selected?

Follow the steps on page WD 15 to select a line.

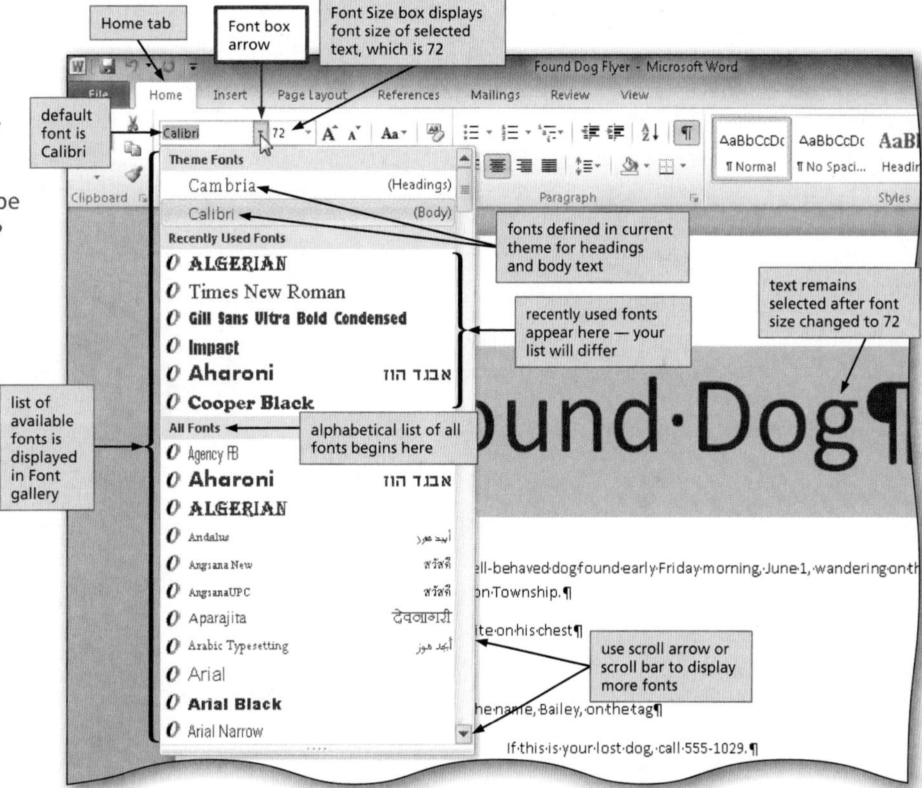

Figure 1–18

2

- Scroll through the Font gallery, if necessary, and then point to Arial Rounded MT Bold (or a similar font) to display a live preview of the selected text in the selected font (Figure 1–19).

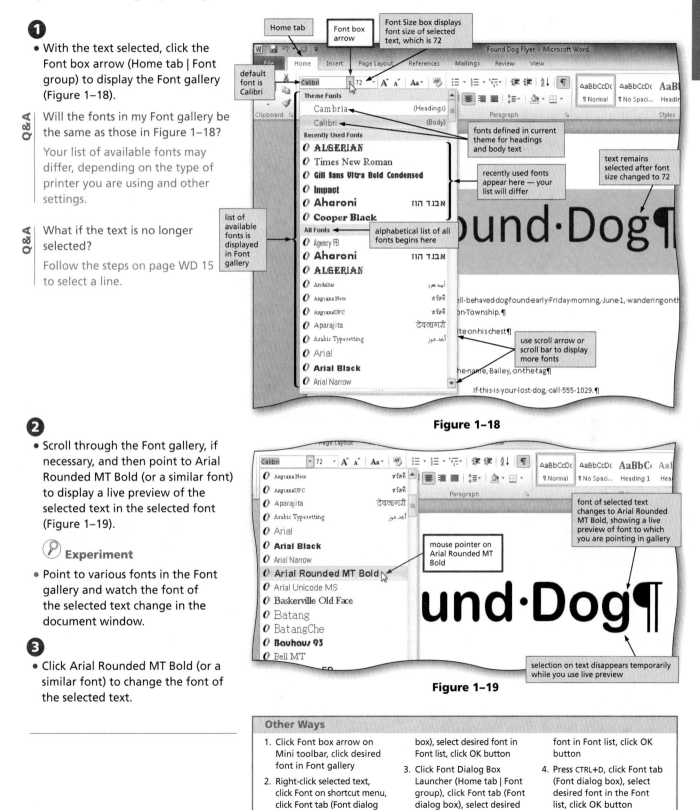 **Experiment**

- Point to various fonts in the Font gallery and watch the font of the selected text change in the document window.

3

- Click Arial Rounded MT Bold (or a similar font) to change the font of the selected text.

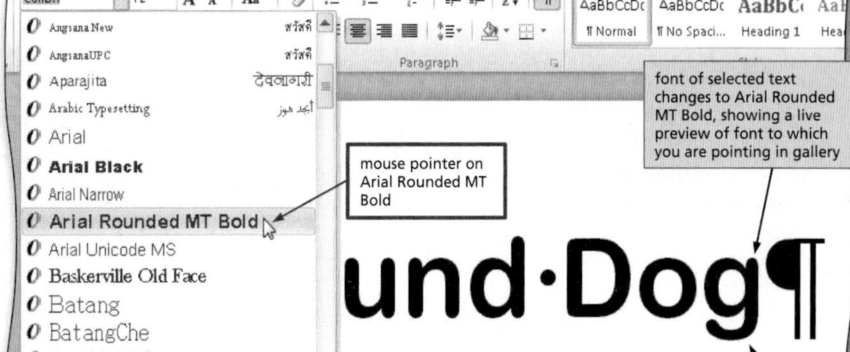

Figure 1–19

Other Ways

1. Click Font box arrow on Mini toolbar, click desired font in Font gallery
2. Right-click selected text, click Font on shortcut menu, click Font tab (Font dialog box), select desired font in Font list, click OK button
3. Click Font Dialog Box Launcher (Home tab | Font group), click Font tab (Font dialog box), select desired font in Font list, click OK button
4. Press CTRL+D, click Font tab (Font dialog box), select desired font in the Font list, click OK button

To Change the Case of Selected Text

The headline currently shows the first letter in each word capitalized, which sometimes is referred to as initial cap. To draw more attention to the headline, you would like the entire line of text to be capitalized, or in uppercase letters. The following steps change the headline to uppercase.

1

- With the text selected, click the Change Case button (Home tab | Font group) to display the Change Case gallery (Figure 1–20).

Home tab
Change Case button
Font box displays font of selected text, which is Arial Rounded MT Bold
Font group
Change Case gallery visually shows the function of each option
UPPERCASE to be selected
text remains selected

Figure 1–20

2

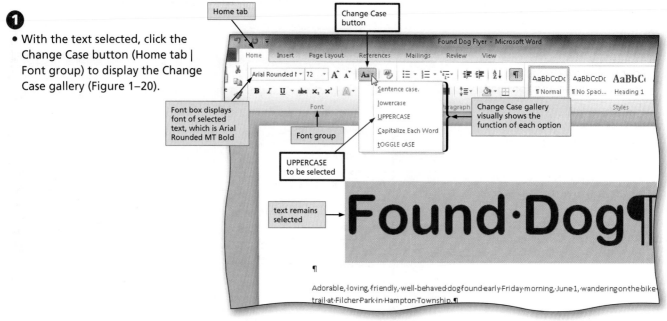

- Click UPPERCASE in the Change Case gallery to change the case of the selected text (Figure 1–21).

Q&A What if a ruler appears on the screen or the mouse pointer shape changes?

Depending on the position of your mouse pointer and locations you click on the screen, a ruler may automatically appear or the mouse pointer shape may change. Simply move the mouse and the ruler should disappear and/or the mouse pointer shape will change.

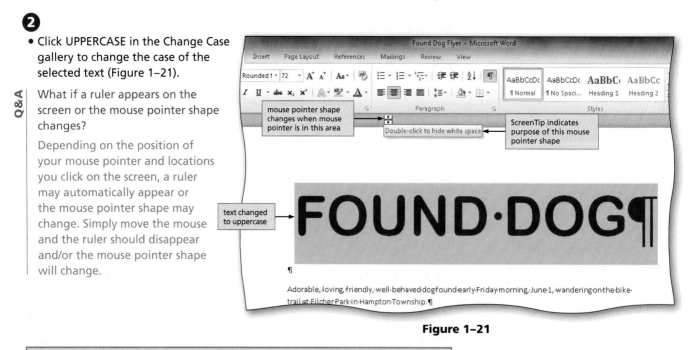

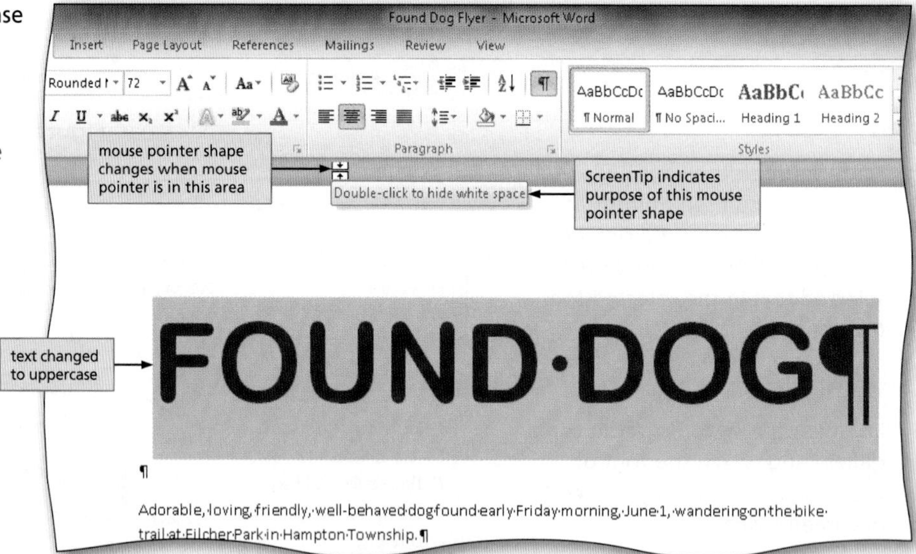

Figure 1–21

Other Ways

1. Right-click selected text, click Font on shortcut menu, click Font tab (Font dialog box), select All caps in Effects area, click OK button
2. Click Font Dialog Box Launcher (Home tab | Font group), click Font tab (Font dialog box), select All caps in Effects area, click OK button
3. Press SHIFT+F3 repeatedly until text is desired case

To Apply a Text Effect to Selected Text

You would like the text in the headline to be even more noticeable. Word provides many text effects to add interest and variety to text. The following steps apply a text effect to the headline.

1

- With the text selected, click the Text Effects button (Home tab | Font group) to display the Text Effects gallery (Figure 1–22).

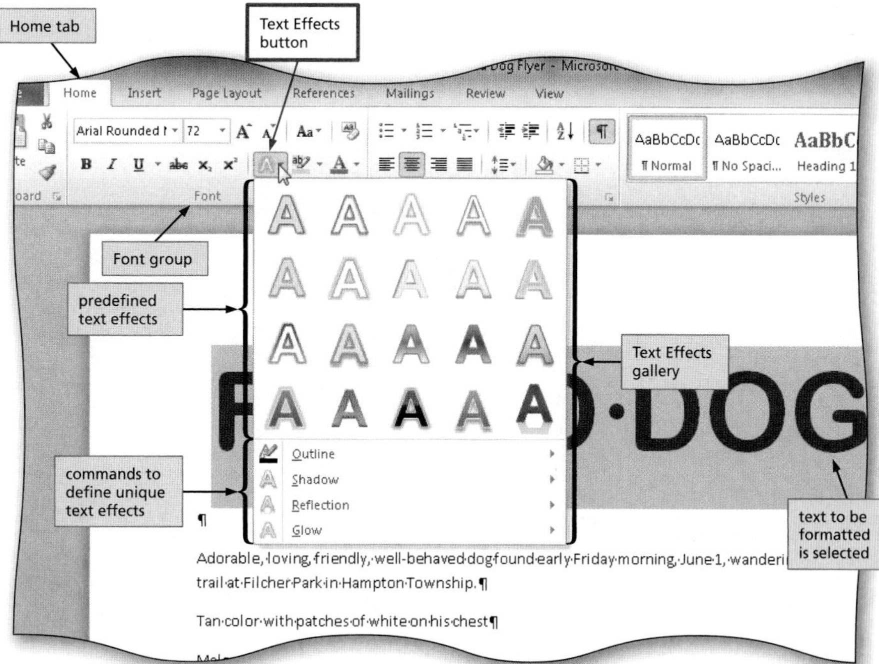

Figure 1–22

- Point to Fill – White, Gradient Outline – Accent 1 (first text effect in third row) to display a live preview of the selected text in the selected text effect (Figure 1–23).

Experiment

- Point to various text effects in the Text Effects gallery and watch the text effects of the selected text change in the document window.

- Click Fill – White, Gradient Outline – Accent 1 to change the text effect of the selected text.

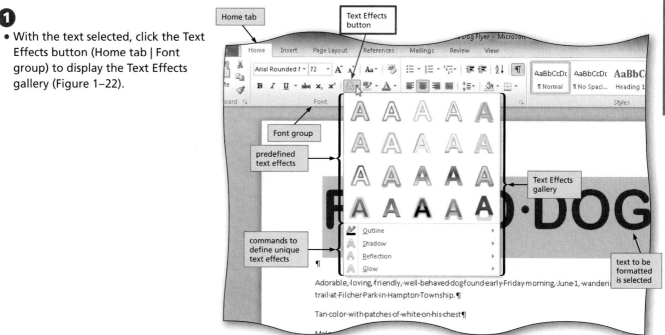

- Click anywhere in the document window to remove the selection from the selected text.

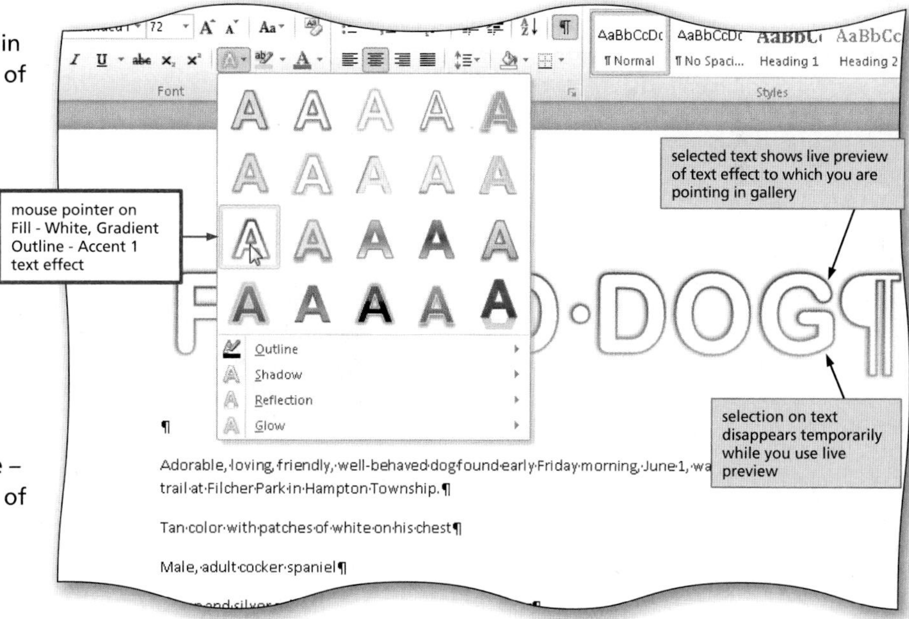

Figure 1–23

Other Ways

1. Right-click selected text, click Font on shortcut menu, click Font tab (Font dialog box), click Text Effects button, select desired text effects (Format Text Effects dialog box), click Close button, click OK button
2. Click Font Dialog Box Launcher (Home tab | Font group), click Font tab (Font dialog box), click Text Effects button, select desired text effects (Format Text Effects dialog box), click Close button, click OK button

To Shade a Paragraph

To make the headline of the flyer more eye-catching, you would like to shade it. When you **shade** text, Word colors the rectangular area behind any text or graphics. If the text to shade is a paragraph, Word shades the area from the left margin to the right margin of the current paragraph. To shade a paragraph, place the insertion point in the paragraph. To shade any other text, you must first select the text to be shaded. This flyer uses brown as the shading color for the headline. The following steps shade a paragraph.

1

- Click somewhere in the paragraph to be shaded (in this case, the headline) to position the insertion point in the paragraph to be formatted.
- Click the Shading button arrow (Home tab | Paragraph group) to display the Shading gallery (Figure 1–24).

Q&A What if I click the Shading button by mistake?

Click the Shading button arrow and proceed with Step 2.

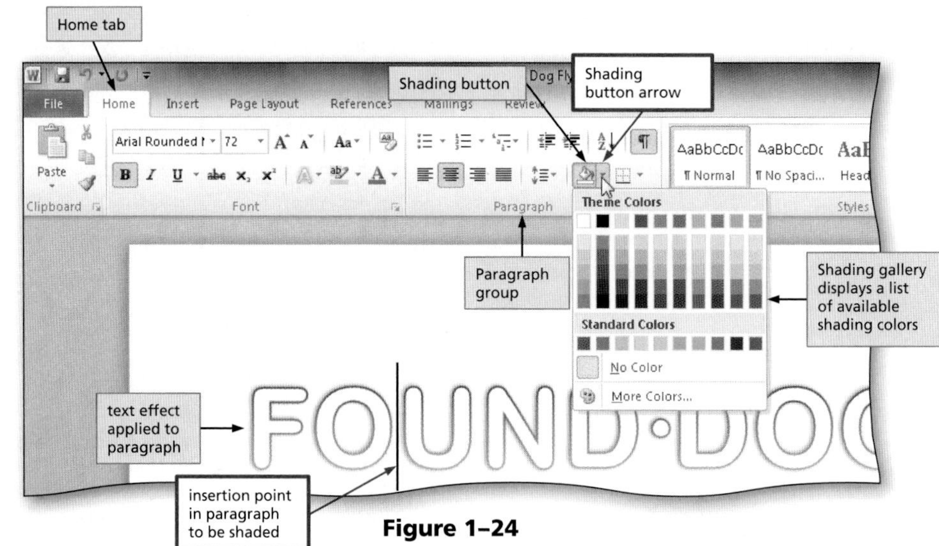

Figure 1–24

2

- Point to Orange, Accent 6, Darker 50% (rightmost color in the sixth row) to display a live preview of the selected shading color (Figure 1–25).

Experiment

- Point to various colors in the Shading gallery and watch the shading color of the current paragraph change.

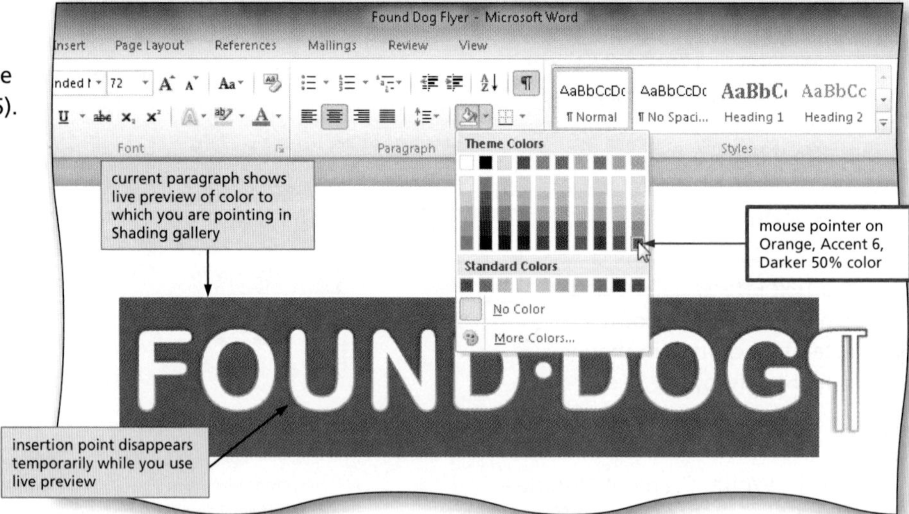

Figure 1–25

3

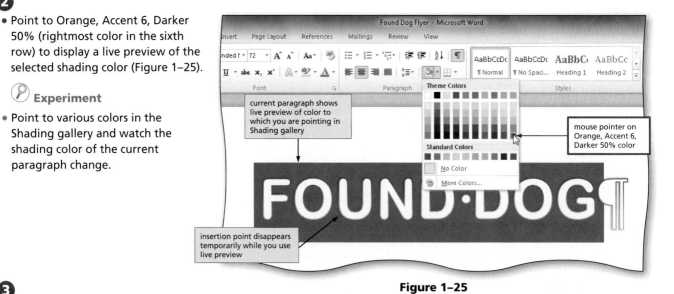

- Click Orange, Accent 6, Darker 50% to shade the current paragraph.

Q&A What if I apply a dark shading color to dark text?

When the font color of text is Automatic, it usually is black. If you select a dark shading color, Word automatically may change the text color to white so that the shaded text is easier to read.

Other Ways

1. Click Border button arrow (Home tab | Paragraph group), click Borders and Shading, click Shading tab (Borders and Shading dialog box), click Fill box arrow, select desired color, click OK button

To Select Multiple Lines

The next formatting step for the flyer is to increase the font size of the characters between the headline and the signature line so that they are easier to read from a distance. To change the font size of the characters in multiple lines, you first must select all the lines to be formatted. The following steps select multiple lines.

- Move the mouse pointer to the left of the first paragraph to be selected until the mouse pointer changes to a right-pointing block arrow (Figure 1–26).

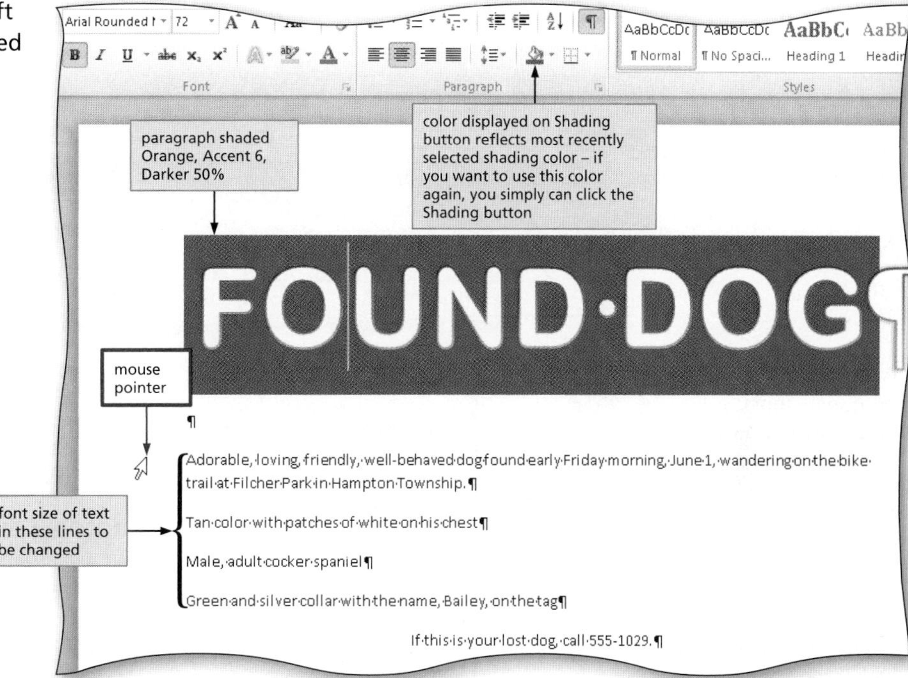
paragraph shaded Orange, Accent 6, Darker 50%
color displayed on Shading button reflects most recently selected shading color – if you want to use this color again, you simply can click the Shading button
FOUND·DOG
mouse pointer
font size of text in these lines to be changed
Adorable, loving, friendly, well-behaved dog found early Friday morning, June 1, wandering on the bike trail at Filcher Park in Hampton Township.
Tan color with patches of white on his chest
Male, adult cocker spaniel
Green and silver collar with the name, Bailey, on the tag
If this is your lost dog, call 555-1029.

Figure 1–26

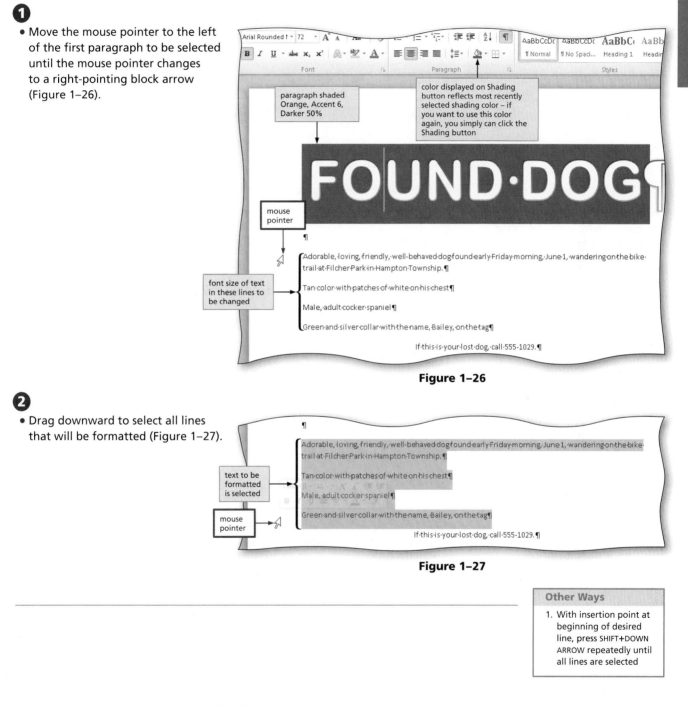

- Drag downward to select all lines that will be formatted (Figure 1–27).

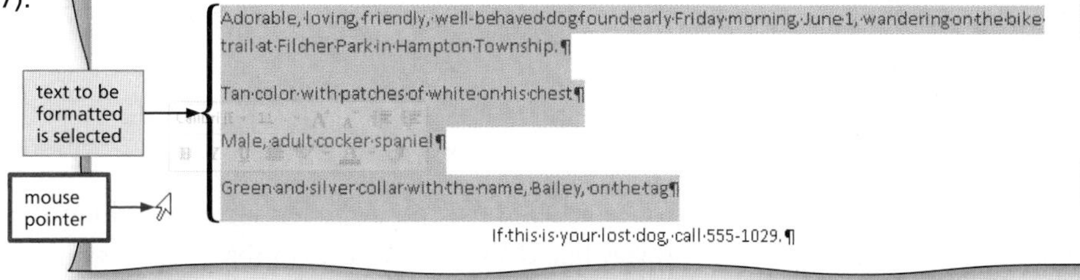
text to be formatted is selected
mouse pointer
Adorable, loving, friendly, well-behaved dog found early Friday morning, June 1, wandering on the bike trail at Filcher Park in Hampton Township.
Tan color with patches of white on his chest
Male, adult cocker spaniel
Green and silver collar with the name, Bailey, on the tag
If this is your lost dog, call 555-1029.

Figure 1–27

Other Ways

1. With insertion point at beginning of desired line, press SHIFT+DOWN ARROW repeatedly until all lines are selected

To Change the Font Size of Selected Text

The characters between the headline and the signature line in the flyer currently are 11 point. To make them easier to read from a distance, this flyer uses 22 point for these characters. The steps on the next page change the font size of the selected text.

1. With the text selected, click the Font Size box arrow (Home tab | Font group) to display the Font Size gallery.
2. Click 22 in the Font Size gallery to increase the font size of the selected text.
3. Click anywhere in the document window to remove the selection from the text.
4. If necessary, scroll so that you can see all the text on the screen (Figure 1–28).

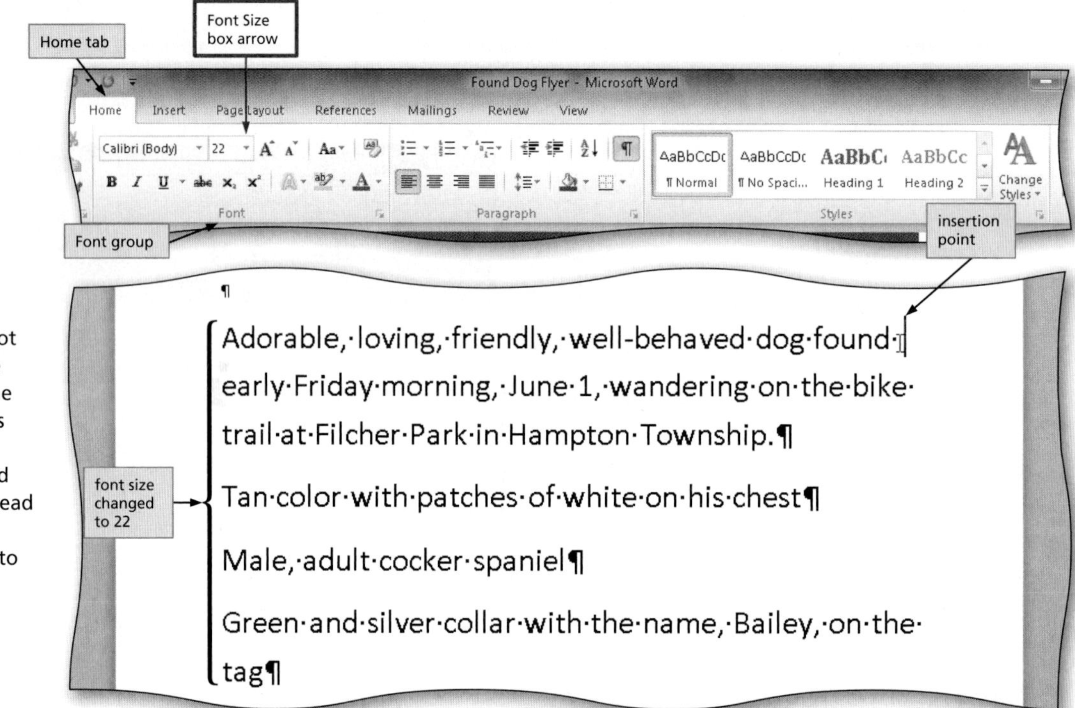
Home tab
Font Size box arrow
Found Dog Flyer - Microsoft Word
Home
Insert
Page Layout
References
Mailings
Review
View
Calibri (Body)
22
AaBbCcDc
¶ Normal
AaBbCcDc
¶ No Spaci...
AaBbC
Heading 1
AaBbCc
Heading 2
Change Styles
Font
Paragraph
Styles
Font group
insertion point
Adorable,·loving,·friendly,·well-behaved·dog·found·
early·Friday·morning,·June·1,·wandering·on·the·bike·
trail·at·Filcher·Park·in·Hampton·Township.¶
font size changed to 22
Tan·color·with·patches·of·white·on·his·chest¶
Male,·adult·cocker·spaniel¶
Green·and·silver·collar·with·the·name,·Bailey,·on·the·
tag¶

Figure 1–28

BTW

Formatting Marks
With some fonts, formatting marks do not display properly on the screen. For example, the raised dot that signifies a blank space between words may be displayed behind a character instead of in the blank space, causing the characters to look incorrect.

To Bullet a List of Paragraphs

The next step is to format as a bulleted list the three paragraphs of identifying information that are above the signature line in the flyer. A **bulleted list** is a series of paragraphs, each beginning with a bullet character.

To format a list of paragraphs with bullets, you first must select all the lines in the paragraphs. The following steps bullet a list of paragraphs.

1

- Move the mouse pointer to the left of the first paragraph to be selected until the mouse pointer changes to a right-pointing block arrow.
- Drag downward until all paragraphs that will be formatted with a bullet character are selected (Figure 1–29).

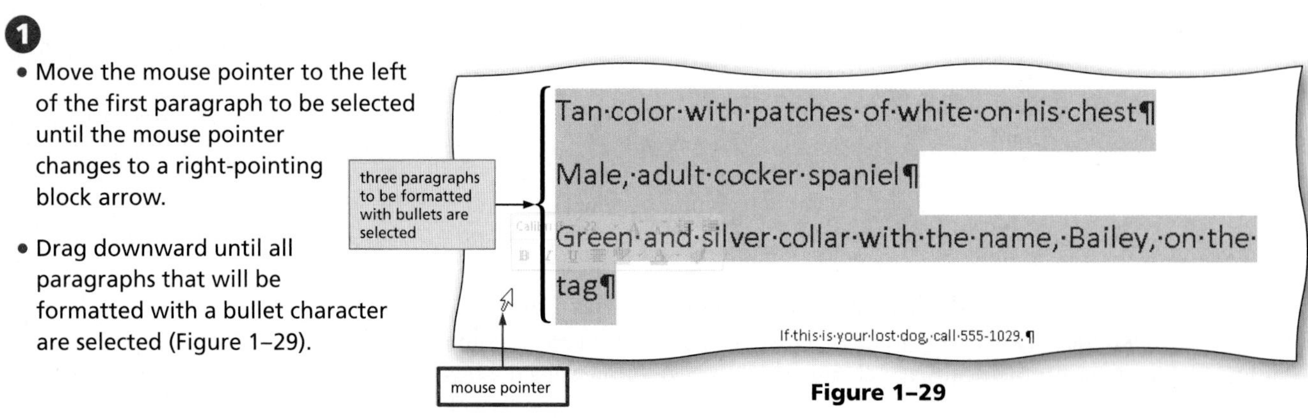
three paragraphs to be formatted with bullets are selected
Tan·color·with·patches·of·white·on·his·chest¶
Male,·adult·cocker·spaniel¶
Green·and·silver·collar·with·the·name,·Bailey,·on·the·
tag¶
If·this·is·your·lost·dog,·call·555-1029.¶
mouse pointer

Figure 1–29

- Click the Bullets button (Home tab | Paragraph group) to place a bullet character at the beginning of each selected paragraph (Figure 1–30).

Q&A How do I remove bullets from a list or paragraph?

Select the list or paragraph and then click the Bullets button again.

Q&A What if I accidentally click the Bullets button arrow?

Press the ESCAPE key to remove the Bullets gallery from the screen and then repeat Step 2.

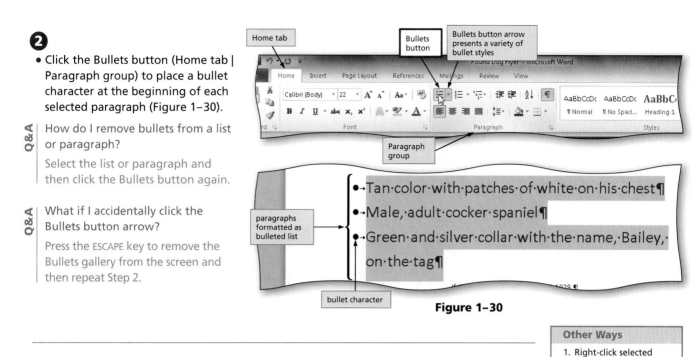

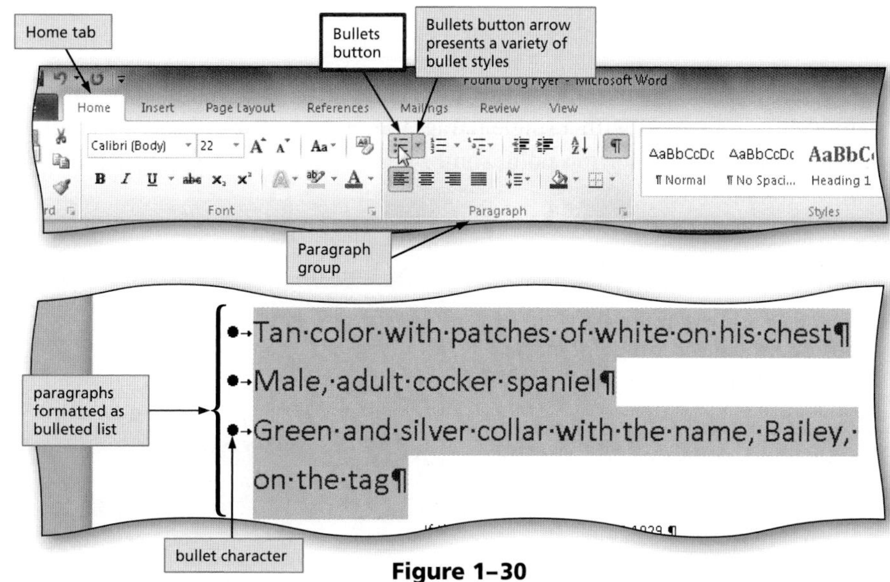

Figure 1–30

Other Ways

1. Right-click selected paragraphs, point to Bullets on shortcut menu, click desired bullet style

To Undo and Redo an Action

Word provides a means of canceling your recent command(s) or action(s). For example, if you format text incorrectly, you can undo the format and try it again. When you point to the Undo button, Word displays the action you can undo as part of a ScreenTip.

If, after you undo an action, you decide you did not want to perform the undo, you can redo the undone action. Word does not allow you to undo or redo some actions, such as saving or printing a document. The next steps undo the bullet format just applied and then redo the bullet format.

- Click the Undo button on the Quick Access Toolbar to reverse your most recent action (in this case, remove the bullets from the paragraphs) (Figure 1–31).

- Click the Redo button on the Quick Access Toolbar to reverse your most recent undo (in this case, place a bullet character on the paragraphs again) (shown in Figure 1–30).

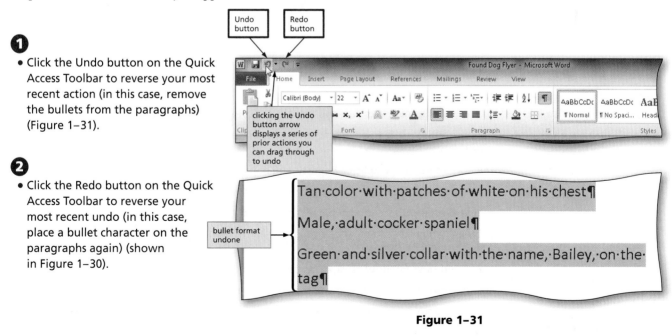

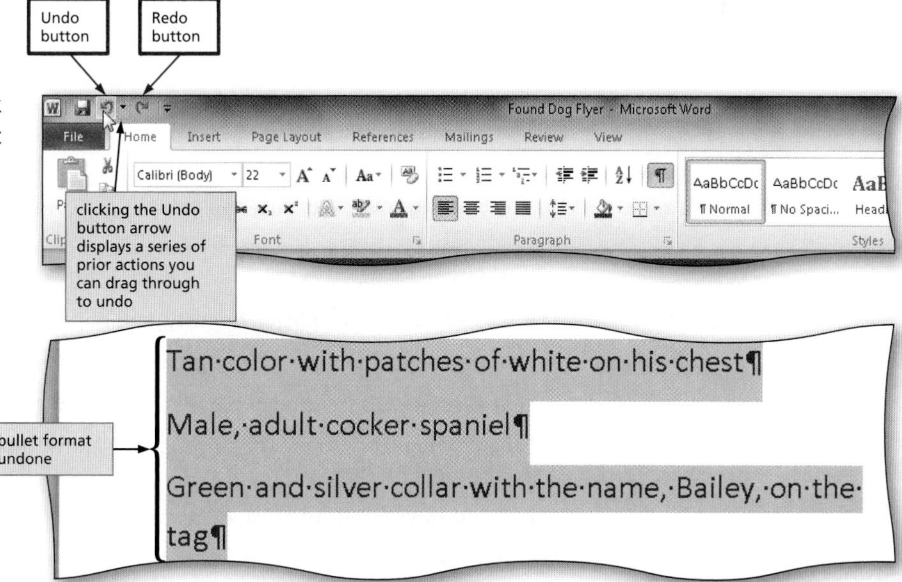

Figure 1–31

Other Ways

1. Press CTRL+Z to undo; press CTRL+Y to redo

To Italicize Text

The next step is to italicize the dog's name, Bailey, in the flyer to further emphasize it. **Italicized** text has a slanted appearance. As with a single paragraph, if you want to format a single word, you do not need to select it. Simply position the insertion point somewhere in the word and apply the desired format. The following step formats a word in italics.

- Click somewhere in the word to be italicized (Bailey, in this case) to position the insertion point in the word to be formatted.
- Click the Italic button (Home tab | Font group) to italicize the word containing the insertion point (Figure 1–32).

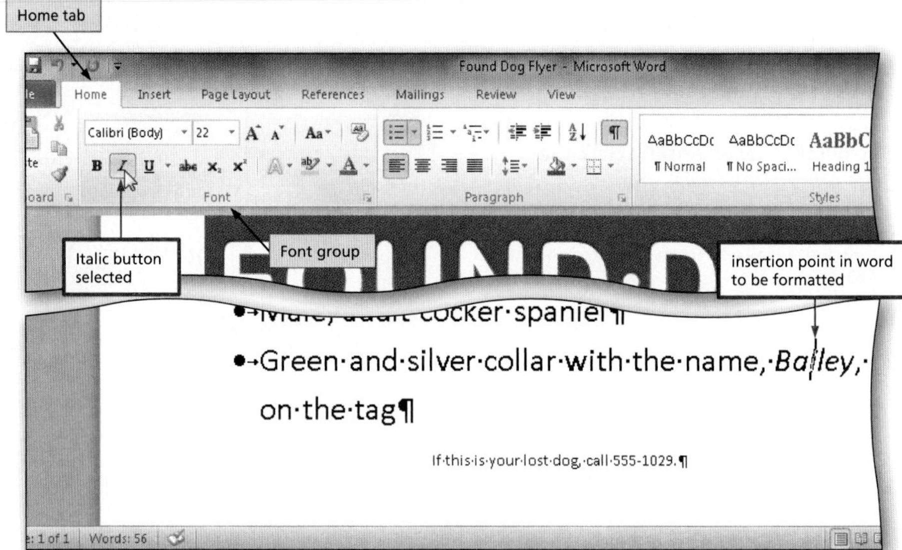

Figure 1–32

Q&A How would I remove an italic format?

You would click the Italic button a second time, or you immediately could click the Undo button on the Quick Access Toolbar or press CTRL+Z.

Q&A How can I tell what formatting has been applied to text?

The selected buttons and boxes on the Home tab show formatting characteristics of the location of the insertion point. With the insertion point in the word, Bailey, the Home tab shows these formats: 22-point Calibri italic font, bulleted paragraph.

Other Ways

1. Click Italic button on Mini toolbar
2. Right-click selected text, click Font on shortcut menu, click Font tab (Font dialog box), click Italic in Font style list, click OK button
3. Click Font Dialog Box Launcher (Home tab | Font group), click Font tab (Font dialog box), click Italic in Font style list, click OK button
4. Press CTRL+I

Plan Ahead

Use color.

When choosing color, associate the meaning of color to your message:

- Red expresses danger, power, or energy, and often is associated with sports or physical exertion.
- Brown represents simplicity, honesty, and dependability.
- Orange denotes success, victory, creativity, and enthusiasm.
- Yellow suggests sunshine, happiness, hope, liveliness, and intelligence.
- Green symbolizes growth, healthiness, harmony, blooming, and healing, and often is associated with safety or money.
- Blue indicates integrity, trust, importance, confidence, and stability.
- Purple represents wealth, power, comfort, extravagance, magic, mystery, and spirituality.
- White stands for purity, goodness, cleanliness, precision, and perfection.
- Black suggests authority, strength, elegance, power, and prestige.
- Gray conveys neutrality and thus often is found in backgrounds and other effects.

BTW

Q&As

For a complete list of the Q&As found in many of the step-by-step sequences in this book, visit the Word 2010 Q&A Web page (scsite.com/wd2010/qa).

To Color Text

To emphasize the dog's name even more, its color is changed to a shade of blue. The following steps change the color of the word, Bailey.

- With the insertion point in the word to format, click the Font Color button arrow (Home tab | Font group) to display the Font Color gallery (Figure 1–33).

Q&A What if I click the Font Color button by mistake?

Click the Font Color button arrow and then proceed with Step 2.

- Point to Blue, Accent 1, Darker 25% (fifth color in the fifth row) to display a live preview of the selected font color.

- Point to various colors in the Font Color gallery and watch the color of the current word change.

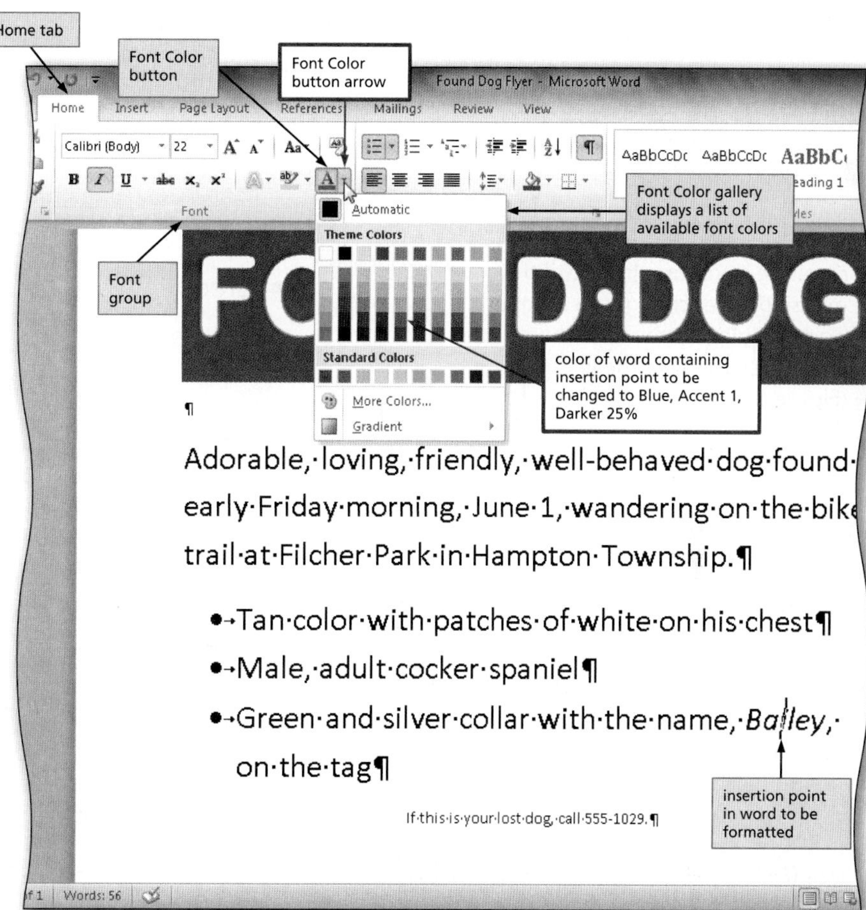
Home tab
Font Color button
Font Color button arrow
Font Color gallery displays a list of available font colors
Font group
color of word containing insertion point to be changed to Blue, Accent 1, Darker 25%
insertion point in word to be formatted
Automatic
Theme Colors
Standard Colors
More Colors...
Gradient
Adorable, loving, friendly, well-behaved dog found early Friday morning, June 1, wandering on the bike trail at Filcher Park in Hampton Township.
Tan color with patches of white on his chest
Male, adult cocker spaniel
Green and silver collar with the name, Bailey, on the tag
If this is your lost dog, call 555-1029.

Figure 1–33

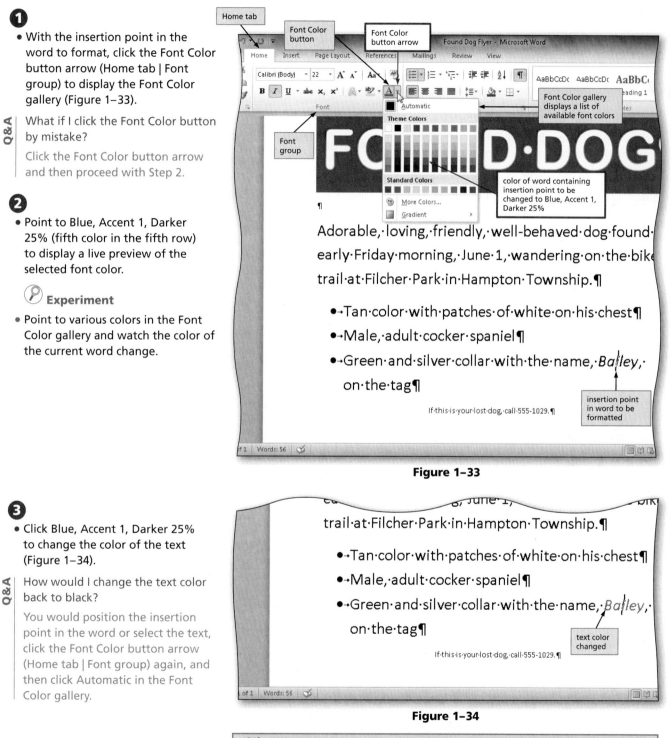

- Click Blue, Accent 1, Darker 25% to change the color of the text (Figure 1–34).

Q&A How would I change the text color back to black?

You would position the insertion point in the word or select the text, click the Font Color button arrow (Home tab | Font group) again, and then click Automatic in the Font Color gallery.

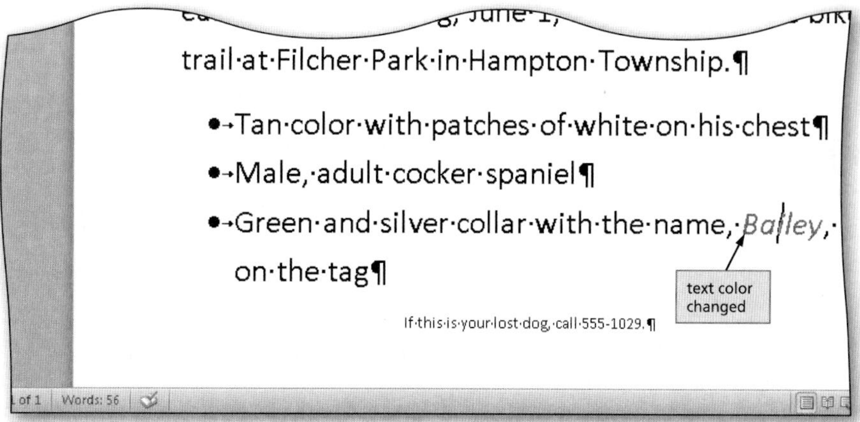
trail at Filcher Park in Hampton Township.
Tan color with patches of white on his chest
Male, adult cocker spaniel
Green and silver collar with the name, Bailey, on the tag
text color changed
If this is your lost dog, call 555-1029.

Figure 1–34

Other Ways

1. Click Font Color button arrow on Mini toolbar, click desired color
2. Right-click selected text, click Font on shortcut menu, click Font tab (Font dialog box), click Font color box arrow, click desired color, click OK button
3. Click Font Dialog Box Launcher (Home tab | Font group), click Font tab (Font dialog box), click Font color box arrow, click desired color, click OK button

To Use the Mini Toolbar to Format Text

Recall from the Office 2010 and Windows 7 chapter at the beginning of this book that the Mini toolbar, which automatically appears based on certain tasks you perform, contains commands related to changing the appearance of text in a document. All commands on the Mini toolbar also exist on the Ribbon.

When the Mini toolbar appears, it initially is transparent. If you do not use the transparent Mini toolbar, it disappears from the screen. The following steps use the Mini toolbar to change the color and font size of text in the signature line of the flyer.

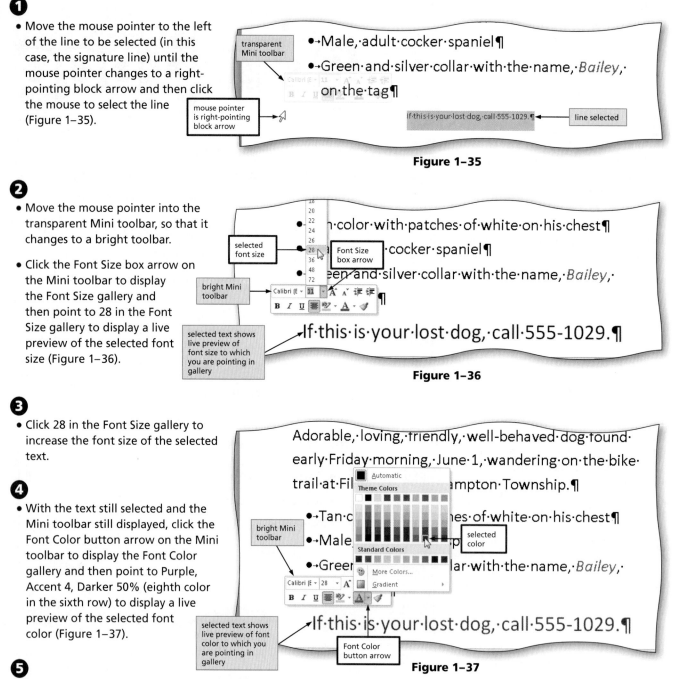

- Move the mouse pointer to the left of the line to be selected (in this case, the signature line) until the mouse pointer changes to a right-pointing block arrow and then click the mouse to select the line (Figure 1–35).

Figure 1–35

2

- Move the mouse pointer into the transparent Mini toolbar, so that it changes to a bright toolbar.
- Click the Font Size box arrow on the Mini toolbar to display the Font Size gallery and then point to 28 in the Font Size gallery to display a live preview of the selected font size (Figure 1–36).

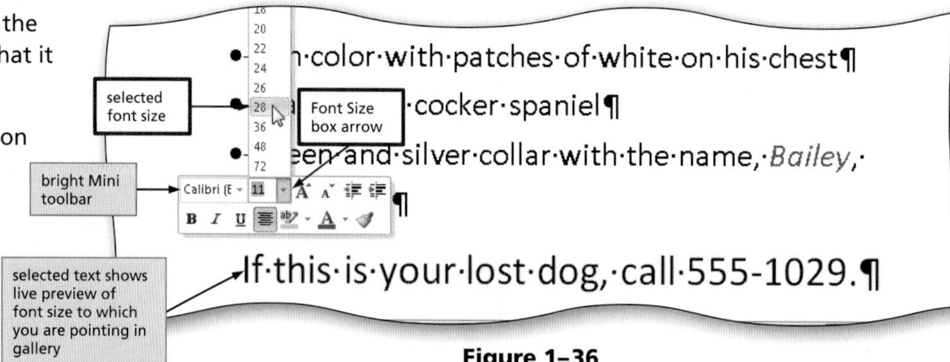

Figure 1–36

- Click 28 in the Font Size gallery to increase the font size of the selected text.

- With the text still selected and the Mini toolbar still displayed, click the Font Color button arrow on the Mini toolbar to display the Font Color gallery and then point to Purple, Accent 4, Darker 50% (eighth color in the sixth row) to display a live preview of the selected font color (Figure 1–37).

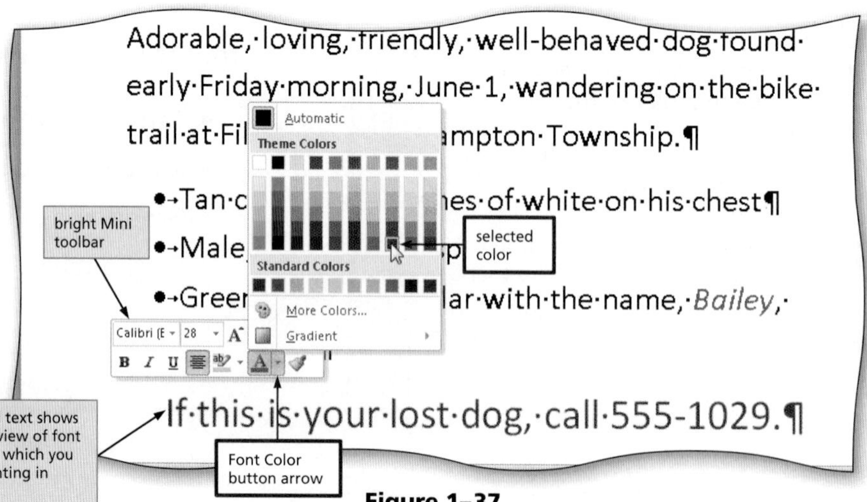

Figure 1–37

5

- Click Purple, Accent 4, Darker 50% to change the color of the text.
- Click anywhere in the document window to remove the selection from the text.

To Select a Group of Words

To emphasize the contact information (call 555-1029), these words are underlined in the flyer. To format a group of words, you first must select them. The following steps select a group of words.

- Position the mouse pointer immediately to the left of the first character of the text to be selected, in this case, the c in call (Figure 1–38).

Q&A

Why did the shape of the mouse pointer change?

The mouse pointer's shape is an I-beam when positioned in unselected text in the document window.

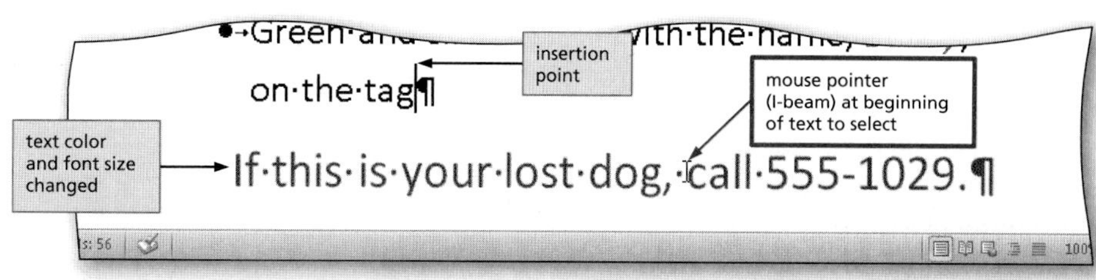

Figure 1–38

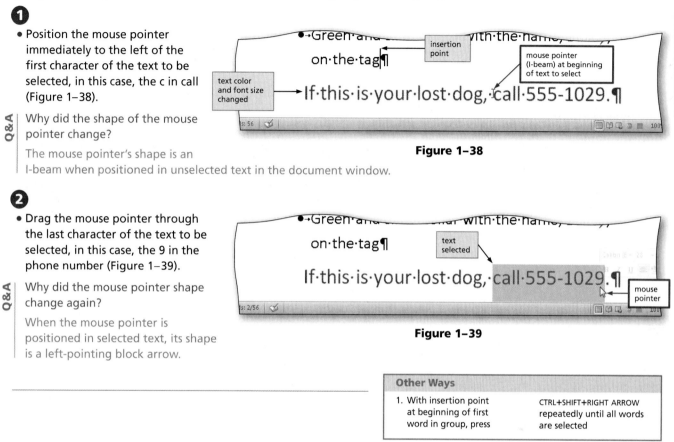

- Drag the mouse pointer through the last character of the text to be selected, in this case, the 9 in the phone number (Figure 1–39).

Q&A

Why did the mouse pointer shape change again?

When the mouse pointer is positioned in selected text, its shape is a left-pointing block arrow.

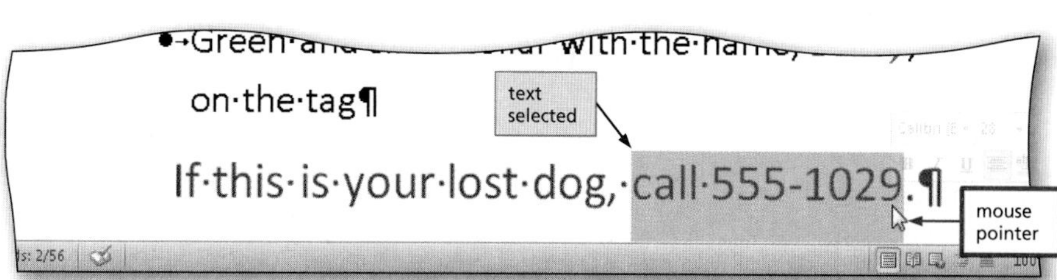

Figure 1–39

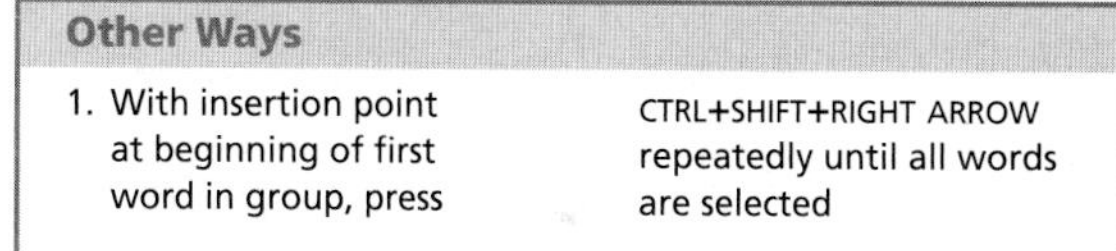

Other Ways

1. With insertion point at beginning of first word in group, press CTRL+SHIFT+RIGHT ARROW repeatedly until all words are selected

To Underline Text

Underlines are used to emphasize or draw attention to specific text. **Underlined** text prints with an underscore (_) below each character. In the flyer, the contact information, call 555-1029, in the signature line is emphasized with an underline. The following step formats selected text with an underline.

- With the text selected, click the Underline button (Home tab | Font group) to underline the selected text (Figure 1–40).

Q&A

How would I remove an underline?

You would click the Underline button a second time, or you immediately could click the Undo button on the Quick Access Toolbar.

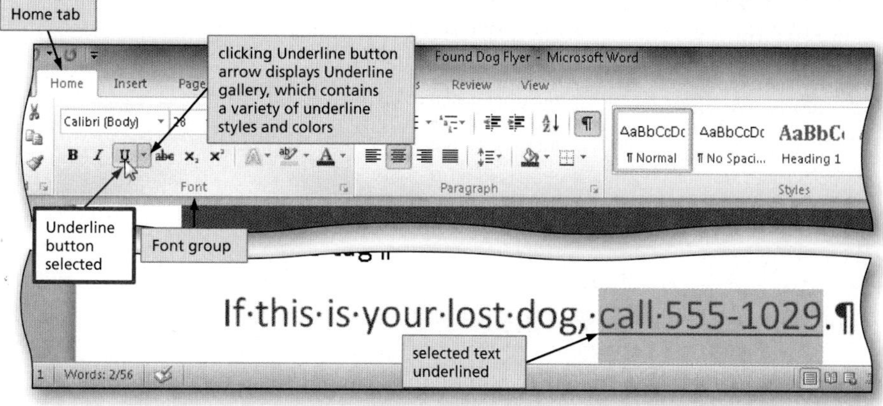

Figure 1–40

Other Ways

1. Right-click text, click Font on shortcut menu, click Font tab (Font dialog box), click Underline style box arrow, click desired underline style, click OK button
2. Click Font Dialog Box Launcher (Home tab | Font group), click Font tab (Font dialog box), click Underline style box arrow, click desired underline style, click OK button
3. Press CTRL+U

To Bold Text

Bold characters appear somewhat thicker and darker than those that are not bold. To further emphasize the signature line, it is bold in the flyer. To format the line, as you have learned previously, you select the line first. The following steps format the signature line bold.

1

- Move the mouse pointer to the left of the line to be selected (in this case, the signature line) until the mouse pointer changes to a right-pointing block arrow and then click the mouse to select the text to be formatted.
- With the text selected, click the Bold button (Home tab | Font group) to bold the selected text (Figure 1–41).

Q&A How would I remove a bold format?

You would click the Bold button a second time, or you immediately could click the Undo button on the Quick Access Toolbar.

2

- Click anywhere in the document window to remove the selection from the screen.

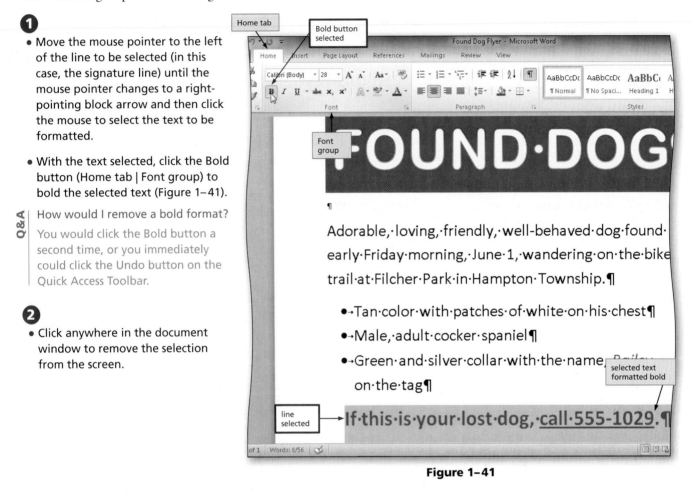

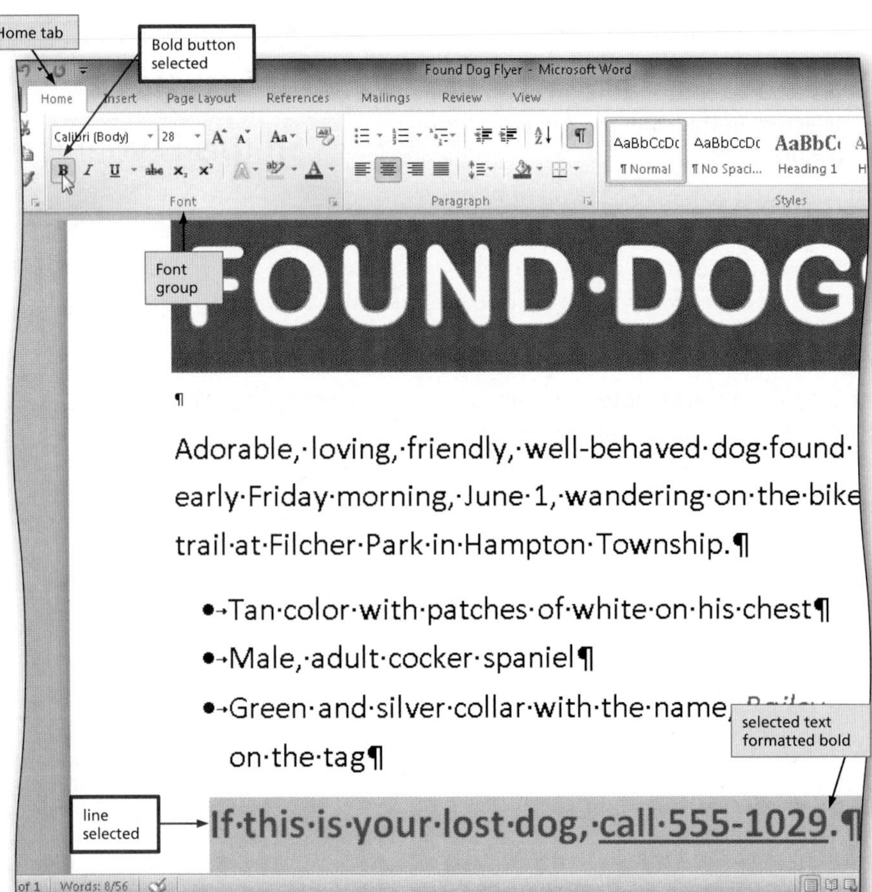
Home tab
Bold button selected
Font group
FOUND·DOG
Adorable,·loving,·friendly,·well-behaved·dog·found· early·Friday·morning,·June·1,·wandering·on·the·bike trail·at·Filcher·Park·in·Hampton·Township.¶
•Tan·color·with·patches·of·white·on·his·chest¶
•Male,·adult·cocker·spaniel¶
•Green·and·silver·collar·with·the·name, on·the·tag¶
selected text formatted bold
line selected
If·this·is·your·lost·dog,·call·555-1029.¶

Figure 1–41

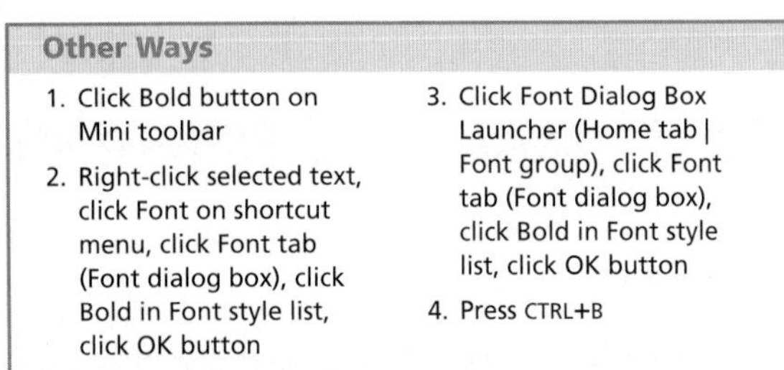

Other Ways

1. Click Bold button on Mini toolbar
2. Right-click selected text, click Font on shortcut menu, click Font tab (Font dialog box), click Bold in Font style list, click OK button
3. Click Font Dialog Box Launcher (Home tab | Font group), click Font tab (Font dialog box), click Bold in Font style list, click OK button
4. Press CTRL+B

To Change Theme Colors

A **color scheme** in Word is a document theme that identifies 12 complementary colors for text, background, accents, and links in a document. With more than 20 predefined color schemes, Word provides a simple way to select colors that work well together.

In the flyer, you want all the colors to convey honesty, dependability, and healing, that is, shades of browns and greens. In Word, the Aspect color scheme uses these colors. Thus, you will change the color scheme from the default, Office, to Aspect. The next steps change theme colors.

- Click the Change Styles button (Home tab | Styles group) to display the Change Styles menu.
- Point to Colors on the Change Styles menu to display the Colors gallery (Figure 1–42).

Experiment

- Point to various color schemes in the Colors gallery and watch the colors change in the document window.

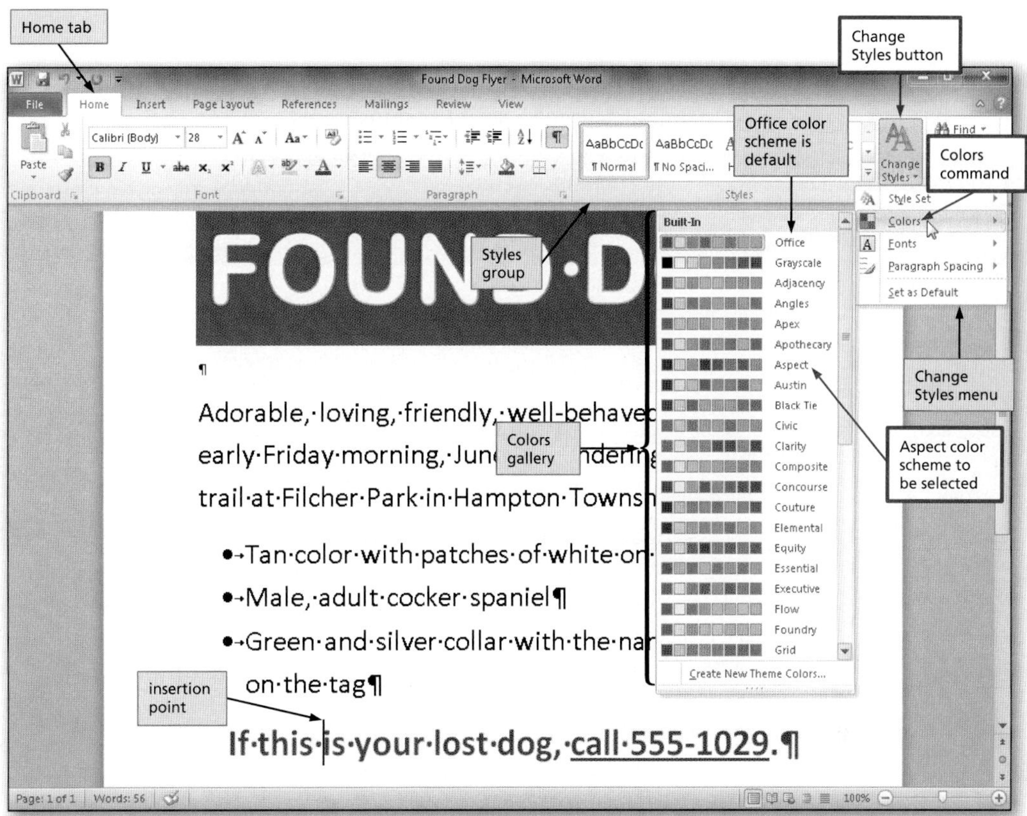

Figure 1–42

- Click Aspect in the Colors gallery to change the document theme colors (Figure 1–43).

Q&A What if I want to return to the original color scheme?

You would click the Change Styles button again, click Colors on the Change Styles menu, and then click Office in the Colors gallery.

Figure 1–43

Other Ways

1. Click Theme Colors button (Page Layout tab | Themes group), select desired color scheme

Selecting Text

In many of the previous steps, you have selected text. Table 1–3 summarizes the techniques used to select various items.

Table 1–3 Techniques for Selecting Text

Item to Select	Mouse	Keyboard (where applicable)
Block of text	Click at beginning of selection, scroll to end of selection, position mouse pointer at end of selection, hold down SHIFT key and then click; or drag through the text.	
Character(s)	Drag through character(s).	SHIFT+RIGHT ARROW or SHIFT+LEFT ARROW
Document	Move mouse to left of text until mouse pointer changes to a right-pointing block arrow and then triple-click.	CTRL+A
Graphic	Click the graphic.	
Line	Move mouse to left of line until mouse pointer changes to a right-pointing block arrow and then click.	HOME, then SHIFT+END or END, then SHIFT+HOME
Lines	Move mouse to left of first line until mouse pointer changes to a right-pointing block arrow and then drag up or down.	HOME, then SHIFT+DOWN ARROW or END, then SHIFT+UP AROW
Paragraph	Triple-click paragraph; or move mouse to left of paragraph until mouse pointer changes to a right-pointing block arrow and then double-click.	CTRL+SHIFT+DOWN ARROW or CTRL+SHIFT+UP ARROW
Paragraphs	Move mouse to left of paragraph until mouse pointer changes to a right-pointing block arrow, double-click, and then drag up or down.	CTRL+SHIFT+DOWN ARROW or CTRL+SHIFT+UP ARROW repeatedly
Sentence	Press and hold down CTRL key and then click sentence.	
Word	Double-click the word.	CTRL+SHIFT+RIGHT ARROW or CTRL+SHIFT+LEFT ARROW
Words	Drag through words.	CTRL+SHIFT+RIGHT ARROW or CTRL+SHIFT+LEFT ARROW repeatedly

To Save an Existing Document with the Same File Name

You have made several modifications to the document since you last saved it. Thus, you should save it again. The following step saves the document again. For an example of the step listed below, refer to the Office 2010 and Windows 7 chapter at the beginning of this book.

 Click the Save button on the Quick Access Toolbar to overwrite the previously saved file.

Break Point: If you wish to take a break, this is a good place to do so. You can quit Word now (refer to page WD 44 for instructions). To resume at a later time, start Word (refer to pages WD 4 and WD 5 for instructions), open the file called Found Dog Flyer (refer to page WD 45 for instructions), and continue following the steps from this location forward.

Inserting and Formatting Pictures in a Word Document

With the text formatted in the flyer, the next step is to insert digital pictures in the flyer and format the pictures. Flyers usually contain graphical images, such as a picture, to attract the attention of passersby. In the following pages, you will perform these tasks:

1. Insert the first digital picture into the flyer and then reduce its size.
2. Insert the second digital picture into the flyer and then reduce its size.
3. Change the look of the first picture and then the second picture.

Plan Ahead

Find the appropriate graphical image.
To use a graphical image, also called a graphic, in a Word document, the image must be stored digitally in a file. Files containing graphical images are available from a variety of sources:

- Word includes a collection of predefined graphical images that you can insert in a document.
- Microsoft has free digital images on the Web for use in a document. Other Web sites also have images available, some of which are free, while others require a fee.
- You can take a picture with a digital camera or camera phone and **download** it, which is the process of copying the digital picture from the camera or phone to your computer.
- With a scanner, you can convert a printed picture, drawing, or diagram to a digital file.

If you receive a picture from a source other than yourself, do not use the file until you are certain it does not contain a virus. A **virus** is a computer program that can damage files and programs on your computer. Use an antivirus program to verify that any files you use are virus free.

Plan Ahead

Establish where to position and how to format the graphical image.
The content, size, shape, position, and format of a graphic should capture the interest of passersby, enticing them to stop and read the flyer. Often, the graphic is the center of attraction and visually the largest element on a flyer. If you use colors in the graphical image, be sure they are part of the document's color scheme.

To Insert a Picture

The next step in creating the flyer is to insert one of the digital pictures of the dog so that it is centered on the blank line below the headline. The picture, which was taken with a camera phone, is available on the Data Files for Students. See the inside back cover of this book for instructions on downloading the Data Files for Students, or contact your instructor for information about accessing the required files.

The following steps insert a centered picture, which, in this example, is located in the Chapter 01 folder in the Word folder in the Data Files for Students folder on a USB flash drive.

1

- Position the insertion point on the blank line below the headline, which is the location where you want to insert the picture.
- Click the Center button (Home tab | Paragraph group) to center the paragraph that will contain the picture.
- Click Insert on the Ribbon to display the Insert tab (Figure 1–44).

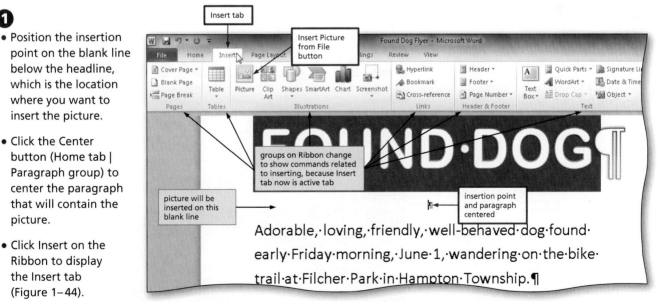

Figure 1–44

2

- With your USB flash drive connected to one of the computer's USB ports, click the Insert Picture from File button (Insert tab | Illustrations group) (shown in Figure 1-44) to display the Insert Picture dialog box (shown in Figure 1-45 on the next page).

3

- Navigate to the picture location (in this case, the Chapter 01 folder in the Word folder in the Data Files for Students folder on a USB flash drive). For a detailed example of this procedure, refer to Steps 3a – 3c in the To Save a File in a Folder section in the Office 2010 and Windows 7 chapter at the beginning of this book.
- Click Dog Picture 1 to select the file (Figure 1–45).

Q&A What if the picture is not on a USB flash drive?

Use the same process, but select the storage location containing the picture.

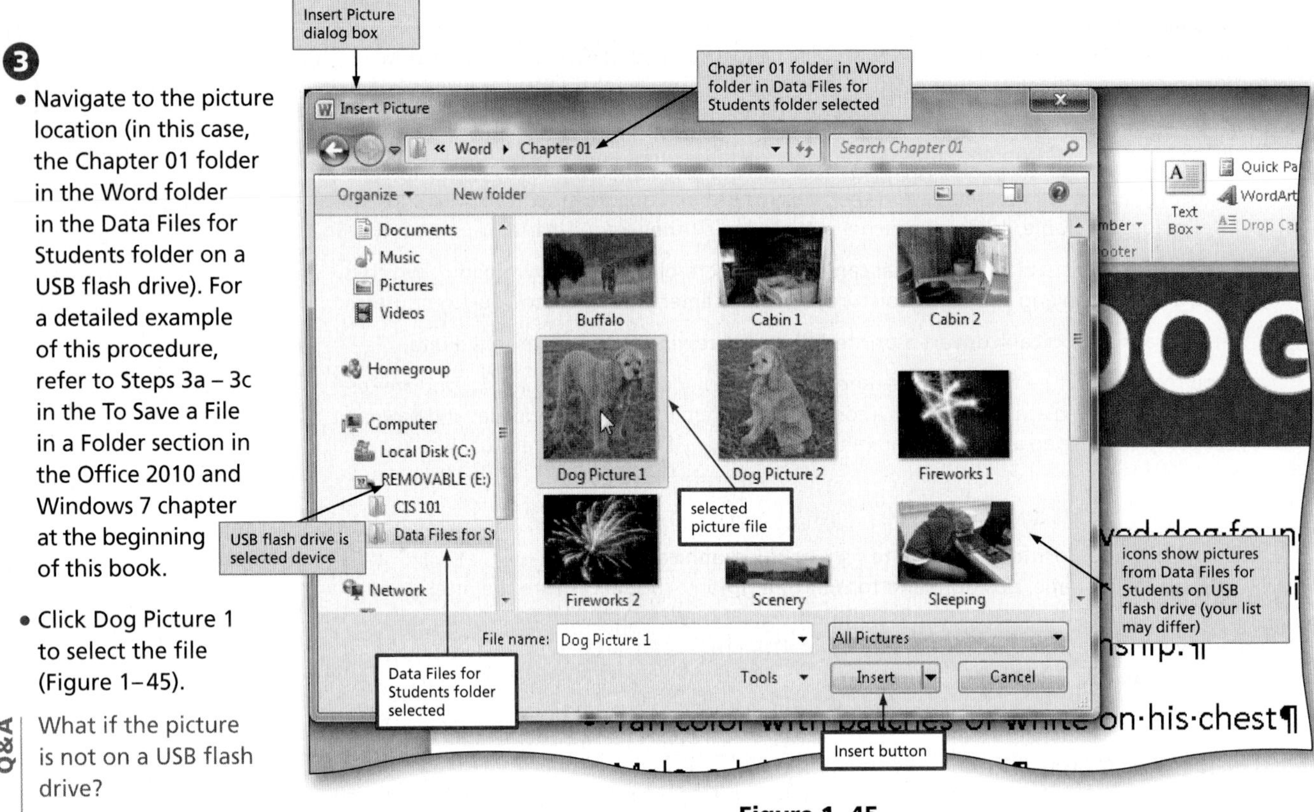

Figure 1–45

4

- Click the Insert button (Insert Picture dialog box) to insert the picture at the location of the insertion point in the document (Figure 1–46).

Q&A What are the symbols around the picture?

A selected graphic appears surrounded by a **selection rectangle**, which has small squares and circles, called **sizing handles**, at each corner and middle location.

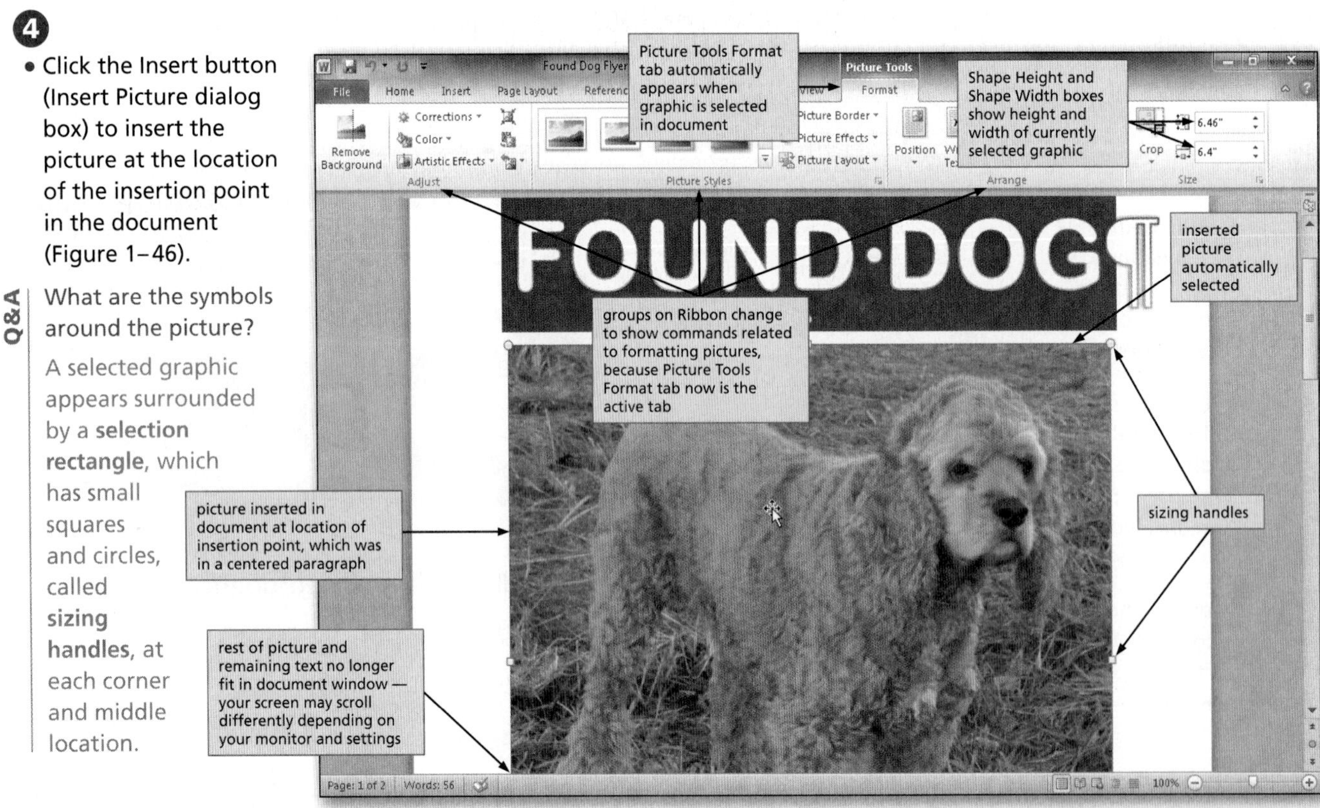

Figure 1–46

To Zoom the Document

The next step is to reduce the size of the picture so that both pictures will fit side-by-side on the same line. With the current picture size, the flyer now has expanded to two pages. The final flyer, however, should fit on a single page. In Word, you can change the zoom so that you can see the entire document (that is, both pages) on the screen at once. Seeing the entire document at once helps you determine the appropriate size for the picture. The following step zooms the document.

1

Experiment

- Repeatedly click the Zoom Out and Zoom In buttons on the status bar and watch the size of the document change in the document window.
- Click the Zoom Out or Zoom In button as many times as necessary until the Zoom button on the status bar displays 50% on its face (Figure 1–47).

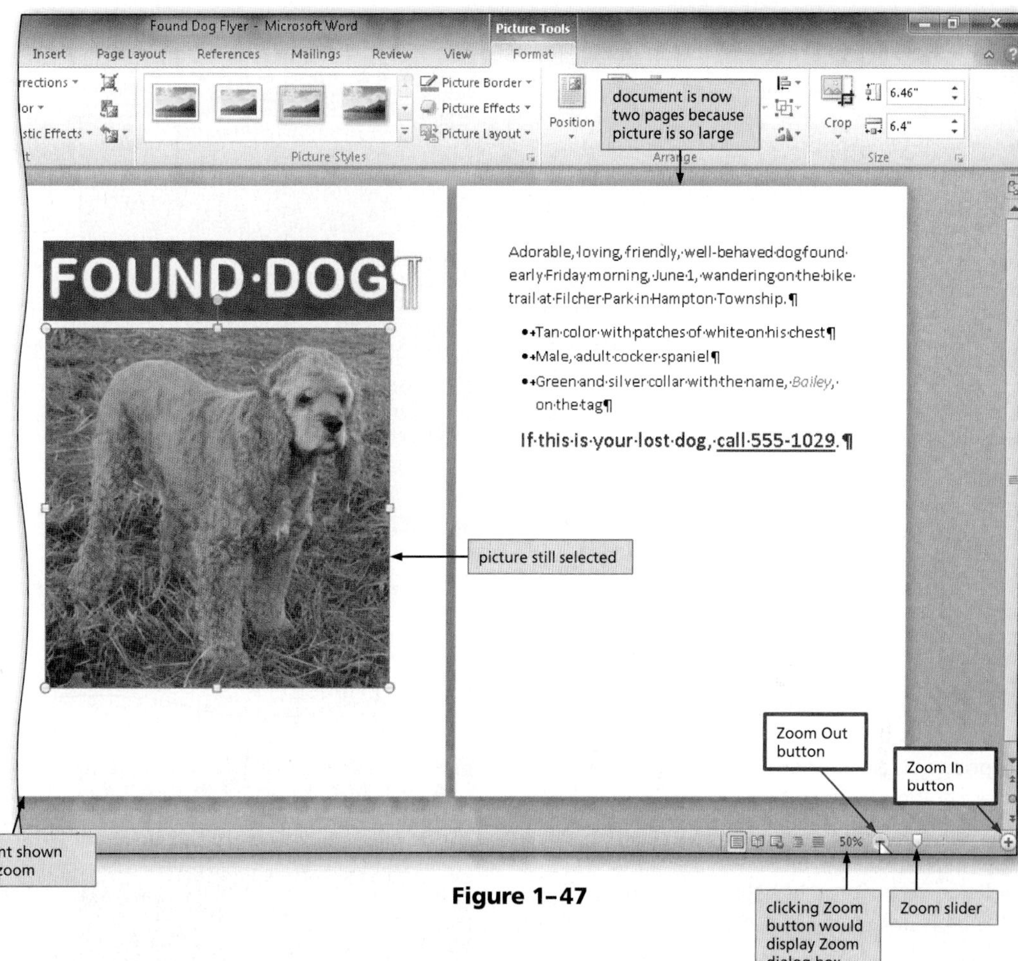

Found Dog Flyer - Microsoft Word
Picture Tools
Insert
Page Layout
References
Mailings
Review
View
Format
Picture Border
Picture Effects
Picture Layout
Picture Styles
Position
Crop
6.46"
6.4"
Size
document is now two pages because picture is so large
FOUND·DOG¶
Adorable,·loving,·friendly,·well-behaved·dog·found·early·Friday·morning,·June·1,·wandering·on·the·bike·trail·at·Filcher·Park·in·Hampton·Township.¶
Tan·color·with·patches·of·white·on·his·chest¶
Male,·adult·cocker·spaniel¶
Green·and·silver·collar·with·the·name,·Bailey,·on·the·tag¶
If·this·is·your·lost·dog,·call·555-1029.¶
picture still selected
Zoom Out button
Zoom In button
document shown at 50% zoom
50%
clicking Zoom button would display Zoom dialog box
Zoom slider

Figure 1–47

Q&A

If I change the zoom percentage, will the document print differently?

Changing the zoom has no effect on the printed document.

Q&A

Are there predefined zoom options?

Yes. Through the View tab | Zoom group or the Zoom dialog box, you can zoom to one page, two pages, many pages, page width, text width, and a variety of set percentages. Page width zoom places the edges of the page at the edges of the Word window, whereas Text width zoom places the contents of the page at the edges of the Word window.

Other Ways

1. Drag Zoom slider on status bar
2. Click Zoom button on status bar, select desired zoom percent or type (Zoom dialog box), click OK button
3. Click Zoom button (View tab | Zoom group), select desired zoom percent or type (Zoom dialog box), click OK button

To Resize a Graphic

The next step is to resize the picture so that both pictures will fit side-by-side on the same line below the headline. **Resizing** includes both enlarging and reducing the size of a graphic. In this flyer, you will reduce the size of the picture. With the entire document displayed in the document window, you will be able to see how the resized graphic will look on the entire page. The following steps resize a selected graphic.

1

- With the graphic still selected, point to the upper-right corner sizing handle on the picture so that the mouse pointer shape changes to a two-headed arrow (Figure 1–48).

Q&A What if my graphic (picture) is not selected?

To select a graphic, click it.

Figure 1–48

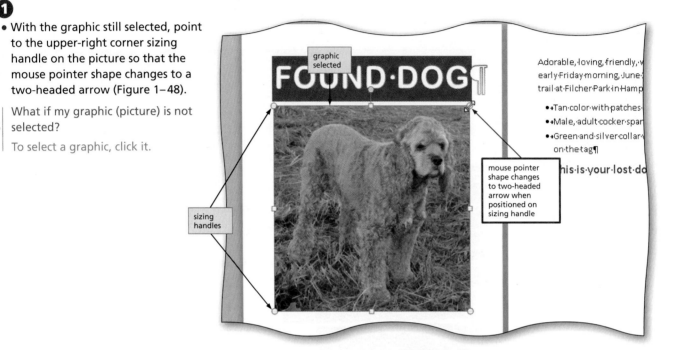

- Drag the sizing handle diagonally inward until the crosshair mouse pointer is positioned approximately as shown in Figure 1–49.

- Release the mouse button to resize the graphic, which in this case should have a height of about 2.74" and a width of about 2.73".

Q&A How can I see the height and width measurements?

Look in the Size group on the Picture Tools Format tab to see the height and width measurements of the currently selected graphic (shown in Figure 1–46 on page WD 32).

Q&A What if the graphic is the wrong size?

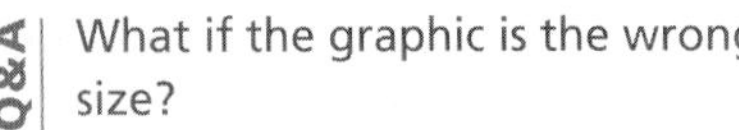

Repeat Steps 1, 2, and 3; or enter the desired height and width values in the Shape Height and Shape Width boxes (Picture Tools Format tab | Size group).

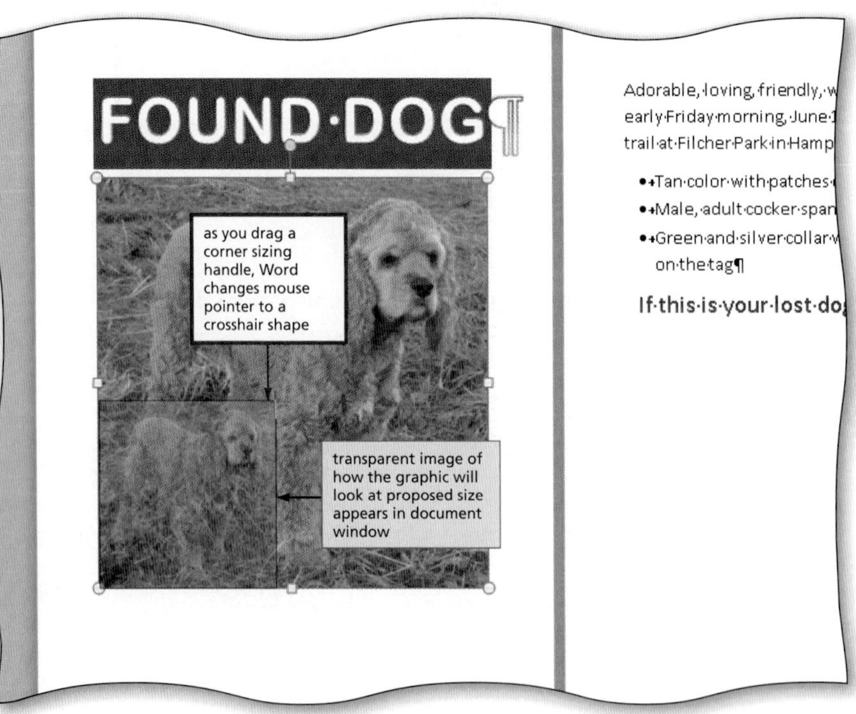

Figure 1–49

4

- Click to the right of the graphic to deselect it (Figure 1–50).

Q&A What happened to the Picture Tools Format tab?

When you click outside of a graphic or press a key to scroll through a document, Word deselects the graphic and removes the Picture Tools Format tab from the screen.

Q&A What if I want to return a graphic to its original size and start again?

With the graphic selected, click the Size Dialog Box Launcher (Picture Tools Format tab | Size group), click the Size tab (Layout dialog box), click the Reset button, and then click the OK button.

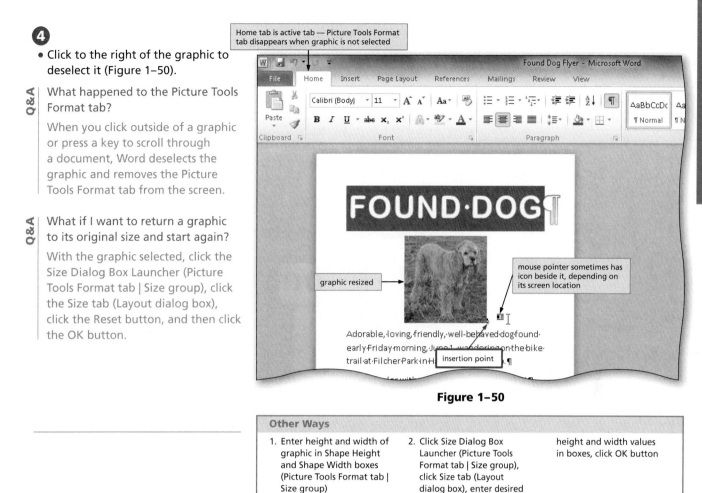

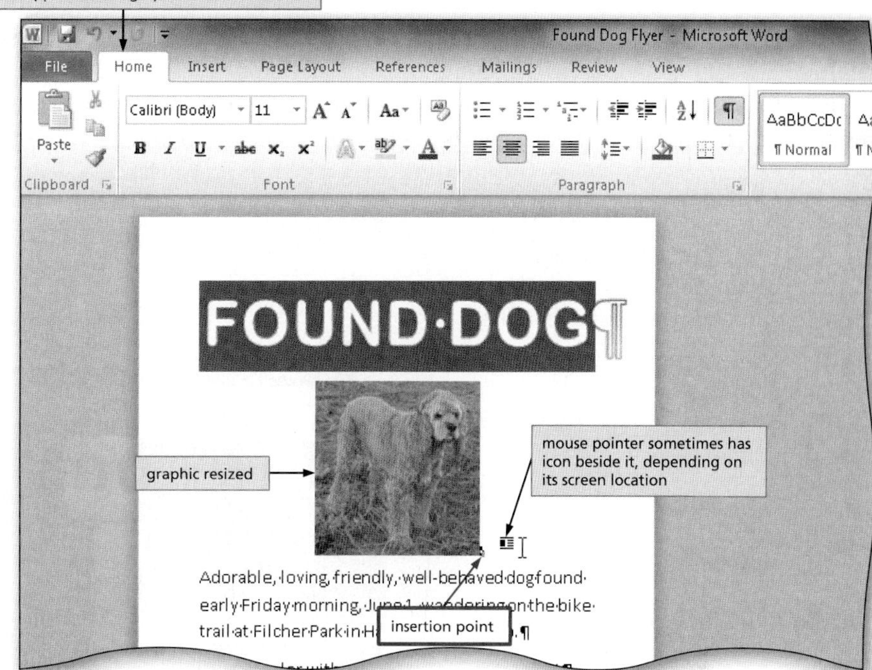

Figure 1–50

Other Ways

1. Enter height and width of graphic in Shape Height and Shape Width boxes (Picture Tools Format tab | Size group)
2. Click Size Dialog Box Launcher (Picture Tools Format tab | Size group), click Size tab (Layout dialog box), enter desired height and width values in boxes, click OK button

To Insert Another Picture

The next step is to insert the other digital picture of the dog immediately to the right of the current picture. This second picture also is available on the Data Files for Students. See the inside back cover of this book for instructions on downloading the Data Files for Students, or contact your instructor for information about accessing the required files.

The following steps insert another picture immediately to the right of the current picture.

1 With the insertion point positioned as shown in Figure 1–50, click Insert on the Ribbon to display the Insert tab.

2 With your USB flash drive connected to one of the computer's USB ports, click the Insert Picture from File button (Insert tab | Illustrations group) to display the Insert Picture dialog box.

3 If necessary, navigate to the picture location (in this case, the Word folder in the CIS 101 folder [or your class folder] on the USB flash drive). For a detailed example of this procedure, refer to Steps 3a – 3c in the To Save a File in a Folder section in the Office 2010 and Windows 7 chapter at the beginning of this book.

4 Click Dog Picture 2 to select the file.

5 Click the Insert button (Insert Picture dialog box) to insert the picture at the location of the insertion point in the document.

BTW **Word Help**
At any time while using Word, you can find answers to questions and display information about various topics through Word Help. Used properly, this form of assistance can increase your productivity and reduce your frustrations by minimizing the time you spend learning how to use Word. For instruction about Word Help and exercises that will help you gain confidence in using it, read the Office 2010 and Windows 7 chapter at the beginning of this book.

To Resize a Graphic by Entering Exact Measurements

The next step is to resize the second picture so that it is the exact same size as the first picture. The height and width measurements of the first graphic are approximately 2.74" and 2.73", respectively. When a graphic is selected, its height and width measurements show in the Size group of the Picture Tools Format tab. The following steps resize a selected graphic by entering its desired exact measurements.

1

- With the second graphic still selected, click the Shape Height box (Picture Tools Format tab | Size group) to select the contents in the box and then type `2.74` as the height.

Q&A What if the Picture Tools Format tab no longer is displayed on my Ribbon?

Double-click the picture to display the Picture Tools Format tab.

Q&A What if the contents of the Shape Height box are not selected?

Triple-click the Shape Height box.

- Click the Shape Width box to select the contents in the box, type `2.73` as the width, and then click the picture to apply the settings.
- If necessary, scroll up to display the entire document in the window (Figure 1–51).

Picture Tools Format tab
Found Dog Flyer - Microsoft Word
Picture Tools
Insert
Page Layout
References
Mailings
Review
View
Format
value entered in Shape Height box may change slightly to preserve proportions
2.74"
2.73"
Picture Styles
Size
Size group
value entered in Shape Width box may change slightly to preserve proportions
FOUND·DOG¶
second dog picture inserted and resized
Adorable,·loving,·friendly,·well-behaved·dog·found·early·Friday·morning,·June·1,·wandering·on·the·bike·trail·at·Filcher·Park·in·Hampton·Township.¶
Tan·color·with·patches·of·white·on·his·chest¶
Male,·adult·cocker·spaniel¶
Green·and·silver·collar·with·the·name,·Bailey,·on·the·tag¶
If·this·is·your·lost·dog,·call·555-1029.¶

Figure 1–51

Q&A Why did my measurements change slightly?

Depending on relative measurements, the height and width values entered may change slightly.

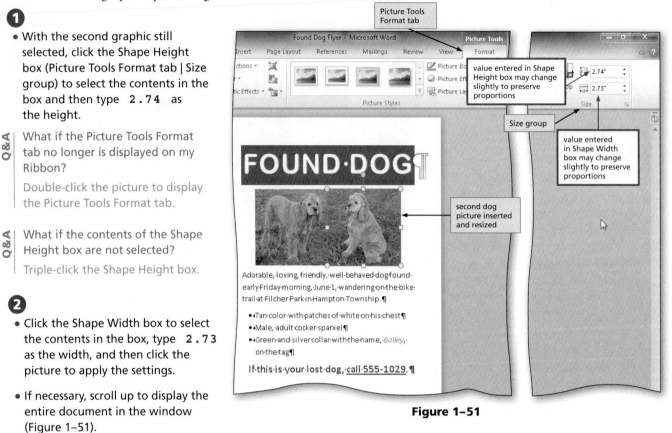

Other Ways

1. Right-click picture, enter shape height and width values in boxes on shortcut menu
2. Right-click picture, click Size and Position on shortcut menu, click Size tab (Layout dialog box), enter shape height and width values in boxes, click OK button

To Zoom the Document

You are finished resizing the graphics and no longer need to view the entire page in the document window. Thus, the following step changes the zoom back to 100 percent.

1 Click the Zoom In button on the status bar as many times as necessary until the Zoom button displays 100% on its face (shown in Figure 1–52).

To Apply a Picture Style

A **style** is a named group of formatting characteristics. Word provides more than 25 picture styles that enable you easily to change a picture's look to a more visually appealing style, including a variety of shapes, angles, borders, and reflections. The flyer in this chapter uses a style that applies soft edges to the picture. The following steps apply a picture style to a picture.

- Click the leftmost dog picture to select it (Figure 1–52).

Q&A What is the green circle attached to the selected graphic?

It is called a rotate handle. When you drag a graphic's rotate handle, the graphic moves in either a clockwise or counterclockwise direction.

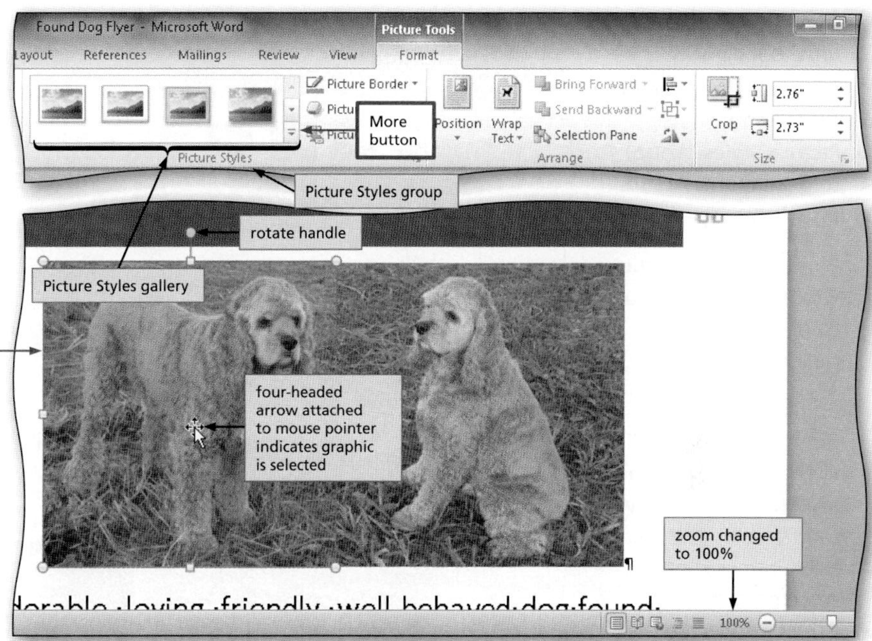

Figure 1–52

- Click the More button in the Picture Styles gallery (Picture Tools Format tab | Picture Styles group) (shown in Figure 1–52) to expand the gallery.
- Point to Soft Edge Rectangle in the Picture Styles gallery to display a live preview of that style applied to the picture in the document (Figure 1–53).

 **Experiment**

- Point to various picture styles in the Picture Styles gallery and watch the style of the picture change in the document window.

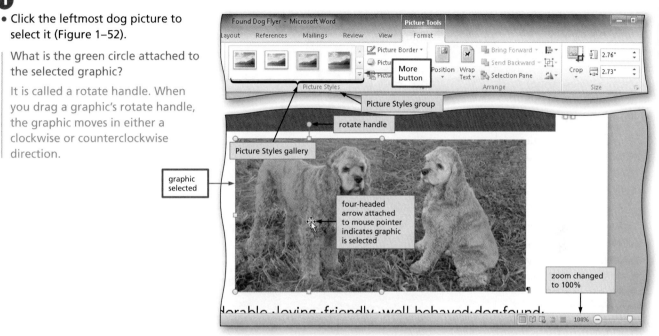

- Click Soft Edge Rectangle in the Picture Styles gallery to apply the style to the selected picture.

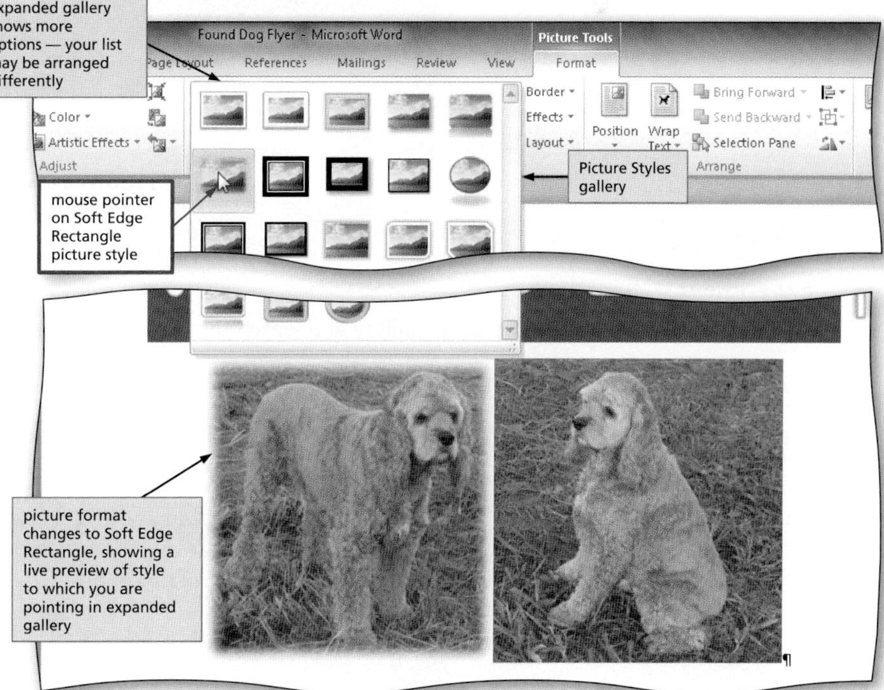

Figure 1–53

To Apply Picture Effects

Word provides a variety of picture effects so that you can further customize a picture. Effects include shadows, reflections, glow, soft edges, bevel, and 3-D rotation. The difference between the effects and the styles is that each effect has several options, providing you with more control over the exact look of the image.

In this flyer, the leftmost dog picture has a slight tan glow effect and is turned inward toward the center of the page. The following steps apply picture effects to the selected picture.

1

- Click the Picture Effects button (Picture Tools Format tab | Picture Styles group) to display the Picture Effects menu.
- Point to Glow on the Picture Effects menu to display the Glow gallery.
- Point to Tan, 5 pt glow, Accent color 6 in the Glow Variations area (rightmost glow in first row) to display a live preview of the selected glow effect applied to the picture in the document window (Figure 1–54).

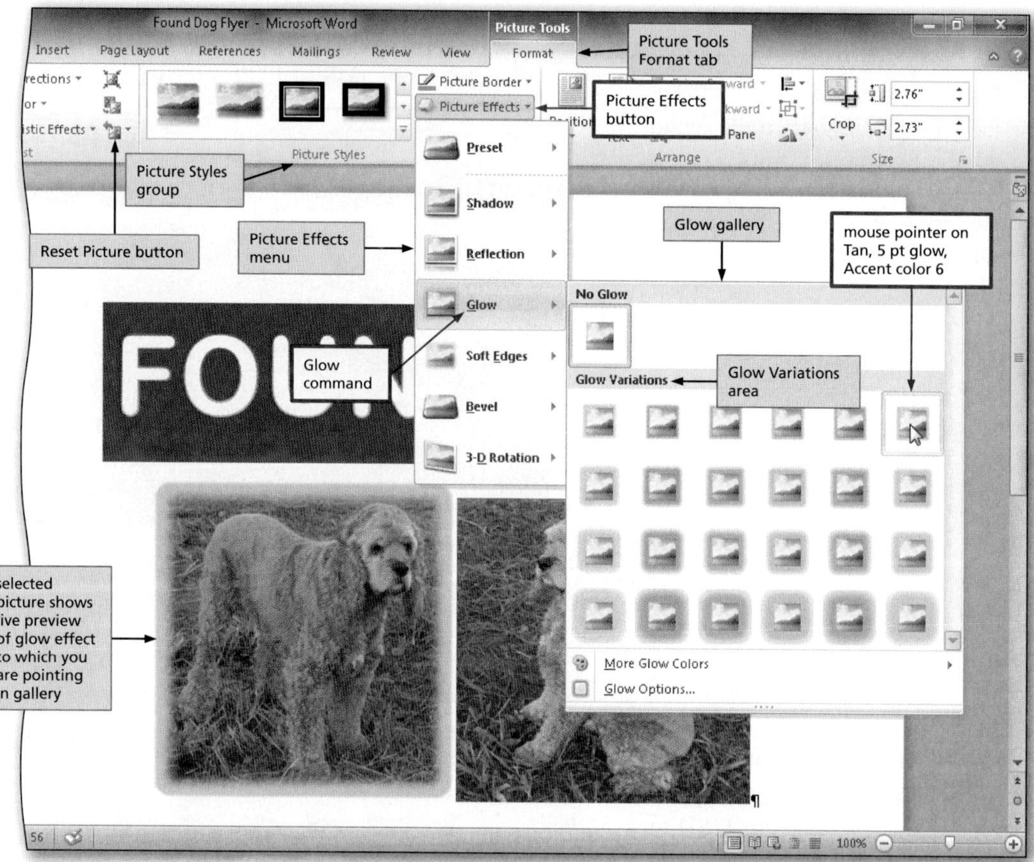

Figure 1–54

Experiment

- Point to various glow effects in the Glow gallery and watch the picture change in the document window.

2

- Click Tan, 5 pt glow, Accent color 6 in the Glow gallery to apply the selected picture effect.

Q&A What if I wanted to discard formatting applied to a picture?

You would click the Reset Picture button (Picture Tools Format tab | Adjust group). To reset formatting and size, you would click the Reset Picture button arrow (Picture Tools Format tab | Adjust group) and then click Reset Picture & Size on the Reset Picture menu.

- Click the Picture Effects button (Picture Tools Format tab | Picture Styles group) to display the Picture Effects menu again.
- Point to 3-D Rotation on the Picture Effects menu to display the 3-D Rotation gallery.
- Point to Off Axis 1 Right in the Parallel area (second rotation in second row) to display a live preview of the selected 3-D effect applied to the picture in the document window (Figure 1–55).

Experiment

- Point to various 3-D rotation effects in the 3-D Rotation gallery and watch the picture change in the document window.

- Click Off Axis 1 Right in the 3-D Rotation gallery to apply the selected picture effect.

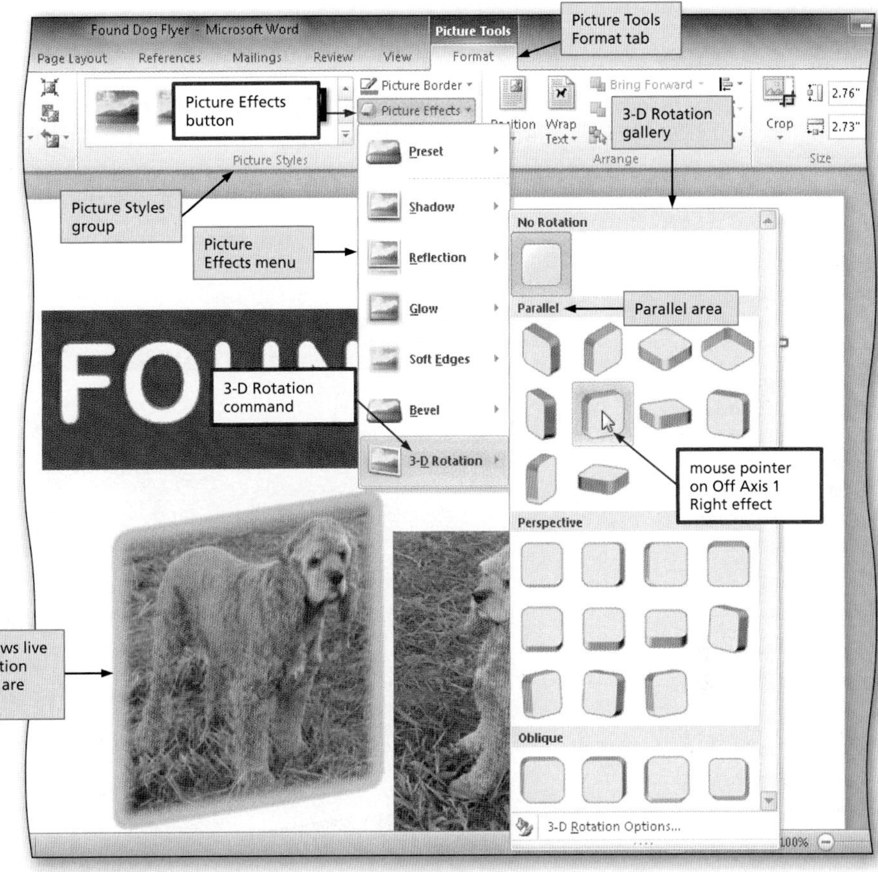

Figure 1–55

Other Ways

1. Right-click picture, click Format Picture on shortcut menu, select desired options (Format Picture dialog box), click Close button
2. Click Format Shape Dialog Box Launcher (Picture Tools Format tab | Picture Styles group), select desired options (Format Picture dialog box), click Close button

To Apply a Picture Style and Effects to Another Picture

In this flyer, the rightmost dog picture also uses the soft edge picture style, has a slight tan glow effect, and is turned inward toward the center of the page. The following steps apply the picture style and picture effects to the picture.

1. Click the rightmost dog picture to select it.
2. Click the More button in the Picture Styles gallery (Picture Tools Format tab | Picture Styles group) to expand the gallery and then click Soft Edge Rectangle in the Picture Styles gallery to apply the selected style to the picture.
3. Click the Picture Effects button (Picture Tools Format tab | Picture Styles group) to display the Picture Effects menu and then point to Glow on the Picture Effects menu to display the Glow gallery.
4. Click Tan, 5 pt glow, Accent color 6 (rightmost glow in first row) in the Glow gallery to apply the picture effect to the picture.

5. Click the Picture Effects button (Picture Tools Format tab | Picture Styles group) to display the Picture Effects menu again and then point to 3-D Rotation on the Picture Effects menu to display the 3-D Rotation gallery.

6. Click Off Axis 2 Left (rightmost rotation in second row) in the Parallel area in the 3-D Rotation gallery to apply the picture effect to the selected picture.

7. Click to the right of the picture to deselect it (Figure 1–56).

BTW
BTWs
For a complete list of the BTWs found in the margins of this book, visit the Word 2010 BTW Web page (scsite .com/wd2010/btw).

Figure 1–56

Enhancing the Page

BTW
Centering Page Contents Vertically
You can center page contents vertically between the top and bottom margins. To do this, click the Page Setup Dialog Box Launcher (Page Layout tab | Page Setup group), click the Layout tab (Page Setup dialog box), click the Vertical alignment box arrow, click Center in the list, and then click the OK button.

With the text and graphics entered and formatted, the next step is to look at the page as a whole and determine if it looks finished in its current state. As you review the page, answer these questions:

- Does it need a page border to frame its contents, or would a page border make it look too busy?
- Is the spacing between paragraphs and graphics on the page adequate? Do any sections of text or graphics look as if they are positioned too closely to the items above or below them?

You determine that a graphical, color-coordinated border would enhance the flyer. You also notice that the flyer would look more proportionate if it had a little more space above and below the pictures. The following pages make these enhancements to the flyer.

To View One Page

Earlier in this chapter, you changed the zoom using the Zoom Out and Zoom In buttons on the status bar. If you want to display an entire page as large as possible in the document window, Word can compute the correct zoom percentage for you. The next steps display a single page in its entirety in the document window as large as possible.

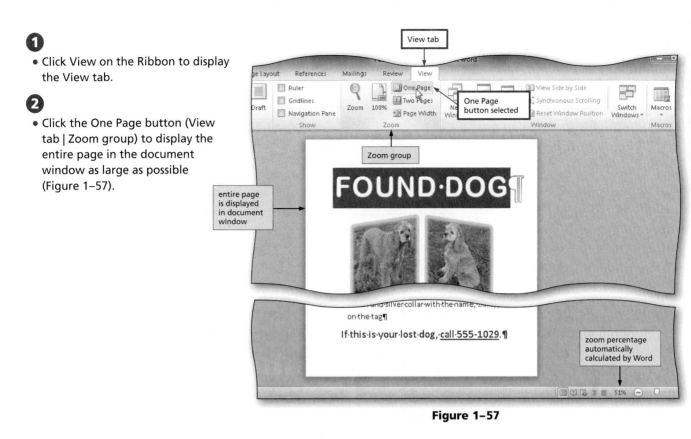

- Click View on the Ribbon to display the View tab.

2

- Click the One Page button (View tab | Zoom group) to display the entire page in the document window as large as possible (Figure 1–57).

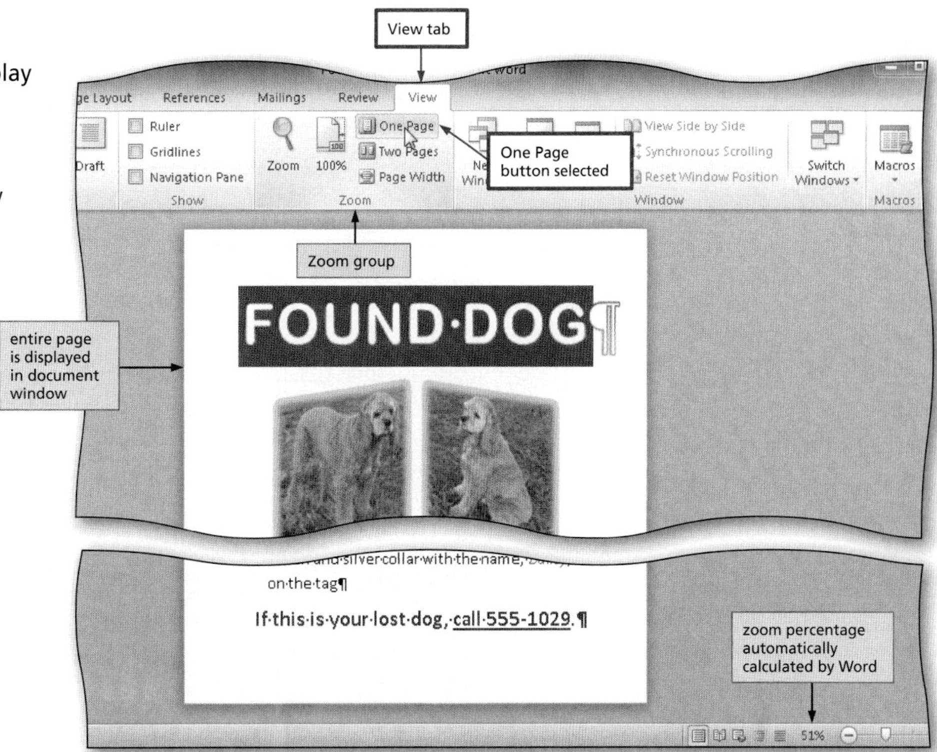

Figure 1–57

To Add a Page Border

In Word, you can add a border around the perimeter of an entire page. The flyer in this chapter has a light green dashed border. The following steps add a page border.

1

- Click Page Layout on the Ribbon to display the Page Layout tab.
- Click the Page Borders button (Page Layout tab | Page Background group) to display the Borders and Shading dialog box (Figure 1–58).

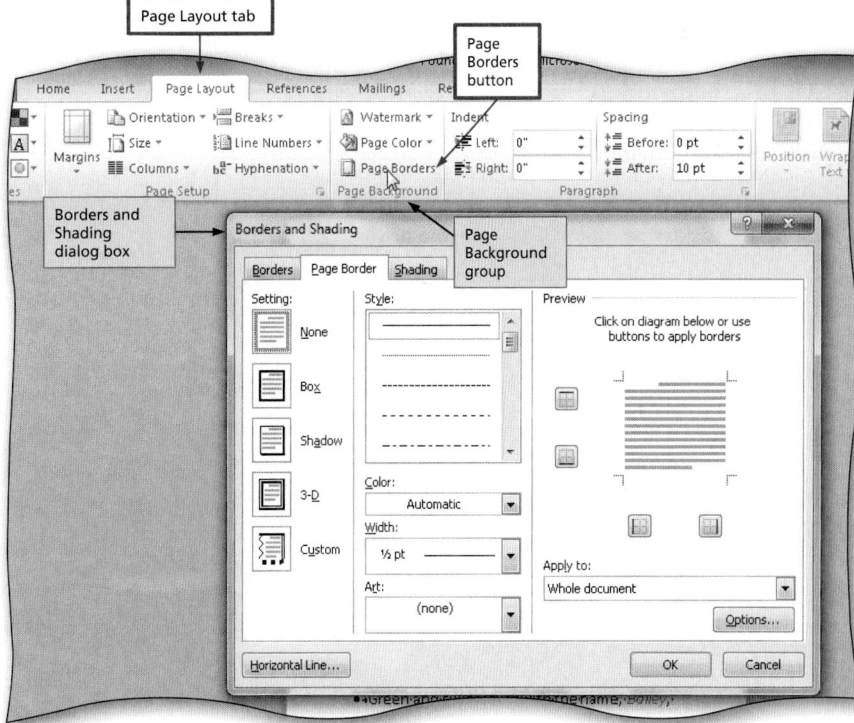

Figure 1–58

2

- Scroll through the Style list (Borders and Shading dialog box) and select the style shown in Figure 1–59.
- Click the Color box arrow to display a Color palette (Figure 1–59).

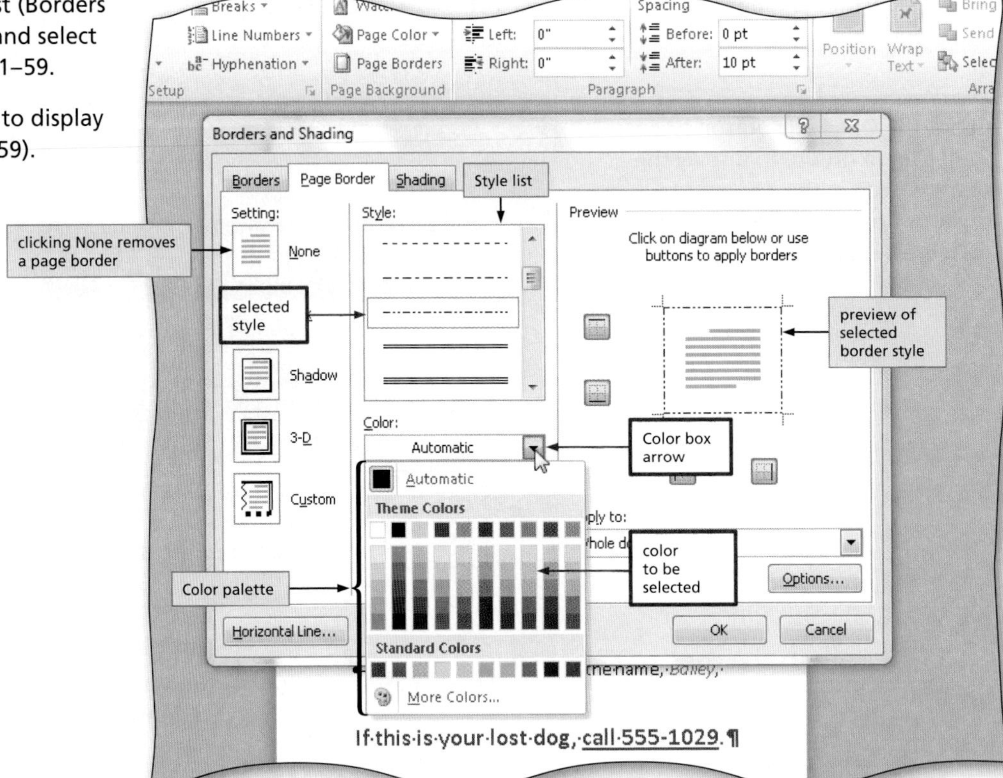

Figure 1–59

- Click Dark Green, Accent 4, Lighter 60% (eighth color in third row) in the Color palette to select the color for the page border.
- Click the Width box arrow and then click 3 pt to select the thickness of the page border (Figure 1–60).

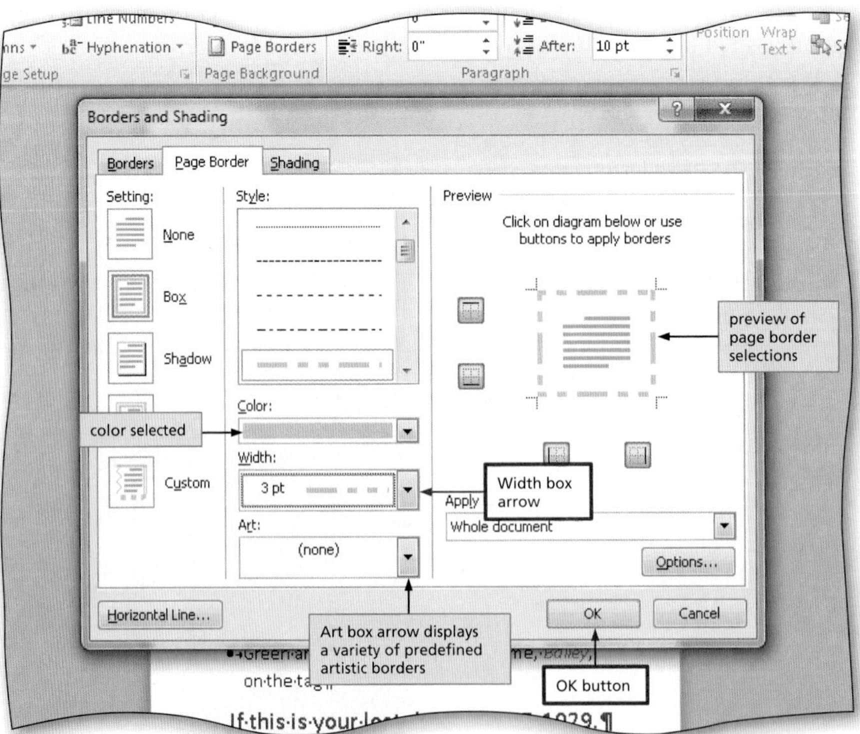

Figure 1–60

4

- Click the OK button to add the border to the page (Figure 1–61).

Q&A What if I wanted to remove the border?

You would click None in the Setting list in the Borders and Shading dialog box.

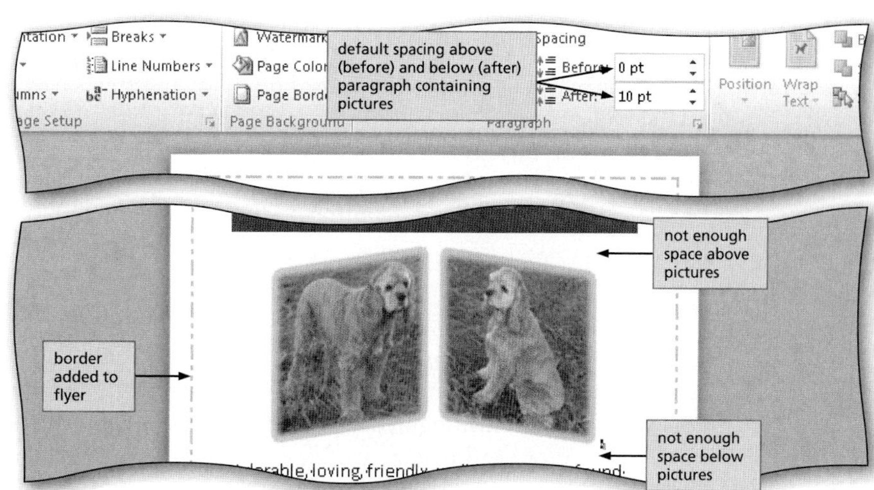

Figure 1–61

To Change Spacing before and after a Paragraph

The default spacing above (before) a paragraph in Word is 0 points and below (after) is 10 points. In the flyer, you want to increase the spacing above and below the paragraph containing the pictures. The following steps change the spacing above and below a paragraph.

- Position the insertion point in the paragraph to be adjusted, in this case, the paragraph containing the pictures.
- Click the Spacing Before box up arrow (Page Layout tab | Paragraph group) as many times as necessary until 24 pt is displayed in the Spacing Before box to increase the space above the current paragraph.

- Click the Spacing After box up arrow (Page Layout tab | Paragraph group) so that 12 pt is displayed in the Spacing After box to increase the space below the current paragraph (Figure 1–62).
- If the text flows to two pages, reduce the spacing above and below paragraphs as necessary.

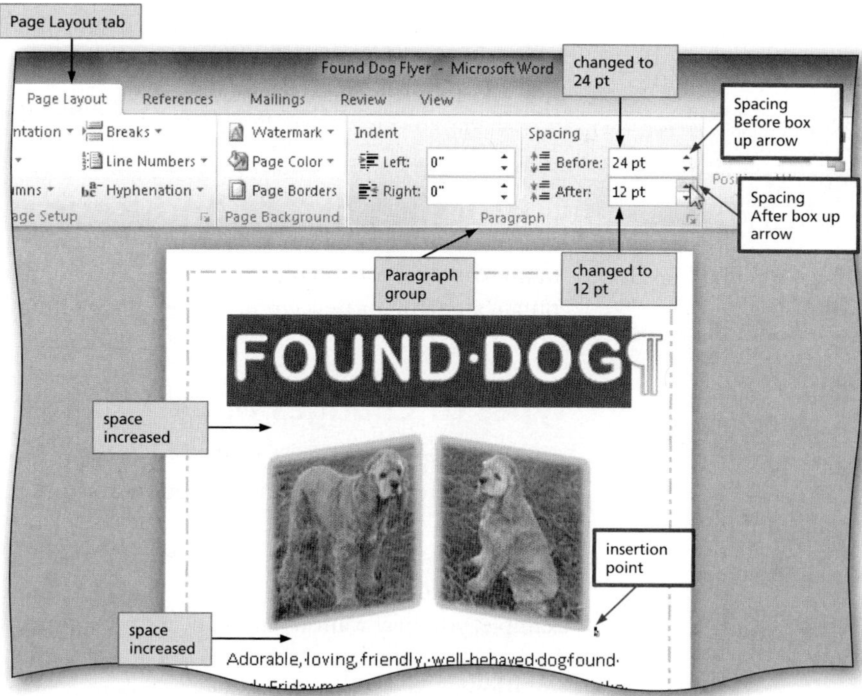

Figure 1–62

Other Ways

1. Right-click paragraph, click Paragraph on shortcut menu, click Indents and Spacing tab (Paragraph dialog box), enter spacing before and after values, click OK button
2. Click Paragraph Dialog Box Launcher (Home tab or Page Layout tab | Paragraph group), click Indents and Spacing tab (Paragraph dialog box), enter spacing before and after values, click OK button

To Save an Existing Document with the Same File Name

You have made several modifications to the document since you last saved it. Thus, you should save it again. The following step saves the document again. For an example of the step listed below, refer to the Office 2010 and Windows 7 chapter at the beginning of this book.

1. Click the Save button on the Quick Access Toolbar to overwrite the previously saved file.

To Quit Word

Although you still need to make some edits to this document, you want to quit Word and resume working on the project at a later time. Thus, the following steps quit Word. For a detailed example of the procedure summarized below, refer to the Office 2010 and Windows 7 chapter at the beginning of this book.

1. If you have one Word document open, click the Close button on the right side of the title bar to close the document and quit Word; or if you have multiple Word documents open, click File on the Ribbon to open the Backstage view and then click Exit in the Backstage view to close all open documents and quit Word.
2. If a Microsoft Word dialog box appears, click the Save button to save any changes made to the document since the last save.

BTW

Certification
The Microsoft Office Specialist (MOS) program provides an opportunity for you to obtain a valuable industry credential — proof that you have the Word 2010 skills required by employers. For more information, visit the Word 2010 Certification Web page (scsite.com/wd2010/cert).

Break Point: If you wish to take a break, this is a good place to do so. To resume at a later time, continue following the steps from this location forward.

Correcting Errors and Revising a Document

After creating a document, you may need to change it. For example, the document may contain an error, or new circumstances may require you to add text to the document.

Types of Changes Made to Documents

The types of changes made to documents normally fall into one of the three following categories: additions, deletions, or modifications.

Additions Additional words, sentences, or paragraphs may be required in a document. Additions occur when you omit text from a document and want to insert it later. For example, you may want to add your e-mail address to the flyer.

Deletions Sometimes, text in a document is incorrect or is no longer needed. For example, you may discover the dog's collar is just green. In this case, you would delete the words, and silver, from the flyer.

Modifications If an error is made in a document or changes take place that affect the document, you might have to revise a word(s) in the text. For example, the dog may have been found in Hampton Village instead of Hampton Township.

To Start Word

Once you have created and saved a document, you may need to retrieve it from your storage medium. For example, you might want to revise the document or print it. The following steps, which assume Windows 7 is running, start Word so that you can open and modify the flyer. You may need to ask your instructor how to start Word for your computer. For a detailed example of the procedure summarized below, refer to the Office 2010 and Windows 7 chapter at the beginning of this book.

1. Click the Start button on the Windows 7 taskbar to display the Start menu.
2. Type `Microsoft Word` as the search text in the 'Search programs and files' text box and watch the search results appear on the Start menu.
3. Click Microsoft Word 2010 in the search results on the Start menu to start Word and display a new blank document in the Word window.
4. If the Word window is not maximized, click the Maximize button next to the Close button on its title bar to maximize the window.

To Open a Document from Word

Earlier in this chapter, you saved your project on a USB flash drive using the file name, Found Dog Flyer. The following steps open the Found Dog Flyer file from the Word folder in the CIS 101 folder on the USB flash drive. For a detailed example of the procedure summarized below, refer to the Office 2010 and Windows 7 chapter at the beginning of this book.

1. With your USB flash drive connected to one of the computer's USB ports, click File on the Ribbon to open the Backstage view.
2. Click Open in the Backstage view to display the Open dialog box.
3. Navigate to the location of the file to be opened (in this case, the Word folder in the CIS 101 folder [or your class folder] on the USB flash drive). For a detailed example of this procedure, refer to Steps 3a – 3c in the To Save a File in a Folder section in the Office 2010 and Windows 7 chapter at the beginning of this book.
4. Click Found Dog Flyer to select the file to be opened.
5. Click the Open button (Open dialog box) to open the selected file and display the opened document in the Word window.

Q&A
Could I have clicked the Recent tab to open the file?
Yes. Because the file was recently closed, it should appear in the Recent Documents list.

To Zoom the Document

While modifying the document, you prefer the document at 100 percent so that it is easier to read. Thus, the following step changes the zoom back to 100 percent.

1. If necessary, click the Zoom In button on the status bar as many times as necessary until the Zoom button displays 100% on its face (shown in Figure 1–63 on the next page).

To Insert Text in an Existing Document

Word inserts text to the left of the insertion point. The text to the right of the insertion point moves to the right and downward to fit the new text. The following steps insert the word, very, to the left of the word, early, in the flyer.

1

- Scroll through the document and then click to the left of the location of text to be inserted (in this case, the e in early) to position the insertion point where text should be inserted (Figure 1–63).

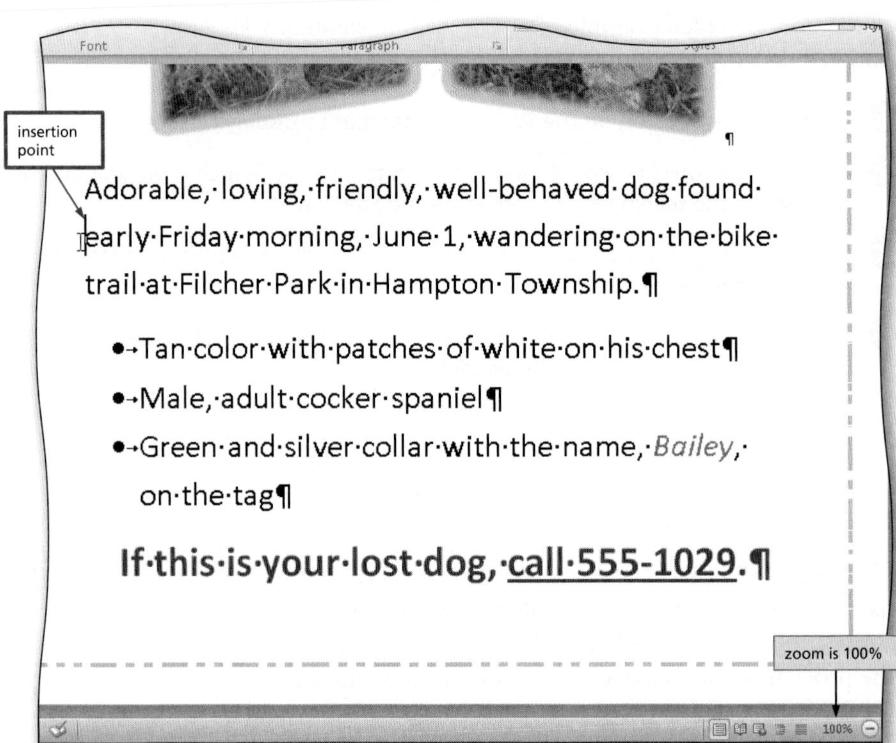
Font
Paragraph
insertion point
Adorable, loving, friendly, well-behaved dog found early Friday morning, June 1, wandering on the bike trail at Filcher Park in Hampton Township.
Tan color with patches of white on his chest
Male, adult cocker spaniel
Green and silver collar with the name, Bailey, on the tag
If this is your lost dog, call 555-1029.
zoom is 100%
100%

Figure 1–63

2

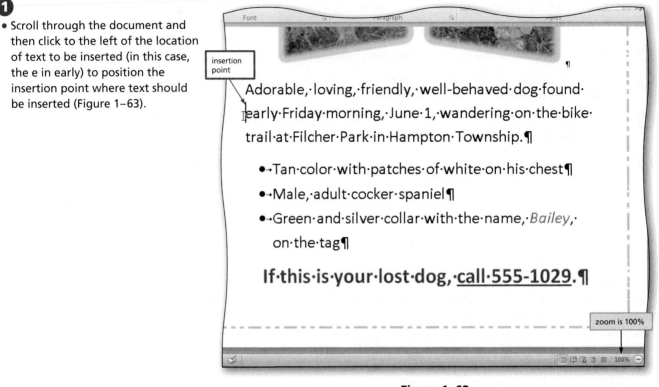

- Type `very` and then press the SPACEBAR to insert the word to the left of the insertion point (Figure 1–64).

Q&A Why did the text move to the right as I typed?

In Word, the default typing mode is **insert mode**, which means as you type a character, Word moves all the characters to the right of the typed character one position to the right.

Adorable, loving, friendly, well-behaved dog found very early Friday morning, June 1, wandering on the bike trail at Filcher Park in Hampton Township.
word inserted
Tan color with patches of white on his chest
Male, adult cocker spaniel
Green and silver collar with the name, Bailey, on the tag
If this is your lost dog, call 555-1029.

Figure 1–64

Deleting Text from a Document

It is not unusual to type incorrect characters or words in a document. As discussed earlier in this chapter, you can click the Undo button on the Quick Access Toolbar to undo a command or action immediately — this includes typing. Word also provides other methods of correcting typing errors.

To delete an incorrect character in a document, simply click next to the incorrect character and then press the BACKSPACE key to erase to the left of the insertion point, or press the DELETE key to erase to the right of the insertion point.

To Delete Text

To delete a word or phrase, you first must select the word or phrase. The following steps select the word, very, that was just added in the previous steps and then delete the selection.

1

- Position the mouse pointer somewhere in the word to be selected (in this case, very) and then double-click to select the word (Figure 1–65).

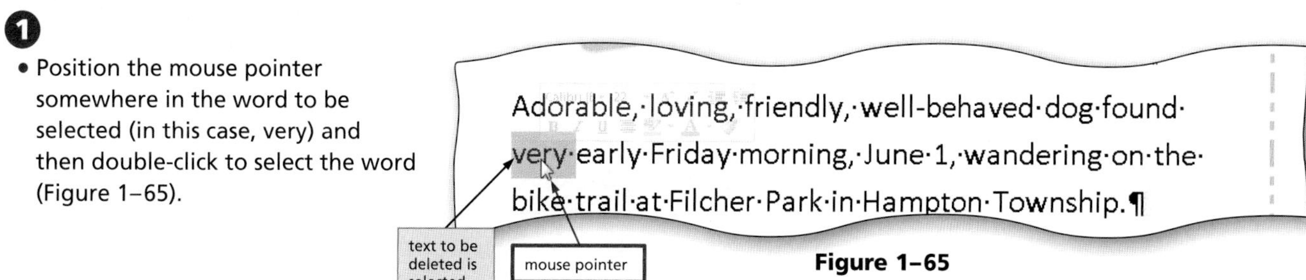

Figure 1–65

2

- With the text selected, press the DELETE key to delete the selected text (shown in Figure 1–63).

To Move Text

While proofreading the flyer, you realize that the body copy would read better if the first two bulleted paragraphs were reversed. An efficient way to move text a short distance, such as reversing two paragraphs, is drag-and-drop editing. With **drag-and-drop editing**, you select the text to be moved and then drag the selected item to the new location and then *drop*, or insert, it there. Another technique for moving text is the cut-and-paste technique, which is discussed in the next chapter. The following steps use drag-and-drop editing to move text.

- Position the mouse pointer in the paragraph to be moved (in this case, the second bulleted item) and then triple-click to select the paragraph.
- With the mouse pointer in the selected text, press and hold down the mouse button, which displays a dotted insertion point and a small dotted box with the mouse pointer (Figure 1–66).

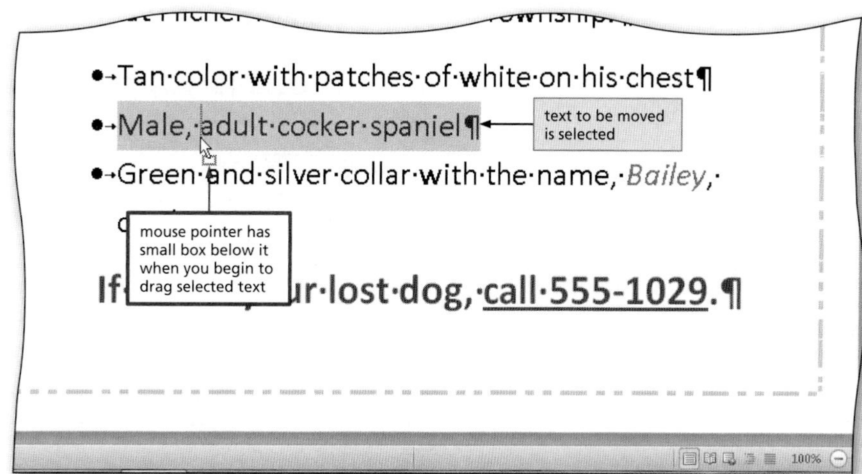

•→Tan·color·with·patches·of·white·on·his·chest¶
•→Male,·adult·cocker·spaniel¶
text to be moved is selected
•→Green·and·silver·collar·with·the·name,·Bailey,·
mouse pointer has small box below it when you begin to drag selected text
r·lost·dog,·call·555-1029.¶
100%

Figure 1–66

2

- Drag the dotted insertion point to the location where the selected text is to be moved, as shown in Figure 1–67.

selected text to be dropped at location of dotted insertion point

Adorable,·loving,·friendly,·well-behaved·dog·found·early·Friday·morning,·June·1,·wandering·on·the·bike·trail·at·Filcher·Park·in·Hampton·Township.¶

- Tan·color·with·patches·of·white·on·his·chest¶
- Male,·adult·cocker·spaniel¶
- Green·and·silver·collar·with·the·name,·*Bailey*,·on·the·tag¶

If·this·is·your·lost·dog,·call·555-1029.¶

Figure 1–67

3

- Release the mouse button to move the selected text to the location of the dotted insertion point (Figure 1–68).

Q&A What if I accidentally drag text to the wrong location?

Click the Undo button on the Quick Access Toolbar and try again.

Q&A Can I use drag-and-drop editing to move any selected item?

Yes, you can select words, sentences, phrases, and graphics and then use drag-and-drop editing to move them.

Q&A What is the purpose of the Paste Options button?

If you click the Paste Options button, a menu appears that allows you to change the format of the item that was moved. The next chapter discusses the Paste Options menu.

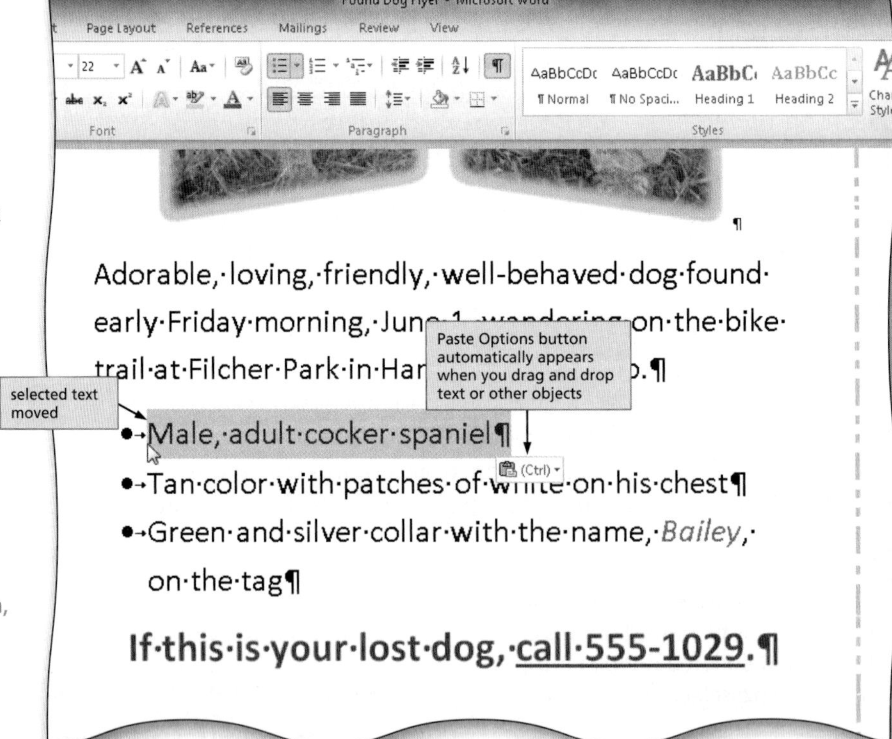

Found Dog Flyer - Microsoft Word
Page Layout
References
Mailings
Review
View
Font
Paragraph
Styles
¶ Normal
¶ No Spaci...
Heading 1
Heading 2
Adorable,·loving,·friendly,·well-behaved·dog·found·
early·Friday·morning,·June
on·the·bike·
trail·at·Filcher·Park·in·Har
Paste Options button automatically appears when you drag and drop text or other objects
selected text moved
•→Male,·adult·cocker·spaniel¶
(Ctrl)
•→Tan·color·with·patches·of·
on·his·chest¶
•→Green·and·silver·collar·with·the·name,·Bailey,·
on·the·tag¶
If·this·is·your·lost·dog,·call·555-1029.¶

Figure 1–68

- Click anywhere in the document window to remove the selection from the bulleted item.

Other Ways

1. Click Cut button (Home tab | Clipboard group), click where text or object is to be pasted, click Paste button (Home tab | Clipboard group)
2. Right-click selected text, click Cut on shortcut menu, right-click where text or object is to be pasted, click Keep Source Formatting on shortcut menu
3. Press CTRL+X, position insertion point where text or object is to be pasted, press CTRL+V

Changing Document Properties

Word helps you organize and identify your files by using **document properties**, which are the details about a file. Document properties, also known as **metadata**, can include information such as the project author, title, subject, and keywords. A **keyword** is a word or phrase that further describes the document. For example, a class name or document topic can describe the file's purpose or content.

Document properties are valuable for a variety of reasons:

- Users can save time locating a particular file because they can view a document's properties without opening the document.
- By creating consistent properties for files having similar content, users can better organize their documents.
- Some organizations require Word users to add document properties so that other employees can view details about these files.

Five different types of document properties exist, but the more common ones used in this book are standard and automatically updated properties. **Standard properties** are associated with all Microsoft Office documents and include author, title, and subject. **Automatically updated properties** include file system properties, such as the date you create or change a file, and statistics, such as the file size.

BTW

Printing Document Properties
To print document properties, click File on the Ribbon to open the Backstage view, click the Print tab in the Backstage view to display the Print gallery, click the first button in the Settings area to display a list of options specifying what you can print, click Document Properties in the list to specify you want to print the document properties instead of the actual document, and then click the Print button in the Print gallery to print the document properties on the currently selected printer.

To Change Document Properties

The **Document Information Panel** contains areas where you can view and enter document properties. You can view and change information in this panel at any time while you are creating a document. Before saving the flyer again, you want to add your name and course information as document properties. The following steps use the Document Information Panel to change document properties.

1

- Click File on the Ribbon to open the Backstage view.
- If necessary, click the Info tab to display the Info gallery (Figure 1–69).

Q&A

How do I close the Backstage view?

Click File on the Ribbon or click the preview of the document in the Info gallery to return to the Word document window.

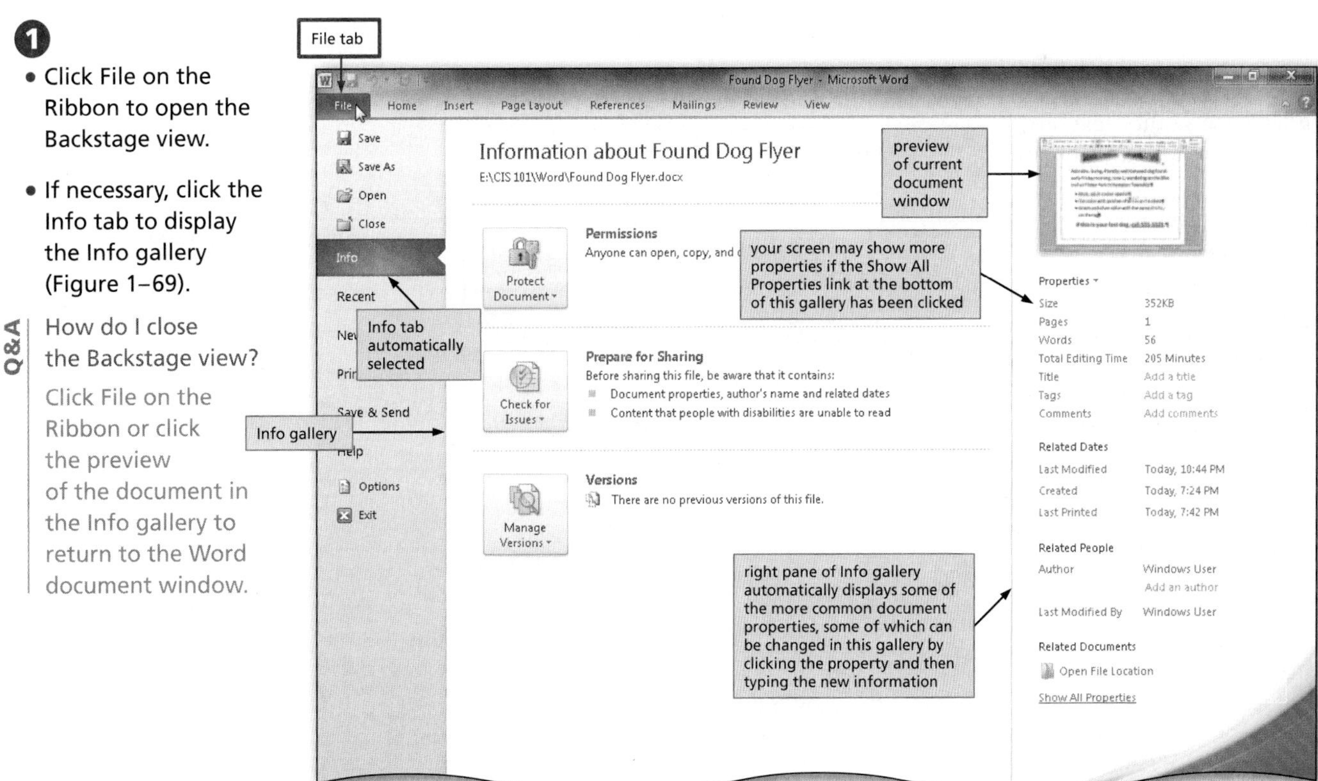

Figure 1–69

2

- Click the Properties button in the right pane of the Info gallery to display the Properties menu (Figure 1–70).

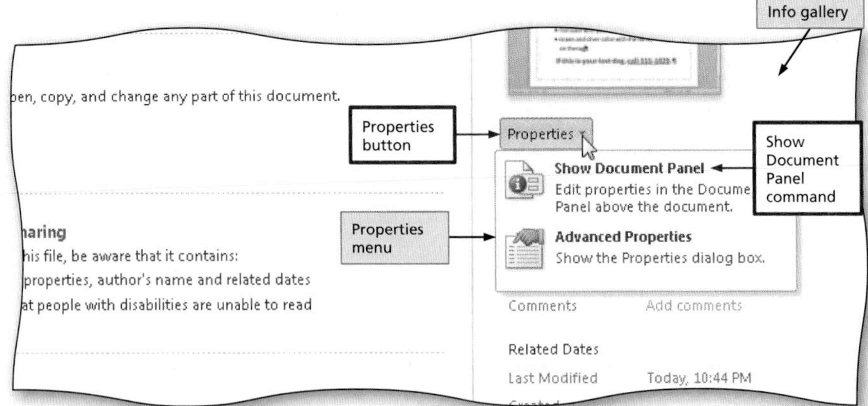

Figure 1–70

3

- Click Show Document Panel on the Properties menu to close the Backstage view and display the Document Information Panel in the Word document window (Figure 1–71).

Why are some of the document properties in my Document Information Panel already filled in?

The person who installed Microsoft Office 2010 on your computer or network may have set or customized the properties.

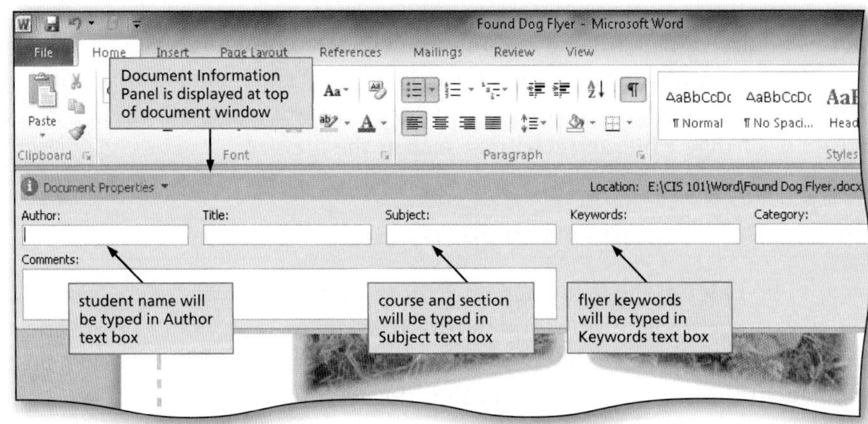

Figure 1–71

4

- Click the Author text box, if necessary, and then type your name as the Author property. If a name already is displayed in the Author text box, delete it before typing your name.
- Click the Subject text box, if necessary delete any existing text, and then type your course and section as the Subject property.
- If an AutoComplete dialog box appears, click its Yes button.

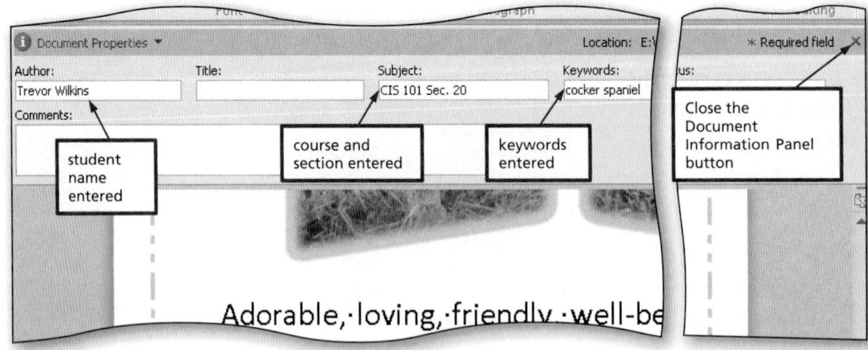

Figure 1–72

- Click the Keywords text box, if necessary delete any existing text, and then type `cocker spaniel` as the Keywords property (Figure 1–72).

What types of document properties does Word collect automatically?

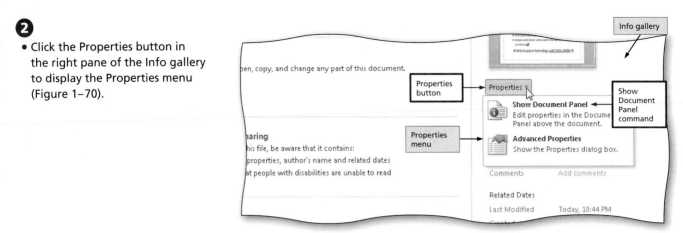

Word records details such as time spent editing a document, the number of times a document has been revised, and the fonts and themes used in a document.

5

- Click the Close the Document Information Panel button so that the Document Information Panel no longer is displayed.

Other Ways

1. Click File on Ribbon, click Info in Backstage view, if necessary click Show All Properties link in Info gallery, click property to change and then type new information, close Backstage view

To Save an Existing Document with the Same File Name

You are finished editing the flyer. Thus, you should save it again. The following step saves the document again. For an example of the step listed below, refer to the Office 2010 and Windows 7 chapter at the beginning of this book.

Click the Save button on the Quick Access Toolbar to overwrite the previously saved file.

Printing a Document

After creating a document, you may want to print it. Printing a document enables you to distribute the document to others in a form that can be read or viewed but typically not edited. It is a good practice to save a document before printing it, in the event you experience difficulties printing.

Determine the best method for distributing the document.

The traditional method of distributing a document uses a printer to produce a hard copy. A **hardcopy** or **printout** is information that exists on a physical medium such as paper. For users that can receive fax documents, you can elect to print a hard copy on a remote fax machine. Hard copies can be useful for the following reasons:

- Many people prefer proofreading a hard copy of a document rather than viewing it on the screen to check for errors and readability.
- Hard copies can serve as reference material if your storage medium is lost or becomes corrupted and you need to recreate the document.

Instead of distributing a hard copy of a document, users can choose to distribute the document as an electronic image that mirrors the original document's appearance. The electronic image of the document can be e-mailed, posted on a Web site, or copied to a portable storage medium such as a USB flash drive. Two popular electronic image formats, sometimes called fixed formats, are PDF by Adobe Systems and XPS by Microsoft. In Word, you can create electronic image files through the Print tab in the Backstage view, the Send & Save tab in the Backstage view, and the Save As dialog box. Electronic images of documents, such as PDF and XPS, can be useful for the following reasons:

- Users can view electronic images of documents without the software that created the original document (e.g., Word). Specifically, to view a PDF file, you use a program called Acrobat Reader, which can be downloaded free from Adobe's Web site. Similarly, to view an XPS file, you use a program called an XPS Viewer, which is included in the latest versions of Windows and Internet Explorer.
- Sending electronic documents saves paper and printer supplies. Society encourages users to contribute to **green computing**, which involves reducing the environmental waste generated when using a computer.

Plan Ahead

BTW

Conserving Ink and Toner

If you want to conserve ink or toner, you can instruct Word to print draft quality documents by clicking File on the Ribbon to open the Backstage view, clicking Options in the Backstage view to display the Word Options dialog box, clicking Advanced in the left pane (Word Options dialog box), scrolling to the Print area in the right pane, placing a check mark in the 'Use draft quality' check box, and then clicking the OK button. Then, use the Backstage view to print the document as usual.

To Print a Document

With the completed document saved, you may want to print it. Because this flyer is being posted, you will print a hard copy on a printer. The steps on the next page print a hard copy of the contents of the saved Found Dog Flyer document.

1

- Click File on the Ribbon to open the Backstage view.
- Click the Print tab in the Backstage view to display the Print gallery (Figure 1–73).

Q&A How can I print multiple copies of my document?

Increase the number in the Copies box in the Print gallery.

Q&A What if I decide not to print the document at this time?

Click File on the Ribbon to close the Backstage view and return to the Word document window.

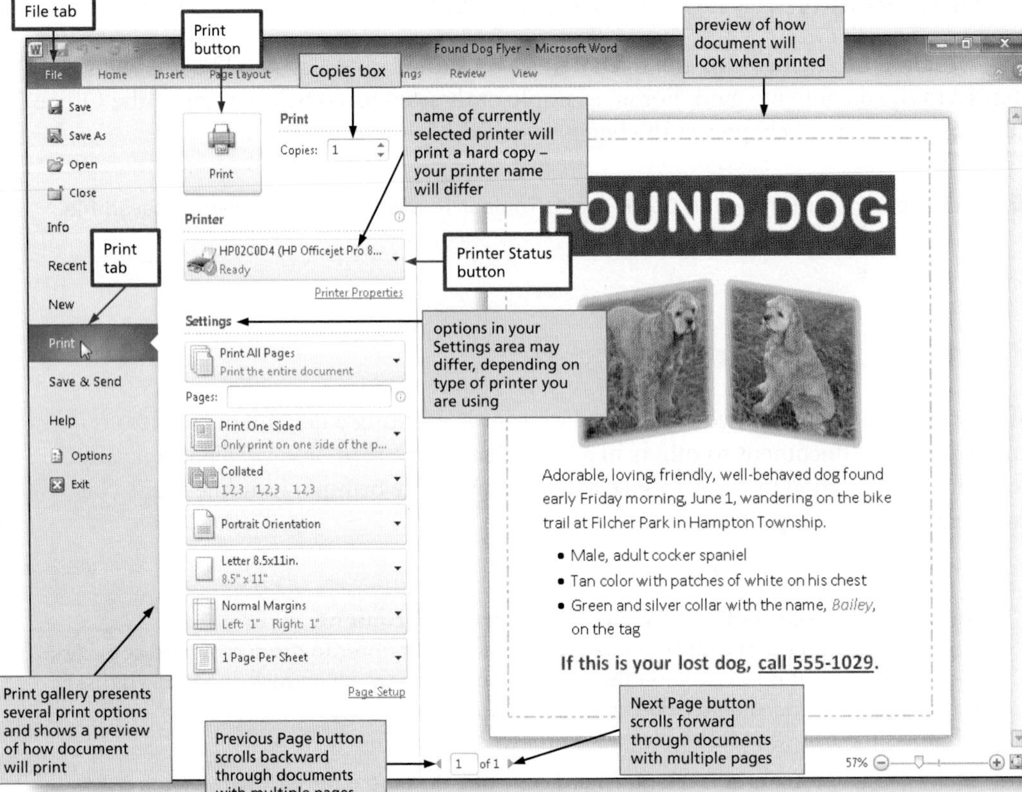

Figure 1–73

2

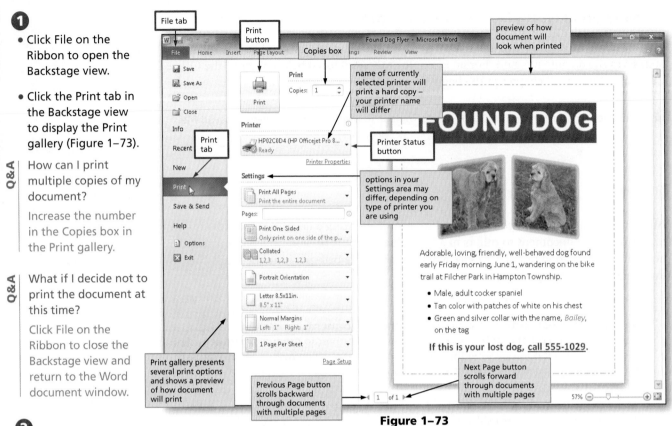

- Verify the printer name that appears on the Printer Status button will print a hard copy of the document. If necessary, click the Printer Status button to display a list of available printer options and then click the desired printer to change the currently selected printer.

3

- Click the Print button in the Print gallery to print the document on the currently selected printer.
- When the printer stops, retrieve the hard copy (Figure 1–74).

Q&A Do I have to wait until my document is complete to print it?

No, you can follow these steps to print a document at any time while you are creating it.

Q&A What if I want to print an electronic image of a document instead of a hard copy?

You would click the Printer Status button in the Print gallery and then select the desired electronic image option such as a Microsoft XPS Document Writer, which would create an XPS file.

Figure 1–74

Other Ways

1. Press CTRL+P, press ENTER

To Quit Word

The project now is complete. Thus, the following steps quit Word. For an example of the step listed below, refer to the Office 2010 and Windows 7 chapter at the beginning of this book.

1. If you have one Word document open, click the Close button on the right side of the title bar to close the document and quit Word; or if you have multiple Word documents open, click File on the Ribbon to open the Backstage view and then click Exit in the Backstage view to close all open documents and quit Word.

2. If a Microsoft Word dialog box appears, click the Save button to save any changes made to the document since the last save.

BTW

Printed Borders
If one or more of your borders do not print, click the Page Borders button (Page Layout tab | Page Background group), click the Options button (Borders and Shading dialog box), click the Measure from box arrow and click Text, change the four text boxes to 15 pt, and then click the OK button in each dialog box. Try printing the document again. If the borders still do not print, adjust the text boxes in the dialog box to a number smaller than 15 point.

Chapter Summary

In this chapter, you have learned how to enter text in a document, format text, insert a picture, format a picture, add a page border, and print a document. The items listed below include all the new Word skills you have learned in this chapter.

1. Start Word (WD 4)
2. Type Text (WD 6)
3. Display Formatting Marks (WD 7)
4. Insert a Blank Line (WD 7)
5. Wordwrap Text as You Type (WD 8)
6. Check Spelling and Grammar as You Type (WD 9)
7. Save a Document (WD 12)
8. Center a Paragraph (WD 14)
9. Select a Line (WD 15)
10. Change the Font Size of Selected Text (WD 16)
11. Change the Font of Selected Text (WD 17)
12. Change the Case of Selected Text (WD 18)
13. Apply a Text Effect to Selected Text (WD 19)
14. Shade a Paragraph (WD 20)
15. Select Multiple Lines (WD 21)
16. Bullet a List of Paragraphs (WD 22)
17. Undo and Redo an Action (WD 23)
18. Italicize Text (WD 24)
19. Color Text (WD 25)
20. Use the Mini Toolbar to Format Text (WD 26)
21. Select a Group of Words (WD 27)
22. Underline Text (WD 27)
23. Bold Text (WD 28)
24. Change Theme Colors (WD 28)
25. Save an Existing Document with the Same File Name (WD 30)
26. Insert a Picture (WD 31)
27. Zoom the Document (WD 33)
28. Resize a Graphic (WD 34)
29. Resize a Graphic by Entering Exact Measurements (WD 36)
30. Apply a Picture Style (WD 37)
31. Apply Picture Effects (WD 38)
32. View One Page (WD 40)
33. Add a Page Border (WD 41)
34. Change Spacing before and after a Paragraph (WD 44)
35. Quit Word (WD 44)
36. Open a Document from Word (WD 45)
37. Insert Text in an Existing Document (WD 46)
38. Delete Text (WD 47)
39. Move Text (WD 47)
40. Change Document Properties (WD 49)
41. Print a Document (WD 51)

If you have a SAM 2010 user profile, your instructor may have assigned an autogradable version of this assignment. If so, log into the SAM 2010 Web site at www.cengage.com/sam2010 to download the instruction and start files.

BTW

Quick Reference
For a table that lists how to complete the tasks covered in this book using the mouse, Ribbon, shortcut menu, and keyboard, see the Quick Reference Summary at the back of this book, or visit the Word 2010 Quick Reference Web page (scsite.com/wd2010/qr).

Learn It Online

Test your knowledge of chapter content and key terms.

Instructions: To complete the Learn It Online exercises, start your browser, click the Address bar, and then enter the Web address **scsite.com/wd2010/learn**. When the Word 2010 Learn It Online page is displayed, click the link for the exercise you want to complete and then read the instructions.

Chapter Reinforcement TF, MC, and SA

A series of true/false, multiple choice, and short answer questions that test your knowledge of the chapter content.

Flash Cards

An interactive learning environment where you identify chapter key terms associated with displayed definitions.

Practice Test

A series of multiple choice questions that test your knowledge of chapter content and key terms.

Who Wants To Be a Computer Genius?

An interactive game that challenges your knowledge of chapter content in the style of a television quiz show.

Wheel of Terms

An interactive game that challenges your knowledge of chapter key terms in the style of the television show *Wheel of Fortune.*

Crossword Puzzle Challenge

A crossword puzzle that challenges your knowledge of key terms presented in the chapter.

Apply Your Knowledge

Reinforce the skills and apply the concepts you learned in this chapter.

Modifying Text and Formatting a Document

Note: To complete this assignment, you will be required to use the Data Files for Students. See the inside back cover of this book for instructions on downloading the Data Files for Students, or contact your instructor for information about accessing the required files.

Instructions: Start Word. Open the document, Apply 1-1 Buffalo Photo Shoot Flyer Unformatted, from the Data Files for Students. The document you open is an unformatted flyer. You are to modify text, format paragraphs and characters, and insert a picture in the flyer.

Perform the following tasks:

1. Delete the word, single, in the sentence of body copy below the headline.
2. Insert the word, Creeks, between the words, Twin Buffalo, in the sentence of body copy below the headline.
3. At the end of the signature line, change the period to an exclamation point.
4. Center the headline and the signature line.
5. Change the theme colors to the Aspect color scheme.
6. Change the font and font size of the headline to 48-point Impact, or a similar font. Change the case of the headline text to all capital letters. Apply the text effect called Gradient Fill – Orange, Accent 1, Outline – White to the headline.
7. Change the font size of body copy between the headline and the signature line to 20 point.
8. Use the Mini toolbar to change the font size of the signature line to 26 point.
9. Select the words, hundreds of buffalo, in the paragraph below the headline and underline them.

10. Italicize the word, every, in the paragraph below the headline. Undo this change and then redo the change.
11. Select the three lines (paragraphs) of text above the signature line and add bullets to the selected paragraphs.
12. Switch the last two bulleted paragraphs. That is, select the Questions bullet and move it so that it is the last bulleted paragraph.
13. Bold the first word of each bulleted paragraph. Change the font color of these same three words to Dark Green, Accent 4, Darker 50%.
14. Bold the text in the signature line. Shade the signature line Dark Green, Accent 4, Darker 50%. If the font color does not automatically change to a lighter color, change it to a shade of white.
15. Change the zoom so that the entire page is visible in the document window.
16. Insert the picture of the buffalo centered on the blank line below the headline. The picture is called Buffalo and is available on the Data Files for Students. Apply the Snip Diagonal Corner, White picture style to the inserted picture. Apply the glow called Dark Green, 5 pt glow, Accent color 4 to the picture.
17. Change the spacing after the headline paragraph to 6 point.
18. The entire flyer now should fit on a single page. If it flows to two pages, resize the picture or decrease spacing before and after paragraphs until the entire flyer text fits on a single page.
19. Change the zoom to text width, then page width, then 100% and notice the differences.
20. Enter the text, Twin Creeks, as the keywords in the document properties. Change the other document properties, as specified by your instructor.
21. Click File on the Ribbon and then click Save As. Save the document using the file name, Apply 1-1 Buffalo Photo Shoot Flyer Formatted.
22. Print the document. Submit the revised document, shown in Figure 1–75, in the format specified by your instructor.
23. Quit Word.

Figure 1–75

Extend Your Knowledge

Extend the skills you learned in this chapter and experiment with new skills. You may need to use Help to complete the assignment.

Modifying Text and Picture Formats and Adding Page Borders

Note: To complete this assignment, you will be required to use the Data Files for Students. See the inside back cover of this book for instructions on downloading the Data Files for Students, or contact your instructor for information about accessing the required files.

Instructions: Start Word. Open the document, Extend 1-1 TVC Cruises Flyer, from the Data Files for Students. You will enhance the look of the flyer shown in Figure 1–76. *Hint:* Remember, if you make a mistake while formatting the picture, you can reset it by clicking the Reset Picture button or Reset Picture button arrow (Picture Tools Format tab | Adjust group).

Perform the following tasks:

1. Use Help to learn about the following formats: remove bullets, grow font, shrink font, art page borders, decorative underline(s), picture bullets, picture border shading, shadow picture effects, and color saturation and tone.
2. Remove the bullet from the paragraph below the picture.
3. Select the text, 10 percent, and use the Grow Font button to increase its font size.
4. Add an art page border to the flyer. If possible, add color to the border.
5. Change the solid underline below the word, cruises, to a decorative underline. Change the color of the underline.
6. Change the style of the bullets to picture bullet(s).
7. Change the color of the picture border. Add a shadow picture effect to the picture.
8. Change the color saturation and color tone of the picture.
9. Change the document properties, including keywords, as specified by your instructor. Save the revised document with a new file name and then submit it in the format specified by your instructor.

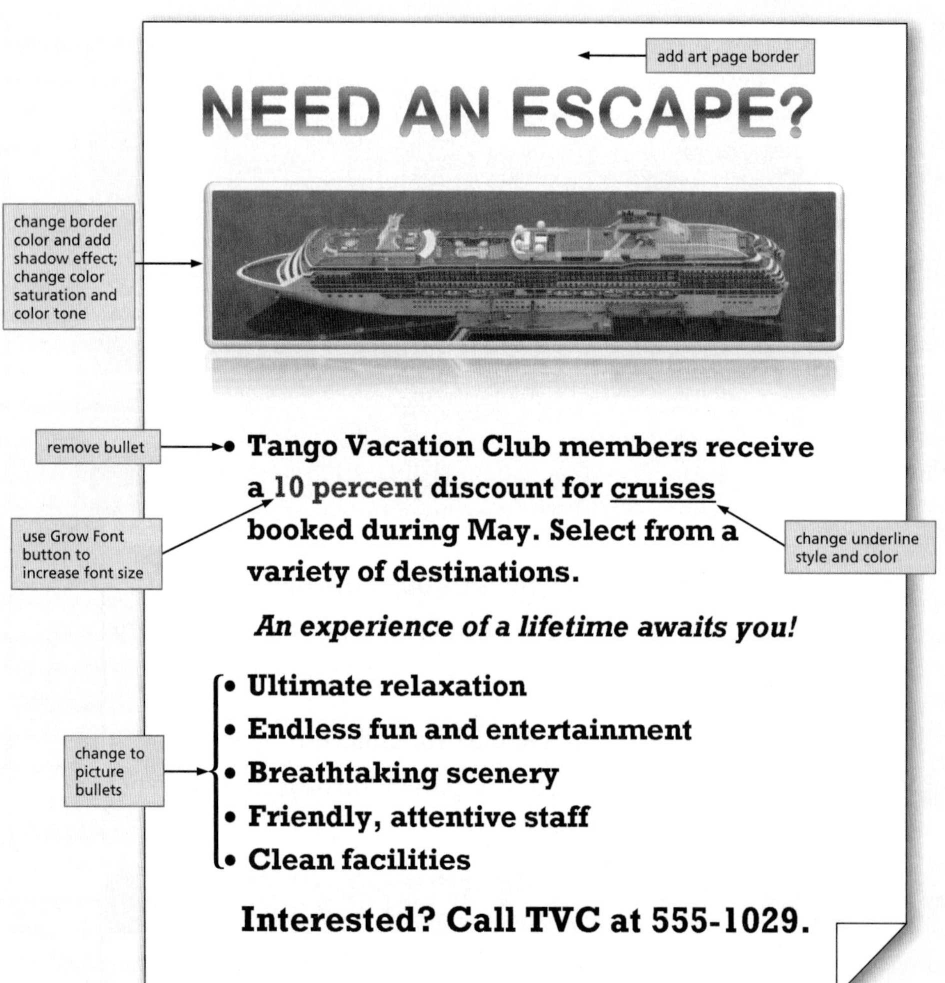

Figure 1–76

Make It Right

Analyze a document and correct all errors and/or improve the design.

Correcting Spelling and Grammar Errors

Note: To complete this assignment, you will be required to use the Data Files for Students. See the inside back cover of this book for instructions on downloading the Data Files for Students, or contact your instructor for information about accessing the required files.

Instructions: Start Word. Open the document, Make It Right 1-1 Karate Academy Flyer Unchecked, from the Data Files for Students. The document is a flyer that contains spelling and grammar errors, as shown in Figure 1–77. You are to correct each spelling (red wavy underline) and grammar error (green and blue wavy underlines) by right-clicking the flagged text and then clicking the appropriate correction on the shortcut menu.

If your screen does not display the wavy underlines, click File on the Ribbon and then click Options in the Backstage view. When the Word Options dialog box is displayed, click Proofing in the left pane, be sure the 'Hide spelling errors in this document only' and 'Hide grammar errors in this document only' check boxes do not contain check marks, and then click the OK button. If your screen still does not display the wavy underlines, redisplay the Word Options dialog box, click Proofing, and then click the Recheck Document button.

Change the document properties, including keywords, as specified by your instructor. Save the revised document with the name, Make It Right 1-1 Karate Academy Flyer, and then submit it in the format specified by your instructor.

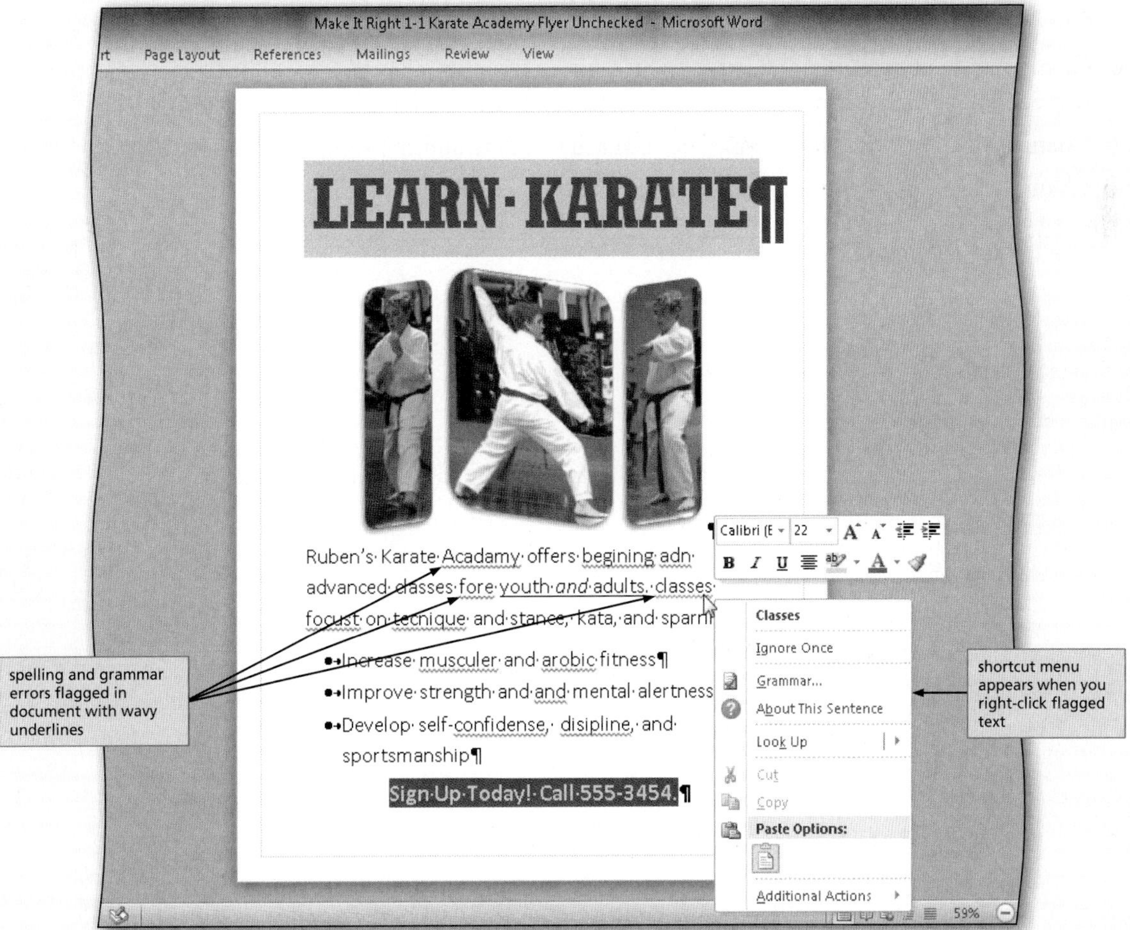

Figure 1–77

In the Lab

Design and/or create a document using the guidelines, concepts, and skills presented in this chapter. Labs are listed in order of increasing difficulty.

Lab 1: Creating a Flyer with a Picture

Problem: As a part-time employee in the Student Services Center at school, you have been asked to prepare a flyer that advertises study habits classes. First, you prepare the unformatted flyer shown in Figure 1–78a, and then you format it so that it looks like Figure 1–78b. *Hint:* Remember, if you make a mistake while formatting the flyer, you can click the Undo button on the Quick Access Toolbar to undo your last action.

Note: To complete this assignment, you will be required to use the Data Files for Students. See the inside back cover of this book for instructions on downloading the Data Files for Students, or contact your instructor for information about accessing the required files.

Instructions: Perform the following tasks:

1. Start Word. Display formatting marks on the screen.
2. Type the flyer text, unformatted, as shown in Figure 1–78a, inserting a blank line between the headline and the body copy. If Word flags any misspelled words as you type, check their spelling and correct them.
3. Save the document using the file name, Lab 1-1 Study Habits Flyer.
4. Center the headline and the signature line.
5. Change the theme colors to Concourse.
6. Change the font size of the headline to 36 point and the font to Ravie, or a similar font. Apply the text effect called Gradient Fill – Dark Red, Accent 6, Inner Shadow.
7. Change the font size of body copy between the headline and the signature line to 20 point.
8. Change the font size of the signature line to 22 point. Bold the text in the signature line.

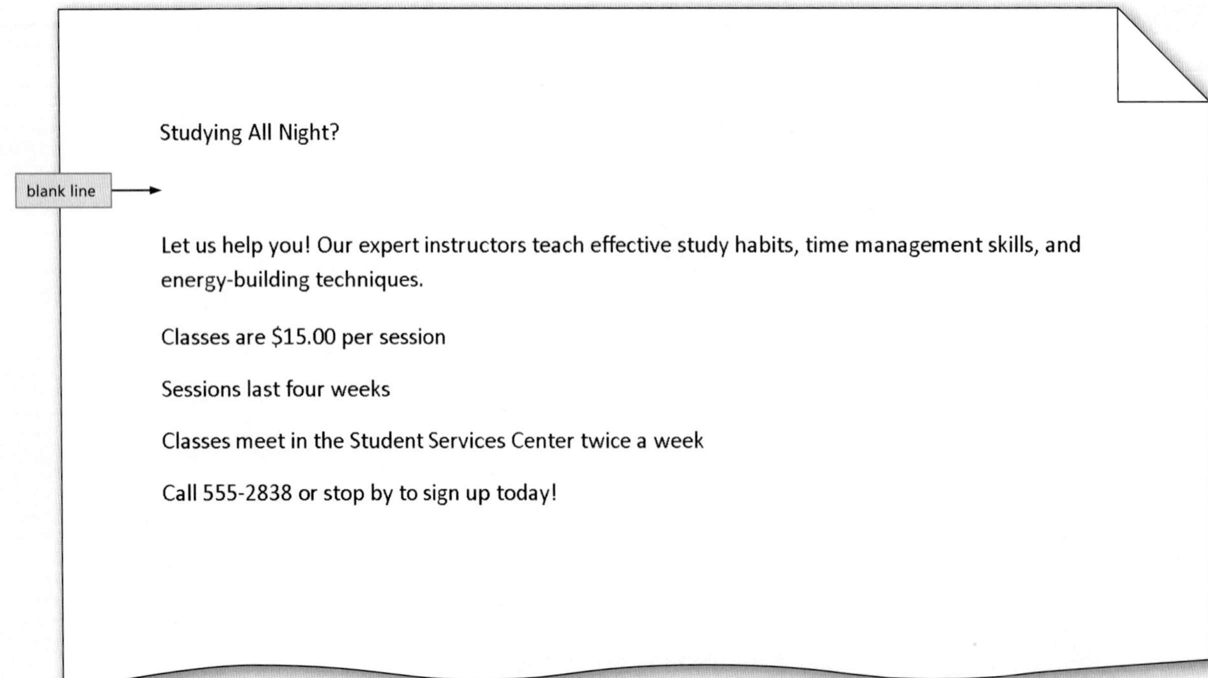

Figure 1–78 (a) Unformatted Flyer

9. Change the font of the body copy and signature line to Rockwell, and change the color of the signature line to Dark Red, Accent 6.
10. Bullet the three lines (paragraphs) of text above the signature line.
11. Bold and capitalize the text, Let us help you!, and change its color to Dark Red, Accent 6.
12. Italicize the word, or, in the signature line.
13. Underline the text, Student Services Center, in the third bulleted paragraph.
14. Change the zoom so that the entire page is visible in the document window.

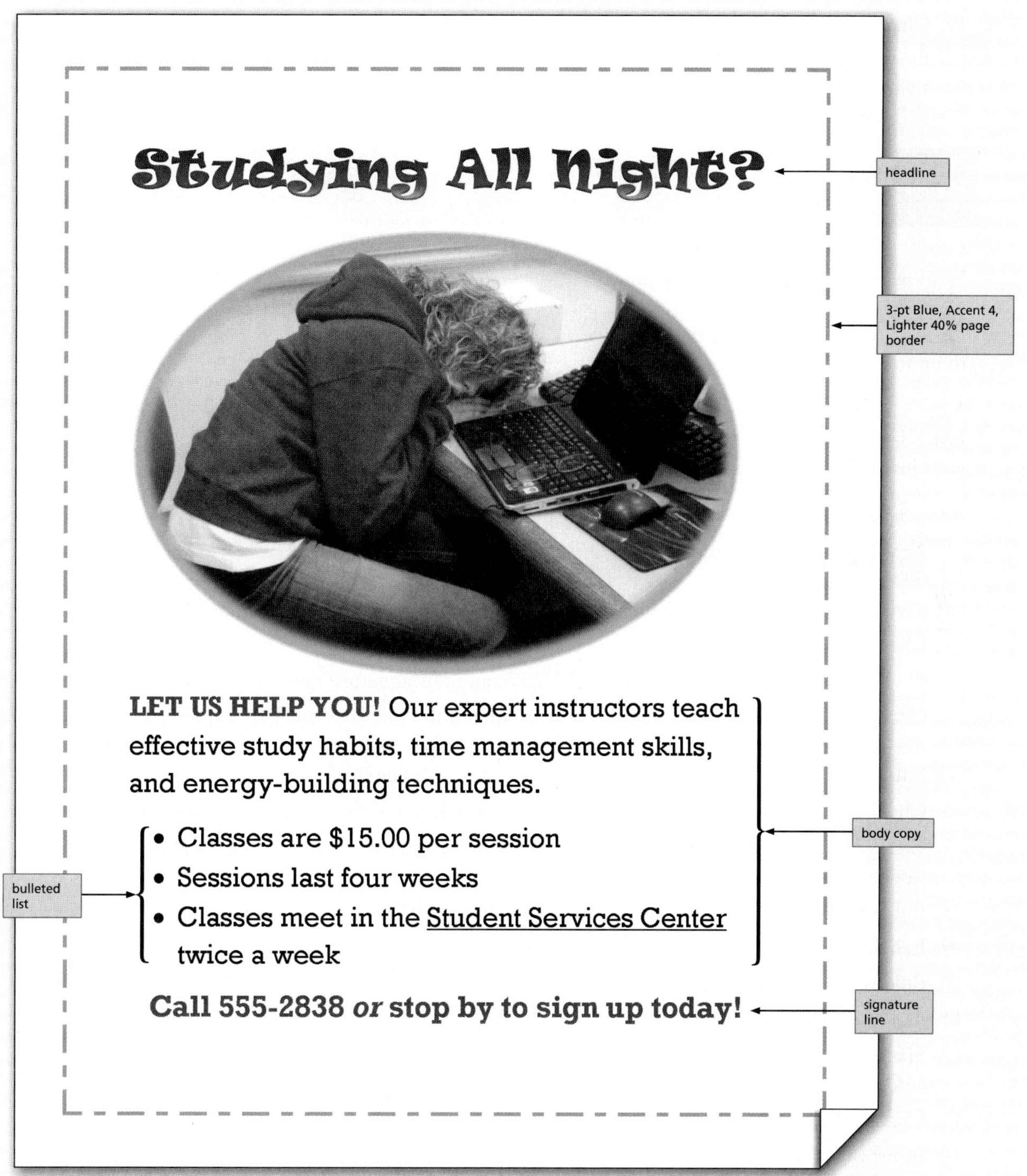

Figure 1–78 (b) Formatted Flyer

Continued >

In the Lab *continued*

15. Insert the picture centered on a blank line below the headline. The picture is called Sleeping and is available on the Data Files for Students.
16. Apply the Soft Edge Oval picture style to the inserted picture. Apply the glow effect called Blue, 5 pt glow, Accent color 4 to the picture.
17. The entire flyer should fit on a single page. If it flows to two pages, resize the picture or decrease spacing before and after paragraphs until the entire flyer text fits on a single page.
18. Add the page border shown in Figure 1–78b on the previous page.
19. Change the document properties, including keywords, as specified by your instructor. Save the flyer again with the same file name. Submit the document, shown in Figure 1–78b, in the format specified by your instructor.

In the Lab

Lab 2: Creating a Flyer with a Resized Picture

Problem: Your boss at Granger Camera House has asked you to prepare a flyer that announces the upcoming photography contest. You prepare the flyer shown in Figure 1–79. *Hint:* Remember, if you make a mistake while formatting the flyer, you can click the Undo button on the Quick Access Toolbar to undo your last action.

Note: To complete this assignment, you will be required to use the Data Files for Students. See the inside back cover of this book for instructions on downloading the Data Files for Students, or contact your instructor for information about accessing the required files.

Instructions: Perform the following tasks:

1. Start Word. Type the flyer text, unformatted. If Word flags any misspelled words as you type, check their spelling and correct them.
2. Save the document using the file name, Lab 1-2 Photography Contest Flyer.
3. Change the theme colors to the Apex color scheme.
4. Center the headline, the line that says RULES, and the signature line.
5. Change the font size of the headline to 36 point and the font to Stencil, or a similar font. Shade the headline paragraph Lavender, Background 2, Darker 50%. Apply the text effect called Fill – Lavender, Accent 6, Outline – Accent 6, Glow – Accent 6.
6. Change the font size of body copy between the headline and the signature line to 18 point.
7. Change the font size of the signature line to 24 point and the font to Stencil. Bold the text in the signature line. Change the font color of the text in the signature line to Gray-50%, Text 2.
8. Bullet the three paragraphs of text above the signature line.
9. Italicize the word, not.
10. Bold the word, landscape.
11. Underline the text, August 31.
12. Shade the line that says RULES to the Gray-50%, Text 2 color. If the font color does not automatically change to a lighter color, change it to White, Background 1.
13. Change the zoom so that the entire page is visible in the document window.
14. Insert the picture on a blank line below the headline. The picture is called Wind Power and is available on the Data Files for Students.

15. Resize the picture so that it is approximately 3.5" × 5.25". Apply the Rotated, White picture style to the inserted picture. Apply the glow effect called Lavender, 5 pt glow, Accent color 6 to the picture.
16. The entire flyer should fit on a single page. If it flows to two pages, resize the picture or decrease spacing before and after paragraphs until the entire flyer text fits on a single page.
17. Add the page border shown in Figure 1–79.
18. Change the document properties, including keywords, as specified by your instructor. Save the flyer again with the same file name. Submit the document, shown in Figure 1–79, in the format specified by your instructor.

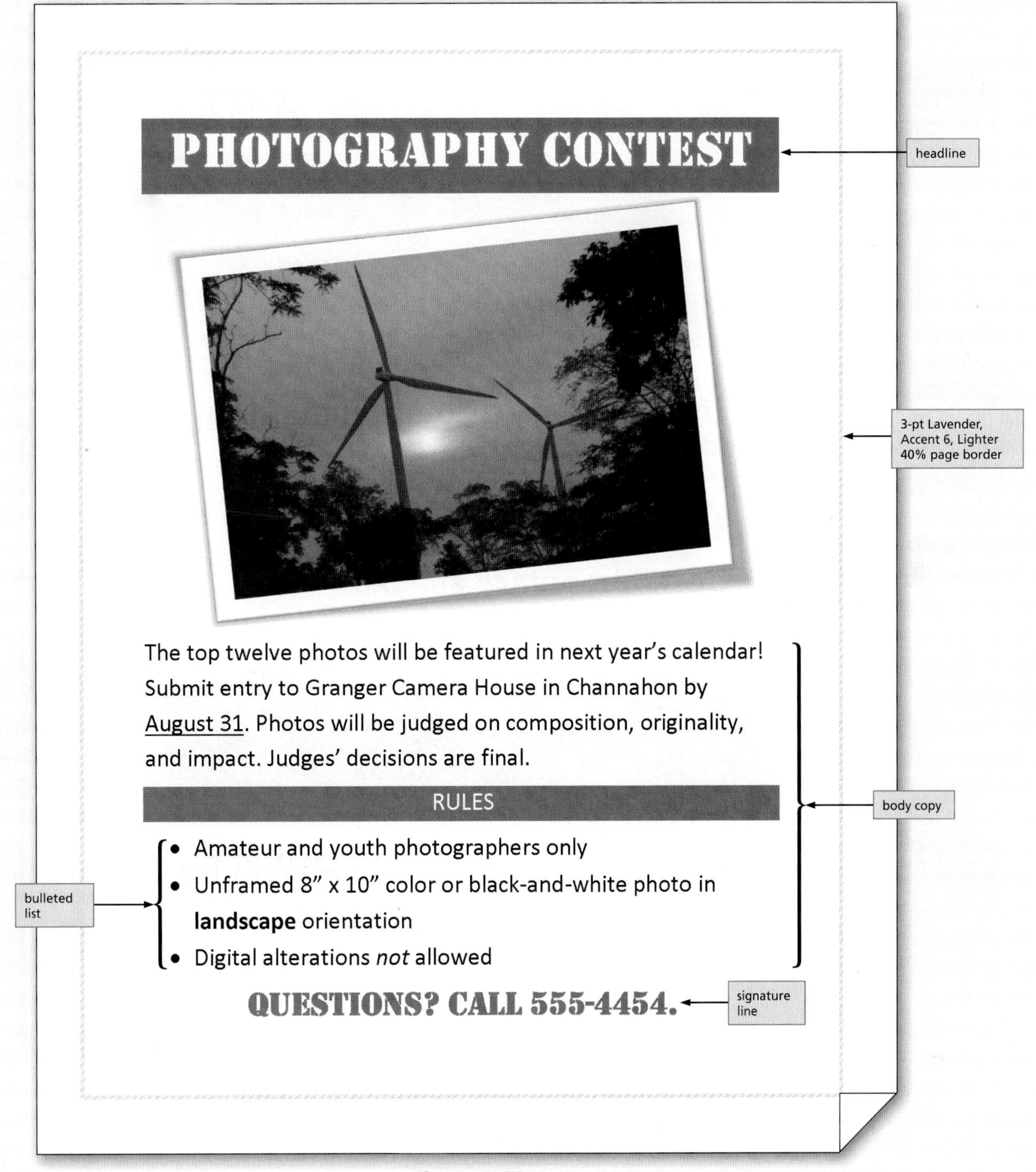

Figure 1–79

STUDENT ASSIGNMENTS

In the Lab

Lab 3: Creating a Flyer with Pictures

Problem: Your boss at Warner Depot has asked you to prepare a flyer that advertises its scenic train ride. You prepare the flyer shown in Figure 1–80.

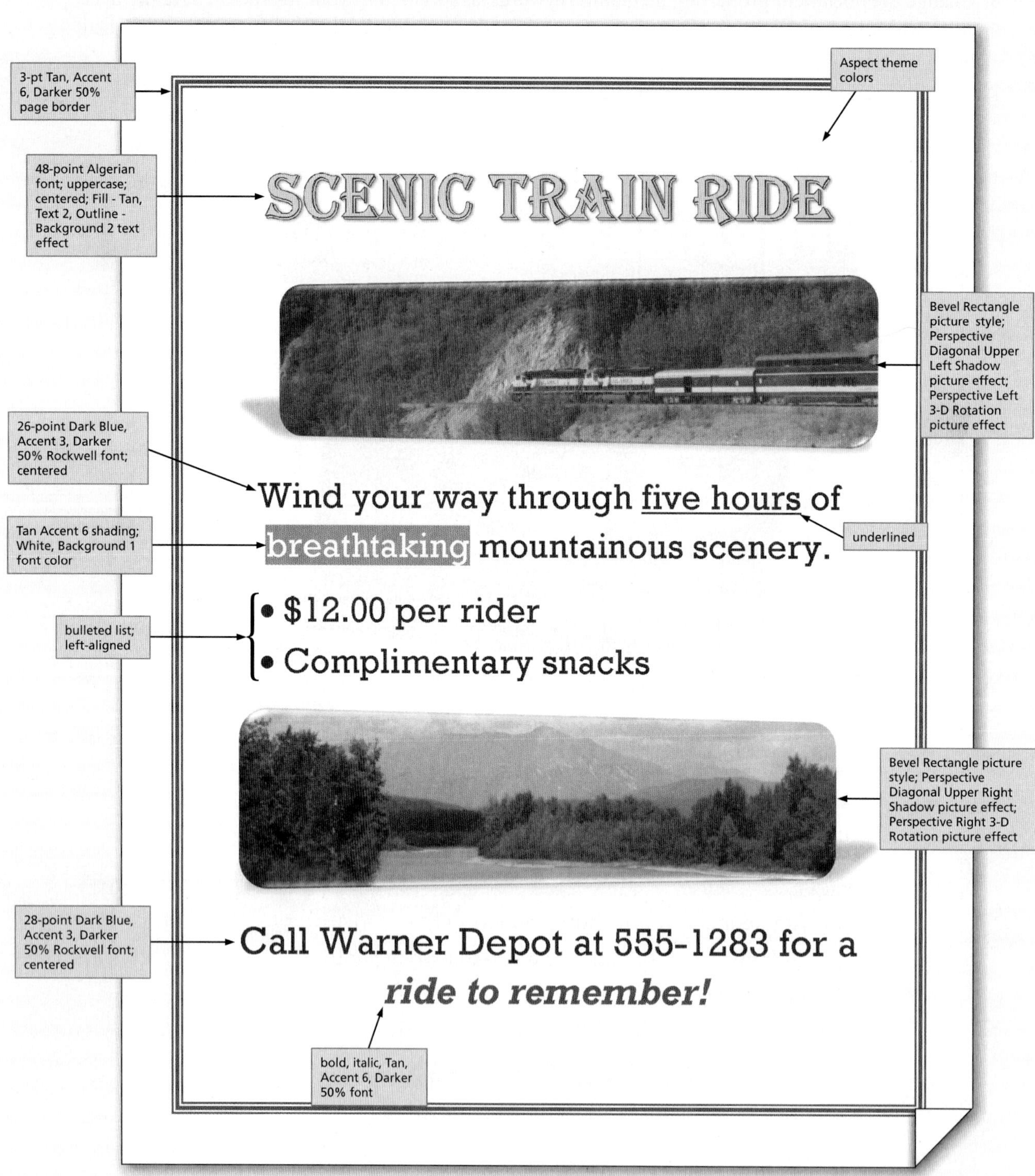

Figure 1–80

Note: To complete this assignment, you will be required to use the Data Files for Students. See the inside back cover of this book for instructions on downloading the Data Files for Students, or contact your instructor for information about accessing the required files.

Instructions: Start Word. Enter the text in the flyer, checking spelling as you type, and then format it as shown in Figure 1–80. The pictures to be inserted are called Train and Scenery and are available on the Data Files for Students. Adjust spacing before and after paragraphs and resize pictures as necessary so that the flyer fits on a single page.

Change the document properties, including keywords, as specified by your instructor. Save the document using the file name, Lab 1-3 Train Ride Flyer. Submit the document, shown in Figure 1–80, in the format specified by your instructor.

Cases and Places

Apply your creative thinking and problem solving skills to design and implement a solution.

Note: To complete these assignments, you may be required to use the Data Files for Students. See the inside back cover of this book for instructions on downloading the Data Files for Students, or contact your instructor for information about accessing the required files.

1: Design and Create a Spring Break Flyer

Academic

As secretary of your school's Student Government Association, you are responsible for creating and distributing flyers for spring break group outings. This year, you have planned a trip to Settlers Resort. The flyer should contain two digital pictures appropriately resized; the Data Files for Students contains two pictures called Cabin 1 and Cabin 2, or you can use your own digital pictures if they are appropriate for the topic of the flyer. The flyer should contain the headline, Feeling Adventurous?, and this signature line: Call Lyn at 555-9901 to sign up. The body copy consists of the following, in any order: Spring Break – Blast to the Past. Settlers Resort is like a page right out of a history textbook! Spend five days living in the 1800s. The bulleted list in the body copy is as follows: One-room cabins with potbelly stoves, Campfire dining with authentic meals, and Horseback riding and much more.

Use the concepts and techniques presented in this chapter to create and format this flyer. Be sure to check spelling and grammar. Submit your assignment in the format specified by your instructor.

2: Design and Create a Yard Sale Flyer

Personal

You are planning a yard sale and would like to create and post flyers around town advertising the upcoming sale. The flyer should contain two digital pictures appropriately resized; the Data Files for Students contains two pictures called Yard Sale 1 and Yard Sale 2, or you can use your own digital pictures if they are appropriate for the topic of the flyer. The flyer should contain the headline, Yard Sale!, and this signature line: Questions? Call 555-9820. The body copy consists of the following, in any order: Hundreds of items for sale. After 20 years, we are moving to a smaller house and are selling anything that won't fit. Everything for sale must go! The bulleted list in the body copy is as follows: When: August 7, 8, 9 from 9:00 a.m. to 7:00 p.m.; Where: 139 Ravel Boulevard; and What: something for everyone – from clothing to collectibles.

Use the concepts and techniques presented in this chapter to create and format this flyer. Be sure to check spelling and grammar. Submit your assignment in the format specified by your instructor.

Continued >

Cases and Places *continued*

3: Design and Create a Village Fireworks Flyer

Professional

As a part-time employee at the Village of Crestwood, your boss has asked you to create and distribute flyers for the upcoming fireworks extravaganza. The flyer should contain two digital pictures appropriately resized; the Data Files for Students contains two pictures called Fireworks 1 and Fireworks 2, or you can use your own digital pictures if they are appropriate for the topic of the flyer. The flyer should contain the headline, Light Up The Sky, and this signature line: Call 555-2983 with questions. The body copy consists of the following, in any order: Join Us! The Village of Crestwood will present its tenth annual Light Up The Sky fireworks extravaganza on August 8 at 9:00 p.m. during the end of summer celebration in Douglas Park. The bulleted list in the body copy is as follows: Pork chop dinners will be sold for $3.00 beginning at 6:00 p.m., Bring chairs and blankets, and Admission is free.

Use the concepts and techniques presented in this chapter to create and format this flyer. Be sure to check spelling and grammar. Submit your assignment in the format specified by your instructor.

2 Creating a Research Paper with Citations and References

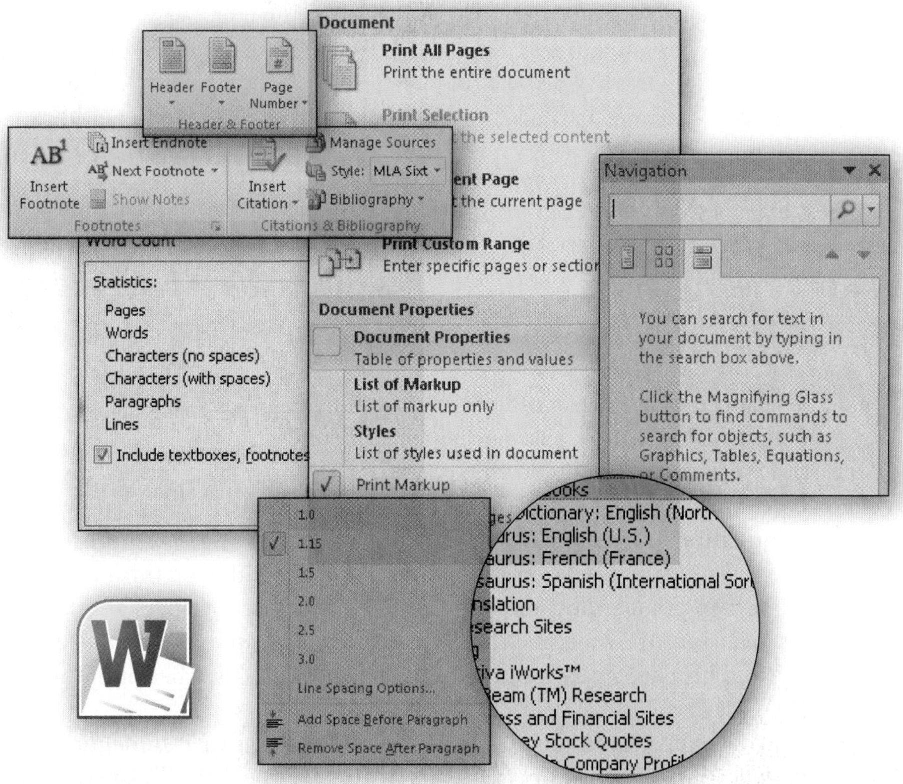

Objectives

You will have mastered the material in this chapter when you can:

- Describe the MLA documentation style for research papers
- Change line and paragraph spacing in a document
- Modify a style
- Use a header to number pages of a document
- Apply formatting using shortcut keys
- Modify paragraph indentation
- Insert and edit citations and their sources
- Add a footnote to a document
- Insert a manual page break
- Create a bibliographical list of sources
- Cut, copy, and paste text
- Find text and replace text
- Find a synonym
- Use the Research task pane to look up information

2 Creating a Research Paper with Citations and References

Introduction

In both academic and business environments, you will be asked to write reports. Business reports range from proposals to cost justifications to five-year plans to research findings. Academic reports focus mostly on research findings.

A **research paper** is a document you can use to communicate the results of research findings. To write a research paper, you learn about a particular topic from a variety of sources (research), organize your ideas from the research results, and then present relevant facts and/or opinions that support the topic. Your final research paper combines properly credited outside information along with personal insights. Thus, no two research papers — even if about the same topic — will or should be the same.

Project — Research Paper

When preparing a research paper, you should follow a standard documentation style that defines the rules for creating the paper and crediting sources. A variety of documentation styles exists, depending on the nature of the research paper. Each style requires the same basic information; the differences in styles relate to requirements for presenting the information. For example, one documentation style uses the term bibliography for the list of sources, whereas another uses references, and yet a third prefers the title works cited. Two popular documentation styles for research papers are the **Modern Language Association of America** (**MLA**) and **American Psychological Association** (**APA**) styles. This chapter uses the MLA documentation style because it is used in a wide range of disciplines.

The project in this chapter follows research paper guidelines and uses Word to create the short research paper shown in Figure 2–1. This paper, which discusses triangulation, follows the MLA documentation style. Each page contains a page number. The first two pages present the name and course information (student name, instructor name, course name, and paper due date), paper title, an introduction with a thesis statement, details that support the thesis, and a conclusion. This section of the paper also includes references to research sources and a footnote. The third page contains a detailed, alphabetical list of the sources referenced in the research paper. All pages include a header at the upper-right edge of the page.

BTW

APA Appendix
If your version of this book includes the Word APA Appendix and you are required to create a research paper using the APA documentation style instead of the MLA documentation style, the appendix shows the steps required to create the research paper in this chapter using the APA guidelines. If your version of this book does not include the Word APA Appendix, see print publications or search the Web for the APA guidelines.

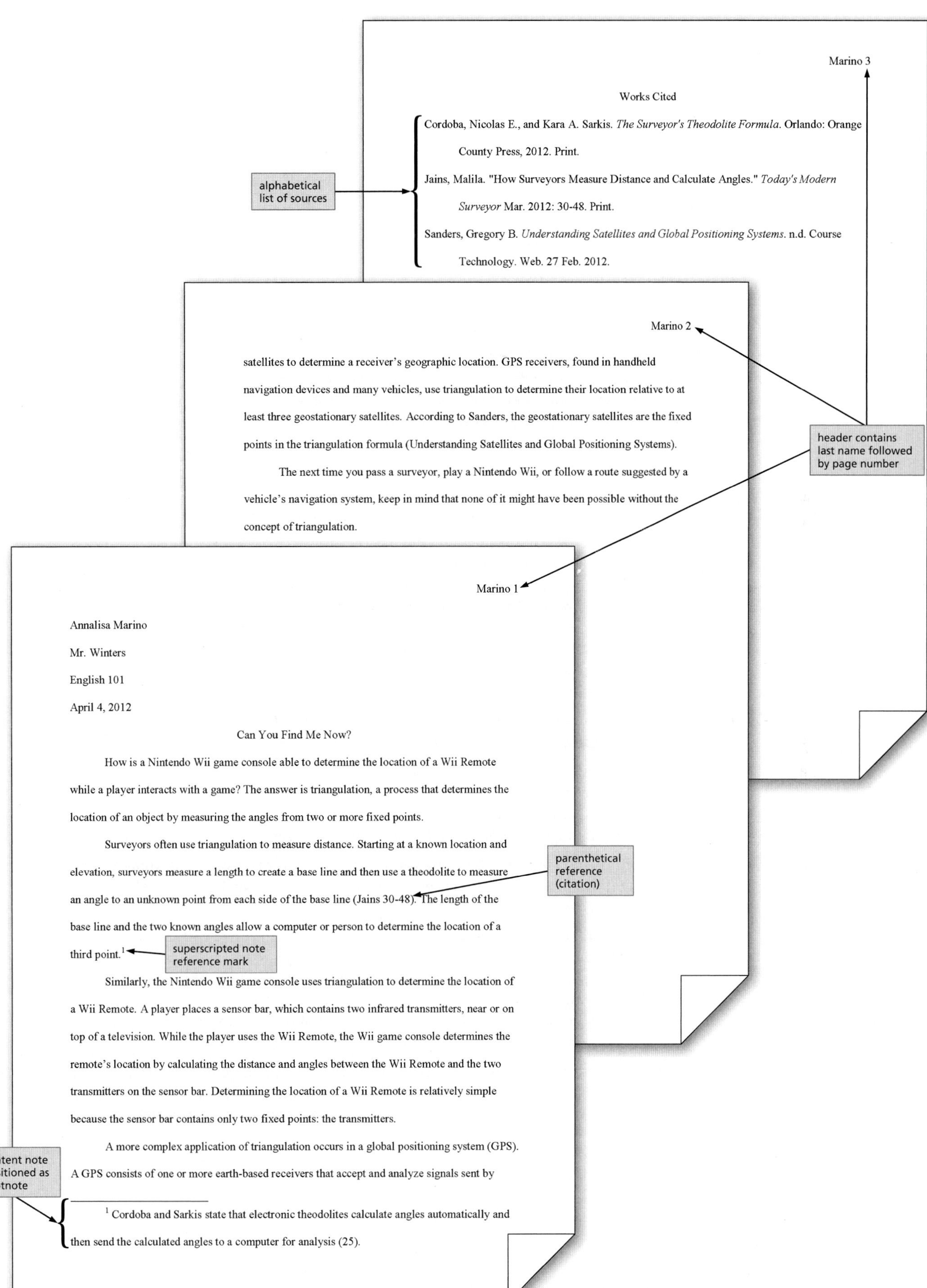

Microsoft Word 2010
Marino 3
Works Cited
Cordoba, Nicolas E., and Kara A. Sarkis. The Surveyor's Theodolite Formula. Orlando: Orange County Press, 2012. Print.
Jains, Malila. "How Surveyors Measure Distance and Calculate Angles." Today's Modern Surveyor Mar. 2012: 30-48. Print.
Sanders, Gregory B. Understanding Satellites and Global Positioning Systems. n.d. Course Technology. Web. 27 Feb. 2012.
alphabetical list of sources
Marino 2
satellites to determine a receiver's geographic location. GPS receivers, found in handheld navigation devices and many vehicles, use triangulation to determine their location relative to at least three geostationary satellites. According to Sanders, the geostationary satellites are the fixed points in the triangulation formula (Understanding Satellites and Global Positioning Systems).
The next time you pass a surveyor, play a Nintendo Wii, or follow a route suggested by a vehicle's navigation system, keep in mind that none of it might have been possible without the concept of triangulation.
header contains last name followed by page number
Marino 1
Annalisa Marino
Mr. Winters
English 101
April 4, 2012
Can You Find Me Now?
How is a Nintendo Wii game console able to determine the location of a Wii Remote while a player interacts with a game? The answer is triangulation, a process that determines the location of an object by measuring the angles from two or more fixed points.
Surveyors often use triangulation to measure distance. Starting at a known location and elevation, surveyors measure a length to create a base line and then use a theodolite to measure an angle to an unknown point from each side of the base line (Jains 30-48). The length of the base line and the two known angles allow a computer or person to determine the location of a third point.[1]
parenthetical reference (citation)
superscripted note reference mark
Similarly, the Nintendo Wii game console uses triangulation to determine the location of a Wii Remote. A player places a sensor bar, which contains two infrared transmitters, near or on top of a television. While the player uses the Wii Remote, the Wii game console determines the remote's location by calculating the distance and angles between the Wii Remote and the two transmitters on the sensor bar. Determining the location of a Wii Remote is relatively simple because the sensor bar contains only two fixed points: the transmitters.
A more complex application of triangulation occurs in a global positioning system (GPS). A GPS consists of one or more earth-based receivers that accept and analyze signals sent by
content note positioned as footnote
[1] Cordoba and Sarkis state that electronic theodolites calculate angles automatically and then send the calculated angles to a computer for analysis (25).

Figure 2–1

Overview

As you read through this chapter, you will learn how to create the research paper shown in Figure 2–1 on the previous page by performing these general tasks:

- Change the document settings.
- Type the research paper.
- Save the research paper.
- Create an alphabetical list of sources.
- Proof and revise the research paper.
- Print the research paper.

Plan Ahead

General Project Guidelines

When creating a Word document, the actions you perform and decisions you make will affect the appearance and characteristics of the finished document. As you create a research paper, such as the project shown in Figure 2–1, you should follow these general guidelines:

1. **Select a topic.** Spend time brainstorming ideas for a topic. Choose one you find interesting. For shorter papers, narrow the scope of the topic; for longer papers, broaden the scope. Identify a tentative thesis statement, which is a sentence describing the paper's subject matter.
2. **Research the topic and take notes.** Gather credible, relevant information about the topic that supports the thesis statement. Sources of research include books, magazines, newspapers, and the Internet. As you record facts and ideas, list details about the source: title, author, place of publication, publisher, date of publication, etc. When taking notes, be careful not to **plagiarize**. That is, do not use someone else's work and claim it to be your own. If you copy information directly, place it in quotation marks and identify its source.
3. **Organize your ideas.** Classify your notes into related concepts. Make an outline from the categories of notes. In the outline, identify all main ideas and supporting details.
4. **Write the first draft, referencing sources.** From the outline, compose the paper. Every research paper should include an introduction containing the thesis statement, supporting details, and a conclusion. Follow the guidelines identified in the required documentation style. Reference all sources of information.
5. **Create the list of sources.** Using the formats specified in the required documentation style, completely list all sources referenced in the body of the research paper in alphabetical order.
6. **Proofread and revise the paper.** If possible, proofread the paper with a fresh set of eyes, that is, at least one to two days after completing the first draft. Proofreading involves reading the paper with the intent of identifying errors (spelling, grammar, etc.) and looking for ways to improve the paper (wording, transitions, flow, etc.). Try reading the paper out loud, which helps to identify unclear or awkward wording. Ask someone else to proofread the paper and give you suggestions for improvements.

When necessary, more specific details concerning the above guidelines are presented at appropriate points in the chapter. The chapter also will identify the actions performed and decisions made regarding these guidelines during the creation of the research paper shown in Figure 2–1.

MLA Documentation Style

The research paper in this project follows the guidelines presented by the MLA. To follow the MLA documentation style, use 12-point Times New Roman, or a similar, font. Double-space text on all pages of the paper using one-inch top, bottom, left, and right margins. Indent the first word of each paragraph one-half inch from the left margin. At the right margin of each page, place a page number one-half inch from the top margin. On each page, precede the page number by your last name.

The MLA documentation style does not require a title page. Instead, place your name and course information in a block at the left margin beginning one inch from the top of the page. Center the title one double-spaced line below your name and course information.

In the text of the paper, place author references in parentheses with the page number(s) of the referenced information. The MLA documentation style uses in-text **parenthetical references** instead of noting each source at the bottom of the page or at the end of the paper. In the MLA documentation style, notes are used only for optional content or bibliographic notes.

If used, content notes elaborate on points discussed in the paper, and bibliographic notes direct the reader to evaluations of statements in a source or provide a means for identifying multiple sources. Use a superscript (raised number) both to signal that a note exists and to sequence the notes (shown in Figure 2-1 on page WD 67). Position notes at the bottom of the page as footnotes or at the end of the paper as endnotes. Indent the first line of each note one-half inch from the left margin. Place one space following the superscripted number before beginning the note text. Double-space the note text (shown in Figure 2–1).

The MLA documentation style uses the term **works cited** to refer to the bibliographic list of sources at the end of the paper. The works cited page alphabetically lists sources that are referenced directly in the paper. Place the list of sources on a separate numbered page. Center the title, Works Cited, one inch from the top margin. Double-space all lines. Begin the first line of each source at the left margin, indenting subsequent lines of the same source one-half inch from the left margin. List each source by the author's last name, or, if the author's name is not available, by the title of the source.

BTW

APA Documentation Style
In the APA documentation style, a separate title page is required instead of placing name and course information on the paper's first page. Double-space all pages of the paper with one-inch top, bottom, left, and right margins. Indent the first word of each paragraph one-half inch from the left margin. In the upper-right margin of each page, including the title page, place a running head that consists of the page number preceded by a brief summary of the paper title.

Changing Document Settings

The MLA documentation style defines some global formats that apply to the entire research paper. Some of these formats are the default in Word. For example, the default left, right, top, and bottom margin settings in Word are one inch, which meets the MLA documentation style. You will modify, however, the font, font size, line and paragraph spacing, and header formats as required by the MLA documentation style.

To Start Word

If you are using a computer to step through the project in this chapter and you want your screens to match the figures in this book, you should change your screen's resolution to 1024 × 768. For information about how to change a computer's resolution, refer to the Office 2010 and Windows 7 chapter at the beginning of this book.

For an introduction to Windows 7 and instruction about how to perform basic Windows 7 tasks, read the Office 2010 and Windows 7 chapter at the beginning of this book, where you can learn how to resize windows, change screen resolution, create folders, move and rename files, use Windows Help, and much more.

BTW

New Document Window
If you wanted to open a new blank document window, you could press CTRL+N or click File on the Ribbon to open the Backstage view, click the New tab to display the New gallery, click the Blank document button, and then click the Create button.

The following steps, which assume Windows 7 is running, start Word based on a typical installation. You may need to ask your instructor how to start Word for your computer. For a detailed example of the procedure summarized below, refer to the Office 2010 and Windows 7 chapter.

1. Click the Start button on the Windows 7 taskbar to display the Start menu.
2. Type `Microsoft Word` as the search text in the 'Search programs and files' text box and watch the search results appear on the Start menu.
3. Click Microsoft Word 2010 in the search results on the Start menu to start Word and display a new blank document in the Word window.
4. If the Word window is not maximized, click the Maximize button next to the Close button on its title bar to maximize the window.
5. If the Print Layout button on the status bar is not selected (shown in Figure 2–2), click it so that your screen is in Print Layout view.
6. If Normal (Home tab | Styles group) is not selected in the Quick Style gallery (shown in Figure 2–2), click it so that your document uses the Normal style.
7. If your zoom percent is not 100, click the Zoom Out or Zoom In button as many times as necessary until the Zoom button displays 100% on its face (shown in Figure 2–2).

BTW

Style Formats
To see the formats assigned to a particular style in a document, click the Styles Dialog Box Launcher (Home tab | Styles group) and then click the Style Inspector button in the Styles task pane. Position the insertion point in the style in the document and then point to the Paragraph formatting or Text level formatting areas in the Style Inspector task pane to display an Enhanced ScreenTip describing formats assigned to the location of the insertion point. You also can click the Reveal Formatting button in the Style Inspector task pane to display the Reveal Formatting task pane.

To Display Formatting Marks

As discussed in Chapter 1, it is helpful to display formatting marks that indicate where in the document you press the ENTER key, SPACEBAR, and other keys. The following steps display formatting marks.

1. If the Home tab is not the active tab, click Home on the Ribbon to display the Home tab.
2. If the Show/Hide ¶ button (Home tab | Paragraph group) is not selected already, click it to display formatting marks on the screen.

Styles

When you create a document, Word formats the text using a particular style. A **style** is a named group of formatting characteristics, including font and font size. The default style in Word is called the **Normal style**, which most likely uses 11-point Calibri font. If you do not specify a style for text you type, Word applies the Normal style to the text. In addition to the Normal style, Word has many other built-in, or predefined, styles that you can use to format text. Styles make it easy to apply many formats at once to text. You can modify existing styles and create your own styles. Styles are discussed as they are used in this book.

To Modify a Style

The MLA documentation style requires that all text in the research paper use 12-point Times New Roman, or a similar, font. If you change the font and font size using buttons on the Ribbon, you will need to make the change many times during the course of creating the paper because Word formats different areas of a document using the Normal style, which uses 11-point Calibri font. For example, body text, headers, and bibliographies all display text based on the Normal style. Thus, instead of changing the font and font size for each of these document elements, a more efficient technique would be to change the Normal style for this document to 12-point Times New Roman. By changing the Normal style, you ensure that all text in the document will use the format required by the MLA. The next steps change the Normal style.

1

- Right-click Normal in the Quick Style gallery (Home tab | Styles group) to display a shortcut menu related to styles (Figure 2–2).

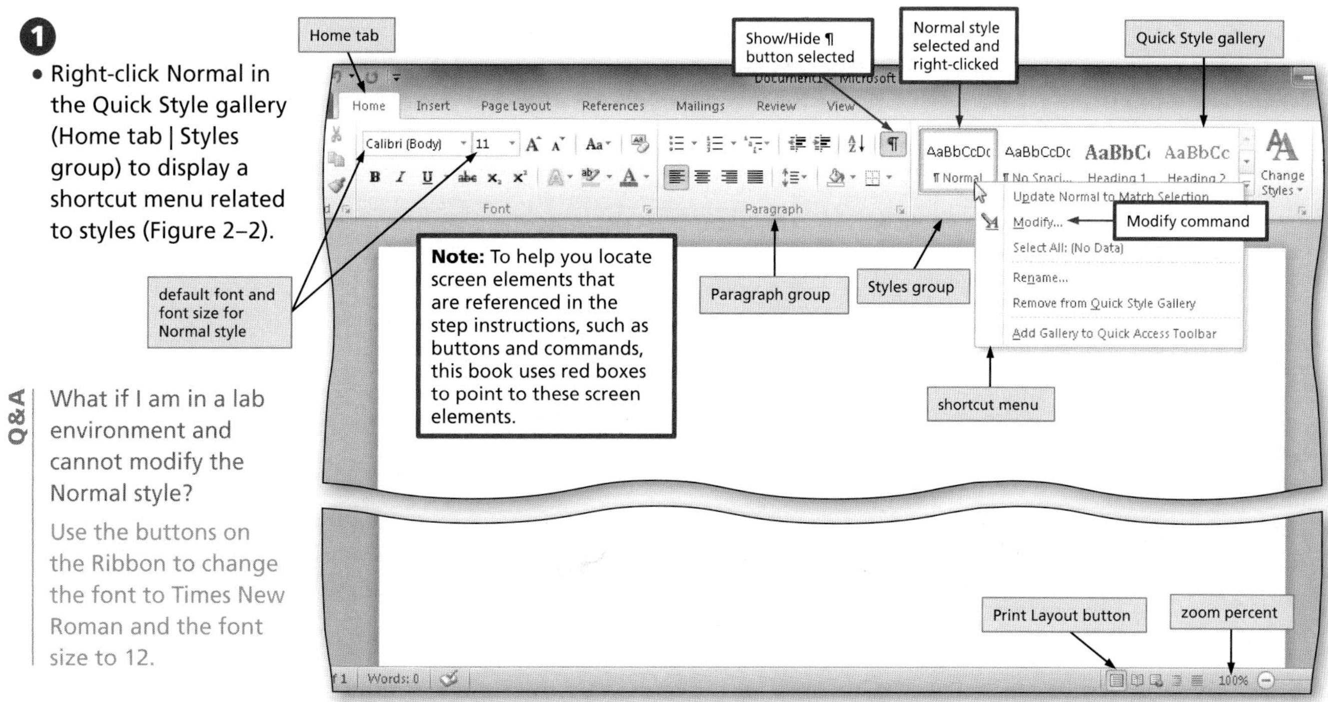

Figure 2–2

Q&A What if I am in a lab environment and cannot modify the Normal style?

Use the buttons on the Ribbon to change the font to Times New Roman and the font size to 12.

2

- Click Modify on the shortcut menu to display the Modify Style dialog box (Figure 2–3).

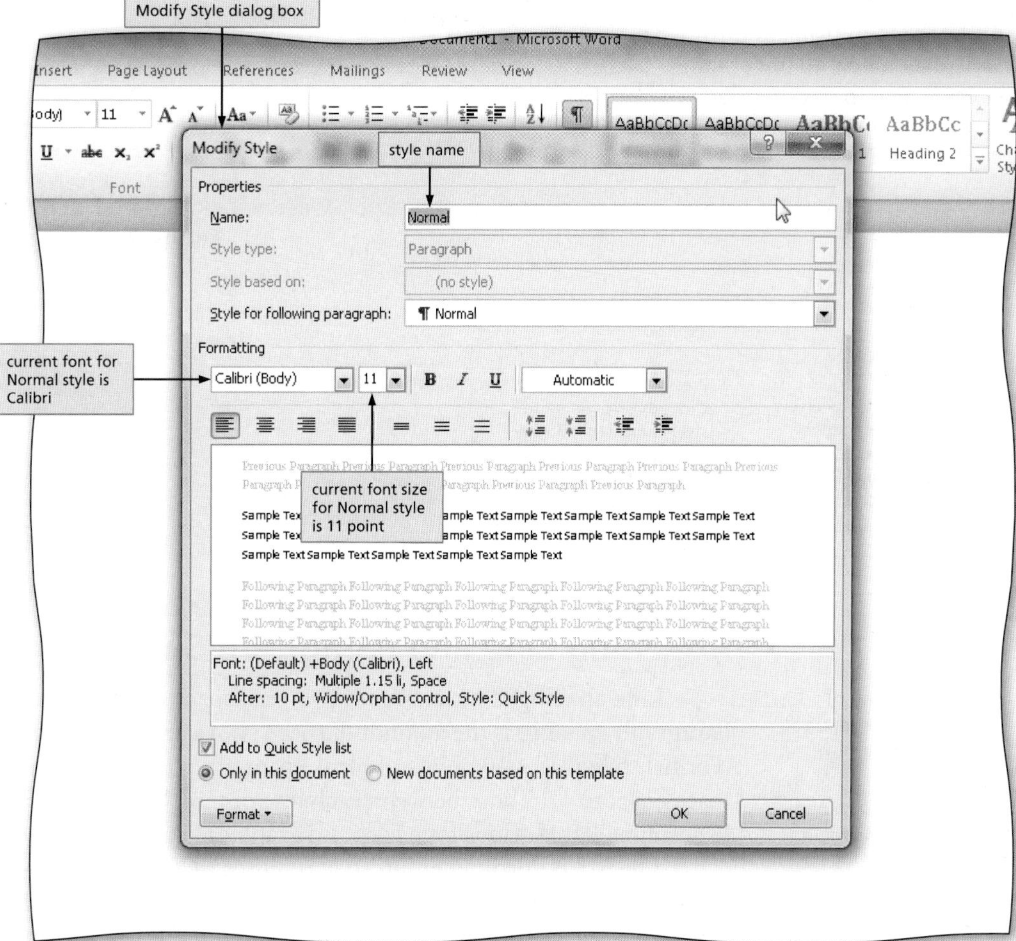

Figure 2–3

3

- Click the Font box arrow (Modify Style dialog box) to display the Font list. Scroll to and then click Times New Roman in the list to change the font for the style being modified.
- Click the Font Size box arrow (Modify Style dialog box) and then click 12 in the Font Size list to change the font size for the style being modified.
- Ensure that the 'Only in this document' option button is selected (Figure 2–4).

Q&A Will all future documents use the new font and font size?

No, because the 'Only in this document' option button is selected. If you want all future documents to use a new setting, you would select the 'New documents based on this template' option button.

- Click the OK button (Modify Style dialog box) to update the Normal style to the specified settings.

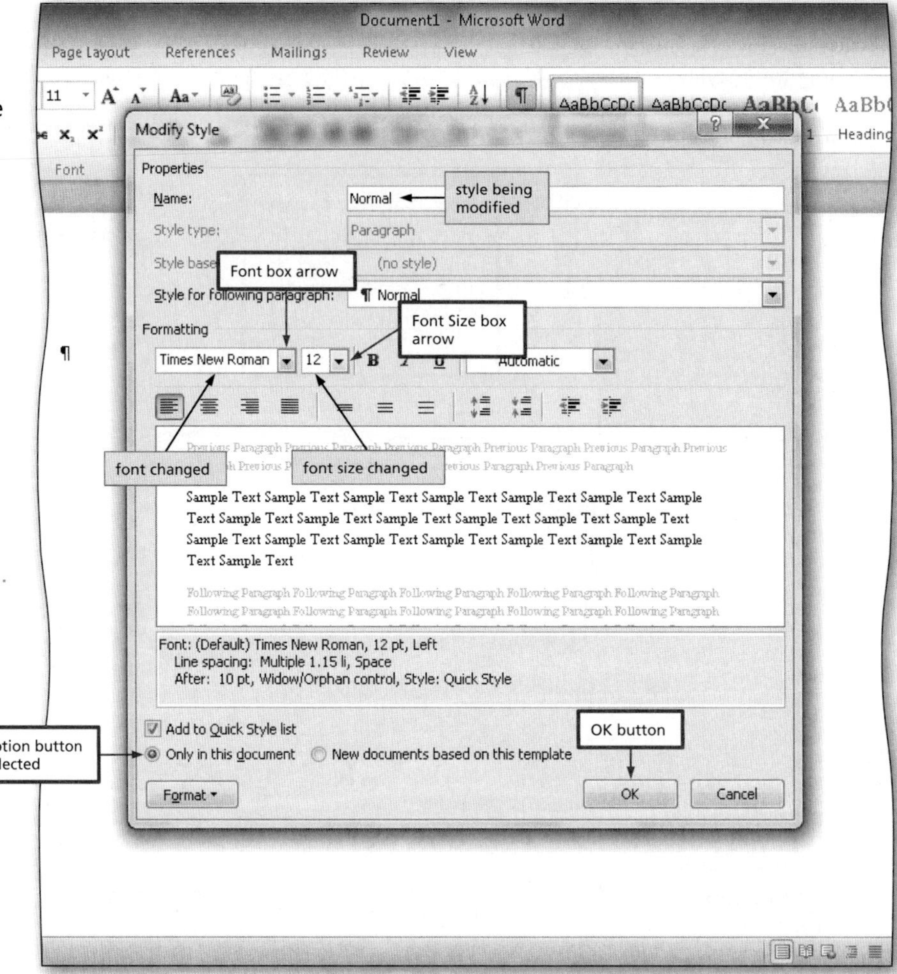

Figure 2–4

Other Ways

1. Click Styles Dialog Box Launcher, click box arrow next to style name, click Modify on menu, change settings (Modify Style dialog box), click OK button
2. Press ALT+CTRL+SHIFT+S, click box arrow next to style name, click Modify on menu, change settings (Modify Style dialog box), click OK button

BTW **Line Spacing**
If the top of a set of characters or a graphical image is chopped off, then line spacing may be set to Exactly. To remedy the problem, change line spacing to 1.0, 1.15, 1.5, 2.0, 2.5, 3.0, or At least (in the Paragraph dialog box), all of which accommodate the largest font or image.

Adjusting Line and Paragraph Spacing

Line spacing is the amount of vertical space between lines of text in a paragraph. **Paragraph spacing** is the amount of space above and below a paragraph. By default, the Normal style places 10 points of blank space after each paragraph and inserts a vertical space equal to 1.15 lines between each line of text. It also automatically adjusts line height to accommodate various font sizes and graphics.

The MLA documentation style requires that you **double-space** the entire research paper. That is, the amount of vertical space between each line of text and above and below paragraphs should be equal to one blank line. The next sets of steps adjust line spacing and paragraph spacing according to the MLA documentation style.

To Change Line Spacing

The lines of the research paper should be double-spaced, according to the MLA documentation style. In Word, you change the line spacing to 2.0 to double-space lines in a paragraph. The following steps change the line spacing to double.

1

- Click the Line and Paragraph Spacing button (Home tab | Paragraph group) to display the Line and Paragraph Spacing gallery (Figure 2–5).

Q&A What do the numbers in the Line and Paragraph Spacing gallery represent?

The default line spacing is 1.15 lines. The options 1.0, 2.0, and 3.0 set line spacing to single, double, and triple, respectively. Similarly, the 1.5 and 2.5 options set line spacing to 1.5 and 2.5 lines. All these options adjust line spacing automatically to accommodate the largest font or graphic on a line.

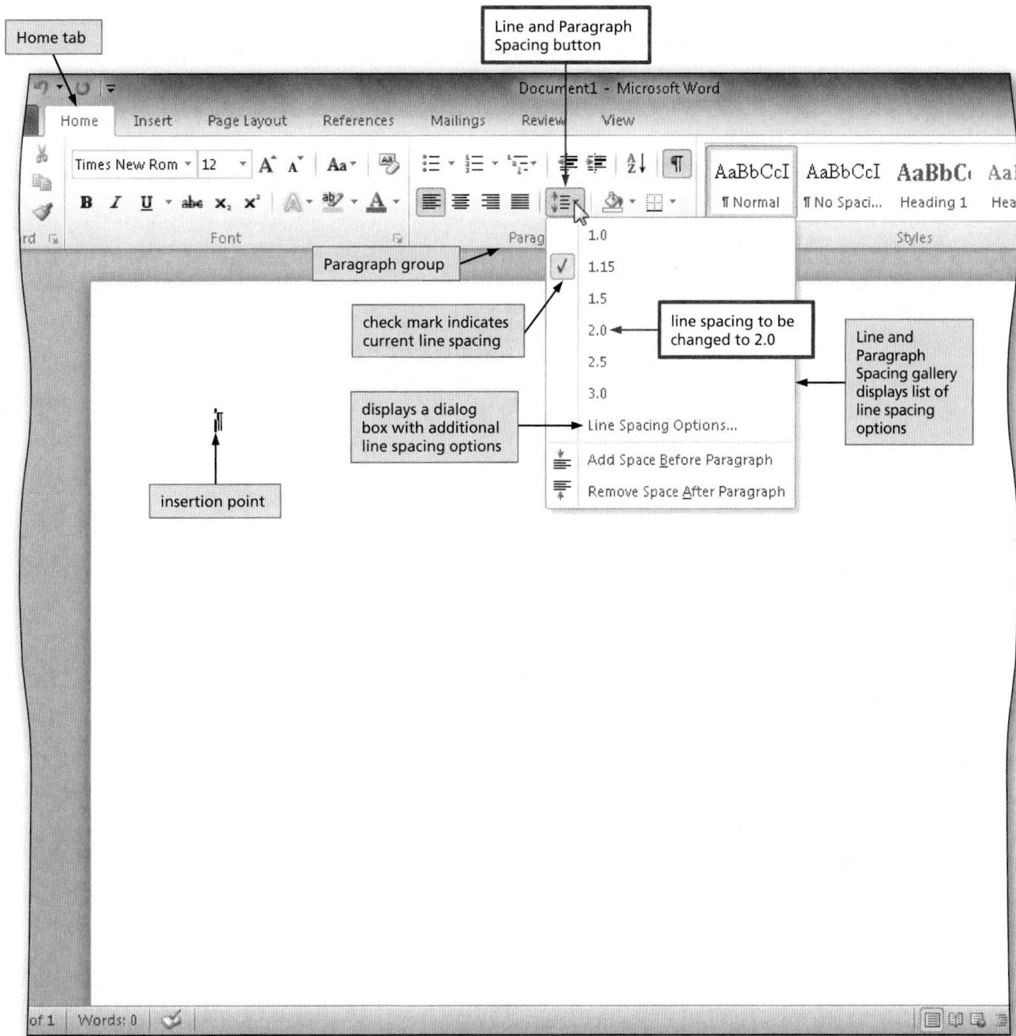

Figure 2–5

2

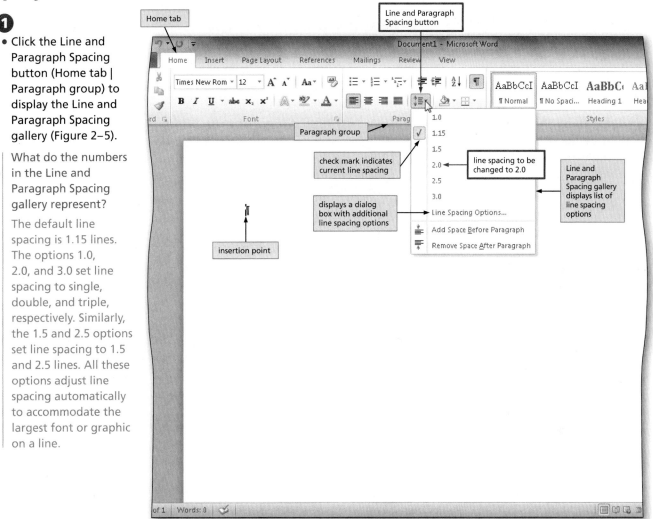

- Click 2.0 in the Line and Paragraph Spacing gallery to change the line spacing at the location of the insertion point.

Q&A Can I change the line spacing of existing text?

Yes. Select the text first and then change the line spacing as described in these steps.

Other Ways

1. Right-click paragraph, click Paragraph on shortcut menu, click Indents and Spacing tab (Paragraph dialog box), click Line spacing box arrow, click desired spacing, click OK button
2. Click Paragraph Dialog Box Launcher (Home tab or Page Layout tab | Paragraph group), click Indents and Spacing tab (Paragraph dialog box), click Line spacing box arrow, click desired spacing, click OK button
3. Press CTRL+2 for double-spacing

To Remove Space after a Paragraph

The research paper should not have additional blank space after each paragraph. The following steps remove space after a paragraph.

- Click the Line and Paragraph Spacing button (Home tab | Paragraph group) to display the Line and Paragraph Spacing gallery (Figure 2–6).

- Click Remove Space After Paragraph in the Line and Paragraph Spacing gallery so that no blank space appears after paragraphs.

Q&A Can I remove space after existing paragraphs?

Yes. Select the paragraphs first and then remove the space as described in these steps.

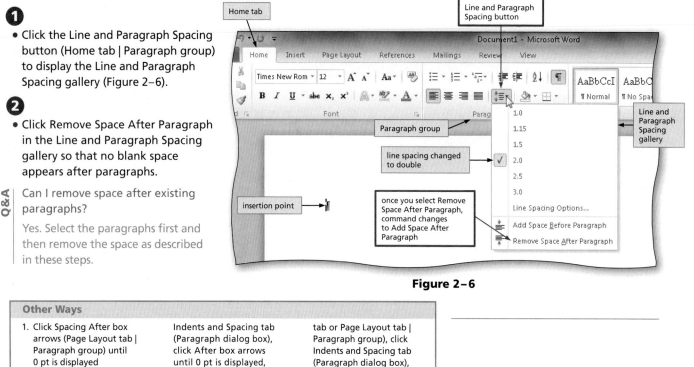

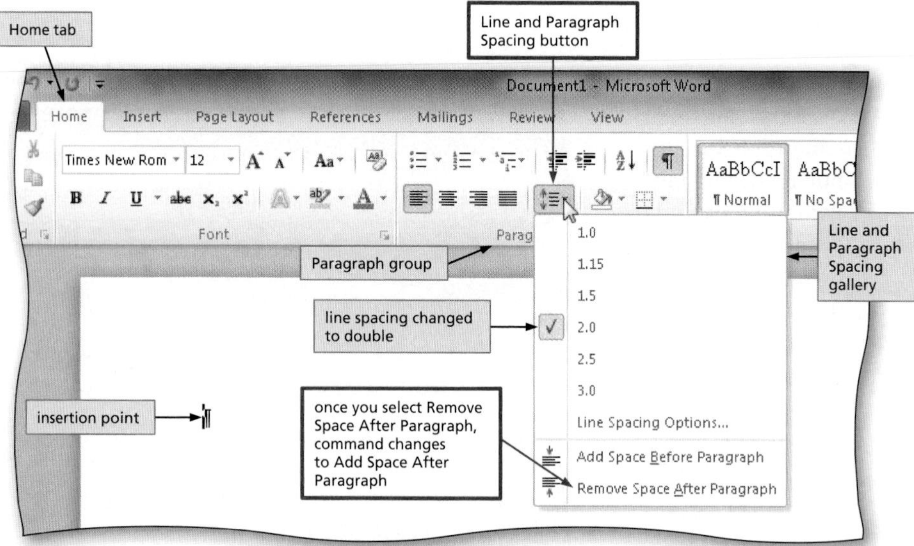

Figure 2–6

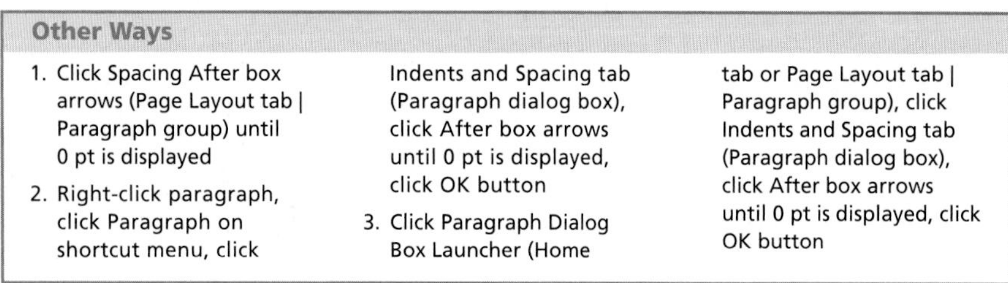

Other Ways

1. Click Spacing After box arrows (Page Layout tab | Paragraph group) until 0 pt is displayed
2. Right-click paragraph, click Paragraph on shortcut menu, click Indents and Spacing tab (Paragraph dialog box), click After box arrows until 0 pt is displayed, click OK button
3. Click Paragraph Dialog Box Launcher (Home tab or Page Layout tab | Paragraph group), click Indents and Spacing tab (Paragraph dialog box), click After box arrows until 0 pt is displayed, click OK button

To Update a Style to Match a Selection

To ensure that all paragraphs in the paper will be double-spaced and do not have space after the paragraphs, you want the Normal style to include the line and paragraph spacing changes made in the previous two sets of steps. You can update a style to reflect the settings of the location of the insertion point or selected text. Because no text has yet been typed in the research paper, you do not need to select text prior to updating the Normal style. The following steps update the Normal style.

- Right-click Normal in the Quick Style gallery (Home tab | Styles group) to display a shortcut menu (Figure 2–7).

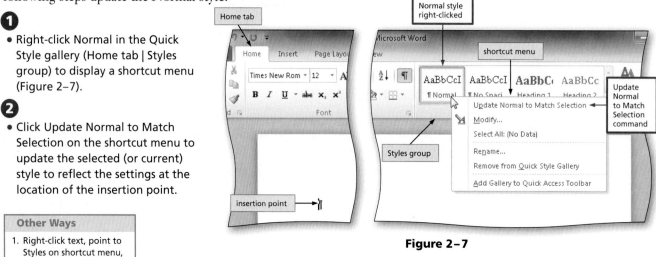

- Click Update Normal to Match Selection on the shortcut menu to update the selected (or current) style to reflect the settings at the location of the insertion point.

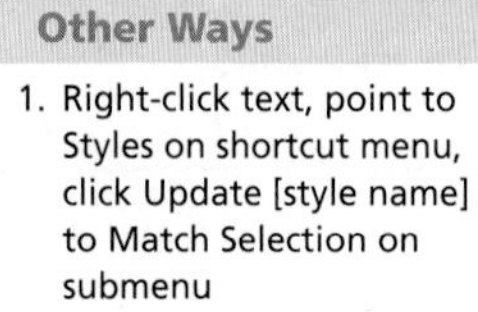

Other Ways

1. Right-click text, point to Styles on shortcut menu, click Update [style name] to Match Selection on submenu

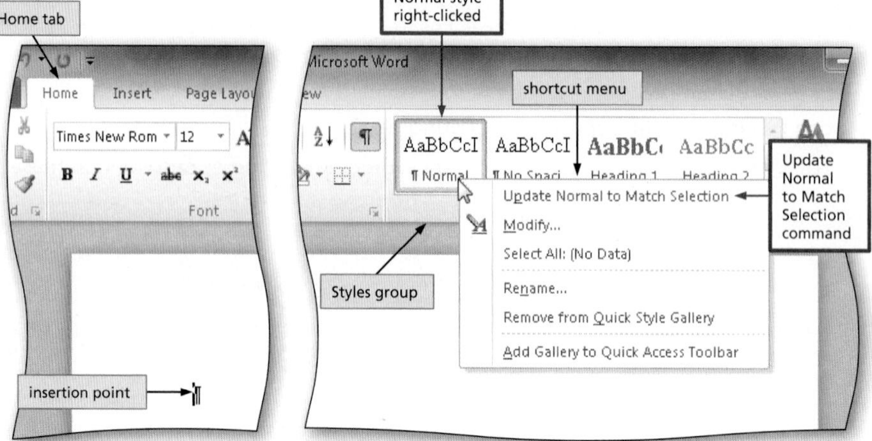

Figure 2–7

Headers and Footers

A **header** is text and graphics that print at the top of each page in a document. Similarly, a **footer** is text and graphics that print at the bottom of every page. In Word, headers print in the top margin one-half inch from the top of every page, and footers print in the bottom margin one-half inch from the bottom of each page, which meets the MLA documentation style. In addition to text and graphics, headers and footers can include document information such as the page number, current date, current time, and author's name.

In this research paper, you are to precede the page number with your last name placed one-half inch from the upper-right edge of each page. The procedures on the following pages enter your name and the page number in the header, as specified by the MLA documentation style.

BTW

The Ribbon and Screen Resolution
Word may change how the groups and buttons within the groups appear on the Ribbon, depending on the computer's screen resolution. Thus, your Ribbon may look different from the ones in this book if you are using a screen resolution other than 1024 x 768.

To Switch to the Header

To enter text in the header, you instruct Word to edit the header. The following steps switch from editing the document text to editing the header.

1

- Click Insert on the Ribbon to display the Insert tab.
- Click the Header button (Insert tab | Header & Footer group) to display the Header gallery (Figure 2–8).

Q&A

Can I use a built-in header for this research paper?

None of the built-in headers adheres to the MLA documentation style. Thus, you enter your own header content, instead of using a built-in header, for this research paper.

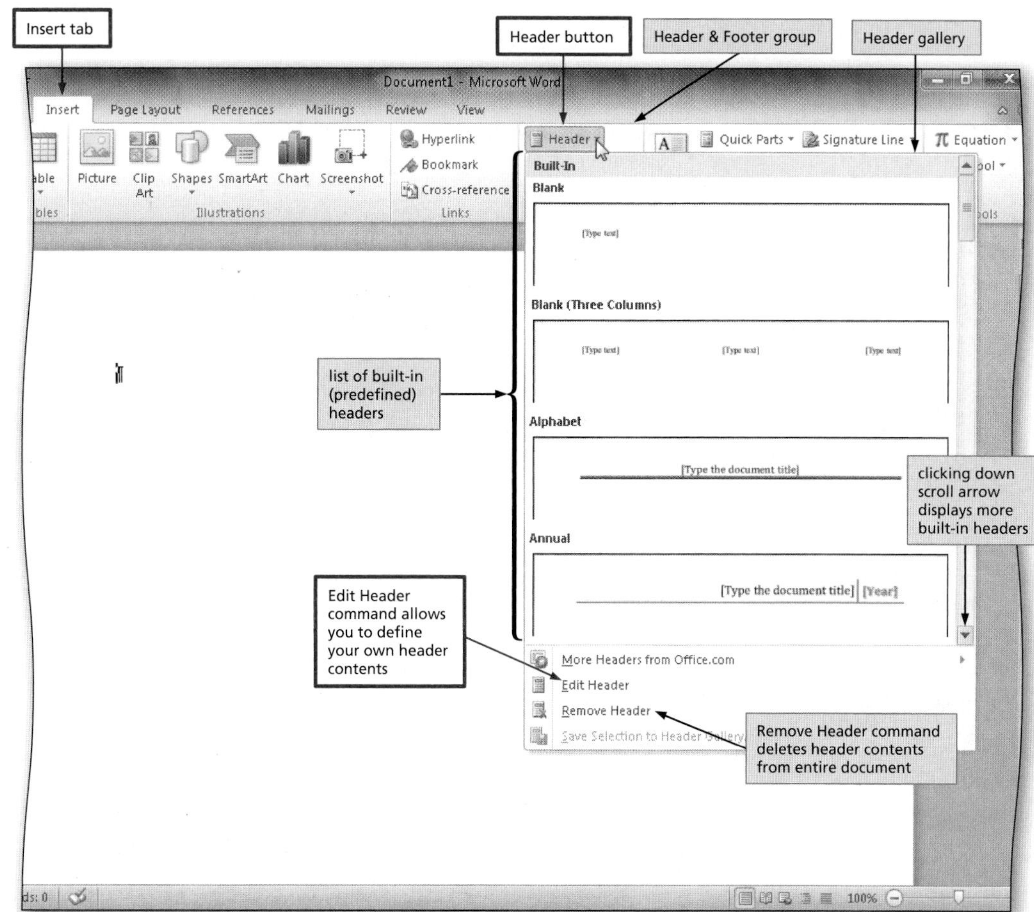

Figure 2–8

Q&A

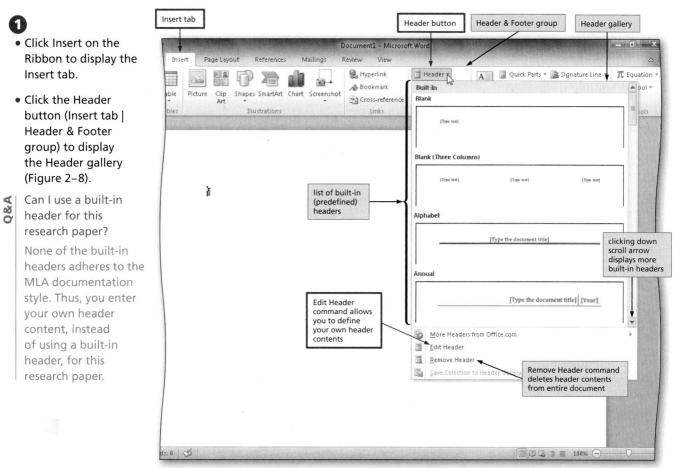

How would I remove a header from a document?

You would click Remove Header in the Header gallery (shown in Figure 2–8). Similarly, to remove a footer, you would click Remove Footer in the Footer gallery.

Experiment

- Click the down scroll arrow in the Header gallery to see the available built-in headers.

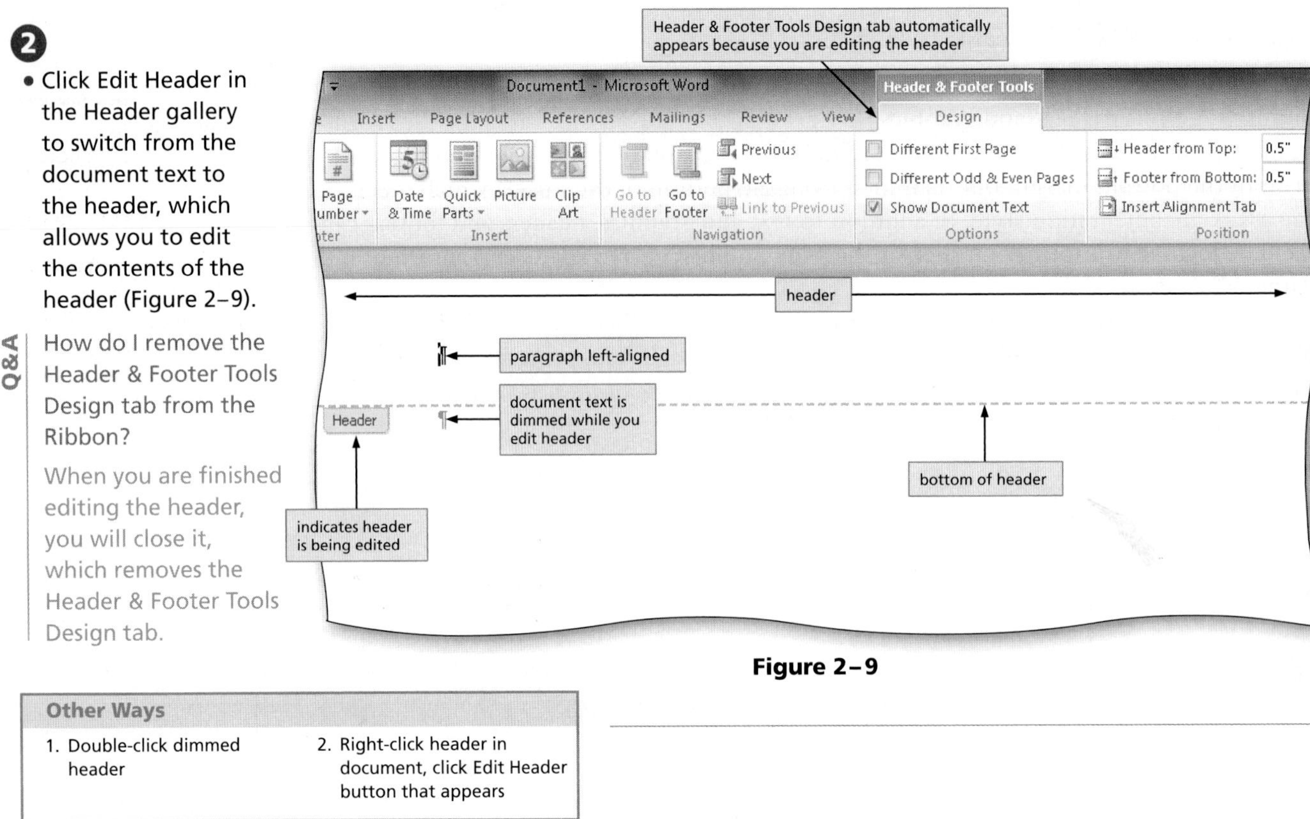

2

- Click Edit Header in the Header gallery to switch from the document text to the header, which allows you to edit the contents of the header (Figure 2–9).

Q&A How do I remove the Header & Footer Tools Design tab from the Ribbon?

When you are finished editing the header, you will close it, which removes the Header & Footer Tools Design tab.

Figure 2–9

Other Ways

1. Double-click dimmed header
2. Right-click header in document, click Edit Header button that appears

To Right-Align a Paragraph

The paragraph in the header currently is left-aligned (Figure 2–9). Your last name and the page number should print **right-aligned**, that is, at the right margin. The following step right-aligns a paragraph.

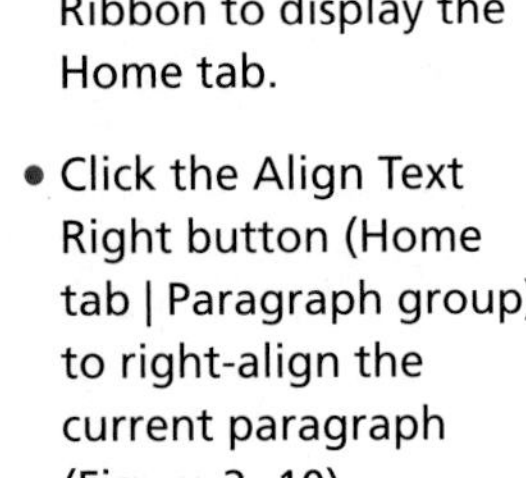

1

- Click Home on the Ribbon to display the Home tab.
- Click the Align Text Right button (Home tab | Paragraph group) to right-align the current paragraph (Figure 2–10).

Q&A What if I wanted to return the paragraph to left-aligned?

Click the Align Text Right button again, or click the Align Text Left button.

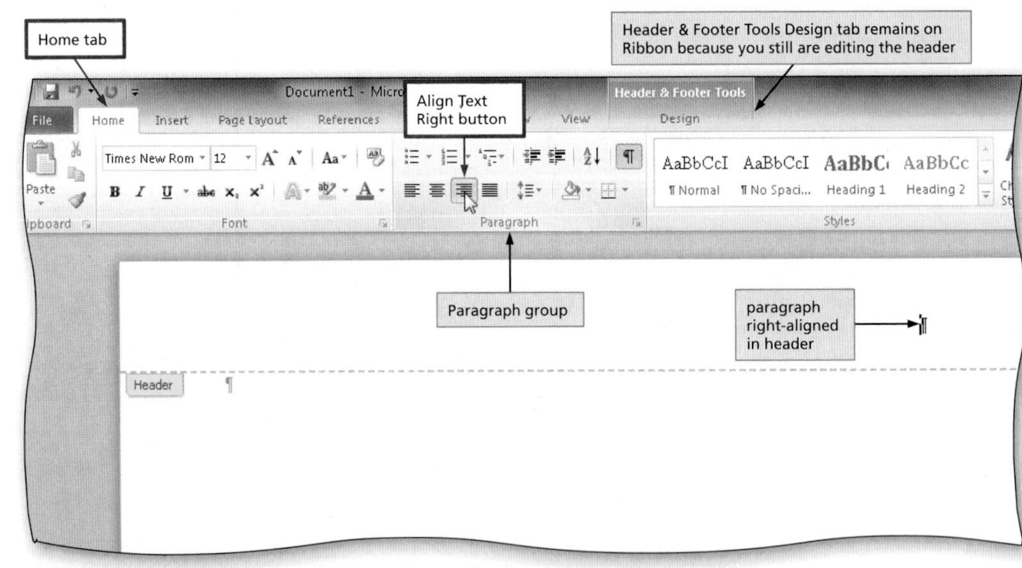

Figure 2–10

Other Ways

1. Right-click paragraph, click Paragraph on shortcut menu, click Indents and Spacing tab (Paragraph dialog box), click Alignment box arrow, click Right, click OK button
2. Click Paragraph Dialog Box Launcher (Home tab or Page Layout tab | Paragraph group), click Indents and Spacing tab (Paragraph dialog box), click Alignment box arrow, click Right, click OK button
3. Press CTRL+R

To Enter Text

The following steps enter your last name right-aligned in the header area.

1. Click Design on the Ribbon to display the Header & Footer Tools Design tab.
2. Type `Marino` and then press the SPACEBAR to enter the last name in the header.

BTW

Footers

If you wanted to create a footer, you would click the Footer button (Insert tab | Header & Footer group) and then select the desired built-in footer or click Edit Footer to create a customized footer; you also could double-click the dimmed footer, or right-click the footer and then click the Edit Footer button that appears.

To Insert a Page Number

The next task is to insert the current page number in the header. The following steps insert a page number at the location of the insertion point.

1

- Click the Insert Page Number button (Header & Footer Tools Design tab | Header & Footer group) to display the Insert Page Number menu.
- Point to Current Position on the Insert Page Number menu to display the Current Position gallery (Figure 2–11).

Experiment

- Click the down scroll arrow in the Current Position gallery to see the available page number formats.

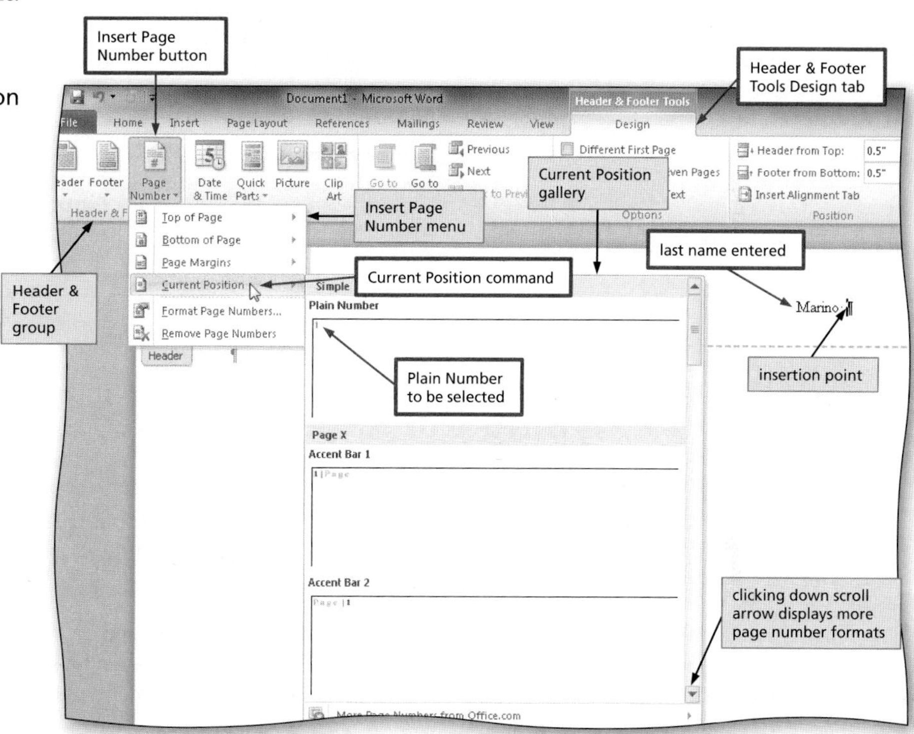

Figure 2–11

2

- If necessary, scroll to the top of the Current Position gallery. Click Plain Number in the Current Position gallery to insert an unformatted page number at the location of the insertion point (Figure 2–12).

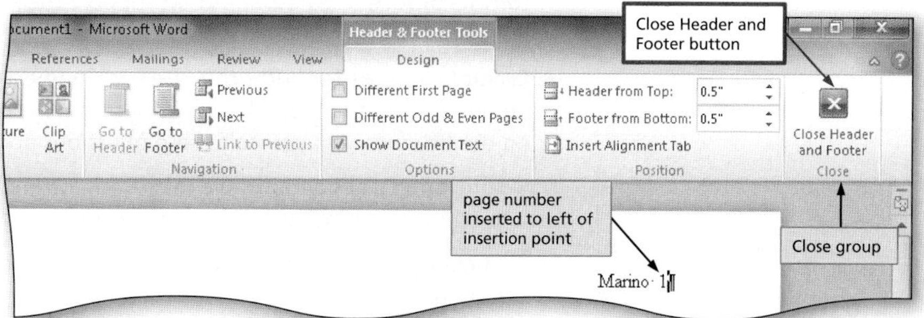

Figure 2–12

Other Ways

1. Click Insert Page Number button (Insert tab | Header & Footer group)
2. Click Quick Parts button (Insert tab | Text group or Header & Footer Tools Design tab | Insert group), click Field on Quick Parts menu, select Page in Field names list (Field dialog box), click OK button

To Close the Header

You are finished entering text in the header. Thus, the next task is to switch back to the document text. The following step closes the header.

- Click the Close Header and Footer button (Header & Footer Tools Design tab | Close group) (shown in Figure 2–12 on the previous page) to close the header and switch back to the document text (Figure 2–13).

Q&A How do I make changes to existing header text?

Switch to the header using the steps described on pages WD 75 and WD 76, edit the header as you would edit text in the document window, and then switch back to the document text.

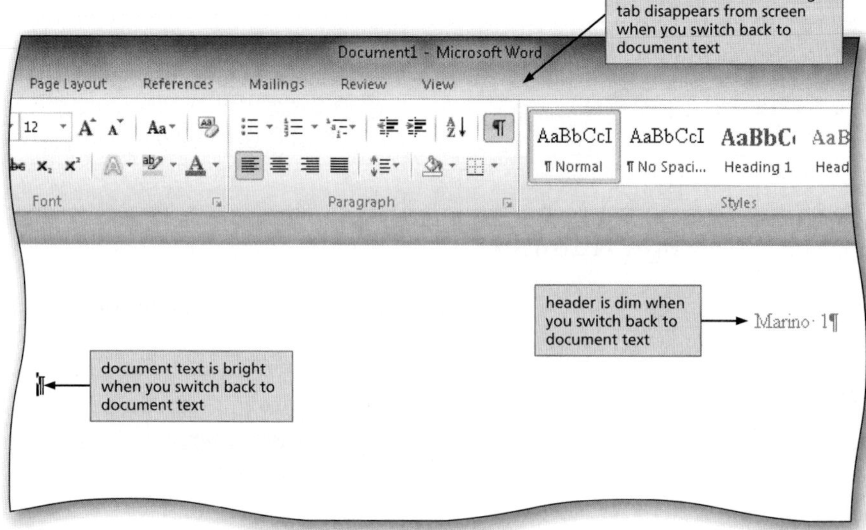

Figure 2–13

Other Ways

1. Double-click dimmed document text

Typing the Research Paper Text

The text of the research paper in this chapter encompasses the first two pages of the paper. You will type the text of the research paper and then modify it later in the chapter, so that it matches Figure 2–1 on page WD 67.

Plan Ahead

Write the first draft, referencing sources.
As you write the first draft of a research paper, be sure it includes the proper components, uses credible sources, and does not contain any plagiarized material.

- **Include an introduction, body, and conclusion.** The first paragraph of the paper introduces the topic and captures the reader's attention. The body, which follows the introduction, consists of several paragraphs that support the topic. The conclusion summarizes the main points in the body and restates the topic.
- **Evaluate sources for authority, currency, and accuracy.** Be especially wary of information obtained from the Web. Any person, company, or organization can publish a Web page on the Internet. Ask yourself these questions about the source:
  - Authority: Does a reputable institution or group support the source? Is the information presented without bias? Are the author's credentials listed and verifiable?
  - Currency: Is the information up to date? Are dates of sources listed? What is the last date revised or updated?
  - Accuracy: Is the information free of errors? Is it verifiable? Are the sources clearly identified?

(continued)

Plan Ahead

(continued)

- **Acknowledge all sources of information; do not plagiarize.** Not only is plagiarism unethical, but it is considered an academic crime that can have severe punishments such as failing a course or being expelled from school.

When you summarize, paraphrase (rewrite information in your own words), present facts, give statistics, quote exact words, or show a map, chart, or other graphical image, you must acknowledge the source. Information that commonly is known or accessible to the audience constitutes common knowledge and does not need to be acknowledged. If, however, you question whether certain information is common knowledge, you should document it — just to be safe.

To Enter Name and Course Information

As discussed earlier in this chapter, the MLA documentation style does not require a separate title page for research papers. Instead, place your name and course information in a block at the top of the page, below the header, at the left margin. The following steps enter the name and course information in the research paper.

1. Type **Annalisa Marino** as the student name and then press the ENTER key.
2. Type **Mr. Winters** as the instructor name and then press the ENTER key.
3. Type **English 101** as the course name and then press the ENTER key.
4. Type **April 4, 2012** as the paper due date and then press the ENTER key (Figure 2–14).

BTW

Date Formats
The MLA documentation style prefers the day-month-year (4 April 2012) or month-day-year (April 4, 2012) format.

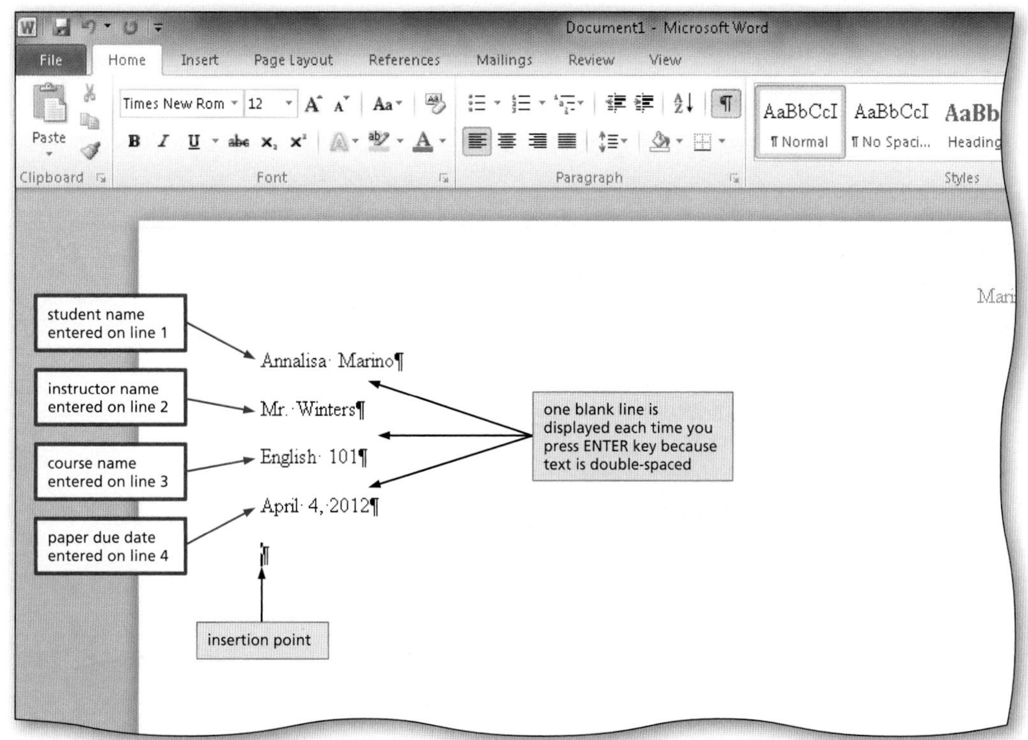

Figure 2–14

To Click and Type

The next step is to enter the title of the research paper centered between the page margins. In Chapter 1, you used the Center button (Home tab | Paragraph group) to center text and graphics. As an alternative, you can use Word's **Click and Type** feature to format and enter text, graphics, and other items. To use Click and Type, you double-click a blank area of the document window. Word automatically formats the item you type or insert according to the location where you double-clicked. The following steps use Click and Type to center and then type the title of the research paper.

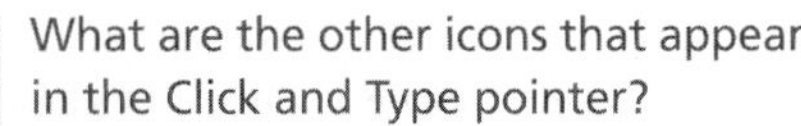

Experiment

- Move the mouse pointer around the document below the entered name and course information and observe the various icons that appear with the I-beam.
- Position the mouse pointer in the center of the document at the approximate location for the research paper title until a center icon appears below the I-beam (Figure 2–15).

Q&A What are the other icons that appear in the Click and Type pointer?

A left-align icon appears to the right of the I-beam when the Click and Type pointer is in certain locations on the left side of the document window. A right-align icon appears to the left of the I-beam when the Click and Type pointer is in certain locations on the right side of the document window.

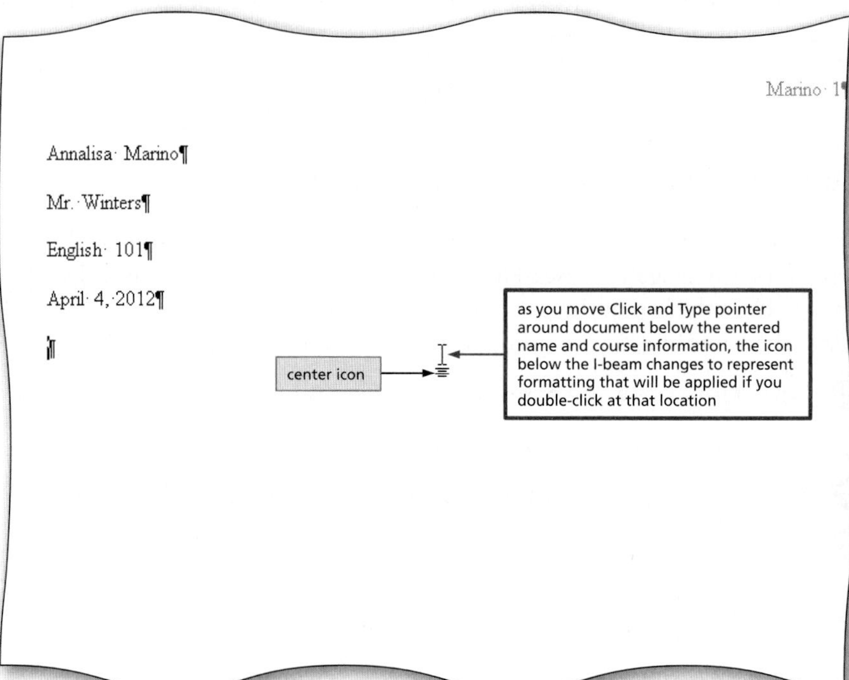

Figure 2–15

- Double-click to center the paragraph mark and insertion point between the left and right margins.
- Type `Can You Find Me Now?` as the paper title and then press the ENTER key to position the insertion point on the next line (Figure 2–16).

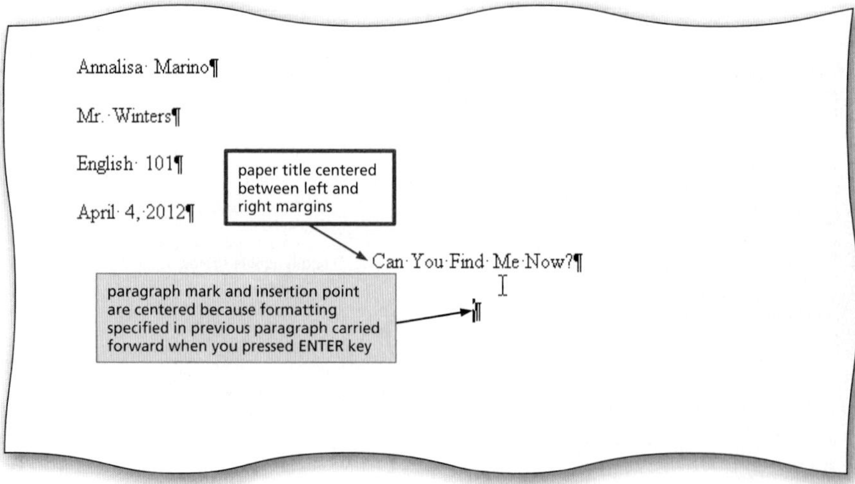

Figure 2–16

Shortcut Keys

Word has many **shortcut keys**, or keyboard key combinations, for your convenience while typing. Table 2–1 lists the common shortcut keys for formatting characters. Table 2–2 lists common shortcut keys for formatting paragraphs.

Table 2–1 Shortcut Keys for Formatting Characters

Character Formatting Task	Shortcut Keys	Character Formatting Task	Shortcut Keys
All capital letters	CTRL+SHIFT+A	Italic	CTRL+I
Bold	CTRL+B	Remove character formatting (plain text)	CTRL+SPACEBAR
Case of letters	SHIFT+F3	Small uppercase letters	CTRL+SHIFT+K
Decrease font size	CTRL+SHIFT+<	Subscript	CTRL+EQUAL SIGN
Decrease font size 1 point	CTRL+[	Superscript	CTRL+SHIFT+PLUS SIGN
Double-underline	CTRL+SHIFT+D	Underline	CTRL+U
Increase font size	CTRL+SHIFT+>	Underline words, not spaces	CTRL+SHIFT+W
Increase font size 1 point	CTRL+]		

Table 2–2 Shortcut Keys for Formatting Paragraphs

Paragraph Formatting	Shortcut Keys	Paragraph Formatting	Shortcut Keys
1.5 line spacing	CTRL+5	Justify paragraph	CTRL+J
Add/remove one line above paragraph	CTRL+0 (zero)	Left-align paragraph	CTRL+L
Center paragraph	CTRL+E	Remove hanging indent	CTRL+SHIFT+T
Decrease paragraph indent	CTRL+SHIFT+M	Remove paragraph formatting	CTRL+Q
Double-space lines	CTRL+2	Right-align paragraph	CTRL+R
Hanging indent	CTRL+T	Single-space lines	CTRL+1
Increase paragraph indent	CTRL+M		

To Format Text Using Shortcut Keys

The paragraphs below the paper title should be left-aligned, instead of centered. Thus, the next step is to left-align the paragraph below the paper title. When your fingers are already on the keyboard, you may prefer using shortcut keys to format text as you type it. The following step left-aligns a paragraph using the shortcut keys CTRL+L. (Recall from Chapter 1 that a notation such as CTRL+L means to press the letter L on the keyboard while holding down the CTRL key.)

1. Press CTRL+L to left-align the current paragraph, that is, the paragraph containing the insertion point (shown in Figure 2–17 on the next page).

Q&A

Why would I use a keyboard shortcut instead of the Ribbon to format text?

Switching between the mouse and the keyboard takes time. If your hands are already on the keyboard, use a shortcut key. If your hand is on the mouse, use the Ribbon.

BTW

Shortcut Keys

To print a complete list of shortcut keys in Word, click the Microsoft Word Help button near the upper-right corner of the Word window, type **shortcut keys** in the 'Type words to search for' text box at the top of the Word Help window, press the ENTER key, click the Keyboard shortcuts for Microsoft Word link, click the Show All link in the upper-right corner of the Help window, click the Print button in the Help window, and then click the Print button in the Print dialog box.

For an introduction to Office 2010 and instruction about how to perform basic tasks in Office 2010 programs, read the Office 2010 and Windows 7 chapter at the beginning of this book, where you can learn how to start a program, use the Ribbon, save a file, open a file, quit a program, use Help, and much more.

To Save a Document

You have performed many tasks while creating this research paper and do not want to risk losing work completed thus far. Accordingly, you should save the document. The following steps assume you already have created folders for storing your files, for example, a CIS 101 folder (for your class) that contains a Word folder (for your assignments). Thus, these steps save the document in the Word folder in the CIS 101 folder on a USB flash drive using the file name, Triangulation Paper.

1. With a USB flash drive connected to one of the computer's USB ports, click the Save button on the Quick Access Toolbar to display the Save As dialog box.
2. Type `Triangulation Paper` in the File name text box to change the file name. Do not press the ENTER key after typing the file name because you do not want to close the dialog box at this time.
3. Navigate to the desired save location (in this case, the Word folder in the CIS 101 folder [or your class folder] on the USB flash drive).
4. Click the Save button (Save As dialog box) to save the document in the selected folder on the selected drive with the entered file name.

To Display the Rulers

According to the MLA documentation style, the first line of each paragraph in the research paper is to be indented one-half inch from the left margin. Although you can use a dialog box to indent paragraphs, Word provides a quicker way through the **horizontal ruler**. This ruler is displayed at the top edge of the document window just below the Ribbon. Word also provides a **vertical ruler** that is displayed along the left edge of the Word window. The following step displays the rulers because you want to use the ruler to indent paragraphs.

1

Experiment

- Repeatedly click the View Ruler button on the vertical scroll bar to see the how this button is used to both show and hide the rulers.

- If the rulers are not displayed, click the View Ruler button on the vertical scroll bar to display the horizontal and vertical rulers on the screen (Figure 2–17).

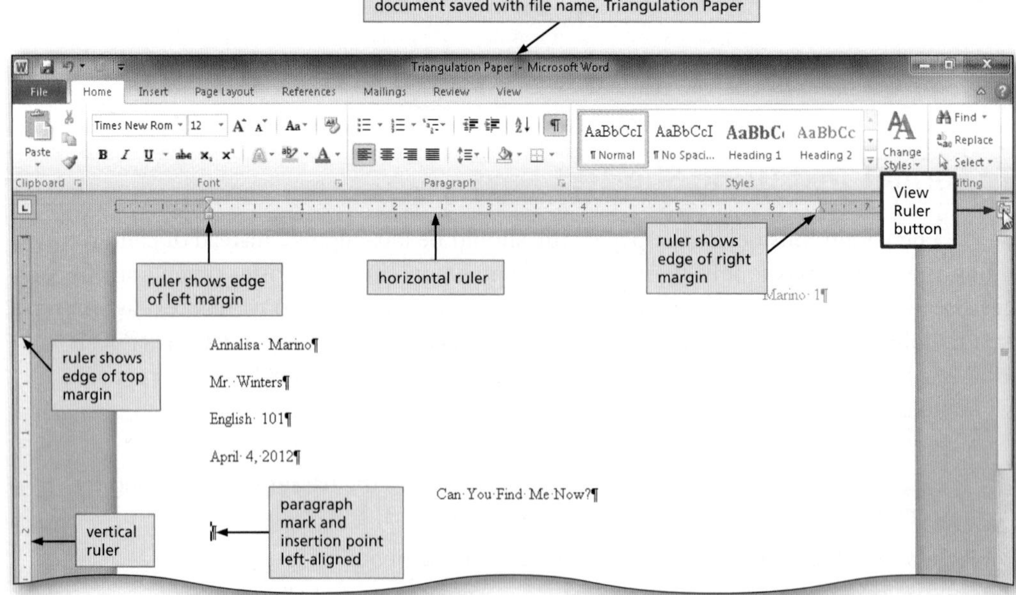

Figure 2–17

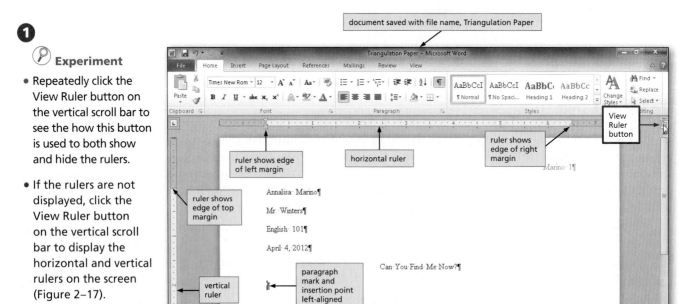

Q&A For what tasks would I use the rulers?

You can use the rulers to indent paragraphs, set tab stops, change page margins, and adjust column widths.

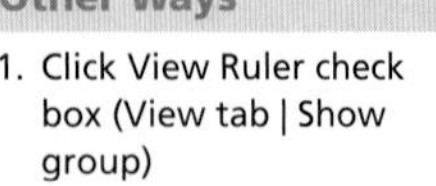

Other Ways

1. Click View Ruler check box (View tab | Show group)

To First-Line Indent Paragraphs

The first line of each paragraph in the research paper is to be indented one-half inch from the left margin. You can use the horizontal ruler, usually simply called the **ruler**, to indent just the first line of a paragraph, which is called a **first-line indent**.

The left margin on the ruler contains two triangles above a square. The **First Line Indent marker** is the top triangle at the 0" mark on the ruler (Figure 2–18). The bottom triangle is discussed later in this chapter. The small square at the 0" mark is the Left Indent marker. The **Left Indent marker** allows you to change the entire left margin, whereas the First Line Indent marker indents only the first line of the paragraph. The following steps first-line indent paragraphs in the research paper.

1

- With the insertion point on the paragraph mark below the research paper title, point to the First Line Indent marker on the ruler (Figure 2–18).

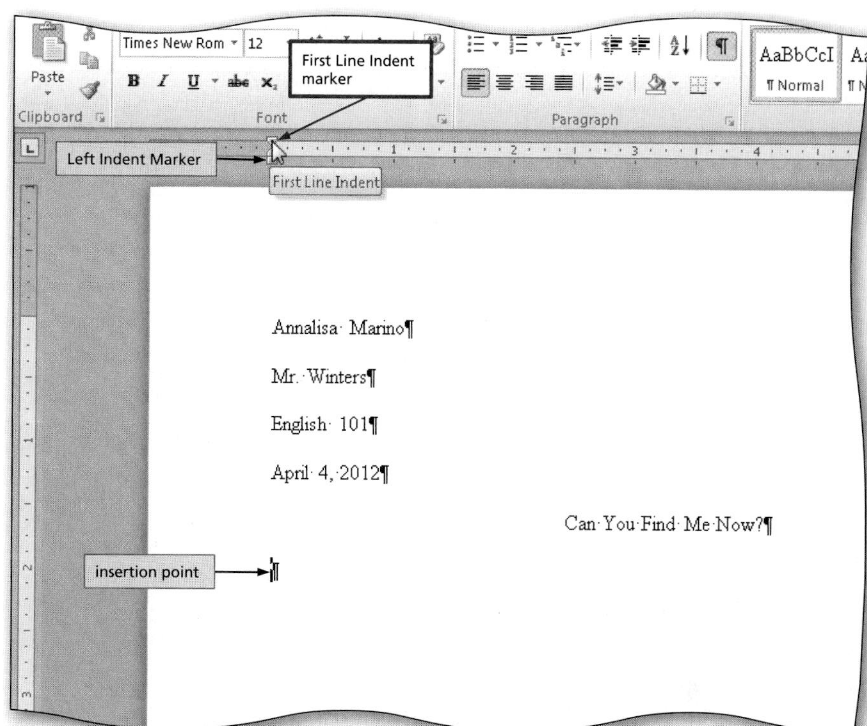

Figure 2–18

2

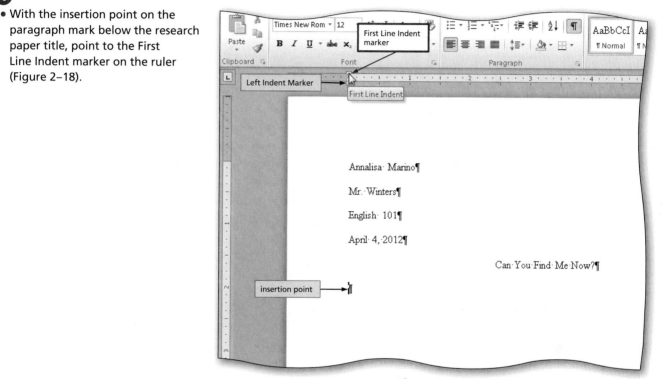

- Drag the First Line Indent marker to the .5" mark on the ruler to display a vertical dotted line in the document window, which indicates the proposed location of the first line of the paragraph (Figure 2–19).

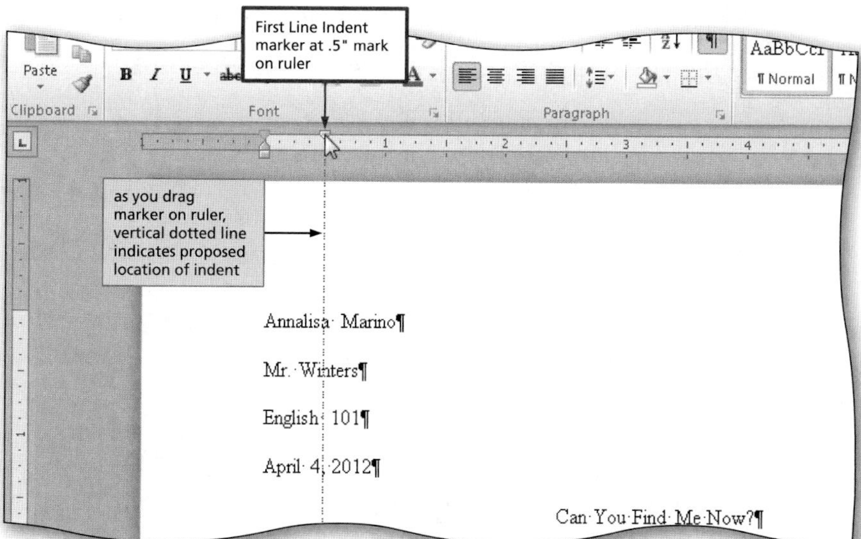

Figure 2–19

- Release the mouse button to place the First Line Indent marker at the .5" mark on the ruler, or one-half inch from the left margin (Figure 2–20).

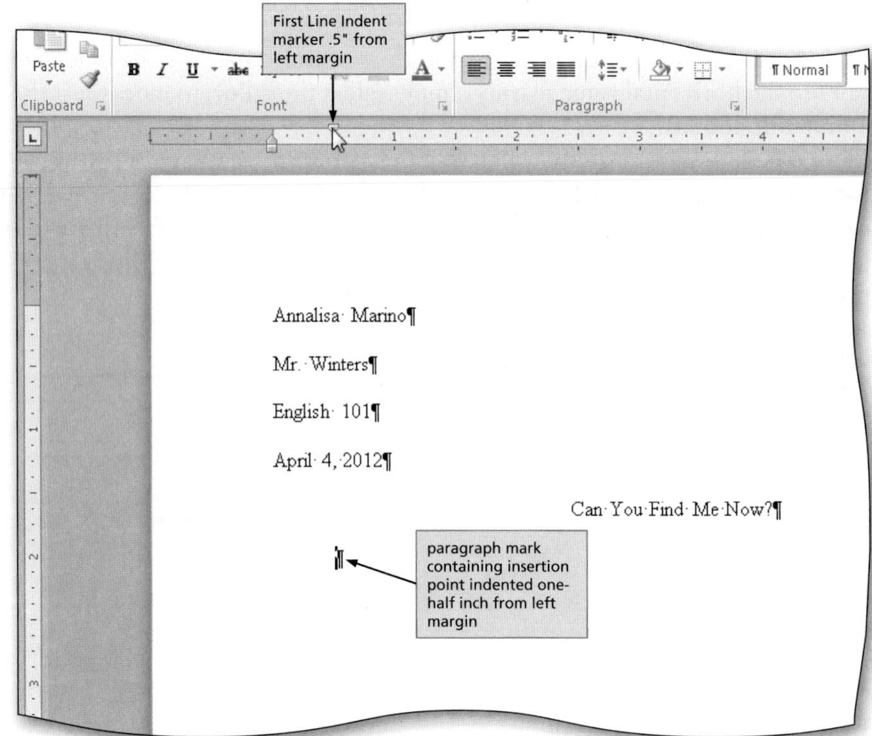

Figure 2–20

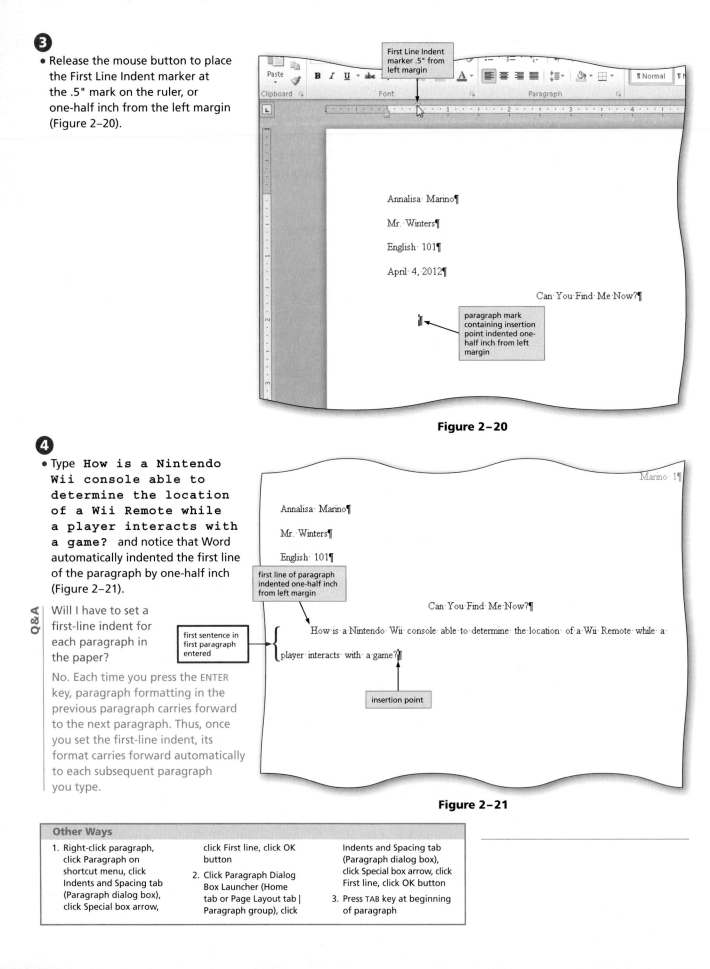

- Type **How is a Nintendo Wii console able to determine the location of a Wii Remote while a player interacts with a game?** and notice that Word automatically indented the first line of the paragraph by one-half inch (Figure 2–21).

Q&A Will I have to set a first-line indent for each paragraph in the paper?

No. Each time you press the ENTER key, paragraph formatting in the previous paragraph carries forward to the next paragraph. Thus, once you set the first-line indent, its format carries forward automatically to each subsequent paragraph you type.

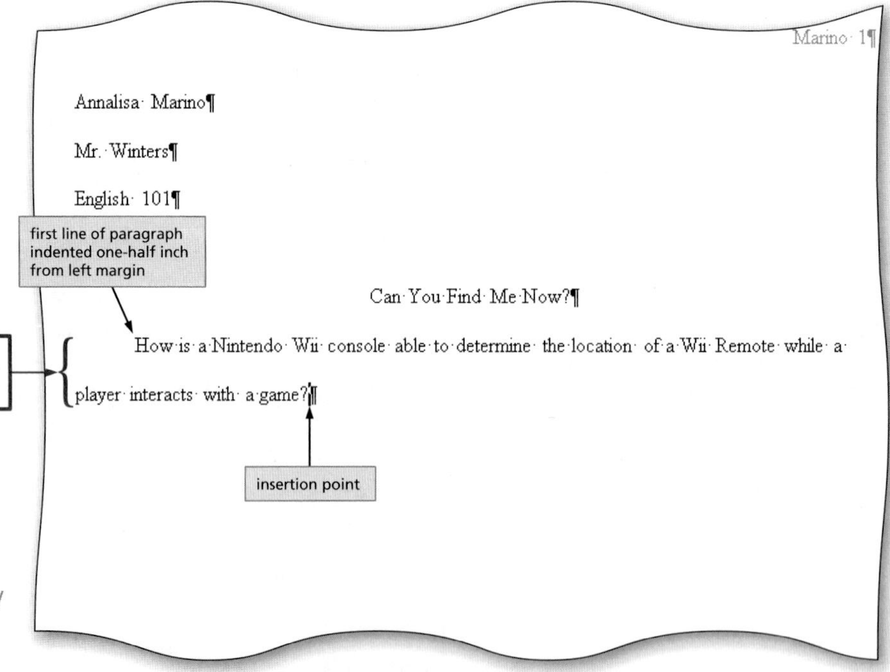

Figure 2–21

Other Ways

1. Right-click paragraph, click Paragraph on shortcut menu, click Indents and Spacing tab (Paragraph dialog box), click Special box arrow, click First line, click OK button
2. Click Paragraph Dialog Box Launcher (Home tab or Page Layout tab | Paragraph group), click Indents and Spacing tab (Paragraph dialog box), click Special box arrow, click First line, click OK button
3. Press TAB key at beginning of paragraph

To AutoCorrect as You Type

As you type, you may make typing, spelling, capitalization, or grammar errors. For this reason, Word provides an **AutoCorrect** feature that automatically corrects these kinds of errors as you type them in the document. For example, if you type ahve, Word automatically changes it to the correct spelling, have, when you press the SPACEBAR or a punctuation mark key such as a period or comma.

Word has predefined many commonly misspelled words, which it automatically corrects for you. The following steps intentionally misspell the word, the, as teh to illustrate the AutoCorrect feature.

- Press the SPACEBAR.
- Type the beginning of the next sentence, misspelling the word, the, as follows: **`The answer is triangulation, a process that determines teh`** (Figure 2–22).

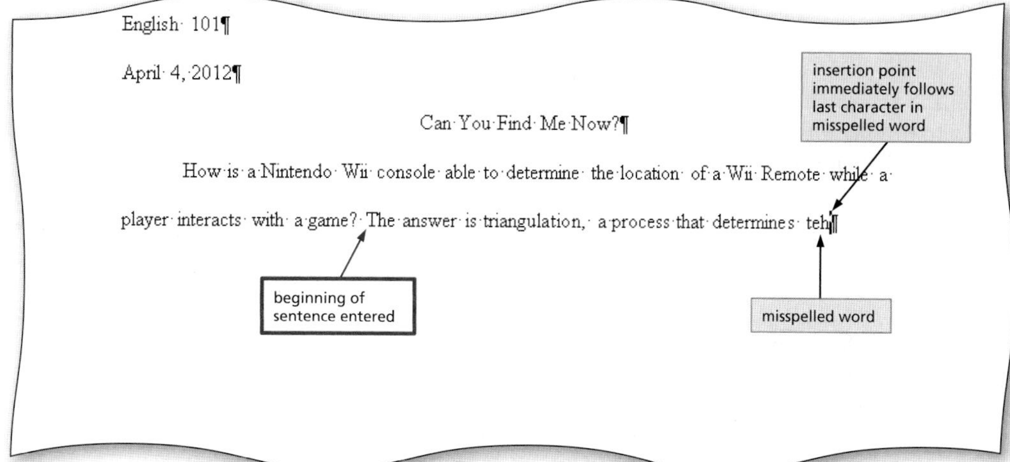

Figure 2–22

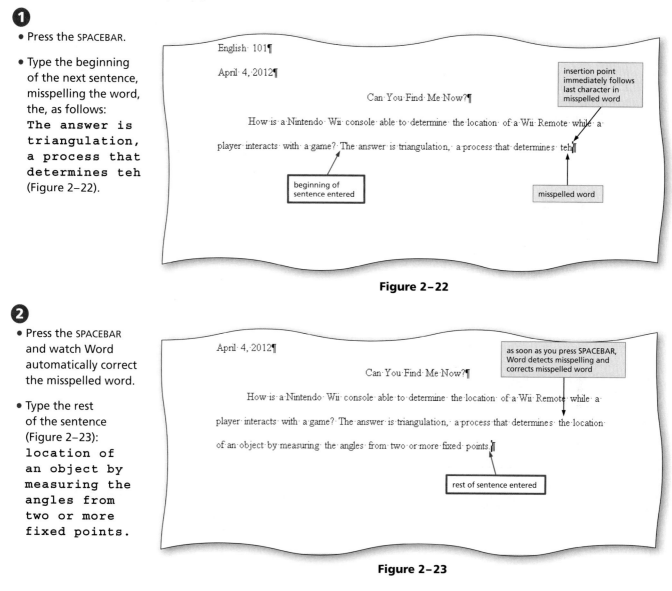

- Press the SPACEBAR and watch Word automatically correct the misspelled word.
- Type the rest of the sentence (Figure 2–23): **`location of an object by measuring the angles from two or more fixed points.`**

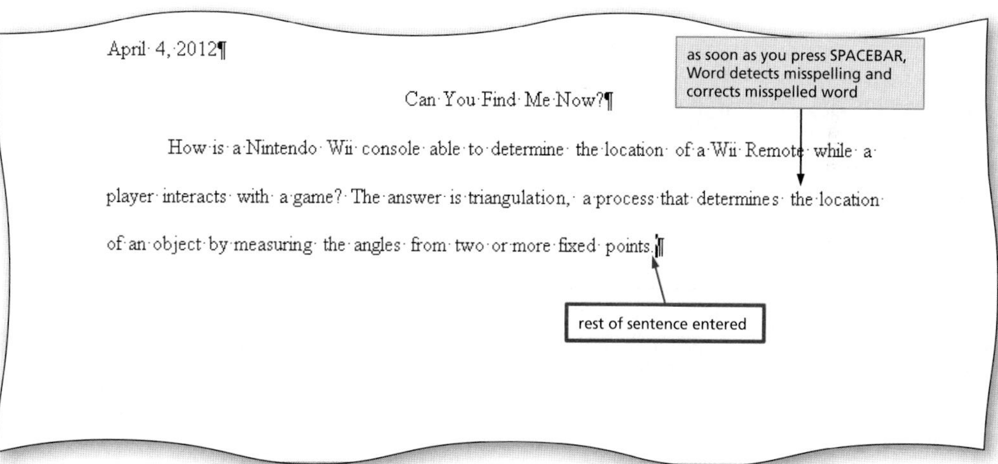

Figure 2–23

To Use the AutoCorrect Options Button

When you position the mouse pointer on text that Word automatically corrected, a small blue box appears below the text. If you point to the small blue box, Word displays the AutoCorrect Options button. When you click the **AutoCorrect Options button**, Word displays a menu that allows you to undo a correction or change how Word handles future automatic corrections of this type. The steps on the next page illustrate the AutoCorrect Options button and menu.

- Position the mouse pointer in the text automatically corrected by Word (the word, the, in this case) to display a small blue box below the automatically corrected word (Figure 2–24).

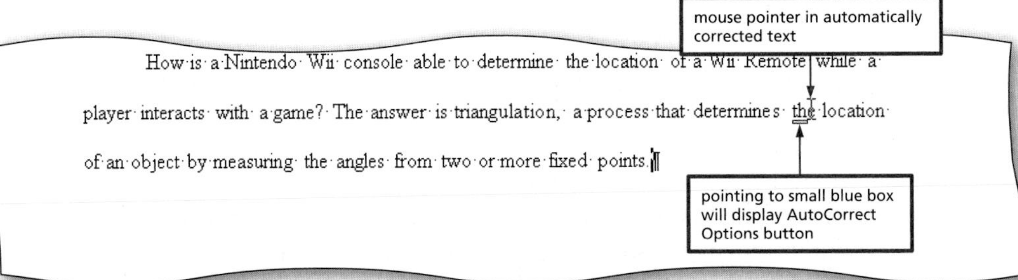

Figure 2–24

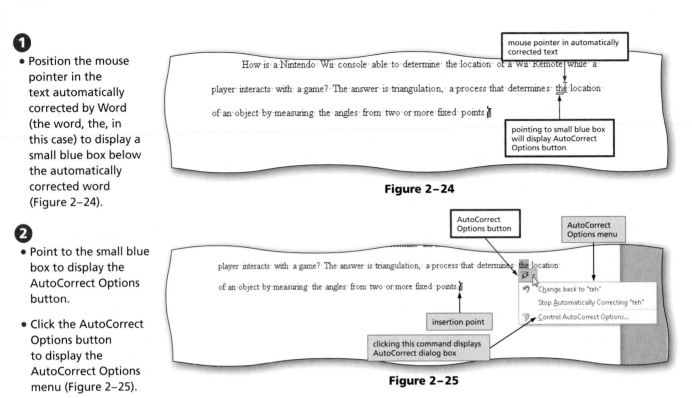

- Point to the small blue box to display the AutoCorrect Options button.
- Click the AutoCorrect Options button to display the AutoCorrect Options menu (Figure 2–25).

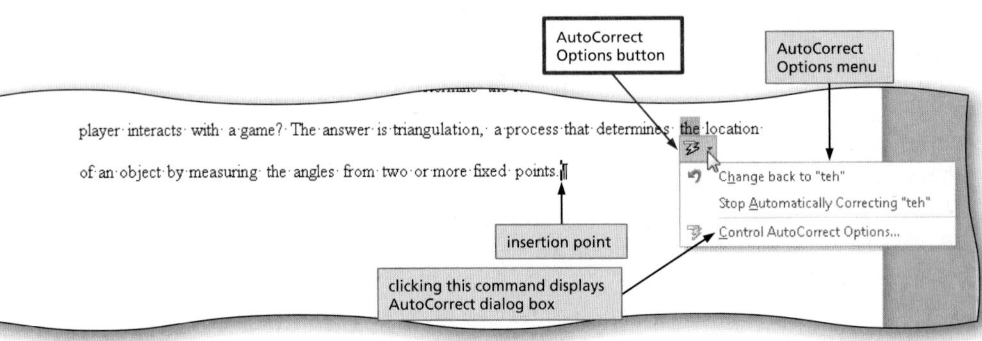

Figure 2–25

- Press the ESCAPE key to remove the AutoCorrect Options menu from the screen.

Q&A Do I need to remove the AutoCorrect Options button from the screen?

No. When you move the mouse pointer, the AutoCorrect Options button will disappear from the screen. If, for some reason, you wanted to remove the AutoCorrect Options button from the screen, you could press the ESCAPE key a second time.

To Create an AutoCorrect Entry

In addition to the predefined list of AutoCorrect spelling, capitalization, and grammar errors, you can create your own AutoCorrect entries to add to the list. For example, if you tend to mistype the word sensor as senser, you should create an AutoCorrect entry for it. The following steps create an AutoCorrect entry.

1

- Click File on the Ribbon to open the Backstage view (Figure 2–26).

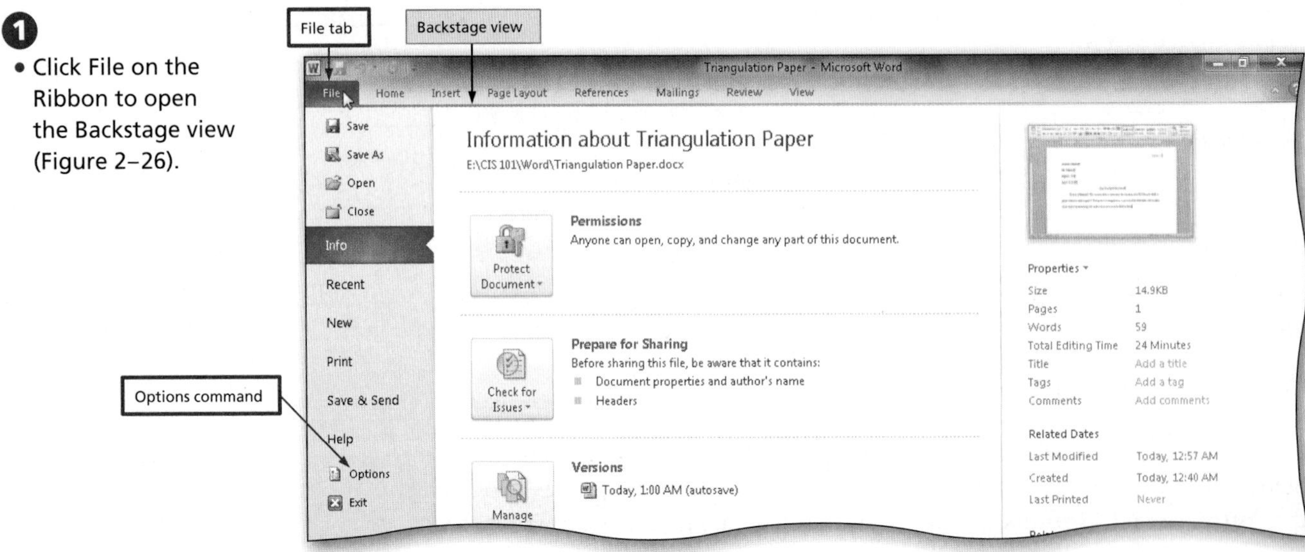

Figure 2–26

2

- Click Options in the Backstage view to display the Word Options dialog box.
- Click Proofing in the left pane (Word Options dialog box) to display proofing options in the right pane.
- Click the AutoCorrect Options button in the right pane to display the AutoCorrect dialog box.
- When Word displays the AutoCorrect dialog box, type **senser** in the Replace text box.
- Press the TAB key and then type **sensor** in the With text box (Figure 2–27).

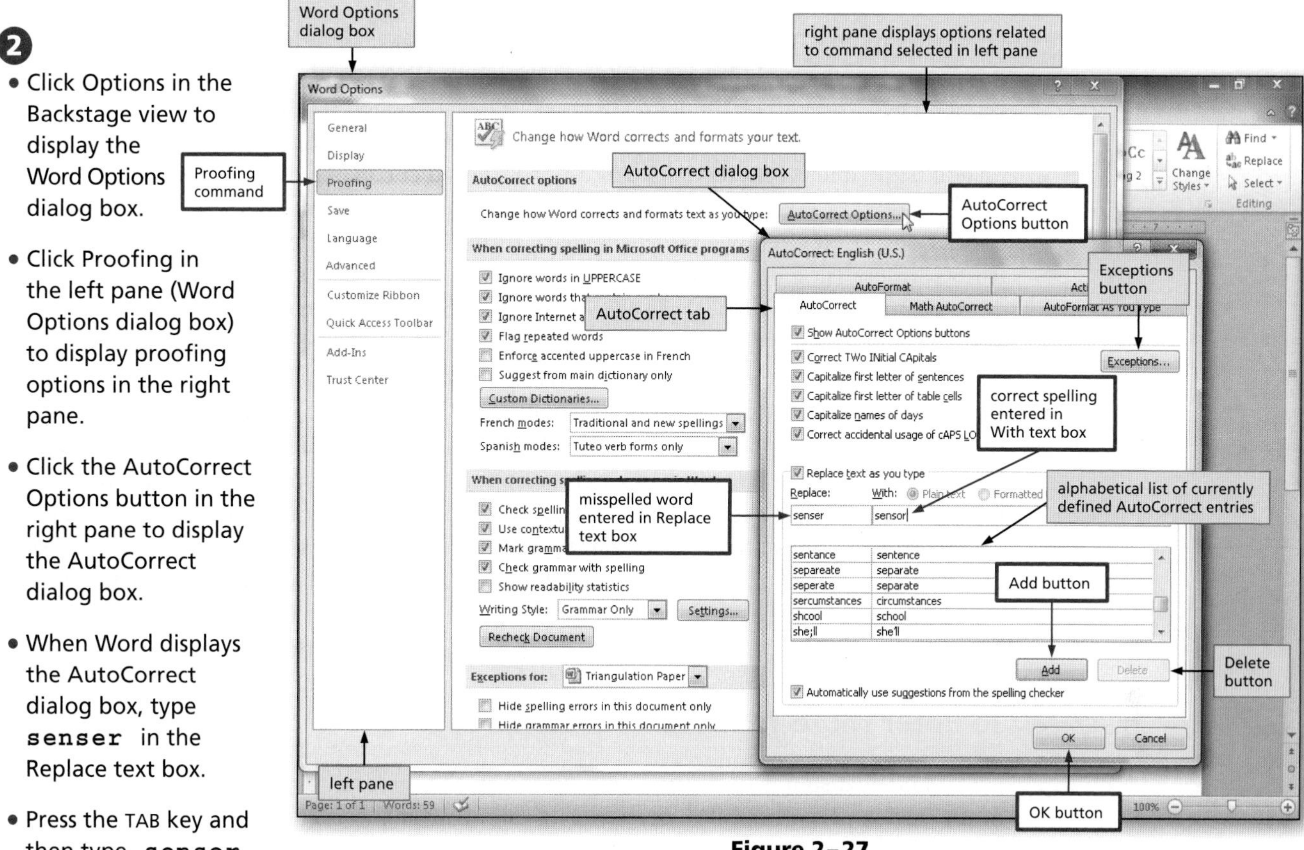

Figure 2–27

Q&A How would I delete an existing AutoCorrect entry?

You would select the entry to be deleted in the list of defined entries in the AutoCorrect dialog box and then click the Delete button.

3

- Click the Add button (AutoCorrect dialog box) to add the entry alphabetically to the list of words to correct automatically as you type. (If your dialog box displays a Replace button instead, click it and then click the Yes button in the Microsoft Word dialog box to replace the previously defined entry.)
- Click the OK button (AutoCorrect dialog box) to close the dialog box.
- Click the OK button (Word Options dialog box) to close the dialog box.

The AutoCorrect Dialog Box

In addition to creating AutoCorrect entries for words you commonly misspell or mistype, you can create entries for abbreviations, codes, and so on. For example, you could create an AutoCorrect entry for asap, indicating that Word should replace this text with the phrase, as soon as possible.

If, for some reason, you do not want Word to correct automatically as you type, you can turn off the 'Replace text as you type' feature by clicking Options in the Backstage view, clicking Proofing in the left pane (Word Options dialog box), clicking the AutoCorrect Options button in the right pane (Figure 2–27), removing the check mark from the 'Replace text as you type' check box, and then clicking the OK button in each open dialog box.

The AutoCorrect sheet in the AutoCorrect dialog box (Figure 2–27) contains other check boxes that correct capitalization errors if the check boxes are selected. If you

BTW **Automatic Corrections**
If you do not want to keep a change automatically made by Word and you immediately notice the automatic correction, you can undo the change by clicking the Undo button on the Quick Access Toolbar or pressing CTRL+Z. You also can undo a correction through the AutoCorrect Options button, which was shown above.

type two capital letters in a row, such as TH, Word makes the second letter lowercase, Th. If you begin a sentence with a lowercase letter, Word capitalizes the first letter of the sentence. If you type the name of a day in lowercase letters, such as tuesday, Word capitalizes the first letter in the name of the day, Tuesday. If you leave the CAPS LOCK key on and begin a new sentence, such as aFTER, Word corrects the typing, After, and turns off the CAPS LOCK key. If you do not want Word to automatically perform any of these corrections, simply remove the check mark from the appropriate check box in the AutoCorrect dialog box.

Sometimes you do not want Word to AutoCorrect a particular word or phrase. For example, you may use the code WD. in your documents. Because Word automatically capitalizes the first letter of a sentence, the character you enter following the period will be capitalized (in the previous sentence, it would capitalize the letter i in the word, in). To allow the code WD. to be entered into a document and still leave the AutoCorrect feature turned on, you would set an exception. To set an exception to an AutoCorrect rule, click Options in the Backstage view, click Proofing in the left pane (Word Options dialog box), click the AutoCorrect Options button in the right pane, click the Exceptions button (Figure 2–27 on the previous page), click the appropriate tab in the AutoCorrect Exceptions dialog box, type the exception entry in the text box, click the Add button, click the Close button (AutoCorrect Exceptions dialog box), and then click the OK button in each of the remaining dialog boxes.

To Enter More Text

BTW **Spacing after Punctuation**
Because word processing documents use variable character fonts, it often is difficult to determine in a printed document how many times someone has pressed the SPACEBAR between sentences. Thus, the rule is to press the SPACEBAR only once after periods, colons, and other punctuation marks.

The next step is to continue typing text in the research paper up to the location of the in-text parenthetical reference. The following steps enter this text.

1. With the insertion point positioned at the end of the first paragraph in the paper, as shown in Figure 2–25 on page WD 86, press the ENTER key, so that you can begin typing the text in the second paragraph.

2. Type `Surveyors often use triangulation to measure distance. Starting at a known location and elevation, surveyors measure a length to create a base line and then use a theodolite to measure an angle to an unknown point from each side of the base line` and then press the SPACEBAR.

Citations

Both the MLA and APA guidelines suggest the use of in-text parenthetical references (placed at the end of a sentence), instead of footnoting each source of material in a paper. These parenthetical references, called citations in Word, guide the reader to the end of the paper for complete information about the source.

Plan Ahead

Reference all sources.
During your research, be sure to record essential publication information about each of your sources. Following is a sample list of types of required information for the MLA documentation style.

- Book: full name of author(s), complete title of book, edition (if available), volume (if available), publication city, publisher name, publication year, publication medium
- Magazine: full name of author(s), complete title of article, magazine title, issue number (if available), date of magazine, page numbers of article, publication medium
- Web site: full name of author(s), title of Web site, Web site publisher or sponsor (if none, write N.p.), publication date (if none, write n.d.), publication medium, date viewed

Word provides tools to assist you with inserting citations in a paper and later generating a list of sources from the citations. With a documentation style selected, Word automatically formats the citations and list of sources according to that style. The process for adding citations in Word is as follows:

1. Modify the documentation style, if necessary.
2. Insert a citation placeholder.
3. Enter the source information for the citation.

You can combine Steps 2 and 3, where you insert the citation placeholder and enter the source information at once. Or, you can insert the citation placeholder as you write and then enter the source information for the citation at a later time. While creating the research paper in this chapter, you will use both methods.

To Change the Bibliography Style

The first step in inserting a citation is to be sure the citations and sources will be formatted using the correct documentation style, called the bibliography style in Word. The following steps change the specified documentation style.

1

- Click References on the Ribbon to display the References tab.
- Click the Bibliography Style box arrow (References tab | Citations & Bibliography group) to display a gallery of predefined documentation styles (Figure 2–28).

2

- Click MLA Sixth Edition in the Bibliography Style gallery to change the documentation style to MLA.

Q&A What if I am using a different edition of a documentation style shown in the Bibliography Style gallery?

Select the closest one and then, if necessary, perform necessary edits before submitting the paper.

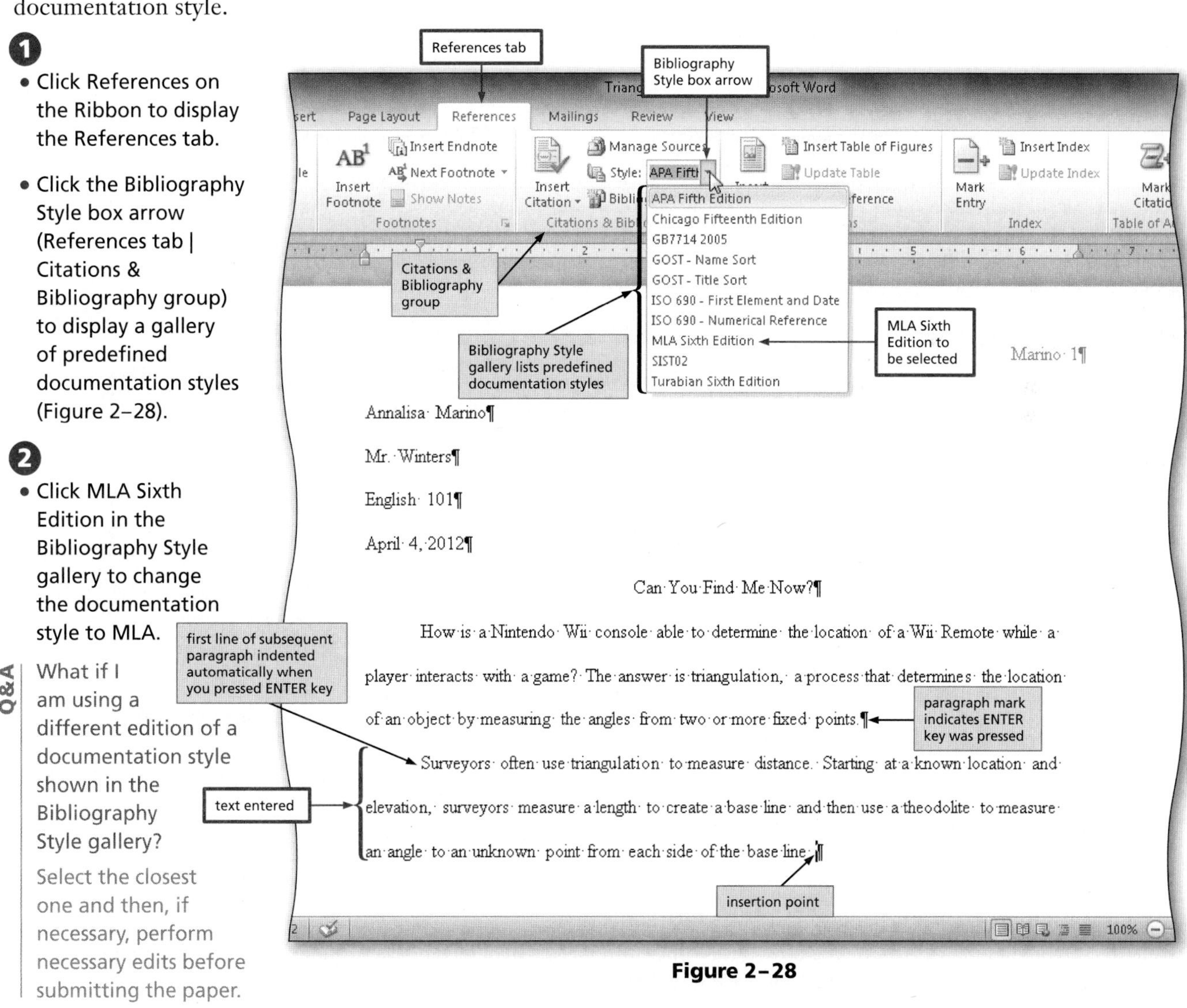

Figure 2–28

To Insert a Citation and Create Its Source

With the documentation style selected, the next task is to insert a citation placeholder and enter the source information for the citation. You can accomplish these steps at once by instructing Word to add a new source. The following steps add a new source for a magazine (periodical) article.

1

- Click the Insert Citation button (References tab | Citations & Bibliography group) to display the Insert Citation menu (Figure 2–29).

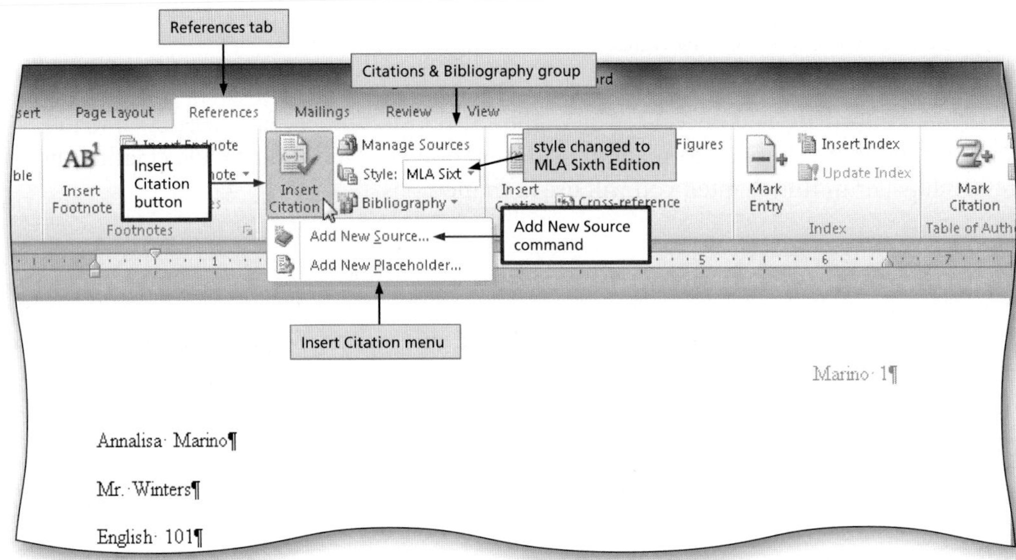

Figure 2–29

2

- Click Add New Source on the Insert Citation menu to display the Create Source dialog box (Figure 2–30).

Q&A What are the Bibliography Fields in the Create Source dialog box?

A **field** is a placeholder for data whose contents can change. You enter data in some fields; Word supplies data for others. In this case, you enter the contents of the fields for a particular source, for example, the author name in the Author field.

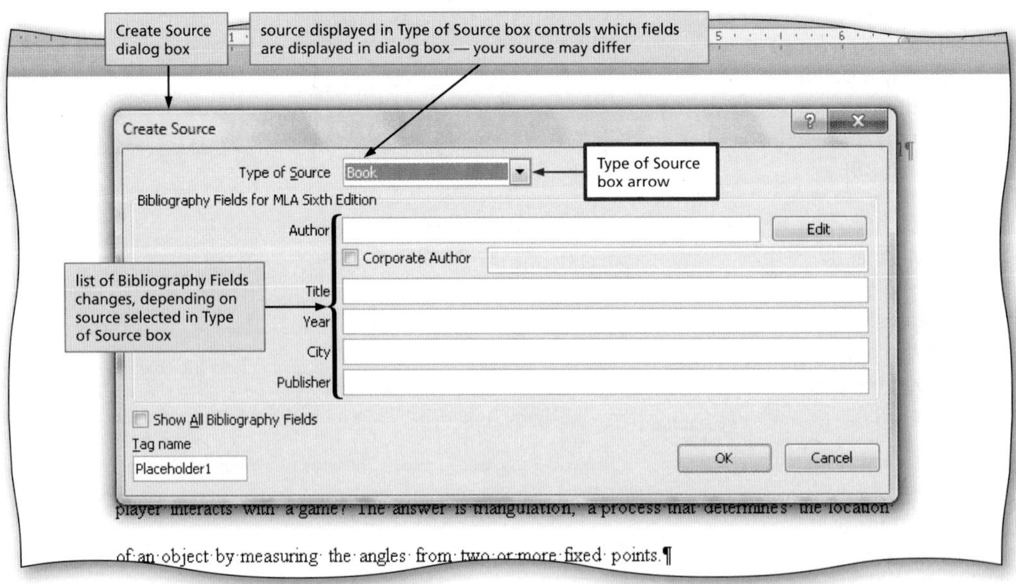

Figure 2–30

 **Experiment**

- Click the Type of Source box arrow and then click one of the source types in the list, so that you can see how the list of fields changes to reflect the type of source you selected.

3

- If necessary, click the Type of Source box arrow (Create Source dialog box) and then click Article in a Periodical, so that the list shows fields required for a magazine (periodical).
- Click the Author text box. Type **Jains, Malila** as the author.
- Click the Title text box. Type **How Surveyors Measure and Calculate Angles** as the article title.
- Press the TAB key and then type **Today's Modern Surveyor** as the periodical title.
- Press the TAB key and then type **2012** as the year.
- Press the TAB key and then type **Mar.** as the month.
- Press the TAB key twice and then type **30-48** as the pages (Figure 2–31).

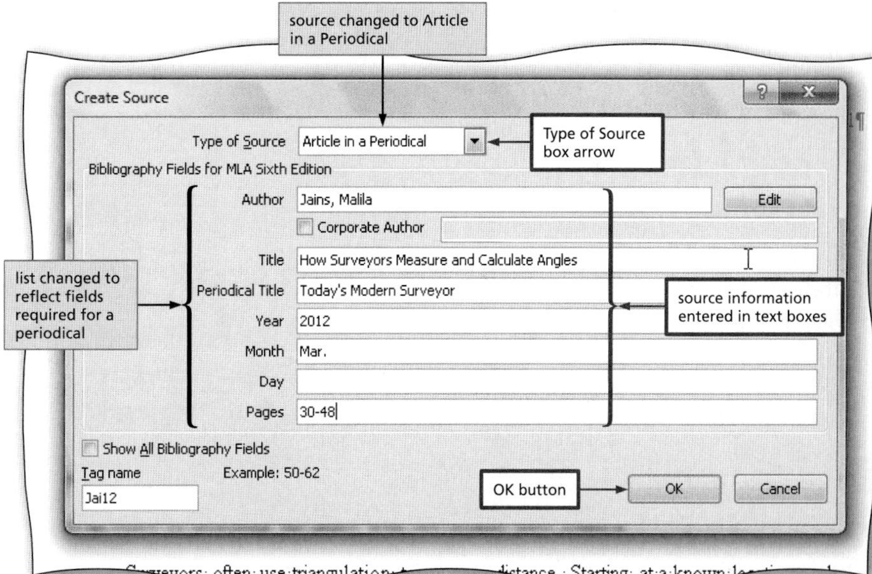

Figure 2–31

- Click the OK button to close the dialog box, create the source, and insert the citation in the document at the location of the insertion point (Figure 2–32).

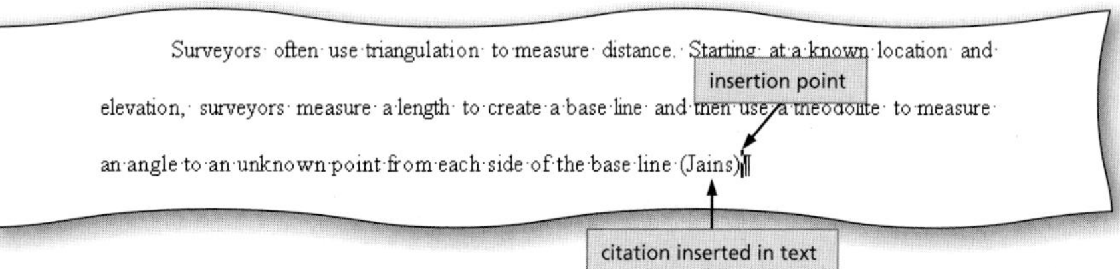

Surveyors often use triangulation to measure distance. Starting at a known location and
insertion point
elevation, surveyors measure a length to create a base line and then use a theodolite to measure
an angle to an unknown point from each side of the base line (Jains)
citation inserted in text

Figure 2–32

To Edit a Citation

In the MLA documentation style, if a source has page numbers, you should include them in the citation. Thus, Word provides a means to enter the page numbers to be displayed in the citation. The following steps edit a citation, so that the page numbers appear in it.

- Click somewhere in the citation to be edited, in this case somewhere in (Jains), which selects the citation and displays the Citation Options box arrow.
- Click the Citation Options box arrow to display the Citation Options menu (Figure 2–33).

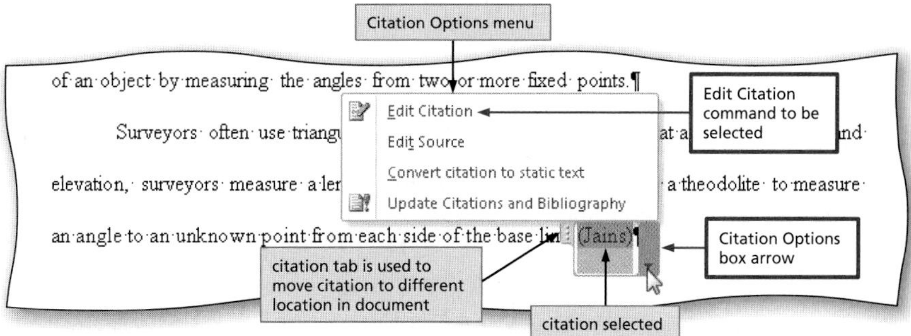

Figure 2–33

Q&A What is the purpose of the tab to the left of the selected citation?

If, for some reason, you wanted to move a citation to a different location in the document, you would select the citation and then drag the citation tab to the desired location.

2

- Click Edit Citation on the Citation Options menu to display the Edit Citation dialog box.
- Type **30-48** in the Pages text box (Edit Citations dialog box) (Figure 2–34).

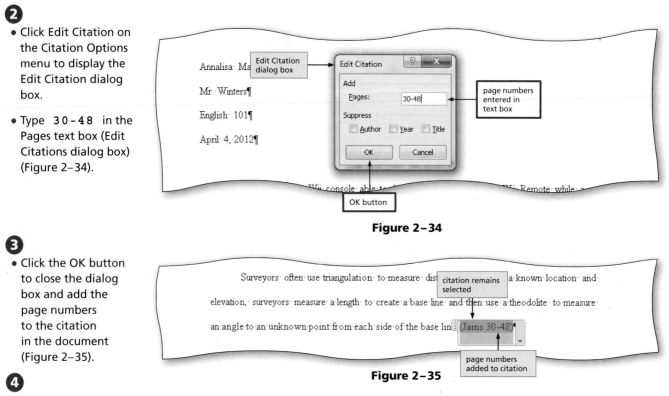

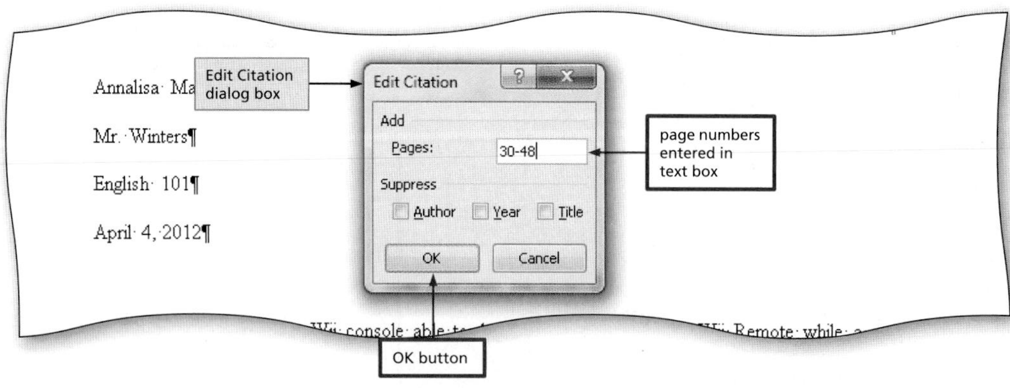
Edit Citation dialog box
Edit Citation
Add
Pages:
30-48
Suppress
Author
Year
Title
OK
Cancel
page numbers entered in text box
OK button
Annalisa Ma
Mr. Winters¶
English 101¶
April 4, 2012¶

Figure 2–34

3

- Click the OK button to close the dialog box and add the page numbers to the citation in the document (Figure 2–35).

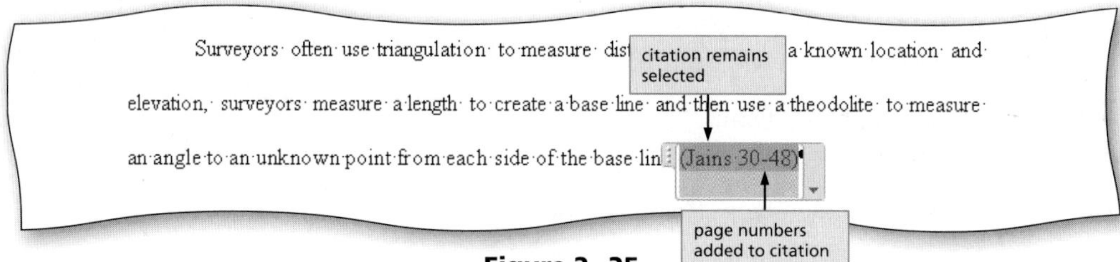
citation remains selected
page numbers added to citation
Surveyors often use triangulation to measure dis
a known location and
elevation, surveyors measure a length to create a base line and then use a theodolite to measure
an angle to an unknown point from each side of the base lin (Jains 30-48)

Figure 2–35

4

- Press the END key to move the insertion point to the end of the line, which also deselects the citation.
- Press the PERIOD key to end the sentence.

BTW

Edit a Source
To edit a source, click somewhere in the citation, click the Citation Options box arrow, and then click Edit Source on the Citation Options menu to display the Edit Source dialog box (which resembles the Create Source dialog box). Make necessary changes and then click the OK button.

To Enter More Text

The next step is to continue typing text in the research paper up to the location of the footnote. The following steps enter this text.

1. Press the SPACEBAR.
2. Type the next sentence (Figure 2–36): **The length of the base line and the two known angles allow a computer or person to determine the location of a third point.**

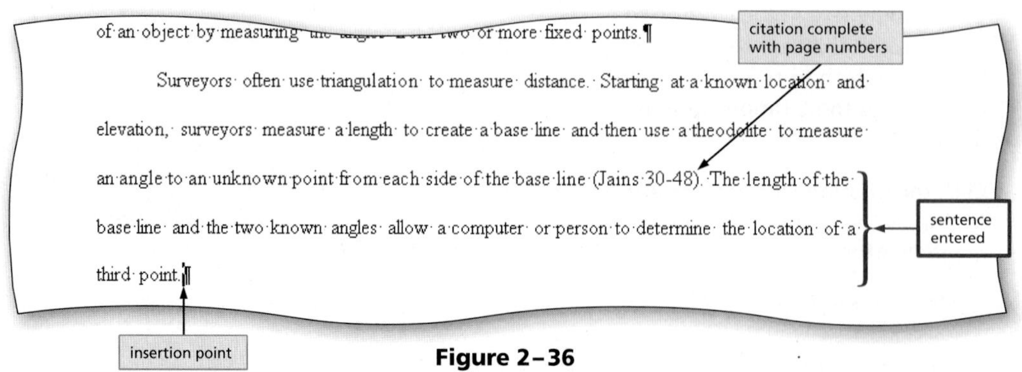
citation complete with page numbers
sentence entered
insertion point
of an object by measuring ... or more fixed points.¶
Surveyors often use triangulation to measure distance. Starting at a known location and
elevation, surveyors measure a length to create a base line and then use a theodolite to measure
an angle to an unknown point from each side of the base line (Jains 30-48). The length of the
base line and the two known angles allow a computer or person to determine the location of a
third point.¶

Figure 2–36

To Save an Existing Document with the Same File Name

You have made several modifications to the document since you last saved it. Thus, you should save it again. The following step saves the document again.

1. Click the Save button on the Quick Access Toolbar to overwrite the previously saved file.

Footnotes

As discussed earlier in this chapter, notes are optional in the MLA documentation style. If used, content notes elaborate on points discussed in the paper, and bibliographic notes direct the reader to evaluations of statements in a source or provide a means for identifying multiple sources. The MLA documentation style specifies that a superscript (raised number) be used for a **note reference mark** to signal that a note exists either at the bottom of the page as a **footnote** or at the end of the document as an **endnote**.

In Word, **note text** can be any length and format. Word automatically numbers notes sequentially by placing a note reference mark both in the body of the document and to the left of the note text. If you insert, rearrange, or remove notes, Word renumbers any subsequent note reference marks according to their new sequence in the document.

To Insert a Footnote Reference Mark

The following step inserts a footnote reference mark in the document at the location of the insertion point and at the location where the footnote text will be typed.

1

- With the insertion point positioned as shown in Figure 2–36, click the Insert Footnote button (References tab | Footnotes group) to display a note reference mark (a superscripted 1) in two places: (1) in the document window at the location of the insertion point and (2) at the bottom of the page where the footnote will be positioned, just below a separator line (Figure 2–37).

Q&A What if I wanted notes to be positioned as endnotes instead of as footnotes?

You would click the Insert Endnote button (References tab | Footnotes group), which places the separator line and the endnote text at the end of the document, instead of the bottom of the page containing the reference.

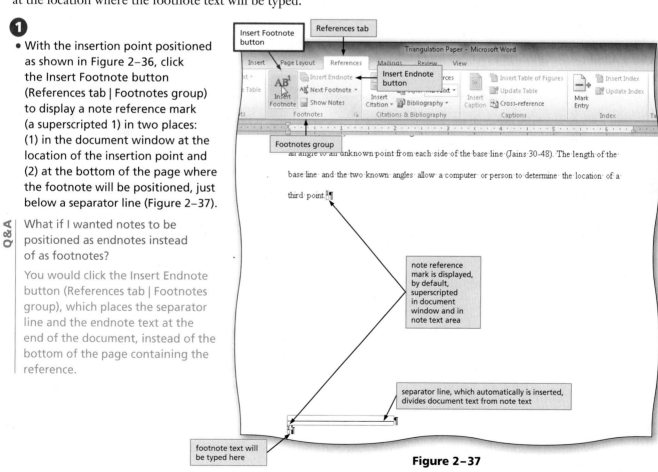

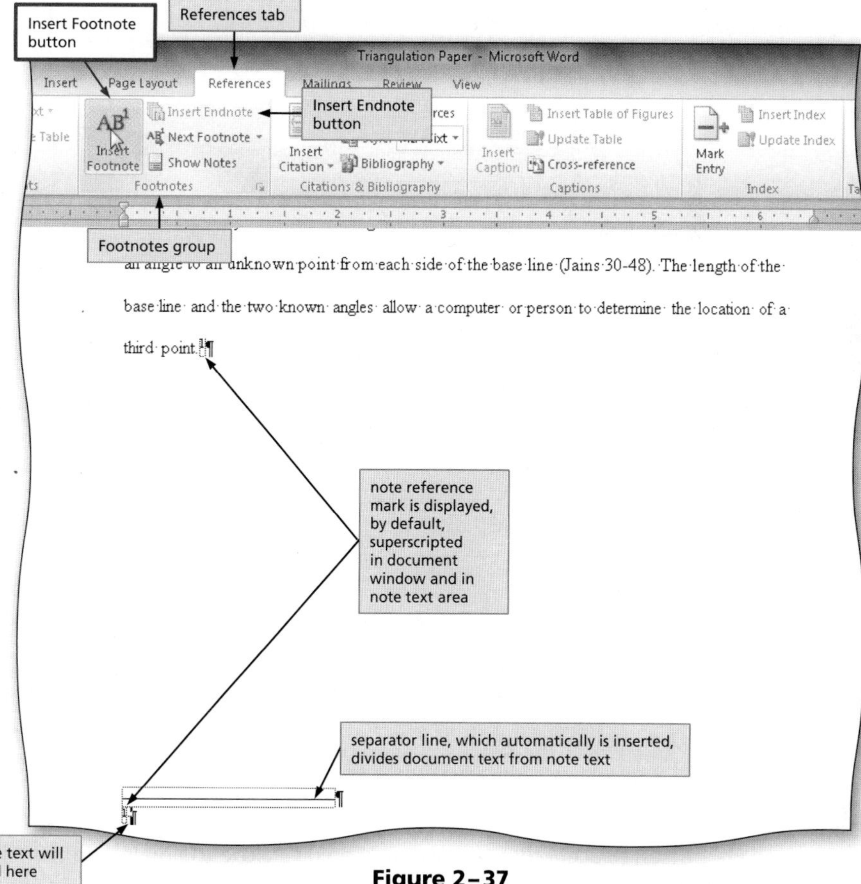

Figure 2–37

Other Ways

1. Press CTRL+ALT+F

To Enter Footnote Text

The following step types the footnote text to the right of the note reference mark below the separator line.

1. Type the footnote text up to the citation: `Cordoba and Sarkis state that electronic theodolites calculate angles automatically and then send the calculated angles to a computer for analysis` and then press the SPACEBAR.

To Insert a Citation Placeholder

Earlier in this chapter, you inserted a citation and its source at once. Sometimes, you may not have the source information readily available and would prefer entering it at a later time.

In the footnote, you will insert a placeholder for the citation and enter the source information later. The following steps insert a citation placeholder.

1

- With the insertion point positioned as shown in Figure 2–38, click the Insert Citation button (References tab | Citations & Bibliography group) to display the Insert Citation menu (Figure 2–38).

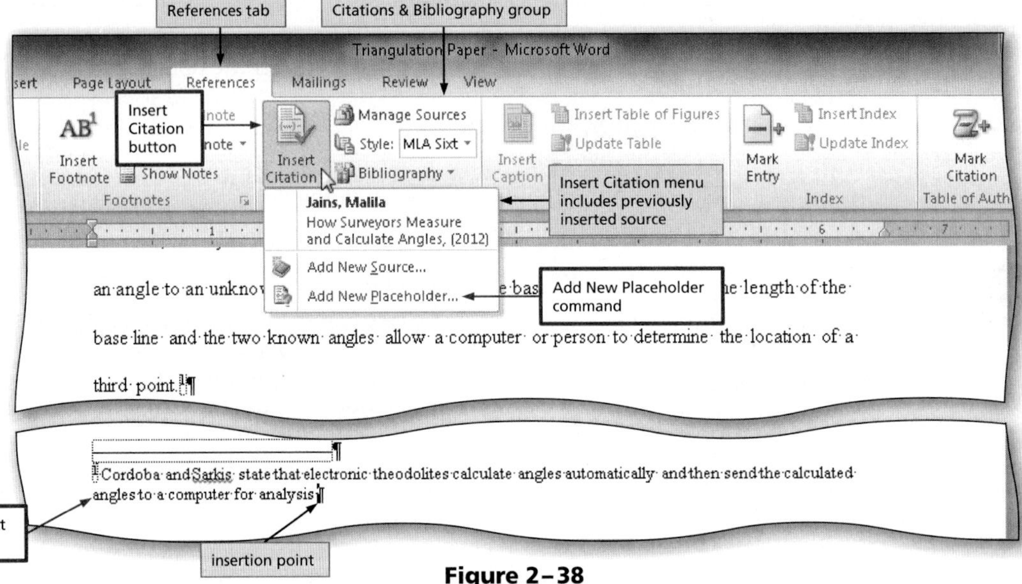

Figure 2–38

2

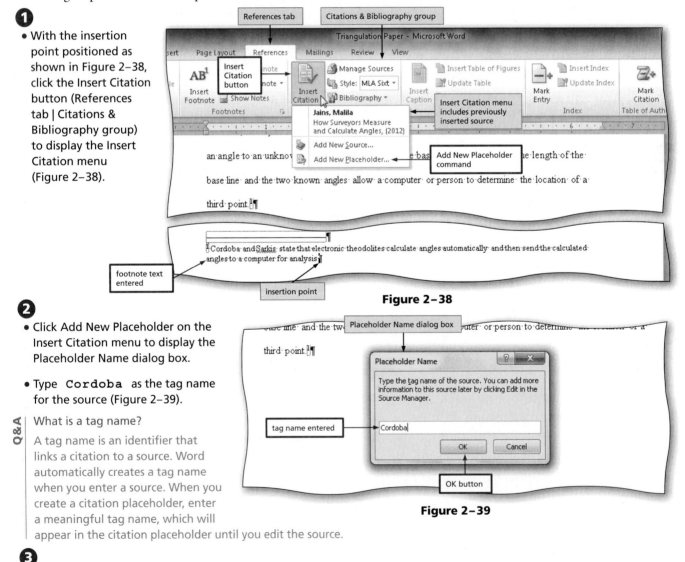

- Click Add New Placeholder on the Insert Citation menu to display the Placeholder Name dialog box.
- Type `Cordoba` as the tag name for the source (Figure 2–39).

Q&A What is a tag name?

A tag name is an identifier that links a citation to a source. Word automatically creates a tag name when you enter a source. When you create a citation placeholder, enter a meaningful tag name, which will appear in the citation placeholder until you edit the source.

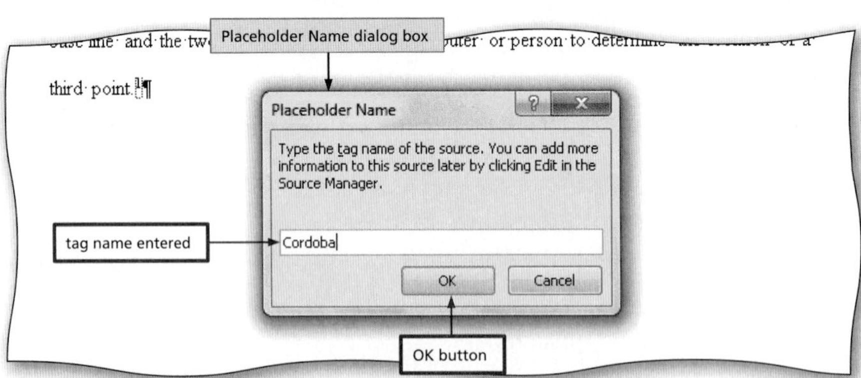

Figure 2–39

3

- Click the OK button (Placeholder Name dialog box) to close the dialog box and insert the entered tag name in the citation placeholder in the document.
- Press the PERIOD key to end the sentence.

Footnote Text Style

When you insert a footnote, Word formats it using the Footnote Text style, which does not adhere to the MLA documentation style. For example, notice in Figure 2–38 that the footnote text is single-spaced, left-aligned, and a smaller font size than the text in the research paper. According to the MLA documentation style, notes should be formatted like all other paragraphs in the paper.

You could change the paragraph formatting of the footnote text to first-line indent and double-spacing and then change the font size from 10 to 12 point. If you use this technique, however, you will need to change the format of the footnote text for each footnote you enter into the document.

A more efficient technique is to modify the format of the Footnote Text style so that every footnote you enter in the document will use the formats defined in this style.

To Modify a Style Using a Shortcut Menu

The Footnote Text style specifies left-aligned single-spaced paragraphs with a 10-point font size for text. To meet MLA documentation style, the footnotes should be double-spaced with a first line indent and a 12-point font size for text. The following steps modify the Footnote Text style.

- Right-click the note text in the footnote to display a shortcut menu related to footnotes (Figure 2–40).

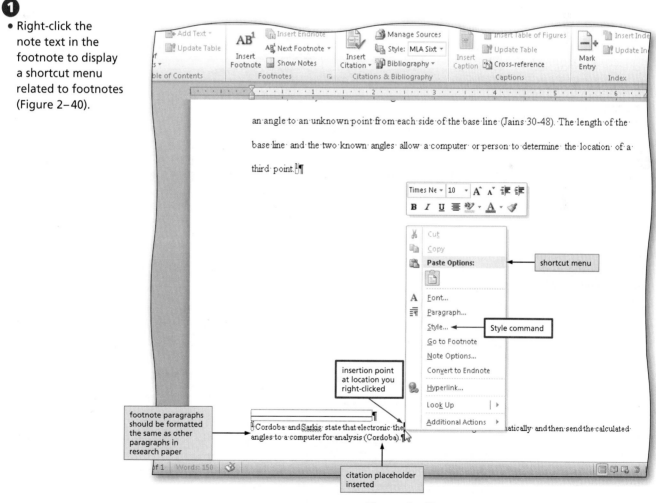

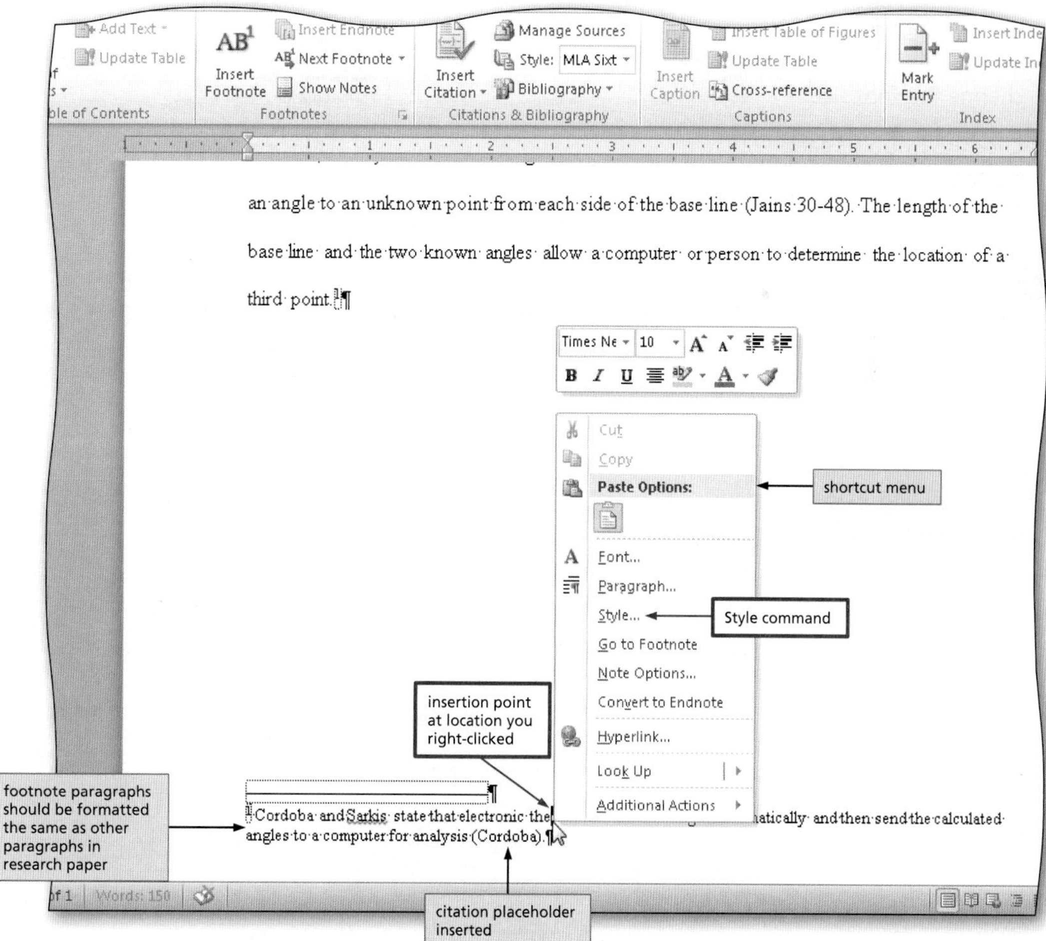

Figure 2–40

2

- Click Style on the shortcut menu to display the Style dialog box. If necessary, click the Category box arrow, click All styles in the Cagetory list, and then click Footnote Text in the Styles list.
- Click the Modify button (Style dialog box) to display the Modify Style dialog box.
- Click the Font Size box arrow (Modify Style dialog box) to display the Font Size list and then click 12 in the Font Size list to change the font size.
- Click the Double Space button to change the line spacing.
- Click the Format button to display the Format menu (Figure 2–41).

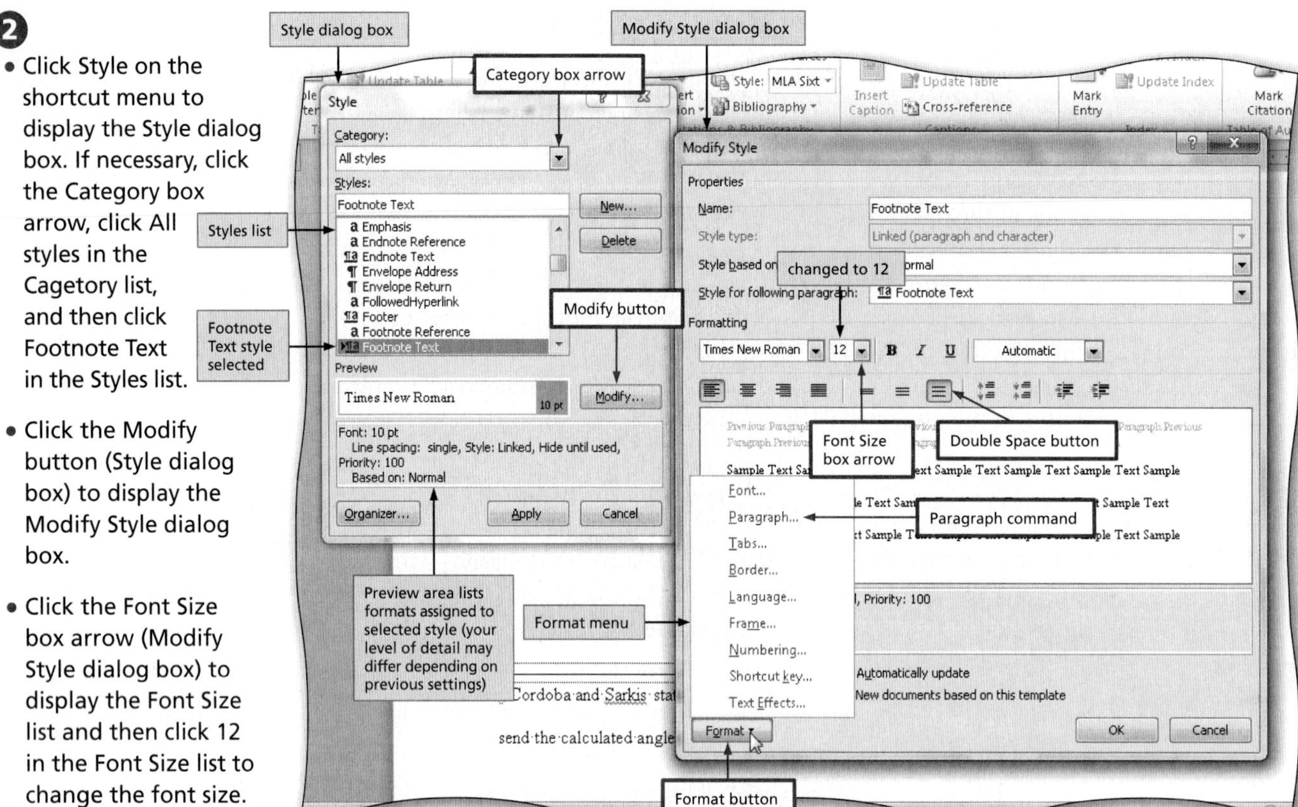

Figure 2–41

3

- Click Paragraph on the Format menu (Modify Style dialog box) to display the Paragraph dialog box.
- Click the Special box arrow (Paragraph dialog box) and then click First line (Figure 2–42).

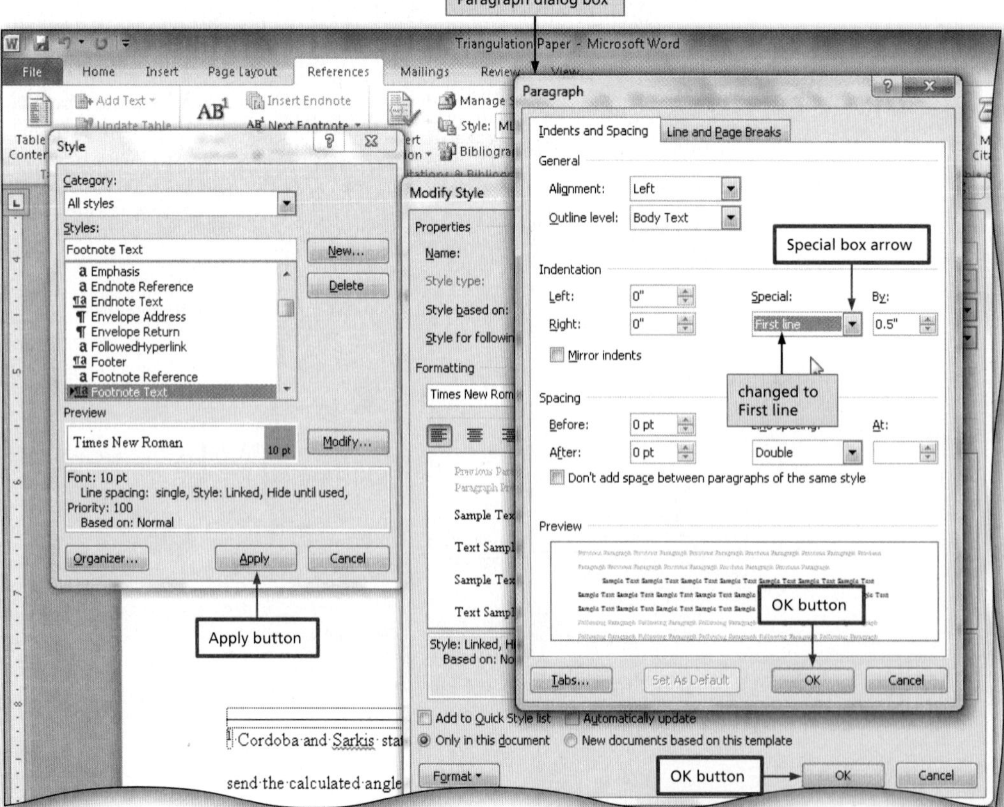

Figure 2–42

- Click the OK button (Paragraph dialog box) to close the dialog box.
- Click the OK button (Modify Style dialog box) to close the dialog box.
- Click the Apply button (Style dialog box) to apply the style changes to the footnote text (Figure 2–43).

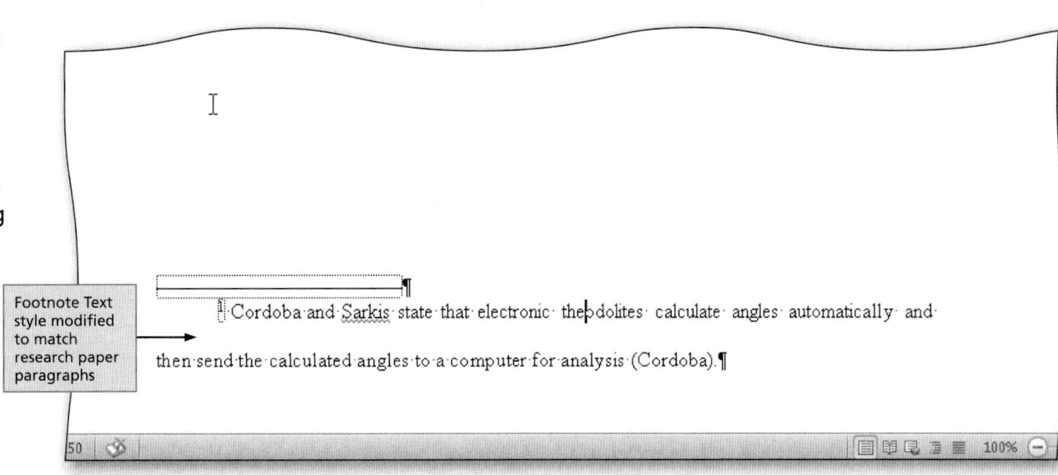

Footnote Text style modified to match research paper paragraphs
Cordoba and Sarkis state that electronic theodolites calculate angles automatically and
then send the calculated angles to a computer for analysis (Cordoba).¶

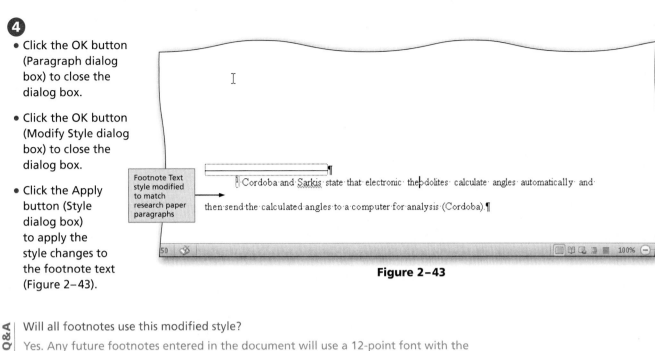

Figure 2–43

Q&A

Will all footnotes use this modified style?

Yes. Any future footnotes entered in the document will use a 12-point font with the paragraphs first-line indented and double-spaced.

Other Ways

1. Click Styles Dialog Box Launcher (Home tab | Styles group), point to style name in list, click style name box arrow, click Modify, change settings (Modify Style dialog box), click OK button
2. Click Styles Dialog Box Launcher (Home tab | Styles group), click Manage Styles button in task pane, select style name in list, click Modify button, change settings (Modify Style dialog box), click OK button in each dialog box

To Edit a Source

When you typed the footnote text for this research paper, you inserted a citation placeholder for the source. Assume you now have the source information and are ready to enter it. The following steps edit a source.

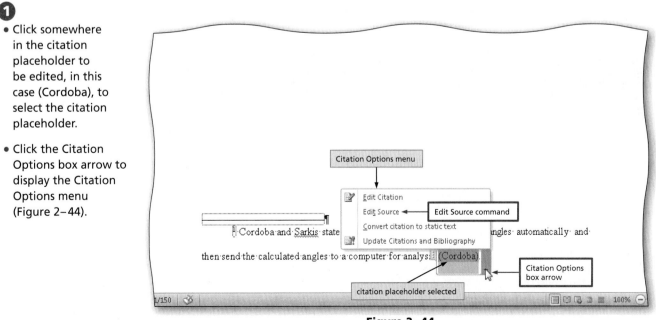

- Click somewhere in the citation placeholder to be edited, in this case (Cordoba), to select the citation placeholder.
- Click the Citation Options box arrow to display the Citation Options menu (Figure 2–44).

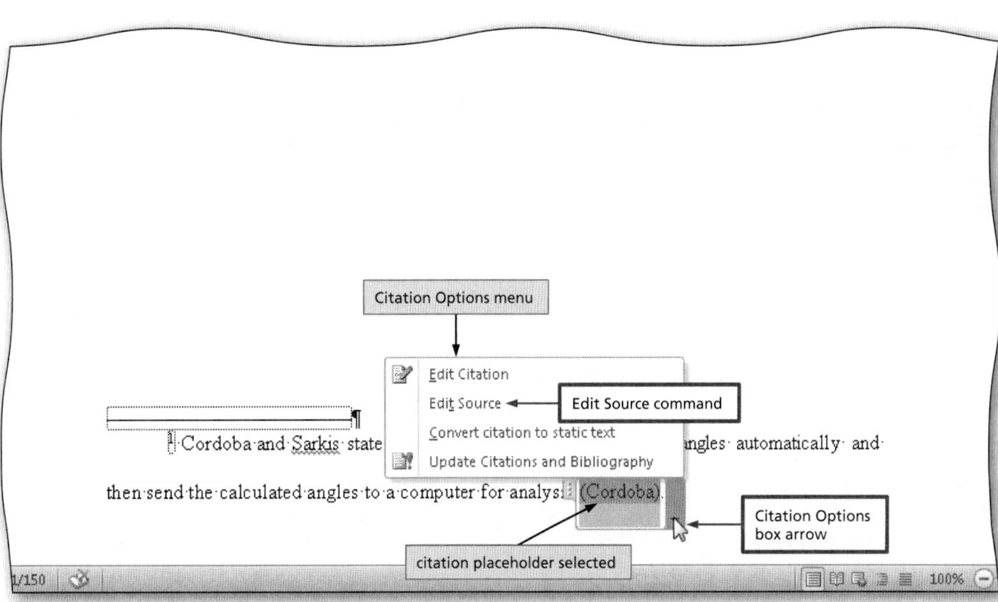

Figure 2–44

2

- Click Edit Source on the Citation Options menu to display the Edit Source dialog box.
- If necessary, click the Type of Source box arrow (Edit Source dialog box) and then click Book, so that the list shows fields required for a book.
- Click the Author text box. Type `Cordoba, Nicolas E.,; Sarkis, Kara A.` as the author.

Q&A What if I do not know how to punctuate the author entry so that Word formats it properly?

Click the Edit button (Edit Source dialog box) to the right of the Author entry for assistance. For example, you should separate multiple author names with a semicolon as shown in this figure.

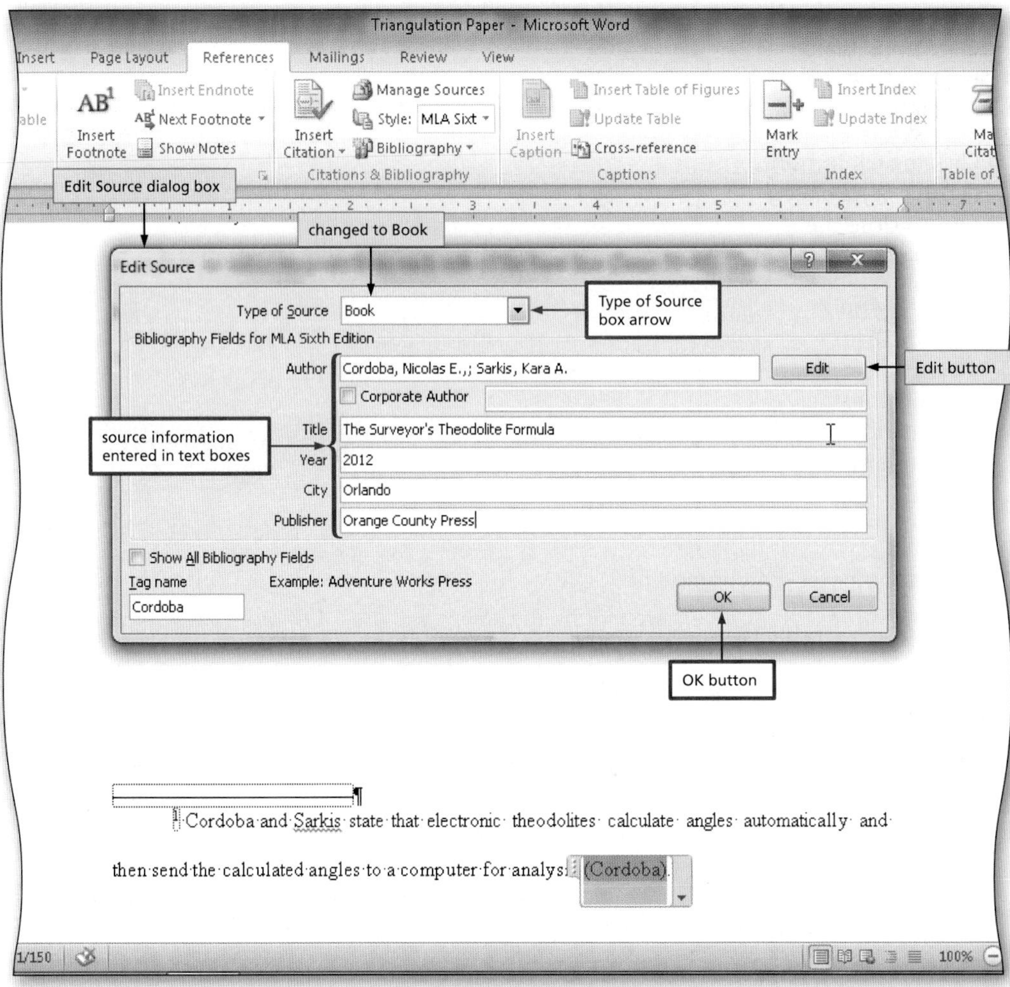

Figure 2–45

- Click the Title text box. Type `The Surveyor's Theodolite Formula` as the book title.
- Press the TAB key and then type `2012` as the year.
- Press the TAB key and then type `Orlando` as the city.
- Press the TAB key and then type `Orange County Press` as the publisher (Figure 2–45).

3

- Click the OK button to close the dialog box and create the source.

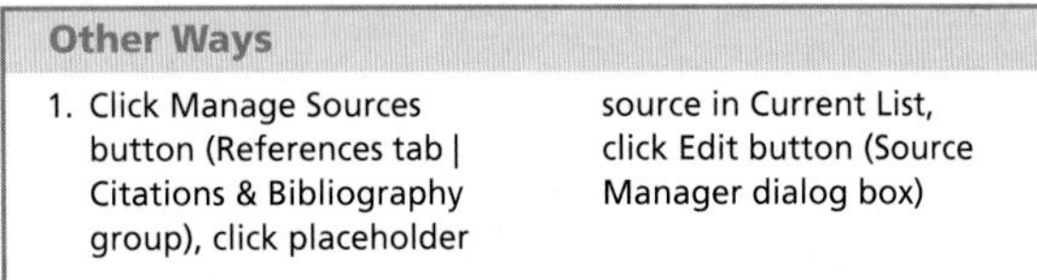

Other Ways

1. Click Manage Sources button (References tab | Citations & Bibliography group), click placeholder source in Current List, click Edit button (Source Manager dialog box)

BTW

Q&As

For a complete list of the Q&As found in many of the step-by-step sequences in this book, visit the Word 2010 Q&A Web page (scsite.com/wd2010/qa).

To Edit a Citation

In the MLA documentation style, if you reference the author's name in the text, you should not list it again in the parenthetical citation. Instead, just list the page number in the citation. To do this, you instruct Word to suppress author and title. The following steps edit the citation, suppressing the author and title but displaying the page numbers.

1. If necessary, click somewhere in the citation to be edited, in this case (Cordoba), to select the citation and display the Citation Options box arrow.
2. Click the Citation Options box arrow to display the Citation Options menu.
3. Click Edit Citation on the Citation Options menu to display the Edit Citation dialog box.
4. Type 25 in the Pages text box (Edit Citation dialog box).
5. Click the Author check box to place a check mark in it.
6. Click the Title check box to place a check mark in it (Figure 2–46).
7. Click the OK button to close the dialog box, remove the author name from the citation in the footnote, suppress the title from showing, and add a page number to the citation (shown in Figure 2-47 on page WD 101).

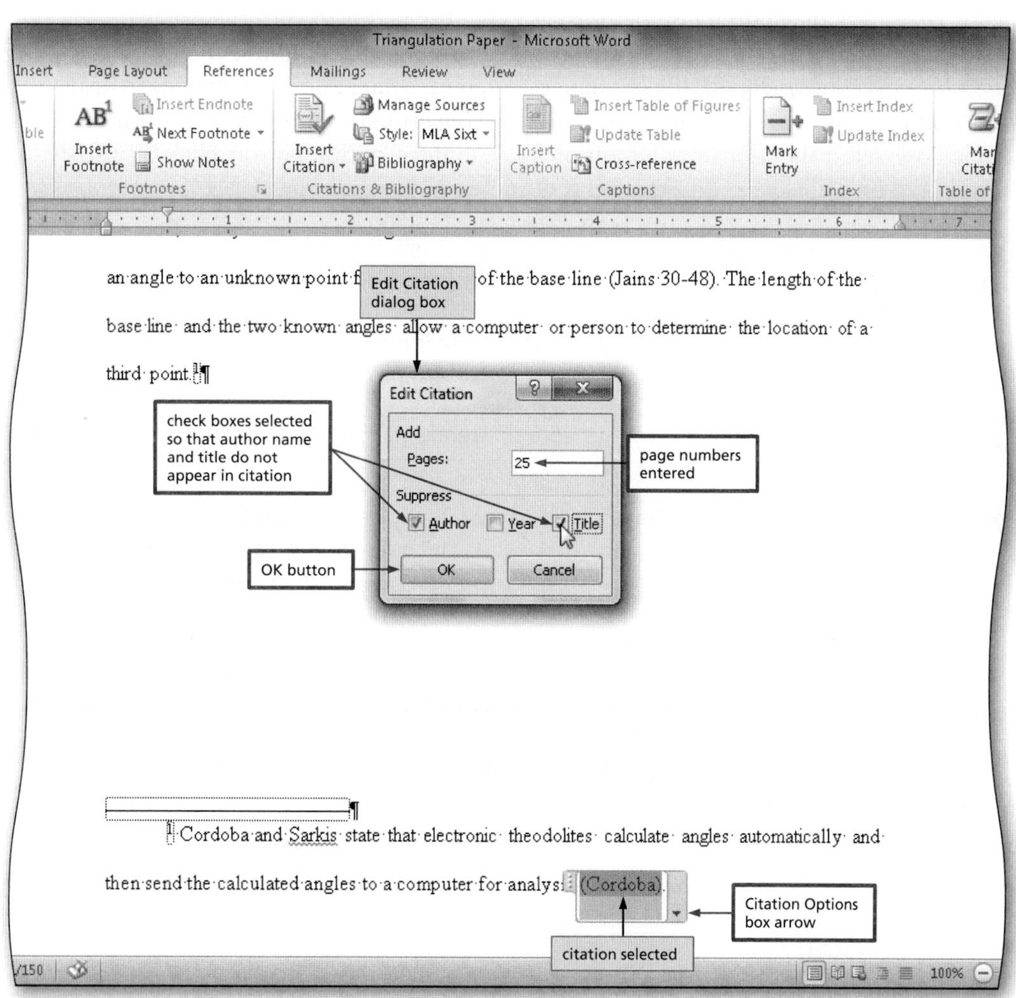

Figure 2–46

BTW

Footnote and Endnote Location
You can change the location of footnotes from the bottom of the page to the end of the text by clicking the Footnotes and Endnote Dialog Box Launcher (References tab | Footnotes group), clicking the Footnotes box arrow (Footnote and Endnote dialog box), and then clicking Below text. Similarly, clicking the Endnotes box arrow (Footnote and Endnote dialog box) enables you to change the location of endnotes from the end of the document to the end of a section. If you wanted to print just the footnotes or endnotes, you could position them at the end of the document on a separate page and then print that page.

BTW

Sending Footnotes or Endnotes to a PowerPoint Presentation
If you wanted footnotes and endnotes, or other headings, to be presented in a PowerPoint slide show, you would perform the following steps. Click the Customize Quick Access Toolbar button on the Quick Access Toolbar. Click More Commands on the Customize Quick Access Toolbar menu. Click the 'Choose commands from' box arrow (Word Options dialog box) and then click All Commands in the list. Scroll through the list of commands and then click Send to Microsoft PowerPoint to select the command. Click the Add button to add the selected command to the Customize Quick Access Toolbar list. Click the OK button to add the button to the Quick Access Toolbar. Then, click the Send to Microsoft PowerPoint button on the Quick Access Toolbar to create a PowerPoint presentation containing the endnotes and footnotes (it may also contain a few additional headings, which you can delete as needed).

Working with Footnotes and Endnotes

You edit footnote text just as you edit any other text in the document. To delete or move a note reference mark, however, the insertion point must be in the document text (not in the footnote text).

To delete a note, select the note reference mark in the document text (not in the footnote text) by dragging through the note reference mark and then click the Cut button (Home tab | Clipboard group). Or, click immediately to the right of the note reference mark in the document text and then press the BACKSPACE key twice, or click immediately to the left of the note reference mark in the document text and then press the DELETE key twice.

To move a note to a different location in a document, select the note reference mark in the document text (not in the footnote text), click the Cut button (Home tab | Clipboard group), click the location where you want to move the note, and then click the Paste button (Home tab | Clipboard group). When you move or delete notes, Word automatically renumbers any remaining notes in the correct sequence.

If you position the mouse pointer on the note reference mark in the document text, the note text is displayed above the note reference mark as a ScreenTip. To remove the ScreenTip, move the mouse pointer.

If, for some reason, you wanted to change the format of note reference marks in footnotes or endnotes (i.e., from 1, 2, 3, to A, B, C), you would click the Footnote & Endnote Dialog Box Launcher (References tab | Footnotes group) to display the Footnote and Endnote dialog box, click the Number format box arrow (Footnote and Endnote dialog box), click the desired number format in the list, and then click the Apply button.

If, for some reason, you wanted to convert footnotes to endnotes, you would click the Footnote & Endnote Dialog Box Launcher (References tab | Footnotes group) to display the Footnote and Endnote dialog box, click the Convert button (Footnote and Endnote dialog box), select the 'Convert all footnotes to endnotes' option button, click the OK button, and then click the Close button (Footnote and Endnote dialog box).

To Enter More Text

The next step is to continue typing text in the body of the research paper. The following steps enter this text.

1. Position the insertion point after the note reference mark in the document and then press the ENTER key.
2. Type the third paragraph of the research paper (Figure 2–47): `Similarly, the Nintendo Wii console uses triangulation to determine the location of a Wii Remote. A player places a sensor bar, which contains two infrared transmitters, near or on top of a television. While the player uses the Wii Remote, the Wii console determines the remote's location by calculating the distance and angles between the Wii Remote and the two transmitters on the sensor bar. Determining the location of a Wii Remote is relatively simple because the sensor bar contains only two fixed points: the transmitters.`

To Count Words

Often when you write papers, you are required to compose the papers with a minimum number of words. The minimum requirement for the research paper in this chapter is 325 words. You can look on the status bar and see the total number of words thus far in a document. For example, Figure 2–47 shows the research paper has 236 words, but you are not sure if that count includes the words in your footnote. The following steps display the Word Count dialog box, so that you can verify the footnote text is included in the count.

1

- Click the Word Count indicator on the status bar to display the Word Count dialog box.
- If necessary, place a check mark in the 'Include textboxes, footnotes and endnotes' check box (Word Count dialog box) (Figure 2–47).

Q&A Why do the statistics in my Word Count dialog box differ from Figure 2–47?

Depending on the accuracy of your typing, your statistics may differ.

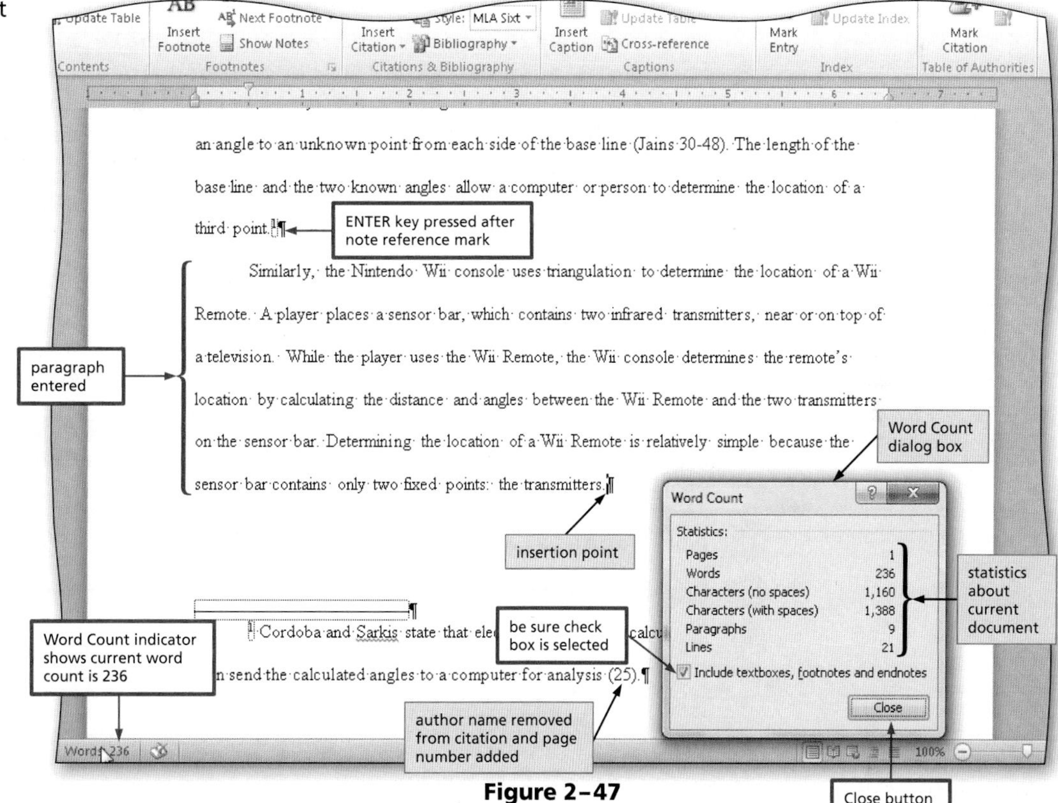

Figure 2–47

2

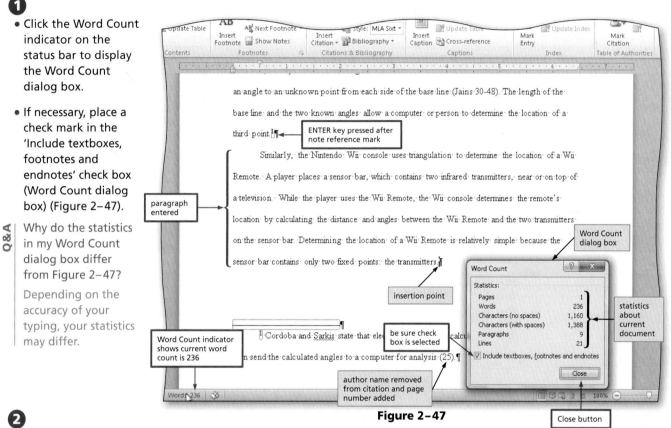

- Click the Close button to close the dialog box.

Q&A Can I display statistics for just a section of the document?

Yes. Select the section and then click the Word Count indicator on the status bar to display statistics about the selected text.

Other Ways

1. Click Word Count button (Review tab | Proofing group)
2. Press CTRL+SHIFT+G

Automatic Page Breaks

As you type documents that exceed one page, Word automatically inserts page breaks, called **automatic page breaks** or **soft page breaks**, when it determines the text has filled one page according to paper size, margin settings, line spacing, and other settings. If you add text, delete text, or modify text on a page, Word recomputes the location of automatic page breaks and adjusts them accordingly.

Word performs page recomputation between the keystrokes, that is, in between the pauses in your typing. Thus, Word refers to the automatic page break task as **background repagination**. The steps on the next page illustrate Word's automatic page break feature.

To Enter More Text and Insert a Citation Placeholder

The next task is to type the fourth paragraph in the body of the research paper. The following steps enter this text and a placeholder.

1. With the insertion point positioned at the end of the third paragraph as shown in Figure 2–47 on the previous page, press the ENTER key.

2. Type the fourth paragraph of the research paper (Figure 2–48): **`A more complex application of triangulation occurs in a global positioning system (GPS). A GPS consists of one or more earth-based receivers that accept and analyze signals sent by satellites to determine a receiver's geographic location. GPS receivers, found in handheld navigation devices and many vehicles, use triangulation to determine their location relative to at least three geostationary satellites. According to Sanders, the satellites are the fixed points in the triangulation formula`** and then press the SPACEBAR.

BTW **Page Break Locations** As you type, your page break may occur at different locations depending on Word settings and the type of printer connected to the computer.

Q&A Why does the text move from the second page to the first page as I am typing?

Word, by default, will not allow the first line of a paragraph to be by itself at the bottom of a page (an orphan) or the last line of a paragraph to be by itself at the top of a page (a widow). As you type, Word adjusts the placement of the paragraph to avoid orphans and widows.

3. Click the Insert Citation button (References tab | Citations & Bibliography group) to display the Insert Citation menu. Click Add New Placeholder on the Insert Citation menu to display the Placeholder Name dialog box.

4. Type **`Sanders`** as the tag name for the source.

5. Click the OK button to close the dialog box and insert the tag name in the citation placeholder.

6. Press the PERIOD key to end the sentence.

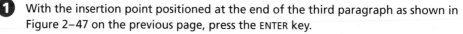

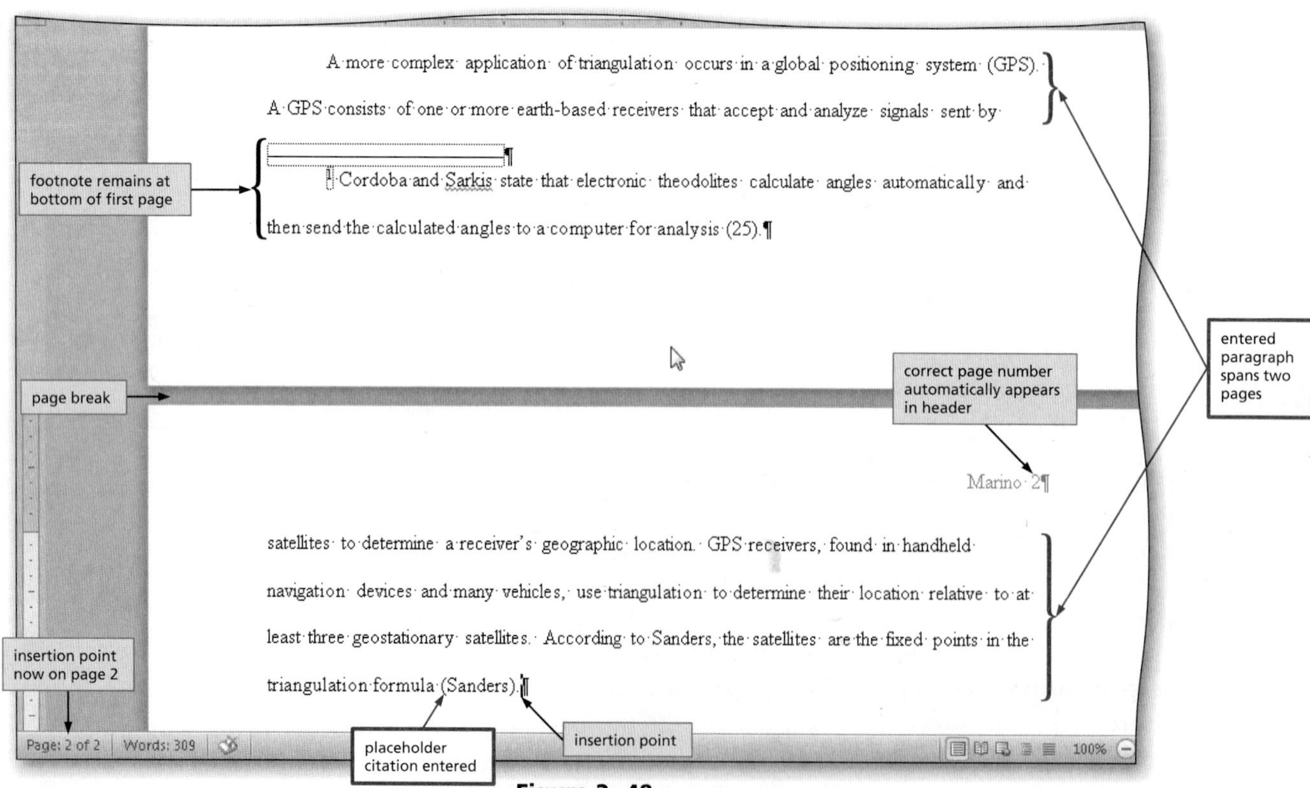
A more complex application of triangulation occurs in a global positioning system (GPS).
A GPS consists of one or more earth-based receivers that accept and analyze signals sent by
Cordoba and Sarkis state that electronic theodolites calculate angles automatically and
then send the calculated angles to a computer for analysis (25).
footnote remains at bottom of first page
page break
correct page number automatically appears in header
entered paragraph spans two pages
Marino 2
satellites to determine a receiver's geographic location. GPS receivers, found in handheld
navigation devices and many vehicles, use triangulation to determine their location relative to at
least three geostationary satellites. According to Sanders, the satellites are the fixed points in the
triangulation formula (Sanders).
insertion point now on page 2
Page: 2 of 2
Words: 309
placeholder citation entered
insertion point
100%

Figure 2–48

To Edit a Source

When you typed the fourth paragraph of the research paper, you inserted a citation placeholder, Sanders, for the source. You now have the source information, which is for a Web site, and are ready to enter it. The following steps edit the source for the Sanders citation placeholder.

1. Click somewhere in the citation placeholder to be edited, in this case (Sanders), to select the citation placeholder.
2. Click the Citation Options box arrow to display the Citation Options menu.
3. Click Edit Source on the Citation Options menu to display the Edit Source dialog box.
4. If necessary, click the Type of Source box arrow (Edit Source dialog box); scroll to and then click Web site, so that the list shows fields required for a Web site.
5. Place a check mark in the Show All Bibliography Fields check box to display more fields related to Web sites.
6. Click the Author text box. Type `Sanders, Gregory B.` as the author.
7. Click the Name of Web Page text box. Type `Understanding Satellites and Global Positioning Systems` as the Web page name.
8. Click the Production Company text box. Type `Course Technology` as the production company.
9. Click the Year Accessed text box. Type `2012` as the year accessed.
10. Press the TAB key and then type `Feb.` as the month accessed.

Q&A What if some of the text boxes disappear as I enter the Web site fields?

With the Show All Bibliography Fields check box selected, the dialog box may not be able to display all Web site fields at the same time. In this case, some may scroll up.

11. Press the TAB key and then type `27` as the day accessed (Figure 2–49).

Q&A Do I need to enter a Web address (URL)?

The latest MLA documentation style update does not require the Web address in the source.

12. Click the OK button to close the dialog box and create the source.

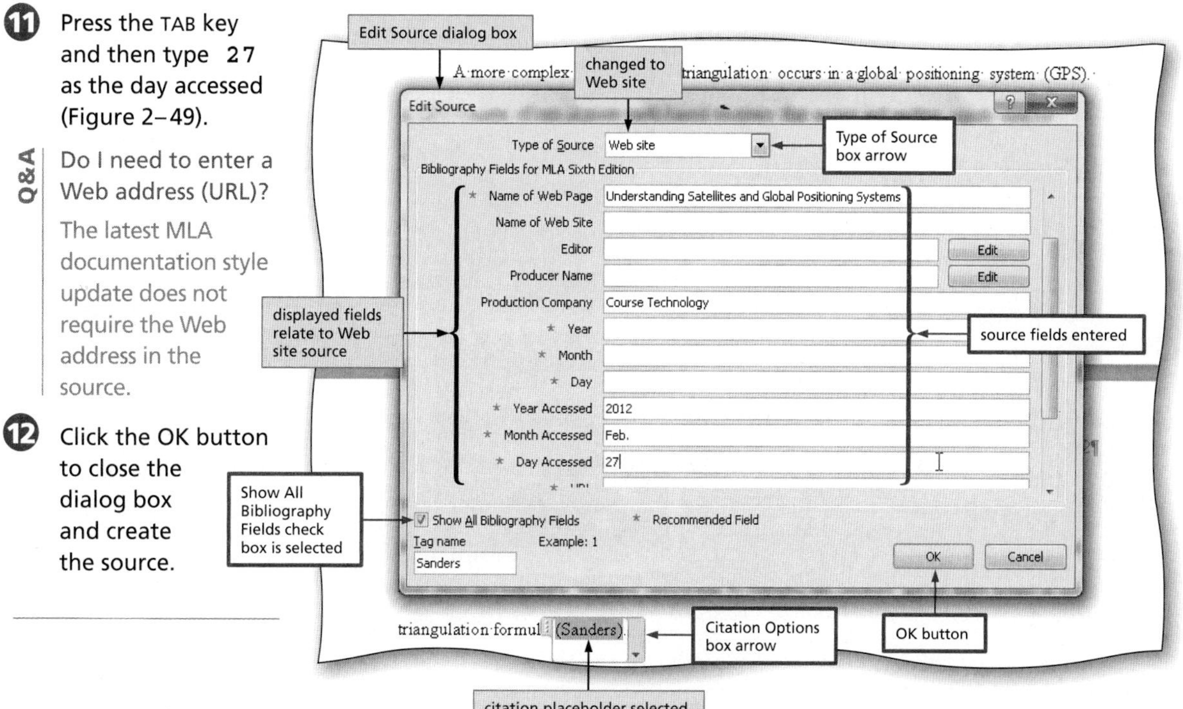

Figure 2–49

To Edit a Citation

As mentioned earlier, if you reference the author's name in the text, you should not list it again in the parenthetical citation. For Web site citations, when you suppress the author's name, the citation shows the Web site name because page numbers do not apply. The following steps edit the citation, suppressing the author and displaying the name of the Web site instead.

1. If necessary, click somewhere in the citation to be edited, in this case (Sanders), to select the citation and display the Citation Options box arrow.
2. Click the Citation Options box arrow and then click Edit Citation on the Citation Options menu to display the Edit Citation dialog box.
3. Click the Author check box (Edit Citation dialog box) to place a check mark in it (Figure 2–50).
4. Click the OK button to close the dialog box, remove the author name from the citation, and show the name of the Web site in the citation (shown in Figure 2–51).

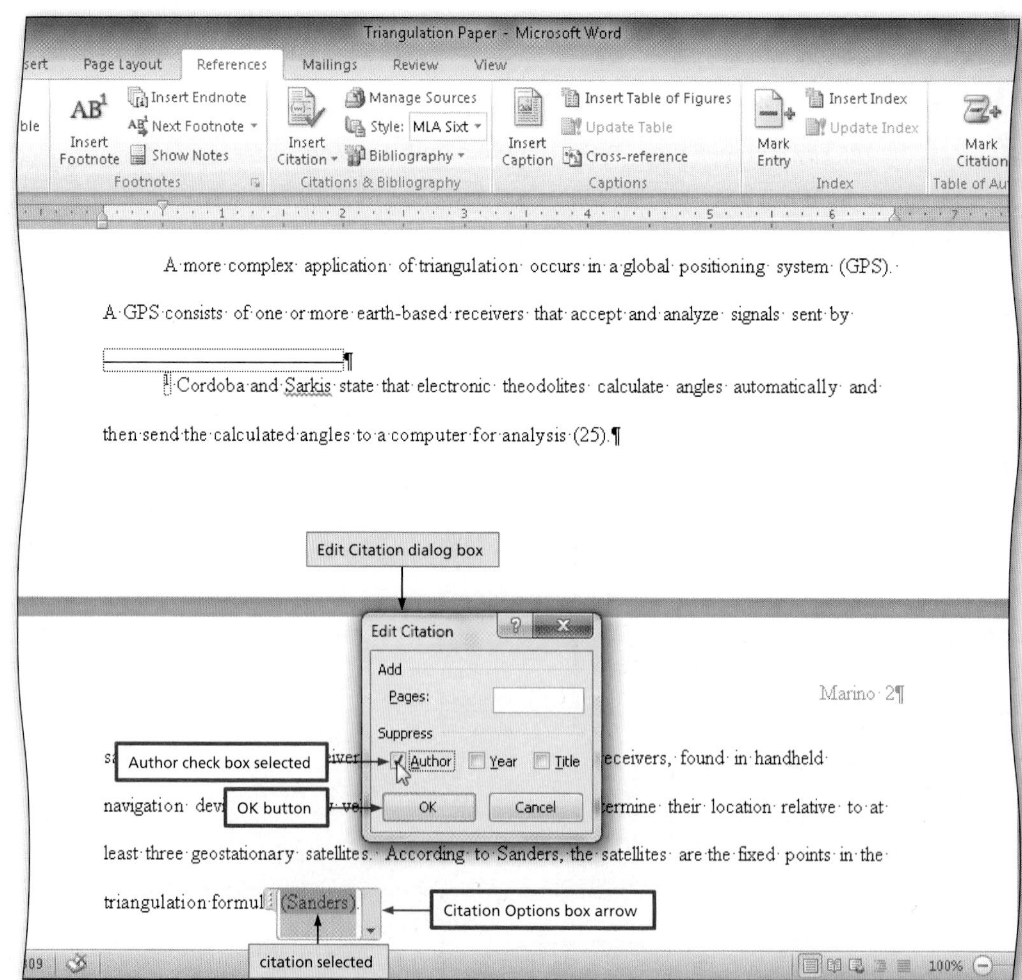

Figure 2–50

BTW

Certification
The Microsoft Office Specialist (MOS) program provides an opportunity for you to obtain a valuable industry credential — proof that you have the Word 2010 skills required by employers. For more information, visit the Word 2010 Certification Web page (scsite.com/wd2010/cert).

To Enter More Text

The next step is to type the last paragraph of text in the research paper. The following steps enter this text.

1. Press the END key to position the insertion point at the end of the fourth paragraph and then press the ENTER key.

2. Type the last paragraph of the research paper (Figure 2–51): **`The next time you pass a surveyor, play a Nintendo Wii, or follow a route prescribed by a vehicle's navigation system, keep in mind that none of it might have been possible without the concept of triangulation.`**

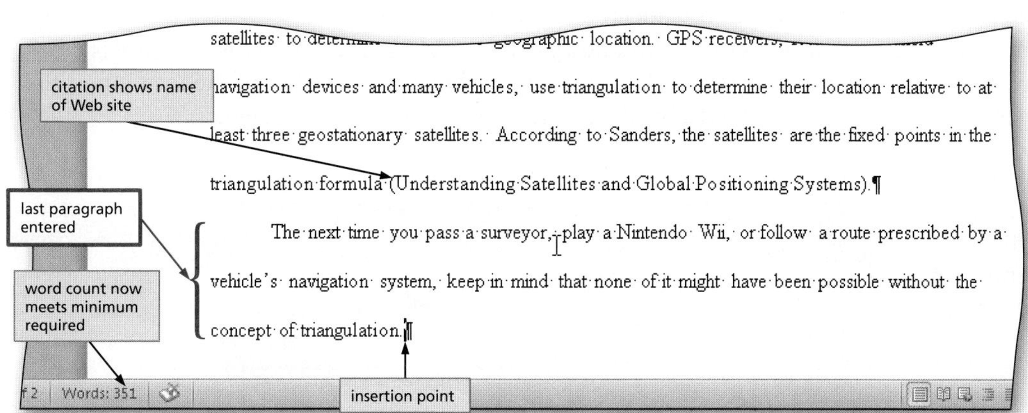

citation shows name of Web site
last paragraph entered
word count now meets minimum required
insertion point
Words: 351
navigation devices and many vehicles, use triangulation to determine their location relative to at least three geostationary satellites. According to Sanders, the satellites are the fixed points in the triangulation formula (Understanding Satellites and Global Positioning Systems).
The next time you pass a surveyor, play a Nintendo Wii, or follow a route prescribed by a vehicle's navigation system, keep in mind that none of it might have been possible without the concept of triangulation.

Figure 2–51

To Save an Existing Document with the Same File Name

You have made several modifications to the document since you last saved it. Thus, you should save it again. The following step saves the document again.

1. Click the Save button on the Quick Access Toolbar to overwrite the previously saved file.

Break Point: If you wish to take a break, this is a good place to do so. You can quit Word now (refer to page WD 125 for instructions). To resume at a later time, start Word (refer to page WD 70 for instructions), open the file called Triangulation Paper (refer to page WD 45 for instructions), and continue following the steps from this location forward.

Creating an Alphabetical Works Cited Page

According to the MLA documentation style, the **works cited page** is a list of sources that are referenced directly in a research paper. You place the list on a separate numbered page with the title, Works Cited, centered one inch from the top margin. The works are to be alphabetized by the author's last name or, if the work has no author, by the work's title. The first line of each entry begins at the left margin. Indent subsequent lines of the same entry one-half inch from the left margin.

Plan Ahead

Create the list of sources.
A **bibliography** is an alphabetical list of sources referenced in a paper. Whereas the text of the research paper contains brief references to the source (the citations), the bibliography lists all publication information about the source. Documentation styles differ significantly in their guidelines for preparing a bibliography. Each style identifies formats for various sources, including books, magazines, pamphlets, newspapers, Web sites, television programs, paintings, maps, advertisements, letters, memos, and much more. You can find information about various styles and their guidelines in printed style guides and on the Web.

To Page Break Manually

The works cited are to be displayed on a separate numbered page. Thus, you must insert a manual page break following the body of the research paper so that the list of sources is displayed on a separate page. A **manual page break**, or **hard page break**, is one that you force into the document at a specific location.

Word never moves or adjusts manual page breaks. Word, however, does adjust any automatic page breaks that follow a manual page break. Word inserts manual page breaks immediately above or to the left of the location of the insertion point. The following step inserts a manual page break after the text of the research paper.

1

- Verify that the insertion point is positioned at the end of the text of the research paper, as shown in Figure 2–51 on the previous page.
- Click Insert on the Ribbon to display the Insert tab.
- Click the Page Break button (Insert tab | Pages group) to insert a manual page break immediately to the left of the insertion point and position the insertion point immediately below the manual page break (Figure 2–52).

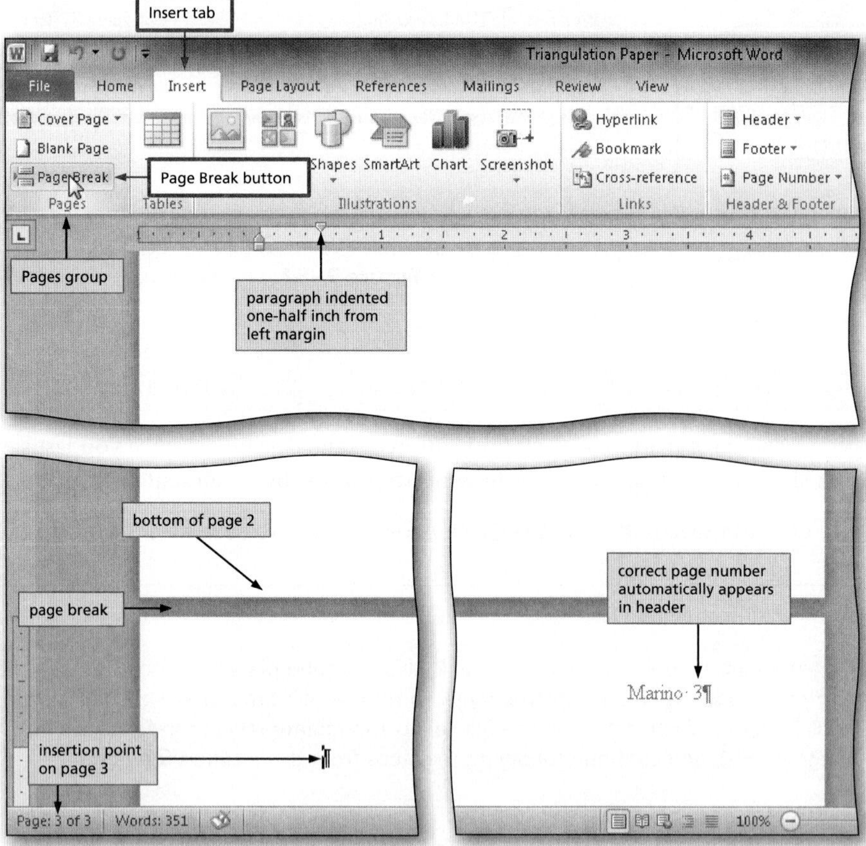

Figure 2–52

Other Ways

1. Press CTRL+ENTER

To Apply a Style

The works cited title is to be centered between the margins of the paper. If you simply issue the Center command, the title will not be centered properly. Instead, it will be one-half inch to the right of the center point because earlier you set the first-line indent for paragraphs to one-half inch.

To properly center the title of the works cited page, you could drag the First Line Indent marker back to the left margin before centering the paragraph, or you could apply the Normal style to the location of the insertion point. Recall that you modified the Normal style for this document to 12-point Times New Roman with double-spaced, left-aligned paragraphs that have no space after the paragraphs.

To apply a style to a paragraph, first position the insertion point in the paragraph and then apply the style. The following step applies the modified Normal style to the location of the insertion point.

1

- Click Home on the Ribbon to display the Home tab.
- With the insertion point on the paragraph mark at the top of page 3 (as shown in Figure 2–52) even if Normal is selected, click Normal in the Quick Style gallery (Home tab | Styles group) to apply the Normal style to the paragraph containing the insertion point (Figure 2–53).

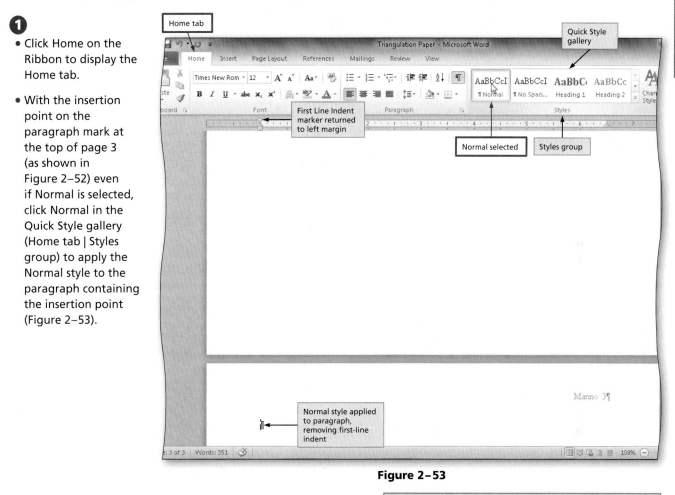

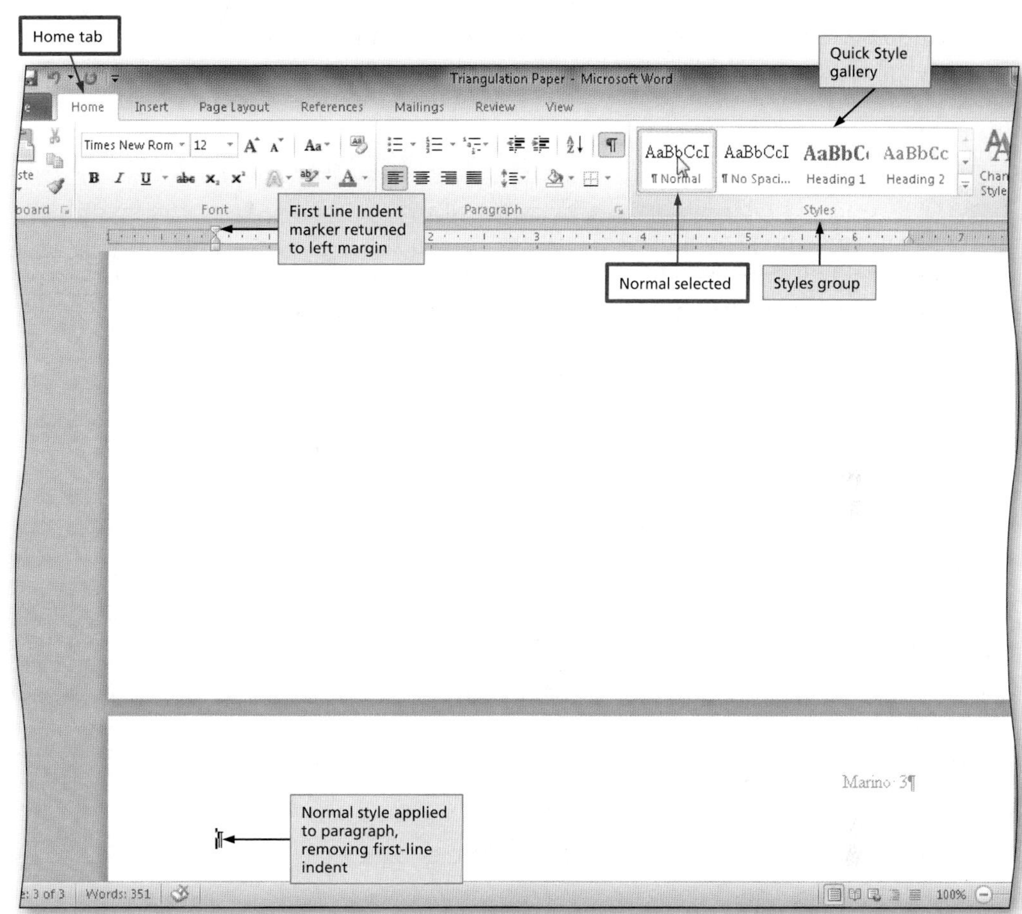

Figure 2–53

Other Ways

1. Click Styles Dialog Box Launcher (Home tab | Styles group), click desired style in Styles task pane
2. Press CTRL+SHIFT+S, click Style Name box arrow in Apply Styles task pane, click desired style in list

To Center Text

The next step is to enter the title, Works Cited, centered between the margins of the paper. The following steps use shortcut keys to format the title.

1. Press CTRL+E to center the paragraph mark.
2. Type **`Works Cited`** as the title.
3. Press the ENTER key.
4. Press CTRL+L to left-align the paragraph mark (shown in Figure 2–54 on the next page).

BTW

BTWs
For a complete list of the BTWs found in the margins of this book, visit the Word 2010 BTW Web page (scsite.com/wd2010/btw).

To Create the Bibliographical List

While typing the research paper, you created several citations and their sources. Word can format the list of sources and alphabetize them in a **bibliographical list**, saving you time looking up style guidelines. That is, Word will create a bibliographical list with each element of the source placed in its correct position with proper punctuation, according to the specified style. For example, in this research paper, the book source will list, in this order, the author name(s), book title, publisher city, publishing company name, and publication year with the correct punctuation between each element according to the MLA documentation style. The following steps create an MLA-styled bibliographical list from the sources previously entered.

- Click References on the Ribbon to display the References tab.
- With the insertion point positioned as shown in Figure 2–54, click the Bibliography button (References tab | Citations & Bibliography group) to display the Bibliography gallery (Figure 2–54).

Q&A Will I select the Works Cited option from the Bibliography gallery?

No. The title it inserts is not formatted according to the MLA documentation style. Thus, you will use the Insert Bibliography command instead.

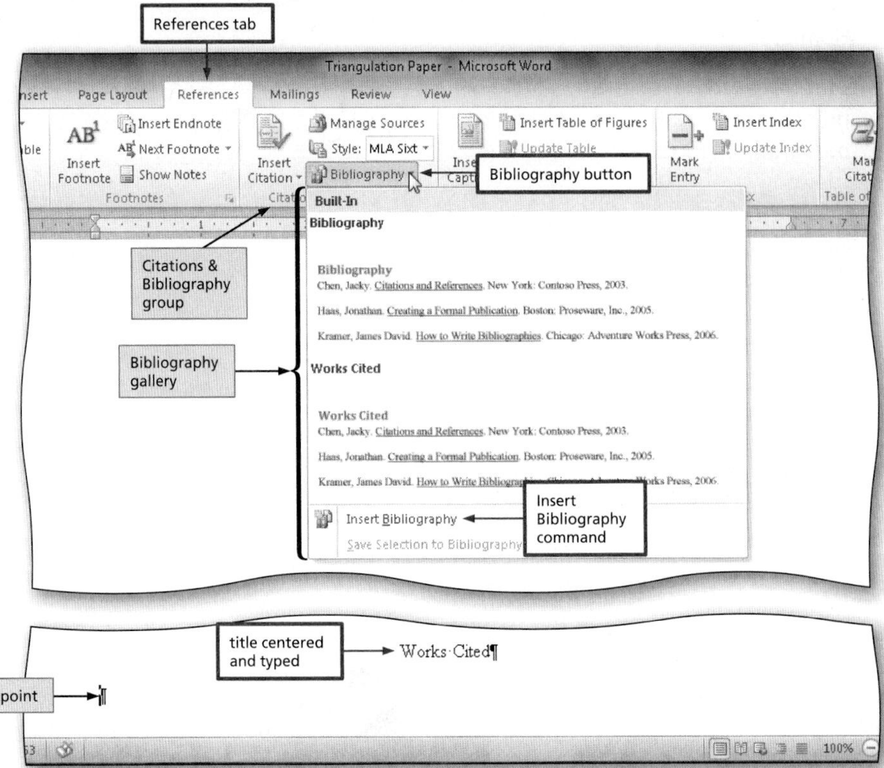

Figure 2–54

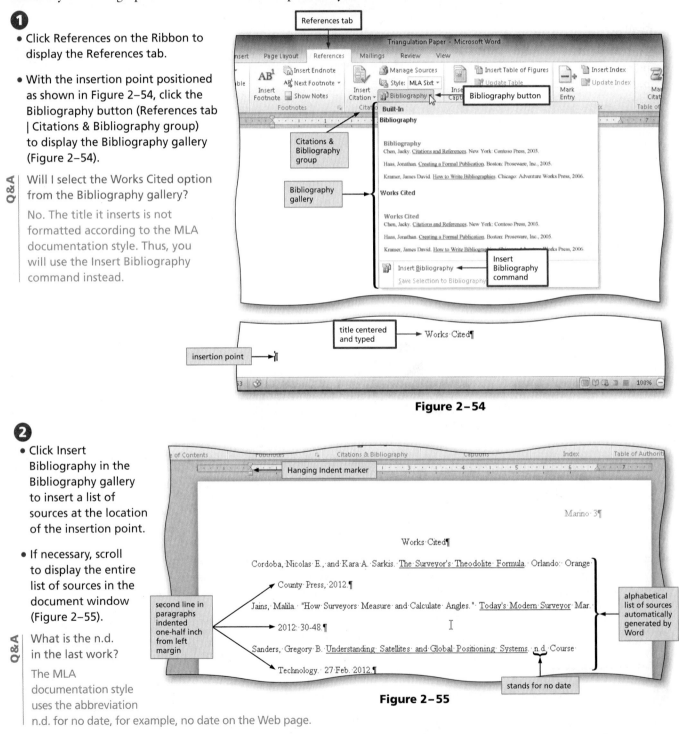

- Click Insert Bibliography in the Bibliography gallery to insert a list of sources at the location of the insertion point.
- If necessary, scroll to display the entire list of sources in the document window (Figure 2–55).

Q&A What is the n.d. in the last work?

The MLA documentation style uses the abbreviation n.d. for no date, for example, no date on the Web page.

Hanging Indent marker

Marino 3¶

Works Cited¶

Cordoba, Nicolas E., and Kara A. Sarkis. The Surveyor's Theodolite Formula. Orlando: Orange County Press, 2012.¶

Jains, Malila. "How Surveyors Measure and Calculate Angles." Today's Modern Surveyor Mar. 2012: 30-48.¶

Sanders, Gregory B. Understanding Satellites and Global Positioning Systems. n.d. Course Technology. 27 Feb. 2012.¶

second line in paragraphs indented one-half inch from left margin

alphabetical list of sources automatically generated by Word

stands for no date

Figure 2–55

To Format Paragraphs with a Hanging Indent

Notice in Figure 2–55 that the first line of each source entry begins at the left margin, and subsequent lines in the same paragraph are indented one-half inch from the left margin. In essence, the first line hangs to the left of the rest of the paragraph; thus, this type of paragraph formatting is called a **hanging indent**. The Bibliography style in Word automatically formats the works cited paragraphs with a hanging indent.

If you wanted to format paragraphs with a hanging indent, you would use one of the following techniques.

- With the insertion point in the paragraph to format, drag the **Hanging Indent marker** (the bottom triangle) on the ruler to the desired mark on the ruler (i.e., .5") to set the hanging indent at that location from the left margin.

or

- Right-click the paragraph to format, click Paragraph on shortcut menu, click Indents and Spacing tab (Paragraph dialog box), click Special box arrow, click Hanging, and then click the OK button.

or

- Click the Paragraph Dialog Box Launcher (Home tab or Page Layout tab | Paragraph group), click Indents and Spacing tab (Paragraph dialog box), click Special box arrow, click Hanging, and then click the OK button.

or

- With the insertion point in the paragraph to format, press CTRL+T.

To Modify a Source and Update the Bibliographical List

If you modify the contents of any source, the list of sources automatically updates because the list is a field. The following steps modify the title of the magazine article.

1

- Click the Manage Sources button (References tab | Citations & Bibliography group) to display the Source Manager dialog box.
- Click the source you wish to edit in the Current List, in this case the article by Jains, to select the source.
- Click the Edit button (Source Manager dialog box) to display the Edit Source dialog box.
- In the Title text box, insert the word, Distance, between the words, Measure and, in the title (Figure 2–56).

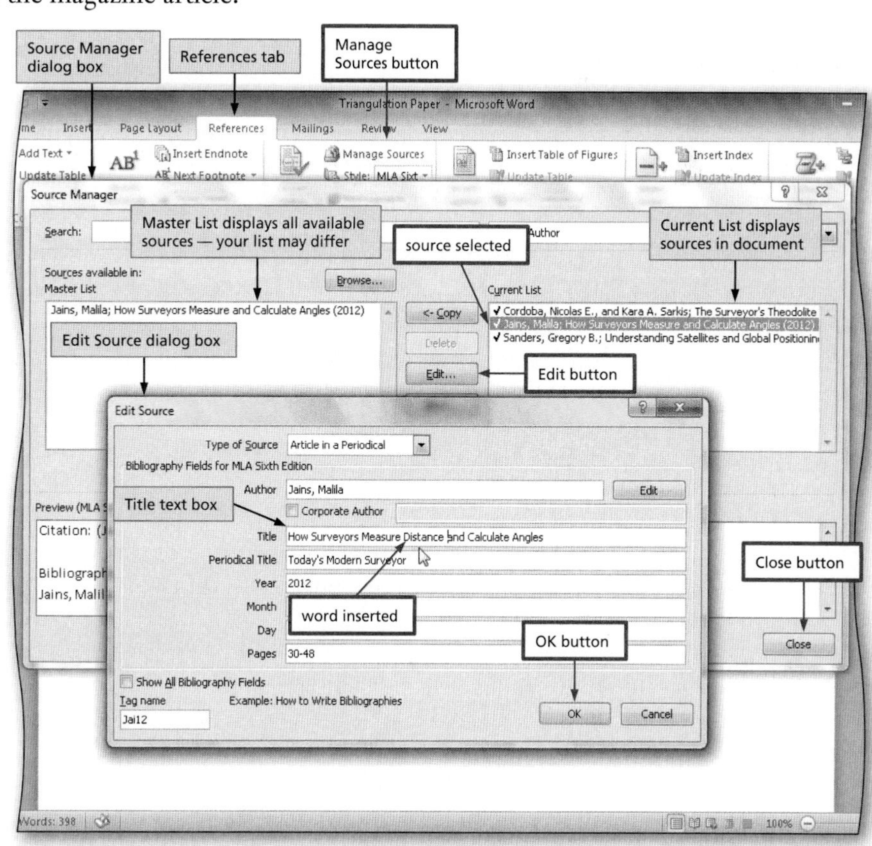

Figure 2–56

- Click the OK button (Edit Source dialog box) to close the dialog box.
- If a Microsoft Word dialog box appears, click its Yes button to update all occurrences of the source.
- Click the Close button (Source Manager dialog box) to update the list of sources in the document and close the dialog box (Figure 2–57).

Q&A What if the list of sources in the document is not updated automatically?

Click in the list of sources and then press the F9 key, which is the shortcut key to update a field.

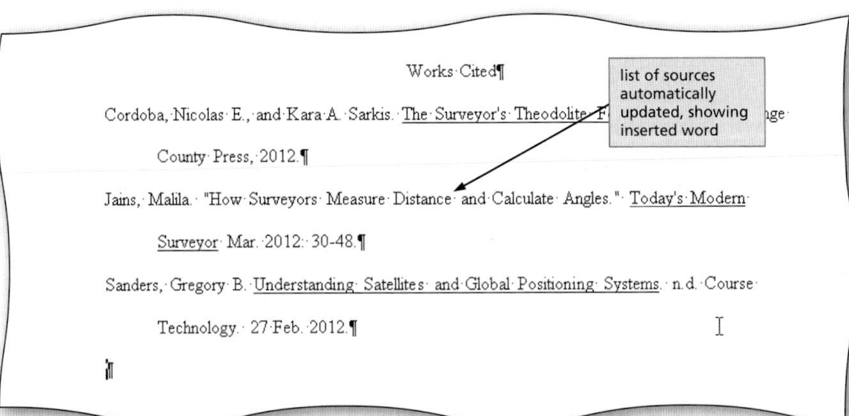

Figure 2–57

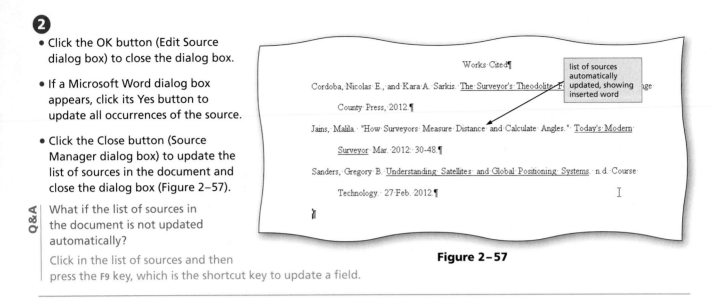

To Convert a Field to Regular Text

Word may use an earlier version of the MLA documentation style to format the bibliography. The latest guidelines for the MLA documentation style, for example, state that titles should be italicized instead of underlined, and each work should identify the source's publication medium (e.g., Print for printed media, Web for online media, etc.). If you format or add text to the bibliography, Word automatically will change it back to the Bibliography style's predetermined formats when the bibliography field is updated. To preserve modifications you make to the format of the bibliography, you can convert the bibliography field to regular text. Keep in mind, though, once you convert the field to regular text, it no longer is a field that can be updated. The following step converts a field to regular text.

- Click somewhere in the field to select it, in this case, somewhere in the bibliography (Figure 2–58).

Q&A What if the bibliography field is not shaded gray?

Click File on the Ribbon to open the Backstage view, click Options in the Backstage view, click Advanced in the left pane (Word Options dialog box), scroll to the 'Show document content' area, click the Field shading box arrow, click When selected, and then click the OK button.

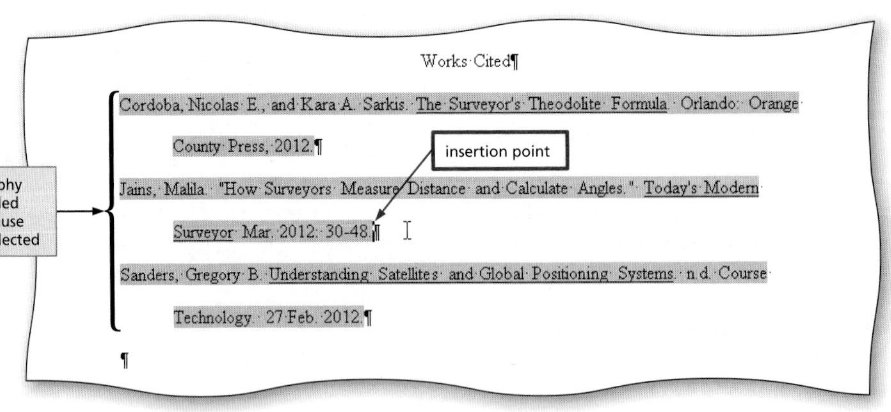

Figure 2–58

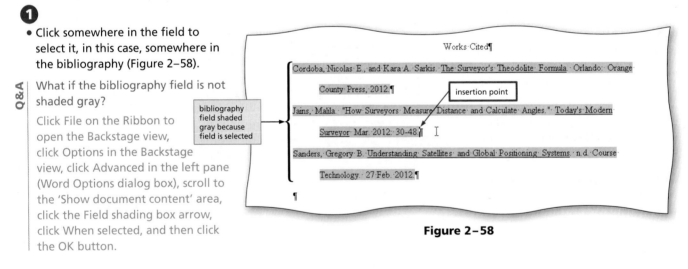

Q&A Why are all the words in the bibliography shaded?

The bibliography field consists of all text in the bibliography.

- Press CTRL+SHIFT+F9 to convert the selected field to regular text.

Q&A Why did the gray shading disappear?

The bibliography no longer is a field, so it is not shaded gray.

- Click anywhere in the document to remove the selection from the text.

To Format the Works Cited to the Latest MLA Documentation Style

As mentioned earlier, the latest the MLA documentation style guidelines state that titles should be italicized instead of underlined, and each work should identify the source's publication medium (e.g., Print, Web, Radio, Television, CD, DVD, Film, etc.). The following steps format and modify the Works Cited as specified by the latest MLA guidelines, if yours are not already formatted this way.

1. Drag through the book title, The Surveyor's Theodolite Formula, to select it.
2. Click Home on the Ribbon to display the Home tab. Click the Underline button (Home tab | Font group) to remove the underline from the selected text and then click the Italic button (Home tab | Font group) to italicize the selected text.
3. Select the magazine title, Today's Modern Surveyor. Remove the underline from the selected title and then italicize the selected title.
4. Select the Web page title, Understanding Satellites and Global Positioning Systems. Remove the underline from the selected title and then italicize the selected title.
5. After the period following the year in the first work, press the SPACEBAR and then type **Print.**
6. After the period following the page range in the second work, press the SPACEBAR and then type **Print.**
7. Before the date in the third work, type **Web.** and then press the SPACEBAR (Figure 2–59).

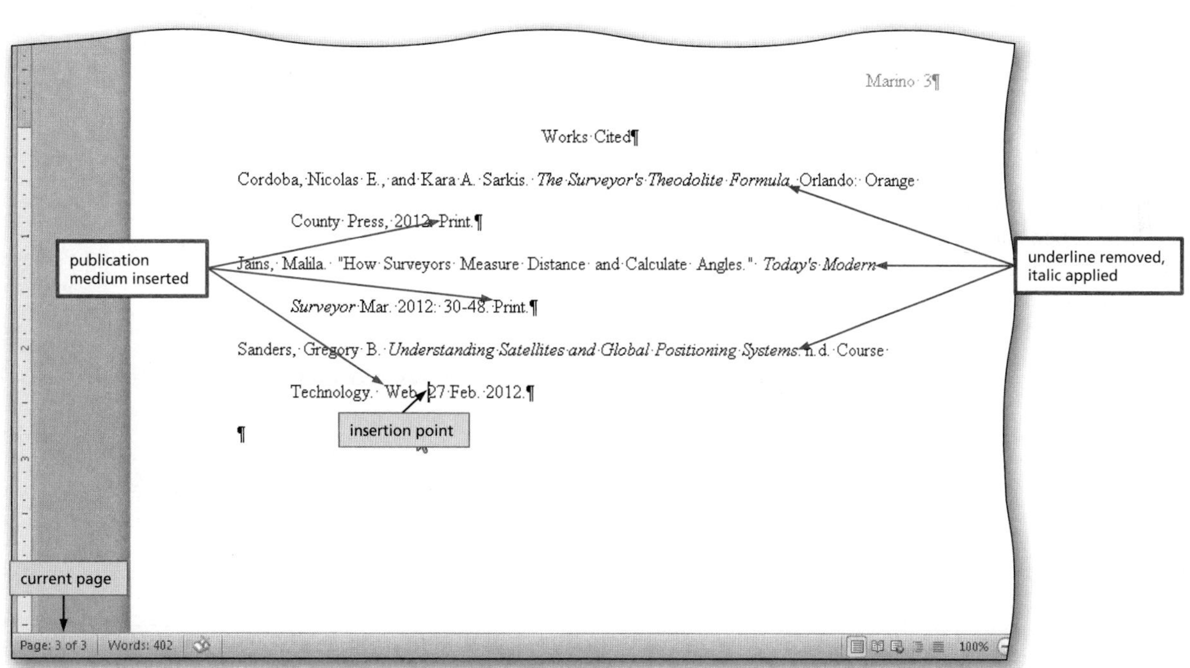

Figure 2–59

To Save an Existing Document with the Same File Name

You have made several modifications to the document since you last saved it. Thus, you should save it again. The following step saves the document again.

1. Click the Save button on the Quick Access Toolbar to overwrite the previously saved file.

Proofing and Revising the Research Paper

As discussed in Chapter 1, once you complete a document, you might find it necessary to make changes to it. Before submitting a paper to be graded, you should proofread it. While **proofreading**, look for grammatical errors and spelling errors. You also should ensure the transitions between sentences flow smoothly and the sentences themselves make sense.

Plan Ahead

Proofread and revise the paper.
As you proofread the paper, look for ways to improve it. Check all grammar, spelling, and punctuation. Be sure the text is logical and transitions are smooth. Where necessary, add text, delete text, reword text, and move text to different locations. Ask yourself these questions:

- Does the title suggest the topic?
- Is the thesis clear?
- Is the purpose of the paper clear?
- Does the paper have an introduction, body, and conclusion?
- Does each paragraph in the body relate to the thesis?
- Is the conclusion effective?
- Are all sources acknowledged?

To assist you with the proofreading effort, Word provides several tools. You can browse through pages, copy text, find text, replace text, insert a synonym, check spelling and grammar, and look up information. The following pages discuss these tools.

To Scroll Page by Page through a Document

The next step is to modify text on the second page of the paper. Currently, the third page is the active page (Figure 2–59 on the previous page). The following step scrolls up one page in the document.

1

- With the insertion point on the third page of the paper, click the Previous Page button on the vertical scroll bar to position the insertion point at the top of the previous page (Figure 2–60).

Q&A The button on my screen shows a ScreenTip different from Previous Page. Why?

By default, the functions of the buttons above and below the Select Browse Object button are Previous Page and Next Page, respectively. You can change the commands associated with these buttons by clicking the Select Browse Object button and then clicking the desired browse object. The Browse by Page command on the Select Browse Object menu, for example, changes the buttons back to Previous Page and Next Page.

Q&A How do I display the next page?

Click the Next Page button on the vertical scroll bar.

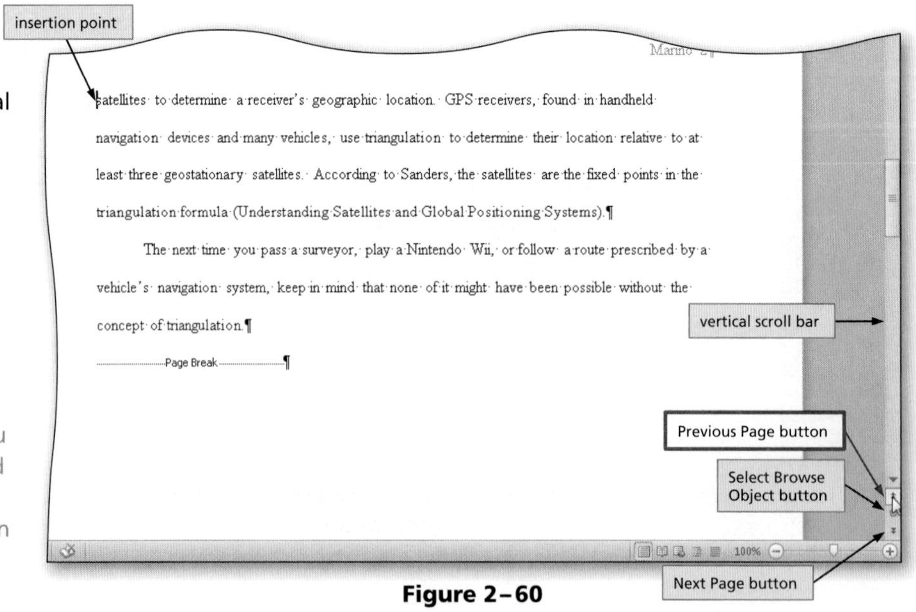

insertion point
Marino 2
satellites to determine a receiver's geographic location. GPS receivers, found in handheld navigation devices and many vehicles, use triangulation to determine their location relative to at least three geostationary satellites. According to Sanders, the satellites are the fixed points in the triangulation formula (Understanding Satellites and Global Positioning Systems).¶
The next time you pass a surveyor, play a Nintendo Wii, or follow a route prescribed by a vehicle's navigation system, keep in mind that none of it might have been possible without the concept of triangulation.¶
Page Break ¶
vertical scroll bar
Previous Page button
Select Browse Object button
Next Page button
100%

Figure 2–60

Other Ways

1. Click Page Number indicator on status bar, click Page in 'Go to what' list (Find and Replace dialog box), type desired page number in 'Enter page number' text box, click Go To button
2. Press CTRL+PAGE UP or CTRL+PAGE DOWN

Copying, Cutting, and Pasting

While proofreading the research paper, you decide it would read better if the word, geostationary, appeared in front of the word, satellites, in the last sentence of the fourth paragraph. You could type the word at the desired location, but because this is a difficult word to spell, you decide to use the Office Clipboard. The **Office Clipboard** is a temporary storage area that holds up to 24 items (text or graphics) copied from any Office program.

Copying is the process of placing items on the Office Clipboard, leaving the item in the document. **Cutting**, by contrast, removes the item from the document before placing it on the Office Clipboard. **Pasting** is the process of copying an item from the Office Clipboard into the document at the location of the insertion point.

To Copy and Paste

In the research paper, you copy a word from one sentence to another. The following steps copy and paste a word.

- Select the item to be copied (the word, geostationary, in this case).
- Click the Copy button (Home tab | Clipboard group) to copy the selected item in the document to the Office Clipboard (Figure 2–61).

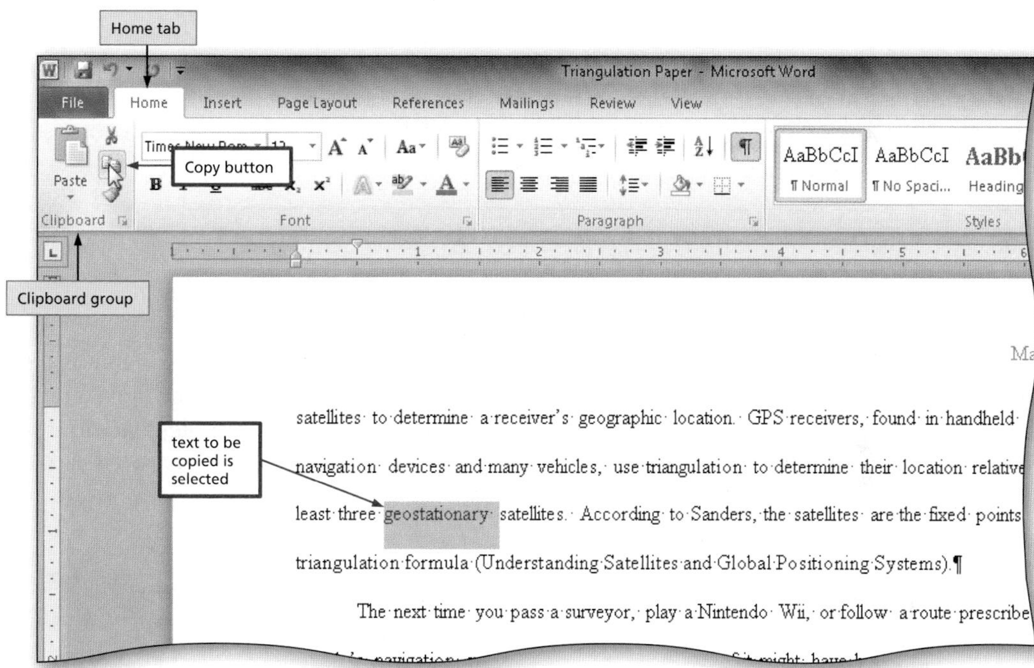
Home tab
Copy button
Clipboard group
text to be copied is selected
Triangulation Paper - Microsoft Word
satellites· to·determine· a·receiver's· geographic· location.· GPS·receivers,· found· in·handheld·
navigation· devices· and·many· vehicles,· use·triangulation· to·determine· their· location· relative
least· three· geostationary· satellites.· According· to·Sanders,·the· satellites· are·the·fixed· points
triangulation·formula·(Understanding·Satellites·and·Global·Positioning·Systems).¶
The·next·time· you·pass·a·surveyor,· play·a·Nintendo· Wii,· or·follow· a·route·prescribe

Figure 2–61

- Position the insertion point at the location where the item should be pasted (immediately to the left of the word, satellites, in this case) (Figure 2–62).

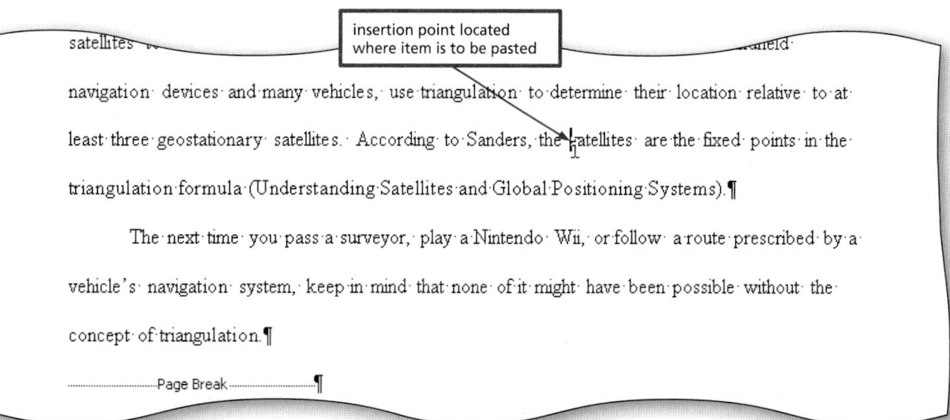
insertion point located where item is to be pasted
navigation· devices· and·many· vehicles,· use·triangulation· to·determine· their· location· relative· to·at·
least·three·geostationary· satellites.· According· to·Sanders,·the·satellites· are·the·fixed· points· in·the·
triangulation·formula·(Understanding·Satellites·and·Global·Positioning·Systems).¶
The·next·time· you·pass·a·surveyor,· play· a·Nintendo· Wii,· or·follow· a·route·prescribed·by·a·
vehicle's· navigation· system,· keep·in·mind· that·none· of·it·might· have·been·possible·without· the·
concept· of·triangulation.¶
Page Break ¶

Figure 2–62

- Click the Paste button (Home tab | Clipboard group) to paste the copied item in the document at the location of the insertion point (Figure 2–63).

Q&A
What if I click the Paste button arrow by mistake?

Click the Paste button arrow again to remove the Paste menu.

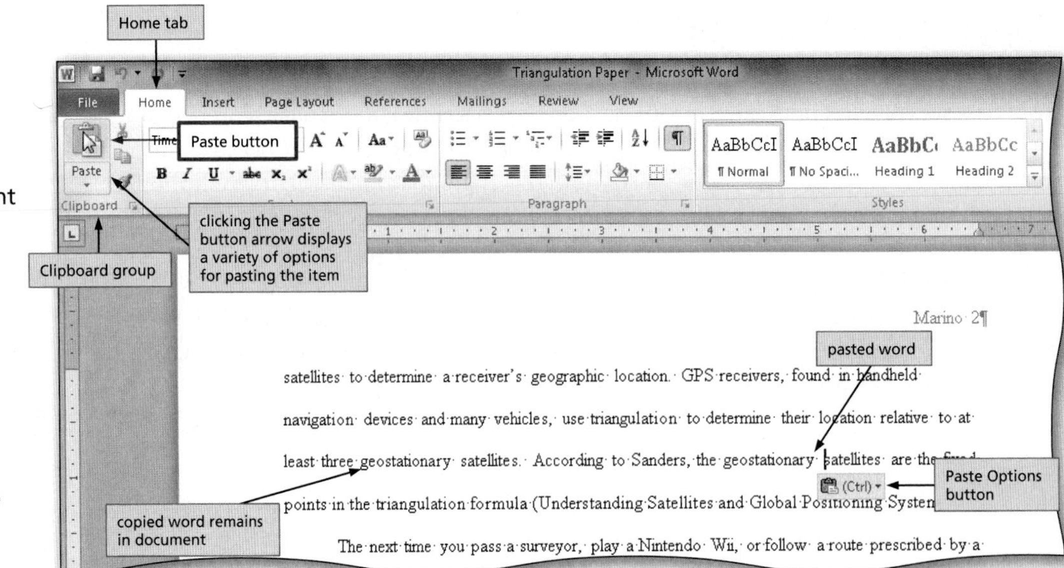

Figure 2–63

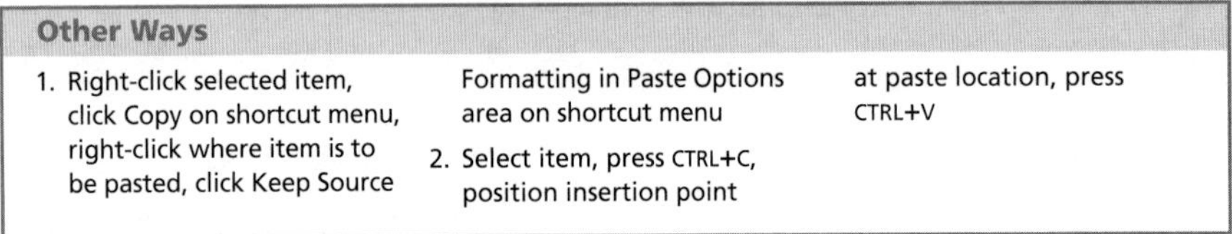

Other Ways

1. Right-click selected item, click Copy on shortcut menu, right-click where item is to be pasted, click Keep Source Formatting in Paste Options area on shortcut menu
2. Select item, press CTRL+C, position insertion point at paste location, press CTRL+V

To Display the Paste Options Menu

When you paste an item or move an item using drag-and-drop editing, which was discussed in the previous chapter, Word automatically displays a Paste Options button near the pasted or moved text (Figure 2–63). The Paste Options button allows you to change the format of a pasted item. For example, you can instruct Word to format the pasted item the same way as where it was copied, or format it the same way as where it is being pasted. The following steps display the Paste Options menu.

- Click the Paste Options button to display the Paste Options menu (Figure 2–64).

Q&A
What are the functions of the buttons on the Paste Options menu?

In general, the left button indicates the pasted item should look the same as it did in its original location. The second button formats the pasted text to match the rest of the item where it was pasted. The third button removes all formatting from the pasted item. The Set Default Paste command displays the Word Options dialog box. Keep in mind that the buttons shown on a Paste Options menu will vary, depending on the item being pasted.

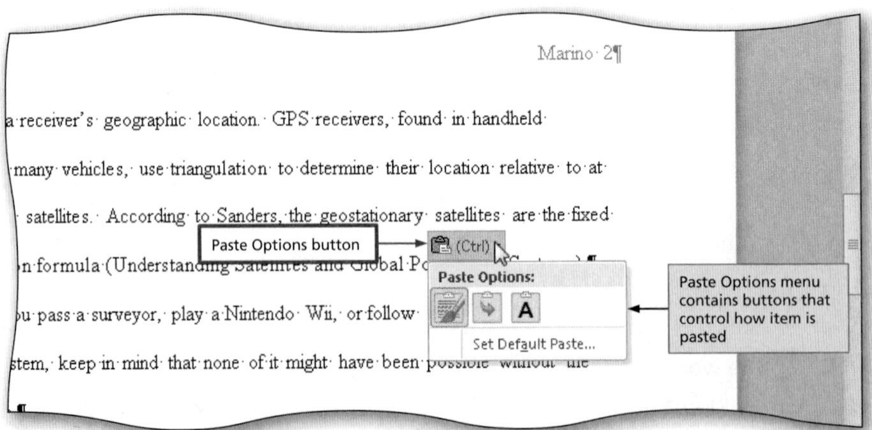

Figure 2–64

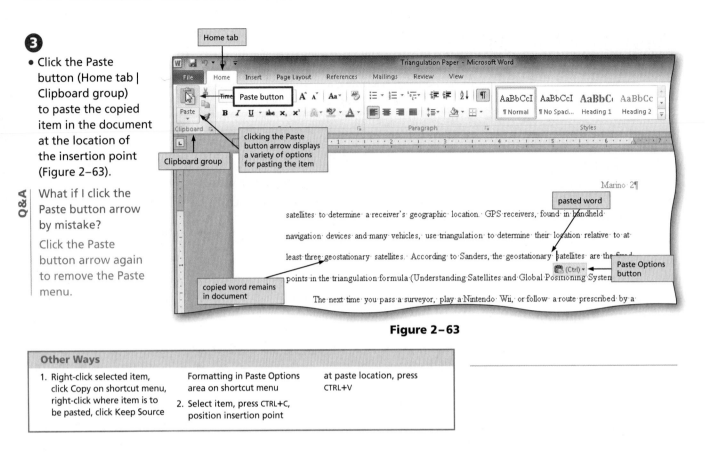

- Press the ESCAPE key to remove the Paste Options menu from the window.

To Find Text

While proofreading the paper, you would like to locate all occurrences of Wii console because you are contemplating changing this text to Wii game console. The following steps find all occurrences of specific text in a document.

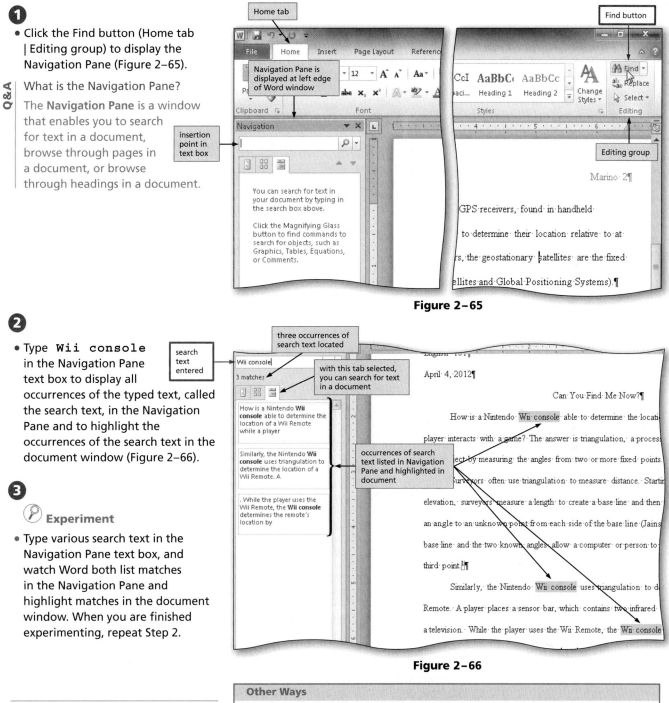

- Click the Find button (Home tab | Editing group) to display the Navigation Pane (Figure 2–65).

Q&A

What is the Navigation Pane?

The **Navigation Pane** is a window that enables you to search for text in a document, browse through pages in a document, or browse through headings in a document.

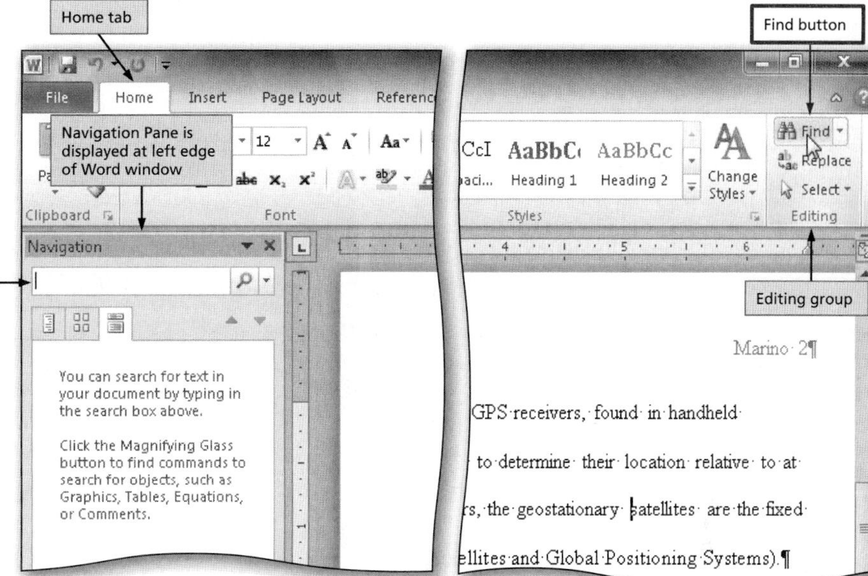

Figure 2–65

- Type **`Wii console`** in the Navigation Pane text box to display all occurrences of the typed text, called the search text, in the Navigation Pane and to highlight the occurrences of the search text in the document window (Figure 2–66).

Experiment

- Type various search text in the Navigation Pane text box, and watch Word both list matches in the Navigation Pane and highlight matches in the document window. When you are finished experimenting, repeat Step 2.

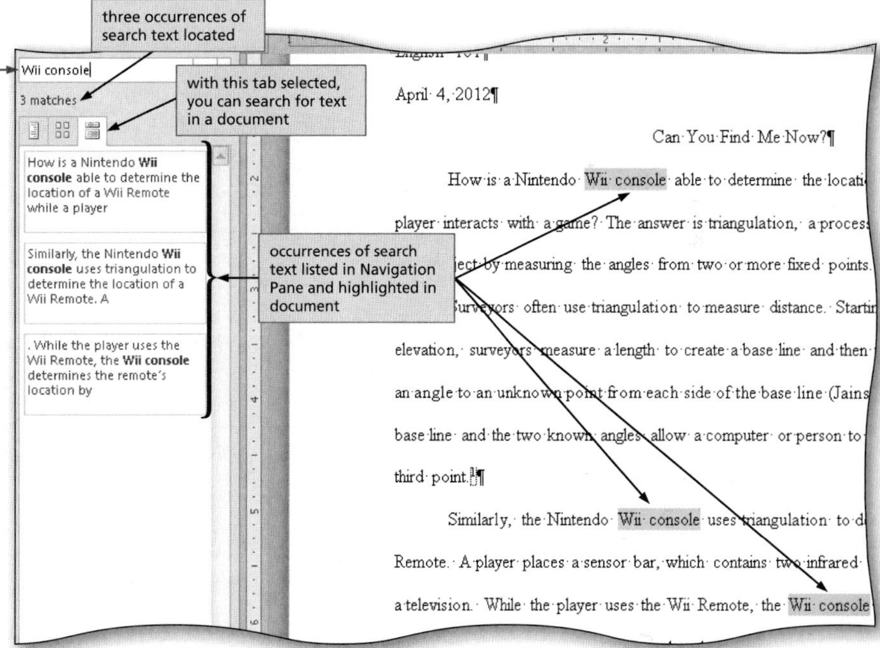

Figure 2–66

Other Ways

1. Click Find button arrow (Home tab | Editing group), click Find on Find menu, enter search text in Navigation Pane
2. Click Select Browse Object button on vertical scroll bar, click Find icon on Select Browse Object menu, enter search text (Find and Replace dialog box), click Find Next button
3. Click Page Number indicator on status bar, click Find tab (Find and Replace dialog box), enter search text, click Find Next button
4. Press CTRL+F

To Replace Text

You decide to change all occurrences of Wii console to Wii game console. To do this, you can use Word's find and replace feature, which automatically locates each occurrence of a word or phrase and then replaces it with specified text. The following steps replace all occurrences of Wii console with Wii game console.

- Click the Replace button (Home tab | Editing group) to display the Replace sheet in the Find and Replace dialog box.
- If necessary, type **Wii console** in the Find what text box (Find and Replace dialog box).
- Press the TAB key. Type **Wii game console** in the Replace with text box (Figure 2–67).

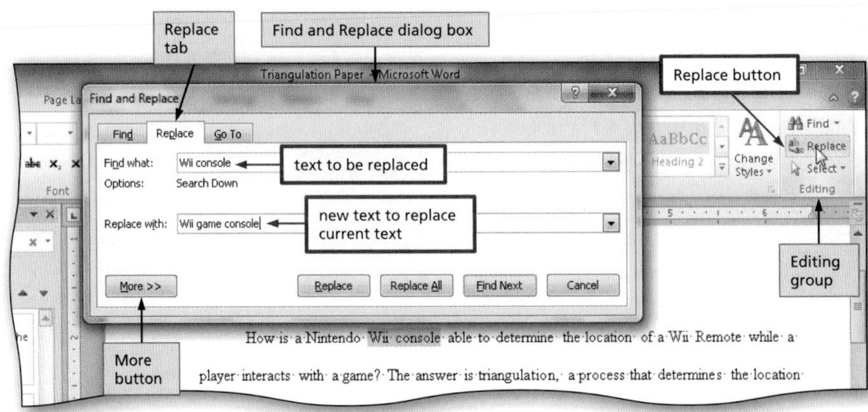

Figure 2–67

- Click the Replace All button to instruct Word to replace all occurrences of the Find what text with the Replace with text (Figure 2–68). If Word displays a dialog box asking if you want to continue searching from the beginning of the document, click the Yes button.

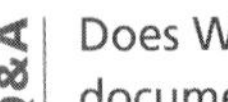

Does Word search the entire document?

If the insertion point is at the beginning of the document, Word searches the entire document; otherwise, Word searches from the location of the insertion point to the end of the document and then displays a dialog box asking if you want to continue searching from the beginning. You also can search a section of text by selecting the text before clicking the Replace button.

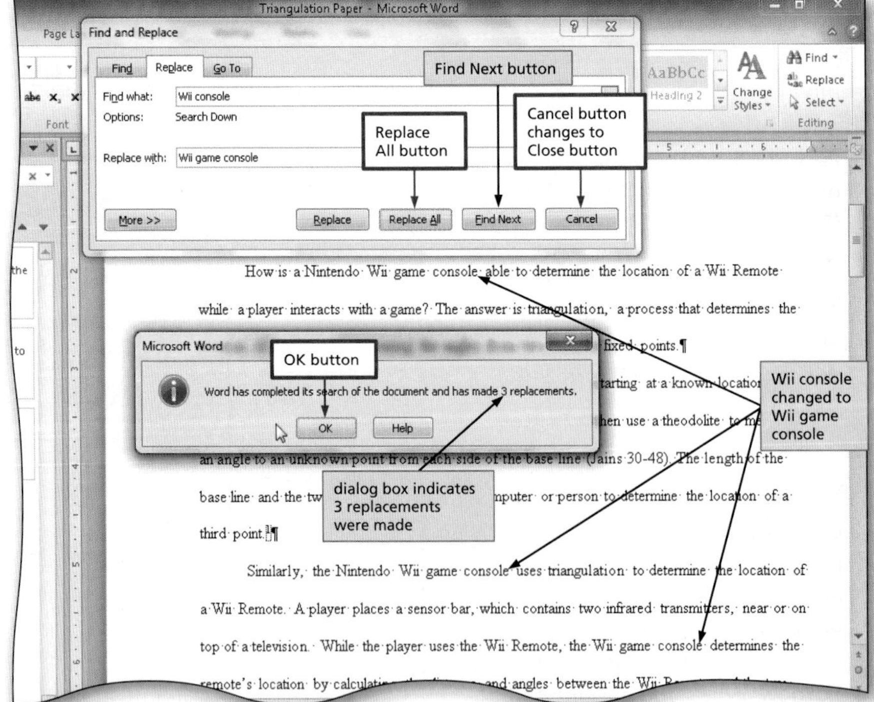

Figure 2–68

3

- Click the OK button (Microsoft Word dialog box) to close the dialog box.
- Click the Close button (Find and Replace dialog box) to close the dialog box.

Other Ways

1. Click Select Browse Object button on vertical scroll bar, click Find icon on Select Browse Object menu, click Replace tab
2. Click Page Number indicator on status bar, click Replace tab (Find and Replace dialog box)
3. Press CTRL+H

Find and Replace Dialog Box

The Replace All button (Find and Replace dialog box) replaces all occurrences of the Find what text with the Replace with text. In some cases, you may want to replace only certain occurrences of a word or phrase, not all of them. To instruct Word to confirm each change, click the Find Next button (Find and Replace dialog box) (Figure 2–68), instead of the Replace All button. When Word locates an occurrence of the text, it pauses and waits for you to click either the Replace button or the Find Next button. Clicking the Replace button changes the text; clicking the Find Next button instructs Word to disregard the replacement and look for the next occurrence of the Find what text.

If you accidentally replace the wrong text, you can undo a replacement by clicking the Undo button on the Quick Access Toolbar. If you used the Replace All button, Word undoes all replacements. If you used the Replace button, Word undoes only the most recent replacement.

BTW

Finding Formatting
To search for formatting or a special character, click the More button (shown in Figure 2–67) to expand the Find dialog box. To find formatting, use the Format button in the expanded Find dialog box. To find a special character, use the Special button.

To Go to a Page

The next step in revising the paper is to change a word on the second page of the document. You could scroll to the location in the document, or as mentioned earlier, you can use the Navigation Pane to browse through pages in a document. The following steps display the top of the second page in the document window and position the insertion point at the beginning of that page.

1

- Click the 'Browse the pages in your document' tab in the Navigation Pane to display thumbnail images of the pages in the document (Figure 2–69).

Q&A

What if the Navigation Pane is not on the screen anymore?

Click View on the Ribbon to display the View tab and then click Navigation Pane (View tab | Show group) to select the check box.

2

- Click the thumbnail of the second page, even if the second page already is selected, to display the top of the selected page in the top of the document window (shown in Figure 2–70 on the next page).

3

- Click the Close button in the Navigation Pane to close the pane.

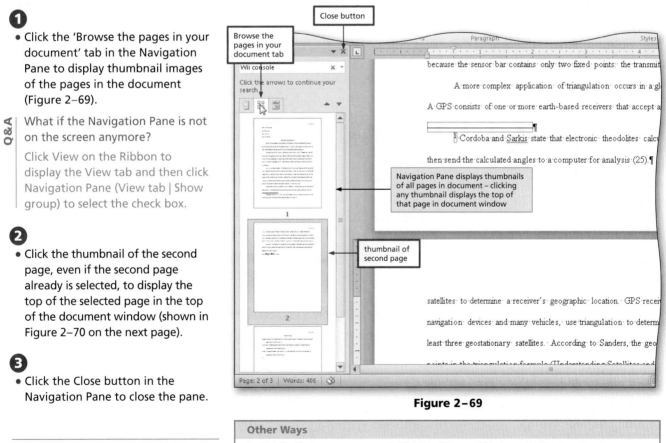

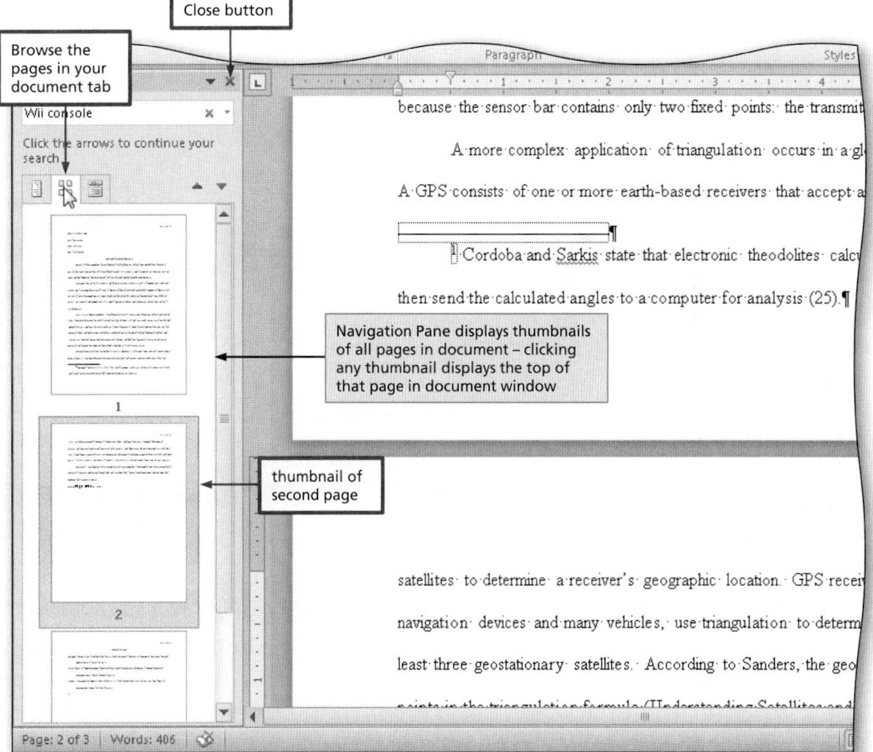

Figure 2–69

Other Ways

1. Click Find button arrow (Home tab | Editing group), click Go To on Find menu, click Go To tab (Find and Replace dialog box), enter page number, click Go To button
2. Click Select Browse Object button on vertical scroll bar, click Go To icon on Select Browse Object menu, enter page number (Find and Replace dialog box), click Go To button
3. Click Page Number indicator on status bar, click Go To tab (Find and Replace dialog box), enter page number, click Go To button
4. Press CTRL+G

To Find and Insert a Synonym

When writing, you may discover that you used the same word in multiple locations or that a word you used was not quite appropriate. In these instances, you will want to look up a **synonym**, or a word similar in meaning, to the duplicate or inappropriate word. A **thesaurus** is a book of synonyms. Word provides synonyms and a thesaurus for your convenience.

In this project, you would like a synonym for the word, prescribed, in the fourth paragraph of the research paper. The following steps find a suitable synonym.

- Locate and then right-click the word for which you want to find a synonym (in this case, prescribed) to display a shortcut menu related to the word you right-clicked.
- Point to Synonyms on the shortcut menu to display a list of synonyms for the word you right-clicked (Figure 2–70).

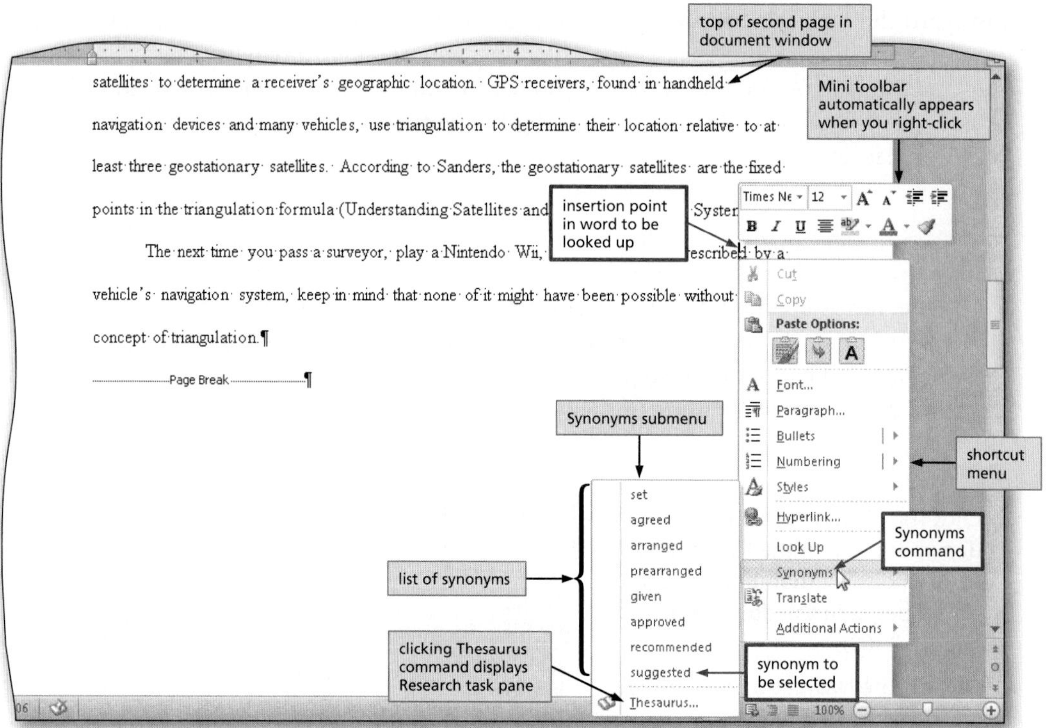

Figure 2–70

2

- Click the synonym you want (in this case, suggested) on the Synonyms submenu to replace the selected word in the document with the selected synonym (Figure 2–71).

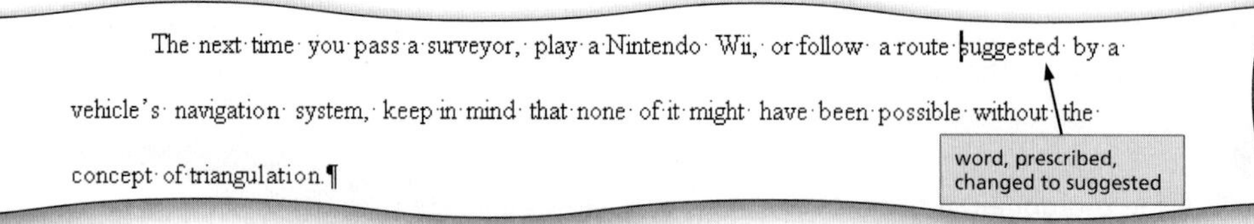

Figure 2–71

Q&A What if the synonyms list on the shortcut menu does not display a suitable word?

You can display the thesaurus in the Research task pane by clicking Thesaurus on the Synonyms submenu. The Research task pane displays a complete thesaurus, in which you can look up synonyms for various meanings of a word. You also can look up an **antonym**, or word with an opposite meaning. The Research task pane is discussed later in this chapter.

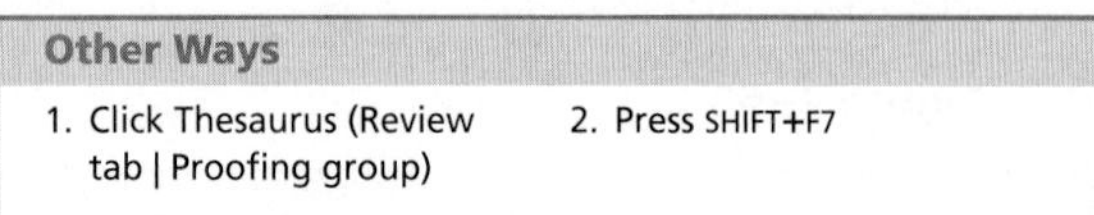

Other Ways

1. Click Thesaurus (Review tab | Proofing group)
2. Press SHIFT+F7

To Check Spelling and Grammar at Once

As discussed in Chapter 1, Word checks spelling and grammar as you type and places a wavy underline below possible spelling or grammar errors. Chapter 1 illustrated how to check these flagged words immediately. As an alternative, you can wait and check the entire document for spelling and grammar errors at once. The next steps check spelling and grammar at once.

Note: In the following steps, the word, theodolite, has been misspelled intentionally as theadalight to illustrate the use of Word's check spelling and grammar at once feature. If you are completing this project on a personal computer, your research paper may contain different misspelled words, depending on the accuracy of your typing.

1

- Press CTRL+HOME because you want the spelling and grammar check to begin from the top of the document.
- Click Review on the Ribbon to display the Review tab.
- Click the Spelling & Grammar button (Review tab | Proofing group) to begin the spelling and grammar check at the location of the insertion point, which in this case, is at the beginning of the document.
- Click the desired spelling in the Suggestions list (theodolite, in this case) (Figure 2–72).

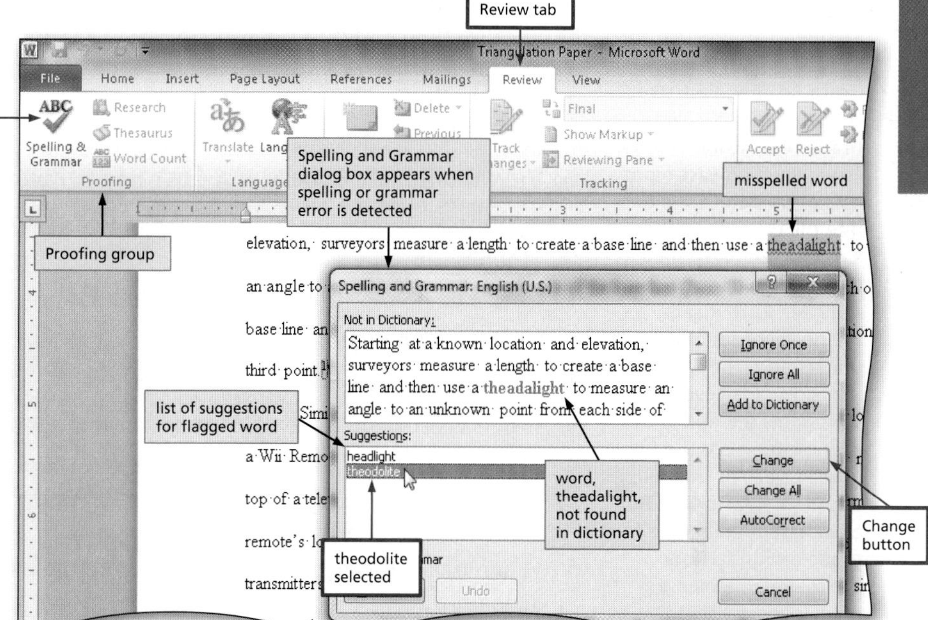

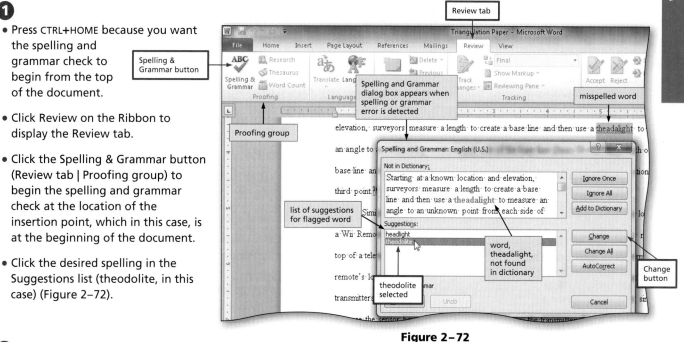

Figure 2–72

2

- With the word, theodolite, selected in the Suggestions list, click the Change button (Spelling and Grammar dialog box) to change the flagged word to the selected suggestion and then continue the spelling and grammar check until the next error is identified or the end of the document is reached (Figure 2–73).

3

- Click the Ignore All button (Spelling and Grammar dialog box) to ignore this and future occurrences of the flagged proper noun and then continue the spelling and grammar check until the next error is identified or the end of the document is reached.

4

- When the spelling and grammar check is finished and Word displays a dialog box, click its OK button.

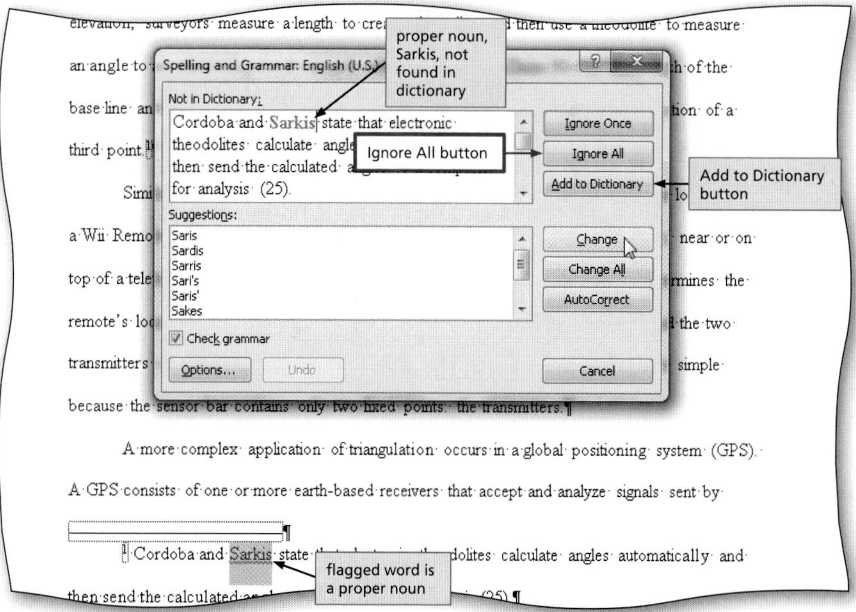

Figure 2–73

Q&A

Can I check spelling of just a section of a document?

Yes, select the text before starting the spelling and grammar check.

Other Ways

1. Click Spelling and Grammar Check icon on status bar, click Spelling on shortcut menu
2. Right-click flagged word, click Spelling on shortcut menu
3. Press F7

BTW

Readability Statistics
You can instruct Word to display readability statistics when it has finished a spelling and grammar check on a document. Three readability statistics presented are the percent of passive sentences, the Flesch Reading Ease score, and the Flesch-Kincaid Grade Level score. The Flesch Reading Ease score uses a 100-point scale to rate the ease with which a reader can understand the text in a document. A higher score means the document is easier to understand. The Flesch-Kincaid Grade Level score rates the text in a document on a U.S. school grade level. For example, a score of 10.0 indicates a student in the tenth grade can understand the material. To show readability statistics when the spelling and grammar check is complete, open the Backstage view, click Options in the Backstage view, click Proofing in the left pane (Word Options dialog box), place a check mark in the 'Show readability statistics' check box, and then click the OK button. Readability statistics will be displayed the next time you check spelling and grammar at once in the document.

The Main and Custom Dictionaries

As shown in the steps on the previous page, Word may flag a proper noun as an error because the proper noun is not in its main dictionary. To prevent Word from flagging proper nouns as errors, you can add the proper nouns to the custom dictionary. To add a correctly spelled word to the custom dictionary, click the Add to Dictionary button (Spelling and Grammar dialog box) or right-click the flagged word and then click Add to Dictionary on the shortcut menu. Once you have added a word to the custom dictionary, Word no longer will flag it as an error.

To View or Modify Entries in a Custom Dictionary

To view or modify the list of words in a custom dictionary, you would follow these steps.

1. Click File on the Ribbon and then click Options in the Backstage view.
2. Click Proofing in the left pane (Word Options dialog box).
3. Click the Custom Dictionaries button.
4. When Word displays the Custom Dictionaries dialog box, place a check mark next to the dictionary name to view or modify. Click the Edit Word List button (Custom Dictionaries dialog box). (In this dialog box, you can add or delete entries to and from the selected custom dictionary.)
5. When finished viewing and/or modifying the list, click the OK button in the dialog box.
6. Click the OK button (Custom Dictionaries dialog box).
7. If the 'Suggest from main dictionary only' check box is selected in the Word Options dialog box, remove the check mark. Click the OK button (Word Options dialog box).

To Set the Default Custom Dictionary

If you have multiple custom dictionaries, you can specify which one Word should use when checking spelling. To set the default custom dictionary, you would follow these steps.

1. Click File on the Ribbon and then click Options in the Backstage view.
2. Click Proofing in the left pane (Word Options dialog box).
3. Click the Custom Dictionaries button.
4. When the Custom Dictionaries dialog box is displayed, place a check mark next to the desired dictionary name. Click the Change Default button (Custom Dictionaries dialog box).
5. Click the OK button (Custom Dictionaries dialog box).
6. If the 'Suggest from main dictionary only' check box is selected in the Word Options dialog box, remove the check mark. Click the OK button (Word Options dialog box).

To Use the Research Task Pane to Look Up Information

From within Word, you can search through various forms of reference information. Earlier, this chapter discussed the Research task pane with respect to looking up a synonym in a thesaurus. Other services available in the Research task pane include a dictionary and, if you are connected to the Web, a search engine and other Web sites that provide information such as stock quotes, news articles, and company profiles.

Assume you want to know more about the word, geostationary. The following steps use the Research task pane to look up a definition of a word.

1

- Locate the word you want to look up.
- While holding down the ALT key, click the word you want to look up (in this case, geostationary) to open the Research task pane and display a dictionary entry for the ALT+clicked word. Release the ALT key.

2

- Click the Search for box arrow in the Research task pane to display a list of search locations (Figure 2–74).

Q&A Why does my Research task pane look different?

Depending on your settings and Microsoft's Web site search settings, your Research task pane may appear different from the figures shown here.

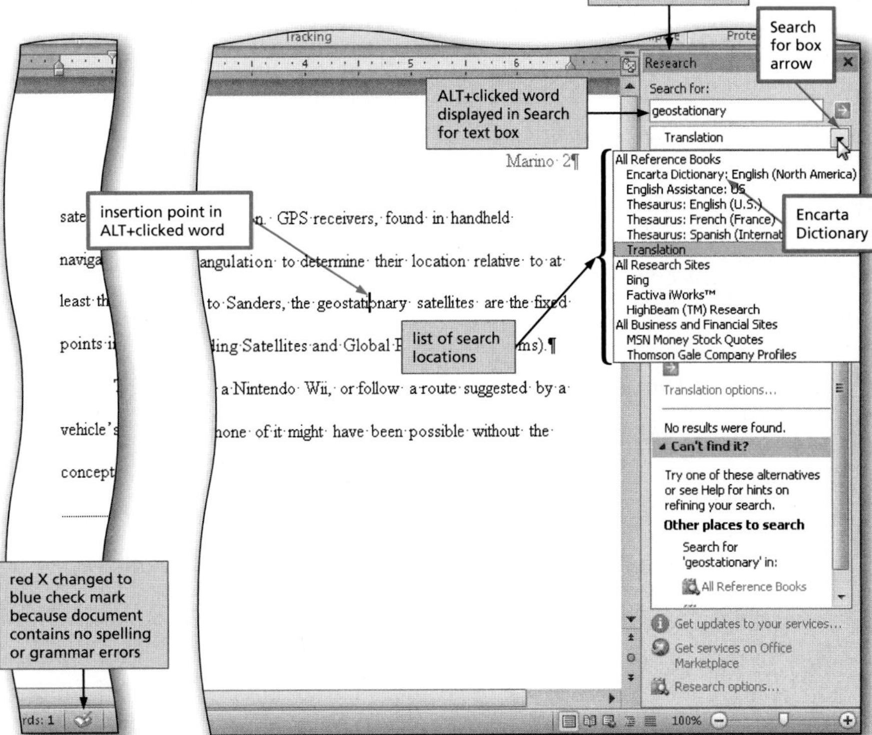

Figure 2–74

- Click Encarta Dictionary in the list to display a definition for the ALT+clicked word (Figure 2–75).

Q&A Can I copy information from the Research task pane into my document?

Yes, you can use the Copy and Paste commands. When using Word to insert material from the Research task pane or any other online reference, however, be careful not to plagiarize.

3

- Click the Close button in the Research task pane.

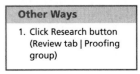

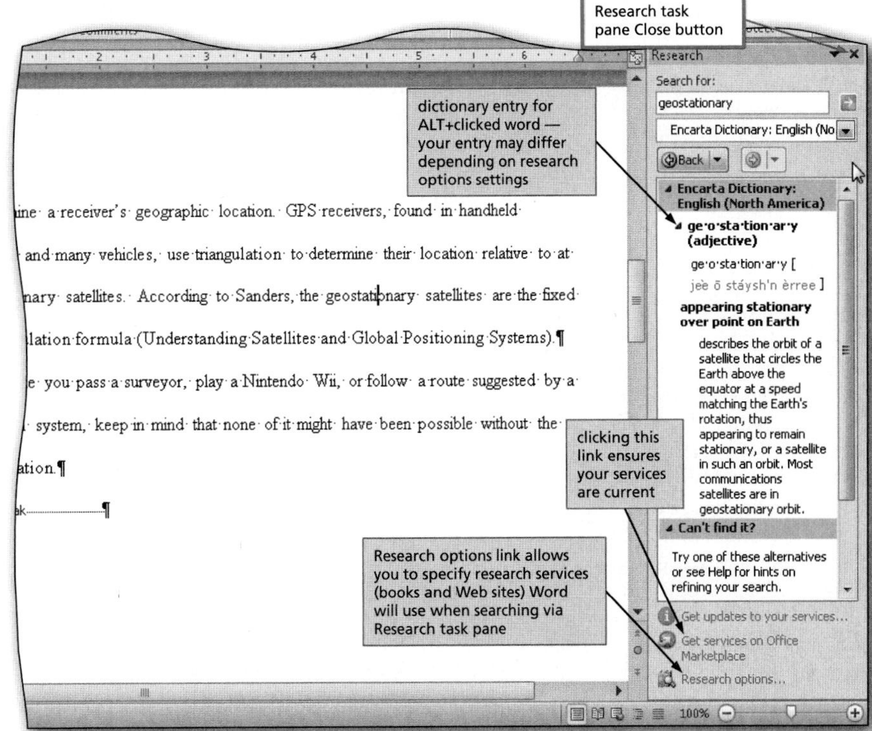

Figure 2–75

Other Ways

1. Click Research button (Review tab | Proofing group)

BTW

Grammar and Style Options
To set grammar and writing style options, click File on the Ribbon to open the Backstage view, click the Options button, and then click Proofing in the left pane (Word Options dialog box) to display a variety of spelling and grammar options that you can select or deselect by placing or removing check marks. To specify how Word checks grammar, click the Settings button in the right pane (Word Options dialog box) and then select the desired settings in the Grammar Settings dialog box.

Research Task Pane Options

When you install Word, it selects a series of services (reference books and Web sites) that it searches through when you use the Research task pane. You can view, modify, and update the list of services at any time.

Clicking the Research options link at the bottom of the Research task pane (shown in Figure 2–75 on the previous page) displays the Research Options dialog box, where you can view or modify the list of installed services. You can view information about any installed service by clicking the service in the list and then clicking the Properties button. To activate an installed service, click the check box to its left; likewise, to deactivate a service, remove the check mark. To add a particular Web site to the list, click the Add Services button, enter the Web address in the Address text box, and then click the Add button (Add Services dialog box). To update or remove services, click the Update/Remove button, select the service in the list, click the Update (or Remove) button (Update or Remove Services dialog box), and then click the Close button. You also can install parental controls through the Parental Control button (Research Options dialog box), for example, if you want to prevent minor children who use Word from accessing the Web.

To Change Document Properties

Before saving the research paper again, you want to add your name, course information, and some keywords as document properties. The following steps use the Document Information Panel to change document properties.

1. Click File on the Ribbon to open the Backstage view and, if necessary, select the Info tab.
2. Click the Properties button in the right pane of the Info gallery to display the Properties menu and then click Show Document Panel on the Properties menu to close the Backstage view and display the Document Information Panel in the Word document window.
3. Click the Author text box, if necessary, and then type your name as the Author property. If a name already is displayed in the Author text box, delete it before typing your name.
4. Click the Subject text box, if necessary delete any existing text, and then type your course and section as the Subject property.
5. Click the Keywords text box, if necessary delete any existing text, and then type **surveyor, Wii, GPS** as the Keywords property.
6. Click the Close the Document Information Panel button so that the Document Information Panel no longer is displayed.

BTW

Conserving Ink and Toner
If you want to conserve ink or toner, you can instruct Word to print draft quality documents by clicking File on the Ribbon to open the Backstage view, clicking Options in the Backstage view to display the Word Options dialog box, clicking Advanced in the left pane (Word Options dialog box), scrolling to the Print area in the right pane, placing a check mark in the 'Use draft quality' check box, and then clicking the OK button. Then, use the Backstage view to print the document as usual.

To Save an Existing Document with the Same File Name

You have made several modifications to the document since you last saved it. Thus, you should save it again. The following step saves the document again.

1. Click the Save button on the Quick Access Toolbar to overwrite the previously saved file.

To Print Document Properties

With the document properties entered and the completed document saved, you may want to print the document properties along with the document. The following steps print the document properties for the Triangulation Paper.

- Click File on the Ribbon to open the Backstage view and then click the Print tab in the Backstage view to display the Print gallery.
- Verify the printer name that appears on the Printer Status button will print a hard copy of the document. If necessary, click the Printer Status button to display a list of available printer options and then click the desired printer to change the currently selected printer.
- Click the first button in the Settings area to display a list of options specifying what you can print (Figure 2–76).

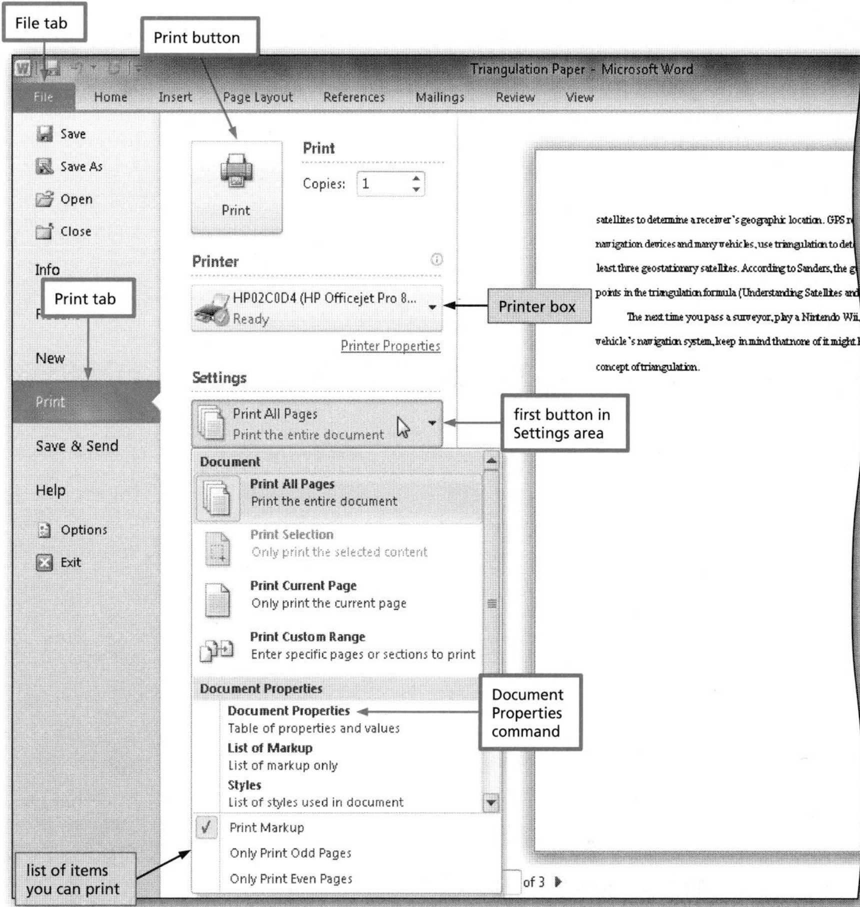

Figure 2–76

- Click Document Properties in the list to specify you want to print the document properties instead of the actual document.
- Click the Print button in the Print gallery to print the document properties on the currently selected printer (Figure 2–77).

Q&A What if the currently updated document properties do not print on the hard copy?

Try closing the document, reopening the document, and then repeating these steps.

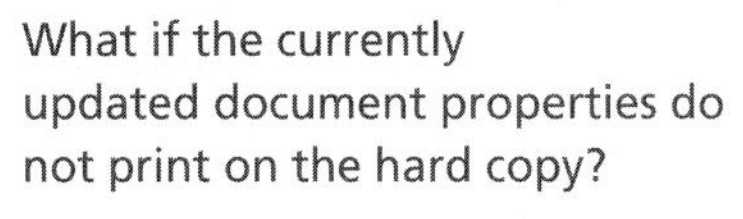

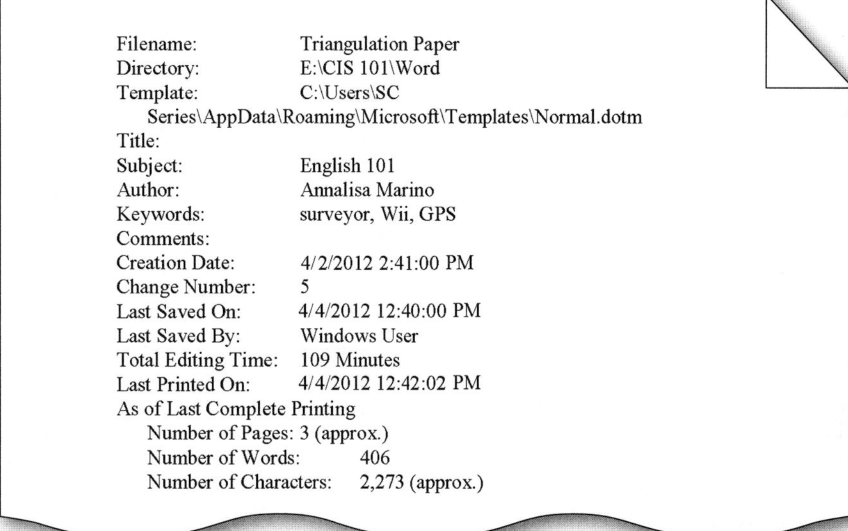

Filename: Triangulation Paper
Directory: E:\CIS 101\Word
Template: C:\Users\SC Series\AppData\Roaming\Microsoft\Templates\Normal.dotm
Title:
Subject: English 101
Author: Annalisa Marino
Keywords: surveyor, Wii, GPS
Comments:
Creation Date: 4/2/2012 2:41:00 PM
Change Number: 5
Last Saved On: 4/4/2012 12:40:00 PM
Last Saved By: Windows User
Total Editing Time: 109 Minutes
Last Printed On: 4/4/2012 12:42:02 PM
As of Last Complete Printing
Number of Pages: 3 (approx.)
Number of Words: 406
Number of Characters: 2,273 (approx.)

Figure 2–77

Other Ways

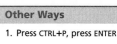

1. Press CTRL+P, press ENTER

To Preview the Document and Then Print It

Before printing the research paper, you want to verify the page layouts. The following steps change the print option to print the document (instead of the document properties), preview the printed pages in the research paper, and then print the document.

- Position the insertion point at the top of the document because you want initially to view the first page in the document.
- Click File on the Ribbon to open the Backstage view and then click the Print tab in the Backstage view to display the Print gallery.
- Verify the printer name that appears on the Printer Status button will print a hard copy of the document. If necessary, select a different printer.
- Click the first button in the Settings area to display a list of options specifying what you can print (Figure 2–78).

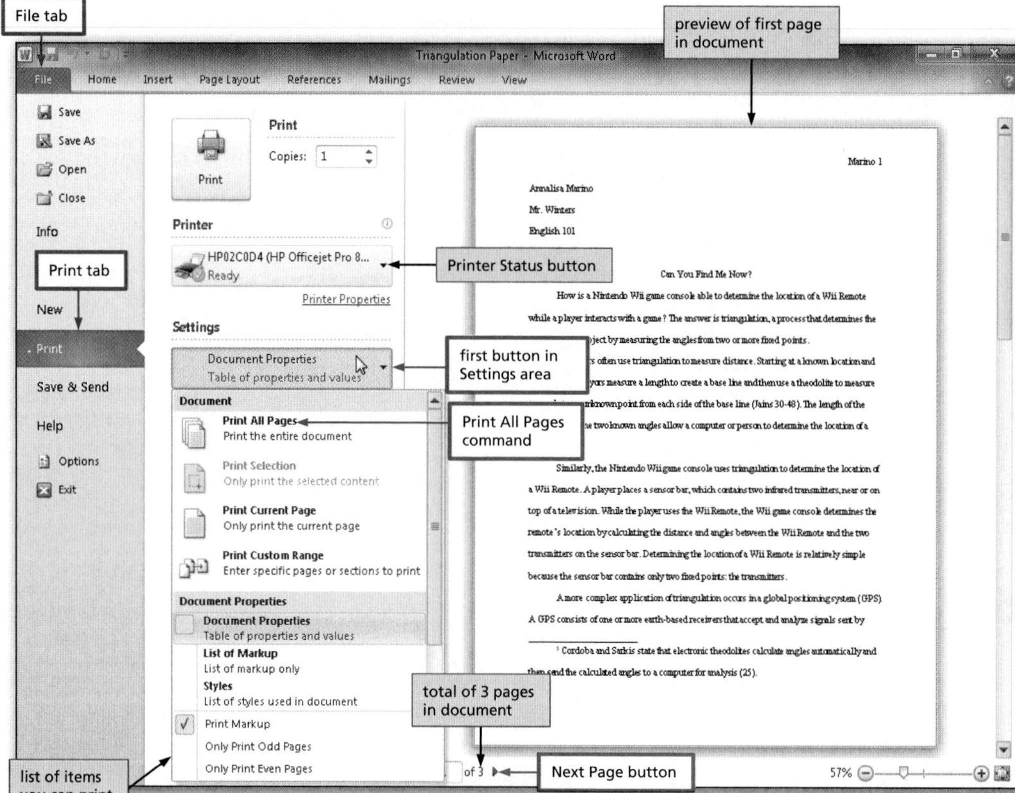

Figure 2–78

- Click Print All Pages in the list to specify you want to print all pages in the actual document.

- Click the Next Page button in the Print gallery to preview the second page of the research paper in the Print gallery.
- Click the Next Page button again to preview the third page of the research paper in the Print gallery (Figure 2–79).

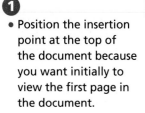

- Click the Print button in the Print gallery to print the research paper on the currently selected printer (shown in Figure 2–1 on page WD 67).

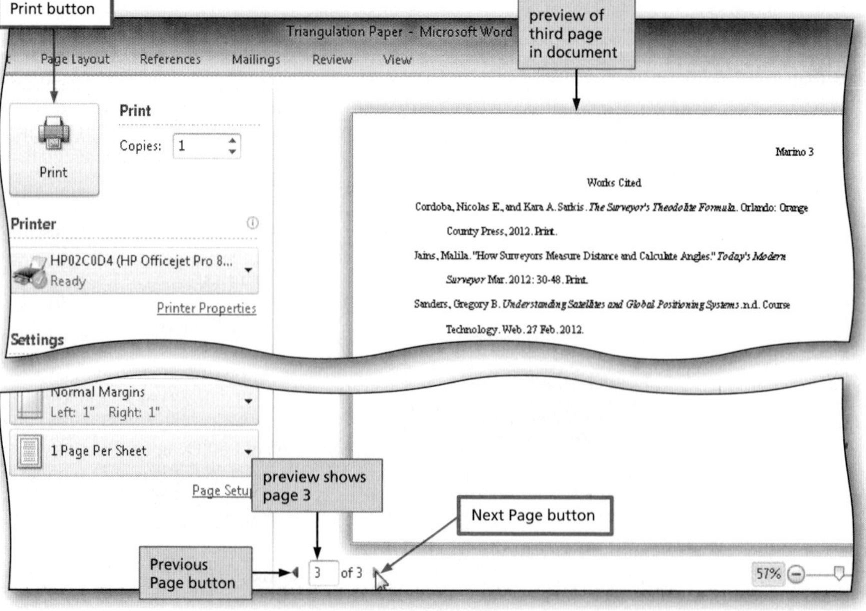

Figure 2–79

Other Ways

1. Press CTRL+P, press ENTER

To Quit Word

This project now is complete. The following steps quit Word. For a detailed example of the procedure summarized below, refer to the Office 2010 and Windows 7 chapter at the beginning of this book.

1. If you have one Word document open, click the Close button on the right side of the title bar to close the document and quit Word; or if you have multiple Word documents open, click File on the Ribbon to open the Backstage view and then click Exit in the Backstage view to close all open documents and quit Word.

2. If a Microsoft Word dialog box appears, click the Save button to save any changes made to the document since the last save.

BTW

Quick Reference
For a table that lists how to complete the tasks covered in this book using the mouse, Ribbon, shortcut menu, and keyboard, see the Quick Reference Summary at the back of this book, or visit the Word 2010 Quick Reference Web page (scsite.com/wd2010/qr).

Chapter Summary

In this chapter, you have learned how to change document settings, use headers to number pages, modify a style, insert and edit citations and their sources, add footnotes, create a bibliographical list of sources, and use the Research task pane. The items listed below include all the new Word skills you have learned in this chapter.

1. Modify a Style (WD 70)
2. Change Line Spacing (WD 73)
3. Remove Space after a Paragraph (WD 74)
4. Update a Style to Match a Selection (WD 74)
5. Switch to the Header (WD 75)
6. Right-Align a Paragraph (WD 76)
7. Insert a Page Number (WD 77)
8. Close the Header (WD 78)
9. Click and Type (WD 80)
10. Display the Rulers (WD 82)
11. First-Line Indent Paragraphs (WD 83)
12. AutoCorrect as You Type (WD 85)
13. Use the AutoCorrect Options Button (WD 85)
14. Create an AutoCorrect Entry (WD 86)
15. Change the Bibliography Style (WD 89)
16. Insert a Citation and Create Its Source (WD 90)
17. Edit a Citation (WD 91)
18. Insert a Footnote Reference Mark (WD 93)
19. Insert a Citation Placeholder (WD 94)
20. Modify a Style Using a Shortcut Menu (WD 95)
21. Edit a Source (WD 97)
22. Count Words (WD 101)
23. Page Break Manually (WD 106)
24. Apply a Style (WD 106)
25. Create the Bibliographical List (WD 108)
26. Format Paragraphs with a Hanging Indent (WD 109)
27. Modify a Source and Update the Bibliographical List (WD 109)
28. Convert a Field to Regular Text (WD 110)
29. Scroll Page by Page through a Document (WD 112)
30. Copy and Paste (WD 113)
31. Display the Paste Options Menu (WD 114)
32. Find Text (WD 115)
33. Replace Text (WD 116)
34. Go to a Page (WD 117)
35. Find and Insert a Synonym (WD 118)
36. Check Spelling and Grammar at Once (WD 118)
37. View or Modify Entries in a Custom Dictionary (WD 120)
38. Set the Default Custom Dictionary (WD 120)
39. Use the Research Task Pane to Look Up Information (WD 120)
40. Print Document Properties (WD 123)
41. Preview the Document and Then Print It (WD 124)

If you have a SAM 2010 user profile, your instructor may have assigned an autogradable version of this assignment. If so, log into the SAM 2010 Web site at www.cengage.com/sam2010 to download the instruction and start files.

STUDENT ASSIGNMENTS

Learn It Online

Test your knowledge of chapter content and key terms.

Instructions: To complete the Learn It Online exercises, start your browser, click the Address bar, and then enter the Web address **scsite.com/wd2010/learn**. When the Word 2010 Learn It Online page is displayed, click the link for the exercise you want to complete and then read the instructions.

Chapter Reinforcement TF, MC, and SA
A series of true/false, multiple choice, and short answer questions that test your knowledge of the chapter content.

Flash Cards
An interactive learning environment where you identify chapter key terms associated with displayed definitions.

Practice Test
A series of multiple choice questions that test your knowledge of chapter content and key terms.

Who Wants To Be a Computer Genius?
An interactive game that challenges your knowledge of chapter content in the style of a television quiz show.

Wheel of Terms
An interactive game that challenges your knowledge of chapter key terms in the style of the television show *Wheel of Fortune*.

Crossword Puzzle Challenge
A crossword puzzle that challenges your knowledge of key terms presented in the chapter.

Apply Your Knowledge

Reinforce the skills and apply the concepts you learned in this chapter.

Revising Text and Paragraphs in a Document

Note: To complete this assignment, you will be required to use the Data Files for Students. See the inside back cover of this book for instructions on downloading the Data Files for Students, or contact your instructor for information about accessing the required files.

Instructions: Start Word. Open the document, Apply 2-1 Space Paragraph Draft, from the Data Files for Students. The document you open contains a paragraph of text. You are to revise the document as follows: move a word, move another word and change the format of the moved word, change paragraph indentation, change line spacing, find all occurrences of a word, replace all occurrences of a word with another word, locate a synonym, and edit the header.

Perform the following tasks:

1. Copy the word, exploration, from the first sentence and paste it in the last sentence after the word, space, so that it is the eighth word in the sentence.
2. Select the underlined word, safe, in the paragraph. Use drag-and-drop editing to move the selected word, safe, so that it is before the word, mission, in the same sentence. Click the Paste Options button that displays to the right of the moved word, safe. Remove the underline format from the moved sentence by clicking Keep Text Only on the Paste Options menu.
3. Display the ruler, if necessary. Use the ruler to indent the first line of the paragraph one-half inch.
4. Change the line spacing of the paragraph to double.
5. Use the Navigation Pane to find all occurrences of the word, sensors. How many are there?
6. Use the Find and Replace dialog box to replace all occurrences of the word, issues, with the word, problems. How many replacements were made?

7. Use Word to find the word, height. Use Word's thesaurus to change the word, height, to the word, altitude.
8. Switch to the header so that you can edit it. In the first line of the header, change the word, Draft, to the word, Modified, so that it reads: Space Paragraph Modified.
9. In the second line of the header, insert the page number (with no formatting) one space after the word, Page.
10. Change the alignment of both lines of text in the header from left-aligned to right-aligned. Switch back to the document text.
11. Change the document properties, as specified by your instructor.
12. Click File on the Ribbon and then click Save As. Save the document using the file name, Apply 2-1 Space Paragraph Modified.
13. Print the document properties and then print the revised document, shown in Figure 2–80.
14. Use the Research task pane to look up the definition of the word, NASA, in the paragraph. Handwrite the definition of the word on your printout, as well as your response to the question in #6.
15. Change the Search for box to All Research Sites. Print an article from one of the sites.
16. Display the Research Options dialog box and, on your printout, handwrite the currently active Reference Books, Research Sites, and Business and Financial Sites. If your instructor approves, activate one of the services.

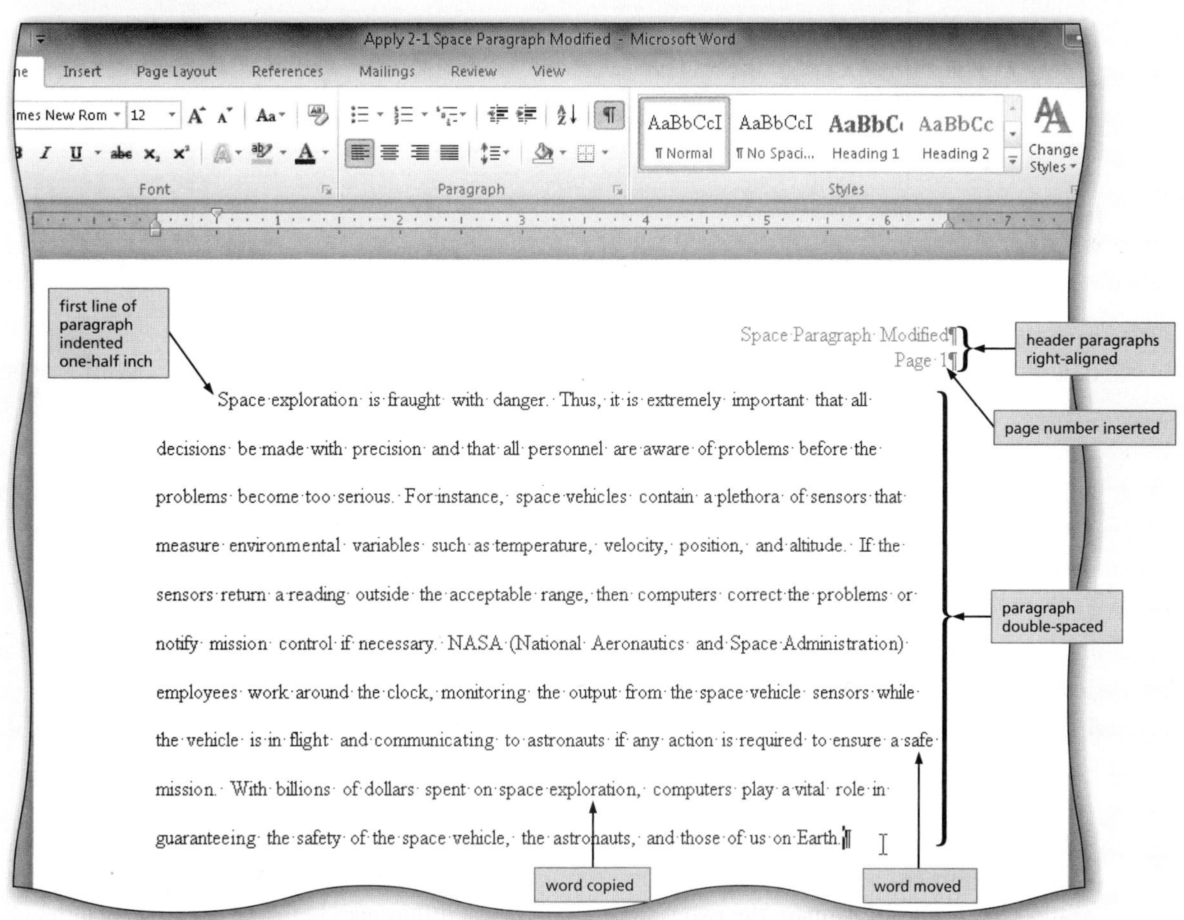

Figure 2–80

Extend Your Knowledge

Extend the skills you learned in this chapter and experiment with new skills. You may need to use Help to complete the assignment.

Working with References and Proofing Tools

Note: To complete this assignment, you will be required to use the Data Files for Students. See the inside back cover of this book for instructions on downloading the Data Files for Students, or contact your instructor for information about accessing the required files.

Instructions: Start Word. Open the document, Extend 2-1 Digital Camera Paper Draft, from the Data Files for Students. You will add another footnote to the paper, use the thesaurus, convert the document from MLA to APA documentation style, convert the footnotes to endnotes, modify the Endnote Text style, change the format of the note reference marks, and translate the document to another language (Figure 2–81).

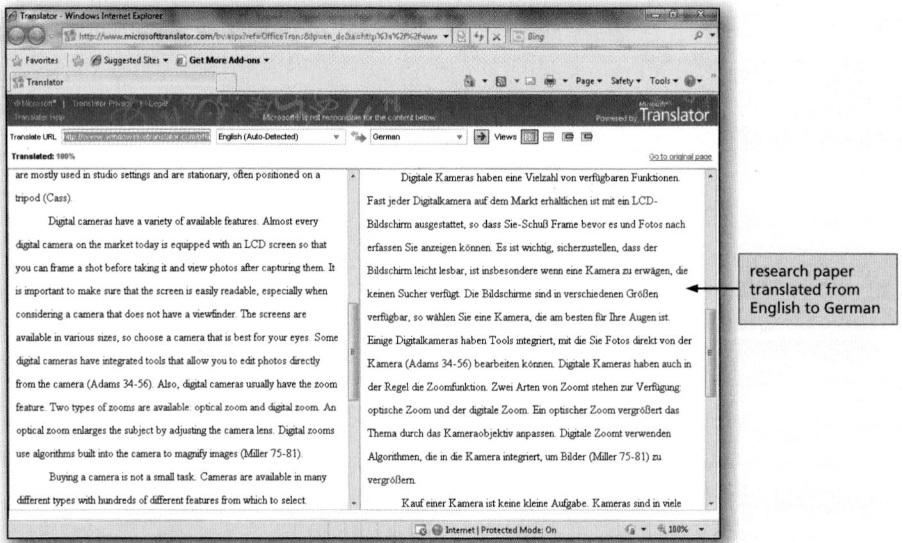

Figure 2–81

Perform the following tasks:

1. Use Help to learn more about footers, footnotes and endnotes, bibliography styles, AutoCorrect, and the Mini Translator.
2. Delete the footer from the document.
3. Insert a second footnote at an appropriate place in the research paper. Use the following footnote text: For instance, Adams states that you may be able to crop photos, change the brightness, or remove red eye effects.
4. Change the location of the footnotes from bottom of page to below text.
5. Use the Find and Replace dialog box to find the word, small, in the document and then replace it with a word of your choice.
6. Save the document with a new file name and then print it. On the printout, write the number of words, characters without spaces, characters with spaces, paragraphs, and lines in the document. Be sure to include footnote text in the statistics.
7. Select the entire document and then change the documentation style of the citations and bibliography from MLA to APA. Save the APA version of the document with a new file name and then print it. Compare the two versions. Circle the differences between the two documents.
8. Convert the footnotes to endnotes.

9. Modify the Endnote Text style to 12-point Times New Roman font, double-spaced text with a hanging-line indent.
10. Change the format of the note reference marks to capital letters (A, B, etc.).
11. Add an AutoCorrect entry that replaces the word, camora, with the word, camera. Add this sentence, A field camora usually is more than sufficient for most users., to the end of the second paragraph, misspelling the word camera to test the AutoCorrect entry. Delete the AutoCorrect entry that replaces camora with the word, camera.
12. Display readability statistics. What are the Flesch-Kincaid Grade Level, the Flesch Reading Ease score, and the percent of passive sentences?
13. Save the revised document with endnotes with a new file name and then print it. On the printout, write your response to the question in #12.
14. If you have an Internet connection, translate the research paper into a language of your choice using the Translate button (Review tab | Language group). Submit the translated document in the format specified by your instructor. Use the Mini Translator to hear how to pronounce three words in your paper.

Make It Right

Analyze a document and correct all errors and/or improve the design.

Inserting Missing Elements in an MLA-Styled Research Paper

Note: To complete this assignment, you will be required to use the Data Files for Students. See the inside back cover of this book for instructions on downloading the Data Files for Students, or contact your instructor for information about accessing the required files.

Instructions: Start Word. Open the document, Make It Right 2-1 Biometrics Paper Draft, from the Data Files for Students. The document is a research paper that is missing several elements. You are to insert these missing elements, all formatted according to the MLA documentation style: header with a page number, name and course information, paper title, footnote, and source information for a citation.

Perform the following tasks:

1. Insert a header with a page number (use your own last name). Also, insert name and course information (your name, your instructor name, your course name, and today's date), and an appropriate paper title, all formatted according to the MLA documentation style.
2. The Jenkins citation placeholder is missing its source information (Figure 2–82). Use the following source information to edit the source: magazine article titled "Fingerprint Readers" written by Arthur D. Jenkins and Marissa K. Weavers, magazine name is *Security Today*, publication date is February 2012, article is on pages 55–60. Edit the citation so that it displays the author name and the page numbers of 55–56 for this reference.

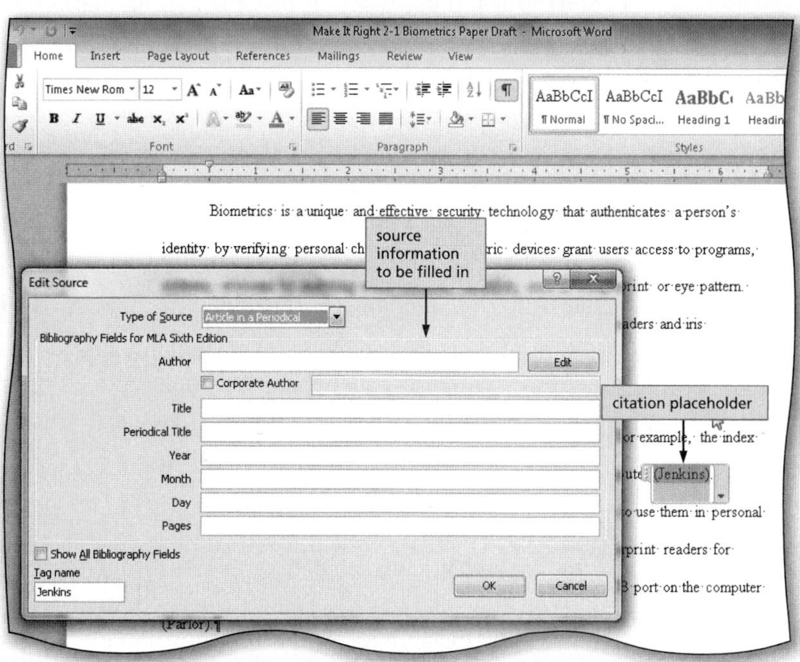

Figure 2–82

Continued >

STUDENT ASSIGNMENTS

Make It Right *continued*

3. Modify the source of the book authored by Carolina Doe, so that the publisher city is Chicago instead of Dallas.
4. Change the Footnote Text style to 12-point Times New Roman, double-spaced paragraphs with a first-line indent.
5. Insert the following footnote with the note reference at an appropriate place in the paper, formatted according to the MLA documentation style: Parlor states that one use of fingerprint readers is for users to log on to programs and Web sites via their fingerprint instead of entering a user name and password.
6. Use the Navigation Pane to display page 3. Use Word to insert the bibliographical list (bibliography). Convert the works cited to regular text. Change the underline format on the titles of the works to the italic format, and insert the correct publication medium for each work.
7. Change the document properties, as specified by your instructor. Save the revised document with the file name, Make It Right 2-1 Biometrics Paper Modified, and then submit it in the format specified by your instructor.

In the Lab

Design and/or create a document using the guidelines, concepts, and skills presented in this chapter. Labs are listed in order of increasing difficulty.

Lab 1: Preparing a Short Research Paper

Problem: You are a college student currently enrolled in an introductory business class. Your assignment is to prepare a short research paper (275–300 words) about video or computer games. The requirements are that the paper be presented according to the MLA documentation style and have three references. One of the three references must be from the Web. You prepare the paper shown in Figure 2–83 on pages WD 131 and WD 132, which discusses game controllers.

Instructions: Perform the following tasks:

1. Start Word. If necessary, display formatting marks on the screen.
2. Modify the Normal style to 12-point Times New Roman font.
3. Adjust line spacing to double.
4. Remove space below (after) paragraphs.
5. Update the Normal style to reflect the adjusted line and paragraph spacing.
6. Create a header to number pages.
7. Type the name and course information at the left margin. Center and type the title.
8. Set a first-line indent to one-half inch for paragraphs in the body of the research paper.
9. Type the research paper as shown in Figures 2–83a and 2–83b. Change the bibliography style to MLA. As you insert citations, enter their source information (shown in Figure 2–83c). The first citation is a book; the second is an article in a periodical; and the third is a Web site. Edit the citations so that they are displayed according to Figures 2–83a and 2–83b.
10. At the end of the research paper text, press the ENTER key and then insert a manual page break so that the Works Cited page begins on a new page. Enter and format the works cited title (Figure 2–83c). Use Word to insert the bibliographical list (bibliography). Convert the bibliography field to text. Change the underline format on the titles of the works to the italic format and insert the correct publication medium for each work (shown in Figure 2–83c).

(b) Page 2

Kimble 2

Game controllers are used primarily to direct movement and actions of on-screen objects. Two popular types are gamepads and motion-sensing game controllers. Games become more enjoyable every day with the use of new and exciting game controllers. What will be next?

(a) Page 1

Kimble 1

Harley Kimble

Ms. Longherst

English 101

April 30, 2012

From One Controller to Another

Video games and computer games use a game controller as the input device that directs movements and actions of on-screen objects. Two commonly used game controllers are gamepads and motion-sensing game controllers (Joyce). Game controllers not only enrich the gaming experience but also aid in the movements and actions of players.

A gamepad is held by the player with both hands, allowing the player to control the movement or actions of the objects in the video or computer games. Players press buttons on the gamepad, often with their thumbs, to carry out actions. Some gamepads have swiveling sticks that also can trigger events during game play (Cortez 20-24). Some gamepads include wireless capabilities; others connect via a cable directly to the game console or a personal computer.

Motion-sensing game controllers allow the user to guide on-screen elements or trigger events by moving a handheld input device in predetermined directions through the air. These controllers communicate with a game console or personal computer via wired or wireless technology. A variety of games, from sports to simulations, use motion-sensing game controllers. Some of these controllers, such as baseball bats and golf clubs, are designed for only one specific kind of game; others are general purpose. A popular, general-purpose, motion-sensing game controller is Nintendo's Wii Remote. Shaped like a television remote control and operated with one hand, the Wii Remote uses Bluetooth wireless technology to communicate with the Wii game console (Bloom 56-59).

Figure 2–83

Continued >

In the Lab *continued*

(c) Page 3

Kimble 3

Works Cited

Bloom, June. *The Gaming Experience.* New York: Buffalo Works Press, 2012. Print.

Cortez, Domiciano Isachar. "Today's Game Controllers." *Gaming, Gaming, Gaming* Jan. 2012: 12-34. Print.

Joyce, Andrea D. *What Gamers Want.* 15 Feb. 2012. Web. 28 Mar. 2012.

11. Check the spelling and grammar of the paper at once.
12. Change the document properties, as specified by your instructor. Save the document using Lab 2-1 Game Controllers Paper as the file name.
13. Print the research paper. Handwrite the number of words, paragraphs, and characters in the research paper above the title of your printed research paper.

In the Lab

Lab 2: Preparing a Research Report with a Footnote

Problem: You are a college student enrolled in an introductory English class. Your assignment is to prepare a short research paper in any area of interest to you. The requirements are that the paper be presented according to the MLA documentation style, contain at least one note positioned as a footnote, and have three references. One of the three references must be from the Internet. You prepare a paper about trends in agriculture (Figure 2–84).

Instructions: Perform the following tasks:

1. Start Word. Modify the Normal style to 12-point Times New Roman font. Adjust line spacing to double and remove space below (after) paragraphs. Update the Normal style to include the adjusted line and paragraph spacing. Create a header to number pages. Type the name and course information at the left margin. Center and type the title. Set a first-line indent for paragraphs in the body of the research paper.
2. Type the research paper as shown in Figures 2–84a and 2–84b. Insert the footnote as shown in Figure 2–84a. Change the Footnote Text style to the format specified in the MLA documentation style. Change the bibliography style to MLA. As you insert citations, use the source information listed below and on page WD 134:
   a. Type of Source: Article in a Periodical
      Author: Barton, Blake
      Title: Computers in Agriculture
      Periodical Title: Agriculture Today and Tomorrow
      Year: 2012
      Month: Feb.
      Pages 53–86
      Publication Medium: Print

(b) Page 2

Gander 2

Brewster, the discovery of pests might trigger a pesticide to discharge in the affected area automatically (Agriculture: Expanding and Growing).

Many farmers use technology on a daily basis to regulate soil moisture and to keep their crops pest free. With technology, farming can be much more convenient and efficient.

(a) Page 1

Gander 1

Samuel Gander

Mr. Dunham

English 102

April 25, 2012

Farming on a Whole New Level

Although people have worked in agriculture for more than 10,000 years, advances in technology assist with maintaining and protecting land, crops, and animals. The demand to keep food prices affordable encourages those working in the agriculture industry to operate as efficiently as possible (Newman and Ruiz 33-47).

Almost all people and companies in this industry have many acres of land they must maintain, and it is not always feasible for farmers to take frequent trips around the property to perform basic tasks such as watering soil in the absence of rain. The number of people-hours required to water soil manually on several thousand acres of land might result in businesses spending thousands of dollars in labor and utility costs. If the irrigation process is automated, sensors detect how much rain has fallen recently, as well as whether the soil is in need of watering. The sensors then send this data to a computer that processes it and decides when and how much to water.[1]

In addition to keeping the soil moist and reducing maintenance costs, computers also can utilize sensors to analyze the condition of crops in the field and determine whether pests or diseases are affecting the crops. If sensors detect pests and/or diseases, computers send a notification to the appropriate individual to take corrective action. In some cases, according to

[1] Barton states that many automated home irrigation systems also are programmable and use rain sensors (67-73).

Figure 2–84

Continued >

In the Lab *continued*

b. Type of Source: Book
   Author: Newman, Albert D., and Carmen W. Ruiz
   Title: The Agricultural Industry Today
   Year: 2012
   City: New York
   Publisher: Alabama Press
   Publication Medium: Print

c. Type of Source: Web site
   Author: Brewster, Letty
   Name of Web page: Agriculture: Expanding and Growing
   Year: 2012
   Month: Jan.
   Day: 3
   Publication Medium: Web
   Year Accessed: 2012
   Month Accessed: Feb.
   Day Accessed: 9

3. At the end of the research paper text, press the ENTER key once and insert a manual page break so that the Works Cited page begins on a new page. Enter and format the works cited title. Use Word to insert the bibliographical list. Convert the bibliography field to text. Change the underline format on the titles of the works to the italic format, and insert the correct publication medium for each work.
4. Check the spelling and grammar of the paper.
5. Save the document using Lab 2-2 Agriculture Paper as the file name.
6. Print the research paper. Handwrite the number of words, including the footnotes, in the research paper above the title of your printed research paper.

In the Lab

Lab 3: Composing a Research Paper from Notes

Problem: You have drafted the notes shown in Figure 2–85. Your assignment is to prepare a short research paper from these notes.

Instructions: Perform the following tasks:

1. Start Word. Review the notes in Figure 2–85 and then rearrange and reword them. Embellish the paper as you deem necessary. Present the paper according to the MLA documentation style.

   Create an AutoCorrect entry that automatically corrects the spelling of the misspelled word, digtal, to the correct spelling, digital. Set an AutoCorrect exception for CD., so that Word does not lowercase the next typed letter.

   Insert a footnote that refers the reader to the Web for more information. Enter citations and their sources as shown.

   Create the works cited page (bibliography) from the listed sources. Convert the bibliography field to text. Change the underline format on the titles of the works to the italic format, and insert the correct publication medium for each work.
2. If necessary, set the default dictionary. Add the word, Flickr, to the dictionary. Check the spelling and grammar of the paper.

3. Use the Research task pane to look up a definition of a word in the paper. Copy and insert the definition into the document as a footnote. Be sure to quote the definition and cite the source. *Hint:* Use a Web site as the type of source.
4. Save the document using Lab 2-3 Cloud Storage Paper as the file name. Print the research paper. Handwrite the number of words, including the footnotes, in the research paper above the title of the printed research paper.

Cloud Storage:

- When storing data using cloud storage, the user must locate the appropriate Web site. Some sites support only certain file types. Other sites provide more than just storage.
- Cloud storage is one of the many different features available on the Internet.
- Cloud storage allows users to store files on Web sites.
- Computer users may use this type of storage if they do not want to store their data locally on a hard disk or other type of media.

Different Web sites provide different types of cloud storage. Three are Google's Gmail, YouTube, and Windows Live SkyDrive (source: "Cloud Storage and the Internet," an article on pages 23-37 in March 2012 issue of *Internet Usage and Trends* by Leona Carter).

- Google's e-mail program, Gmail, is cloud storage that stores e-mail messages.
- YouTube is different from Gmail, however, because it stores only digital videos (source: pages 22-24 in a book called *Working with the Internet: Cloud Storage* by Robert M. Gaff, published at Jane Lewis Press in New York in 2012).
- Windows Live SkyDrive is a cloud storage provider that accepts any type of file. This type of Web site is used mainly for backup or additional storage space.

Some cloud storage Web sites also provide other services (source: a Web site titled *The Internet: Cloud Storage* by Rebecca A. Ford and Harry I. Garland of Course Technology dated January 2, 2012, viewed on March 7, 2012).

- Flickr provides cloud storage for digital photos and also enables users to manage their photos and share them with others.
- Facebook provides cloud storage for a number of different file types including digital photos, digital videos, messages, and personal information. Facebook also provides a means of social networking.
- Google Docs not only stores documents, spreadsheets, and presentations in its cloud, it also enables its users to create these documents.

Figure 2–85

Cases and Places

Apply your creative thinking and problem solving skills to design and implement a solution.

Note: To complete these assignments, you may be required to use the Data Files for Students. See the inside back cover of this book for instructions on downloading the Data Files for Students, or contact your instructor for information about accessing the required files.

1: Create a Research Paper about Preparing for a Career in the Computer Industry

Academic

As a student in an introductory computer class, your instructor has assigned a research paper that discusses educational options available for students pursuing a career in the computer industry. The source for the text in your research paper is in a file called Preparing for a Career in the Computer Industry, which is located on the Data Files for Students. In addition to this source, if your instructor requests, use the Research task pane to obtain information from another source. Include a note positioned as a footnote. Add an AutoCorrect entry to correct a word you commonly mistype.

Using the concepts and techniques presented in this chapter, along with the text in the file on the Data Files for Students, create and format this research paper according to the MLA documentation style. Be sure to check spelling and grammar of the finished paper. Submit your assignment in the format specified by your instructor.

2: Create a Research Paper about Computer Viruses

Personal

The computer you recently purchased included an antivirus program. Because you need practice writing research papers and you want to learn more about computer viruses, you decide to write a paper about computer viruses. The source for the text in your research paper is in a file called Computer Viruses, which is located on the Data Files for Students. In addition to this source, if your instructor requests, use the Research task pane to obtain information from another source. Include a note positioned as a footnote. Add an AutoCorrect entry to correct a word you commonly mistype.

Using the concepts and techniques presented in this chapter, along with the text in the file on the Data Files for Students, create and format this research paper according to the MLA documentation style. Be sure to check spelling and grammar of the finished paper. Submit your assignment in the format specified by your instructor.

3: Create a Research Paper about a Disaster Recovery Plan

Professional

Your boss has asked you to research the components of a disaster recovery plan. Because you learned in college how to write research papers, you decide to present your findings in a research paper. The source for the text in your research paper is in a file called Disaster Recovery Plan, which is located on the Data Files for Students. In addition to this source, if your instructor requests, use the Research task pane to obtain information from another source. Include a note positioned as a footnote. Add an AutoCorrect entry to correct a word you commonly mistype.

Using the concepts and techniques presented in this chapter, along with the text in the file on the Data Files for Students, create and format this research paper according to the MLA documentation style. Be sure to check spelling and grammar of the finished paper. Submit your assignment in the format specified by your instructor.

3 Creating a Business Letter with a Letterhead and Table

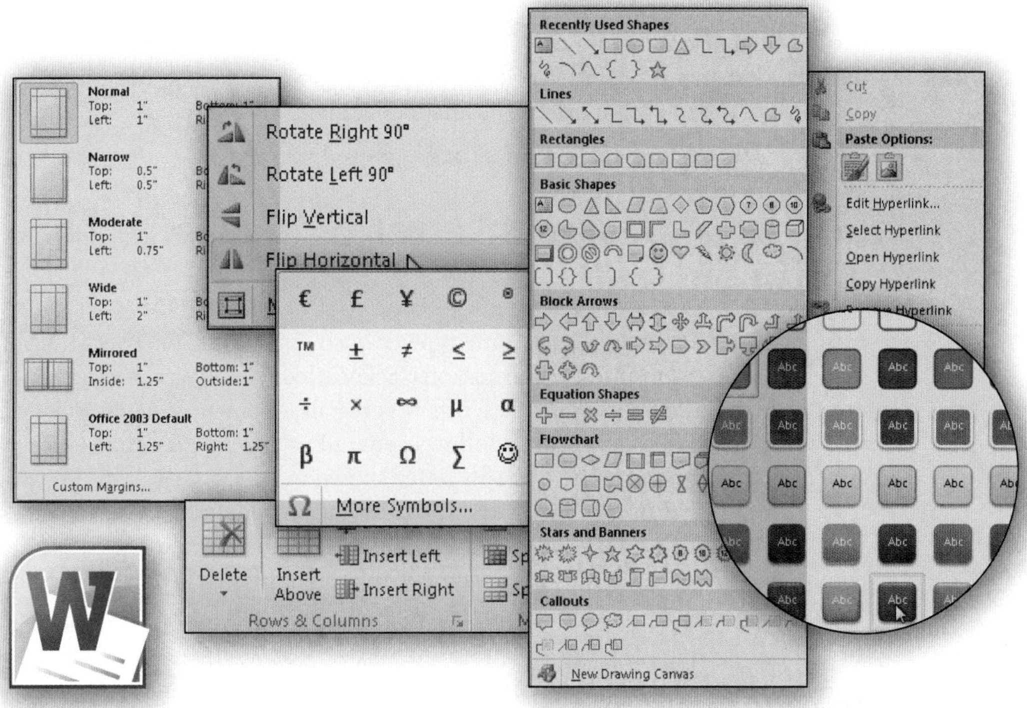

Objectives

You will have mastered the material in this chapter when you can:

- Change margins
- Insert and format a shape
- Change text wrapping
- Insert and format a clip art image
- Insert a symbol
- Add a border to a paragraph
- Clear formatting
- Convert a hyperlink to regular text
- Create a file from an existing file
- Apply a Quick Style
- Set and use tab stops
- Insert the current date
- Create, insert, and modify a building block
- Insert a Word table, enter data in the table, and format the table
- Address and print an envelope

3 Creating a Business Letter with a Letterhead and Table

Introduction

In a business environment, people use documents to communicate with others. Business documents can include letters, memos, newsletters, proposals, and resumes. An effective business document clearly and concisely conveys its message and has a professional, organized appearance. You can use your own creative skills to design and compose business documents. Using Word, for example, you can develop the content and decide on the location of each item in a business document.

Project — Business Letter with a Letterhead and Table

At some time, you will prepare some type of business letter. Contents of business letters include requests, inquiries, confirmations, acknowledgements, recommendations, notifications, responses, invitations, offers, referrals, complaints, and more.

The project in this chapter follows generally accepted guidelines for writing letters and uses Word to create the business letter shown in Figure 3–1. This business letter to a potential advertiser (Wilcox Tractor Restorations) includes a custom letterhead, as well as all essential business letter components: date line, inside address, salutation, body, complimentary close, and signature block. To easily present the advertisement rates, this information appears in a table, and the discounts are in a bulleted list.

Overview

As you read through this chapter, you will learn how to create the business letter in Figure 3–1 by performing these general tasks:

- Design and create a letterhead.
- Compose a business letter.
- Print the business letter.
- Address and print an envelope.

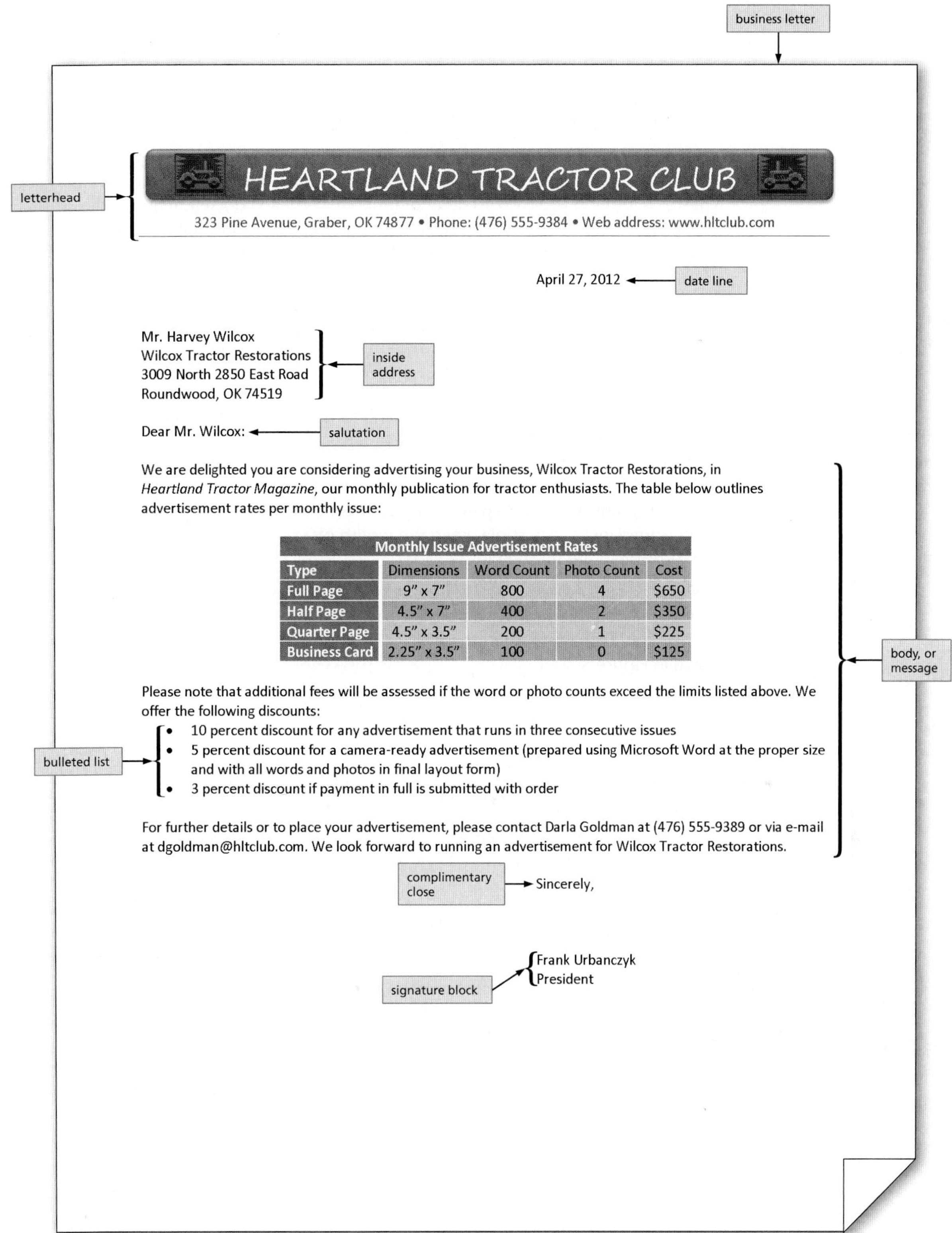

HEARTLAND TRACTOR CLUB

323 Pine Avenue, Graber, OK 74877 • Phone: (476) 555-9384 • Web address: www.hltclub.com

April 27, 2012

Mr. Harvey Wilcox
Wilcox Tractor Restorations
3009 North 2850 East Road
Roundwood, OK 74519

Dear Mr. Wilcox:

We are delighted you are considering advertising your business, Wilcox Tractor Restorations, in *Heartland Tractor Magazine*, our monthly publication for tractor enthusiasts. The table below outlines advertisement rates per monthly issue:

Monthly Issue Advertisement Rates				
Type	Dimensions	Word Count	Photo Count	Cost
Full Page	9" x 7"	800	4	$650
Half Page	4.5" x 7"	400	2	$350
Quarter Page	4.5" x 3.5"	200	1	$225
Business Card	2.25" x 3.5"	100	0	$125

Please note that additional fees will be assessed if the word or photo counts exceed the limits listed above. We offer the following discounts:

- 10 percent discount for any advertisement that runs in three consecutive issues
- 5 percent discount for a camera-ready advertisement (prepared using Microsoft Word at the proper size and with all words and photos in final layout form)
- 3 percent discount if payment in full is submitted with order

For further details or to place your advertisement, please contact Darla Goldman at (476) 555-9389 or via e-mail at dgoldman@hltclub.com. We look forward to running an advertisement for Wilcox Tractor Restorations.

Sincerely,

Frank Urbanczyk
President

Figure 3-1

Plan Ahead

General Project Guidelines

When creating a Word document, the actions you perform and decisions you make will affect the appearance and characteristics of the finished document. As you create a business letter, such as the project shown in Figure 3–1 on the previous page, you should follow these general guidelines:

1. **Determine how to create a letterhead.** A **letterhead** is the section of a letter that identifies an organization or individual. Often, the letterhead appears at the top of a letter. Although you can design and print a letterhead yourself, many businesses pay an outside firm to design and print their letterhead, usually on higher-quality paper. They then use the professionally preprinted paper for external business communications.
2. **If you do not have preprinted letterhead paper, design a creative letterhead.** Use text, graphics, formats, and colors that reflect the organization or individual. Include the organization's or individual's name, postal mailing address, and telephone number. If the organization or individual has an e-mail address and Web address, you may include those as well.
3. **Compose an effective business letter.** A finished business letter should look like a symmetrically framed picture with evenly spaced margins, all balanced below an attractive letterhead. The letter should be well-written, properly formatted, logically organized, and use visuals where appropriate. The content of a letter should contain proper grammar, correct spelling, logically constructed sentences, flowing paragraphs, and sound ideas. If possible, keep the length of a business letter to one page. Be sure to proofread the finished letter carefully.

When necessary, more specific details concerning the above guidelines are presented at appropriate points in the chapter. The chapter also will identify the actions performed and decisions made regarding these guidelines during the creation of the business letter shown in Figure 3–1.

For an introduction to Windows 7 and instruction about how to perform basic Windows 7 tasks, read the Office 2010 and Windows 7 chapter at the beginning of this book, where you can learn how to resize windows, change screen resolution, create folders, move and rename files, use Windows Help, and much more.

To Start Word and Display Formatting Marks

If you are using a computer to step through the project in this chapter and you want your screens to match the figures in this book, you should change your screen's resolution to 1024 × 768. For information about how to change a computer's resolution, refer to the Office 2010 and Windows 7 chapter at the beginning of this book.

The following steps start Word and display formatting marks.

1. Start Word. If necessary, maximize the Word window.
2. If the Print Layout button on the status bar is not selected (shown in Figure 3–2), click it so that your screen is in Print Layout view.
3. Change your zoom to 110% (or a percent where the document is large enough for you easily to see its contents).
4. If the Show/Hide ¶ button (Home tab | Paragraph group) is not selected already, click it to display formatting marks on the screen.

For an introduction to Office 2010 and instruction about how to perform basic tasks in Office 2010 programs, read the Office 2010 and Windows 7 chapter at the beginning of this book, where you can learn how to start a program, use the Ribbon, save a file, open a file, quit a program, use Help, and much more.

To Change Theme Colors

Recall that Word provides document themes that contain a variety of color schemes to assist you in selecting complementary colors in a document. In a letter, select a color scheme that adequately reflects the organization or person. The letter in this chapter uses the Executive color scheme. The following steps change theme colors.

1. Click the Change Styles button (Home tab | Styles group) to display the Change Styles menu and then point to Colors on the Change Styles menu to display the Colors gallery.

2. Click Executive in the Colors gallery to change the document theme colors to the selected color scheme.

BTW

The Ribbon and Screen Resolution
Word may change how the groups and buttons within the groups appear on the Ribbon, depending on the computer's screen resolution. Thus, your Ribbon may look different from the ones in this book if you are using a screen resolution other than 1024 × 768.

To Change Margin Settings

Word is preset to use standard 8.5-by-11-inch paper, with 1-inch top, bottom, left, and right margins. If you change the default (preset) margin settings, the new margin settings affect every page in the document. If you wanted the margins to affect just a portion of the document, you would divide the document into sections (discussed in a later chapter), which enables you to specify different margin settings for each section.

The business letter in this chapter uses .75-inch left and right margins and 1-inch top and bottom margins, so that more text can fit from left to right on the page. The following steps change margin settings.

1

- Display the Page Layout tab.
- Click the Margins button (Page Layout tab | Page Setup group) to display the Margins gallery (Figure 3–2).

2

- Click Moderate in the Margins gallery to change the margins to the specified settings.

Q&A

What if the margin settings I want are not in the Margins gallery?

You can click Custom Margins in the Margins gallery and then enter your desired margin values in the top, bottom, left, and right text boxes in the dialog box.

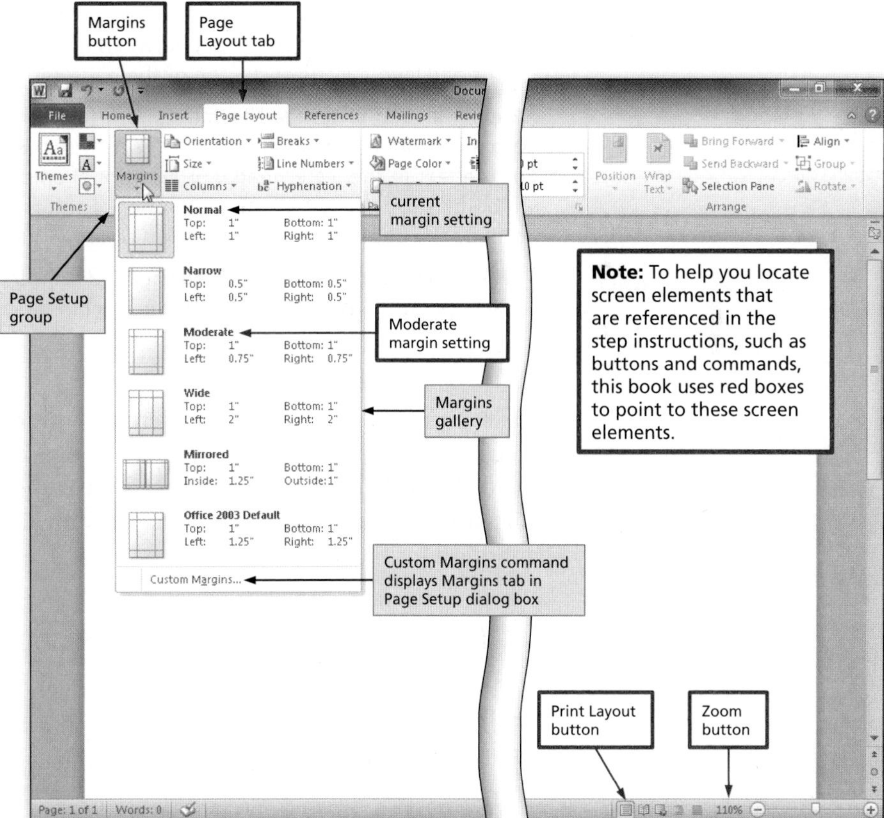

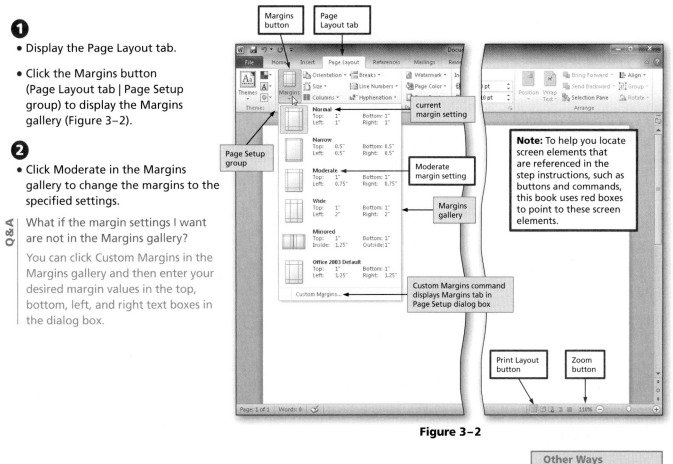

Figure 3–2

Other Ways

1. Position mouse pointer on margin boundary on ruler; when mouse pointer changes to two-headed arrow, drag margin boundary on ruler

Creating a Letterhead

The cost of preprinted letterhead can be high. Thus, an alternative is to create your own letterhead and save it in a file. When you want to create a letter at a later time using the letterhead, simply create a new document from the letterhead file. In this chapter, you create a letterhead and then save it in a file for future use.

Plan Ahead

Design a creative letterhead.
A letterhead often is the first section a reader notices on a letter. Thus, it is important the letterhead appropriately reflect the essence of the business or individual (i.e., formal, technical, creative, etc.). The letterhead should leave ample room for the contents of the letter. When designing a letterhead, consider its contents, placement, and appearance.

- **Contents of letterhead.** A letterhead should contain these elements:
  - Complete legal name of the individual, group, or company
  - Complete mailing address: street address including building, room, suite number, or post office box, along with city, state, and postal code
  - Telephone number(s) and fax number, if one exists

  Many letterheads also include a Web address, an e-mail address, and a logo or other image. If you use an image, select one that expresses your personality or goals.
- **Placement of elements in the letterhead.** Many letterheads center their elements across the top of the page. Others align some or all of the elements with the left or right margins. Sometimes, the elements are split between the top and bottom of the page. For example, a name and logo may be at the top of the page with the address at the bottom of the page.
- **Appearance of letterhead elements.** Use fonts that are easy to read. Give the organization or individual name impact by making its font size larger than the rest of the text in the letterhead. For additional emphasis, consider formatting the name in bold, italic, or a different color. Choose colors that complement each other and convey the goals of the organization or individual.

When finished designing the letterhead, determine if a divider line would help to visually separate the letterhead from the remainder of the letter.

The letterhead for the business letter in this chapter consists of the organization name, appropriate graphics, postal address, telephone number, and Web address. The name and graphics are enclosed in a rectangular shape (Figure 3–1 on page WD 139), and the contact information is below the shape. You will follow these general steps to create the letterhead for the business letter:

1. Insert and format a shape.
2. Enter and format the organization name in the shape.
3. Insert, format, and position the images in the shape.
4. Enter the contact information below the shape.
5. Add a border below the contact information.

To Insert a Shape

The first step is in creating the letterhead in this chapter is to draw a rectangular shape. Word has a variety of predefined shapes, which are a type of drawing object, that you can insert in documents. A **drawing object** is a graphic that you create using Word. Examples of shape drawing objects include rectangles, circles, triangles, arrows, flowcharting symbols, stars, banners, and callouts. The next steps insert a rounded rectangle shape.

1

- Display the Insert tab.
- Click the Shapes button (Insert tab | Illustrations group) to display the Shapes gallery (Figure 3–3).

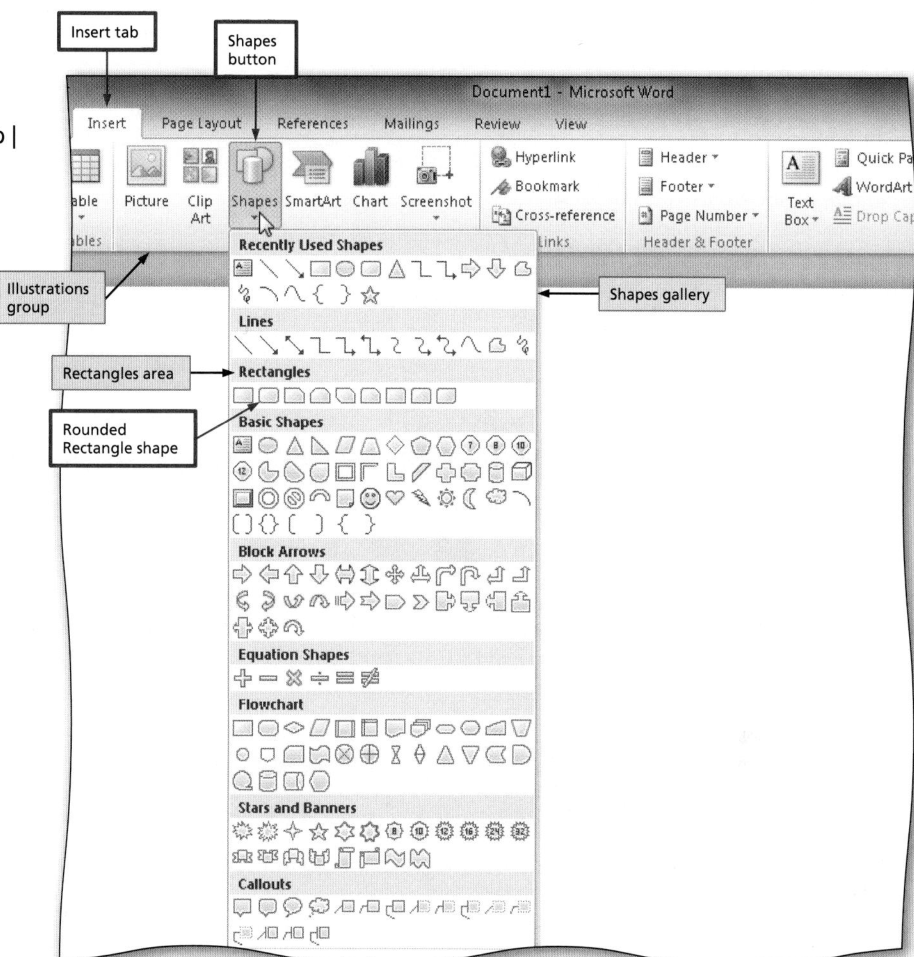

Figure 3–3

2

- Click the Rounded Rectangle shape in the Rectangles area of the Shapes gallery, which removes the gallery and changes the mouse pointer to the shape of a crosshair.
- Position the mouse pointer (a crosshair) by the insertion point in the document window, as shown in Figure 3–4, which is the location for the upper-left corner of the desired shape.

Q&A What is the purpose of the crosshair mouse pointer?

In the document window, you will drag the crosshair mouse pointer from the upper-left corner to the lower-right corner to form the desired location and size of the shape.

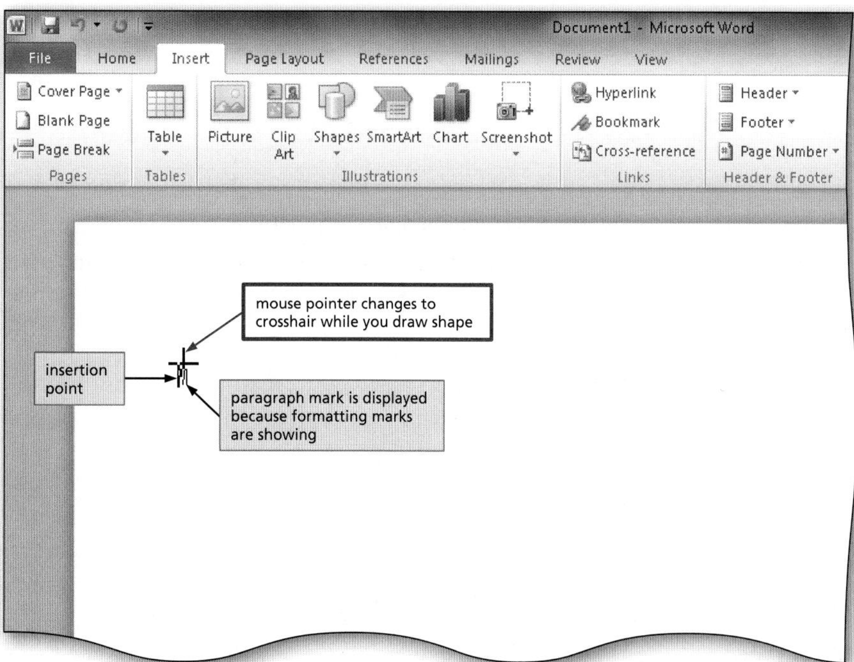

Figure 3–4

- Drag the mouse to the right and downward to form the boundaries of the shape, as shown in Figure 3–5. Do not release the mouse button.

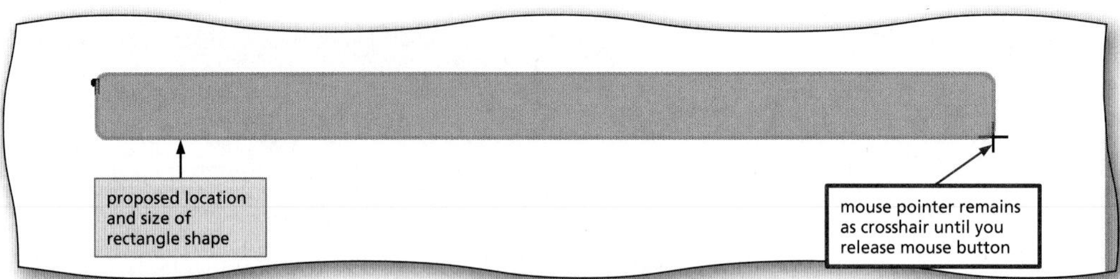

Figure 3–5

- Release the mouse button so that Word draws the shape according to your drawing in the document window.
- Verify your shape is the same approximate height and width as the one in this project by clicking the Size button (Drawing Tools Format tab | Size group) and then, if necessary, changing the values in the Shape Height box and Shape Width boxes to 0.5"and 7", respectively (Figure 3–6). When finished, click the Size button again to remove the Shape Height and Shape Width boxes.

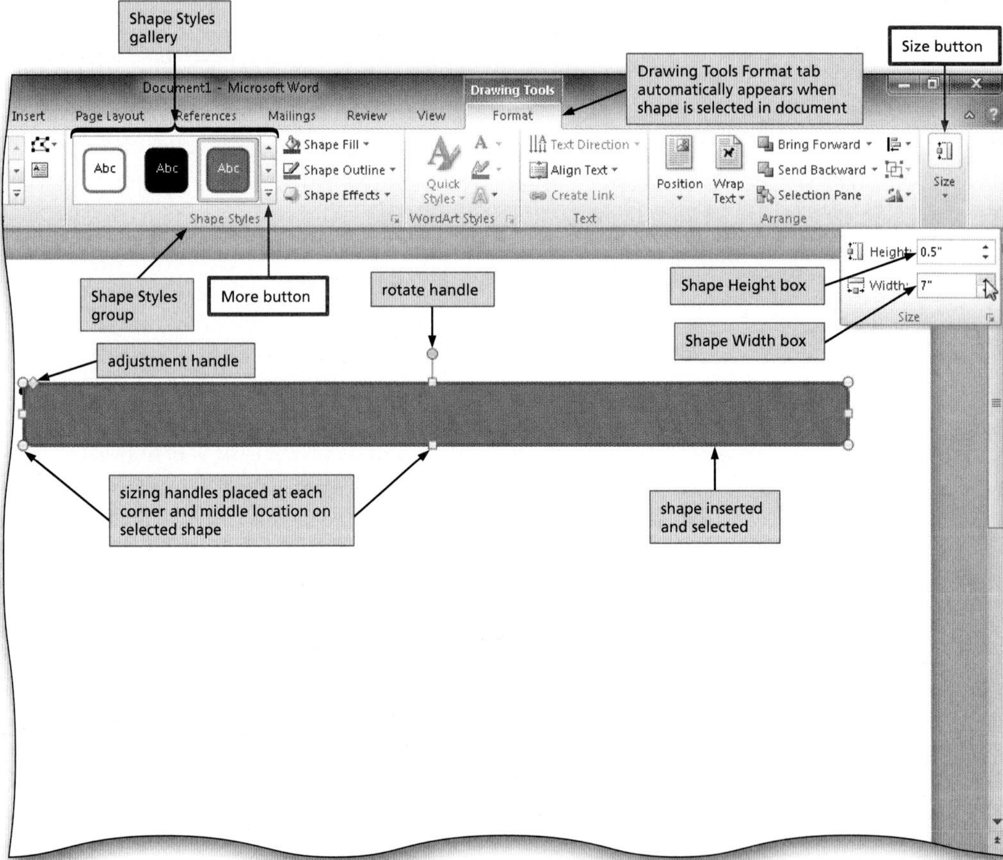

Figure 3–6

Q&A What is the purpose of the rotate and adjustment handles?

When you drag an object's **rotate handle**, which is the green circle, Word rotates the object in the direction you drag the mouse. When you drag an object's **adjustment handle**, which is the yellow diamond, Word changes the object's shape.

Q&A What if I wanted to delete a shape and start over?

With the shape selected, you would press the DELETE key.

To Apply a Shape Style

Word provides a Shape Styles gallery, allowing you to change the appearance of the shape. Because the organization in this project, Heartland Tractor Club, supports many different tractor manufacturers, its letterhead should use a color that is not commonly associated with a particular tractor manufacturer. The next steps apply a shape style that uses a shade of brown.

1

- With the shape still selected, click the More button (shown in Figure 3–6) in the Shape Styles gallery (Drawing Tools Format tab | Shape Styles group) to expand the gallery.

Q&A What if my shape is no longer selected?

Click the shape to select it.

- Point to Intense Effect - Brown, Accent 4 in the Shape Styles gallery to display a live preview of that style applied to the shape in the document (Figure 3–7).

Experiment

- Point to various styles in the Shape Styles gallery and watch the style of the shape change in the document.

2

- Click Intense Effect - Brown, Accent 4 in the Shape Styles gallery to apply the selected style to the shape.

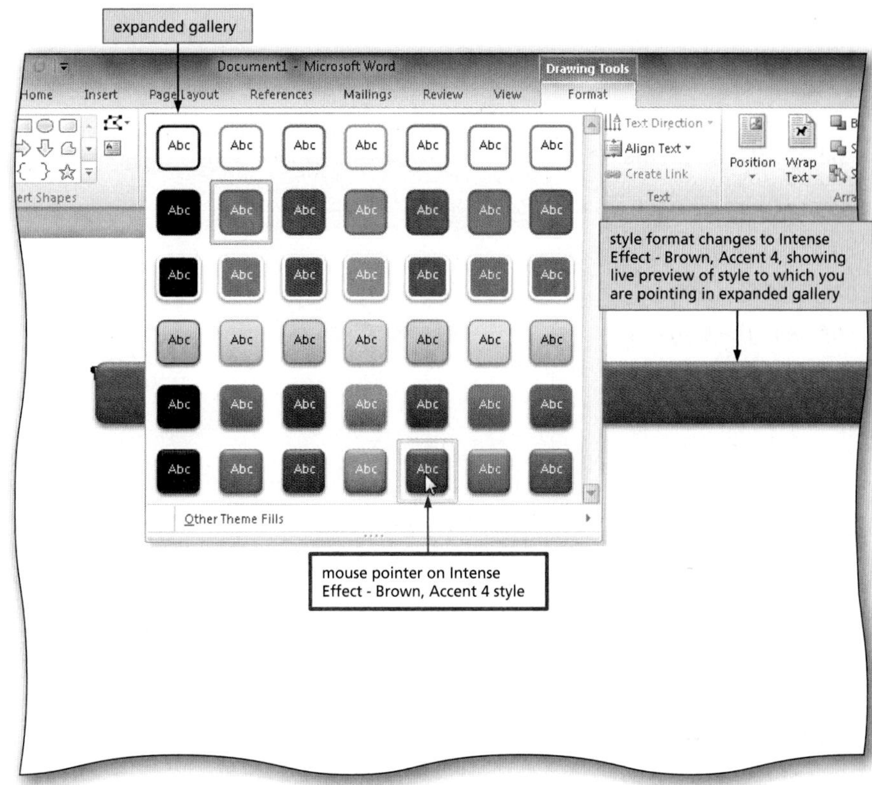

Figure 3–7

Other Ways

1. Click Format Shape Dialog Box Launcher (Drawing Tools Format tab | Shape Styles group), click Picture Color in left pane (Format Shape dialog box), select desired colors, click Close button
2. Right-click shape, click Format Shape on shortcut menu, click Picture Color in left pane (Format Shape dialog box), select desired colors, click Close button

To Add Text to a Shape

The next step is to add the organization name to the shape. The following steps add text to a shape.

1

- Right-click the shape to display a shortcut menu and the Mini toolbar (Figure 3–8).

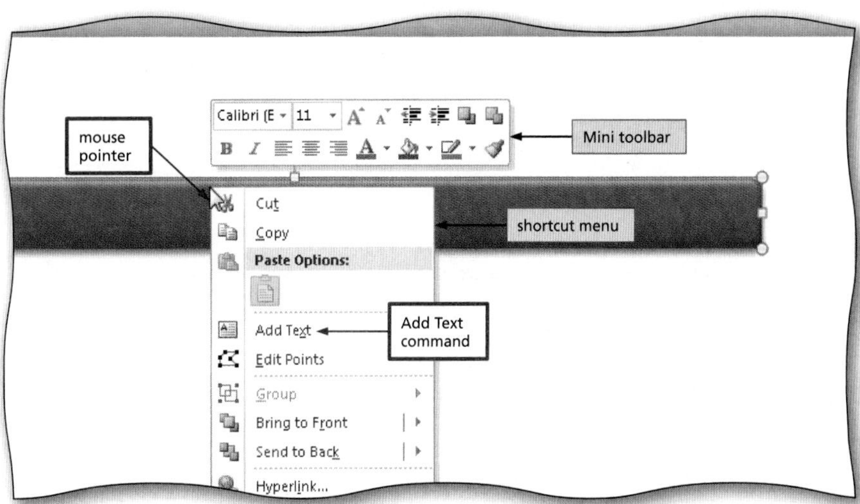

Figure 3–8

- Click Add Text on the shortcut menu to place an insertion point centered in the shape.
- Type **HEARTLAND TRACTOR CLUB** as the organization name in the shape (Figure 3–9).

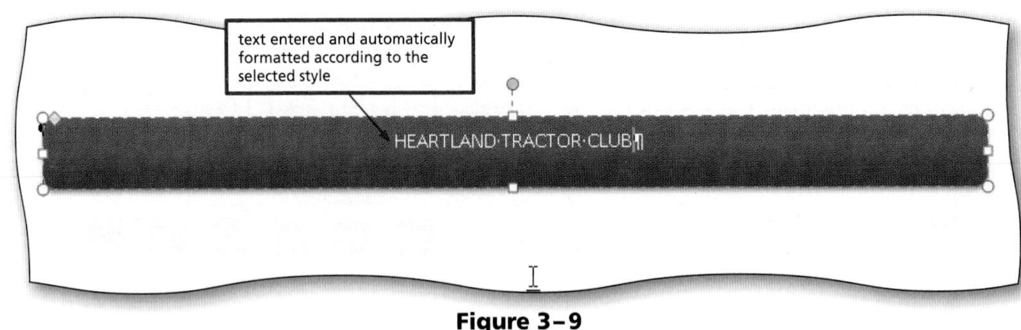

Figure 3–9

To Use the Grow Font Button to Increase Font Size

You want the font size of the organization name to be much larger in the shape. In previous chapters, you used the Font Size box arrow (Home tab | Font group) to change the font size of text. Word also provides a Grow Font button (Home tab | Font group), which increases the font size of selected text each time you click the button. The following steps use the Grow Font button to increase the font size of the organization name to 22 point.

1

- Drag through the organization name in the shape to select the text to be formatted.

2

- Display the Home tab.
- Repeatedly click the Grow Font button (Home tab | Font group) until the Font Size box displays 22 to increase the font size of the selected text (Figure 3–10).

Q&A

What if I click the Grow Font button (Home tab | Font group) too many times, causing the font size to be too big?

Click the Shrink Font button (Home tab | Font group) until the desired font size is displayed.

Experiment

- Repeatedly click the Grow Font and Shrink Font buttons (Home tab | Font group) and watch the font size of the selected name change in the document window. When you are finished experimenting with these two buttons, set the font size to 22.

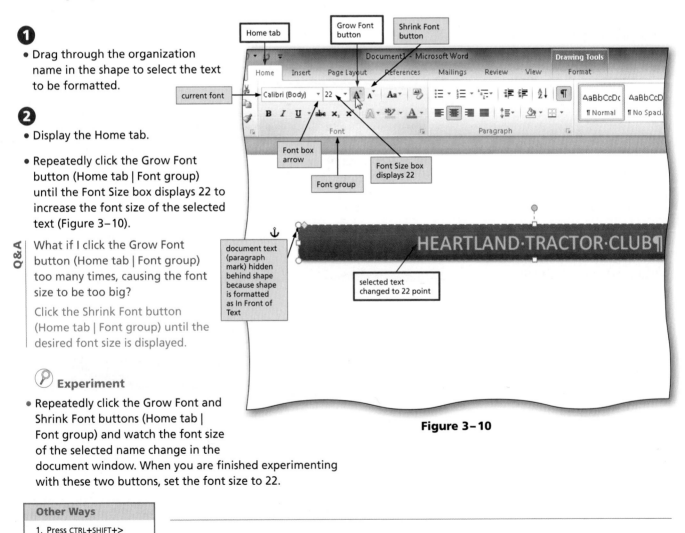

Figure 3–10

Other Ways

1. Press CTRL+SHIFT+>

To Change the Font of Selected Text

The font of the organization name currently is Calibri. To make the organization name stand out even more, change the font of the name in the letterhead to a font different from the rest of the letter. The following steps change the font of the selected text.

1. With the text selected, click the Font box arrow (Home tab | Font group) to display the Font gallery.
2. Scroll to and then click Segoe Script in the Font gallery to change the font of the selected text (shown in Figure 3–11 on the next page).
3. Click anywhere in the text in the shape to remove the selection and place the insertion point in the shape.

Floating versus Inline Objects

When you insert an object, such as a shape, in a document, Word inserts it as either an inline object or a floating object. An **inline object** is an object that is part of a paragraph. With inline objects, you change the location of the object by setting paragraph options, such as centered, right-aligned, and so on. A **floating object** is an object that can be positioned at a specific location in a document or in a layer over or behind text in a document. You have more flexibility with floating objects because you can position a floating object anywhere on the page.

In addition to changing an object from inline to floating and vice versa, Word provides several floating options. All of these options affect how text wraps with the object. Table 3–1 lists the various text wrapping options and explains the function of each one.

Table 3–1 Text Wrapping Options

Text Wrapping Option	Object Type	How It Works
In Line with Text	Inline	Object positioned according to paragraph formatting; for example, if paragraph is centered, object will be centered with any text in the paragraph.
Square	Floating	Text wraps around object, with text forming a box around the object.
Tight	Floating	Text wraps around object, with text forming to shape of the object.
Through	Floating	Object appears at beginning, middle, or end of text. Moving object changes location of text.
Top and Bottom	Floating	Object appears above or below text. Moving object changes location of text.
Behind Text	Floating	Object appears behind text.
In Front of Text	Floating	Object appears in front of text and may cover the text.

BTW

Positioning Objects
If you want to use the Square text wrapping option, you can specify where the object should be positioned on the page. To specify the position, select the object, click the Object Position button (Picture Tools Format tab | Arrange group), and then click the desired location in the Object Position gallery.

To Change an Object's Text Wrapping

When you insert a shape in a Word document, the default text wrapping is In Front of Text, which means the object will cover any text behind it. Because you want the letterhead above the contents of the letter, instead of covering the contents of the letter, you change the text wrapping for the shape to Top and Bottom. The following steps change a shape's text wrapping.

1

- Click the edge of the shape to select the shape.
- Display the Drawing Tools Format tab.
- Click the Wrap Text button (Drawing Tools Format tab | Arrange group) to display the Wrap Text gallery (Figure 3–11).

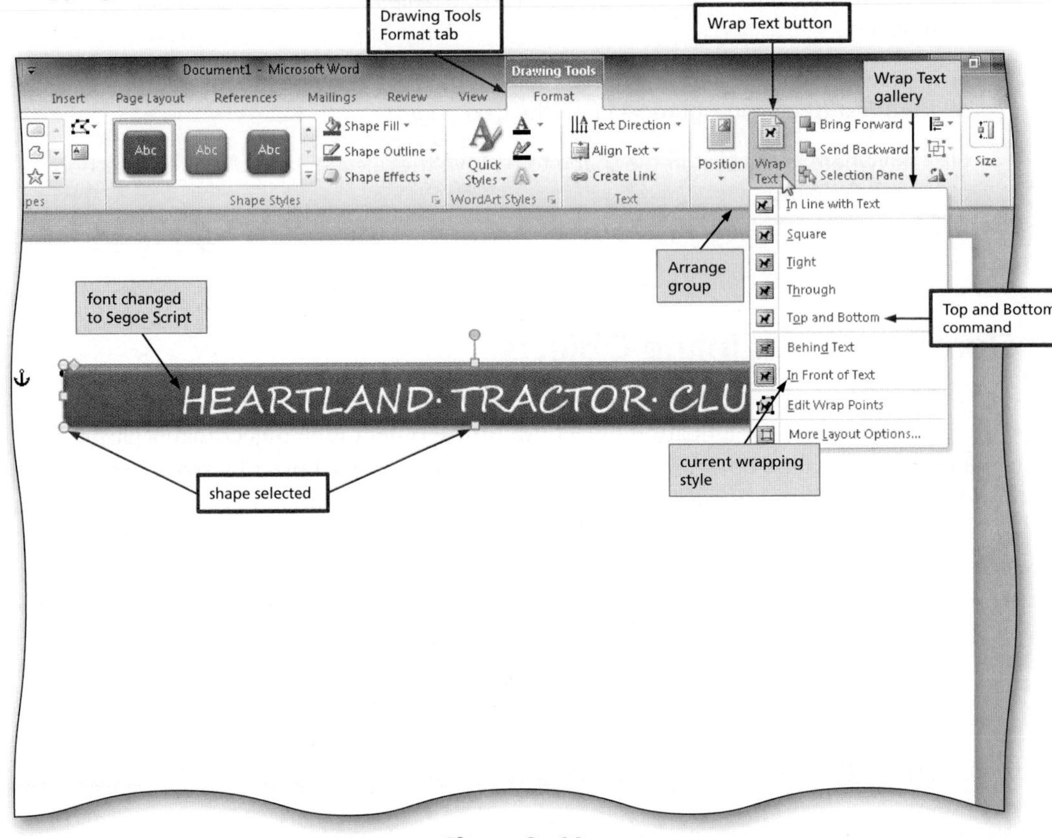

Figure 3–11

Experiment

- Point to various text wrapping options in the Wrap Text gallery and watch the shape configure to the selected wrapping option, which in this case, moves the paragraph mark to different locations in the document.

- Click Top and Bottom in the Wrap Text gallery so that the object does not cover the document text.

Other Ways

1. Right-click object, point to Wrap Text on shortcut menu, click desired wrapping style

To Insert Clip Art

Files containing graphical images, or graphics, are available from a variety of sources. In the Chapter 1 document, you inserted a digital picture taken with a camera phone. In this project, you insert **clip art**, which is a predefined graphic. In Microsoft Office programs, clip art is located in the **Clip Organizer**, which contains a collection of clip art, photos, animations, sounds, and videos.

The letterhead in this project contains clip art of a tractor (Figure 3–1 on page WD 139). Thus, the next steps insert a clip art image on the line below the shape in the document.

- Click the paragraph mark below the shape to position the insertion point where you want to insert the clip art image.
- Display the Insert tab.
- Click the Clip Art button (Insert tab | Illustrations group) to display the Clip Art pane (Figure 3–12).

Q&A

What is a pane?

Recall from the Office 2010 and Windows 7 chapter at the beginning of this book that a pane, or task pane, is a separate window that enables you to carry out some Word tasks more efficiently.

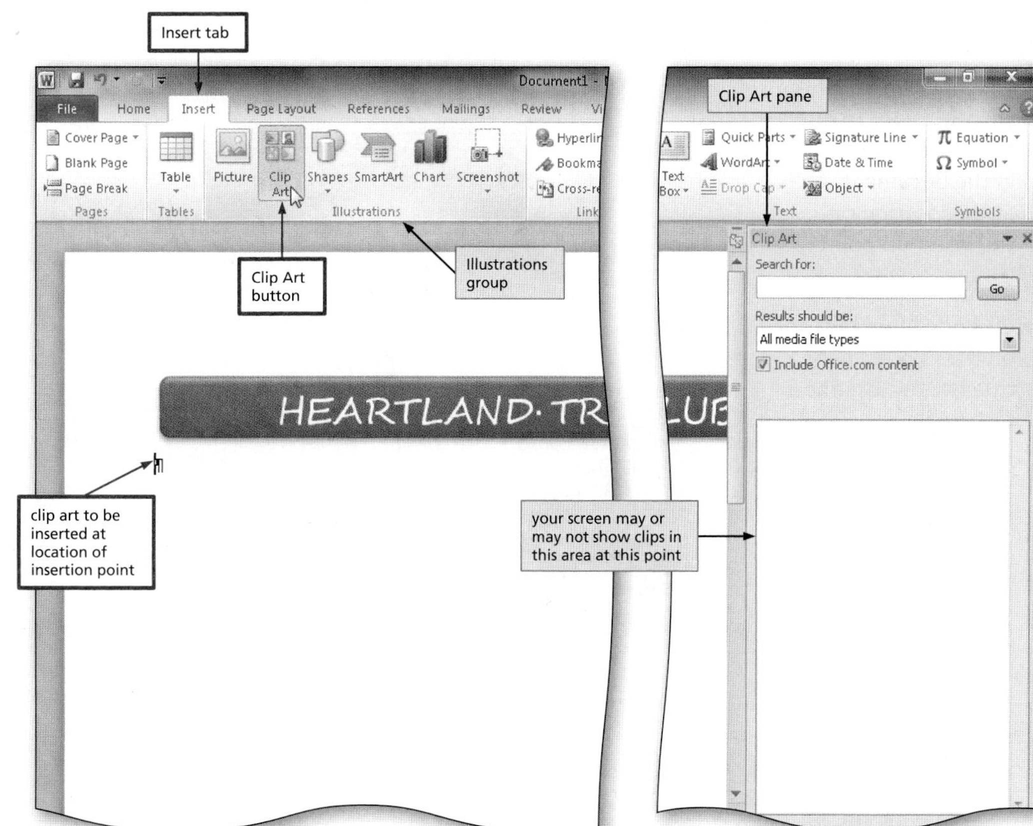

Figure 3–12

- If the Search for text box displays text, drag through the text to select it.
- Type `tractor` in the Search for text box to specify the search text, which in this case indicates the type of image you wish to locate.
- Click the Go button to display a list of clips that match the entered search text (Figure 3–13).

Q&A

Why is my list of clips different from Figure 3–13?

If your Include Office.com content check box is selected and you are connected to the Internet, the Clip Art pane displays clips from the Web as well as those installed on your hard disk.

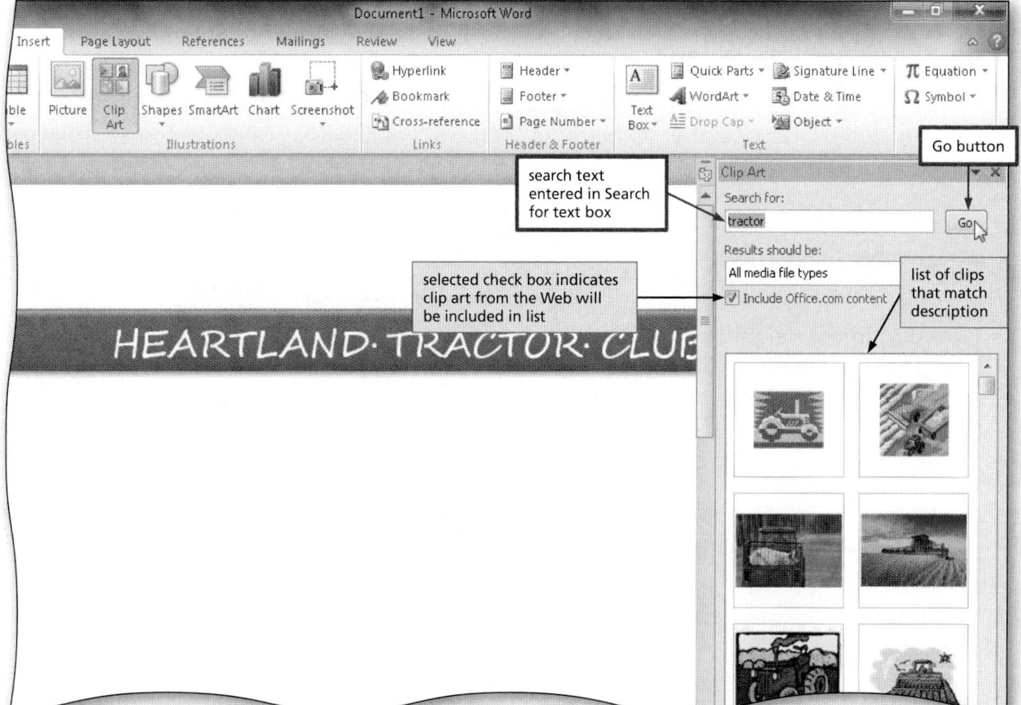

Figure 3–13

- Click the clip art of the yellow tractor to insert this clip art image in the document at the location of the insertion point (Figure 3–14).
- Click the Close button on the Clip Art pane title bar to close the task pane.

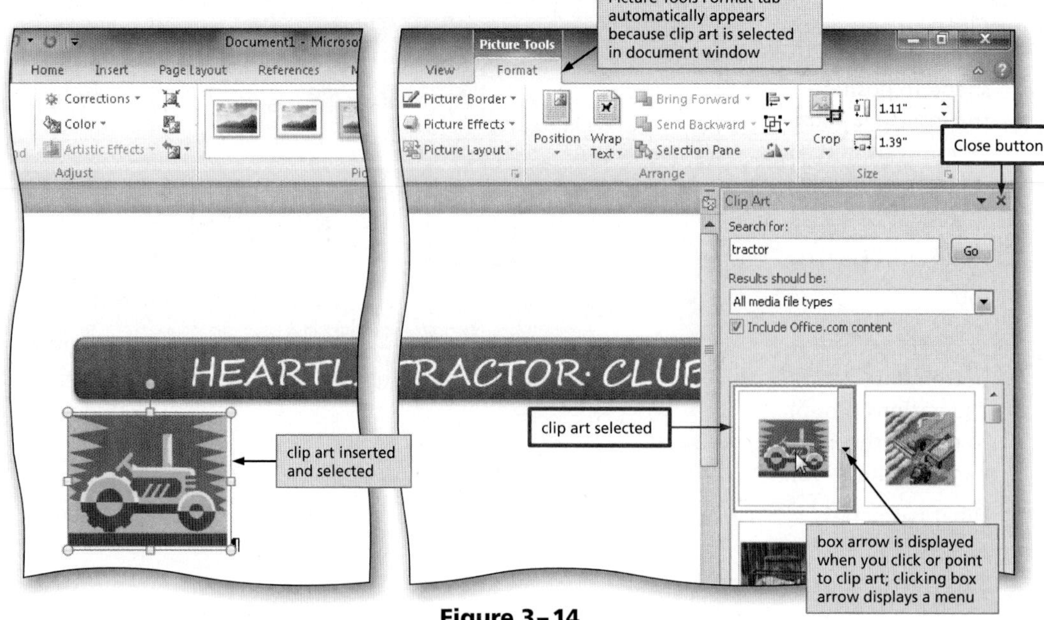

Figure 3–14

To Resize a Graphic to a Percent of the Original

In this project, the graphic is 35 percent of its original size. Instead of dragging a sizing handle to change the graphic's size, as you learned in Chapter 1, you can set exact size percentages. The following steps resize a graphic to a percent of the original.

- With the graphic still selected, click the Advanced Layout: Size Dialog Box Launcher (Picture Tools Format tab | Size group) to display the Layout dialog box.

Q&A What if the graphic is not selected or the Picture Tools Format tab is not on the Ribbon?

Click the graphic to select it or double-click the graphic to make the Picture Tools Format tab the active tab.

2

- In the Scale area (Layout dialog box), double-click the current value in the Height box to select it.
- Type **35** in the Height box and then press the TAB key to display the same percent value in the Width box (Figure 3–15).

Figure 3–15

Q&A Why did Word automatically fill in the value in the Width box?

When the 'Lock aspect ratio' check box (Layout dialog box) is selected, Word automatically maintains the size proportions of the graphic.

Q&A How do I know to use 35 percent for the resized graphic?

The larger graphic consumed too much room on the page. Try various percentages to determine the size that works best in the letterhead design.

- Click the OK button to close the dialog box and resize the selected graphic (Figure 3–16).

Figure 3–16

Other Ways

1. Right-click graphic, click Size and Position on shortcut menu, enter values (Layout dialog box), click OK button

To Change the Color of a Graphic

In Word, you can change the color of a graphic. The clip art currently consists of shades of yellow and brown. Because the clip art in this project will be placed in a rectangle shape, you prefer to use colors that blend better with the current color scheme. The following steps change the color of the graphic to a shade in the current color scheme that matches the color of the shape.

- With the graphic still selected (shown in Figure 3–16), click the Color button (Picture Tools Format tab | Adjust group) to display the Color gallery.
- Point to Orange, Accent color 3 Dark in the Color gallery (fourth color in second row) to display a live preview of that color applied to the selected graphic in the document (Figure 3–17).

Experiment

- Point to various colors in the Color gallery and watch the color of the graphic change in the document.

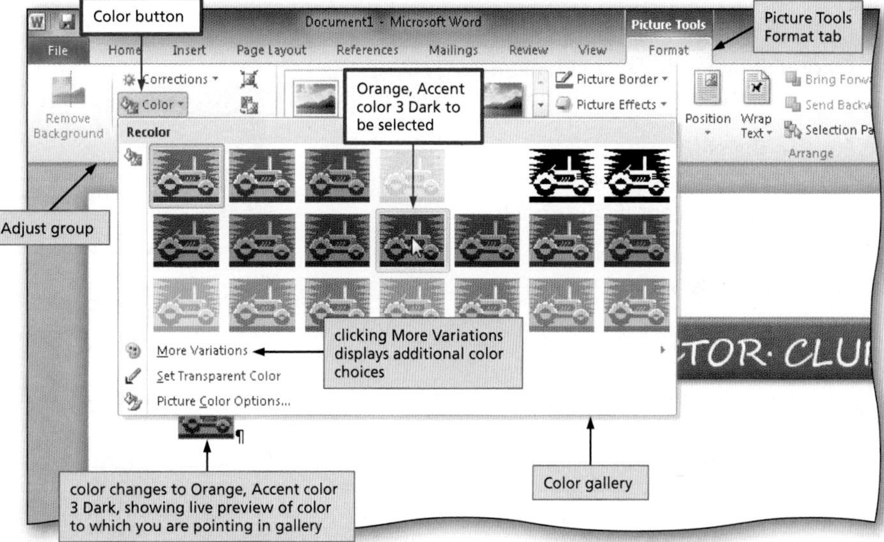

Figure 3–17

- Click Orange, Accent color 3 Dark in the Color gallery to change the color of the selected graphic.

Q&A How would I change a graphic back to its original colors?

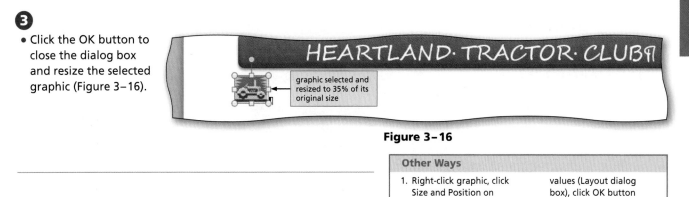

With the graphic selected, you would click No Recolor in the Color gallery (upper-left color).

Other Ways

1. Right-click graphic, click Format Picture on shortcut menu, click Picture Color button in left pane (Format Picture dialog box), select color, click Close button

To Set a Transparent Color in a Graphic

In Word, you can make one color in a graphic transparent, that is, remove the color. You would make a color transparent if you wanted to remove part of a graphic or see text or colors behind a graphic. In this project, you will remove the lighter brown from the edges of the tractor graphic so that when you move the graphic on the rectangular shape, the color of the shape can be seen in the transparent locations. The following steps set a transparent color in a graphic.

1

- With the graphic still selected, click the Color button (Picture Tools Format tab | Adjust group) to display the Color gallery (Figure 3–18).

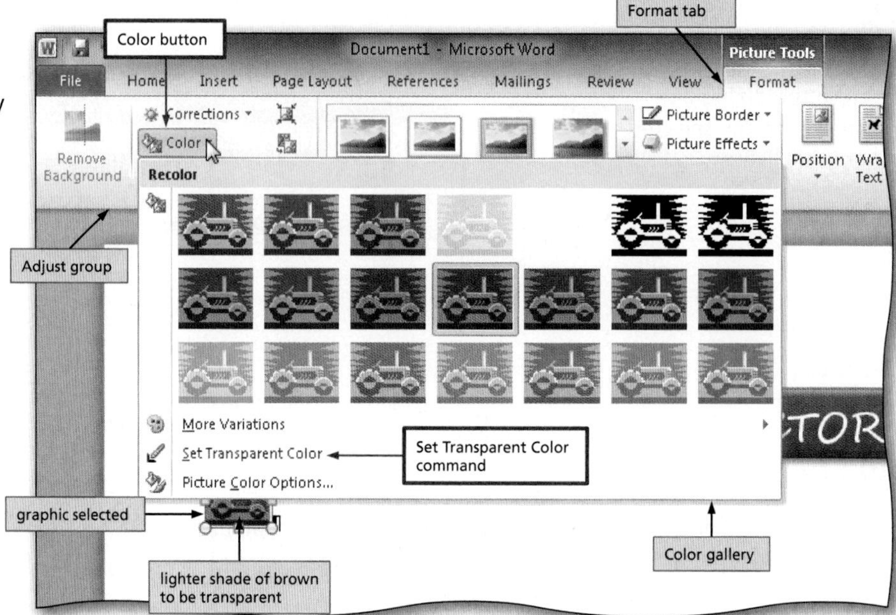

Figure 3–18

2

- Click Set Transparent Color in the Color gallery to display a pen mouse pointer in the document window.
- Position the pen mouse pointer in the graphic where you want to make the color transparent (Figure 3–19).

Q&A Can I make multiple colors in a graphic transparent?

No, you can make only one color transparent.

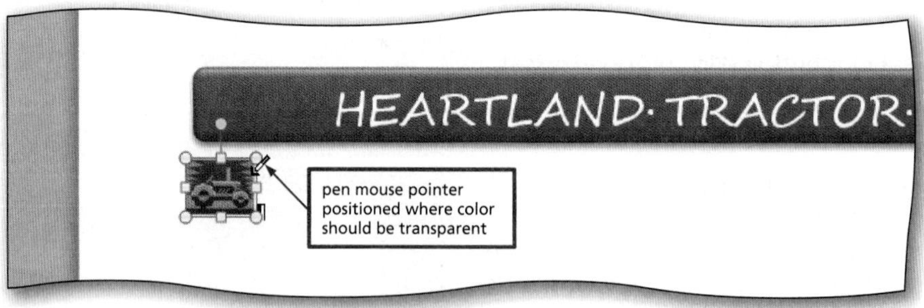

Figure 3–19

3

- Click the location in the graphic where you want the color to be transparent (Figure 3–20).

Q&A What if I make the wrong color transparent?

Click the Undo button on the Quick Access Toolbar, or press CTRL+Z, and then repeat these steps.

Figure 3–20

To Adjust the Brightness and Contrast of a Graphic

In Word, you can adjust the lightness (brightness) of a graphic and also contrast, which is the difference between the lightest and darkest areas of the graphic. The following steps decrease the brightness and contrast of the tractor graphic, each by 20%.

1

- With the graphic still selected (shown in Figure 3–20), click the Corrections button (Picture Tools Format tab | Adjust group) to display the Corrections gallery (Figure 3–21).

Q&A Does live preview work in this gallery?

Yes, but the graphic is covered by the gallery in this case. To see the live preview, you would need to position the graphic so that you can see it while the gallery is displayed.

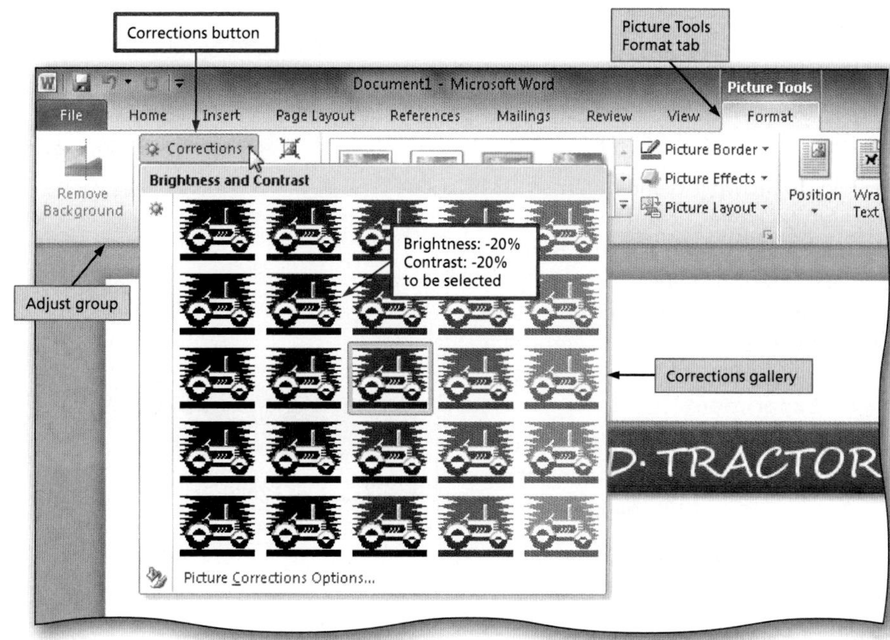

Figure 3–21

2

- Click Brightness: −20% Contrast: −20% in the Corrections gallery (second image in second row) to change the brightness and contrast of the selected graphic (Figure 3–22).

Q&A Can I remove all formatting applied to a graphic and start over?

Yes. With the graphic selected, you would click the Reset Picture button (Picture Tools Format tab | Adjust group).

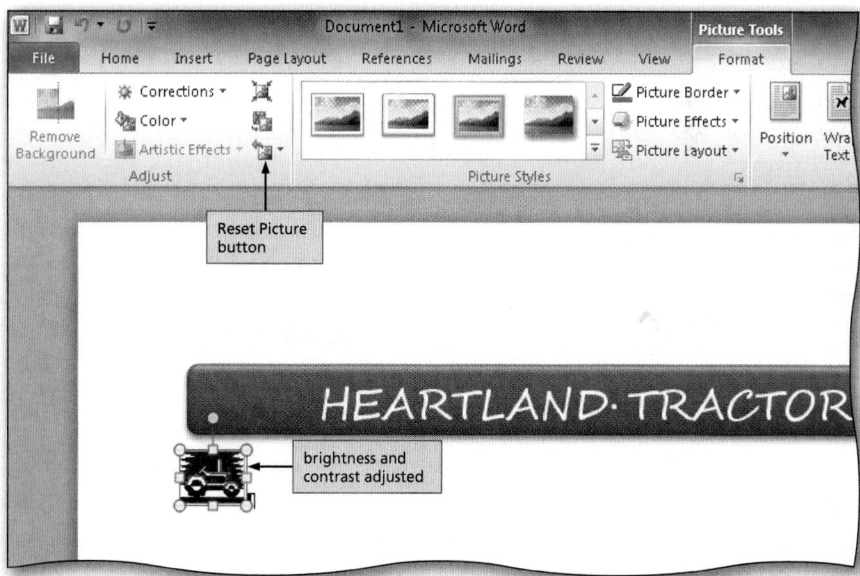

Figure 3–22

Other Ways

1. Right-click graphic, click Format Picture on shortcut menu, click Picture Corrections button in left pane (Format Picture dialog box), adjust settings, click Close button

To Change the Border Color on a Graphic

The tractor graphic currently has no border (outline). You would like the graphic to have a brown border. The following steps change the border color on a graphic.

1

- Click the Picture Border button arrow (Picture Tools Format tab | Picture Styles group) to display the Picture Border gallery.
- Point to Brown, Accent 4, Darker 50% (eighth theme color from left in the sixth row) in the Picture Border gallery to display a live preview of that border color around the picture (Figure 3–23).

Experiment

- Point to various colors in the Picture Border gallery and watch the border color on the picture change in the document window.

2

- Click Brown, Accent 4, Darker 50% in the Picture Border gallery to change the picture border color.

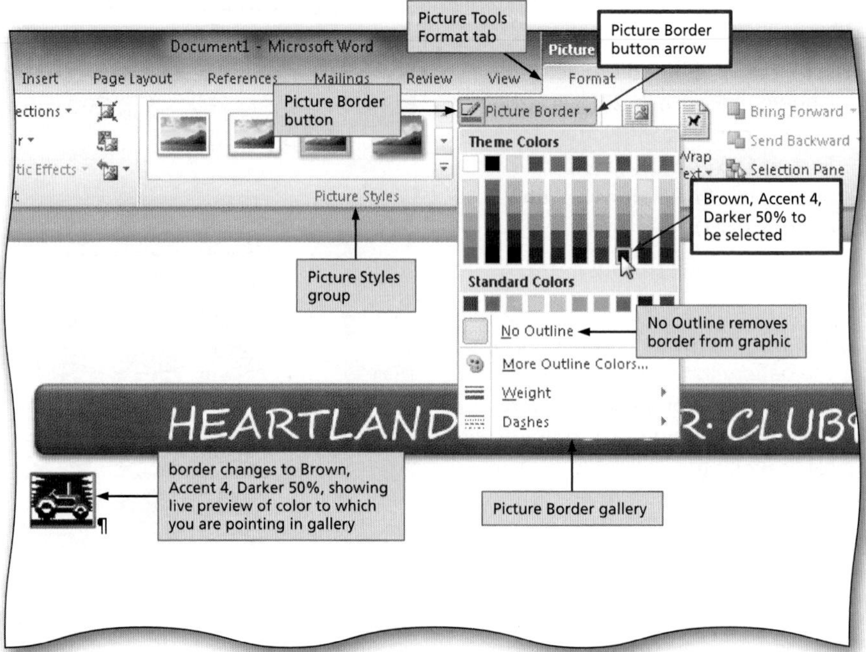

Figure 3–23

Q&A How would I remove a border from a graphic?
With the graphic selected, you would click the No Outline in the Picture Border gallery.

BTW Clip Organizer
To make a Web clip available on your hard disk, point to the clip in the Clip Art pane, click its box arrow, click Make Available Offline, select the collection to store the clip (Copy to Collection dialog box) or click the New button to define a new collection, and then click the OK button. You can use the Clip Organizer to create, rename, or delete collections; add clips to a collection from the Web, a camera, or a scanner; delete, move, and copy clips; and search for existing clips. Start the Clip Organizer by clicking the Start button on the taskbar, clicking All Programs on the Start menu, clicking the Microsoft Office folder to its contents, clicking the Microsoft Office 2010 Tools folder to display its contents, and then clicking Microsoft Clip Organizer.

To Change an Object's Text Wrapping

The tractor graphic is to be positioned to the left of the organization name in the shape. Clip art, by default, is formatted as an inline graphic, which cannot be moved into a shape. To move the graphic in the shape so that it is not covered by any text, you format it as a floating object with In Front of Text wrapping. The following steps change a graphic's text wrapping.

1. If necessary, click the graphic to select it. If necessary, display the Picture Tools Format tab.
2. Click the Wrap Text button (Picture Tools Format tab | Arrange group) to display the Wrap Text gallery.

Q&A Do both the Picture Tools Format and Drawing Tools Format tabs have a Wrap Text button?
Yes. You can specify how to wrap text with both pictures and drawings.

3. Click In Front of Text in the Wrap Text gallery so that you can position the object on top of any item in the document, in this case, on top of the rectangular shape.

To Move a Graphic

The next step is to move the tractor graphic up so that it is positioned to the left of the text on the rectangle shape. The following steps move a graphic.

- Position the mouse pointer in the graphic so that the mouse pointer has a four-headed arrow attached to it (Figure 3–24).

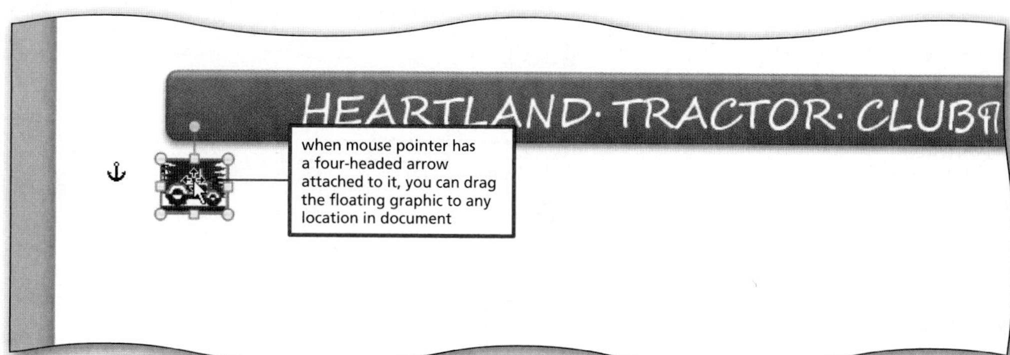

Figure 3–24

- Drag the graphic to the location shown in Figure 3–25.

What if I moved the graphic to the wrong location?

Repeat these steps. You can drag a floating graphic to any location in a document.

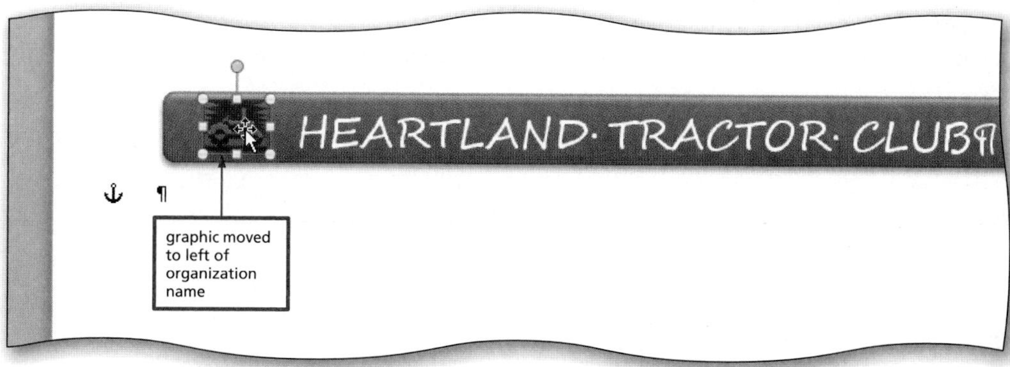

Figure 3–25

To Copy a Graphic

In this project, the same tractor graphic is to be placed to the right of the organization name in the shape. Instead of performing the same steps to insert and format another tractor graphic, you can copy the graphic to the Office Clipboard, paste the graphic from the Office Clipboard, and then move the graphic to the desired location.

You use the same steps to copy a graphic as you used in Chapter 2 to copy text. The following steps copy a graphic.

1. If necessary, click the graphic to select it.
2. Display the Home tab.
3. Click the Copy button, shown in Figure 3–26 on the next page, (Home tab | Clipboard group) to copy the selected item to the Office Clipboard.

To Use Paste Options

The next step is to paste the copied graphic in the document. The following steps paste a graphic using the Paste Options gallery.

- Click the Paste button arrow (Home tab | Clipboard group) to display the Paste gallery.

Q&A What if I accidentally click the Paste button?

Click the Paste Options button below the graphic pasted in the document to display a Paste Options gallery.

- Point to the Keep Source Formatting button in the Paste gallery to display a live preview of that paste option (Figure 3–26).

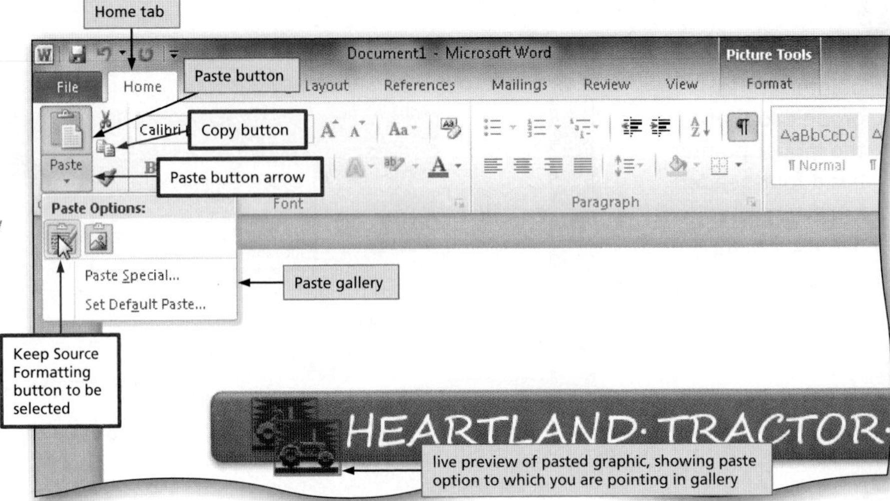

Figure 3–26

Experiment

- Point to the two buttons in the Paste gallery and watch the appearance of the pasted graphic change.

Q&A What do the buttons in the Paste gallery mean?

The Keep Source Formatting button indicates the pasted graphic should have the same formats as it did in its original location. The second button removes all formatting from the graphic.

Q&A Why are these paste buttons different from the ones in Chapter 2?

The buttons that appear in the Paste gallery differ depending on the item you are pasting. Use live preview to see how the pasted object will look in the document.

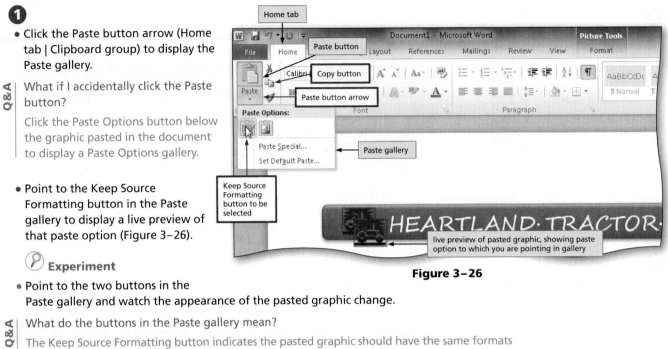

- Click the Keep Source Formatting button in the Paste gallery to paste the object using the same formatting as the original.

To Move a Graphic

The next step is to move the second tractor graphic so that it is positioned to the right of the text in the rectangle shape. The following step moves a graphic.

1 Position the mouse pointer in the graphic so that the mouse pointer has a four-headed arrow attached to it and then drag the graphic to the location shown in Figure 3–27.

Q&A Why does my graphic not look like it is positioned the same as the graphic on the left?

The paragraph mark at the end of the organization name may be obstructing your view. To determine if the graphic is positioned properly, you can temporarily turn off formatting marks by clicking the Show/Hide ¶ button (Home tab | Paragraph group).

Figure 3–27

To Flip a Graphic

The next step is to flip the clip art image on the right so that the tractor is facing the opposite direction. The following steps flip a graphic horizontally.

- If necessary, display the Picture Tools Format tab.
- With the graphic still selected, click the Rotate button (Picture Tools Format tab | Arrange group) to display the Rotate gallery.
- Point to Flip Horizontal in the Rotate gallery to display a live preview of the selected rotate option applied to the selected graphic (Figure 3–28).

Experiment

- Point to the rotate options in the Rotate gallery and watch the picture rotate in the document window.

- Click Flip Horizontal in the Rotate gallery, so that Word flips the graphic to display its mirror image.

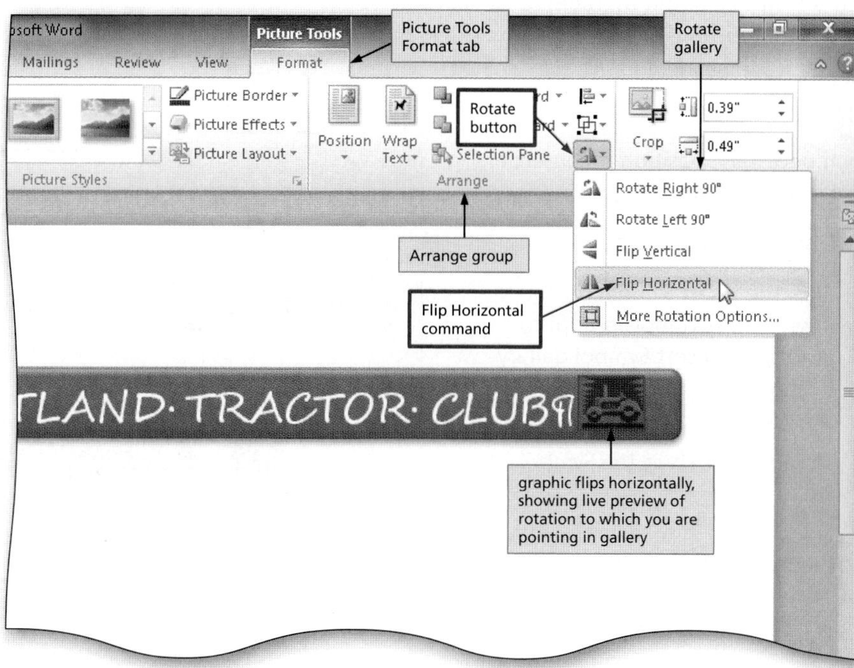

Figure 3–28

Q&A

Can I flip a graphic vertically?

Yes, you would click Flip Vertical in the Rotate gallery. You also can rotate a graphic clockwise or counterclockwise by clicking the Rotate Right 90° and Rotate Left 90° commands, respectively, in the Rotate gallery.

To Specify Formatting before Typing and Then Enter Text

The contact information for the organization in this project is located on the line below the organization name. The following steps format and then enter the postal address in the letterhead.

1. Position the insertion point on the line below the shape containing the organization name.
2. If necessary, display the Home tab. Click the Center button (Home tab | Paragraph group) to center the paragraph.
3. Click the Font Color button arrow (Home tab | Font group) to display the Font Color gallery and then click Orange, Accent 3, Darker 50% (seventh color in sixth row) in the Font Color gallery to change the font color.
4. Type `323 Pine Avenue, Graber, OK 74877` and then press the SPACEBAR (shown in Figure 3–29 on the next page).

BTW

Q&As

For a complete list of the Q&As found in many of the step-by-step sequences in this book, visit the Word 2010 Q&A Web page (scsite.com/wd2010/qa).

To Insert a Symbol from the Symbol Dialog Box

In the letterhead in this chapter, a small round dot separates the postal address and phone number, and the same type of dot separates the phone number and Web address information. This special symbol (the round dot) is not on the keyboard. Thus, Word provides a method of inserting dots and other symbols, such as letters in the Greek alphabet and mathematical characters.

The following steps insert a dot symbol, called a bullet symbol, between the postal address and phone number in the letterhead.

1

- If necessary, position the insertion point as shown in Figure 3–29.
- Display the Insert tab.
- Click the Insert Symbol button (Insert tab | Symbols group) to display the Insert Symbol gallery (Figure 3–29).

Q&A What if the symbol I want to insert already appears in the Symbol gallery?

You can click any symbol shown in the Symbol gallery to insert it in the document.

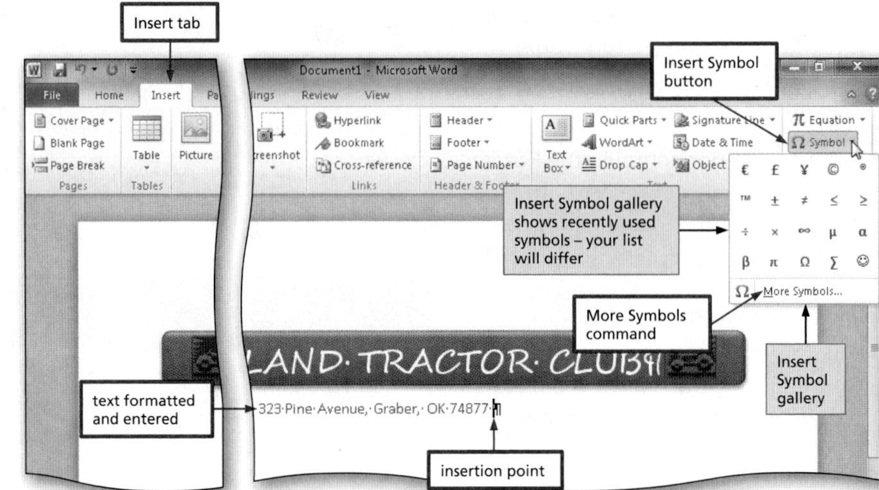

Figure 3–29

2

- Click More Symbols in the Insert Symbol gallery to display the Symbol dialog box.
- If the font in the Font box is not (normal text), click the Font box arrow (Symbol dialog box) and then scroll to (normal text) and click it to select this font.
- If the subset in the Subset box is not General Punctuation, click the Subset box arrow and then scroll to General Punctuation and click it to select this subset.
- In the list of symbols, if necessary, scroll to the bullet symbol shown in Figure 3–30 and then click the symbol to select it.

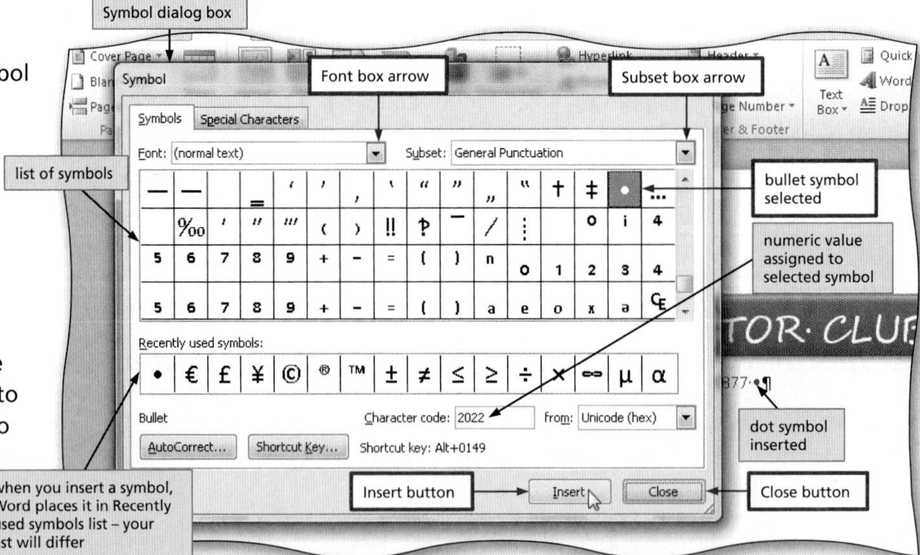

Figure 3–30

- Click the Insert button (Symbol dialog box) to place the selected symbol in the document to the left of the insertion point (Figure 3–30).

Q&A Why is the Symbol dialog box still open?

The Symbol dialog box remains open, allowing you to insert additional symbols.

3

- Click the Close button (Symbol dialog box) to close the dialog box.

To Insert a Symbol from the Symbol Gallery

In the letterhead, another bullet symbol separates the phone number from the Web address information. Once you insert a symbol using the Symbol dialog box, Word adds that symbol to the Symbol gallery so that it is more readily available. The following steps use the Symbol gallery to insert a bullet symbol between the phone number and Web address.

1

- Press the SPACEBAR, type **`Phone: (476) 555-9384`** and then press the SPACEBAR.

2

- Click the Insert Symbol button (Insert tab | Symbols group) to display the Insert Symbol gallery (Figure 3–31).

Q&A Why is the bullet symbol now in the Insert Symbol gallery?

When you insert a symbol from the Symbol dialog box, Word automatically adds the symbol to the Insert Symbol gallery.

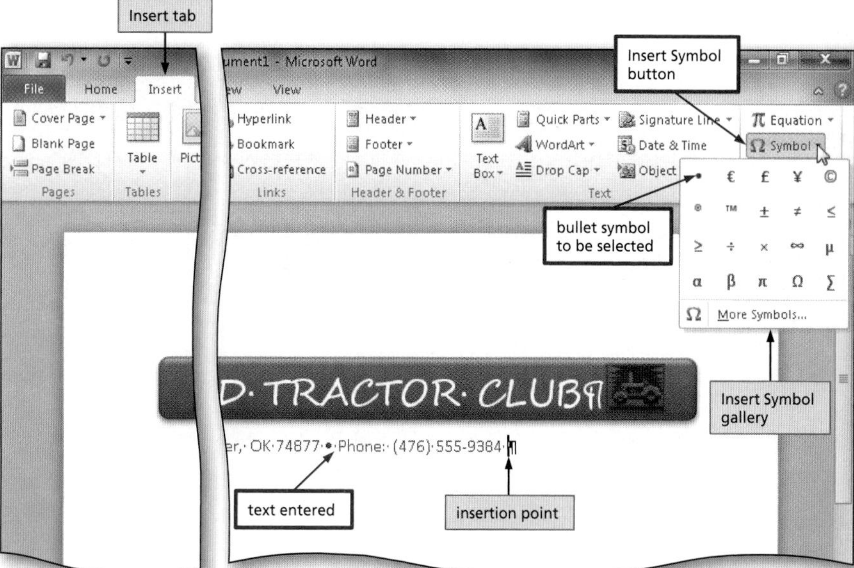

Figure 3–31

3

- Click the bullet symbol in the Insert Symbol gallery to insert the symbol at the location of the insertion point (shown in Figure 3–32).

To Enter Text

The following steps enter the Web address in the letterhead.

1. Press the SPACEBAR.
2. Type **`Web address: www.hltclub.com`** to finish the text in the letterhead (Figure 3–32).

BTW

Inserting Special Characters

In addition to symbols, you can insert a variety of special characters including dashes, hyphens, spaces, apostrophes, and quotation marks. Click the Special Characters tab in the Symbols dialog box (Figure 3–30), click the desired character in the Character list, click the Insert button, and then click the Close button.

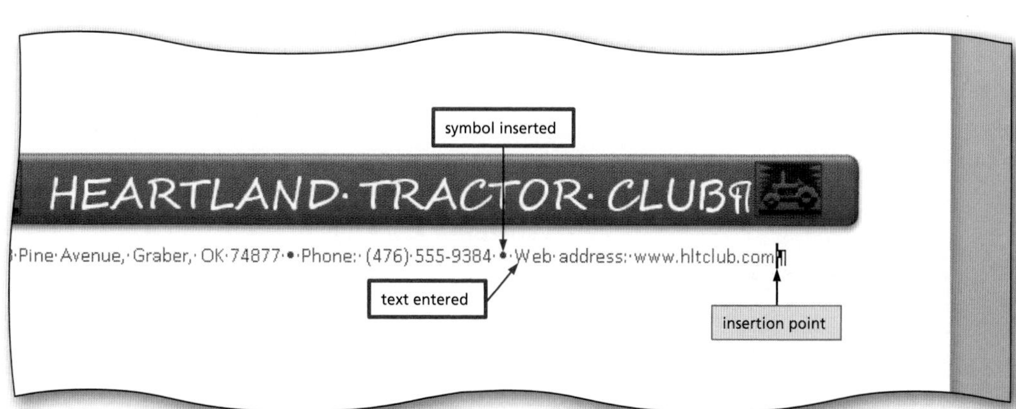

Figure 3–32

To Bottom Border a Paragraph

The letterhead in this project has a horizontal line that extends from the left margin to the right margin immediately below the address, phone, and Web address information, which separates the letterhead from the rest of the letter. In Word, you can draw a solid line, called a **border**, at any edge of a paragraph. That is, borders may be added above or below a paragraph, to the left or right of a paragraph, or in any combination of these sides. The following steps add a bottom border to the paragraph containing address, phone, and Web information.

- Display the Home tab.
- With the insertion point in the paragraph to border, click the Border button arrow (Home tab | Paragraph group) to display the Border gallery (Figure 3–33).

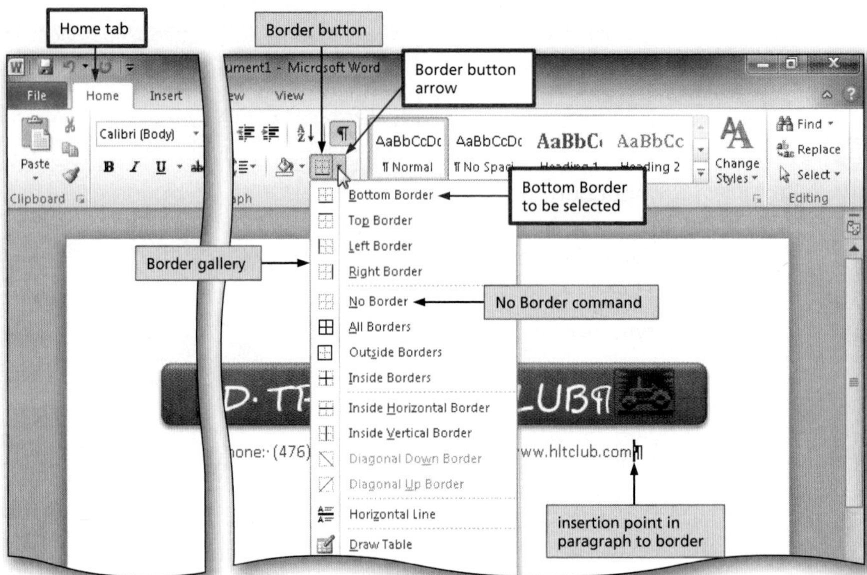

Figure 3–33

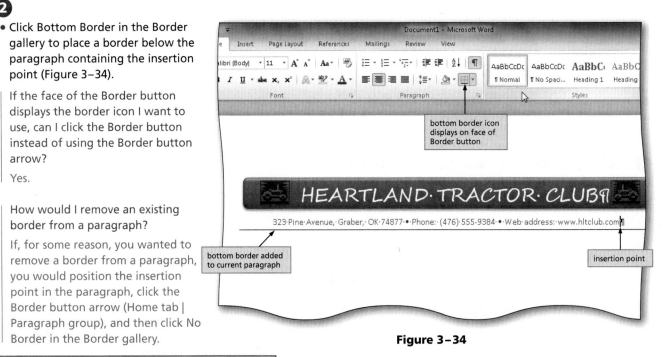

- Click Bottom Border in the Border gallery to place a border below the paragraph containing the insertion point (Figure 3–34).

Q&A If the face of the Border button displays the border icon I want to use, can I click the Border button instead of using the Border button arrow?

Yes.

Q&A How would I remove an existing border from a paragraph?

If, for some reason, you wanted to remove a border from a paragraph, you would position the insertion point in the paragraph, click the Border button arrow (Home tab | Paragraph group), and then click No Border in the Border gallery.

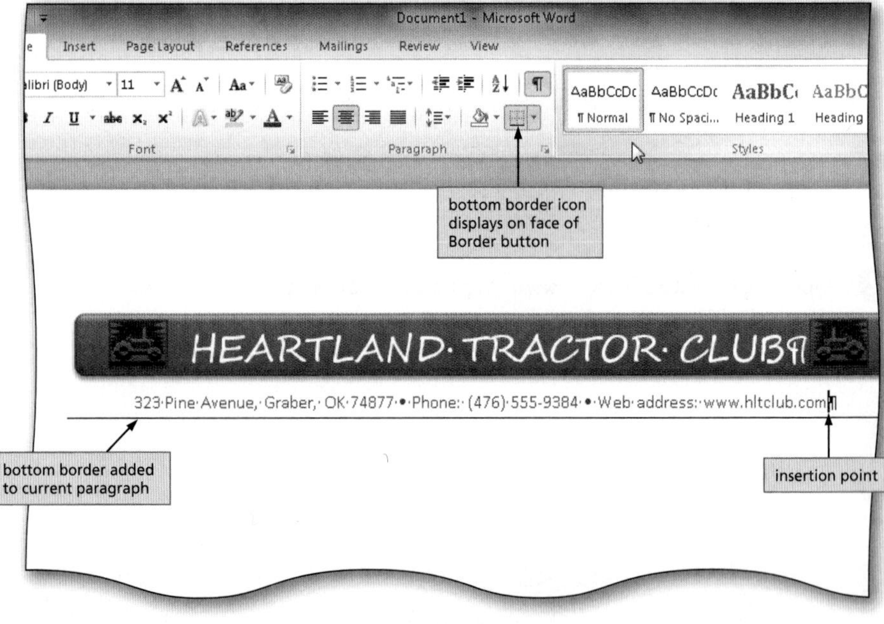

Figure 3–34

Other Ways

1. Click Page Borders button (Page Layout tab | Page Background group), click Borders tab (Borders and Shading dialog box), select desired border options, click OK button

To Clear Formatting

The next step is to position the insertion point below the letterhead, so that you can type the contents of the letter. When you press the ENTER key at the end of a paragraph containing a border, Word moves the border forward to the next paragraph. The paragraph also retains all current settings, such as the center format. Instead, you want the paragraph and characters on the new line to use the Normal style: black font with no border.

In Word, the term, **clear formatting**, refers to returning the formatting to the Normal style. The following steps clear formatting at the location of the insertion point.

1

- With the insertion point between the Web address and paragraph mark at the end of the line (as shown in Figure 3–34), press the ENTER key to move the insertion point and paragraph to the next line (Figure 3–35).

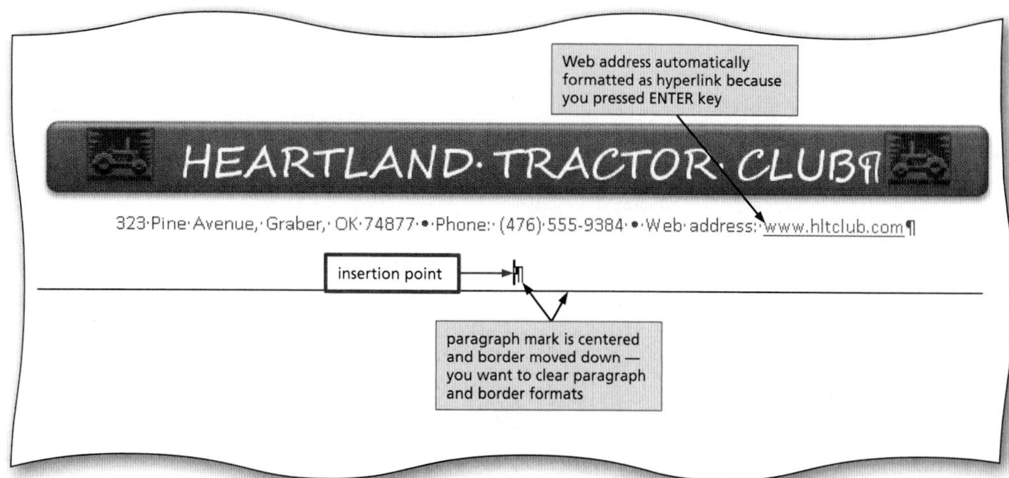

Figure 3–35

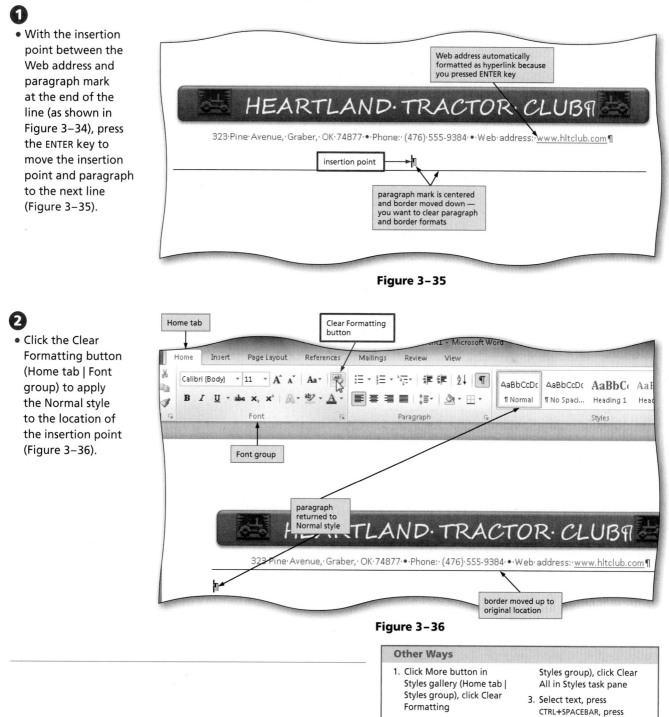

2

- Click the Clear Formatting button (Home tab | Font group) to apply the Normal style to the location of the insertion point (Figure 3–36).

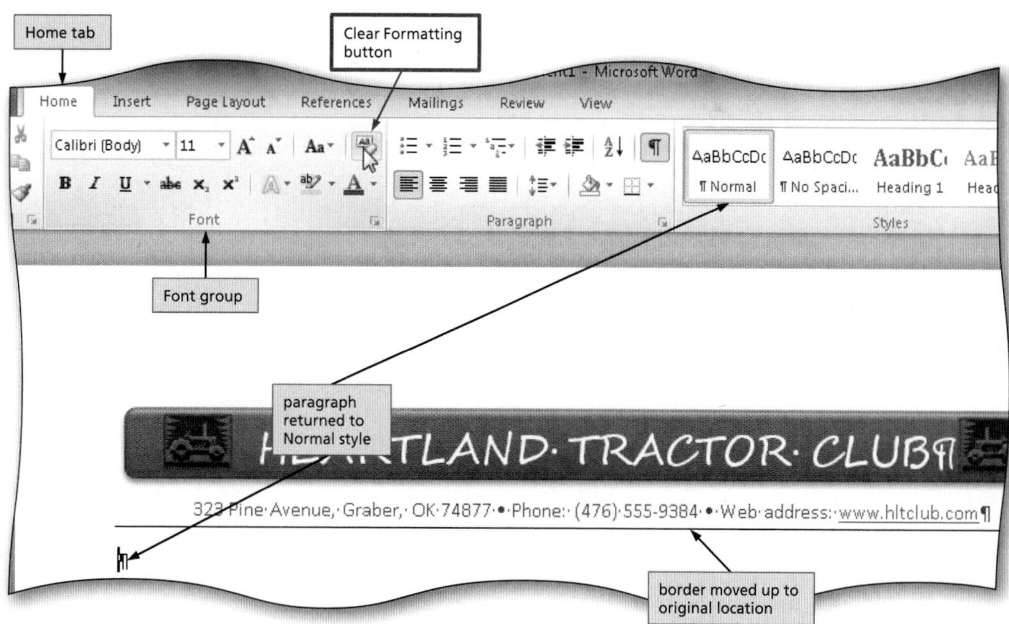

Figure 3–36

Other Ways

1. Click More button in Styles gallery (Home tab | Styles group), click Clear Formatting
2. Click Styles Dialog Box Launcher (Home tab | Styles group), click Clear All in Styles task pane
3. Select text, press CTRL+SPACEBAR, press CTRL+Q

AutoFormat as You Type

As you type text in a document, Word automatically formats some of it for you. For example, when you press the ENTER key or SPACEBAR after typing an e-mail address or Web address, Word automatically formats the address as a hyperlink, that is, colored blue and underlined. In Figure 3–35 on the previous page, for example, Word formatted the Web address as a hyperlink because you pressed the ENTER key at the end of the line. Table 3–2 outlines commonly used AutoFormat As You Type options and their results.

Table 3–2 Commonly Used AutoFormat As You Type Options

Typed Text	AutoFormat Feature	Example
Quotation marks or apostrophes	Changes straight quotation marks or apostrophes to curly ones	"the" becomes “the”
Text, a space, one hyphen, one or no spaces, text, space	Changes the hyphen to an en dash	ages 20 - 45 becomes ages 20 – 45
Text, two hyphens, text, space	Changes the two hyphens to an em dash	Two types--yellow and red becomes Two types—yellow and red
Web or e-mail address followed by SPACEBAR or ENTER key	Formats Web or e-mail address as a hyperlink	www.scsite.com becomes www.scsite.com
Three hyphens, underscores, equal signs, asterisks, tildes, or number signs and then ENTER key	Places a border above a paragraph	--- This line becomes __________ This line
Number followed by a period, hyphen, right parenthesis, or greater than sign and then a space or tab followed by text	Creates a numbered list	1. Word 2. PowerPoint becomes 1. Word 2. PowerPoint
Asterisk, hyphen, or greater than sign and then a space or tab followed by text	Creates a bulleted list	* Home tab * Insert tab becomes • Home tab • Insert tab
Fraction and then a space or hyphen	Condenses the fraction entry so that it consumes one space instead of three	1/2 becomes ½
Ordinal and then a space or hyphen	Makes part of the ordinal a superscript	3rd becomes 3rd

BTW

AutoFormat Settings
Before you can use them, AutoFormat options must be enabled. To check if an AutoFormat option is enabled, click File on the Ribbon to open the Backstage view, click Options in the Backstage view, click Proofing in the left pane (Word Options dialog box), click the AutoCorrect Options button, click the AutoFormat As You Type tab, select the appropriate check boxes, and then click the OK button in each open dialog box.

To Convert a Hyperlink to Regular Text

The Web address in the letterhead should be formatted as regular text; that is, it should not be blue or underlined. Thus, the following steps remove the hyperlink format from the Web address in the letterhead.

1

- Right-click the hyperlink (in this case, the Web address) to display the Mini toolbar and a shortcut menu (Figure 3–37).

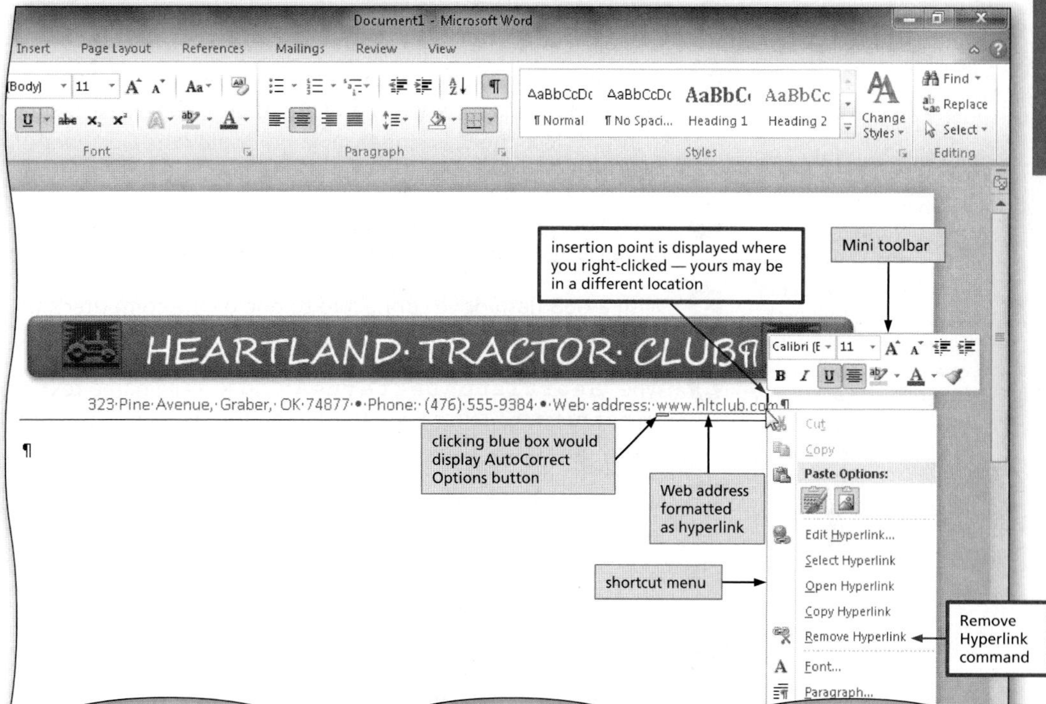

Figure 3–37

2

- Click Remove Hyperlink on the shortcut menu to remove the hyperlink format from the text.
- Position the insertion point on the paragraph mark below the border because you are finished with the letterhead (Figure 3–38).

Figure 3–38

Q&A

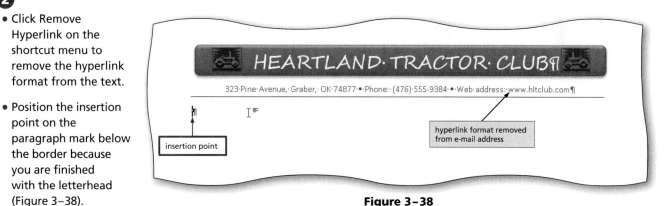

Could I have used the AutoCorrect Options button instead of the Remove Hyperlink command?

Yes. Alternatively, you could have pointed to the small blue box at the beginning of the hyperlink, clicked the AutoCorrect Options button, and then clicked Undo Hyperlink on the AutoCorrect Options menu.

Other Ways

1. With insertion point in hyperlink, click Hyperlink button (Insert tab | Links group), click Remove Link button

BTW

Saving a Template
As an alternative to saving the letterhead as a Word document, you could save it as a template. To do so, click File on the Ribbon to open the Backstage view, click the Save & Send tab to display the Save & Send gallery, click Change File Type, click Template in the right pane, click the Save As button, enter the template name (Save As dialog box), if necessary select the Templates folder, and then click the Save button in the dialog box. To use the template, click File on the Ribbon to open the Backstage view, click the New tab to display the New gallery, click My templates, and then double-click the template icon or name.

To Change Document Properties, Then Save and Close a File

The letterhead now is complete. Thus, you should save it in a file. The following steps assume you already have created folders for storing your files, for example, a CIS 101 folder (for your class) that contains a Word folder (for your assignments). Thus, these steps change document properties, save the file in the Word folder in the CIS 101 folder on a USB flash drive using the file name, Heartland Letterhead, and then close the file.

1. Click File on the Ribbon to open the Backstage view and then, if necessary, select the Info tab. Display the Properties menu and then click Show Document Panel on the Properties menu to close the Backstage view and display the Document Information Panel in the Word document window.
2. Enter your name in the Author property, and enter your course and section in the Subject property. Close the Document Information Panel.
3. With a USB flash drive connected to one of the computer's USB ports, click the Save button on the Quick Access Toolbar to display the Save As dialog box.
4. Type `Heartland Letterhead` in the File name text box to change the file name. Do not press the ENTER key after typing the file name because you do not want to close the dialog box at this time.
5. Navigate to the desired save location (in this case, the Word folder in the CIS 101 folder [or your class folder] on the USB flash drive).
6. Click the Save button (Save As dialog box) to save the file in the selected folder on the selected drive with the entered file name.
7. Click File on the Ribbon to open the Backstage view and then click Close in the Backstage view to close the document.

Break Point: If you wish to take a break, this is a good place to do so. To resume at a later time, start Word and continue following the steps from this location forward.

Creating a Business Letter

You have created a letterhead for the business letter. The next step is to compose the rest of the content in the business letter. The following pages use Word to create a business letter that contains a table and a bulleted list.

Plan Ahead

Compose an effective business letter.
When composing a business letter, you need to be sure to include all essential elements and to decide which letter style to use.

- **Include all essential letter elements, properly spaced and sized.** All business letters contain the same basic elements, including the date line, inside address, message, and signature block (shown in Figure 3–1 on page WD 139). If a business letter does not use a letterhead, then the top of the letter should include return address information in a heading.
- **Use proper spacing and formats for the contents of the letter below the letterhead.** Use a font that is easy to read, in a size between 8 and 12 point. Add emphasis with bold, italic, and bullets where appropriate, and use tables to present numeric information. Paragraphs should be single-spaced, with double-spacing between paragraphs.
- **Determine which letter style to use.** You can follow many different styles when creating business letters. A letter style specifies guidelines for the alignment and spacing of elements in the business letter.

To Create a New File from an Existing File

The top of the business letter in this chapter contains the letterhead, which you saved in a separate file. You could open the letterhead file and then save it with a new name, so that the letterhead file remains intact for future use. A more efficient technique is to create a new file from the letterhead file. Doing this enables you to save the document the first time using the Save button on the Quick Access Toolbar instead of requiring you to use the Save As command in the Backstage view. The following steps create a new file from an existing file.

1

- Click File on the Ribbon to open the Backstage view.
- Click the New tab in the Backstage view to display the New gallery (Figure 3–39).

Q&A What are the templates in the New gallery?

A template is a document that includes prewritten text and/or formatting common to documents of the specified type. Word provides many templates to simplify the task of creating documents.

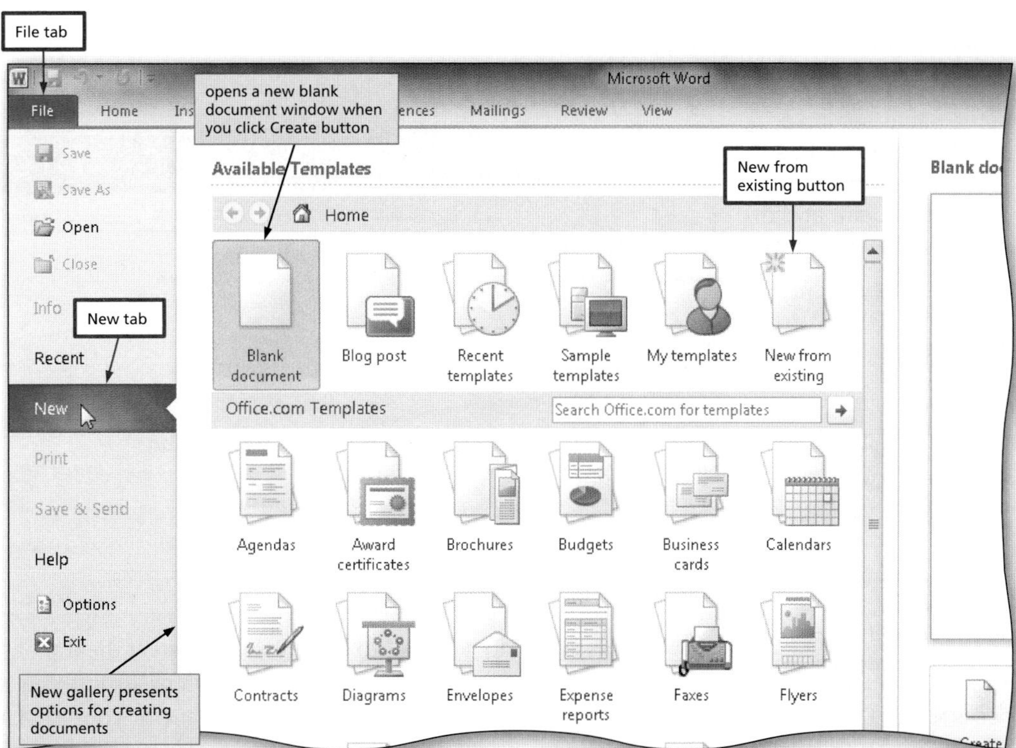

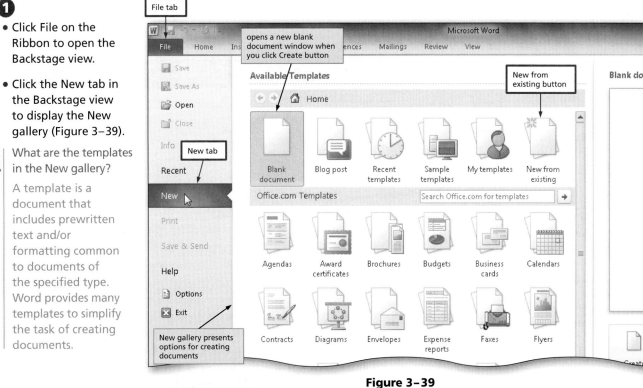

Figure 3–39

2

- Click the 'New from existing' button in the New gallery to display the New from Existing Document dialog box.
- If necessary, navigate to the location of the saved Heartland Letterhead file (in this case, the Word folder in the CIS 101 folder on the USB flash drive).
- Click Heartland Letterhead to select the file (Figure 3–40).

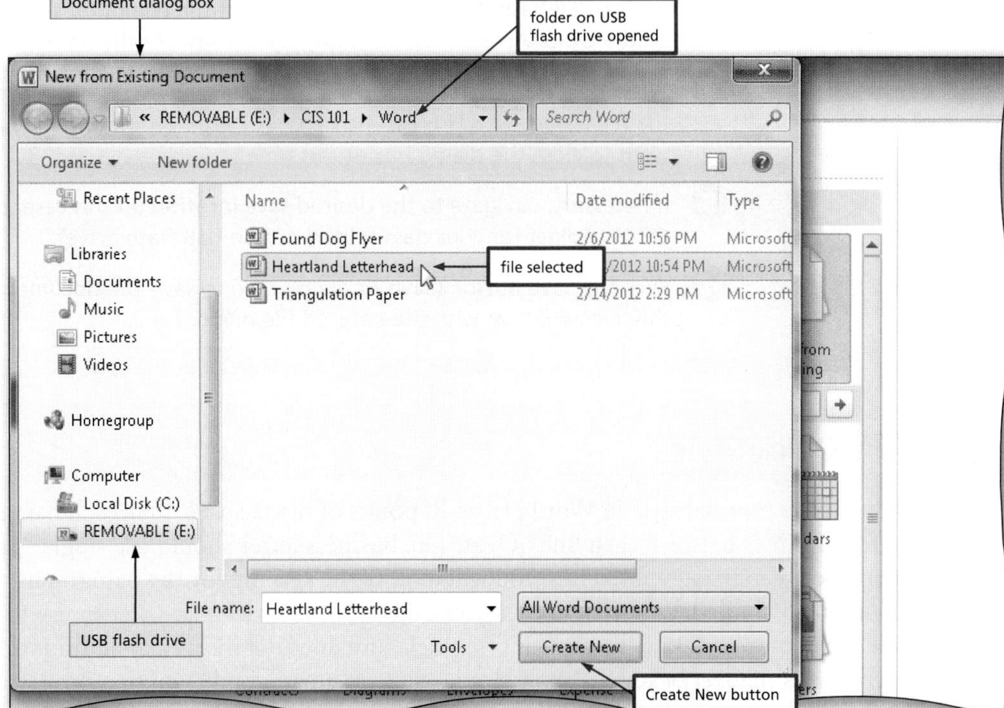

Figure 3–40

- Click the Create New button (New from Existing Document dialog box) to open a new document window that contains the contents of the selected file.
- If necessary, click the paragraph mark below the letterhead to position the insertion point at that location (Figure 3–41).

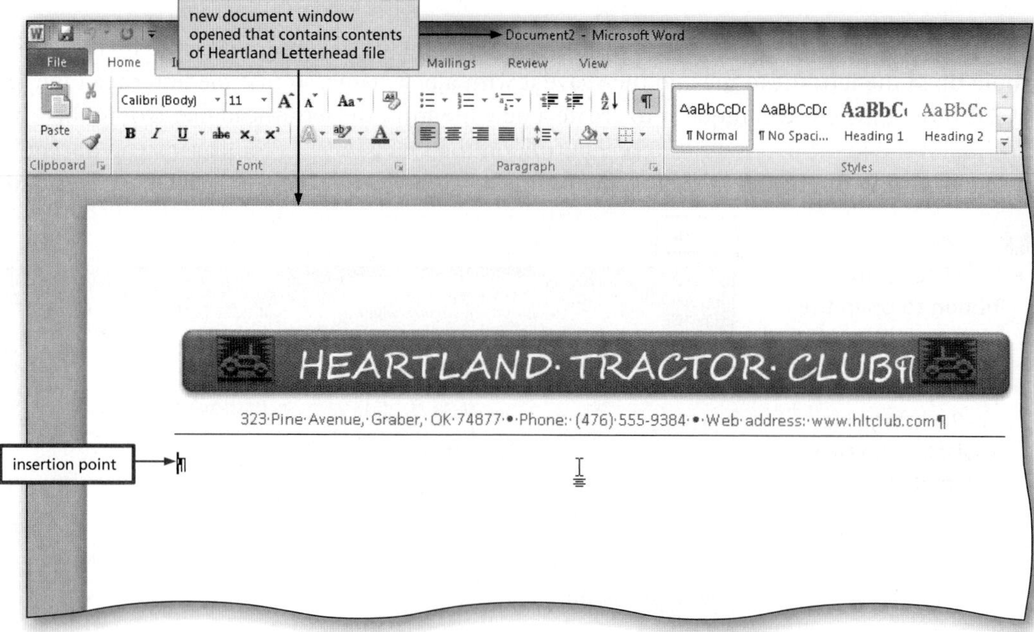

Figure 3–41

BTW

New Document Window
If you wanted to open a new blank document window, you could press CTRL+N or click File on the Ribbon to open the Backstage view, click the New tab to display the New gallery, click the Blank document button, and then click the Create button.

To Save a Document

Because you do not want to lose the letterhead at the top of this document, you should save the letter before continuing. The following steps assume you already have created folders for storing your files, for example, a CIS 101 folder (for your class) that contains a Word folder (for your assignments). Thus, these steps save the document in the Word folder in the CIS 101 folder on a USB flash drive using the file name, Heartland Advertisement Letter.

1. With a USB flash drive connected to one of the computer's USB ports, click the Save button on the Quick Access Toolbar to display the Save As dialog box.
2. Type `Heartland Advertisement Letter` in the File name text box to change the file name. Do not press the ENTER key after typing the file name because you do not want to close the dialog box at this time.
3. If necessary, navigate to the desired save location (in this case, the Word folder in the CIS 101 folder [or your class folder] on the USB flash drive).
4. Click the Save button (Save As dialog box) to save the document in the selected folder on the selected drive with the entered file name.

To Apply a Quick Style

Recall that the Normal style in Word places 10 points of blank space after each paragraph and inserts a vertical space equal to 1.15 lines between each line of text. The business letter should use single spacing for paragraphs and double spacing between paragraphs. Thus, you will modify the spacing for the paragraphs.

Word has many built-in, or predefined, styles called Quick Styles that you can use to format text. The No Spacing style, for example, defines line spacing to single and does not insert any additional blank space between lines when you press the ENTER key. To apply a quick style to a paragraph, you first position the insertion point in the paragraph and then apply the style. The next step applies the No Spacing quick style to a paragraph.

1

- With the insertion point positioned in the paragraph to be formatted, click No Spacing in the Quick Style gallery (Home tab | Styles group) to apply the selected style to the current paragraph (Figure 3–42).

Q&A Will this style be used in the rest of the document?

Yes. The paragraph formatting, which includes the style, will carry forward to subsequent paragraphs each time you press the ENTER key.

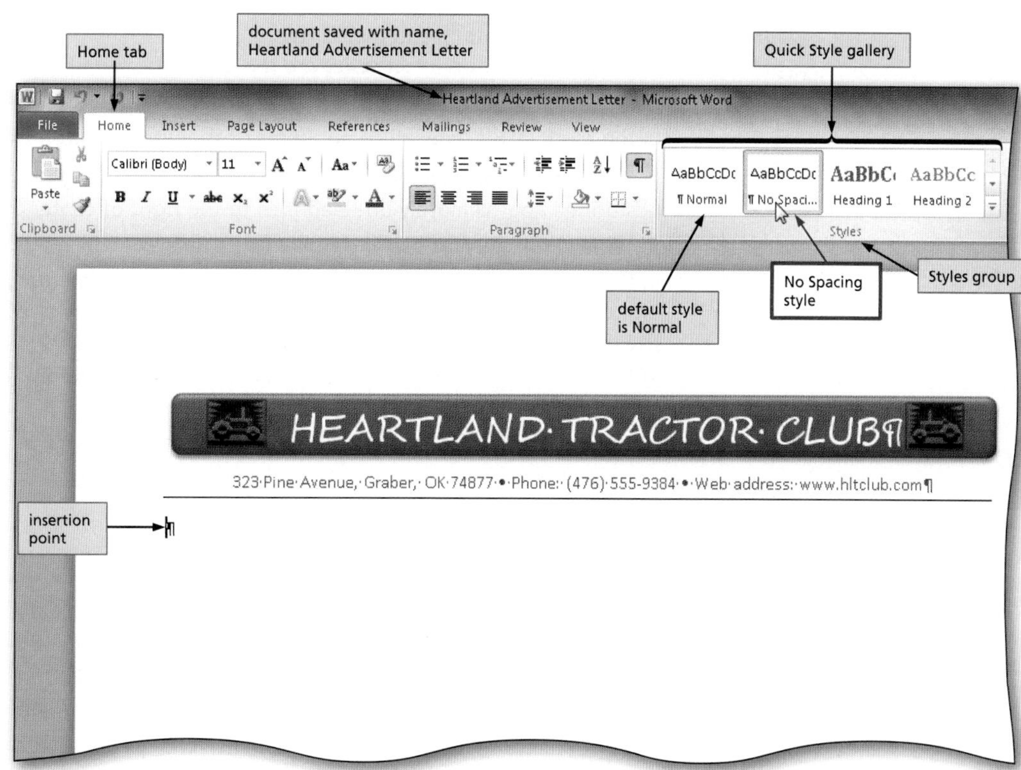

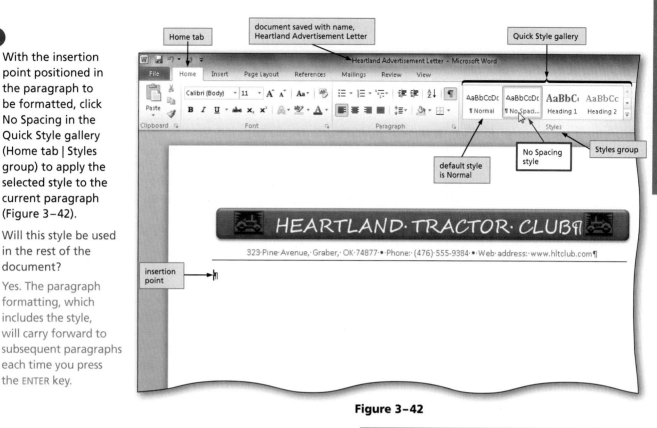

Figure 3–42

Other Ways

1. Click Styles Dialog Box Launcher (Home tab | Styles group), click desired style in Styles task pane
2. Press CTRL+SHIFT+S, click Style Name box arrow in Apply Styles task pane, click desired style in list

Plan Ahead

Include all essential letter elements.

Be sure to include all essential business letter elements, properly spaced, in your letter.

- The **date line**, which consists of the month, day, and year, is positioned two to six lines below the letterhead.
- The **inside address**, placed three to eight lines below the date line, usually contains the addressee's courtesy title plus full name, job title, business affiliation, and full geographical address.
- The **salutation**, if present, begins two lines below the last line of the inside address. If you do not know the recipient's name, avoid using the salutation "To whom it may concern" — it is impersonal. Instead, use the recipient's title in the salutation, e.g., Dear Personnel Director. In a business letter, use a colon (:) at the end of the salutation; in a personal letter, use a comma.
- The body of the letter, the **message**, begins two lines below the salutation. Within the message, paragraphs are single-spaced with one blank line between paragraphs.
- Two lines below the last line of the message, the **complimentary close** is displayed. Capitalize only the first word in a complimentary close.
- Type the **signature block** at least four blank lines below the complimentary close, allowing room for the author to sign his or her name.

Plan Ahead

Determine which letter style to use.
Three common business letter styles are the block, the modified block, and the modified semi-block. Each style specifies different alignments and indentations.

- In the block letter style, all components of the letter begin flush with the left margin.
- In the modified block letter style, the date, complimentary close, and signature block are positioned approximately one-half inch to the right of center or at the right margin. All other components of the letter begin flush with the left margin.
- In the modified semi-block letter style, the date, complimentary close, and signature block are centered, positioned approximately one-half inch to the right of center or at the right margin. The first line of each paragraph in the body of the letter is indented one-half to one inch from the left margin. All other components of the letter begin flush with the left margin.

The business letter in this project follows the modified block style.

Using Tab Stops to Align Text

A **tab stop** is a location on the horizontal ruler that tells Word where to position the insertion point when you press the TAB key on the keyboard. Word, by default, places a tab stop at every one-half inch mark on the ruler. These default tab stops are indicated at the bottom of the horizontal ruler by small vertical tick marks (shown in Figure 3–43). You also can set your own custom tab stops. Tab settings are a paragraph format. Thus, each time you press the ENTER key, any custom tab stops are carried forward to the next paragraph.

To move the insertion point from one tab stop to another, press the TAB key on the keyboard. When you press the TAB key, a **tab character** formatting mark appears in the empty space between the tab stops.

When you set a custom tab stop, you specify how the text will align at a tab stop. The tab marker on the ruler reflects the alignment of the characters at the location of the tab stop. Table 3–3 shows types of tab stop alignments in Word and their corresponding tab markers.

BTW

Tabs Dialog Box
You can use the Tabs dialog box to set, change the alignment of, and remove custom tab stops. To display the Tabs dialog box, click the Paragraph Dialog Box Launcher (Home tab or Page Layout tab | Paragraph group) and then click the Tabs button (Paragraph dialog box), or double-click a tab marker on the ruler. To set a custom tab stop, enter the desired position (Tabs dialog box) and then click the Set button. To change the alignment of a custom tab stop, click the tab stop position to be changed, click the new alignment, and then click the Set button. To remove an existing tab stop, click the tab stop position to be removed and then click the Clear button. To remove all tab stops, click the Clear All button in the Tabs dialog box.

Table 3–3 Types of Tab Stop Alignments

Tab Stop Alignment	Tab Marker	Result of Pressing TAB Key	Example
Left Tab	└	Left-aligns text at the location of the tab stop	toolbar ruler
Center Tab	┴	Centers text at the location of the tab stop	toolbar ruler
Right Tab	┘	Right-aligns text at the location of the tab stop	toolbar ruler
Decimal Tab	┴.	Aligns text on decimal point at the location of the tab stop	45.72 223.75
Bar Tab	ǀ	Aligns text at a bar character at the location of the tab stop	| toolbar | ruler

To Display the Ruler

One way to set custom tab stops is by using the horizontal ruler. Thus, the following step displays the ruler in the document window.

If the rulers are not displayed already, click the View Ruler button on the vertical scroll bar (shown in Figure 3–43).

Q&A What if the View Ruler button is not visible on the vertical scroll bar?
Display the View tab and then place a check mark in the Ruler check box.

To Set Custom Tab Stops

The first required element of the business letter is the date line, which in this letter is positioned two lines below the letterhead. The date line contains the month, day, and year, and begins four inches from the left margin, which is approximately one-half inch to the right of center. Thus, you should set a custom tab stop at the 4" mark on the ruler. The following steps set a left-aligned tab stop.

1

- With the insertion point on the paragraph mark below the border (shown in Figure 3–42 on page WD 167), press the ENTER key so that a blank line appears above the insertion point.
- If necessary, click the tab selector at the left edge of the horizontal ruler until it displays the type of tab you wish to use, which is the Left Tab icon in this case.
- Position the mouse pointer on the 4" mark on the ruler, which is the location of the desired custom tab stop (Figure 3–43).

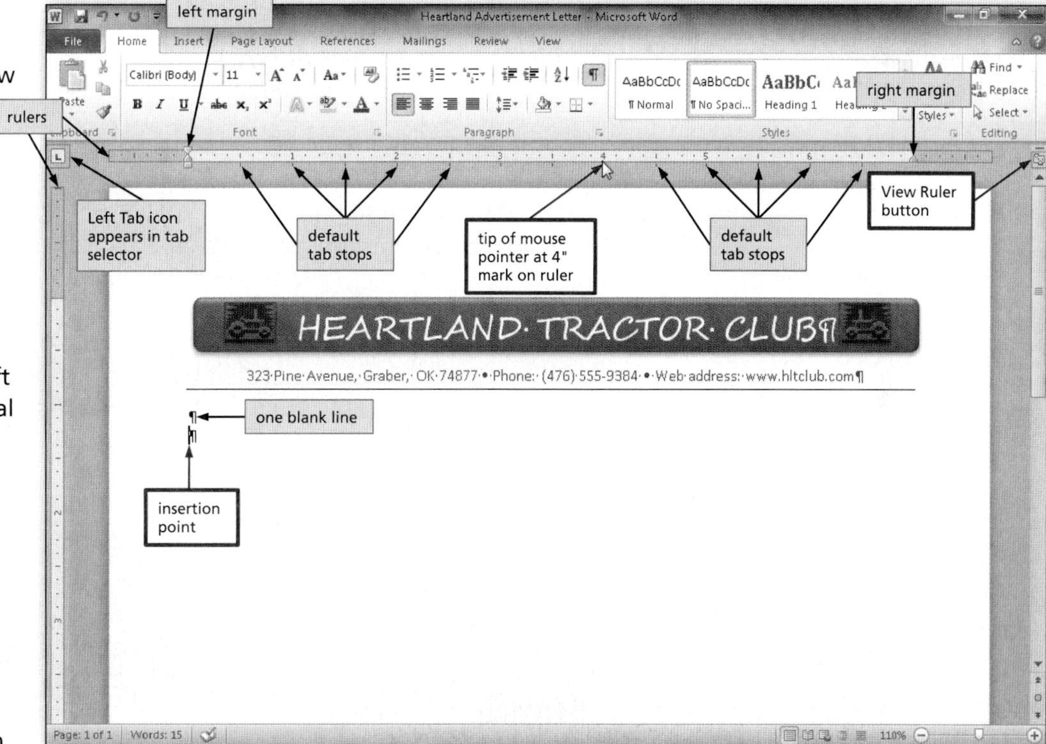

Figure 3–43

Q&A What is the purpose of the tab selector?
Before using the ruler to set a tab stop, ensure the correct tab stop icon appears in the tab selector. Each time you click the tab selector, its icon changes. The Left Tab icon is the default. For a list of the types of tab stops, see Table 3–3.

2

- Click the 4" mark on the ruler to place a tab marker at that location (Figure 3–44).

Q&A What if I click the wrong location on the ruler?

You can move a custom tab stop by dragging the tab marker to the desired location on the ruler. Or, you can remove an existing custom tab stop by pointing to the tab marker on the ruler and then dragging the tab marker down and out of the ruler.

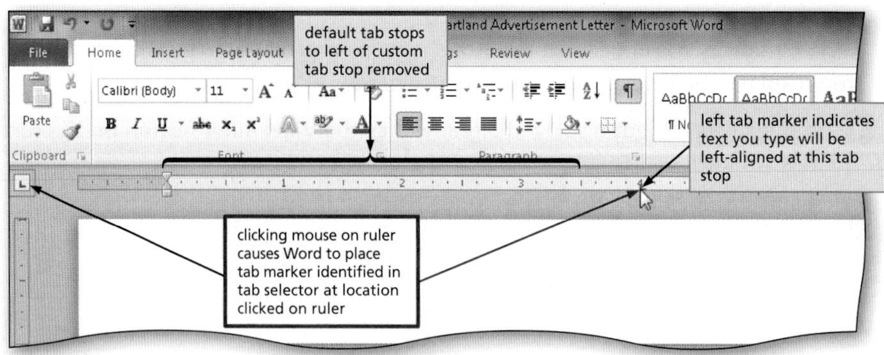

Figure 3–44

Q&A What happened to all the default tab stops on the ruler?

When you set a custom tab stop, Word clears all default tab stops to the left of the newly set custom tab stop on the ruler.

Other Ways

1. Click Paragraph Dialog Box Launcher (Home tab or Page Layout tab | Paragraph group), click Tabs button (Paragraph dialog box), type tab stop position (Tabs dialog box), click Set button, click OK button

To Insert the Current Date in a Document

The next step is to enter the current date at the 4" tab stop in the document, as specified in the guidelines for a modified block style letter. In Word, you can insert a computer's system date in a document. The following steps insert the current date in the letter.

1

- Press the TAB key to position the insertion point at the location of the tab stop in the current paragraph.
- Display the Insert tab.
- Click the Insert Date and Time button (Insert tab | Text group) to display the Date and Time dialog box.
- Select the desired format (Date and Time dialog box), in this case April 27, 2012.
- If the Update automatically check box is selected, click the check box to remove the check mark (Figure 3–45).

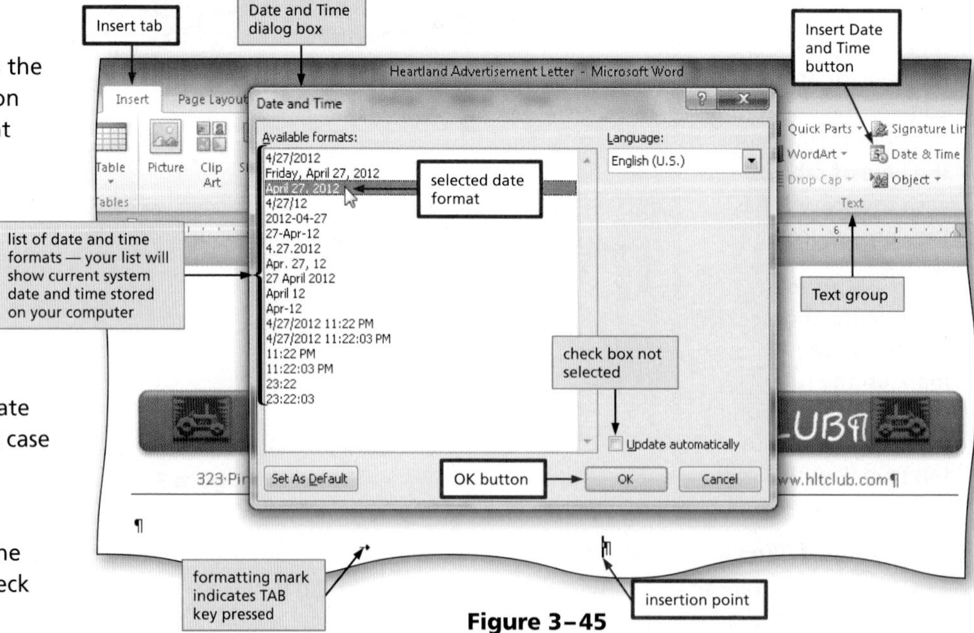

Figure 3–45

Q&A Why should the Update automatically check box not be selected?

In this project, the date at the top of the letter always should show today's date (for example, April 27, 2012). If, however, you wanted the date always to change to reflect the current computer date (for example, showing the date you open or print the letter), then you would place a check mark in this check box.

2

- Click the OK button to insert the current date at the location of the insertion point (Figure 3–46).

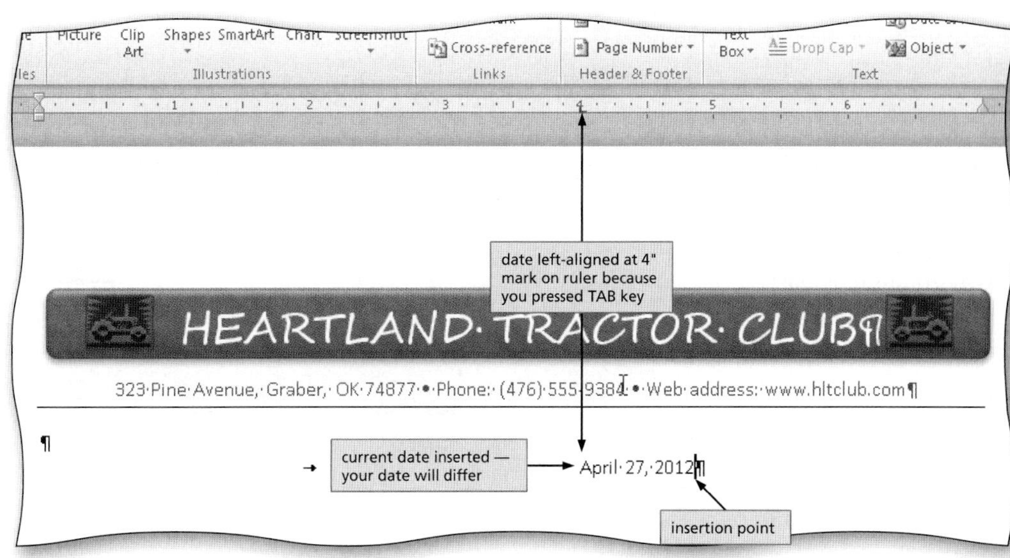

Figure 3–46

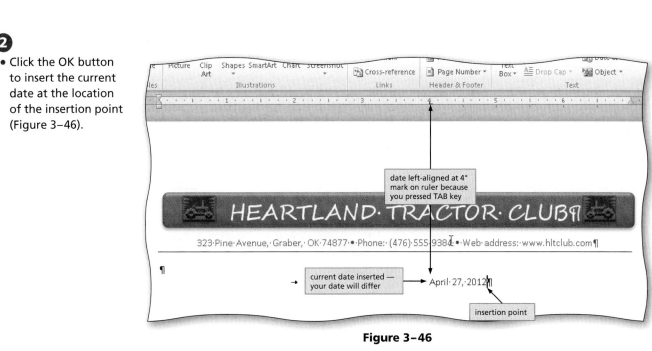

To Enter the Inside Address and Salutation

The next step in composing the business letter is to type the inside address and salutation. The following steps enter this text.

1. With the insertion point at the end of the date (shown in Figure 3–46), press the ENTER key three times.
2. Type **`Mr. Harvey Wilcox`** and then press the ENTER key.
3. Type **`Wilcox Tractor Restorations`** and then press the ENTER key.
4. Type **`3009 North 2850 East Road`** and then press the ENTER key.
5. Type **`Roundwood, OK 74519`** and then press the ENTER key twice.
6. Type **`Dear Mr. Wilcox:`** to complete the inside address and salutation entries (Figure 3–47).

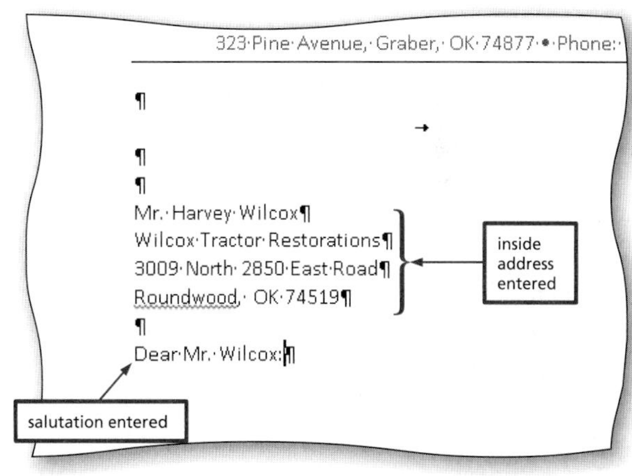

Figure 3–47

To Create a Building Block

If you use the same text or graphic frequently, you can store the text or graphic as a **building block** and then insert the stored building block entry in the open document, as well as in future documents. That is, you can create the entry once as a building block and then insert the building block when you need it. In this way, you avoid entering the text or graphics inconsistently or incorrectly in different locations throughout the same or multiple documents.

The steps on the next page create a building block for the prospective advertiser's name, Wilcox Tractor Restorations. Later, you will insert the building block in the document instead of typing the advertiser's name.

1

- Select the text to be a building block, in this case Wilcox Tractor Restorations. Do not select the paragraph mark at the end of the text because you do not want the paragraph to be part of the building block.

Q&A Why is the paragraph mark not part of the building block?

Select the paragraph mark only if you want to store paragraph formatting, such as indentation and line spacing, as part of the building block.

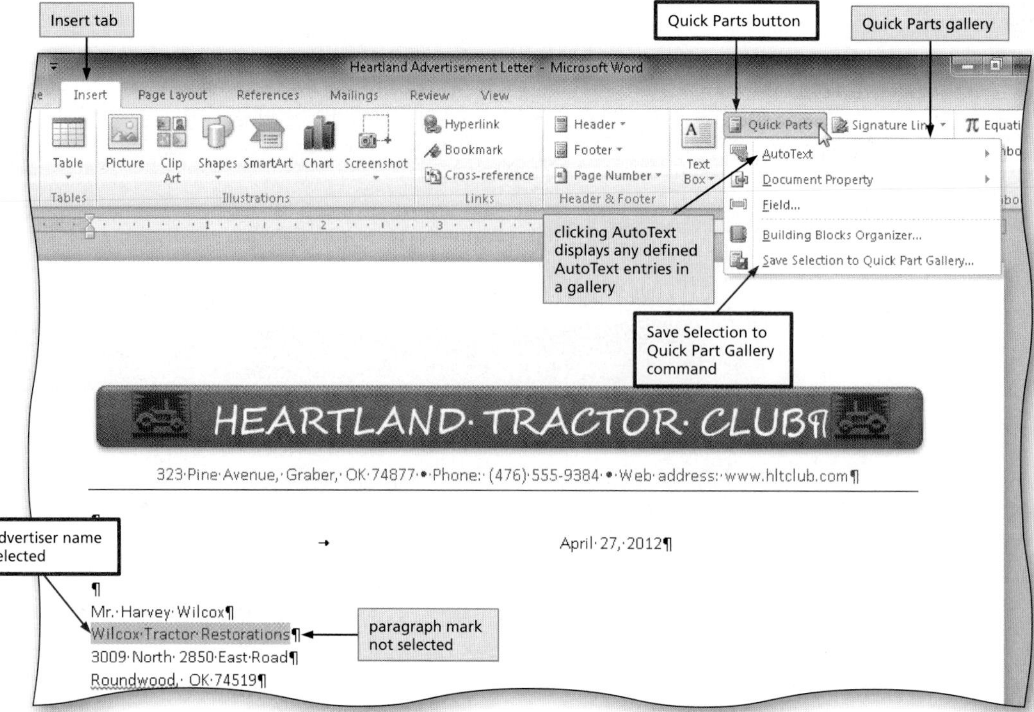

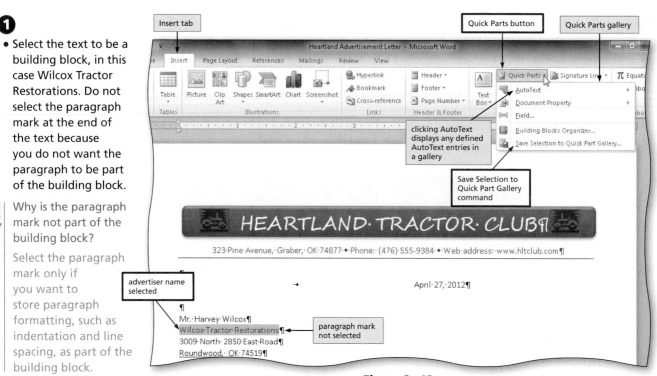

Figure 3–48

- Click the Quick Parts button (Insert tab | Text group) to display the Quick Parts gallery (Figure 3–48).

2

- Click Save Selection to Quick Part Gallery in the Quick Parts gallery to display the Create New Building Block dialog box.
- Type **wtr** in the Name text box (Create New Building Block dialog box) to replace the proposed building block name (Wilcox Tractor, in this case) with a shorter building block name (Figure 3–49).

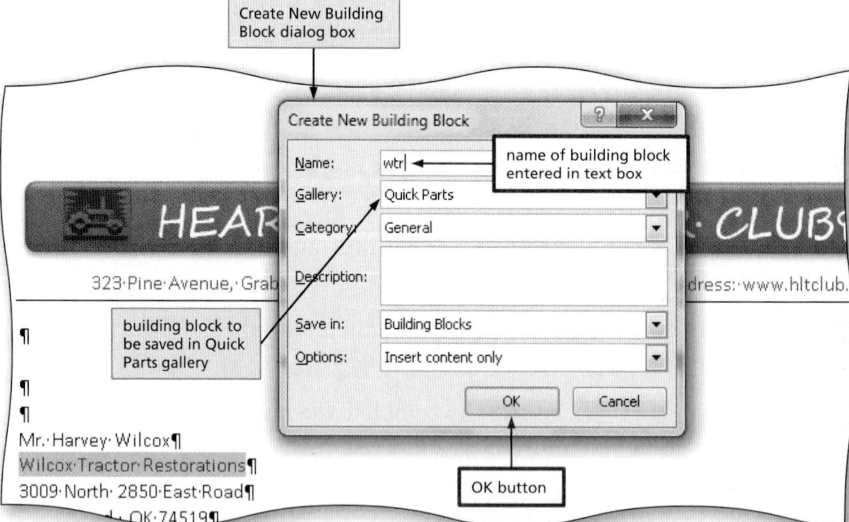

Figure 3–49

3

- Click the OK button to store the building block entry and close the dialog box.
- If Word displays another dialog box, click the Yes button, to save changes to the building blocks.

Q&A Will this building block be available in future documents?

When you quit Word, a dialog box may appear asking if you want to save changes to the "Building Blocks". Click the Save button if you want to use the new building block in future documents.

Other Ways
1. Select text, press ALT+F3

To Modify a Building Block

When you save a building block in the Quick Parts gallery, it is displayed at the top of the Quick Parts gallery. If the building block is a text entry, you can place it in the AutoText gallery instead, which also is accessible through the Quick Parts gallery.

When you point to the building block in the Quick Parts gallery, a ScreenTip displays the building block name. If you want to display more information when the user points to the building block, you can include a description as an Enhanced ScreenTip. The following steps modify a building block to include a description and change its category to AutoText.

- Click the Quick Parts button (Insert tab | Text group) to display the Quick Parts gallery.
- Right-click the Wilcox Tractor Restorations building block to display a shortcut menu (Figure 3–50).

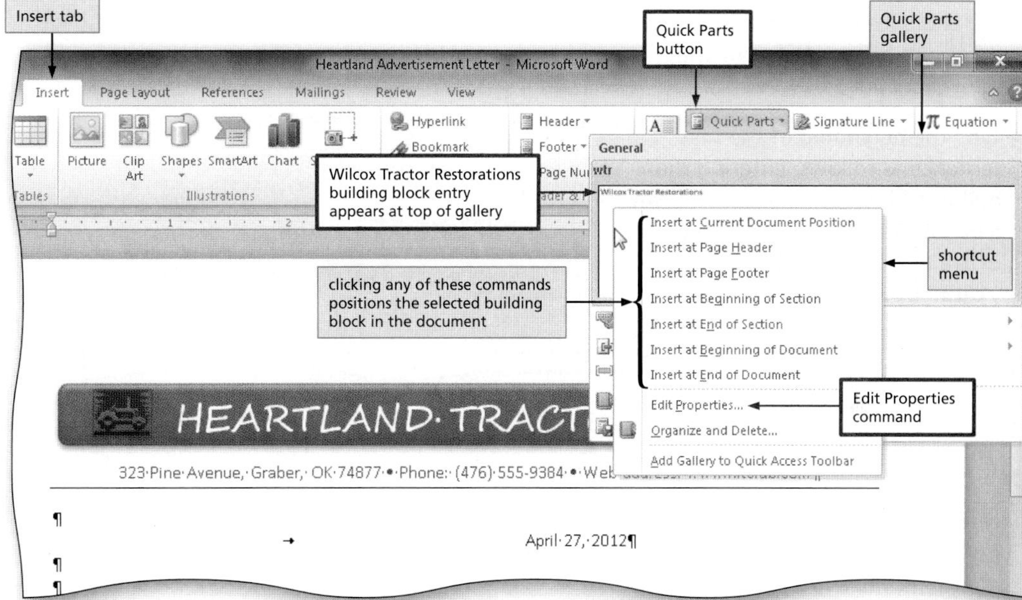

Figure 3–50

- Click Edit Properties on the shortcut menu to display the Modify Building Block dialog box, filled in with information related to the selected building block.
- Click the Gallery box arrow (Modify Building Block dialog box) and then click AutoText to change the gallery in which the building block will be displayed.
- Type **Potential Advertiser** in the Description text box (Figure 3–51).

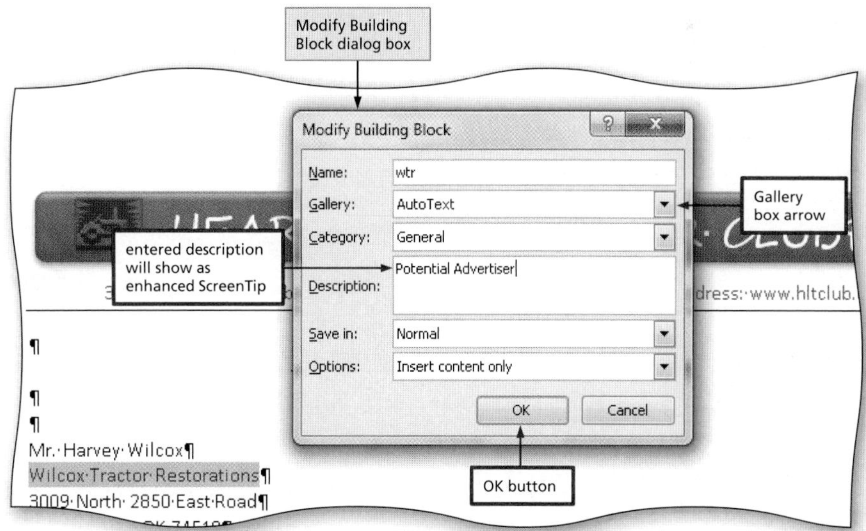

Figure 3–51

- Click the OK button to store the building block entry and close the dialog box.
- Click the Yes button when asked if you want to redefine the building block entry.

To Insert a Building Block

In the first sentence in the body of the letter, you want the prospective advertiser name, Wilcox Tractor Restorations, to be displayed. Recall that you stored a building block name of wtr for Wilcox Tractor Restorations. Thus, you will type the building block name and then instruct Word to replace a building block name with the stored building block entry. The following steps insert a building block.

- Click to the right of the colon in the salutation and then press the ENTER key twice to position the insertion point one blank line below the salutation.
- Type the beginning of the first sentence as follows, entering the building block name as shown: `We are delighted you are considering advertising your business, wtr` (Figure 3–52).

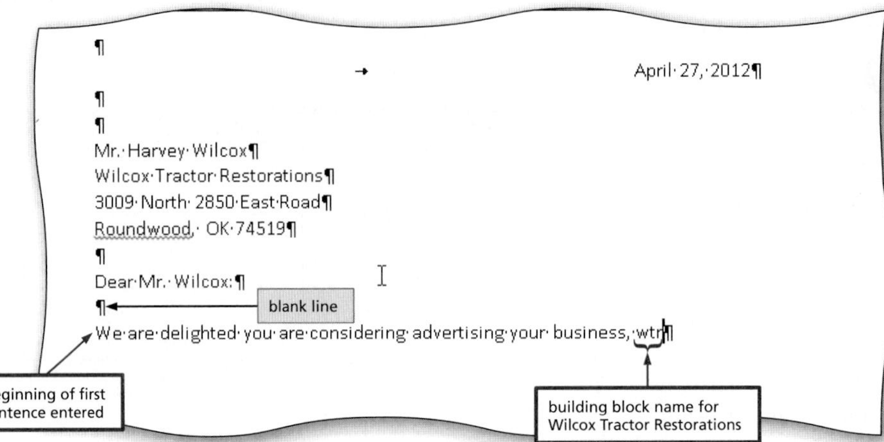
April·27,·2012¶
Mr.·Harvey·Wilcox¶
Wilcox·Tractor·Restorations¶
3009·North·2850·East·Road¶
Roundwood,·OK·74519¶
Dear·Mr.·Wilcox:¶
blank line
We·are·delighted·you·are·considering·advertising·your·business,·wtr¶
beginning of first sentence entered
building block name for Wilcox Tractor Restorations

Figure 3–52

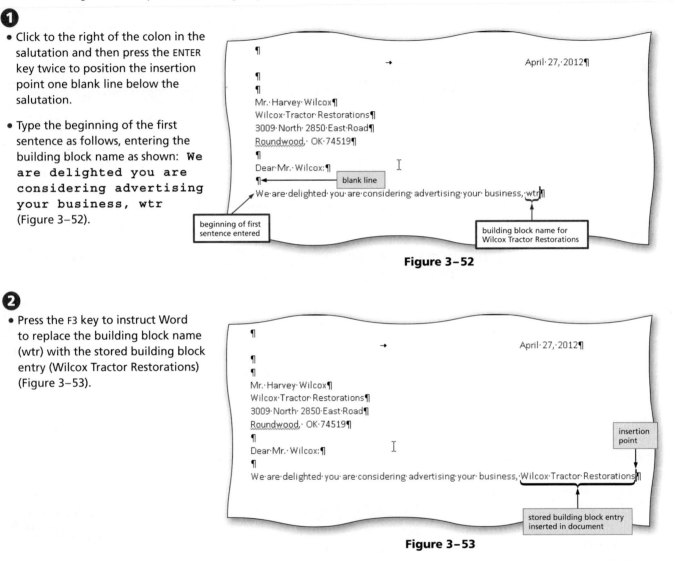

- Press the F3 key to instruct Word to replace the building block name (wtr) with the stored building block entry (Wilcox Tractor Restorations) (Figure 3–53).

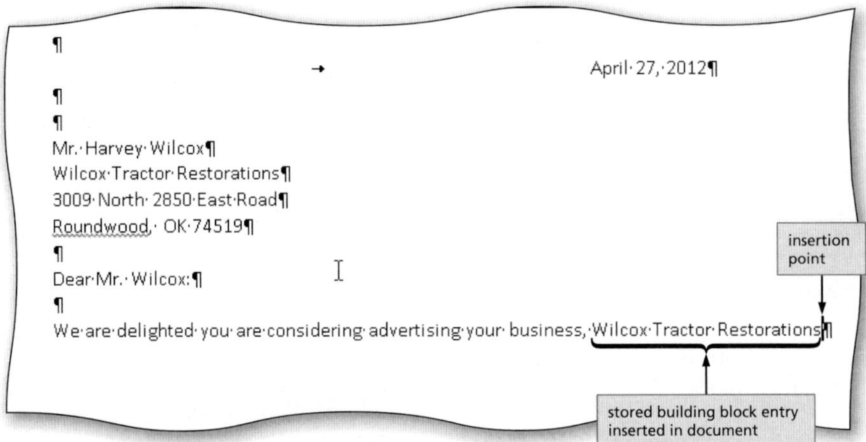
April·27,·2012¶
Mr.·Harvey·Wilcox¶
Wilcox·Tractor·Restorations¶
3009·North·2850·East·Road¶
Roundwood,·OK·74519¶
Dear·Mr.·Wilcox:¶
insertion point
We·are·delighted·you·are·considering·advertising·your·business,·Wilcox·Tractor·Restorations¶
stored building block entry inserted in document

Figure 3–53

Other Ways

1. Click Quick Parts button (Insert tab | Text group), if necessary point to AutoText, click desired building block

Building Blocks versus AutoCorrect

In Project 2, you learned how to use the AutoCorrect feature, which enables you to insert and create AutoCorrect entries, similarly to how you created and inserted building blocks in this chapter. The difference between an AutoCorrect entry and a building block entry is that the AutoCorrect feature makes corrections for you automatically as soon as you press the SPACEBAR or type a punctuation mark, whereas you must instruct Word to insert a building block. That is, you enter the building block name and then press the F3 key, or click the Quick Parts button and select the building block from one of the galleries.

To Insert a Nonbreaking Space

Some compound words, such as proper nouns, dates, units of time and measure, abbreviations, and geographic destinations, should not be divided at the end of a line. These words either should fit as a unit at the end of a line or be wrapped together to the next line.

Word provides two special characters to assist with this task: the nonbreaking space and the nonbreaking hyphen. A **nonbreaking space** is a special space character that prevents two words from splitting if the first word falls at the end of a line. Similarly, a **nonbreaking hyphen** is a special type of hyphen that prevents two words separated by a hyphen from splitting at the end of a line.

The following steps insert a nonbreaking space between the words in the magazine name.

1

- With the insertion point at the end of the building block entry in the document (as shown in Figure 3–53), press the COMMA key and then press the SPACEBAR.
- Type `in` and then press the SPACEBAR. Press CTRL+I to turn on italics because magazine names should be italicized.
- Type `Heartland` as the first word in the magazine name and then press CTRL+SHIFT+SPACEBAR to insert a nonbreaking space after the entered word (Figure 3–54).

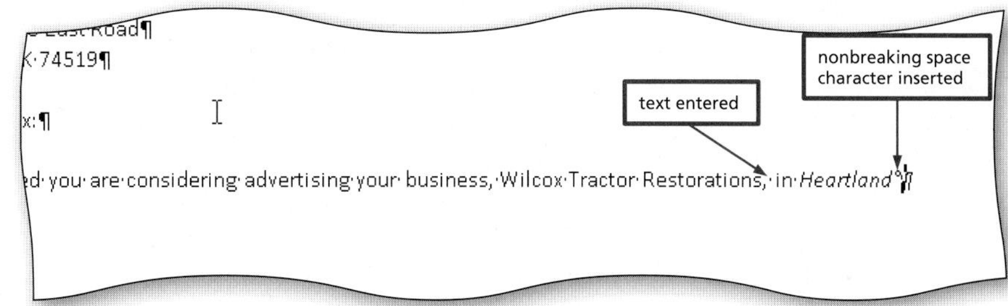

Figure 3–54

2

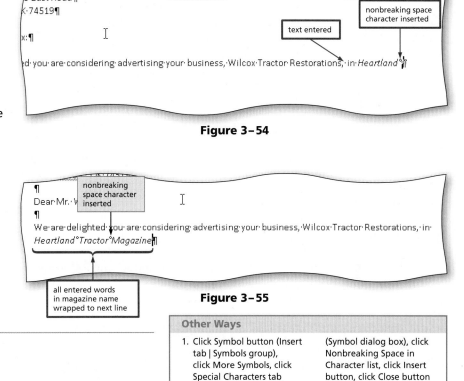

- Type `Tractor` and then press CTRL+SHIFT+SPACEBAR to insert another nonbreaking space after the entered word.
- Type `Magazine` and then press CTRL+I to turn off italics (Figure 3–55).

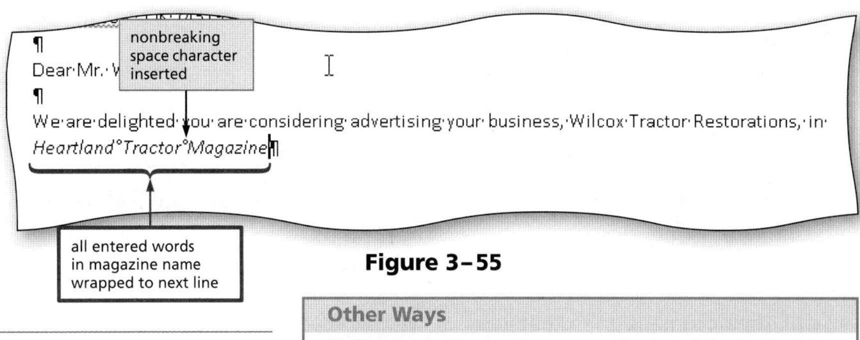

Figure 3–55

Other Ways

1. Click Symbol button (Insert tab | Symbols group), click More Symbols, click Special Characters tab (Symbol dialog box), click Nonbreaking Space in Character list, click Insert button, click Close button

To Enter Text

The next step in creating the letter is to enter the rest of the text in the first paragraph. The following steps enter this text.

1. Press the COMMA key and then press the SPACEBAR.
2. Type this text: `our monthly publication for tractor enthusiasts. The table below outlines advertisement rates per monthly issue:`
3. Press the ENTER key twice to place a blank line between paragraphs (shown in Figure 3–56 on the next page).

Q&A Why does my document wrap on different words?

Differences in wordwrap may relate to the printer connected to your computer. Thus, it is possible that the same document could wordwrap differently if associated with a different printer.

BTW **Nonbreaking Hyphen**
If you wanted to insert a nonbreaking hyphen, you would press CTRL+SHIFT+HYPHEN.

To Save an Existing Document with the Same File Name

You have made several modifications to the document since you last saved it. Thus, you should save it again. The following step saves the document again.

Click the Save button on the Quick Access Toolbar to overwrite the previously saved file.

Break Point: If you wish to take a break, this is a good place to do so. You can quit Word now. To resume at a later time, start Word, open the file called Heartland Advertisement Letter, and continue following the steps from this location forward.

Tables

The next step in composing the business letter is to place a table listing the rates for various types of advertisements (shown in Figure 3–1 on page WD 139). A Word **table** is a collection of rows and columns. The intersection of a row and a column is called a **cell**, and cells are filled with data.

The first step in creating a table is to insert an empty table in the document. When inserting a table, you must specify the total number of rows and columns required, which is called the **dimension** of the table. The table in this project has five columns. You often do not know the total number of rows in a table. Thus, many Word users create one row initially and then add more rows as needed. In Word, the first number in a dimension is the number of columns, and the second is the number of rows. For example, in Word, a 5 × 1 (pronounced "five by one") table consists of five columns and one row.

To Insert an Empty Table

The next step is to insert an empty table in the letter. The following steps insert a table with five columns and one row at the location of the insertion point.

1

- Scroll the document up so that you will be able to see the table in the document window.
- With the insertion point positioned as shown in Figure 3–56, click the Table button (Insert tab | Tables group) to display the Table gallery (Figure 3–56).

Experiment

- Point to various cells on the grid to see a preview of various table dimensions in the document window.

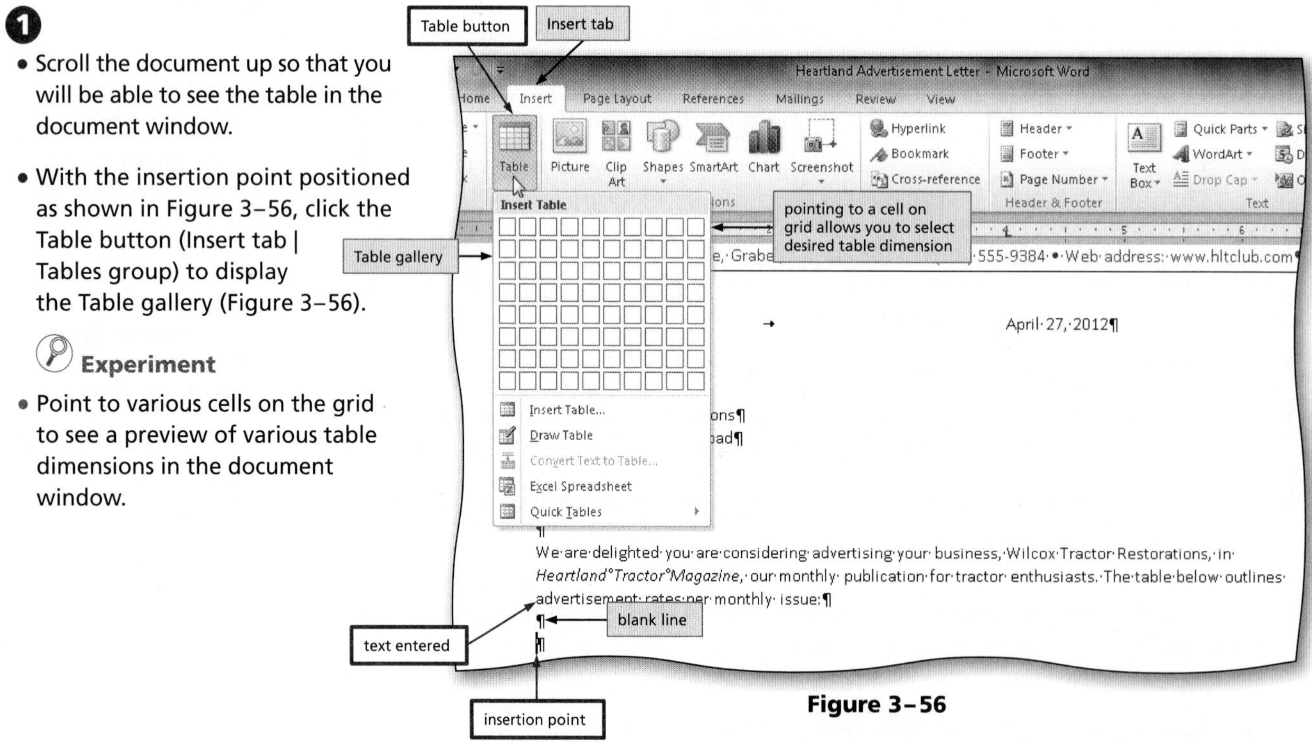

Figure 3–56

- Position the mouse pointer on the cell in the first row and fifth column of the grid to preview the desired table dimension (Figure 3–57).

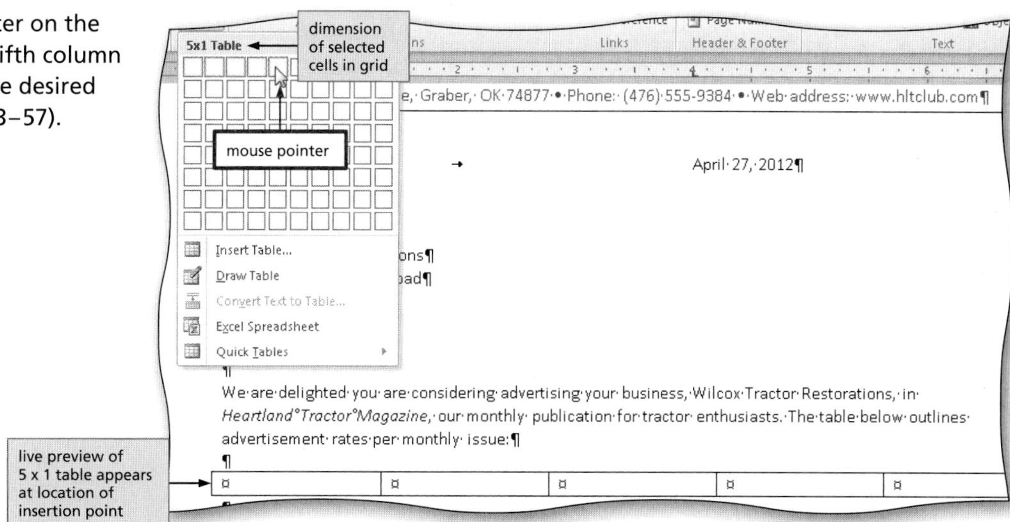

Figure 3–57

3

- Click the cell in the first row and fifth column of the grid to insert an empty table with one row and five columns in the document.
- If necessary, scroll the table up in the document window (Figure 3–58).

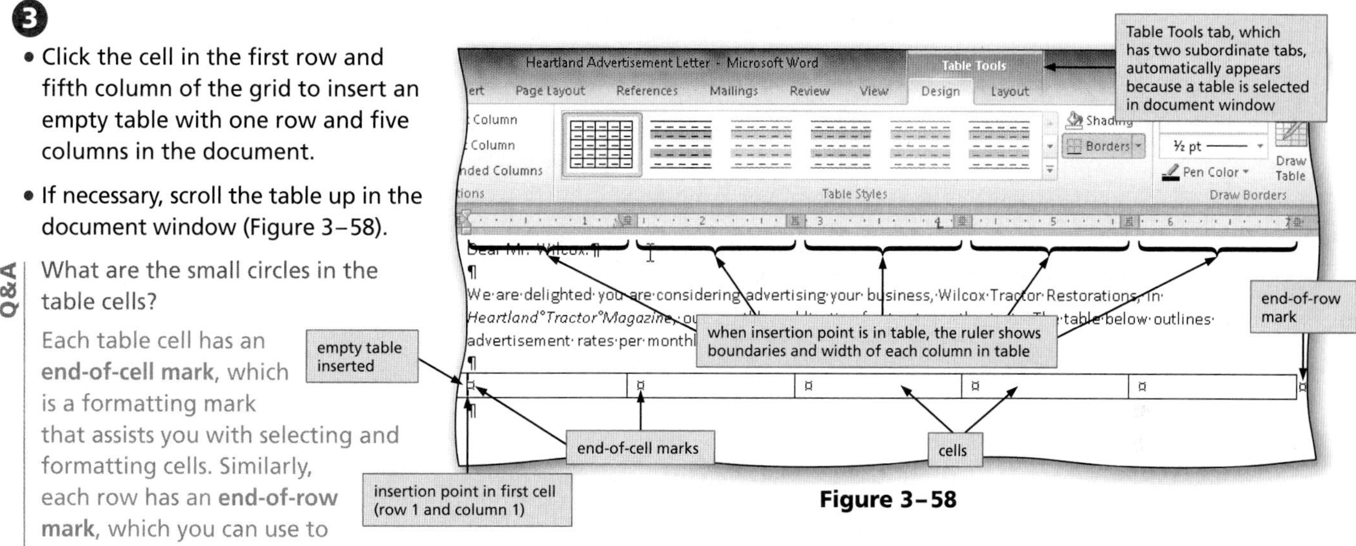

Figure 3–58

Q&A What are the small circles in the table cells?

Each table cell has an **end-of-cell mark**, which is a formatting mark that assists you with selecting and formatting cells. Similarly, each row has an **end-of-row mark**, which you can use to add columns to the right of a table. Recall that formatting marks do not print on a hard copy. The end-of-cell marks currently are left-aligned, that is, positioned at the left edge of each cell.

Other Ways

1. Click Table (Insert tab | Tables group), click Insert Table in Table gallery, enter number of columns and rows (Insert Table dialog box), click OK button

To Enter Data in a Table

The next step is to enter data in the cells of the empty table. The data you enter in a cell wordwraps just as text wordwraps between the margins of a document. To place data in a cell, you click the cell and then type.

To advance rightward from one cell to the next, press the TAB key. When you are at the rightmost cell in a row, press the TAB key to move to the first cell in the next row; do not press the ENTER key. The ENTER key is used to begin a new paragraph within a cell. One way to add new rows to a table is to press the TAB key when the insertion point is positioned in the bottom-right corner cell of the table. The step on the next page enters data in the first row of the table and then inserts a blank second row.

1

- With the insertion point in the left cell of the table, type **Type** and then press the TAB key to advance the insertion point to the next cell.
- Type **Dimensions** and then press the TAB key to advance the insertion point to the next cell.
- Type **Word Count** and then press the TAB key to advance the insertion point to the next cell.
- Type **Photo Count** and then press the TAB key to advance the insertion point to the next cell.
- Type **Cost** and then press the TAB key to insert a second row at the end of the table and position the insertion point in the first column of the new row (Figure 3–59).

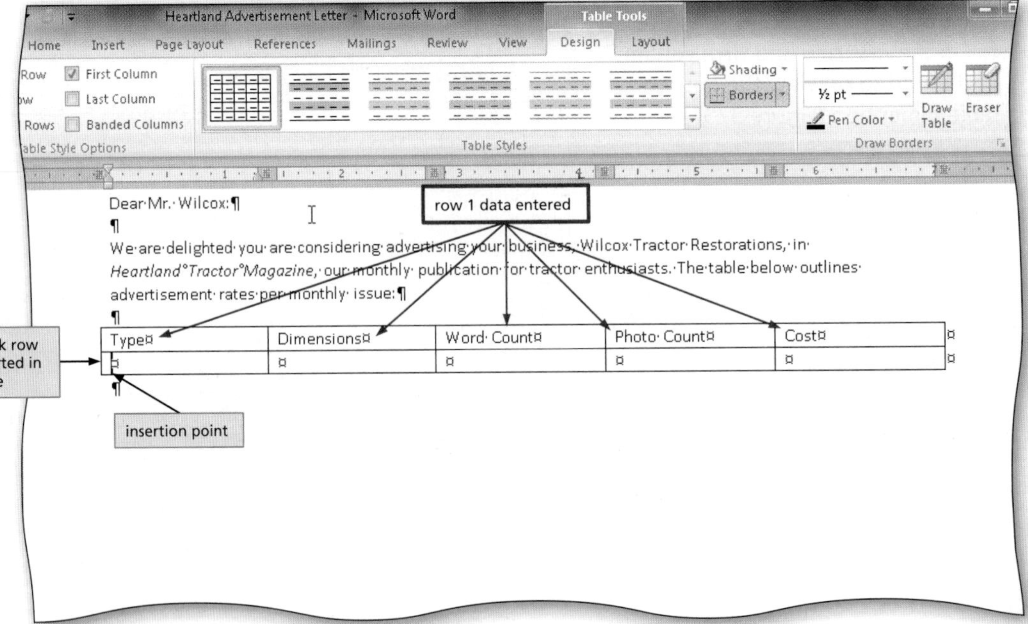

Figure 3–59

Q&A
How do I edit cell contents if I make a mistake?

Click in the cell and then correct the entry.

To Enter Data in a Table

The following steps enter the remaining data in the table.

1 Type **Full Page** and then press the TAB key to advance the insertion point to the next cell. Type **9" x 7"** and then press the TAB key to advance the insertion point to the next cell. Type **800** and then press the TAB key to advance the insertion point to the next cell. Type **4** and then press the TAB key to advance the insertion point to the next cell. Type **$650** and then press the TAB key to insert a row at the end of the table and position the insertion point in the first column of the new row.

2 In the third row, type **Half Page** in the first column, **4.5" x 7"** as the dimensions, **400** as the word count, **2** as the photo count, and **$350** as the cost. Press the TAB key to position the insertion point in the first column of a new row.

3 In the fourth row, type **Quarter Page** in the first column, **4.5" x 3.5"** as the dimensions, **200** as the word count, **1** as the photo count, and **$225** as the cost. Press the TAB key.

4 In the fifth row, type **Business Card** in the first column, **2.25" x 3.5"** as the dimensions, **100** as the word count, **0** as the photo count, and **$125** as the cost (Figure 3–60).

BTW
Tables
For simple tables, such as the one just created, Word users often select the table dimension in the Table gallery to create the table. For a more complex table, such as one with a varying number of columns per row, Word has a Draw Table feature that allows users to draw a table in the document using a pencil pointer. To use this feature, click the Table button (Insert tab | Tables group) and then click Draw Table.

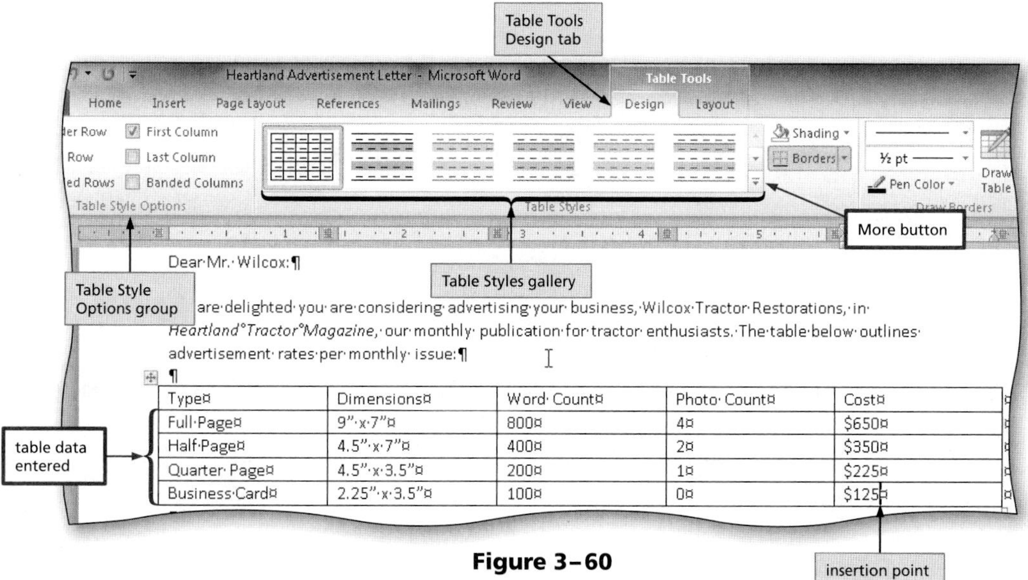

Figure 3–60

To Apply a Table Style

The next step is to apply a table style to the table. Word provides a Table Styles gallery, allowing you to change the basic table format to a more visually appealing style. Word provides a gallery of more than 90 table styles, which include a variety of colors and shading. The following steps apply a table style to the table in the letter.

- With the insertion point in the table, be sure the check marks match those in the Table Style Options group (Table Tools Design tab) as shown in Figure 3–60.

Q&A What if the Table Tools Design tab no longer is the active tab?

Click in the table and then display the Table Tools Design tab.

Q&A What do the options in the Table Style Options group mean?

When you apply table styles, if you want the top row of the table (header row), a row containing totals (total row), first column, or last column to be formatted differently, select those check boxes. If you want the rows or columns to alternate with colors, select Banded Rows or Banded Columns, respectively.

2

- Click the More button in the Table Styles gallery (shown in Figure 3–60) (Table Tools Design tab | Table Styles group) to expand the gallery.
- Scroll and then point to Medium Grid 3 - Accent 4 in the Table Styles gallery to display a live preview of that style applied to the table in the document (Figure 3–61).

Experiment

- Point to various table styles in the Table Styles gallery and watch the format of the table change in the document window.

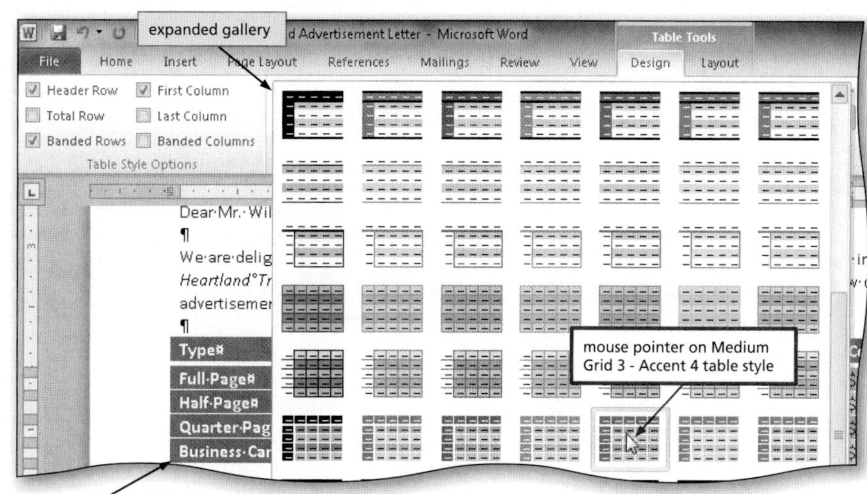

Figure 3–61

3

- Click Medium Grid 3 - Accent 4 in the Table Styles gallery to apply the selected style to the table (Figure 3–62).

Experiment

- Select and remove check marks from various check boxes in the Table Style Options group and watch the format of the table change in the document window. When finished experimenting, be sure the check marks match those shown in Figure 3–62.

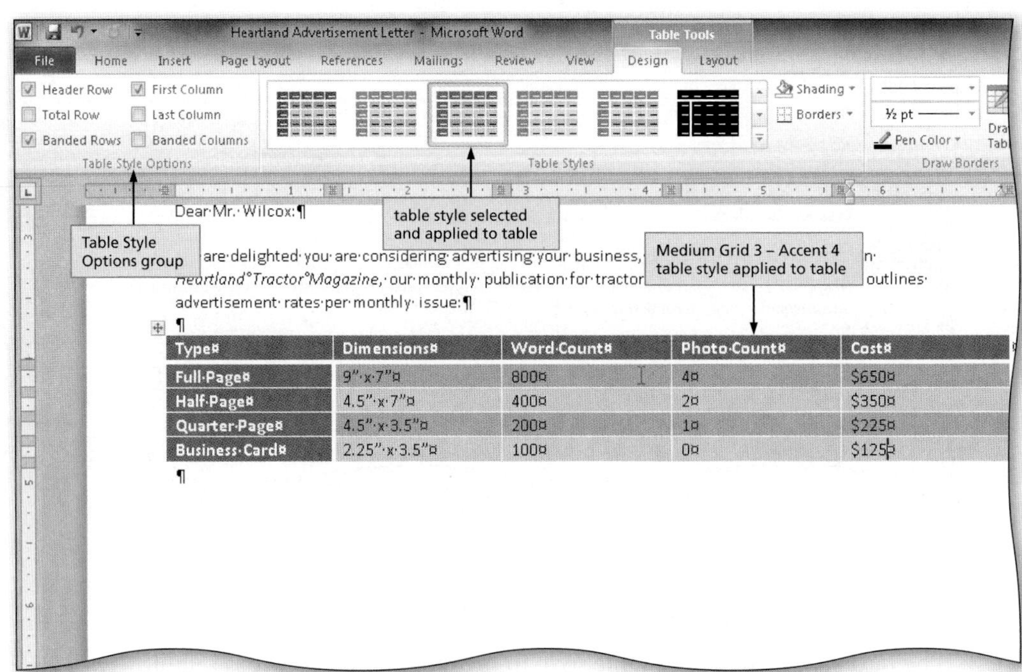

Figure 3–62

To Resize Table Columns to Fit Table Contents

The table in this project currently extends from the left margin to the right margin of the document. You want each column to be only as wide as the longest entry in the table. That is, the first column must be wide enough to accommodate the words, Business Card, and the second column should be only as wide as the title, Dimensions, and so on. The following steps instruct Word to fit the width of the columns to the contents of the table automatically.

- With the insertion point in the table, display the Table Tools Layout tab.
- Click the AutoFit button (Table Tools Layout tab | Cell Size group) to display the AutoFit menu (Figure 3–63).

Q&A

What causes the table move handle and table resize handle to appear and disappear from the table?

They appear whenever you position the mouse pointer in the table.

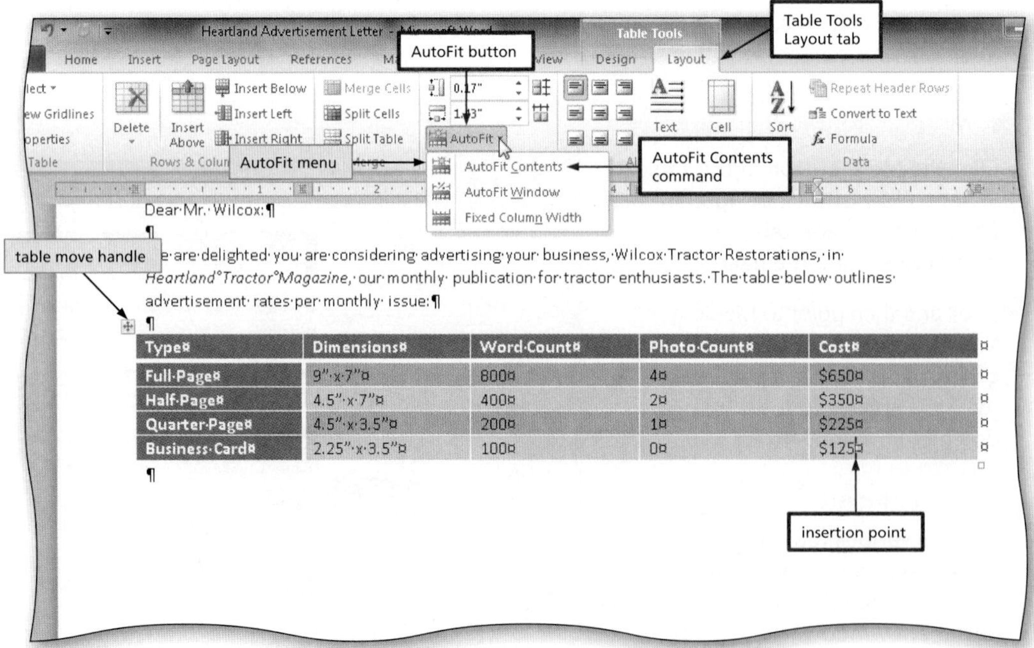

Figure 3–63

2

- Click AutoFit Contents on the AutoFit menu, so that Word automatically adjusts the widths of the columns based on the text in the table (Figure 3–64).

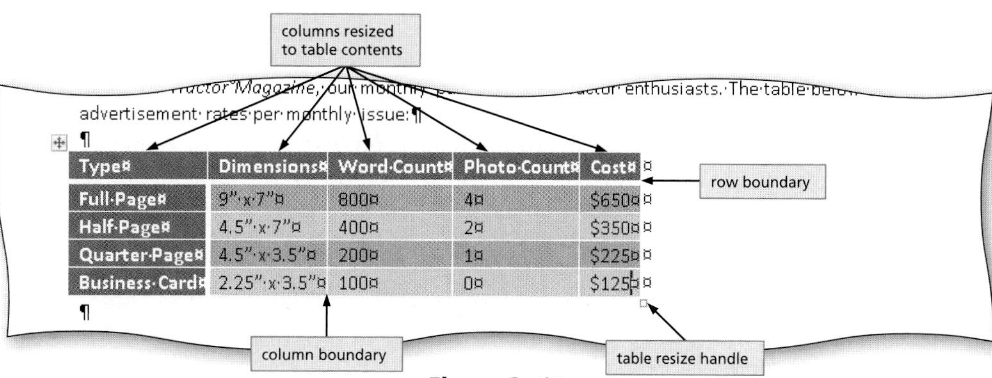

Figure 3–64

Q&A

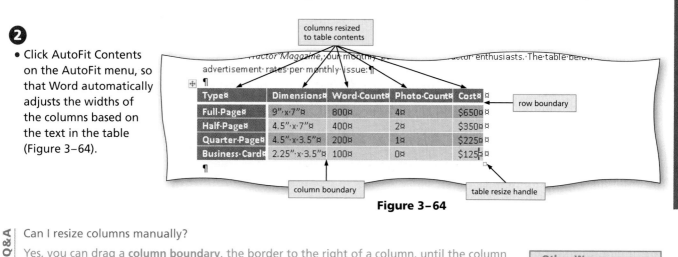

Can I resize columns manually?

Yes, you can drag a **column boundary**, the border to the right of a column, until the column is the desired width. Similarly, you can resize a row by dragging the **row boundary**, the border at the bottom of a row, until the row is the desired height. You also can resize the entire table by dragging the **table resize handle**, which is a small square that appears when you point to a corner of the table (shown in Figure 3–63).

Other Ways

1. Right-click table, point to AutoFit on shortcut menu, click AutoFit to Contents
2. Double-click column boundary

Selecting Table Contents

When working with tables, you may need to select the contents of cells, rows, columns, or the entire table. Table 3–4 identifies ways to select various items in a table.

BTW

Resizing Table Columns and Rows

To change the width of a column or height of a row to an exact measurement, hold down the ALT key while dragging markers on the ruler. Or, enter values in the Table Column Width or Table Row Height text boxes (Table Tools Layout tab | Cell Size group).

Table 3–4 Selecting Items in a Table

Item to Select	Action
Cell	Point to left edge of cell and click when the mouse pointer changes to a small solid upward angled pointing arrow. Or, position insertion point in cell, click Select button (Table Tools Layout tab | Table group), and then click Select Cell on the Select menu.
Column	Point to border at top of column and click when the mouse pointer changes to a small solid downward-pointing arrow. Or, position insertion point in column, click Select button (Table Tools Layout tab | Table group), and then click Select Column on the Select menu.
Row	Point to the left of the row and click when mouse pointer changes to a right-pointing block arrow. Or, position insertion point in row, click Select button (Table Tools Layout tab | Table group), and then click Select Row on the Select menu.
Multiple cells, rows, or columns adjacent to one another	Drag through cells, rows, or columns.
Multiple cells, rows, or columns not adjacent to one another	Select first cell, row, or column (as described above) and then hold down CTRL key while selecting next cell, row, or column.
Next cell	Press TAB key.
Previous cell	Press SHIFT+TAB.
Table	Point somewhere in table and then click table move handle that appears in upper-left corner of table. Or, position insertion point in table, click Select button (Table Tools Layout tab | Table group), and then click Select Table on the Select menu.

BTW

Tab Character in Tables

In a table, the TAB key advances the insertion point from one cell to the next. To insert a tab character in a cell, you must press CTRL+TAB.

To Align Data in Cells

The next step is to change the alignment of the data in cells in the second, third, fourth, and fifth columns of the table. In addition to aligning text horizontally in a cell (left, center, or right), you can align it vertically within a cell (top, center, bottom). When the height of the cell is close to the same height as the text, however, differences in vertical alignment are not readily apparent, which is the case for this table. The following steps center data in cells.

- Select the cells in the second, third, fourth, and fifth columns using one of the techniques described in Table 3–4 on the previous page (Figure 3–65).

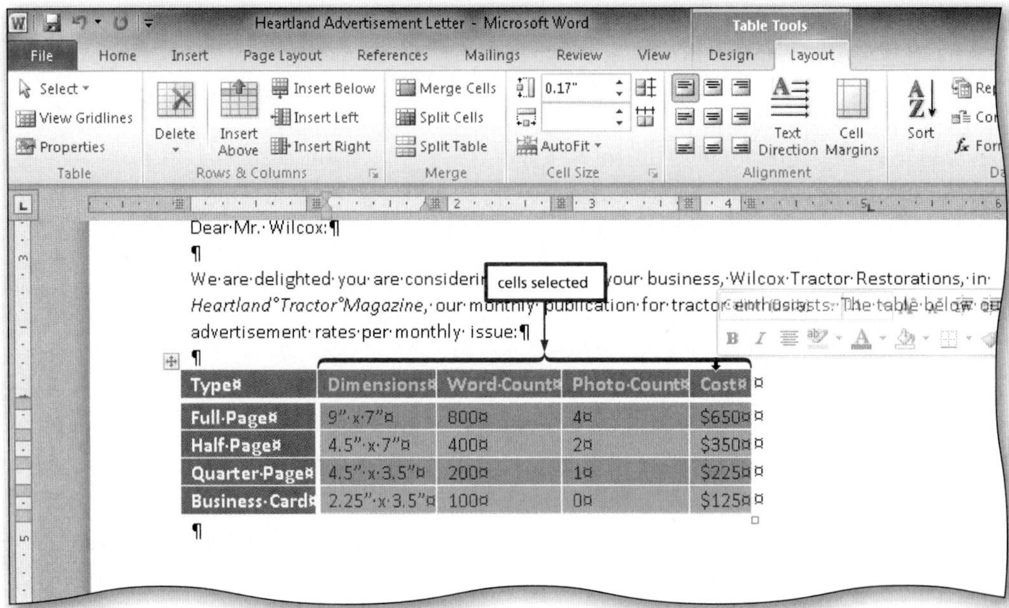

Figure 3–65

2

- Click the Align Top Center button (Table Tools Layout tab | Alignment group) to center the contents of the selected cells.
- Click in the table to remove the selection (Figure 3–66).

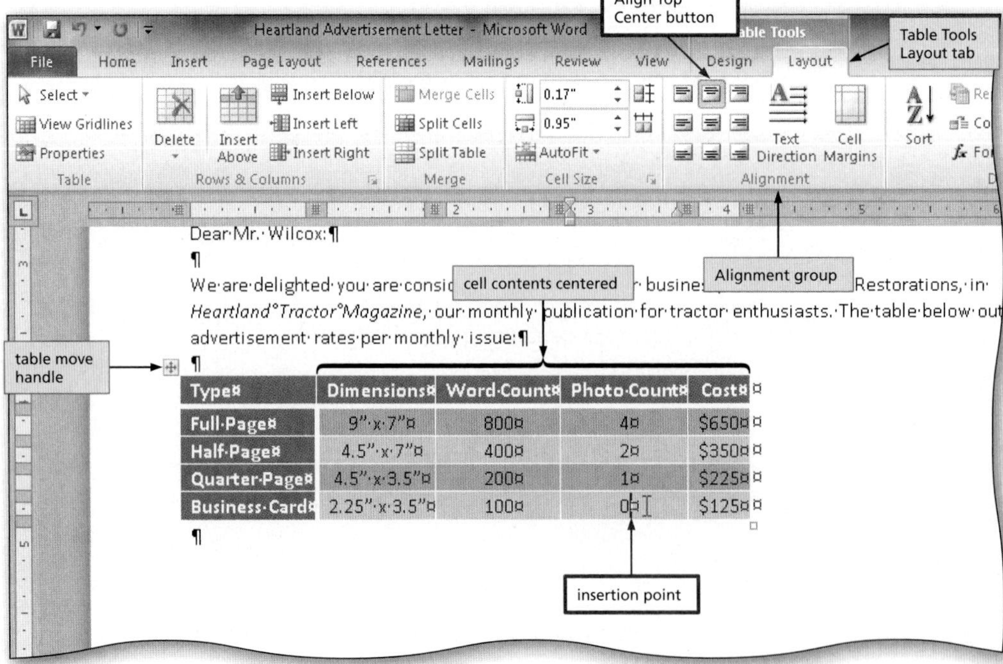

Figure 3–66

To Center a Table

When you first create a table, it is left-aligned, that is, flush with the left margin. In this letter, the table should be centered between the margins. To center a table, you first select the entire table. The following steps select and center a table using the Mini toolbar.

1

- Position the mouse pointer in the table so that the table move handle appears (shown in Figure 3–66).

Q&A What if the table move handle does not appear?

You also can select a table by clicking the Select button (Table Tools Layout tab | Table group) and then clicking Select Table on the menu.

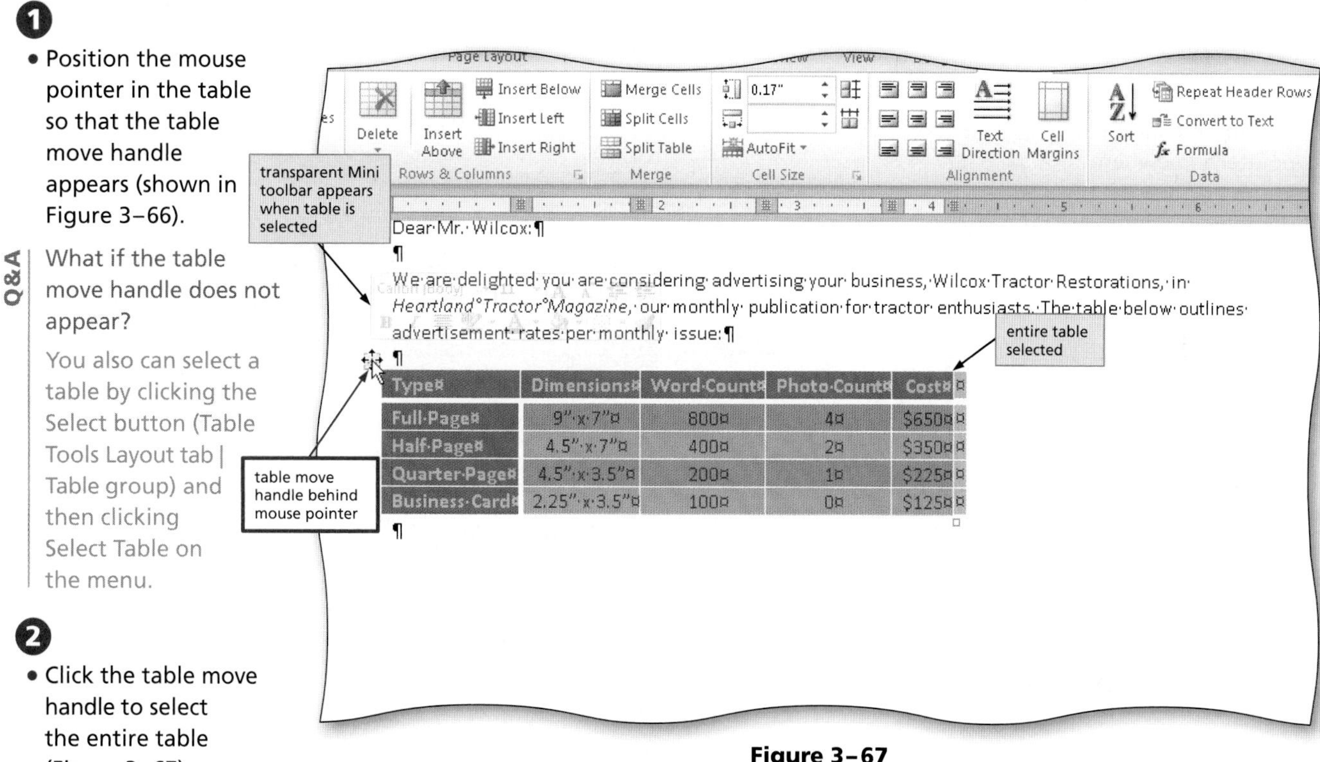

transparent Mini toolbar appears when table is selected
entire table selected
table move handle behind mouse pointer
Dear Mr. Wilcox:
We are delighted you are considering advertising your business, Wilcox Tractor Restorations, in Heartland Tractor Magazine, our monthly publication for tractor enthusiasts. The table below outlines advertisement rates per monthly issue:
Type | Dimensions | Word Count | Photo Count | Cost
Full Page | 9" x 7" | 800 | 4 | $650
Half Page | 4.5" x 7" | 400 | 2 | $350
Quarter Page | 4.5" x 3.5" | 200 | 1 | $225
Business Card | 2.25" x 3.5" | 100 | 0 | $125

2

- Click the table move handle to select the entire table (Figure 3–67).

Figure 3–67

3

- Move the mouse pointer into the Mini toolbar, so that the toolbar changes to a bright toolbar. Click the Center button on the Mini toolbar to center the selected table between the left and right margins (Figure 3–68).

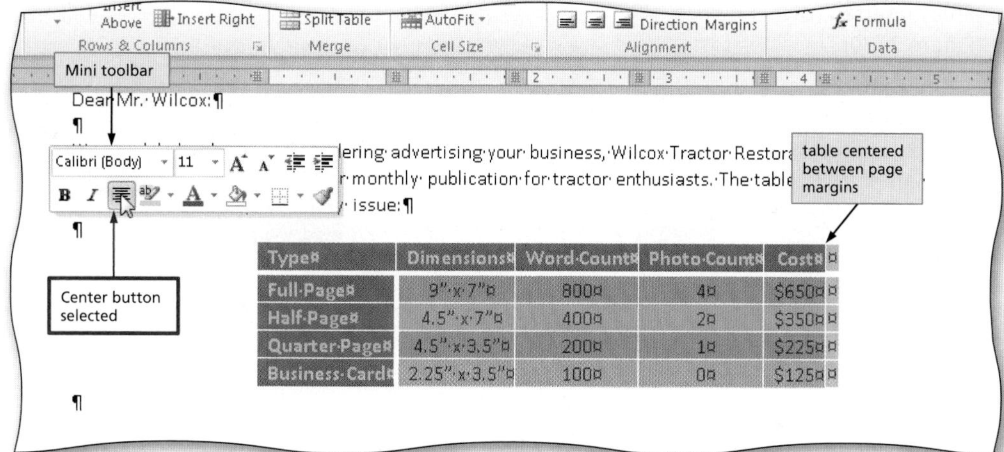

Figure 3–68

Q&A Could I have clicked the Center button on the Home tab?

Yes. If the command you want to use is not on the currently displayed tab on the Ribbon and it is available on the Mini toolbar, use the Mini toolbar instead of switching to a different tab. This technique minimizes mouse movement.

To Insert a Row in a Table

The next step is to insert a row at the top of the table because you want to place a title on the table. As discussed earlier, you can insert a row at the end of a table by positioning the insertion point in the bottom-right corner cell and then pressing the TAB key. You cannot use the TAB key to insert a row at the beginning or middle of a table. Instead, you use the Insert Rows Above or Insert Rows Below command. The following steps insert a row in a table.

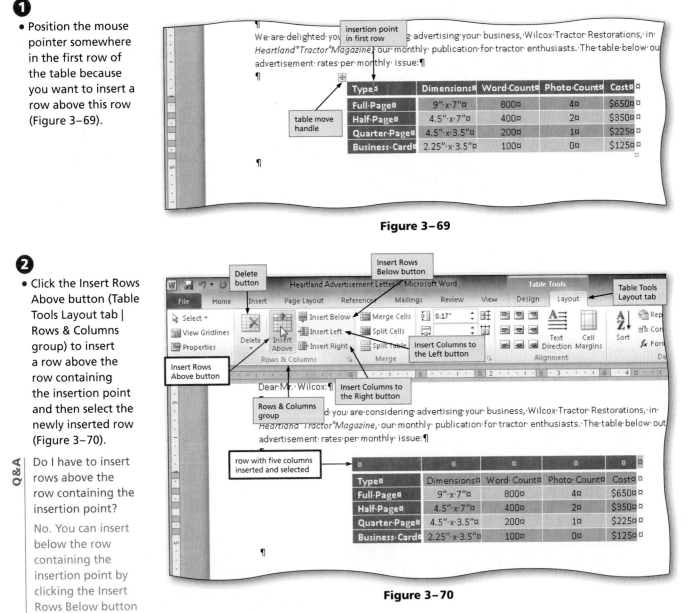

- Position the mouse pointer somewhere in the first row of the table because you want to insert a row above this row (Figure 3–69).

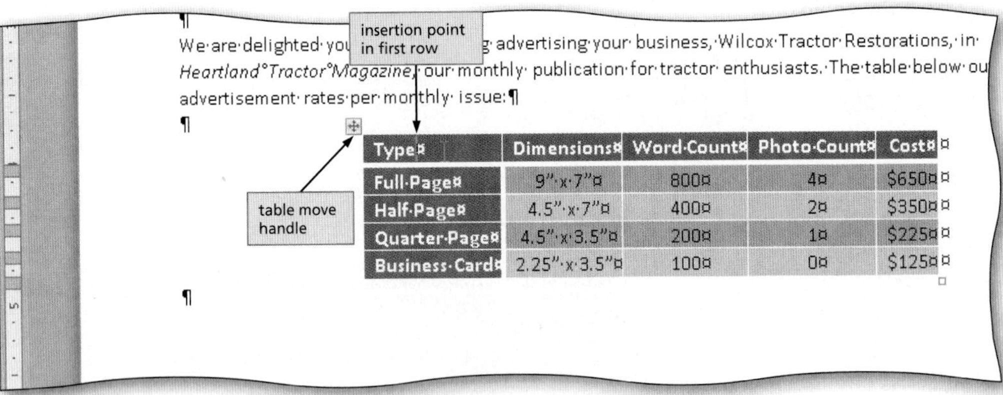

Figure 3–69

- Click the Insert Rows Above button (Table Tools Layout tab | Rows & Columns group) to insert a row above the row containing the insertion point and then select the newly inserted row (Figure 3–70).

Q&A Do I have to insert rows above the row containing the insertion point?

No. You can insert below the row containing the insertion point by clicking the Insert Rows Below button (Table Tools Layout tab | Rows & Columns group).

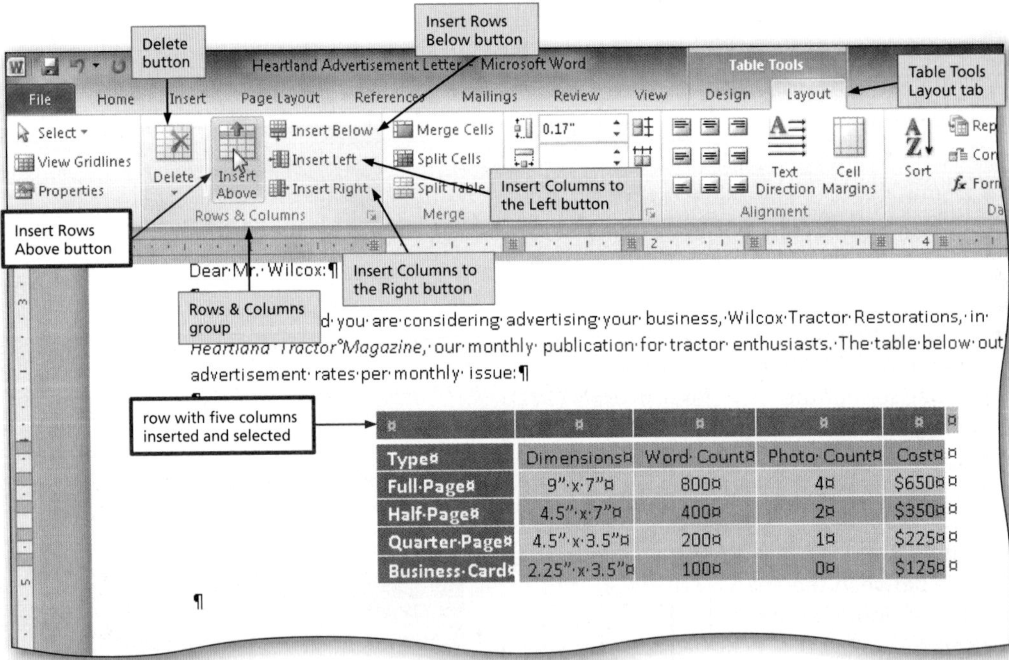

Figure 3–70

Q&A Why did the colors in the second row change?

The table style specifies to format the Header row differently, which is the first row.

Other Ways

1. Right-click row, point to Insert on shortcut menu, click desired command on Insert submenu

To Insert a Column in a Table

If, instead of inserting rows, you wanted to insert a column in a table, you would perform the following steps.

1. Position the insertion point in the column to the left or right of where you want to insert the column.
2. Click the Insert Columns to the Left button (Table Tools Layout tab | Rows & Columns group) to insert a column to the left of the current column, or click the Insert Columns to the Right button (Table Tools Layout tab | Rows & Columns group) to insert a column to the right of the current column. Or you could right-click the table, point to Insert on the shortcut menu, and click Insert Columns to the Left or Insert Columns to the Right on the Insert submenu.

BTW

Moving Tables

If you wanted to move a table to a new location, you would point to the upper-left corner of the table until the table move handle appears (shown in Figure 3–69), point to the table move handle, and the drag it to move the entire table to a new location.

BTW

Moving Columns and Rows

You can use drag-and-drop or cut-and-paste techniques/methods to move table columns and rows. First, you select the column(s) or row(s) to be moved. Next, press and hold down the mouse button, which displays a dotted insertion point and a small dotted box with the mouse pointer. Then, drag the dotted insertion point to the location where the selected column or row is to be moved. Or, you can select the column or row to be moved, click the Cut button (Home tab | Clipboard group), click where the column or row is to be moved, and then click the Paste button (Home tab | Clipboard group).

Deleting Table Data

If you want to delete row(s) or delete column(s) from a table, position the insertion point in the row(s) or column(s) to delete, click the Delete button (Table Tools Layout tab | Rows & Columns group), and then click Delete Rows or Delete Columns on the Delete menu. Or, select the row or column to delete, right-click the selection, and then click Delete Rows or Delete Columns on the shortcut menu.

To delete the contents of a cell, select the cell contents and then press the DELETE or BACKSPACE key. You also can drag and drop or cut and paste the contents of cells. To delete an entire table, select the table, click the Delete button (Table Tools Layout tab | Rows & Columns group), and then click Delete Table on the Delete menu. To delete the contents of a table and leave an empty table, you would select the table and then press the DELETE key.

To Merge Cells

The top row of the table is to contain the table title, which should be centered above the columns of the table. The row just inserted has one cell for each column, in this case, five cells (shown in Figure 3–70). The title of the table, however, should be in a single cell that spans all rows. Thus, the following steps merge the five cells into a single cell.

- With the cells to merge selected (as shown in Figure 3–70), click the Merge Cells button (Table Tools Layout tab | Merge group) to merge the five cells into one cell (Figure 3–71).

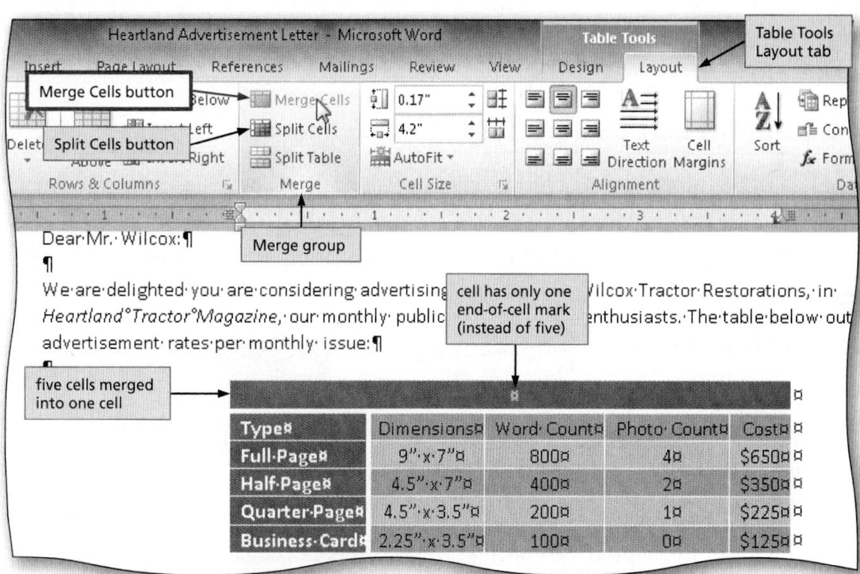

Figure 3–71

- Position the insertion point in the first row and then type **Monthly Issue Advertisement Rates** as the table title (Figure 3–72).

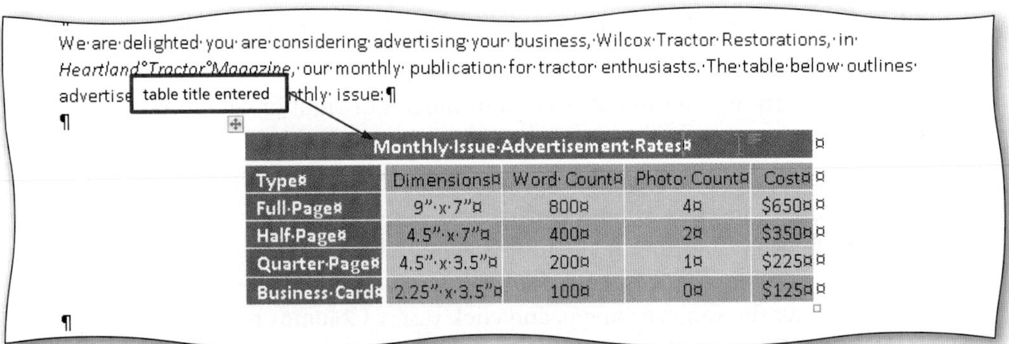

We are delighted you are considering advertising your business, Wilcox Tractor Restorations, in Heartland Tractor Magazine, our monthly publication for tractor enthusiasts. The table below outlines advertis… …thly issue:
table title entered
Monthly Issue Advertisement Rates

Type	Dimensions	Word Count	Photo Count	Cost
Full Page	9" x 7"	800	4	$650
Half Page	4.5" x 7"	400	2	$350
Quarter Page	4.5" x 3.5"	200	1	$225
Business Card	2.25" x 3.5"	100	0	$125

Figure 3–72

Other Ways

1. Right-click selected cells to merge, click Merge Cells on shortcut menu

To Split Table Cells

Instead of merging multiple cells into a single cell, sometimes you want to split a single cell into multiple cells. If you wanted to split cells, you would perform the following steps.

1. Position the insertion point in the cell to split.
2. Click the Split Cells button (Table Tools Layout tab | Merge group), or right-click the cell and then click Split Cells on the shortcut menu, to display the Split Cells dialog box.
3. Enter the number of columns and rows into which you want the cell split (Split Cells dialog box).
4. Click the OK button.

To Add More Text

The table now is complete. The next step is to enter text below the table. The following steps enter text.

1. Position the insertion point on the paragraph mark below the table and then press the ENTER key.
2. Type **Please note that additional fees will be assessed if the word or photo counts exceed the limits listed above. We offer the following discounts:** and then press the ENTER key (shown in Figure 3–73).

To Bullet a List as You Type

In Chapter 1, you learned how to apply bullets to existing paragraphs. If you know before you type that a list should be bulleted, you can use Word's AutoFormat As You Type feature to bullet the paragraphs as you type them (see Table 3–2 on page WD 162). The following steps add bullets to a list as you type.

1

- Press the ASTERISK key (*) as the first character on the line (Figure 3–73).

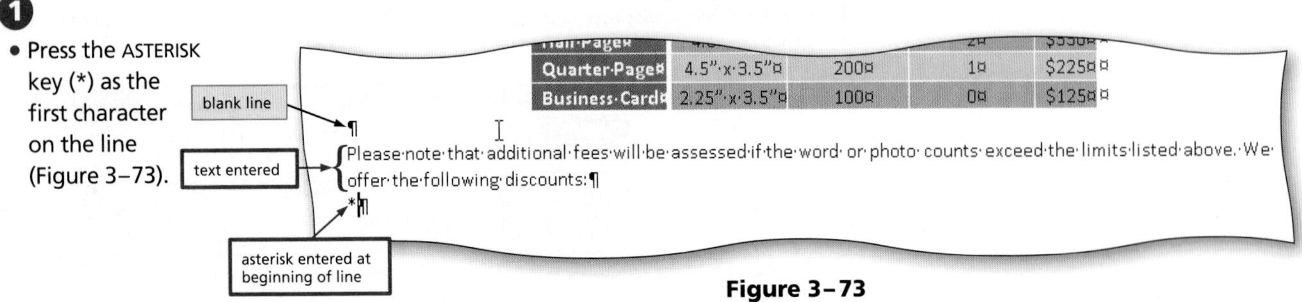

Quarter Page 4.5" x 3.5" 200 1 $225
Business Card 2.25" x 3.5" 100 0 $125
blank line
text entered
Please note that additional fees will be assessed if the word or photo counts exceed the limits listed above. We offer the following discounts:
asterisk entered at beginning of line

Figure 3–73

2

- Press the SPACEBAR to convert the asterisk to a bullet character.

Q&A What if I did not want the asterisk converted to a bullet character?

You could undo the AutoFormat by clicking the Undo button, pressing CTRL+Z, clicking the AutoCorrect Options button that appears to the left of the bullet character as soon as you press the SPACEBAR, and then clicking Undo Automatic Bullets on the AutoCorrect Options menu, or by clicking the Bullets button (Home tab | Paragraph group).

- Type `10 percent discount for any advertisement that runs in three consecutive issues` as the first bulleted item.
- Press the ENTER key to place another bullet character at the beginning of the next line (Figure 3–74).

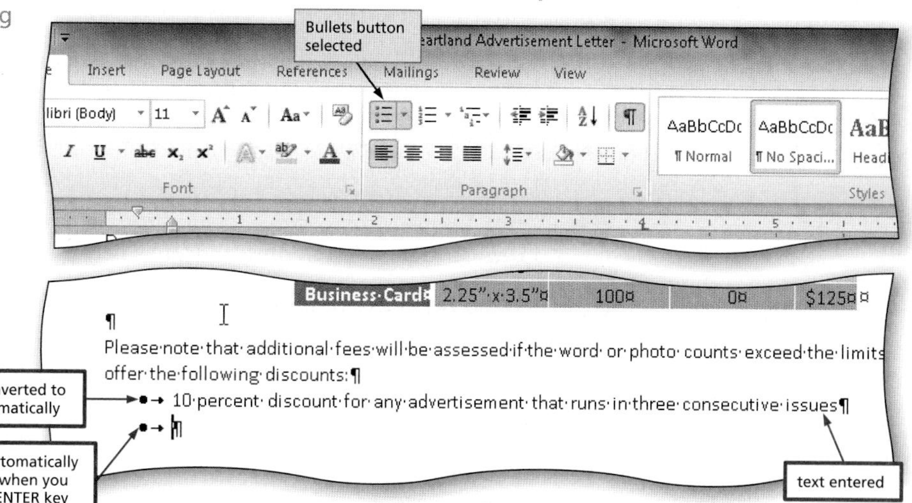

Figure 3–74

3

- Type `5 percent discount for a camera-ready advertisement (prepared using Microsoft Word at the proper size and with all words and photos in final layout form)` and then press the ENTER key.
- Type `3 percent discount if payment in full is submitted with order` and then press the ENTER key.
- Press the ENTER key to turn off automatic bullets as you type (Figure 3–75).

Q&A Why did automatic bullets stop?

When you press the ENTER key without entering any text after the automatic bullet character, Word turns off the automatic bullets feature.

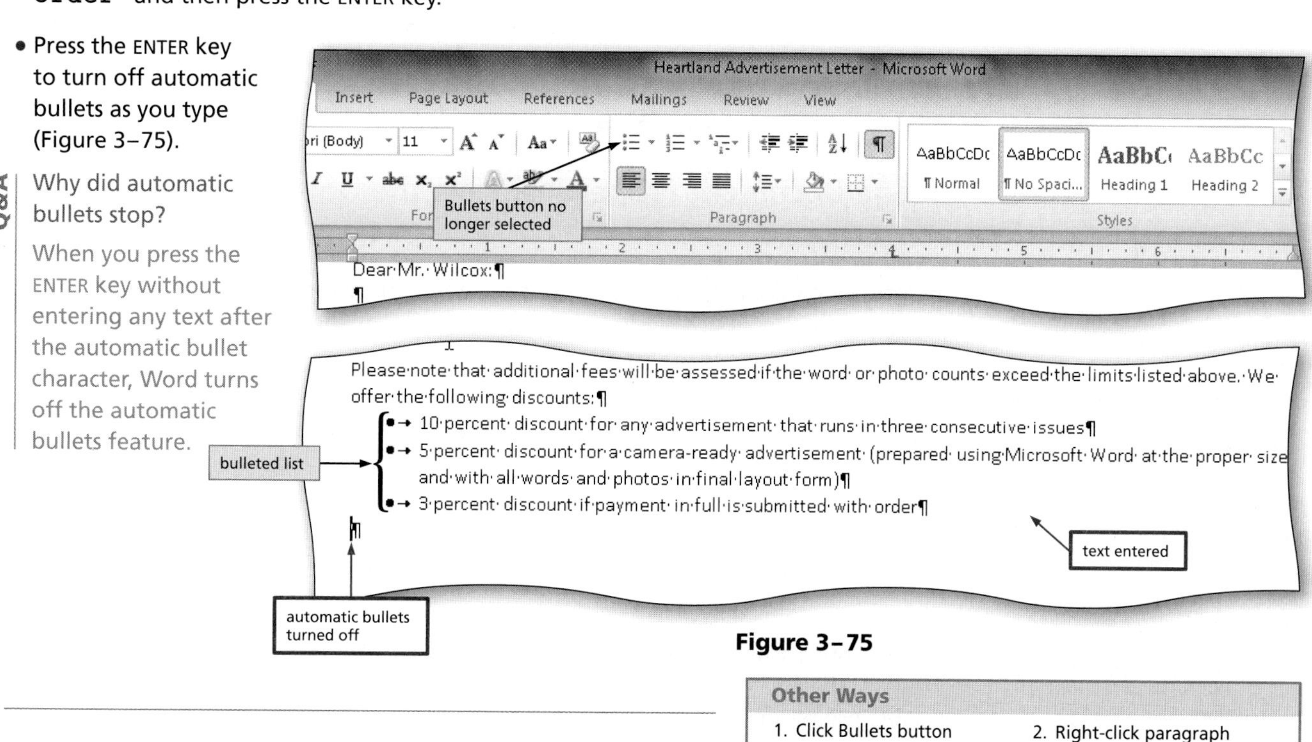

Figure 3–75

Other Ways

1. Click Bullets button (Home tab | Paragraph group)
2. Right-click paragraph to be bulleted, point to Bullets on shortcut menu, click desired bullet style

BTW **Certification**
The Microsoft Office Specialist (MOS) program provides an opportunity for you to obtain a valuable industry credential — proof that you have the Word 2010 skills required by employers. For more information, visit the Word 2010 Certification Web page (scsite.com/wd2010/cert).

To Enter More Text

The following steps enter the remainder of text in the letter.

1. Press the ENTER key and then type the paragraph shown in Figure 3–76, making certain you use the building block name, wtr, to insert the advertiser name.
2. If necessary, remove the hyperlink from the e-mail address by right-clicking the e-mail address and then clicking Remove Hyperlink on the shortcut menu. Press the END key to position the insertion point at the end of the line.
3. Press the ENTER key twice. Press the TAB key to position the insertion point at the 4" mark on the ruler. Type `Sincerely,` and then press the ENTER key four times.
4. Press the TAB key to position the insertion point at the 4" mark on the ruler. Type `Frank Urbanczyk` and then press the ENTER key.
5. Press the TAB key to position the insertion point at the 4" mark on the ruler. Type `President` as the final text in the business letter (Figure 3–76).

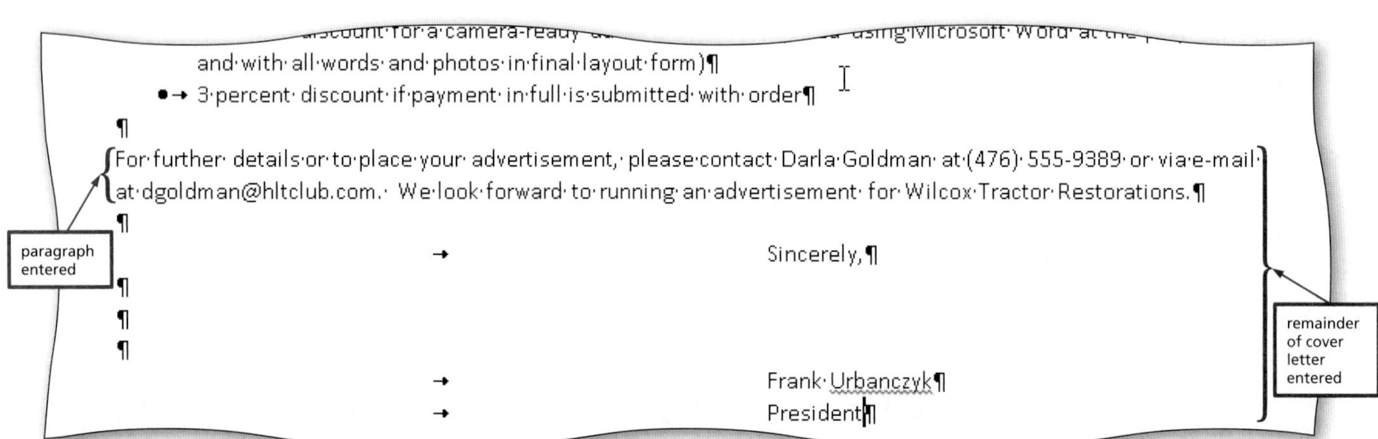

Figure 3–76

To Change Document Properties, Save the Document Again, and Print It

BTW **Conserving Ink and Toner**
If you want to conserve ink or toner, you can instruct Word to print draft quality documents by clicking File on the Ribbon to open the Backstage view, clicking Options in the Backstage view to display the Word Options dialog box, clicking Advanced in the left pane (Word Options dialog box), scrolling to the Print area in the right pane, placing a check mark in the 'Use draft quality' check box, and then clicking the OK button. Then, use the Backstage view to print the document as usual.

Before saving the letter again, you want to add your name and course and section as document properties. The following steps change document properties, save the document again, and then print the document.

1. Display the Document Information Panel in the Word document window. If necessary, enter your name in the Author property, and enter your course and section in the Subject property. Close the Document Information Panel.
2. Click the Save button on the Quick Access Toolbar to overwrite the previously saved file.
3. Open the Backstage view and then click the Print tab in the Backstage view to display the Print gallery.
4. Verify the printer name that appears on the Printer Status button will print a hard copy of the document. If necessary, click the Printer Status button to display a list of available printer options and then click the desired printer to change the currently selected printer.
5. Click the Print button in the Print gallery to print the letter on the currently selected printer (shown in Figure 3–1 on page WD 139).

Addressing and Printing Envelopes and Mailing Labels

With Word, you can print address information on an envelope or on a mailing label. Computer-printed addresses look more professional than handwritten ones.

BTW

BTWs
For a complete list of the BTWs found in the margins of this book, visit the Word 2010 BTW Web page (scsite.com/wd2010/btw).

To Address and Print an Envelope

The following steps address and print an envelope. If you are in a lab environment, check with your instructor before performing these steps.

- Scroll through the letter to display the inside address in the document window.
- Drag through the inside address to select it (Figure 3–77).

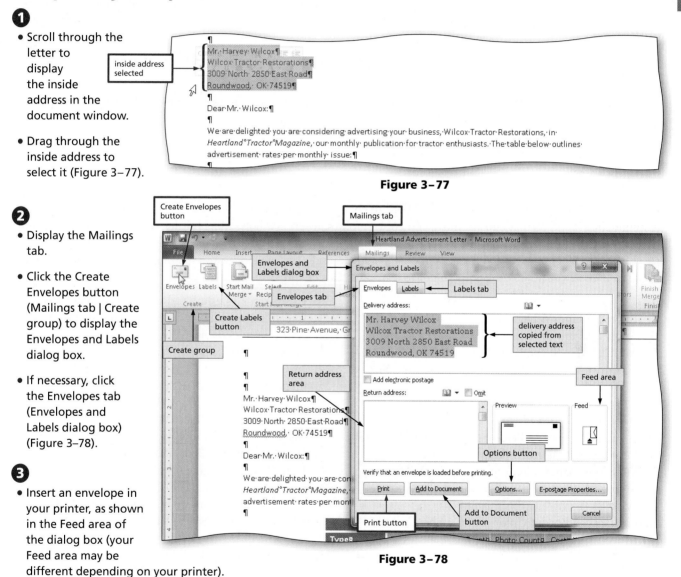

inside address selected
Mr. Harvey Wilcox
Wilcox Tractor Restorations
3009 North 2850 East Road
Roundwood, OK 74519
Dear Mr. Wilcox:
We are delighted you are considering advertising your business, Wilcox Tractor Restorations, in Heartland Tractor Magazine, our monthly publication for tractor enthusiasts. The table below outlines advertisement rates per monthly issue:

Figure 3–77

- Display the Mailings tab.
- Click the Create Envelopes button (Mailings tab | Create group) to display the Envelopes and Labels dialog box.
- If necessary, click the Envelopes tab (Envelopes and Labels dialog box) (Figure 3–78).

- Insert an envelope in your printer, as shown in the Feed area of the dialog box (your Feed area may be different depending on your printer).
- Click the Print button (Envelopes and Labels dialog box) to print the envelope.

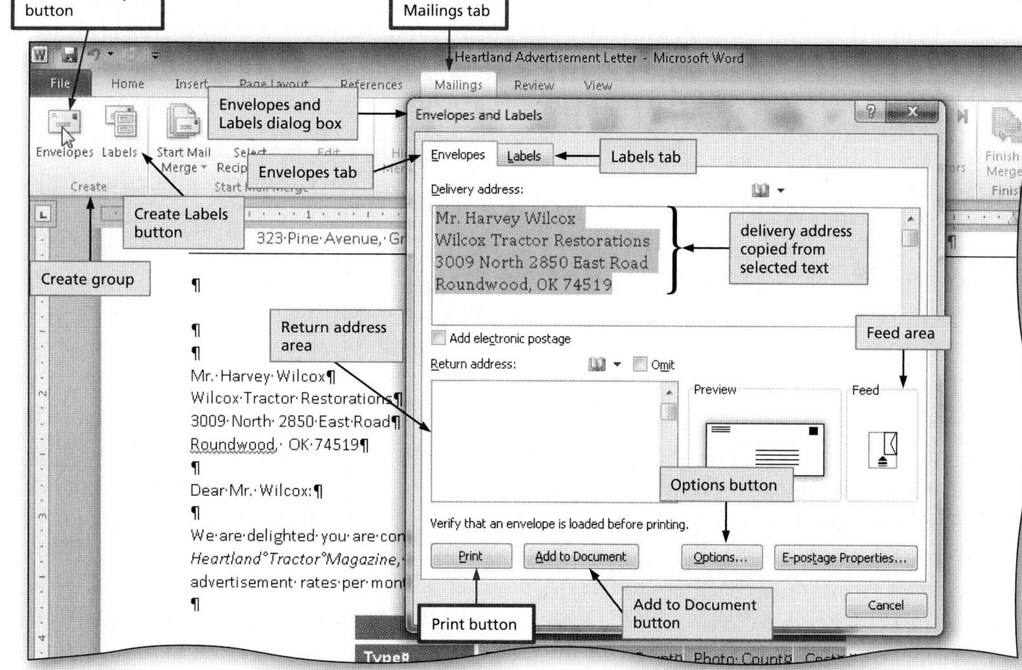

Figure 3–78

Envelopes and Labels

Instead of printing the envelope immediately, you can add it to the document by clicking the Add to Document button (Envelopes and Labels dialog box). To specify a different envelope or label type (identified by a number on the box of envelopes or labels), click the Options button (Envelopes and Labels dialog box).

Instead of printing an envelope, you can print a mailing label. To do this, click the Create Labels button (Mailings tab | Create group) (shown in Figure 3–78 on the previous page). Type the delivery address in the Delivery address box. To print the same address on all labels on the page, click 'Full page of the same label' in the Print area. Click the Print button (Envelopes and Labels dialog box) to print the label(s).

To Quit Word

This project now is complete. The following steps quit Word.

BTW

Quick Reference
For a table that lists how to complete the tasks covered in this book using the mouse, Ribbon, shortcut menu, and keyboard, see the Quick Reference Summary at the back of this book, or visit the Word 2010 Quick Reference Web page (scsite.com/wd2010/qr).

1. If you have one Word document open, click the Close button on the right side of the title bar to close the document and quit Word; or if you have multiple Word documents open, click File on the Ribbon to open the Backstage view and then click Exit in the Backstage view to close all open documents and quit Word.
2. If a Microsoft Word dialog box appears, click the Save button to save any changes made to the document since the last save.
3. If Word displays a dialog box asking if you want to save modified "Building Blocks", click the Save button.

Chapter Summary

In this chapter, you have learned how to use Word to change margins, insert and format a shape, change text wrapping, insert and format clip art, move and copy graphics, insert symbols, add a border, clear formatting, convert a hyperlink to regular text, create a file from an existing file, set and use tab stops, insert the current date, create and insert building blocks, insert and format tables, and address and print envelopes and mailing labels. The items listed below include all the new Word skills you have learned in this chapter.

1. Change Margin Settings (WD 141)
2. Insert a Shape (WD 142)
3. Apply a Shape Style (WD 144)
4. Add Text to a Shape (WD 145)
5. Use the Grow Font Button to Increase Font Size (WD 146)
6. Change an Object's Text Wrapping (WD 148)
7. Insert Clip Art (WD 148)
8. Resize a Graphic to a Percent of the Original (WD 150)
9. Change the Color of a Graphic (WD 151)
10. Set a Transparent Color in a Graphic (WD 152)
11. Adjust the Brightness and Contrast of a Graphic (WD 153)
12. Change the Border Color on a Graphic (WD 154)
13. Move a Graphic (WD 155)
14. Use Paste Options (WD 156)
15. Flip a Graphic (WD 157)
16. Insert a Symbol from the Symbol Dialog Box (WD 158)
17. Insert a Symbol from the Symbol Gallery (WD 159)
18. Bottom Border a Paragraph (WD 160)
19. Clear Formatting (WD 161)
20. Convert a Hyperlink to Regular Text (WD 163)
21. Create a New File from an Existing File (WD 165)
22. Apply a Quick Style (WD 166)
23. Set Custom Tab Stops (WD 169)
24. Insert the Current Date in a Document (WD 170)
25. Create a Building Block (WD 171)
26. Modify a Building Block (WD 173)
27. Insert a Building Block (WD 174)
28. Insert a Nonbreaking Space (WD 175)
29. Insert an Empty Table (WD 176)
30. Enter Data in a Table (WD 177)
31. Apply a Table Style (WD 179)
32. Resize Table Columns to Fit Table Contents (WD 180)
33. Align Data in Cells (WD 182)
34. Center a Table (WD 183)
35. Insert a Row in a Table (WD 184)
36. Insert a Column in a Table (WD 185)
37. Merge Cells (WD 185)
38. Split Table Cells (WD 186)
39. Bullet a List as You Type (WD 186)
40. Address and Print an Envelope (WD 189)

If you have a SAM 2010 user profile, your instructor may have assigned an autogradable version of this assignment. If so, log into the SAM 2010 Web site at www.cengage.com/sam2010 to download the instruction and start files.

Learn It Online

Test your knowledge of chapter content and key terms.

Instructions: To complete the Learn It Online exercises, start your browser, click the Address bar, and then enter the Web address **scsite.com/wd2010/learn**. When the Word 2010 Learn It Online page is displayed, click the link for the exercise you want to complete and then read the instructions.

Chapter Reinforcement TF, MC, and SA

A series of true/false, multiple choice, and short answer questions that test your knowledge of the chapter content.

Flash Cards

An interactive learning environment where you identify chapter key terms associated with displayed definitions.

Practice Test

A series of multiple choice questions that test your knowledge of chapter content and key terms.

Who Wants To Be a Computer Genius?

An interactive game that challenges your knowledge of chapter content in the style of a television quiz show.

Wheel of Terms

An interactive game that challenges your knowledge of chapter key terms in the style of the television show *Wheel of Fortune.*

Crossword Puzzle Challenge

A crossword puzzle that challenges your knowledge of key terms presented in the chapter.

Apply Your Knowledge

Reinforce the skills and apply the concepts you learned in this chapter.

Working with Tabs and a Table

Note: To complete this assignment, you will be required to use the Data Files for Students. See the inside back cover of this book for instructions on downloading the Data Files for Students, or contact your instructor for information about accessing the required files.

Instructions: Start Word. Create a new document from the file called Apply 3-1 Projected College Expenses Draft, located on the Data Files for Students. The document is a Word table that you are to edit and format. The revised table is shown in Figure 3–79.

Projected College Expenses

	Freshman	Sophomore	Junior	Senior
Room & Board	3390.00	3627.30	3881.21	4152.90
Tuition & Books	4850.50	5189.50	5552.72	5941.46
Entertainment	635.00	679.45	727.01	777.90
Cell Phone	359.88	365.78	372.81	385.95
Miscellaneous	325.00	347.75	372.09	398.14
Clothing	540.25	577.80	618.29	661.52
Total	$10,100.63	$10,787.58	$11,524.13	$12,317.87

Figure 3–79

Continued >

Apply Your Knowledge *continued*

Perform the following tasks:

1. In the line containing the table title, Projected College Expenses, remove the tab stop at the 1" mark on the ruler.
2. Set a centered tab at the 3" mark on the ruler.
3. Bold the characters in the title. Use the Grow Font button to increase their font size to 14. Change their color to Dark Blue, Text 2, Darker 25%.
4. In the table, delete the row containing the Food expenses.
5. Insert a new row at the bottom of the table. In the first cell of the new row, enter Total in the cell. Enter these values in the next three cells: Freshman – $10,100.63; Sophomore – $10,787.58; Senior – $12,317.87.
6. Insert a column between the Sophomore and Senior columns. Fill in the column as follows: Column Title – Junior; Room & Board – 3881.21; Tuition & Books – 5552.72; Entertainment – 727.01; Cell Phone – 372.81; Miscellaneous – 372.09; Clothing – 618.29; Total – $11,524.13.
7. In the Table Style Options group (Table Tools Design tab), these check boxes should have check marks: Header Row, Total Row, Banded Rows, and First Column. The Last Column and Banded Columns check boxes should not be selected.
8. Apply the Medium Grid 3 - Accent 2 style to the table.
9. Make all columns as wide as their contents (AutoFit Contents).
10. Center the cells containing the column headings.
11. Right-align all cells containing numbers in the table.
12. Center the table between the left and right margins of the page.
13. Change the document properties, as specified by your instructor.
14. Save the document using the file name, Apply 3-1 Projected College Expenses Modified and submit it in the format specified by your instructor.

Extend Your Knowledge

Extend the skills you learned in this chapter and experiment with new skills. You may need to use Help to complete the assignment.

Working with Formulas, Clip Art, Sorting, Picture Bullets, Tabs, and Mailing Labels

Note: To complete this assignment, you will be required to use the Data Files for Students. See the inside back cover of this book for instructions on downloading the Data Files for Students, or contact your instructor for information about accessing the required files.

Instructions: Start Word. Create a new document from the file called Extend 3-1 Herbals Letter Draft, located on the Data Files for Students. You will enter formulas in the table, change the clip art to Web clip art, change the table style, sort paragraphs, use picture bullets, move tabs, print mailing labels, and work with the Clip Organizer.

Perform the following tasks:

1. Use Help to learn about entering formulas, clip art from the Web, sorting, picture bullets, and printing mailing labels.
2. Use the Formula dialog box (Figure 3–80) to add formulas to the last column in the table so that the total due displays for each item; be sure to enter a number format so that the products are

displayed with dollar signs. Then, add formulas to the last row in the table so that the total quantity and total due are displayed, also with dollar signs. Write down the formulas that Word uses to find the product of values in the rows and to sum the values in a column.

3. Delete the current clip art images in the letterhead. Use the Clip Art pane to locate appropriate clip art from the Web, make the clip available offline, and insert an image on each side of the business name in the letterhead.
4. Change the table style. One at a time, select and deselect each check box in the Table Style Options group. Write down the function of each check box: Header Row, Total Row, Banded Rows, First Column, Last Column, and Banded Columns. Select the check boxes you prefer for the table.
5. Sort the paragraphs in the bulleted list.
6. Change the bullets in the bulleted list to picture bullets.
7. Move the tab stops in the date line, complimentary close, and signature block from the 3.5" mark to the 4" mark on the ruler.
8. Change the document properties, as specified by your instructor. Save the revised document and then submit it in the format specified by your instructor.
9. Print a single mailing label for the letter.
10. Print a full page of mailing labels, each containing the address shown in Figure 3–80.
11. If your instructor approves, start the Clip Organizer. How many collections appear? Expand the Office Collections. Copy one of the Academic clips to the Favorites folder in the My Collections folder. Locate the clip you made available offline in Step 3 and then preview it. What are five of its properties? Add a keyword to the clip. Delete the clip you made available offline.

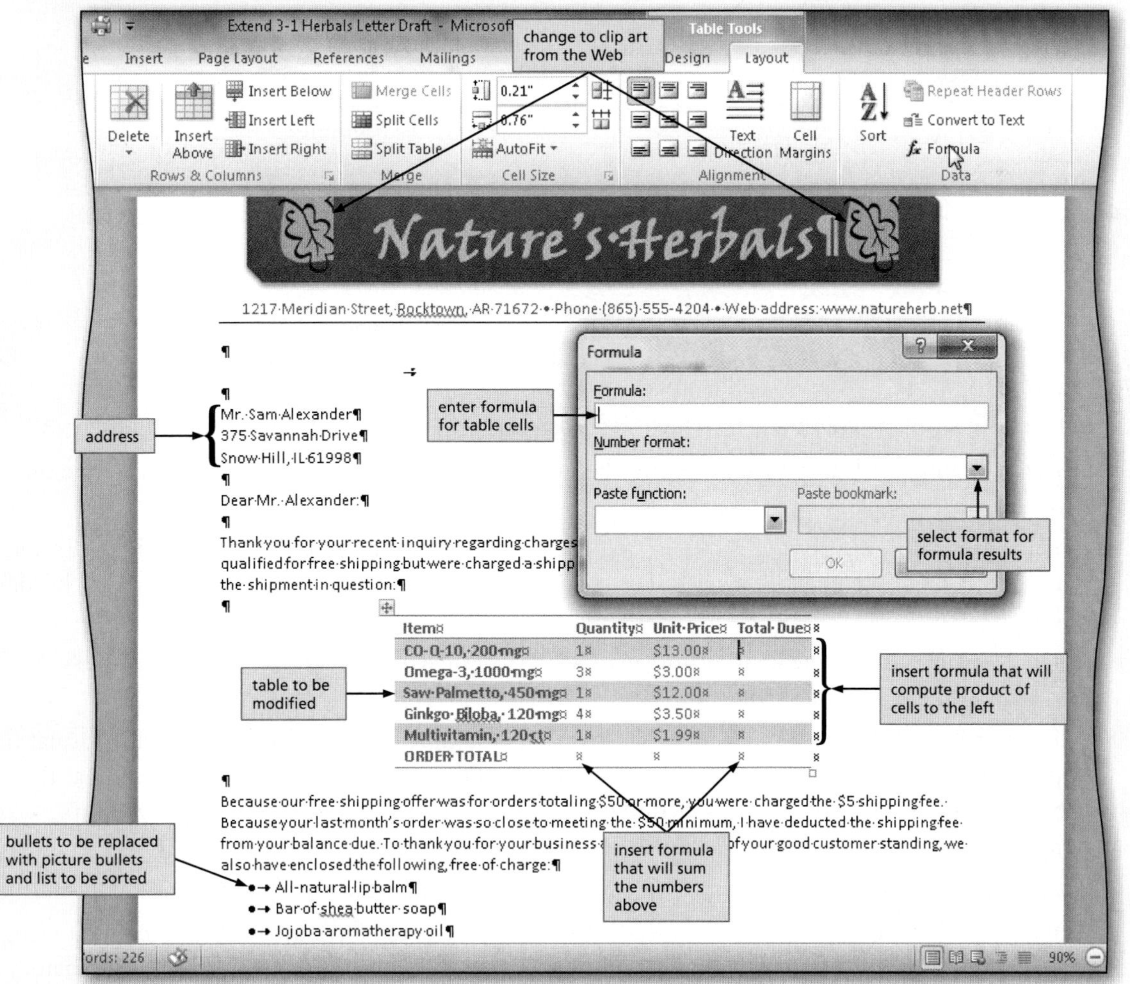

Figure 3–80

STUDENT ASSIGNMENTS

Make It Right

Analyze a document and correct all errors and/or improve the design.

Formatting a Business Letter

Note: To complete this assignment, you will be required to use the Data Files for Students. See the inside back cover of this book for instructions on downloading the Data Files for Students, or contact your instructor for information about accessing the required files.

Instructions: Start Word. Create a new document from the file called Make It Right 3-1 Scholarship Letter Draft, located on the Data Files for Students. The document is a business letter that is missing elements and is formatted poorly or incorrectly (Figure 3–81). You are to insert and format clip art in the letterhead, change the color of the text and graphic(s), insert symbols, remove a hyperlink, change the letter style from block to modified block, and format the table.

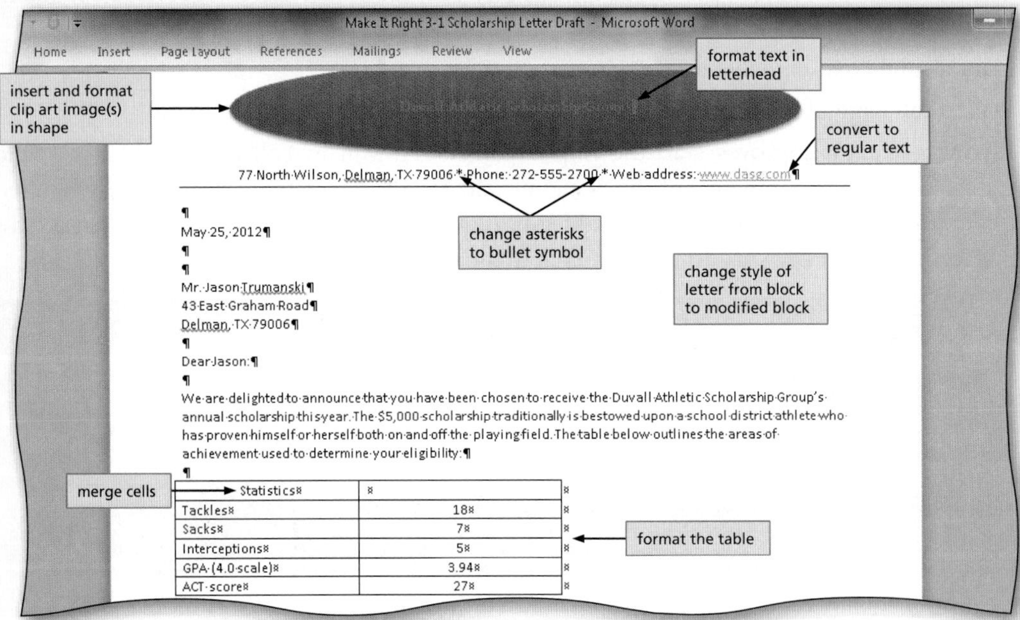

Figure 3–81

Perform the following tasks:

1. Increase the font size of the text in the letterhead. Change the color of the text in the letterhead.
2. Locate and insert at least one appropriate clip art image in the letterhead. If necessary, resize the graphic(s). Move the graphic(s) into the shape.
3. Change the color of the graphic to match the color of the text or shape. Adjust the brightness and contrast of the graphic. Format one color in the graphic as transparent. Change the picture border color.
4. Change the asterisks in the contact information to the dot symbol. Convert the Web address hyperlink to regular text.
5. The letter currently is the block letter style. It should be the modified block letter style. Format the appropriate paragraphs by setting custom tab stops and then positioning those paragraphs at the tab stops. Be sure to position the insertion point in the paragraph before setting the tab stop.
6. Merge the two cells in the first row of the table to one cell and then center the title in the cell. Center the entire table between the page margins. Apply a table style of your choice.
7. Change the document properties, as specified by your instructor. Save the revised document using the file name, Make It Right 3-1 Scholarship Letter Modified, and then submit it in the format specified by your instructor.

In the Lab

Design and/or create a document using the guidelines, concepts, and skills presented in this chapter. Labs are listed in order of increasing difficulty.

Lab 1: Creating a Letter with a Letterhead

Problem: As a consultant for DataLock Storage, you respond to queries from potential customers. One letter you prepare is shown in Figure 3–82.

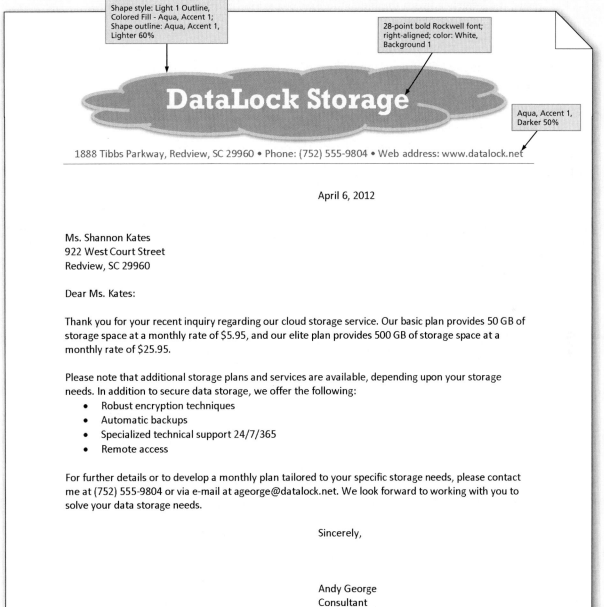

April 6, 2012

Ms. Shannon Kates
922 West Court Street
Redview, SC 29960

Dear Ms. Kates:

Thank you for your recent inquiry regarding our cloud storage service. Our basic plan provides 50 GB of storage space at a monthly rate of $5.95, and our elite plan provides 500 GB of storage space at a monthly rate of $25.95.

Please note that additional storage plans and services are available, depending upon your storage needs. In addition to secure data storage, we offer the following:

- Robust encryption techniques
- Automatic backups
- Specialized technical support 24/7/365
- Remote access

For further details or to develop a monthly plan tailored to your specific storage needs, please contact me at (752) 555-9804 or via e-mail at ageorge@datalock.net. We look forward to working with you to solve your data storage needs.

Sincerely,

Andy George
Consultant

Figure 3–82

Continued >

In the Lab *continued*

Perform the following tasks:

1. Change the theme colors to Technic.
2. Create the letterhead shown at the top of Figure 3–82 on the previous page, following these guidelines:
   a. Insert the cloud shape at an approximate height of 0.95" and width of 5.85". Change text wrapping for the shape to Top and Bottom. Add the company name, DataLock Storage, to the shape. Format the shape and its text as indicated in the figure.
   b. Insert the bullet symbols as shown in the contact information. Remove the hyperlink format from the Web address. If necessary, clear formatting after entering the bottom border.
   c. Save the letterhead with the file name, Lab 3-1 Cloud Storage Letterhead.
3. Create the letter shown in Figure 3–82 using the modified block letter style, following these guidelines:
   a. Apply the No Spacing Quick Style to the document text (below the letterhead).
   b. Set a left-aligned tab stop at the 3.5" mark on the ruler for the date line, complimentary close, and signature block. Insert the current date.
   c. Bullet the list as you type it.
   d. Convert the e-mail address to regular text.
   e. Check the spelling of the letter. Change the document properties, as specified by your instructor. Save the letter with Lab 3-1 Cloud Storage Letter as the file name.
4. If your instructor permits, address and print an envelope or a mailing label for the letter.

In the Lab

Lab 2: Creating a Letter with a Letterhead and Table

Problem: As head librarian at Jonner Public Library, you are responsible for sending confirmation letters for class registrations. You prepare the letter shown in Figure 3–83.

Perform the following tasks:

1. Change the theme colors to Trek. Change the margins to 1" top and bottom and .75" left and right.
2. Create the letterhead shown at the top of Figure 3–83, following these guidelines:
   a. Insert the down ribbon shape at an approximate height of 1" and width of 7". Change text wrapping for the shape to Top and Bottom. Add the library name to the shape. Format the shape and its text as indicated in the figure.
   b. Insert the clip art image, resize it, change text wrapping to Top and Bottom, move it to the left of the shape, and format it as indicated in the figure. Copy the clip art image and move the copy of the image to the right of the shape, as shown in the figure. Flip the copied image horizontally.
   c. Insert the black small square symbols as shown in the contact information. Remove the hyperlink format from the Web address. If necessary, clear formatting after entering the bottom border.
   d. Save the letterhead with the file name, Lab 3-2 Library Letterhead.
3. Create the letter shown in Figure 3–83, following these guidelines:
   a. Apply the No Spacing Quick Style to the document text (below the letterhead).
   b. Set a left-aligned tab stop at the 4" mark on the ruler for the date line, complimentary close, and signature block. Insert the current date.
   c. Insert and center the table. Format the table as specified in the figure.
   d. Bullet the list as you type it. Convert the e-mail address to regular text.
   e. Check the spelling of the letter. Change the document properties, as specified by your instructor. Save the letter with Lab 3-2 Library Letter as the file name.
4. If your instructor permits, address and print an envelope or a mailing label for the letter.

Shape style: Colored Fill - Orange, Accent 1

24-point bold Harrington font, centered

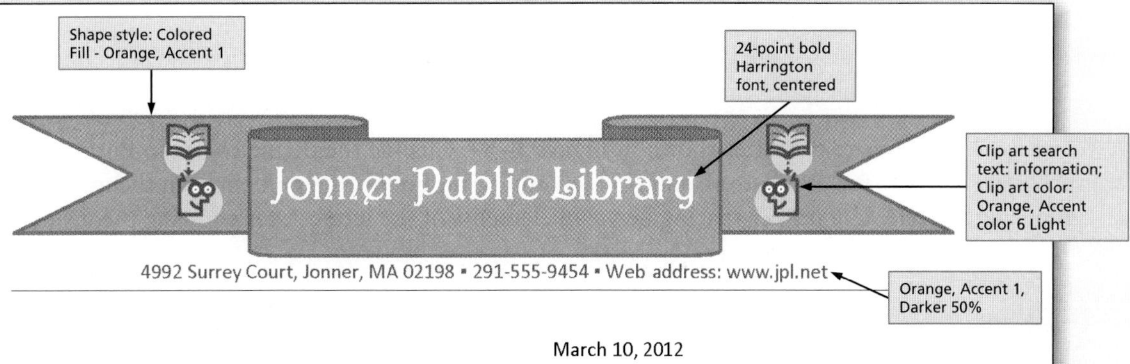

Clip art search text: information; Clip art color: Orange, Accent color 6 Light

4992 Surrey Court, Jonner, MA 02198 ▪ 291-555-9454 ▪ Web address: www.jpl.net

Orange, Accent 1, Darker 50%

March 10, 2012

Mr. Brent Jackson
5153 Anlyn Drive
Jonner, MA 02198

Dear Mr. Jackson:

Thank you for registering online for our spring classes. As a library patron, you are aware that we offer a great deal more than books and magazines. The table below outlines the classes for which you have registered, along with the dates and locations:

Table style: Medium Grid 3 - Accent 1; Table style options: Header Row and Banded Columns

Class	Date	Location
Intro to Windows 7	April 10	Room 10B
eBay Basics	April 18	Room 24C
Genealogy Searches	April 24	Room 10B
Overview of Office 2010	April 28	Room 22A

Note that all classes, regardless of date, begin at 10:00 a.m. and last four hours. Although no materials or textbooks are required for the classes, you are strongly encouraged to bring the following items:

- Pens, pencils, or other writing implements
- Blank CD or DVD to store documents and notes created during class
- Notebook or loose-leaf binder for handwritten notes
- Your valid library card to verify enrollment eligibility

Please note that no food or drinks are allowed in any of our computer facilities. If you have any questions or would like to register for additional courses, please contact me at (291) 555-9454 or via e-mail at mtlawrence@jpl.net.

Again, thank you for your interest in and continued patronage of Jonner Public Library. We look forward to seeing you when your first class begins.

Sincerely,

Marcia Lawrence
Head Librarian

Figure 3–83

In the Lab

Lab 3: Creating a Letter with a Letterhead and Table

Problem: As president of the County Education Board, you communicate with schools in your district. One of the schools has just been awarded a four-star rating.

Instructions: Prepare the letter shown in Figure 3–84. Change the theme colors to Pushpin. Change the margins to 1" top and bottom and .75" left and right. Follow the guidelines in the modified semi-block letter style. Use proper spacing between elements of the letter. After entering the inside address,

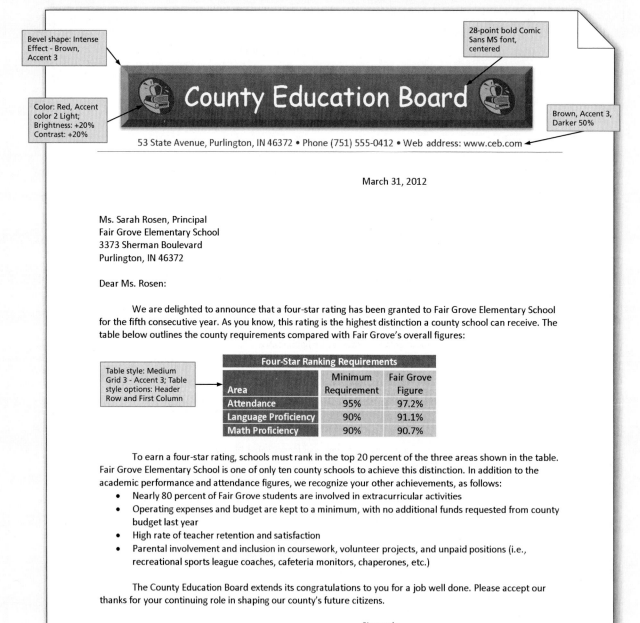

53 State Avenue, Purlington, IN 46372 • Phone (751) 555-0412 • Web address: www.ceb.com

March 31, 2012

Ms. Sarah Rosen, Principal
Fair Grove Elementary School
3373 Sherman Boulevard
Purlington, IN 46372

Dear Ms. Rosen:

We are delighted to announce that a four-star rating has been granted to Fair Grove Elementary School for the fifth consecutive year. As you know, this rating is the highest distinction a county school can receive. The table below outlines the county requirements compared with Fair Grove's overall figures:

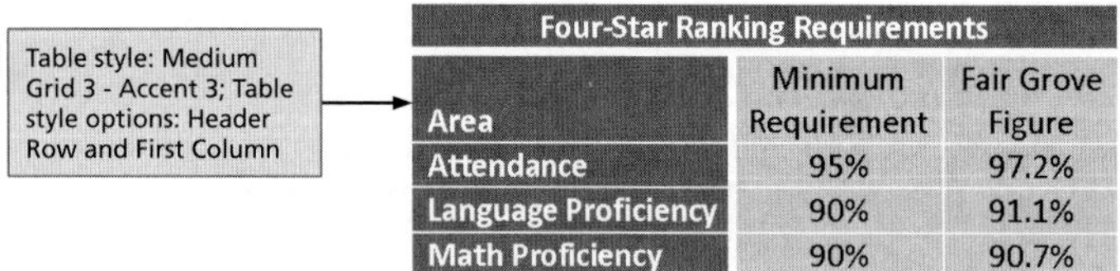

Four-Star Ranking Requirements		
Area	Minimum Requirement	Fair Grove Figure
Attendance	95%	97.2%
Language Proficiency	90%	91.1%
Math Proficiency	90%	90.7%

To earn a four-star rating, schools must rank in the top 20 percent of the three areas shown in the table. Fair Grove Elementary School is one of only ten county schools to achieve this distinction. In addition to the academic performance and attendance figures, we recognize your other achievements, as follows:

- Nearly 80 percent of Fair Grove students are involved in extracurricular activities
- Operating expenses and budget are kept to a minimum, with no additional funds requested from county budget last year
- High rate of teacher retention and satisfaction
- Parental involvement and inclusion in coursework, volunteer projects, and unpaid positions (i.e., recreational sports league coaches, cafeteria monitors, chaperones, etc.)

The County Education Board extends its congratulations to you for a job well done. Please accept our thanks for your continuing role in shaping our county's future citizens.

Sincerely,

Walt Andreas
President

Figure 3–84

create a building block for Fair Grove Elementary School and insert the building block whenever you have to enter the school name. Resize table columns to fit contents. Check the spelling of the letter. Change the document properties, as specified by your instructor. Save the letter with Lab 3-3 Education Board Letter as the file name.

Cases and Places

Apply your creative thinking and problem solving skills to design and implement a solution.

Note: To complete these assignments, you may be required to use the Data Files for Students. See the inside back cover of this book for instructions on downloading the Data Files for Students, or contact your instructor for information about accessing the required files.

1: Create a Letter to a Potential Employer

Academic

As a student about to graduate, you are actively seeking employment in your field and have located an advertisement for a job in which you are interested. You decide to write a letter to the potential employer: Ms. Janice Tremont at Home Health Associates, 554 Mountain View Lane, Blue Dust, MO 64319.

The draft wording for the letter is as follows: I am responding to your advertisement for the nursing position in the *Blue Dust Press*. I have tailored my activities and education for a career in geriatric medicine. This month, I will graduate with concentrations in Geriatric Medicine (24 hours), Osteopathic Medicine (12 hours), and Holistic Nursing (9 hours). In addition to receiving my bachelor degree in nursing, I have enhanced my education by participating in the following activities: volunteered at Blue Dust's free health care clinic; attended several continuing education and career-specific seminars, including An Aging Populace, Care of the Homebound, and Special Needs of the Elderly; completed one-semester internship at Blue Dust Community Hospital in spring semester of 2012; completed Certified Nursing Assistant (CNA) program at Blue Dust Community College; and worked as nurse's aide for two years during college. I look forward to an interview so that we can discuss the position you offer and my qualifications. With my background and education, I am confident that I will make a positive contribution to Home Health Associates.

The letter should contain a letterhead that uses a shape and clip art, a table (use a table to present the areas of concentration), and a bulleted list (use a bulleted list to present the activities). Insert nonbreaking spaces in the newspaper name. Use the concepts and techniques presented in this chapter to create and format a letter according to the modified block style, creating appropriate paragraph breaks and rewording the draft as necessary. Use your personal information for contact information in the letter. Be sure to check the spelling and grammar of the finished letter. Submit your assignment in the format specified by your instructor.

2: Create a Letter Requesting Donations

Personal

As an alumnus of your historic high school, you are concerned that the building is being considered for demolition. You decide to write a letter to another graduate: Mr. Jim Lemon, 87 Travis Parkway, Vigil, CT 06802.

The draft wording for the letter is as follows: As a member of the class of 1988, you, like many others, probably have many fond memories of our alma mater, Vigil East High School. I recently learned that the building is being considered for demolition because of its age and structural integrity.

Continued >

Cases and Places *continued*

As a result, I have decided to call upon the many graduating classes of the school to band together and save the historic building from demolition. According to the documents I have reviewed and information from meetings I have attended, a minimum of $214,000 is necessary to save the school and bring it up to code. Once the repairs are made, I plan to start the process of having it declared an historic landmark. You can help by donating your time, skills, or money. We need skilled tradesmen, including carpenters, roofers, plumbers, and electricians, as well as laborers. In addition, we are asking for monetary donations, as follows, although donations in any amount will be accepted gladly: a donation of $100 categorizes you as a Save Our School Friend, $250 a Patron, and $500 a Benefactor. Once our monetary goal has been reached, the necessary repairs and replacements will be made as follows: Phase I: roof and exterior, Phase II: electrical and plumbing, and Phase III: interior walls, trim, flooring, and fixtures. I hope you will join our conservation efforts so that Vigil East High School will continue to stand proudly for many more years. If you have questions, please contact me at the phone number or e-mail address above. I hope to hear from you soon.

The letter should contain a letterhead that uses a shape and clip art, a table (use a table to present the Save Our School donor categories), and a bulleted list (use a bulleted list to present the phases). Use the concepts and techniques presented in this chapter to create and format a letter according to the modified block style, creating appropriate paragraph breaks and rewording the draft as necessary. Use your personal information for contact information in the letter and Save Our School as the text in the letterhead. Be sure to check spelling and grammar of the finished letter. Submit your assignment in the format specified by your instructor.

3: Create a Confirmation Letter

Professional

As coordinator for Condor Parks and Recreation, you send letters to confirm registration for activities. You write a confirmation letter to this registrant: Ms. Tracey Li, 52 West 15th Street, Harpville, KY 42194. Condor Parks and Recreation is located at 2245 Community Place, Harpville, KY 42194; phone number is (842) 555-0444; and Web address is www.condorparks.com.

The draft wording for the letter is as follows: Thank you for your interest in our new spring activities recently listed in the *Condor Daily Press*. The courses for which you have enrolled, along with their dates and times are Introductory Golf Clinic on May 5 – 6 from 4:00 – 6:00 p.m. at a cost of $25, Recreational League Volleyball on April 30 – May 28 from 7:30 – 9:00 p.m. at a cost of $130, Pilates on May 30 – June 27 from 8:00 – 9:00 p.m. at a cost of $75, and Intermediate Golf Clinic on June 9 – 10 from 12:00 – 2:00 p.m. at a cost of $30. By paying your annual $25 parks and recreation fee, you also are entitled to the following benefits: free access to racquetball and tennis courts, on a first-come-first-served basis; attendance at any park-sponsored events, including plays, musical performances, and festivals; and free parking at any parks and recreation facility. Please confirm your registration by calling me at [enter your phone number here] or via e-mail at [enter your e-mail address here]. Thank you for your interest in Condor Parks and Recreation offerings. We look forward to seeing you at upcoming events.

The letter should contain a letterhead that uses a shape and clip art, a table (use a table to present the courses enrolled), and a bulleted list (use a bulleted list to present the benefits). Insert nonbreaking spaces in the newspaper name. Use the concepts and techniques presented in this chapter to create and format a letter according to the modified block style, creating appropriate paragraph breaks and rewording the draft as necessary. Be sure to check spelling and grammar of the finished letter. Submit your assignment in the format specified by your instructor.

NOTES

NOTES

NOTES

NOTES

Appendix A

Project Planning Guidelines

Using Project Planning Guidelines

The process of communicating specific information to others is a learned, rational skill. Computers and software, especially Microsoft Office 2010, can help you develop ideas and present detailed information to a particular audience.

Using Microsoft Office 2010, you can create projects such as Word documents, PowerPoint presentations, Excel spreadsheets, and Access databases. Productivity software such as Microsoft Office 2010 minimizes much of the laborious work of drafting and revising projects. Some communicators handwrite ideas in notebooks, others compose directly on the computer, and others have developed unique strategies that work for their own particular thinking and writing styles.

No matter what method you use to plan a project, follow specific guidelines to arrive at a final product that presents information correctly and effectively (Figure A–1). Use some aspects of these guidelines every time you undertake a project, and others as needed in specific instances. For example, in determining content for a project, you may decide that a chart communicates trends more effectively than a paragraph of text. If so, you would create this graphical element and insert it in an Excel spreadsheet, a Word document, or a PowerPoint slide.

Determine the Project's Purpose

Begin by clearly defining why you are undertaking this assignment. For example, you may want to track monetary donations collected for your club's fund-raising drive. Alternatively, you may be urging students to vote for a particular candidate in the next election. Once you clearly understand the purpose of your task, begin to draft ideas of how best to communicate this information.

PROJECT PLANNING GUIDELINES

1. DETERMINE THE PROJECT'S PURPOSE
Why are you undertaking the project?

2. ANALYZE YOUR AUDIENCE
Who are the people who will use your work?

3. GATHER POSSIBLE CONTENT
What information exists, and in what forms?

4. DETERMINE WHAT CONTENT TO PRESENT TO YOUR AUDIENCE
What information will best communicate the project's purpose to your audience?

Figure A–1

Analyze Your Audience

Learn about the people who will read, analyze, or view your work. Where are they employed? What are their educational backgrounds? What are their expectations? What questions do they have?

Design experts suggest drawing a mental picture of these people or finding photos of people who fit this profile so that you can develop a project with the audience in mind.

By knowing your audience members, you can tailor a project to meet their interests and needs. You will not present them with information they already possess, and you will not omit the information they need to know.

Example: Your assignment is to raise the profile of your college's nursing program in the community. How much do they know about your college and the nursing curriculum? What are the admission requirements? How many of the applicants admitted complete the program? What percent pass the state board exams?

Gather Possible Content

Rarely are you in a position to develop all the material for a project. Typically, you would begin by gathering existing information that may reside in spreadsheets or databases. Web sites, pamphlets, magazine and newspaper articles, and books could provide insights of how others have approached your topic. Personal interviews often provide perspectives not available by any other means. Consider video and audio clips as potential sources for material that might complement or support the factual data you uncover.

Determine What Content to Present to Your Audience

Experienced designers recommend writing three or four major ideas you want an audience member to remember after reading or viewing your project. It also is helpful to envision your project's endpoint, the key fact you wish to emphasize. All project elements should lead to this ending point.

As you make content decisions, you also need to think about other factors. Presentation of the project content is an important consideration. For example, will your brochure be printed on thick, colored paper or posted on the Web? Will your PowerPoint presentation be viewed in a classroom with excellent lighting and a bright projector, or will it be viewed on a notebook computer monitor? Determine relevant time factors, such as the length of time to develop the project, how long readers will spend reviewing your project, or the amount of time allocated for your speaking engagement. Your project will need to accommodate all of these constraints.

Decide whether a graph, photo, or artistic element can express or emphasize a particular concept. The right hemisphere of the brain processes images by attaching an emotion to them, so audience members are more apt to recall these graphics long term rather than just reading text.

As you select content, be mindful of the order in which you plan to present information. Readers and audience members generally remember the first and last pieces of information they see and hear, so you should place the most important information at the top or bottom of the page.

Summary

When creating a project, it is beneficial to follow some basic guidelines from the outset. By taking some time at the beginning of the process to determine the project's purpose, analyze the audience, gather possible content, and determine what content to present to the audience, you can produce a project that is informative, relevant, and effective.

Appendix B

Publishing Office 2010 Web Pages Online

With Office 2010 programs, you use the Save As command in the Backstage view to save a Web page to a Web site, network location, or FTP site. **File Transfer Protocol** (**FTP**) is an Internet standard that allows computers to exchange files with other computers on the Internet.

You should contact your network system administrator or technical support staff at your Internet access provider to determine if their Web server supports Web folders, FTP, or both, and to obtain necessary permissions to access the Web server.

Using an Office Program to Publish Office 2010 Web Pages

When publishing online, someone first must assign the necessary permissions for you to publish the Web page. If you are granted access to publish online, you must obtain the Web address of the Web server, a user name, and possibly a password that allows you to connect to the Web server. The steps in this appendix assume that you have access to an online location to which you can publish a Web page.

To Connect to an Online Location

To publish a Web page online, you first must connect to the online location. To connect to an online location using Windows 7, you would perform the following steps.

1. Click the Start button on the Windows 7 taskbar to display the Start menu.
2. Click Computer in the right pane of the Start menu to open the Computer window.
3. Click the 'Map network drive' button on the toolbar to display the Map Network Drive dialog box. (If the 'Map network drive' button is not visible on the toolbar, click the 'Display additional commands' button on the toolbar and then click 'Map network drive' in the list to display the Map Network Drive dialog box.)
4. Click the 'Connect to a Web site that you can use to store your documents and pictures' link (Map Network Drive dialog box) to start the Add Network Location wizard.
5. Click the Next button (Add Network Location dialog box).
6. Click 'Choose a custom network location' and then click the Next button.
7. Type the Internet or network address specified by your network or system administrator in the text box and then click the Next button.
8. Click 'Log on anonymously' to deselect the check box, type your user name in the User name text box, and then click the Next button.
9. If necessary, enter the name you want to assign to this online location and then click the Next button.
10. Click to deselect the Open this network location when I click Finish check box, and then click the Finish button.

11. Click the Cancel button to close the Map Network Drive dialog box.
12. Close the Computer window.

To Save a Web Page to an Online Location

The online location now can be accessed easily from Windows programs, including Microsoft Office programs. After creating a Microsoft Office file you wish to save as a Web page, you must save the file to the online location to which you connected in the previous steps. To save a Microsoft Word document as a Web page, for example, and publish it to the online location, you would perform the following steps.

1. Click File on the Ribbon to display the Backstage view and then click Save As in the Backstage view to display the Save As dialog box.
2. Type the Web page file name in the File name text box (Save As dialog box). Do not press the ENTER key because you do not want to close the dialog box at this time.
3. Click the 'Save as type' box arrow and then click Web Page to select the Web Page format.
4. If necessary, scroll to display the name of the online location in the navigation pane.
5. Double-click the online location name in the navigation pane to select that location as the new save location and display its contents in the right pane.
6. If a dialog box appears prompting you for a user name and password, type the user name and password in the respective text boxes and then click the Log On button.
7. Click the Save button (Save As dialog box).

The Web page now has been published online. To view the Web page using a Web browser, contact your network or system administrator for the Web address you should use to connect to the Web page.

Appendix C

Saving to the Web Using Windows Live SkyDrive

Introduction

Windows Live SkyDrive, also referred to as **SkyDrive**, is a free service that allows users to save files to the Web, such as documents, presentations, spreadsheets, databases, videos, and photos. Using SkyDrive, you also can save files in folders, providing for greater organization. You then can retrieve those files from any computer connected to the Internet. Some Office 2010 programs including Word, PowerPoint, and Excel can save files directly to an Internet location such as SkyDrive. SkyDrive also facilitates collaboration by allowing users to share files with other SkyDrive users (Figure C–1).

Figure C–1

Note: An Internet connection is required to perform the steps in this appendix.

To Save a File to Windows Live SkyDrive

You can save files directly to SkyDrive from within Word, PowerPoint, and Excel using the Backstage view. The following steps save an open Word document (Koala Exhibit Flyer, in this case) to SkyDrive. These steps require you to have a Windows Live account. Contact your instructor if you do not have a Windows Live account.

1

- Start Word and then open a document you want to save to the Web (in this case, the Koala Exhibit Flyer).
- Click File on the Ribbon to display the Backstage view (Figure C–2).

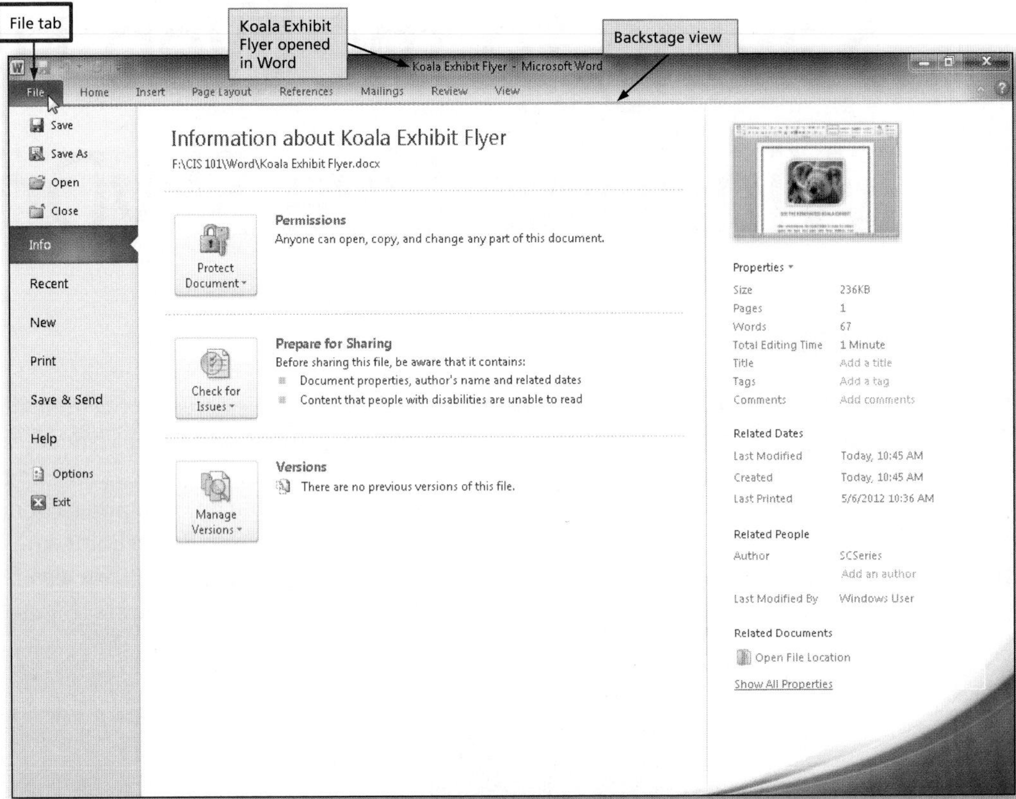

Figure C–2

2

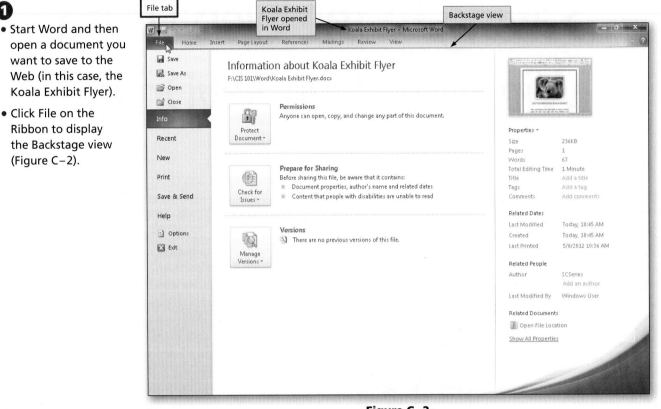

- Click the Save & Send tab to display the Save & Send gallery (Figure C–3).

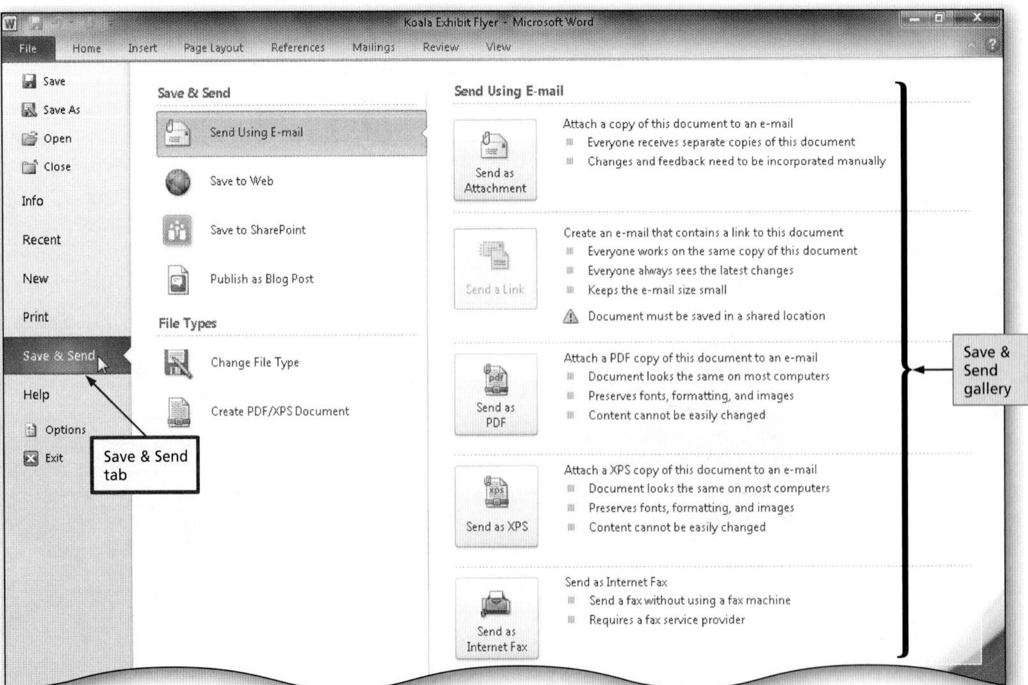

Figure C–3

3

- Click Save to Web in the Save & Send gallery to display information about saving a file to the Web (Figure C–4).

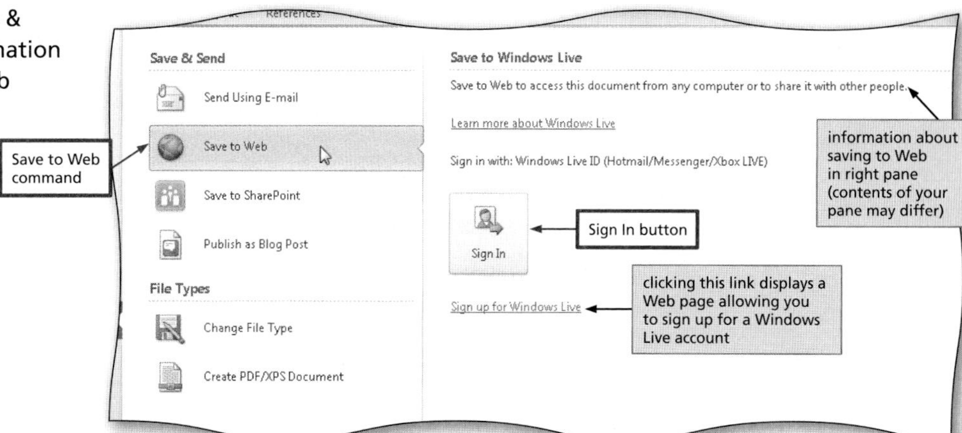

Figure C–4

4

- Click the Sign In button to display a Windows Live login dialog box that requests your e-mail address and password (Figure C–5).

Q&A What if the Sign In button does not appear?

If you already are signed into Windows Live, the Sign In button will not be displayed. Instead, the contents of your Windows Live SkyDrive will be displayed. If you already are signed into Windows Live, proceed to Step 6.

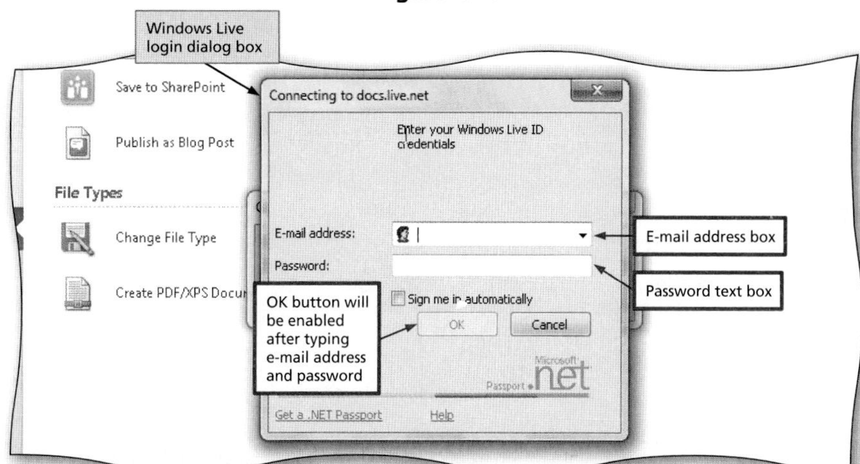

Figure C–5

5

- Enter your Windows Live e-mail address in the E-mail address box (Windows Live login dialog box).
- Enter your Windows Live password in the Password text box.
- Click the OK button to sign into Windows Live and display the contents of your Windows Live SkyDrive in the right pane of the Save & Send gallery.
- If necessary, click the My Documents folder to set the save location for the document (Figure C–6).

Figure C–6

Q&A What if the My Documents folder does not exist?

Click another folder to select it as the save location. Record the name of this folder so that you can locate and retrieve the file later in this appendix.

Q&A My SkyDrive shows personal and shared folders. What is the difference?

Personal folders are private and are not shared with anyone. Shared folders can be viewed by SkyDrive users to whom you have assigned the necessary permissions.

6

- Click the Save As button in the right pane of the Save & Send gallery to contact the SkyDrive server (which may take some time, depending on the speed of your Internet connection) and then display the Save As dialog box (Figure C–7).

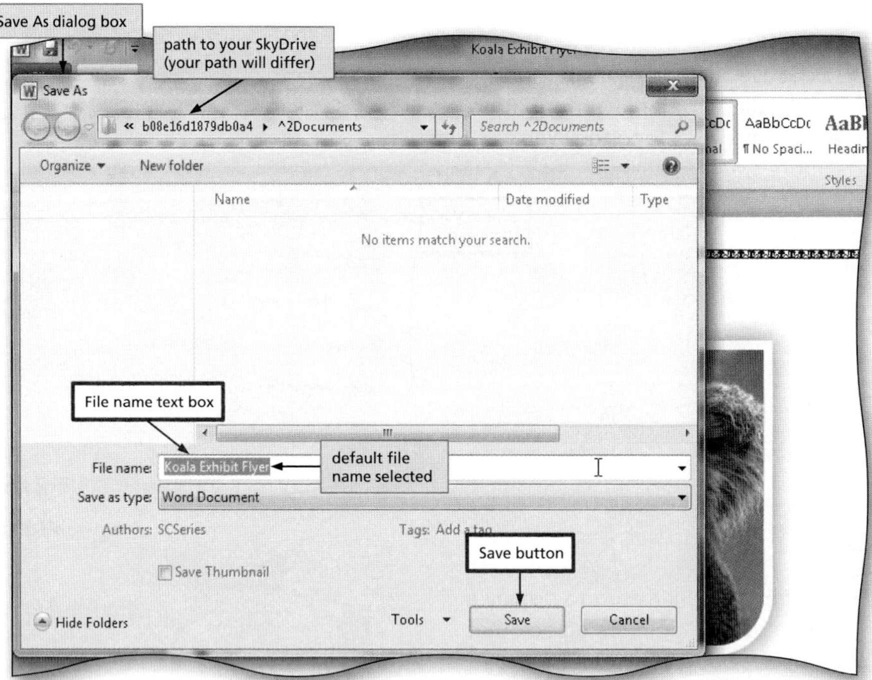

Figure C–7

7

- Type `Koala Exhibit Web` in the File name text box to enter the file name and then click the Save button (Save As dialog box) to save the file to Windows Live SkyDrive (Figure C–8).

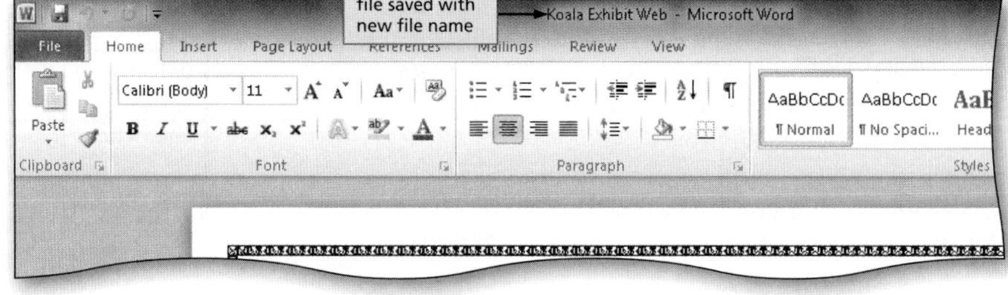

Figure C–8

Q&A

Is it necessary to rename the file?

It is good practice to rename the file. If you download the file from SkyDrive to your computer, having a different file name will preserve the original file.

8

- If you have one Word document open, click the Close button on the right side of the title bar to close the document and quit Word; or if you have multiple Word documents open, click File on the Ribbon to open the Backstage view and then click Exit in the Backstage view to close all open documents and quit Word.

Web Apps

Microsoft has created a scaled-down, Web-based version of its Microsoft Office suite, called **Microsoft Office Web Apps,** or **Web Apps**. Web Apps contains Web-based versions of Word, PowerPoint, Excel, and OneNote that can be used to view and edit files that are saved to SkyDrive. Web Apps allows users to continue working with their files even while they are not using a computer with Microsoft Office installed. In addition to working with files located on SkyDrive, Web Apps also enables users to create new Word documents, PowerPoint presentations, Excel spreadsheets, and OneNote notebooks. After returning to a computer with the Microsoft Office suite, some users choose to download files from SkyDrive and edit them using the associated Microsoft Office program.

Note: As with all Web applications, SkyDrive and Office Web Apps are subject to change. Consequently, the steps required to perform the actions in this appendix might be different from those shown.

To Download a File from Windows Live SkyDrive

Files saved to SkyDrive can be downloaded from a Web browser using any computer with an Internet connection. The following steps download the Koala Exhibit Web file using a Web browser.

- Click the Internet Explorer program button pinned on the Windows 7 taskbar to start Internet Explorer.
- Type **skydrive.live.com** in the Address bar and then press the ENTER key to display a SkyDrive Web page requesting you sign in to your Windows Live account (Figure C–9). (If the contents of your SkyDrive are displayed instead, you already are signed in and can proceed to Step 3 on the next page.)

Q&A Why does the Web address change after I enter it in the Address bar?

The Web address changes because you are being redirected to sign into Windows Live before you can access SkyDrive.

Q&A Can I open the file from Microsoft Word instead of using the Web browser?

If you are opening the file on the same computer from which you saved it to the SkyDrive, click File on the Ribbon to open the Backstage view. Click the Recent tab and then click the desired file name (Koala Exhibit Web, in this case) in the Recent Documents list, or click Open and then navigate to the location of the saved file (for a detailed example of this procedure, refer to the Office 2010 and Windows 7 chapter at the beginning of this book).

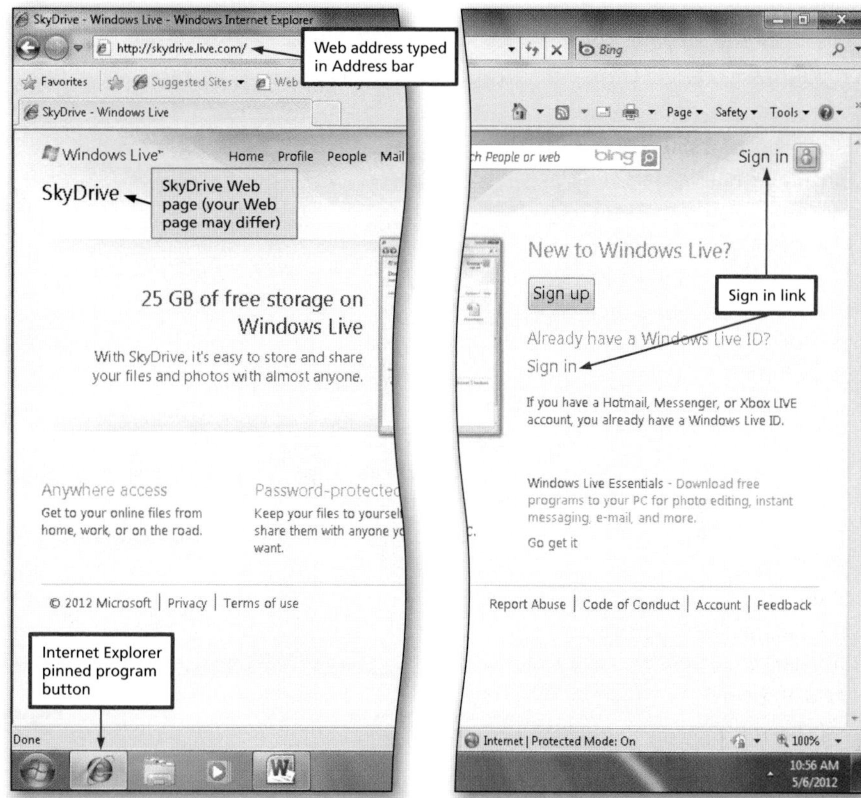

Figure C–9

- Click the Sign in link to display the Windows Live ID and Password text boxes (Figure C–10).

Q&A Why can I not locate the Sign in link?

If your computer remembers your Windows Live sign in credentials from a previous session, your e-mail address already may be displayed on the SkyDrive Web page. In this case, point to your e-mail address to display the Sign in button, click the Sign in button, and then proceed to Step 3. If you cannot locate your e-mail address or Sign in link, click the Sign in with a different Windows Live ID link and then proceed to Step 3.

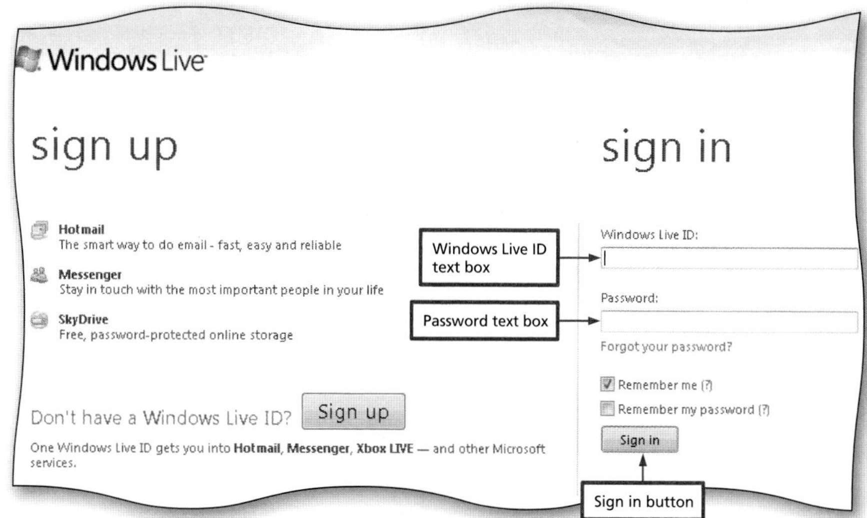

Figure C–10

- If necessary, enter your Windows Live ID and password in the appropriate text boxes and then click the Sign in button to sign into Windows Live and display the contents of your SkyDrive (Figure C–11).

Q&A What if my screen shows the contents of a particular folder, instead of all folders?

To display all folders on your SkyDrive, point to Windows Live in the upper-left corner of the window and then click SkyDrive on the Windows Live menu.

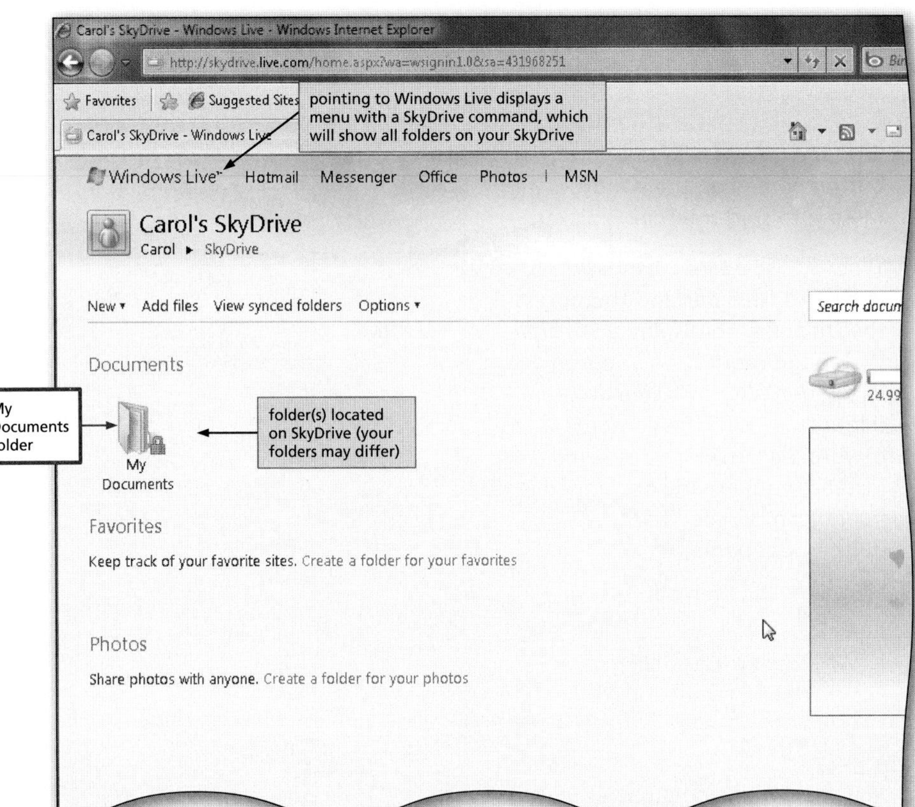

Figure C–11

- Click the My Documents folder, or the link corresponding to the folder containing the file you wish to open, to select the folder and display its contents (Figure C–12).

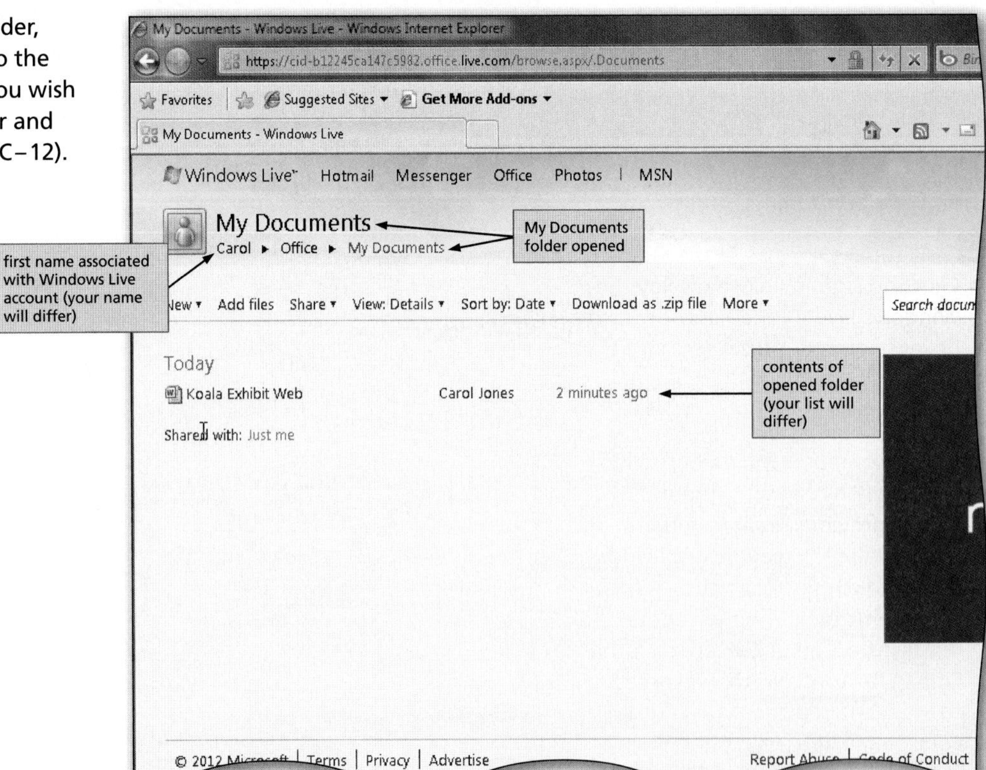

Figure C–12

- Point to the Koala Exhibit Web file to select the file and display commands associated with the file.
- Click the More link to display the More menu (Figure C–13).

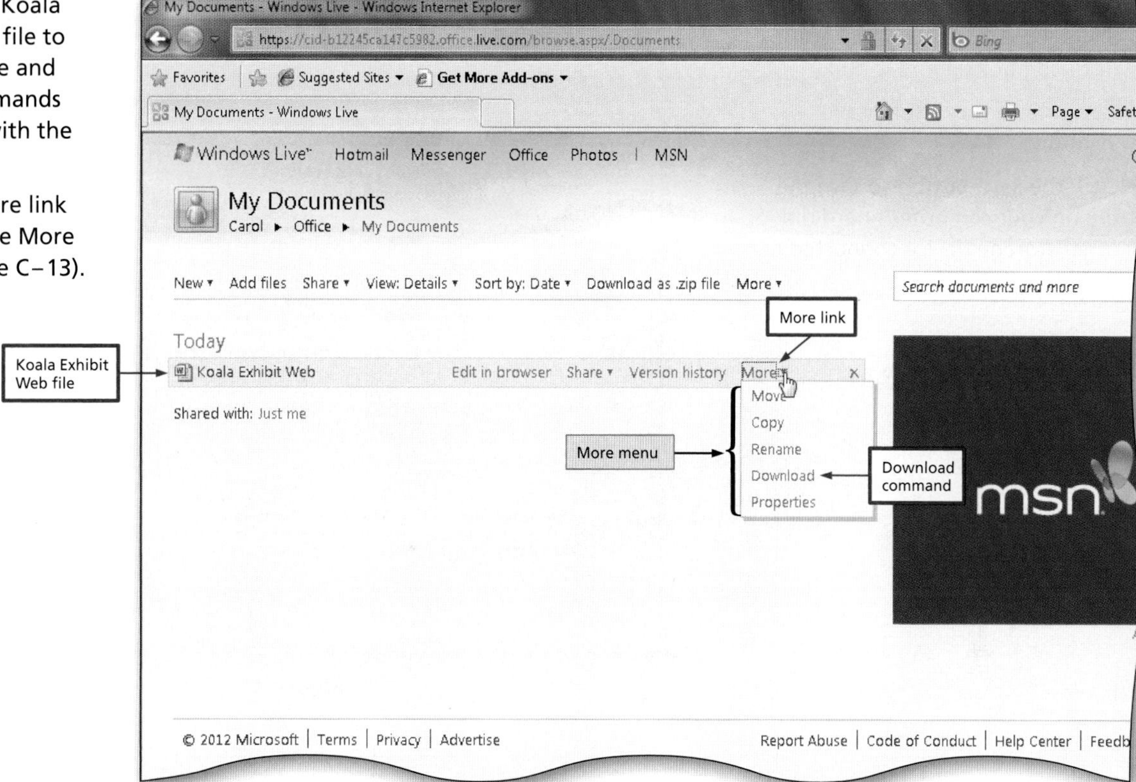

Figure C–13

- Click Download on the More menu to display the File Download dialog box (Figure C–14).

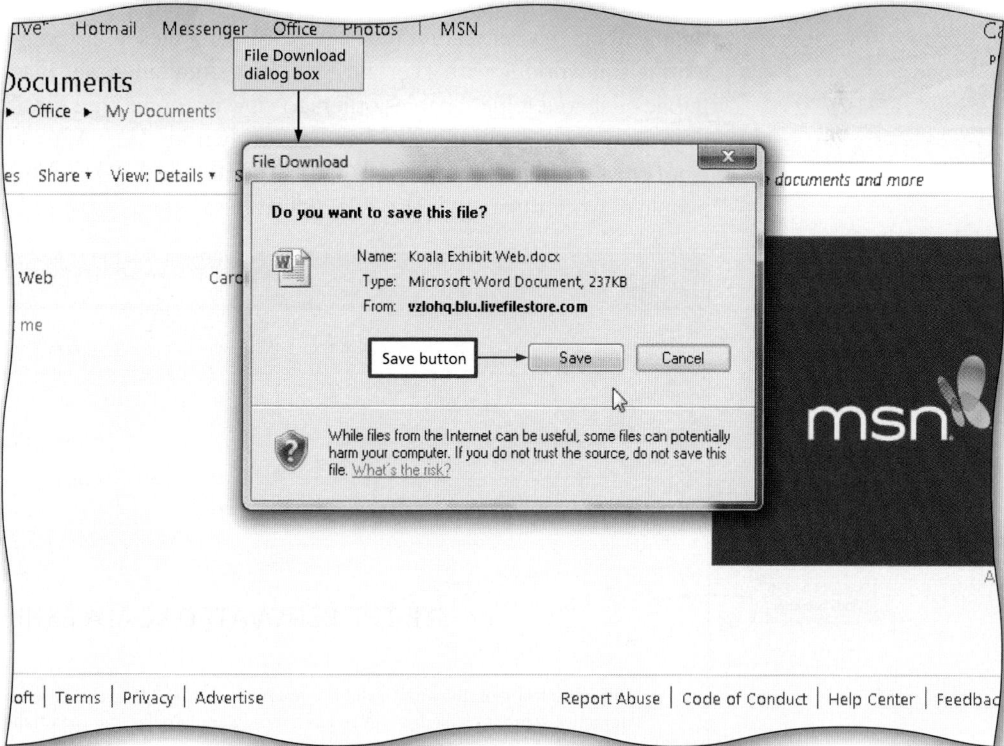

Figure C–14

- Click the Save button (File Download dialog box) to display the Save As dialog box (Figure C–15).
- Navigate to the desired save location.
- Click the Save button to save the file on your computer's hard disk or other storage device connected to the computer.

Figure C–15

Collaboration

In today's workplace, it is common to work with others on projects. Collaborating with the members of your team often requires sharing files. It also can involve multiple people editing and working with a certain set of files simultaneously. Placing files on SkyDrive in a public or shared folder enables others to view or modify the files. The members of the team then can view and edit the files simultaneously using Web Apps, enabling the team to work from one set of files (Figure C–16). Collaboration using Web Apps not only enables multiple people to work together, it also can reduce the amount of time required to complete a project.

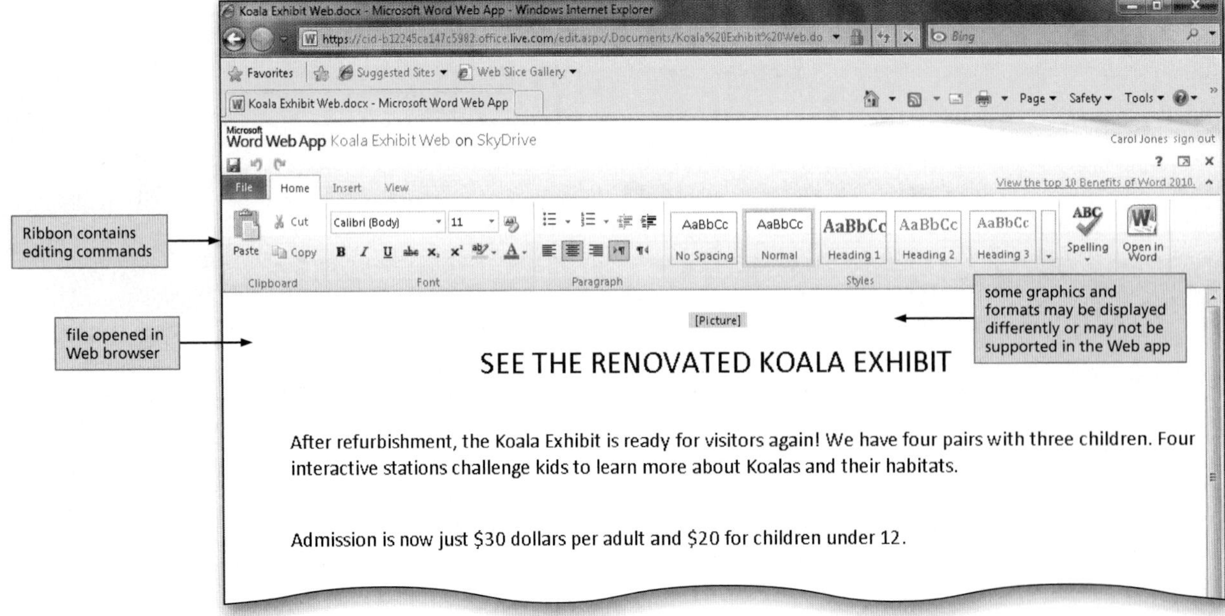

Figure C–16

Appendix D

APA Research Paper — Chapter 2 Supplement

Project — Research Paper Based on APA Documentation Style

As described in Chapter 2, two popular documentation styles for research papers are the Modern Language Association of America (MLA) and American Psychological Association (APA). This appendix creates the same research paper shown in Chapter 2, except it uses the APA documentation style instead of the MLA documentation style (Figure D–1 on the next page).

This appendix is intended as a supplement for Chapter 2. It assumes you have completed the Chapter 2 project and thus presents only the steps required to create the research paper following the APA guidelines. That is, this appendix does not repeat background, explanations, boxes, or steps from Chapter 2 that are not required specifically to create the APA version of the research paper. For example, this appendix does not present proofing tools, citation placeholders, footnotes, copy and paste, Research task pane, etc. You should know the material presented in Chapter 2 because it will help you to complete later chapters in the book successfully and if you intend to take the Word Certification exam.

APA Documentation Style

The research paper in this appendix follows the guidelines presented by the APA. To follow the APA documentation style, format the text to 12-point Times New Roman or a similar font. Double-space text on all pages of the paper using one-inch top, bottom, left, and right margins. Indent the first word of each paragraph in the body of the paper, and in footnotes if they are used, one-half inch from the left margin. At the top of each page, place a left-aligned running head and a right-aligned page number. The **running head** consists of the text, Running head:, followed by an abbreviated paper title (no more than 50 characters) in all capital letters.

The APA documentation style requires a title page. In addition to the running head and page number at the top of the page, the title page contains the complete paper title, author name, and institutional affiliation, all centered on separate lines in the upper-half of the page. The paper title should not exceed 12 words and should be written so that it easily can be shortened to an abbreviated title for the running head. The author name, also

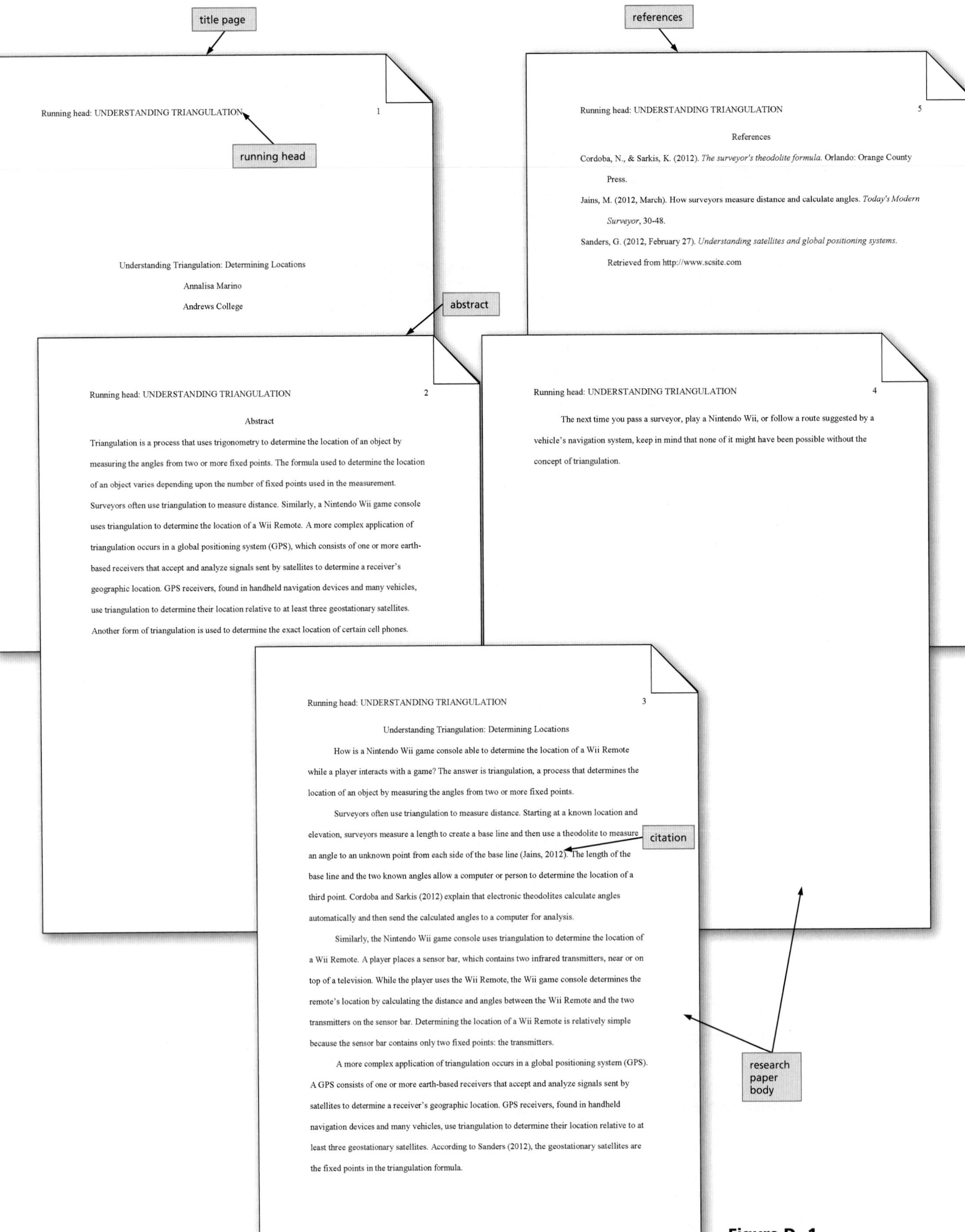

Running head: UNDERSTANDING TRIANGULATION 1

Understanding Triangulation: Determining Locations

Annalisa Marino

Andrews College

Running head: UNDERSTANDING TRIANGULATION 2

Abstract

Triangulation is a process that uses trigonometry to determine the location of an object by measuring the angles from two or more fixed points. The formula used to determine the location of an object varies depending upon the number of fixed points used in the measurement. Surveyors often use triangulation to measure distance. Similarly, a Nintendo Wii game console uses triangulation to determine the location of a Wii Remote. A more complex application of triangulation occurs in a global positioning system (GPS), which consists of one or more earth-based receivers that accept and analyze signals sent by satellites to determine a receiver's geographic location. GPS receivers, found in handheld navigation devices and many vehicles, use triangulation to determine their location relative to at least three geostationary satellites. Another form of triangulation is used to determine the exact location of certain cell phones.

Running head: UNDERSTANDING TRIANGULATION 3

Understanding Triangulation: Determining Locations

How is a Nintendo Wii game console able to determine the location of a Wii Remote while a player interacts with a game? The answer is triangulation, a process that determines the location of an object by measuring the angles from two or more fixed points.

Surveyors often use triangulation to measure distance. Starting at a known location and elevation, surveyors measure a length to create a base line and then use a theodolite to measure an angle to an unknown point from each side of the base line (Jains, 2012). The length of the base line and the two known angles allow a computer or person to determine the location of a third point. Cordoba and Sarkis (2012) explain that electronic theodolites calculate angles automatically and then send the calculated angles to a computer for analysis.

Similarly, the Nintendo Wii game console uses triangulation to determine the location of a Wii Remote. A player places a sensor bar, which contains two infrared transmitters, near or on top of a television. While the player uses the Wii Remote, the Wii game console determines the remote's location by calculating the distance and angles between the Wii Remote and the two transmitters on the sensor bar. Determining the location of a Wii Remote is relatively simple because the sensor bar contains only two fixed points: the transmitters.

A more complex application of triangulation occurs in a global positioning system (GPS). A GPS consists of one or more earth-based receivers that accept and analyze signals sent by satellites to determine a receiver's geographic location. GPS receivers, found in handheld navigation devices and many vehicles, use triangulation to determine their location relative to at least three geostationary satellites. According to Sanders (2012), the geostationary satellites are the fixed points in the triangulation formula.

Running head: UNDERSTANDING TRIANGULATION 4

The next time you pass a surveyor, play a Nintendo Wii, or follow a route suggested by a vehicle's navigation system, keep in mind that none of it might have been possible without the concept of triangulation.

Running head: UNDERSTANDING TRIANGULATION 5

References

Cordoba, N., & Sarkis, K. (2012). *The surveyor's theodolite formula.* Orlando: Orange County Press.

Jains, M. (2012, March). How surveyors measure distance and calculate angles. *Today's Modern Surveyor*, 30-48.

Sanders, G. (2012, February 27). *Understanding satellites and global positioning systems.* Retrieved from http://www.scsite.com

Figure D–1

called an author byline, should not contain any title (e.g., Professor) or degrees (e.g., PhD). If the author is not affiliated with an institution, list the author's city and state of residence. The title page also can include an author note centered at the bottom of the page, which can contain separate paragraphs identifying the author's departmental affiliation, changes in affiliation during research, acknowledgments, and contact information. If the title page contains an author note, the text, Author Note, should be centered above the notes.

Research papers that follow the APA documentation style include an abstract. The **abstract** is a one-paragraph summary (usually 250 words or fewer) of the most important topics in the paper. The abstract appears after the title page on its own numbered page, which includes the running head. The title, Abstract, is centered above a single paragraph that is double-spaced and not indented.

The APA documentation style cites references in the text of the paper, called **citations**, instead of noting each source at the bottom of the page or at the end of the paper. This documentation style uses the term, **references,** to refer to the bibliographic list of sources at the end of the paper. The references page alphabetically lists sources that are cited in the paper. Place the list of sources on a separate numbered page. Center the title, References, one inch from the top margin. Double-space all entries and format them with a **hanging indent**, in which the first line of a paragraph begins at the left margin and subsequent lines in the same paragraph are indented. The APA guidelines specify the hanging indent should be one-half inch from the left margin. List each source by the author's last name, or, if the author's name is not available, by the title of the source. Capitalize only the first letter of the first word in a title, along with any proper nouns.

To Start Word

If you are using a computer to step through the project in this appendix and you want your screens to match the figures in this appendix, you should change your screen's resolution to 1024 × 768. For information about how to change a computer's resolution, refer to the Office 2010 and Windows 7 chapter at the beginning of this book.

The following steps, which assume Windows 7 is running, start Word based on a typical installation. You may need to ask your instructor how to start Word for your computer.

1. Click the Start button on the Windows 7 taskbar to display the Start menu.
2. Type `Microsoft Word` as the search text in the 'Search programs and files' text box and watch the search results appear on the Start menu.
3. Click Microsoft Word 2010 in the search results on the Start menu to start Word and display a new blank document in the Word window.
4. If the Word window is not maximized, click the Maximize button next to the Close button on its title bar to maximize the window.
5. If the Print Layout button on the status bar is not selected (shown in Figure D–2 on the next page), click it so that your screen is in Print Layout view.
6. If Normal (Home tab | Styles group) is not selected in the Quick Style gallery (shown in Figure D–2), click it so that your document uses the Normal style.
7. If your zoom percent is not 100, click the Zoom Out or Zoom In button on the status bar as many times as necessary until the Zoom button displays 100% on its face (shown in Figure D–2).

To Display Formatting Marks

As discussed in Chapter 1, it is helpful to display formatting marks that indicate where in the document you press the ENTER key, SPACEBAR, and other keys. The following steps display formatting marks.

1. If the Home tab is not the active tab, click Home on the Ribbon to display the Home tab.
2. If the Show/Hide ¶ button (Home tab | Paragraph group) is not selected already, click it to display formatting marks on the screen.

To Modify the Normal Style for the Current Document

The APA documentation style requires that all text in the research paper use 12-point Times New Roman, or a similar, font. If you change the font and font size using buttons on the Ribbon, you may need to make the change many times during the course of creating the paper because Word formats different areas of a document using the Normal style, which uses 11-point Calibri font. By changing the Normal style, you ensure that all text in the document will use the format required by the APA. The following steps change the Normal style.

1.
- Right-click Normal in the Quick Style gallery (Home tab | Styles group) to display a shortcut menu (Figure D–2).

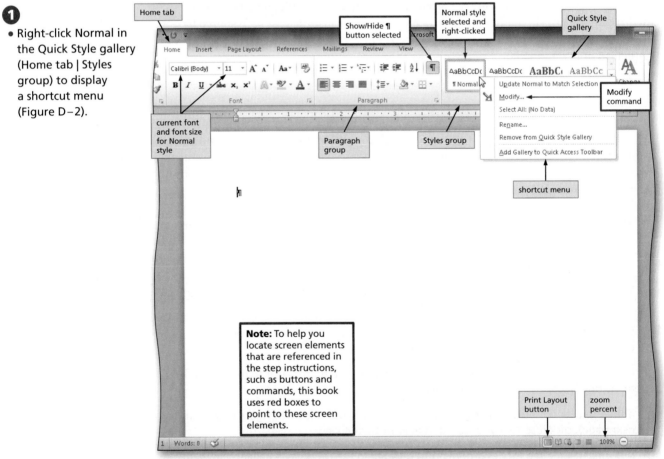

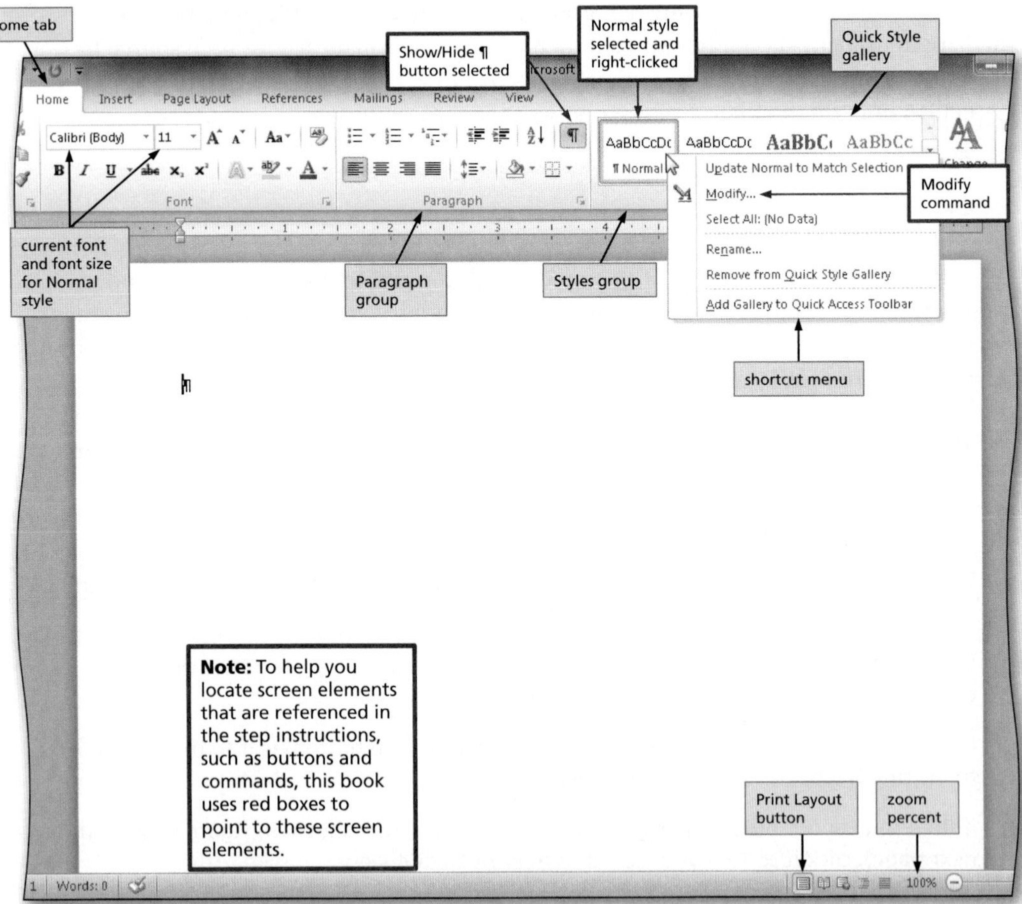

Figure D–2

- Click Modify on the shortcut menu to display the Modify Style dialog box.
- Click the Font box arrow (Modify Style dialog box) to display the Font list. Scroll to and then click Times New Roman in the Font list to change the font for the selected style.
- Click the Font Size box arrow (Modify Style dialog box) and then click 12 in the Font Size list to change the font size for the selected style.
- Ensure that the 'Only in this document' option button is selected (Figure D–3).

- Click the OK button (Modify Style dialog box) to update the selected style (in this case, the Normal style) to the specified settings.

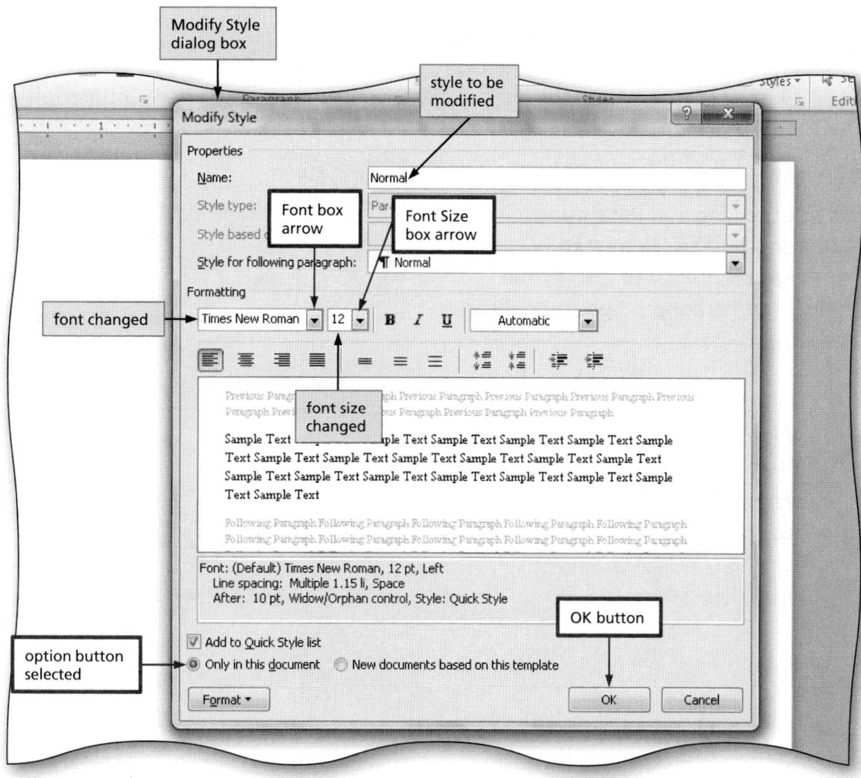

Figure D–3

To Change Line Spacing to Double

The APA documentation style requires that you double-space the entire research paper. That is, the amount of vertical space between each line of text and above and below paragraphs should be equal to one blank line. The following steps change the line spacing to 2.0, which double-spaces the lines in the research paper.

- Click the Line and Paragraph Spacing button (Home tab | Paragraph group) to display the Line and Paragraph Spacing gallery (Figure D–4).

- Click 2.0 in the Line and Paragraph Spacing gallery to change the line spacing for the paragraph containing the insertion point.

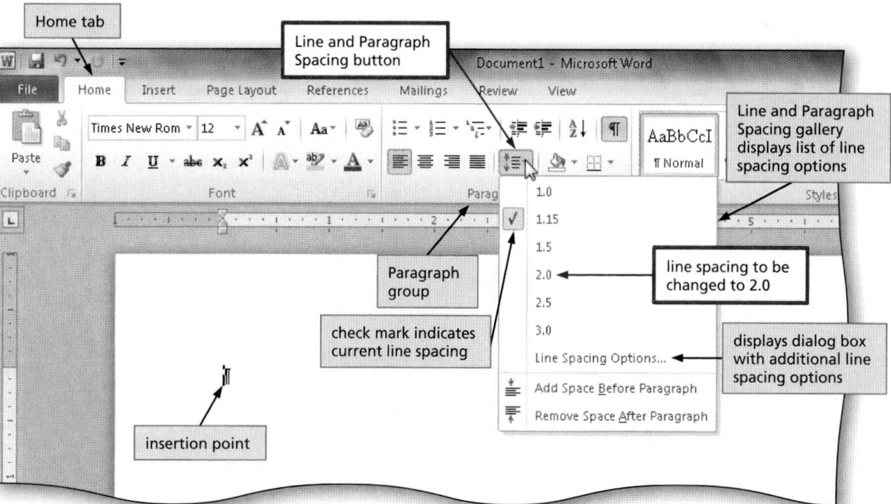

Figure D–4

To Remove Space after a Paragraph

The research paper should not have additional blank space after each paragraph. The following steps remove the blank space after a paragraph.

- Click the Line and Paragraph Spacing button (Home tab | Paragraph group) to display the Line and Paragraph Spacing gallery (Figure D–5).

- Click Remove Space After Paragraph in the Line and Paragraph Spacing gallery so that no blank space appears after paragraphs.

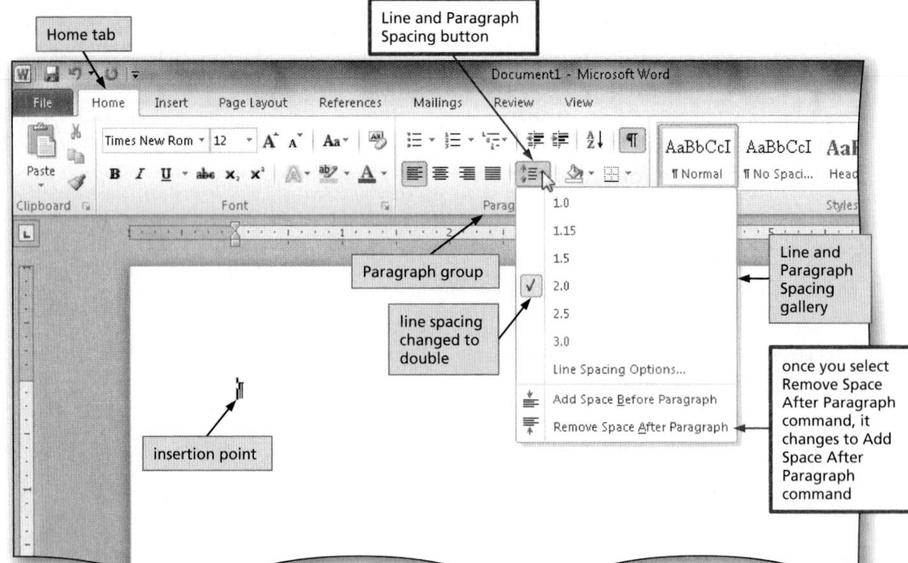

Figure D–5

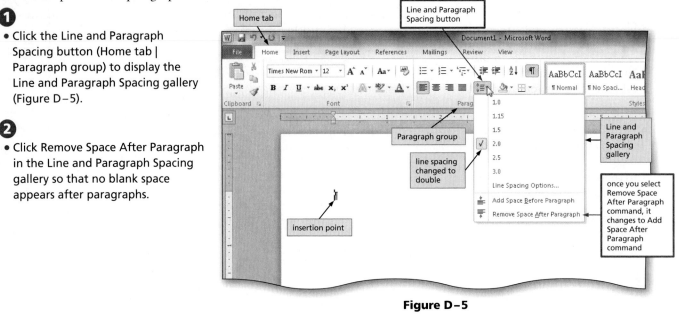

To Update a Style to Match a Selection

To ensure that all paragraphs in the paper will be double-spaced and do not have space after the paragraphs, you want the Normal style to include the line and paragraph spacing changes made in the previous two sets of steps. Because no text has yet been typed in the research paper, you do not need to select text prior to updating the Normal style. The following steps update the Normal style.

- Right-click Normal in the Quick Style gallery (Home tab | Styles group) to display a shortcut menu (Figure D–6).

- Click Update Normal to Match Selection on the shortcut menu to update the current style to reflect the settings at the location of the insertion point.

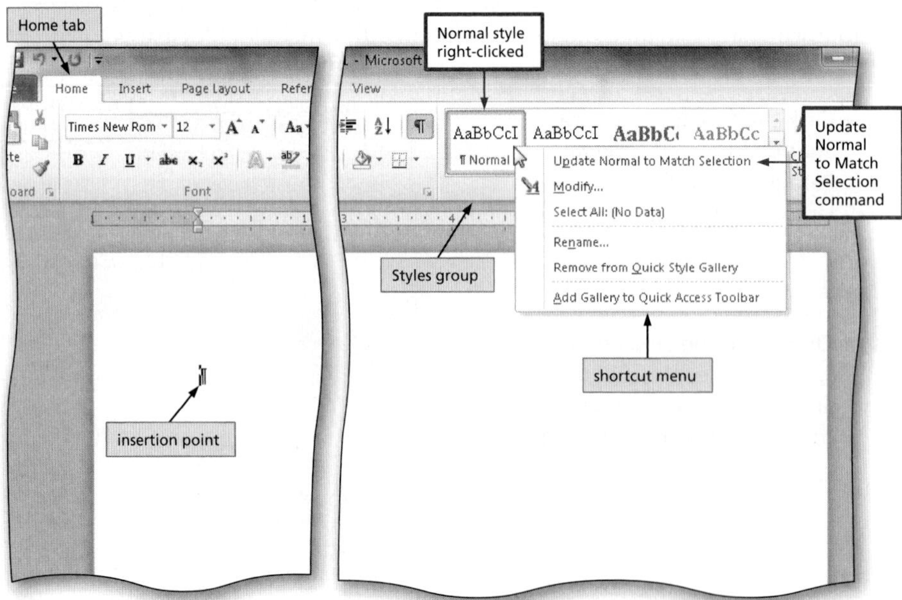

Figure D–6

To Insert a Formatted Header and Switch to the Header

In this research paper, the running head is to be placed at the left margin and the page number at the right margin, both on the same line one-half inch from the top of each page. Because the APA documentation style requires text at both the left and right margins, you can insert a formatted header that contains placeholders for text at the left, center, and right locations of the header. The following steps insert a formatted header and then switch from editing the document text to editing the header.

- Click Insert on the Ribbon to display the Insert tab.
- Click the Header button (Insert tab | Header & Footer group) to display the Header gallery (Figure D–7).

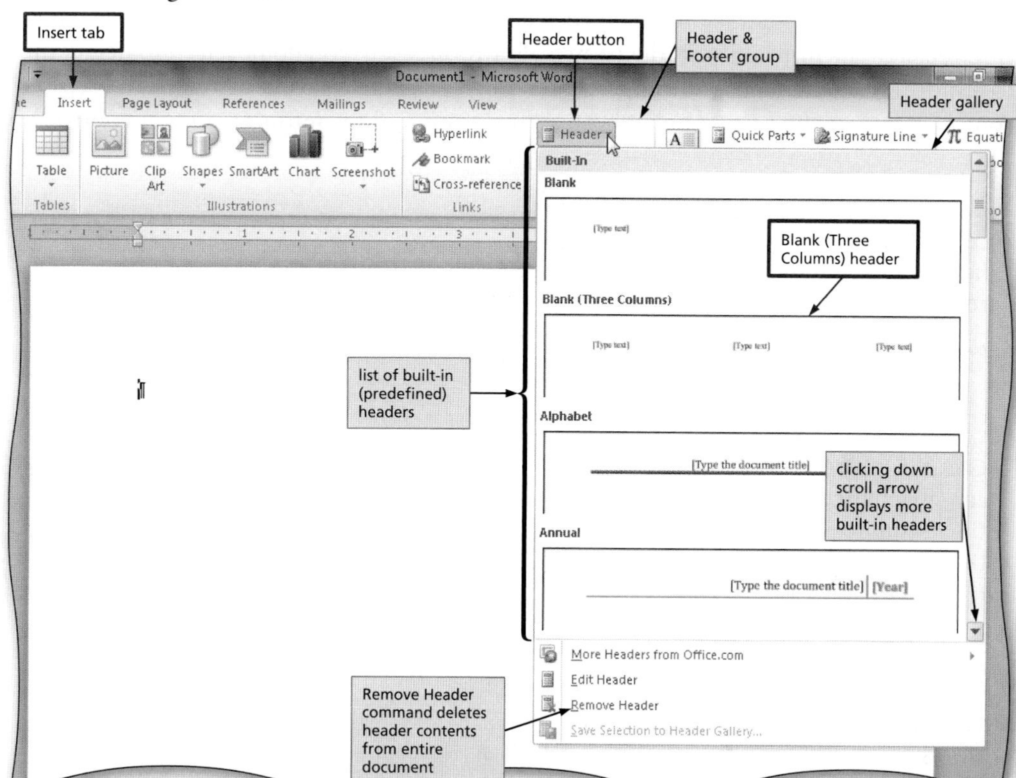

Figure D–7

- Click Blank (Three Columns) in the Header gallery to insert the selected header design in the document and switch from the document text to the header, which allows you to edit the contents of the header (Figure D–8).

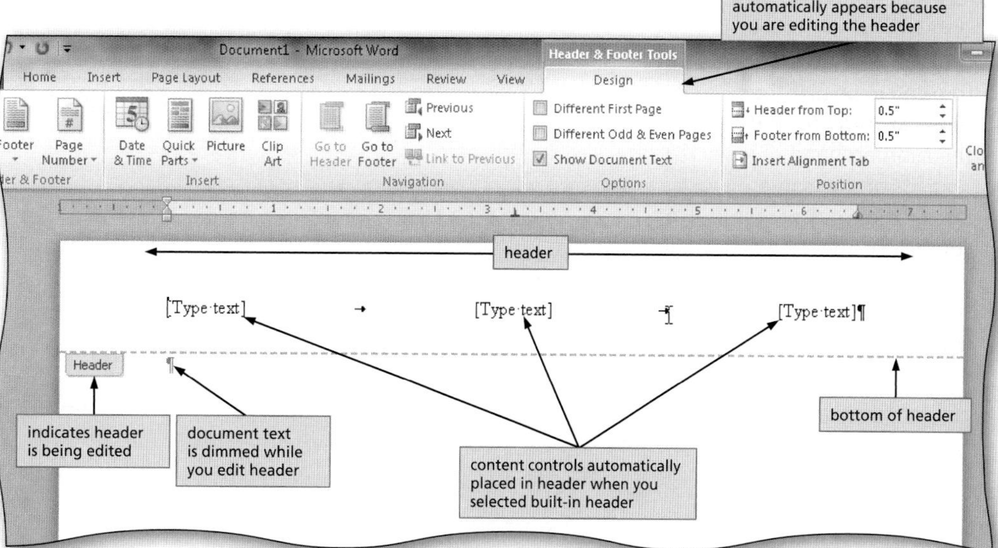

Figure D–8

To Enter Text in a Header Content Control

The formatted header contains three content controls (one at the left margin, one centered, and one at the right margin) with a tab character between each content control. A **content control** contains instructions for filling areas of text or graphics. The tab characters, which are formatting marks that indicate the TAB key has been pressed, are displayed because Word uses tab stops to align these content controls. Chapter 3 discusses tab stops in more depth.

To select a content control, you click it. As soon as you begin typing in a selected content control, the text you type replaces the instruction in the control. For this reason, you do not need to delete the selection unless you wish to remove the content control and not enter any replacement text. The following steps delete the centered content control and then enter the running head at the location of the leftmost content control in the header.

- Click the centered content control in the header to select the content control.
- Press the DELETE key to delete the selected content control.
- Click the leftmost content control in the header to select the content control (Figure D–9).

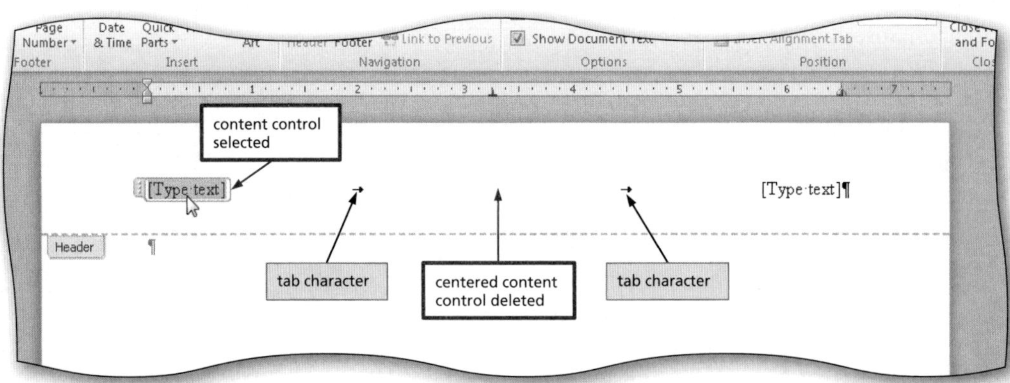

Figure D–9

2

- Type **`Running head: UNDERSTANDING TRIANGULATION`** as the text in the leftmost content control and then press the DELETE key twice to remove one of the tab characters so that the running head text fits on the same line as the rightmost content control, which will contain the page number (Figure D–10).

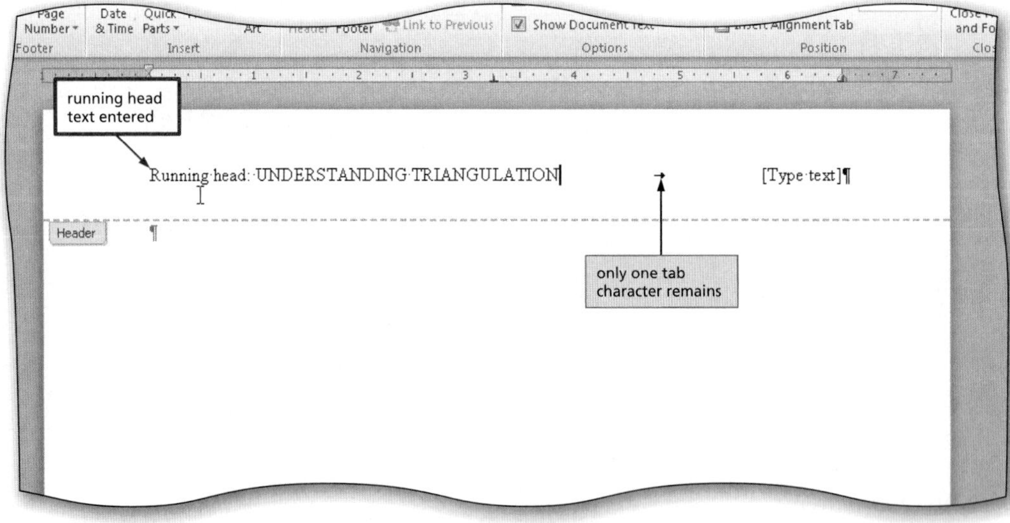

Figure D–10

To Count Characters

The running head should be no more than 50 characters, according to the APA documentation style. The next steps count the characters in the running head.

- Drag through the running head text, UNDERSTANDING TRIANGULATION, to select the text.
- With the running head selected, click the Word Count indicator on the status bar to display the Word Count dialog box (Figure D–11).

2

- Click the Close button (Word Count dialog box) to close the dialog box.

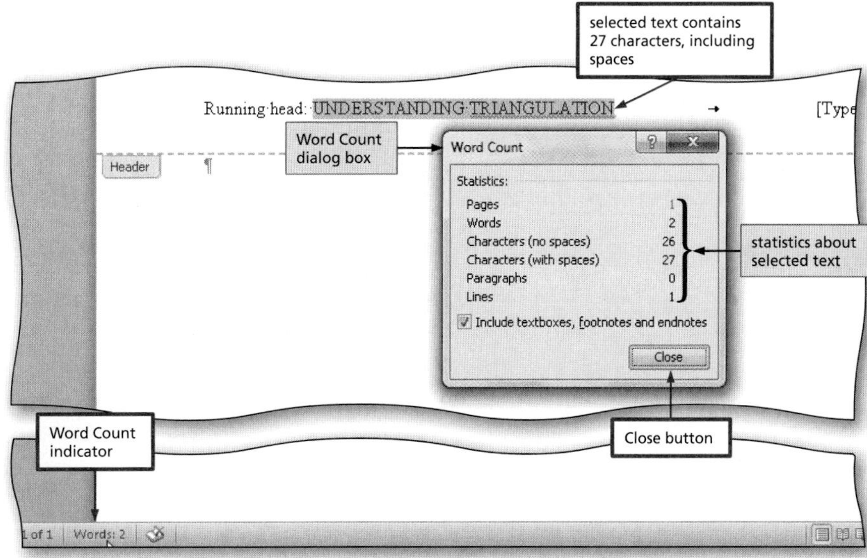

Figure D–11

To Insert a Page Number in a Header Content Control

The next task is to insert the current page number in the header. The following steps insert a page number at the location of the rightmost content control in the header.

1

- Click the rightmost content control in the header to select the content control.
- Click the Insert Page Number button (Header & Footer Tools Design tab | Header & Footer group) to display the Insert Page Number menu.
- Point to Current Position on the Insert Page Number menu to display the Current Position gallery (Figure D–12).

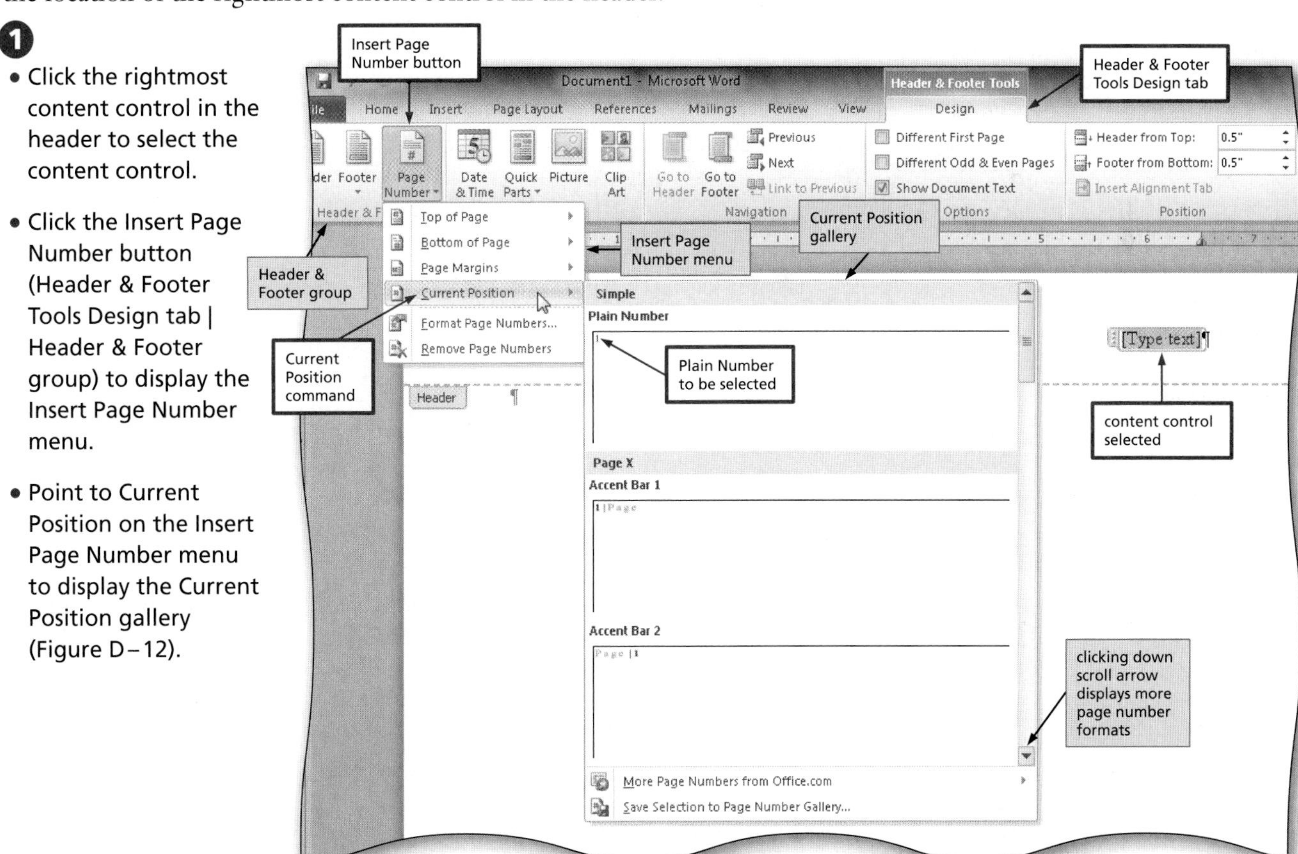

Figure D–12

2

- Click Plain Number in the Current Position gallery to insert an unformatted page number at the location of the selected content control in the header (Figure D–13).

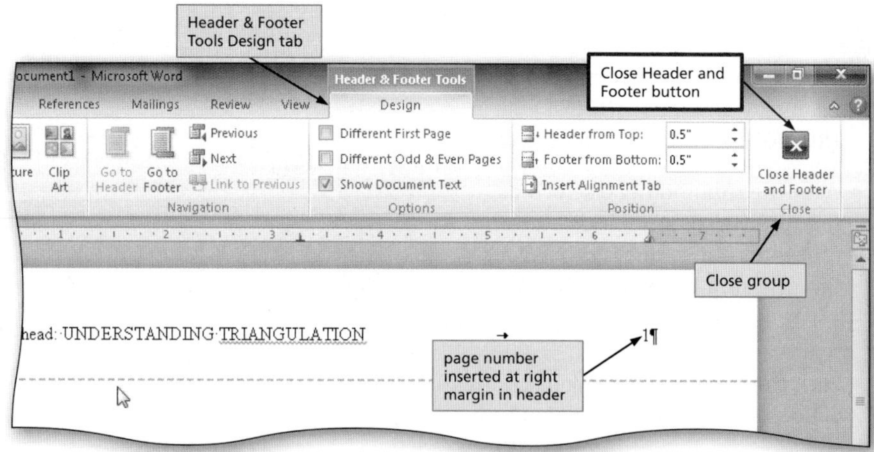

Figure D–13

To Close the Header

The header is complete. Thus, the next task is to switch back to the document text. The following step closes the header.

1

- Click the Close Header and Footer button (Header & Footer Tools Design tab | Close group) (shown in Figure D–13) to close the header and switch back to the document text (Figure D–14).

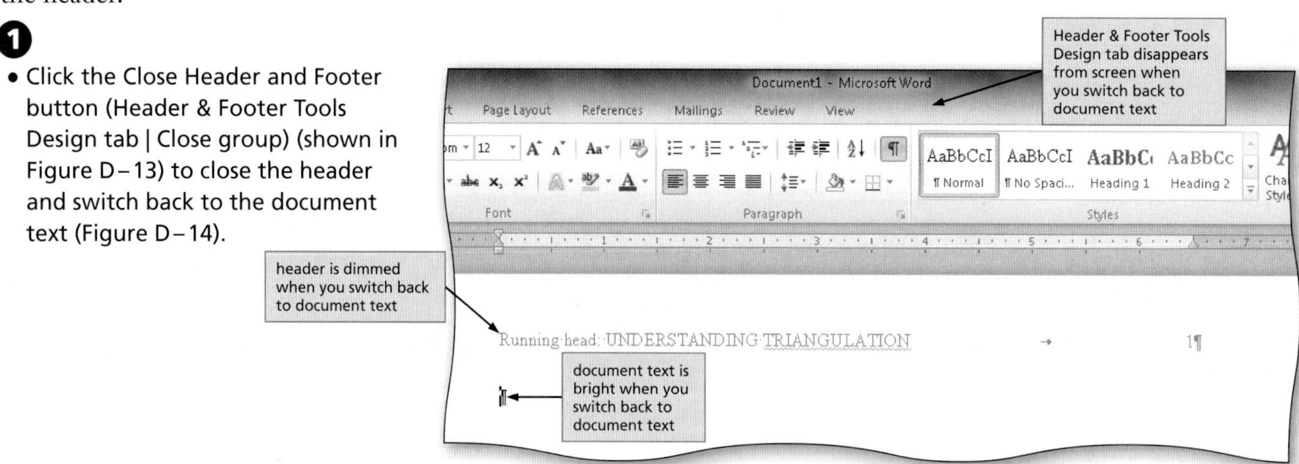

Figure D–14

To Type the Title Page Text

In addition to the header, which appears on every page in the paper, the title page for this research paper should contain the complete paper title, author name, and institutional affiliation, all centered on separate lines in the upper-half of the page. The following steps type the title page text.

1. With the insertion point at the top of the document, press the ENTER key six times.
2. Click the Center button (Home tab | Paragraph group) to center the insertion point.
3. Type `Understanding Triangulation: Determining Locations` and then press the ENTER key.
4. Type `Annalisa Marino` and then press the ENTER key.
5. Type `Andrews College` and then press the ENTER key (Figure D–15).

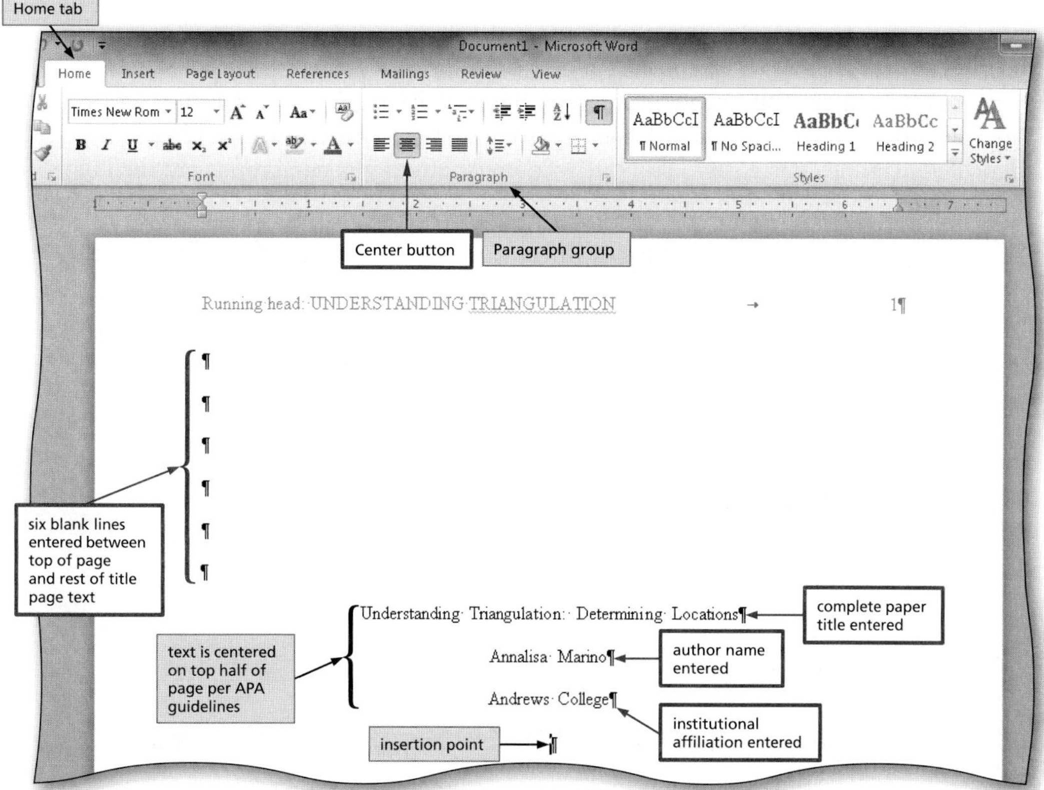

Figure D–15

To Page Break Manually

The title page is complete, and the abstract for the research paper will begin on a new page. To move the insertion point to the next page, you insert a manual page break. A **manual page break**, or **hard page break**, is one that you force into the document at a specific location.

Word never moves or adjusts manual page breaks; however, Word adjusts any automatic page breaks that follow a manual page break. Word inserts manual page breaks immediately above or to the left of the location of the insertion point. The following step inserts a manual page break after the title page.

1

- Verify the insertion point is positioned below the college name on the title page (shown in Figure D–15), which is the location for the page break.
- Click Insert on the Ribbon to display the Insert tab.
- Click the Page Break button (Insert tab | Pages group) to insert a manual page break immediately to the left of the insertion point and position the insertion point immediately below the manual page break (Figure D–16).

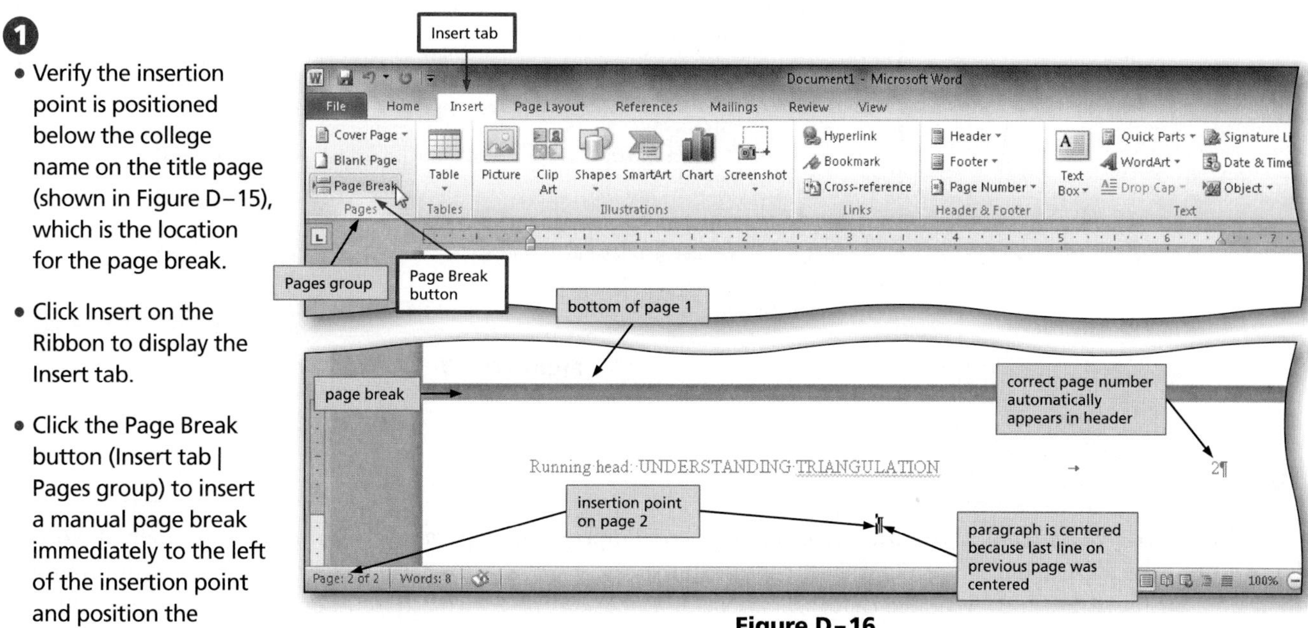

Figure D–16

To Type the Abstract

The abstract is a one-page summary of the most important points in the research paper. The title should be centered, and the paragraph below the title should be left-aligned. The following steps type the title centered, left-align a paragraph, and then type the abstract in the research paper.

1. Type **`Abstract`** and then press the ENTER key to enter the title for the page containing the abstract.
2. Press CTRL+L to left-align the current paragraph, that is, the paragraph containing the insertion point. (Recall from Chapter 1 that a notation such as CTRL+L means to press the letter L on the keyboard while holding down the CTRL key.)
3. Type the abstract text as shown in Figure D–17.

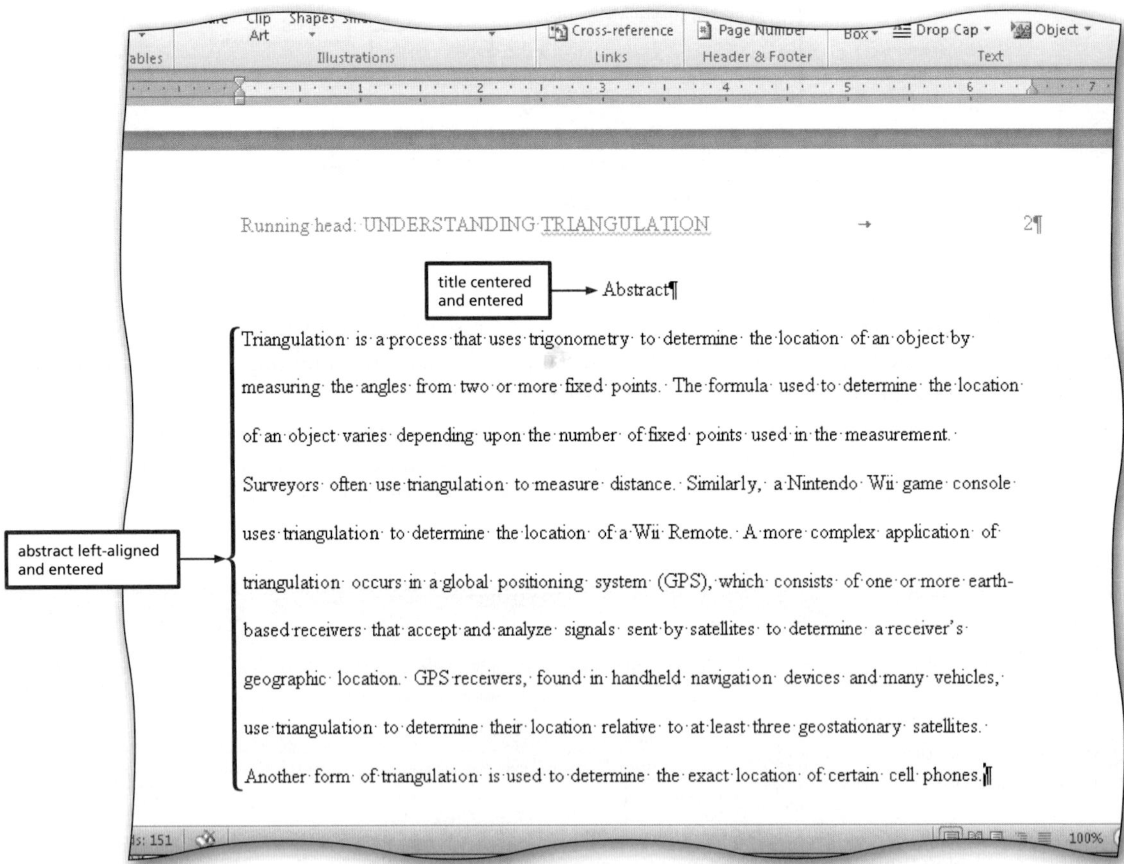

Figure D–17

To Count Words

When you write papers, you often are required to compose the papers with a minimum number of words. In addition, the APA documentation style specifies that the abstract in a research paper should contain no more than 250 words, sometimes no more than 150 words. The next steps verify the number of words in the abstract.

1

- Position the mouse pointer in the paragraph containing the abstract and then triple-click to select the paragraph.
- Verify the number of words in the selected text by looking at the Word Count indicator on the status bar (Figure D–18).

2

- Click anywhere in the abstract to remove the selection from the text.

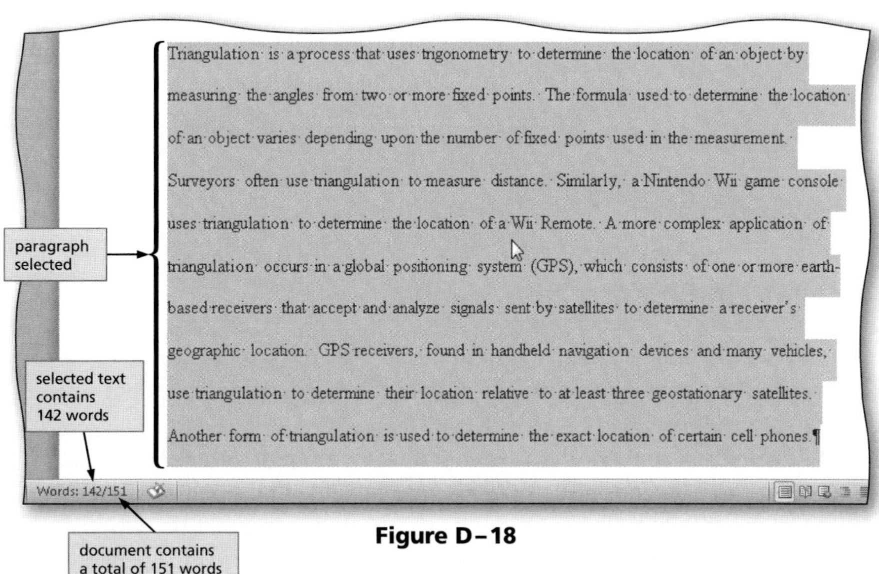

Figure D–18

To Page Break Manually

The abstract is complete, and the text for the research paper should begin on a new page. The following steps insert a manual page break after the abstract.

1. Press CTRL+END to position the insertion point at the end of the document, which is the end of the abstract in this case.

2. Click the Page Break button (Insert tab | Pages group) to insert a manual page break immediately to the left of the insertion point and position the insertion point immediately below the manual page break.

To Enter the Paper Title

The following steps enter the title of the research paper centered between the page margins.

1. Center the insertion point.

2. Type **`Understanding Triangulation: Determining Locations`** and then press the ENTER key to enter the title of the paper (Figure D–19).

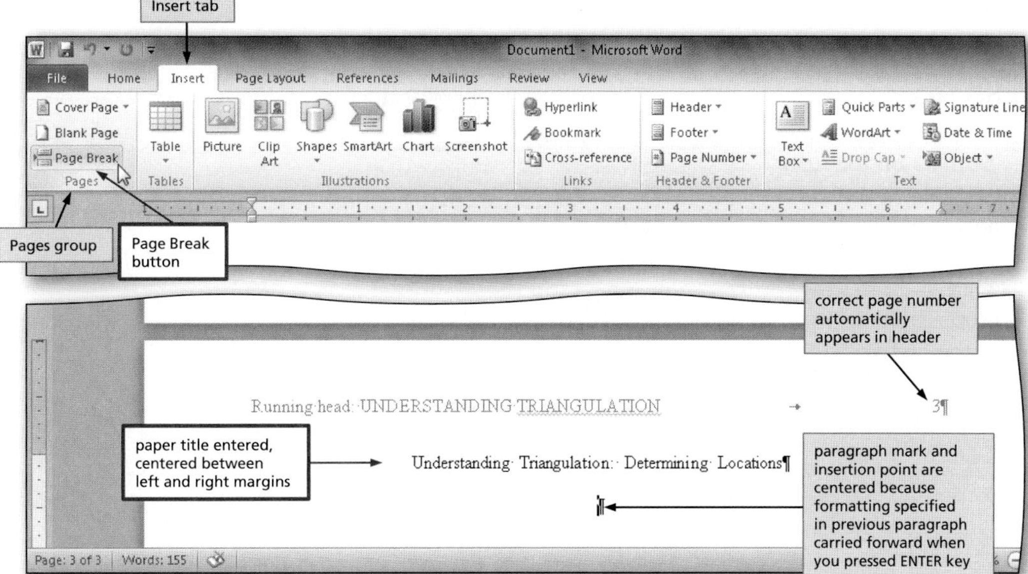

Figure D–19

To Format Text

The paragraphs below the paper title should be left-aligned, instead of centered. Thus, the following step left-aligns the paragraph below the paper title.

1. Press CTRL+L to left-align the current paragraph, that is, the paragraph containing the insertion point.

To First-Line Indent Paragraphs

The first line of each paragraph in the research paper is to be indented one-half inch from the left margin. You can use the horizontal ruler, usually simply called the **ruler**, to indent just the first line of a paragraph, which is called a **first-line indent**.

The left margin on the ruler contains two triangles above a square. The **First Line Indent marker** is the top triangle at the 0" mark on the ruler (Figure D–20). The small square at the 0" mark is the Left Indent marker. The **Left Indent marker** allows you to change the entire left margin, whereas the First Line Indent marker indents only the first line of the paragraph. The following steps first-line indent paragraphs in the research paper.

1

- If the rulers are not displayed, click the View Ruler button on the vertical scroll bar to display the horizontal and vertical rulers on the screen.
- With the insertion point on the paragraph mark below the research paper title, point to the First Line Indent marker on the ruler (Figure D–20).

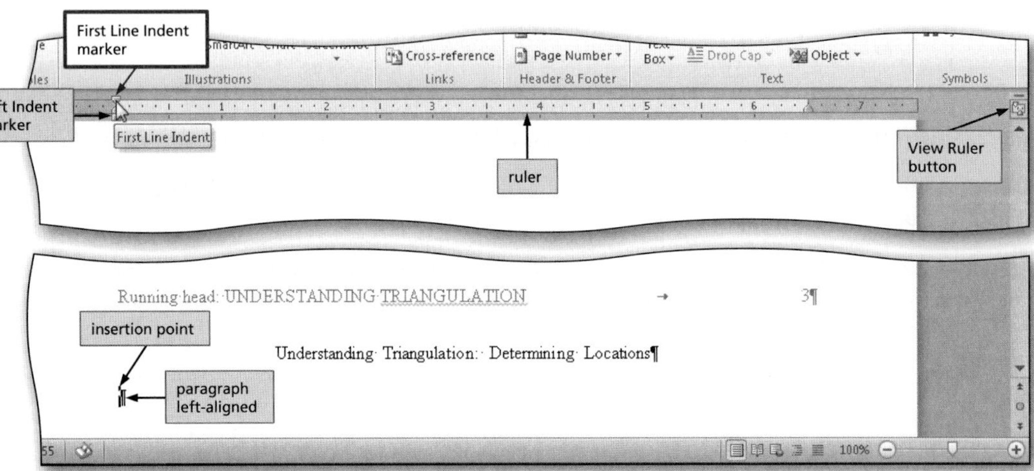

Figure D–20

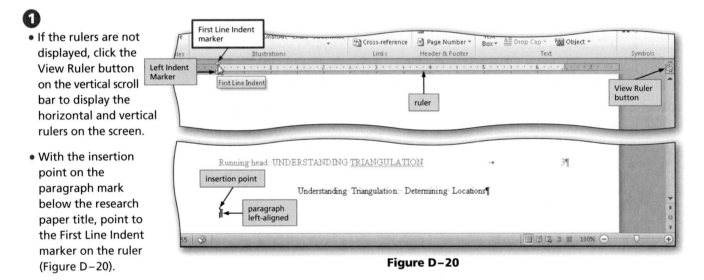

- Drag the First Line Indent marker to the .5" mark on the ruler to display a vertical dotted line in the document window, which indicates the proposed location of the first line of the paragraph (Figure D–21).

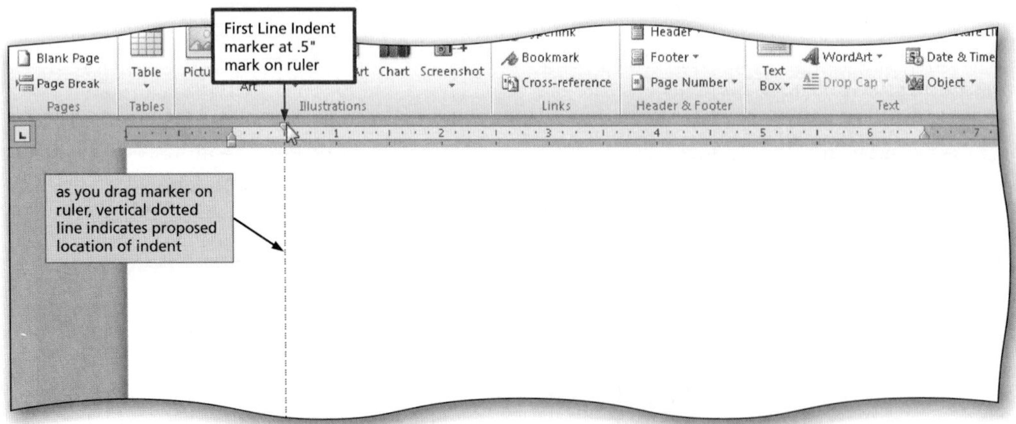

Figure D–21

3

- Release the mouse button to place the First Line Indent marker at the .5" mark on the ruler, or one-half inch from the left margin (Figure D–22).

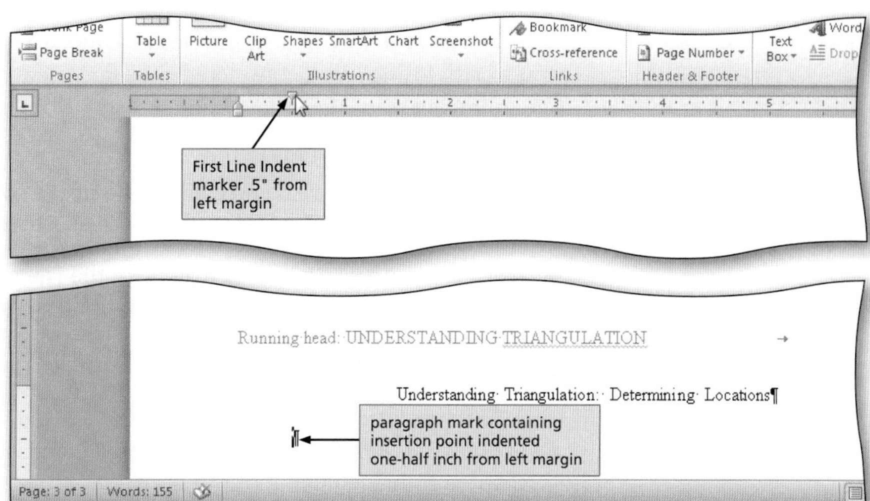
Page Break
Pages
Table
Tables
Picture
Clip Art
Shapes
SmartArt
Chart
Screenshot
Illustrations
Bookmark
Cross-reference
Links
Page Number
Header & Footer
Text Box
First Line Indent marker .5" from left margin
Running head: UNDERSTANDING TRIANGULATION
Understanding Triangulation: Determining Locations¶
paragraph mark containing insertion point indented one-half inch from left margin
Page: 3 of 3
Words: 155

Figure D–22

To Type the First and Second Paragraphs

The following steps type the first and second paragraphs of the research paper.

1 Type the first paragraph of the research paper as shown in Figure D–23 and then press the ENTER key.

2 Type the second paragraph of the research paper as shown in Figure D–23.

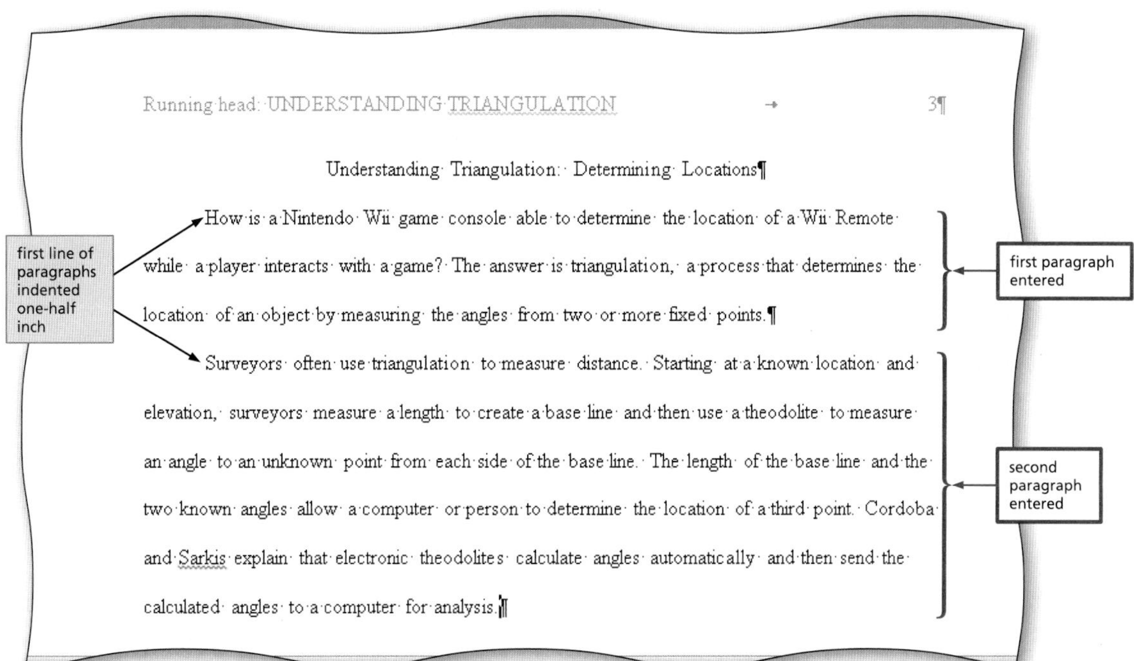
Running head: UNDERSTANDING TRIANGULATION
3¶
Understanding Triangulation: Determining Locations¶
How is a Nintendo Wii game console able to determine the location of a Wii Remote while a player interacts with a game? The answer is triangulation, a process that determines the location of an object by measuring the angles from two or more fixed points.¶
Surveyors often use triangulation to measure distance. Starting at a known location and elevation, surveyors measure a length to create a base line and then use a theodolite to measure an angle to an unknown point from each side of the base line. The length of the base line and the two known angles allow a computer or person to determine the location of a third point. Cordoba and Sarkis explain that electronic theodolites calculate angles automatically and then send the calculated angles to a computer for analysis.¶
first line of paragraphs indented one-half inch
first paragraph entered
second paragraph entered

Figure D–23

To Save a Document

You have performed several tasks while creating this research paper and do not want to risk losing work completed thus far. Accordingly, you should save the document. The following steps save the document on a USB flash drive using the file name, Triangulation Paper.

1. With a USB flash drive connected to one of the computer's USB ports, click the Save button on the Quick Access Toolbar to display the Save As dialog box.
2. Type `Triangulation Paper` in the File name text box to change the file name. Do not press the ENTER key after typing the file name because you do not want to close the dialog box at this time.
3. Navigate to the desired save location (in this case, the Word folder in the CIS 101 folder [or your class folder] on the USB flash drive). For a detailed example of this procedure, refer to Steps 3a – 3c in the To Save a File in a Folder section in the Office 2010 and Windows 7 chapter at the beginning of this book.
4. Click the Save button (Save As dialog box) to save the document in the selected folder on the selected drive with the entered file name.

To Change the Bibliography Style

The APA guidelines suggest the use of in-text citations instead of footnoting each source of material in a paper. These parenthetical acknowledgments guide the reader to the end of the paper for complete information about the source.

The first step in inserting a citation is to be sure the citations and sources will be formatted using the correct documentation style, called the bibliography style in Word. The following steps change the specified documentation style.

- Click References on the Ribbon to display the References tab.
- Click the Bibliography Style box arrow (References tab | Citations & Bibliography group) to display a gallery of predefined documentation styles (Figure D–24).

2

- Click APA Fifth Edition in the Bibliography Style gallery to change the documentation style to APA.

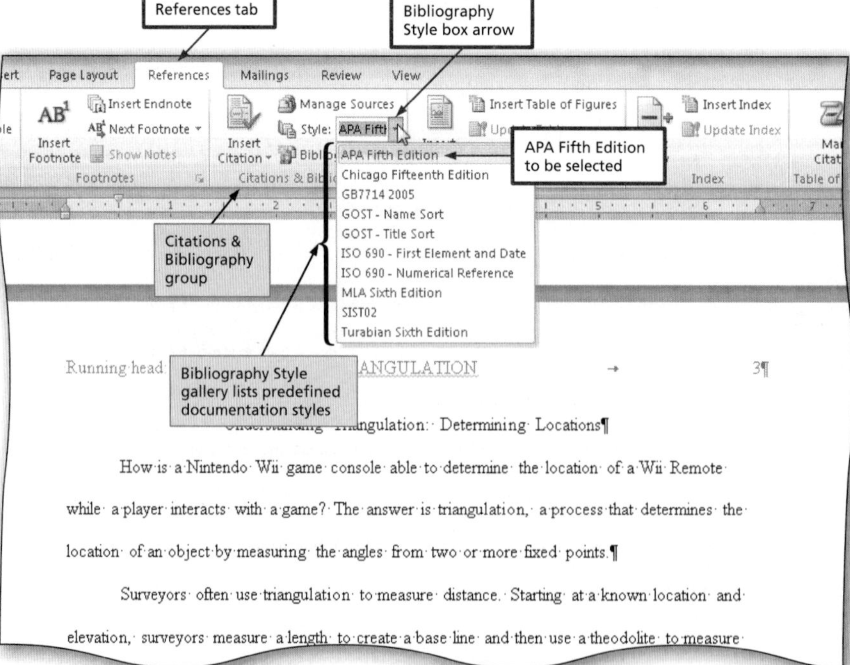

Figure D–24

To Insert a Citation and Create Its Source

With the documentation style selected, the next task is to insert a citation placeholder and enter the source information. You can accomplish these steps at once by instructing Word to add a new source. The following steps add a new source for a magazine (periodical) article.

1

- Position the insertion point to the right of the word, line, at the end of the second sentence in the second paragraph, before the period, and then press the SPACEBAR because you want a space between the end of the sentence and the citation.
- Click the Insert Citation button (References tab | Citations & Bibliography group) to display the Insert Citation menu (Figure D–25).

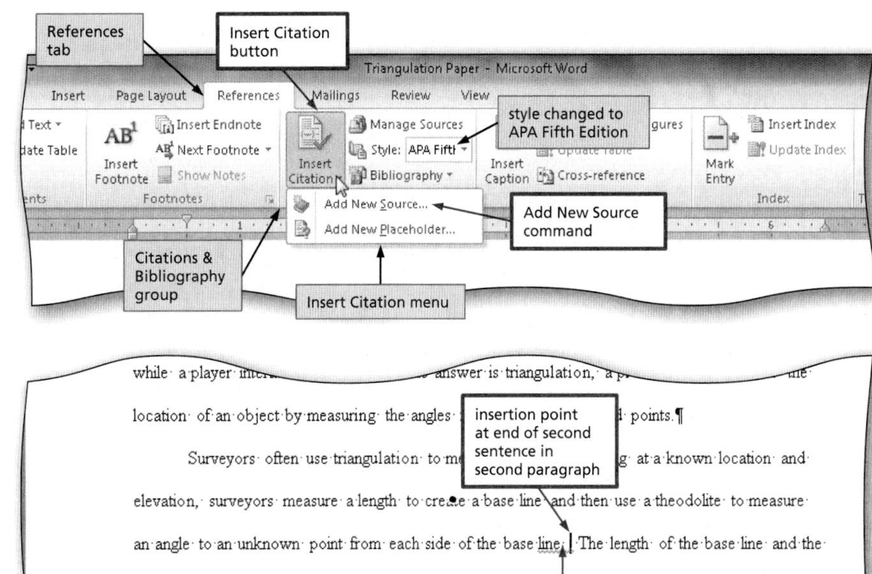

Figure D–25

2

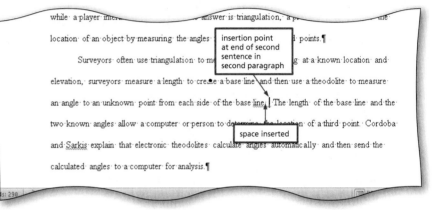

- Click Add New Source on the Insert Citation menu to display the Create Source dialog box (Figure D–26).

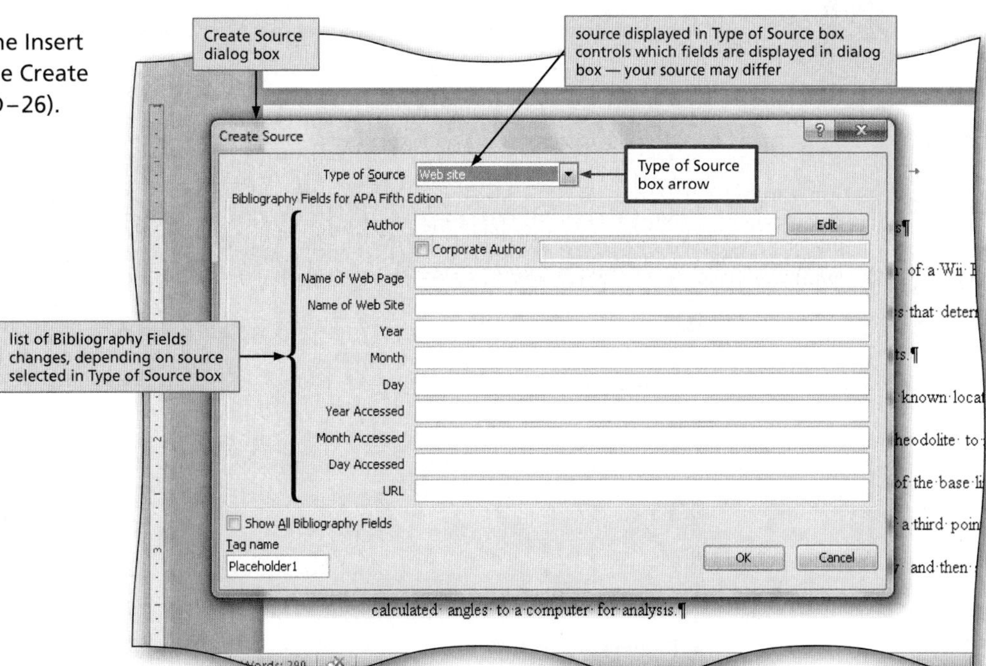

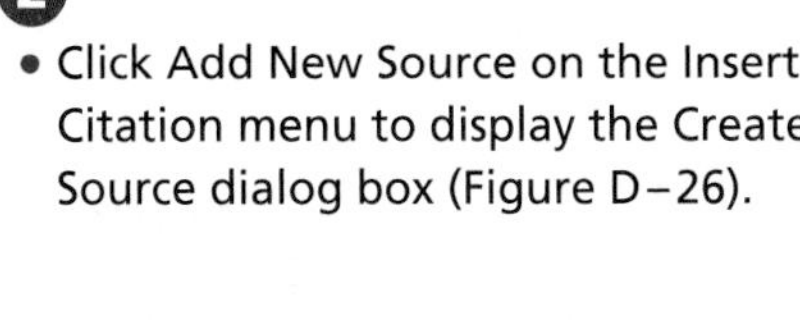

Figure D–26

3

- If necessary, click the Type of Source box arrow (Create Source dialog box) and then click Article in a Periodical, so that the list shows fields required for a magazine (periodical).
- Type `Jains, M.` in the Author text box.
- Type `How surveyors measure distance and calculate angles` in the Title text box.
- Type `Today's Modern Surveyor` in the Periodical Title text box.
- Type `2012` in the Year text box.
- Type `March` in the Month text box.
- Type `30-48` in the Pages text box (Figure D–27).

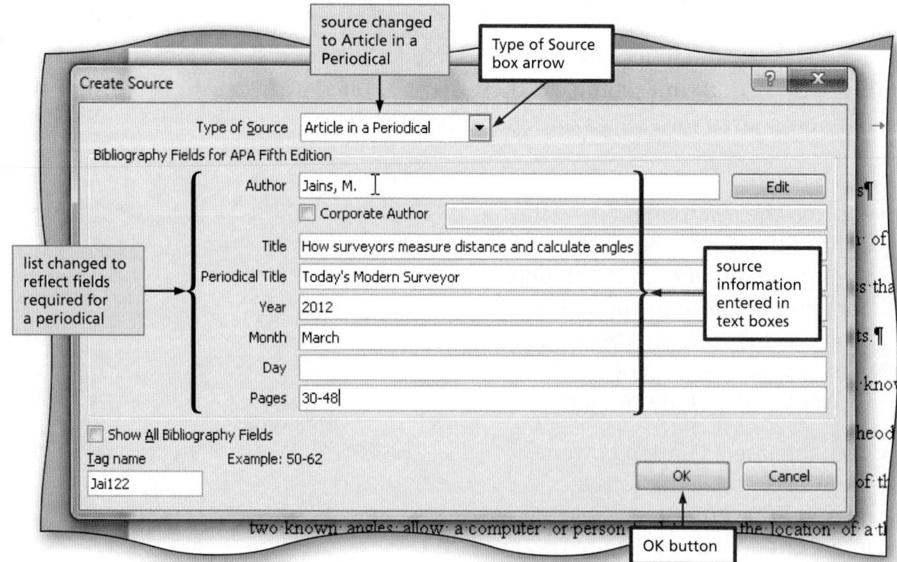

Figure D–27

4

- Click the OK button to close the dialog box, create the source, and insert the citation in the document at the location of the insertion point (Figure D–28).

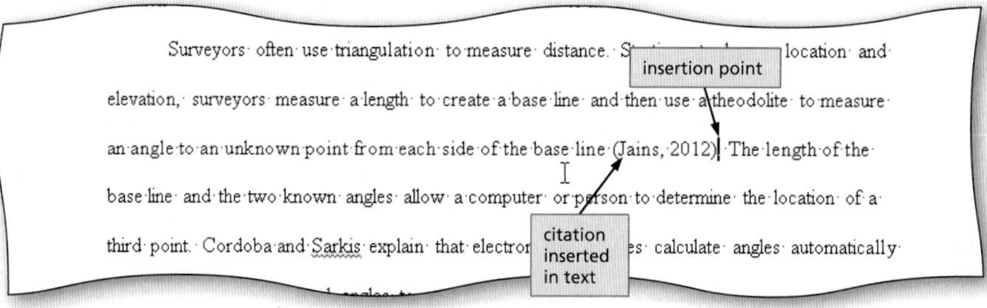

Figure D–28

To Insert Another Citation and Create Its Source

The following steps add a new source for a book.

1. Position the insertion point at the location for the citation (in this case, after the name, Sarkis, in the last sentence of the second paragraph) and then press the SPACEBAR (shown in Figure D–29).
2. Click the Insert Citation button (References tab | Citations & Bibliography group) to display the Insert Citation menu.
3. Click Add New Source on the Insert Citation menu to display the Create Source dialog box.
4. If necessary, click the Type of Source box arrow (Create Source dialog box) and then click Book, so that the list shows fields required for a Book.
5. Type `Cordoba, N.; Sarkis, K.` in the Author text box.
6. Type `The surveyor's theodolite formula` in the Title text box.
7. Type `2012` in the Year text box.

8 Type `Orlando` in the City text box.

9 Type `Orange County Press` in the Publisher text box (Figure D–29).

10 Click the OK button to close the dialog box, create the source, and insert the citation in the document at the location of the insertion point.

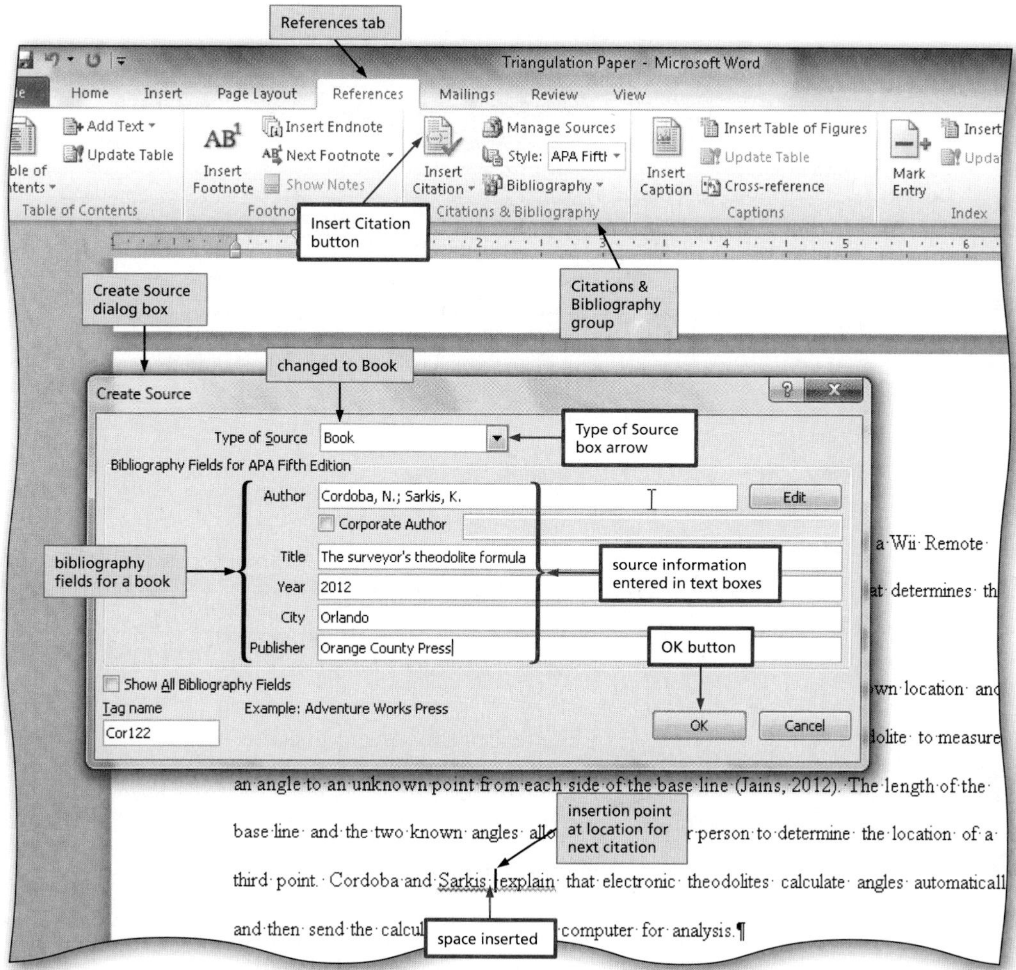

Figure D–29

To Edit a Citation

In the APA documentation style, if you reference the author's name in the text, you should not list it again in the citation. Instead, just list the publication year in the citation. To do this, instruct Word to suppress the author and title. The following steps edit the citation, suppressing the author and title but displaying the page numbers.

1

- Click somewhere in the citation to be edited, in this case somewhere in (Cordoba & Sarkis, 2012), which selects the citation and displays the Citation Options box arrow.
- Click the Citation Options box arrow to display the Citation Options menu (Figure D–30).

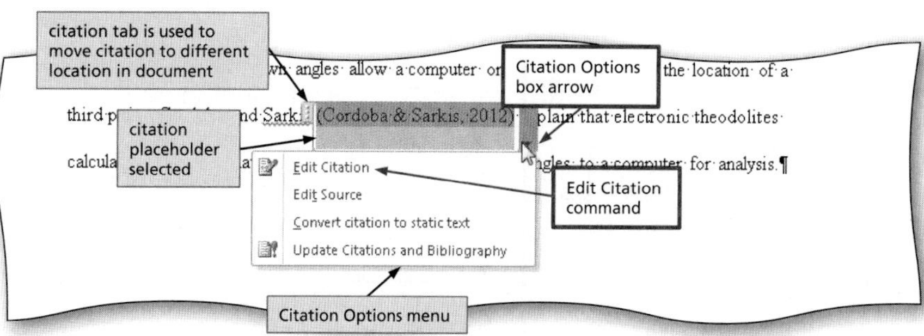

Figure D–30

- Click Edit Citation on the Citation Options menu to display the Edit Citation dialog box.
- In the Suppress area (Edit Citation dialog box), click the Author check box to place a check mark in it.
- In the Suppress area, click the Title check box to place a check mark in it (Figure D–31).

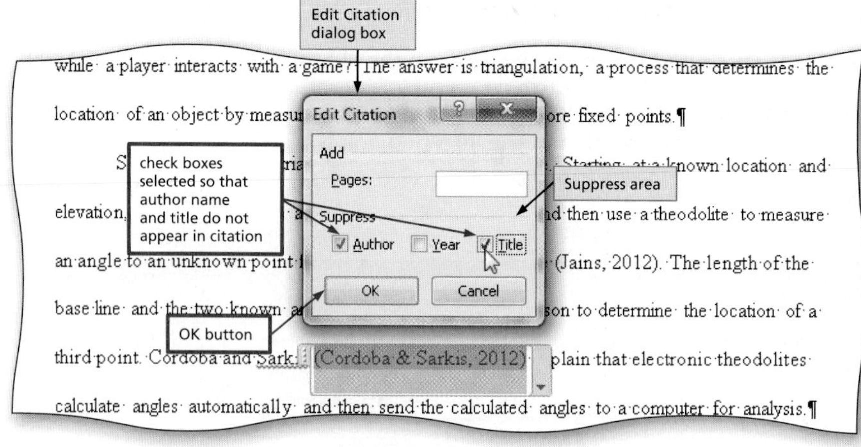

Figure D–31

- Click the OK button to close the dialog box, remove the author name from the citation, and suppress the title from showing.
- Press CTRL+END to move the insertion point to the end of the document, which also removes the selection from the citation (Figure D–32).

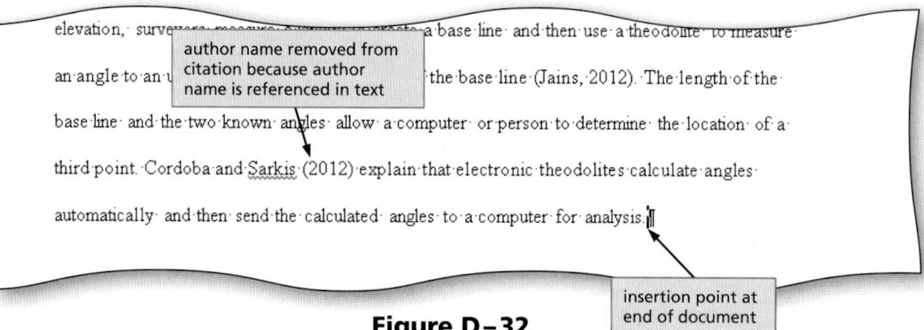

Figure D–32

To Type the Third and Fourth Paragraphs

The following steps continue typing text in the research paper.

1. With the insertion point positioned as shown in Figure D-32, press the ENTER key and then type the third paragraph of the research paper as shown in Figure D–33.
2. Press the ENTER key and then type the fourth paragraph of the research paper as shown in Figure D–33.

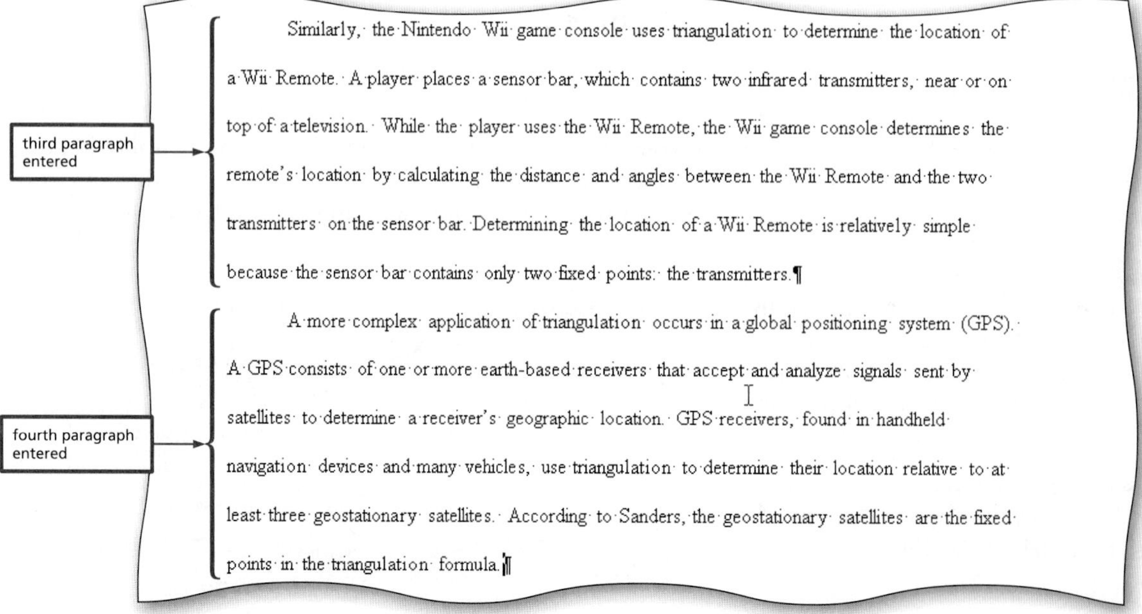

Figure D–33

To Insert Another Citation and Create Its Source

The following steps add a new source for a Web site.

1. Position the insertion point at the location for the citation (in this case, after the name, Sanders, in the last sentence of the fourth paragraph) and then press the SPACEBAR to insert a space before the comma.
2. Click the Insert Citation button (References tab | Citations & Bibliography group) to display the Insert Citation menu.
3. Click Add New Source on the Insert Citation menu to display the Create Source dialog box.
4. If necessary, click the Type of Source box arrow (Create Source dialog box) and then click Web site, so that the list shows fields required for a Web site.
5. Type **Sanders, G.** in the Author text box.
6. Type **Understanding satellites and global positioning systems** in the Name of Web Page text box.
7. Type **2012** in the Year text box.
8. Type **February** in the Month text box.
9. Type **27** in the Day text box.
10. Type **http://www.scsite.com** in the URL text box (Figure D–34).
11. Click the OK button to close the dialog box, create the source, and insert the citation in the document at the location of the insertion point.

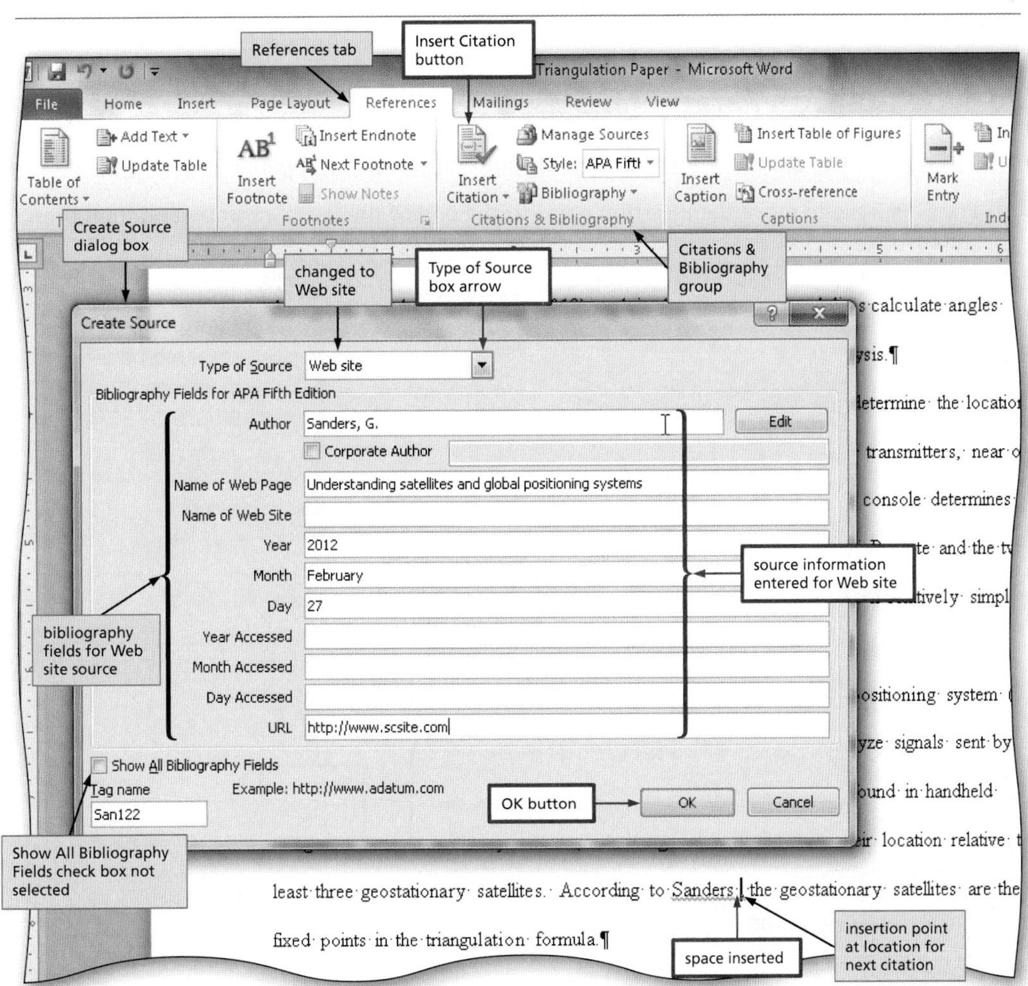

Figure D–34

To Edit a Citation

As previously mentioned, if you reference the author's name in the text, you should not list it again in the citation. Instead, just list the page number in the citation. The following steps edit the citation, suppressing the author but displaying the year.

1. If necessary, click somewhere in the citation to be edited, in this case somewhere in (Sanders, 2012), to select the citation and display the Citation Options box arrow.
2. Click the Citation Options box arrow to display the Citation Options menu.

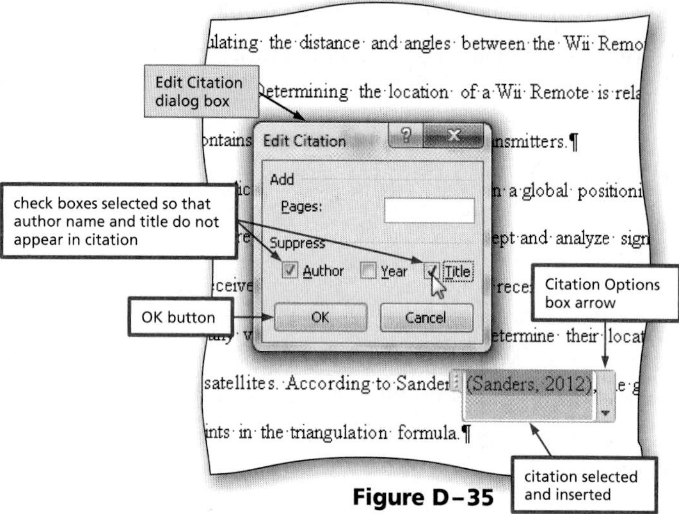

Figure D–35

3. Click Edit Citation on the Citation Options menu to display the Edit Citation dialog box.
4. In the Suppress area (Edit Citation dialog box), click the Author check box to place a check mark in it.
5. In the Suppress area, click the Title check box to place a check mark in it (Figure D–35).
6. Click the OK button to close the dialog box and remove the author name from the citation.

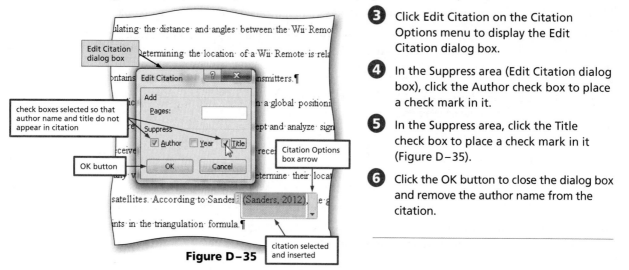

To Type the Fifth Paragraph

The following steps type the last paragraph in the research paper.

1. Press CTRL+END to move the insertion point to the end of the last paragraph and then press the ENTER key.
2. Type the fifth paragraph of the research paper as shown in Figure D–36.

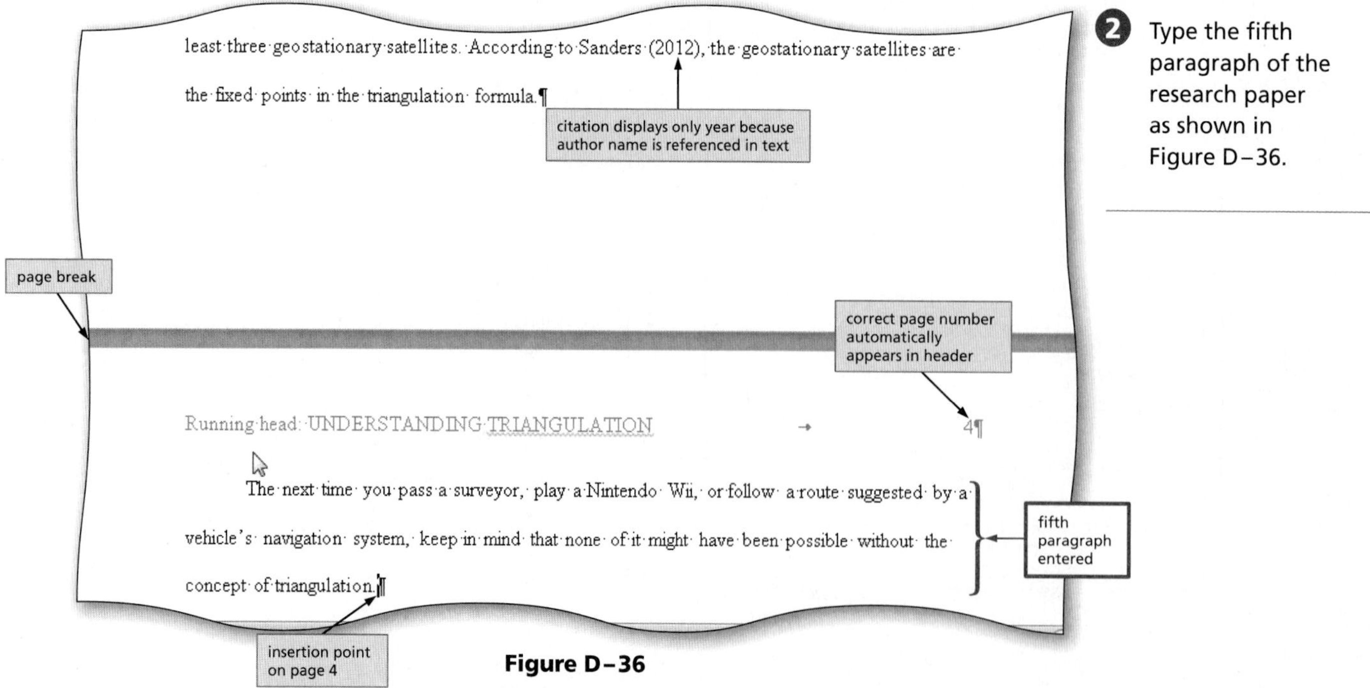

least three geostationary satellites. According to Sanders (2012), the geostationary satellites are the fixed points in the triangulation formula.
citation displays only year because author name is referenced in text
page break
correct page number automatically appears in header
Running head: UNDERSTANDING TRIANGULATION
4
The next time you pass a surveyor, play a Nintendo Wii, or follow a route suggested by a vehicle's navigation system, keep in mind that none of it might have been possible without the concept of triangulation.
fifth paragraph entered
insertion point on page 4

Figure D–36

To Save an Existing Document with the Same File Name

You have made several modifications to the research paper since you last saved it. Thus, you should save it again. The following step saves the document again.

1. Click the Save button on the Quick Access Toolbar to overwrite the previously saved file.

To Page Break Manually

The research paper text is complete. The next step is to create the references on a separate numbered page. The following steps insert a manual page break.

1. Click Insert on the Ribbon to display the Insert tab.
2. Click the Page Break button (Insert tab | Pages group) to insert a manual page break immediately to the left of the insertion point and position the insertion point immediately below the manual page break (shown in Figure D–37).

To Apply the Normal Style

The references title is to be centered between the margins of the paper. If you simply issue the Center command, the title will not be centered properly. Instead, it will be one-half inch to the right of the center point because earlier you set the first-line indent for paragraphs to one-half inch from the left margin.

So that you can properly center the title of the reference page, you will apply the Normal style to the location of the insertion point. Recall that you modified the Normal style for this document to 12-point Times New Roman with double-spaced, left-aligned paragraphs that have no space after the paragraphs.

To apply a style to a paragraph, first position the insertion point in the paragraph and then apply the style. The following step applies the modified Normal style to the location of the insertion point.

1.
- Click Home on the Ribbon to display the Home tab.
- With the insertion point on the paragraph mark at the top of page 5, as shown in Figure D–37, even if Normal is selected, click Normal in the Quick Style gallery (Home tab | Styles group) to apply the selected style to the paragraph containing the insertion point (Figure D–37).

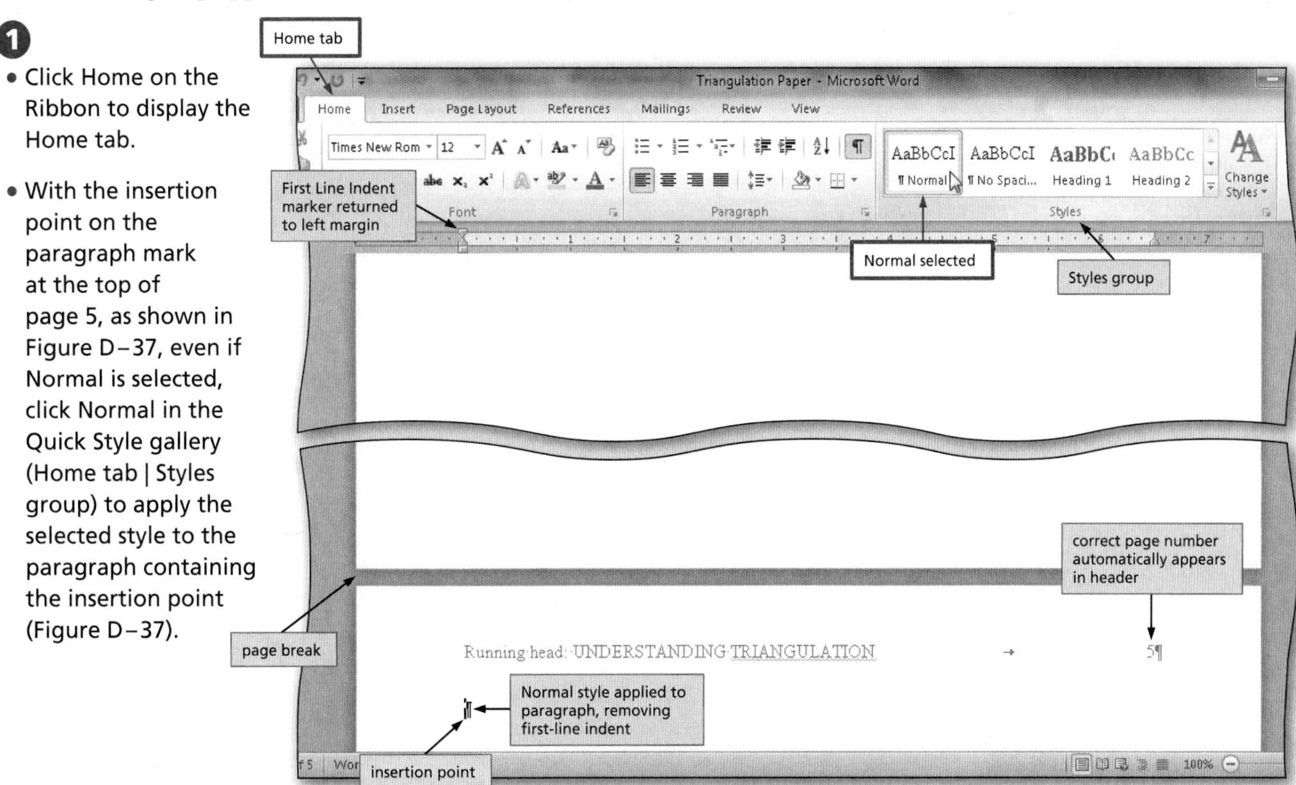

Figure D–37

To Enter the References Page Title

The next step is to enter the title, References, centered between the margins of the paper. The following steps use shortcut keys to format the title.

1. Press CTRL+E to center the paragraph mark.
2. Type `References` as the title.
3. Press the ENTER key.
4. Press CTRL+L to left-align the paragraph mark (shown in Figure D–38).

To Create the Bibliographical List

While typing the research paper, you created several citations and their sources. Word can format the list of sources and alphabetize them in a **bibliographical list**, which spares you the task of looking up style guidelines. That is, Word will create a bibliographical list with each element of the source placed in its correct position with proper punctuation, according to the specified style. For example, in this research paper, the book source will list, in this order, the author name(s), publication year, book title, publisher city, and publishing company name with the book title italicized and the correct punctuation between each element according to the specified APA documentation style. The following steps create an APA-styled bibliographical list from the sources previously entered.

1
- Click References on the Ribbon to display the References tab.
- With the insertion point positioned as shown in Figure D–38, click the Bibliography button (References tab | Citations & Bibliography group) to display the Bibliography gallery (Figure D–38).

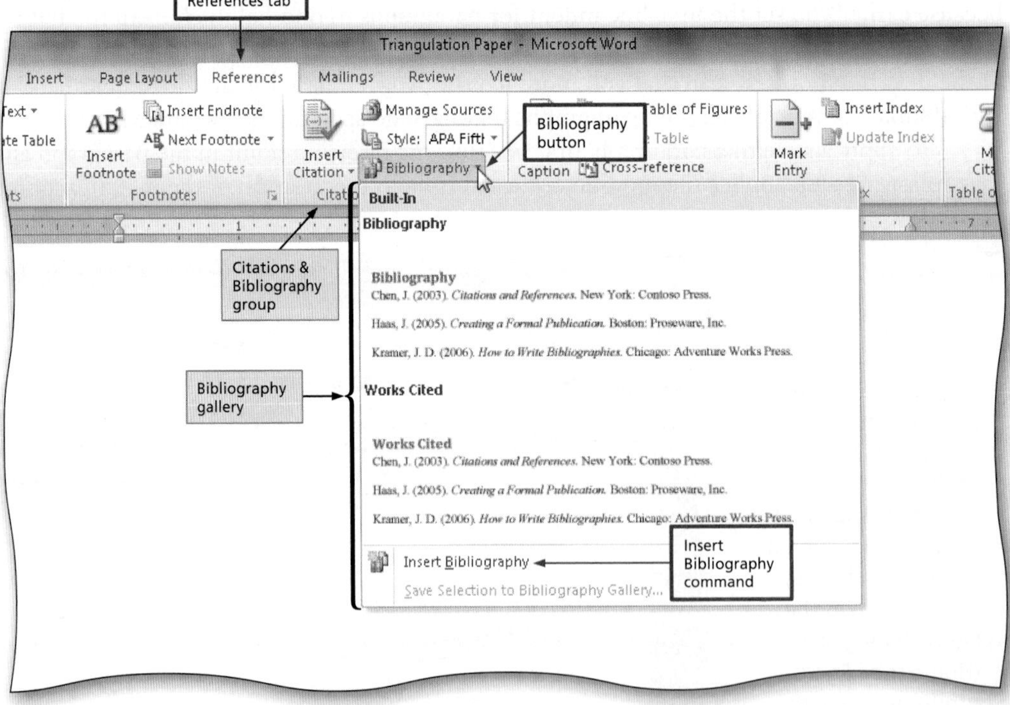

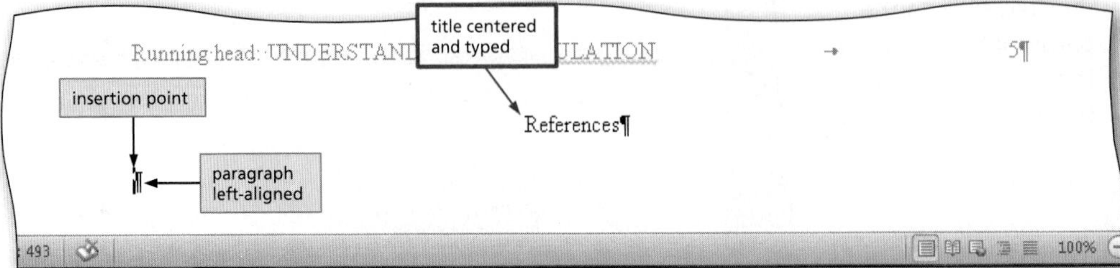

Figure D–38

2

- Click Insert Bibliography in the Bibliography gallery to insert a list of sources at the location of the insertion point.
- If necessary, scroll to display the entire list of sources in the document window (Figure D–39).

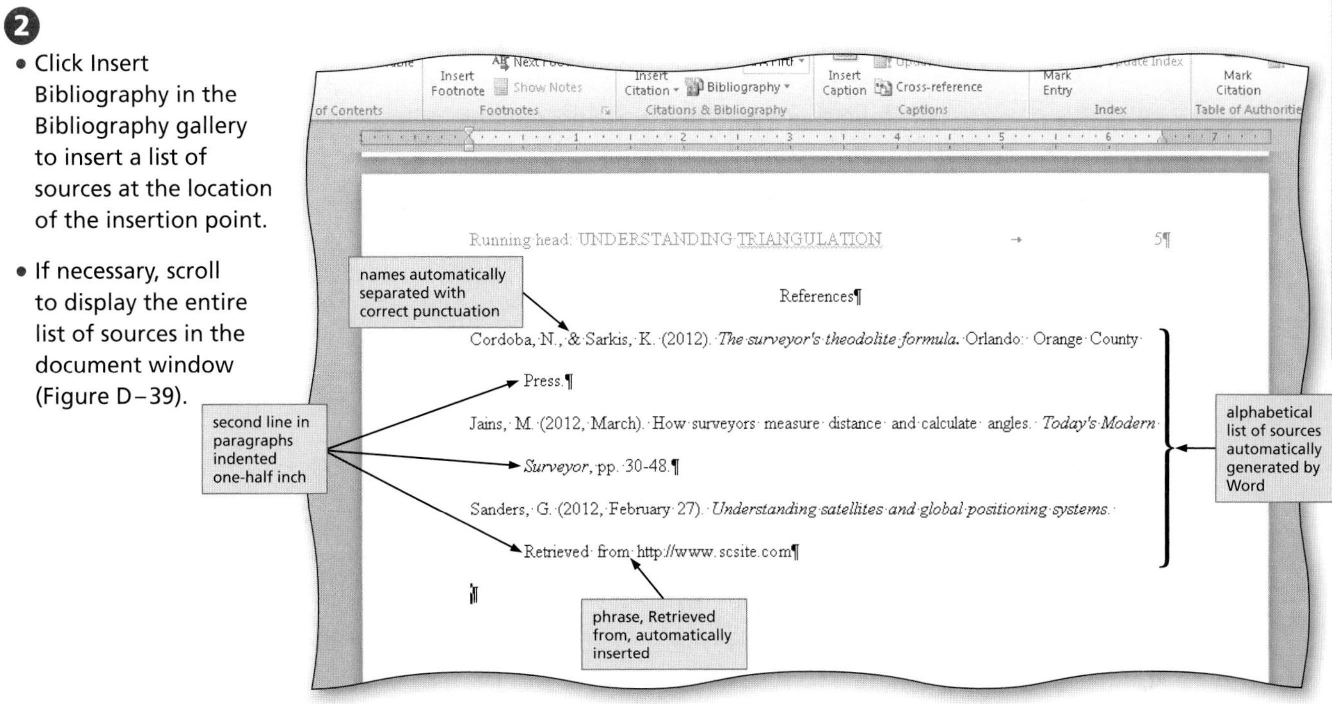

Figure D–39

To Convert a Field to Regular Text

Word may use an earlier version of the APA documentation style to format the bibliography. The latest guidelines for the APA documentation style, for example, state that the page number in magazine articles should not be preceded with the pp. notation. If you edit the bibliography, Word automatically will change it back to the Bibliography style's predetermined text and formats when the bibliography field is updated. To preserve modifications you make to the format of the bibliography, you can convert the bibliography field to regular text. Keep in mind, though, once you convert the field to regular text, it no longer is a field that can be updated. The following step converts a field to regular text.

1

- Click somewhere in the field to select it, in this case, somewhere in the bibliography (Figure D–40).

2

- Press CTRL+SHIFT+F9 to convert the selected field to regular text.
- Click anywhere in the document to remove the selection from the text.

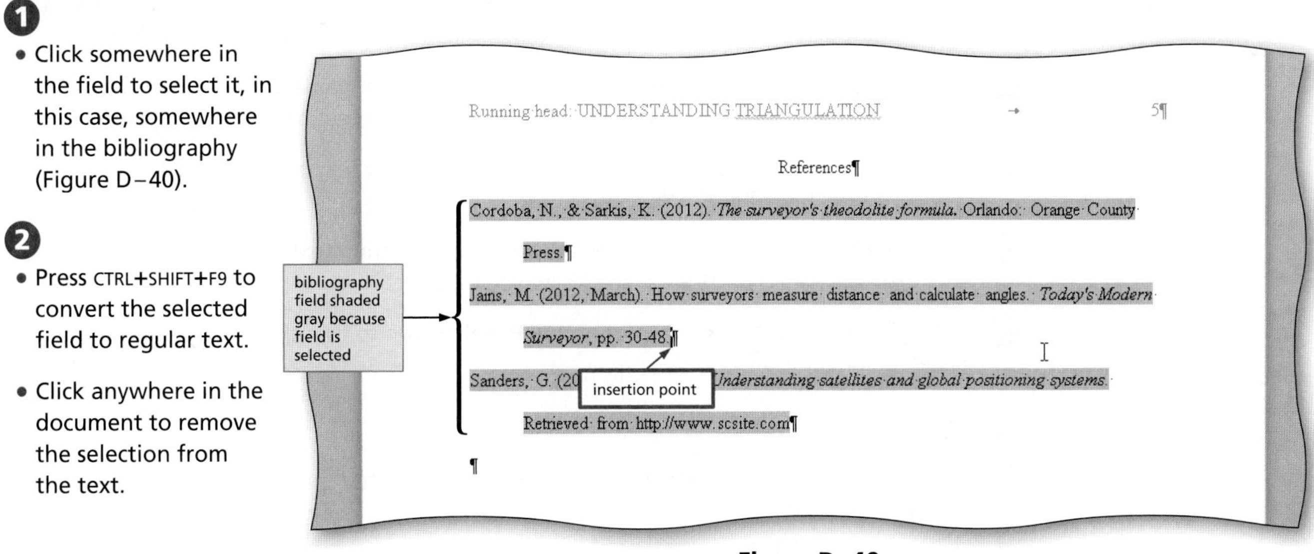

Figure D–40

To Format the References as Specified by the Latest APA Documentation Style

The following steps remove the pp. notation in front of the page number, as specified by the latest APA guidelines.

1. Drag through the pp. notation in the magazine entry to select it.
2. Press the DELETE key to delete the selected text (Figure D–41).

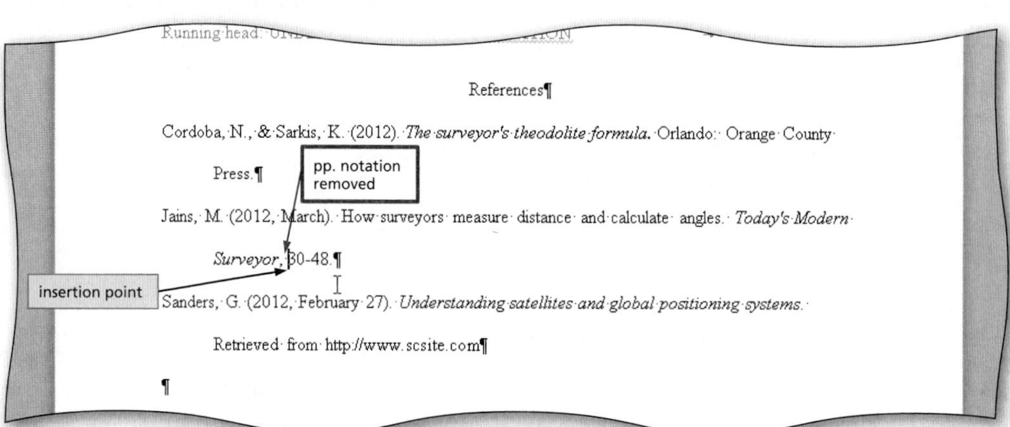

Figure D–41

To Change Document Properties

Before saving the research paper again, you will add your name, course information, and some keywords as document properties. The following steps use the Document Information Panel to change document properties.

1. Click File on the Ribbon to open the Backstage view and, if necessary, select the Info tab.
2. Click the Properties button in the right pane of the Info gallery to display the Properties menu and then click Show Document Panel on the Properties menu to close the Backstage view and display the Document Information Panel in the Word document window.
3. Click the Author text box, if necessary, and then type your name as the Author property. If a name already is displayed in the Author text box, delete it before typing your name.
4. Click the Subject text box, if necessary delete any existing text, and then type your course and section as the Subject property.
5. Click the Keywords text box, if necessary delete any existing text, and then type **`surveyor, Wii, GPS`** as the Keywords property.
6. Click the Close the Document Information Panel button so that the Document Information Panel no longer is displayed.

To Save an Existing Document, Print the Document, and Quit Word

The document now is complete. You should save the research paper again before quitting Word. The next steps save the document again and then quit Word.

1. Click the Save button on the Quick Access Toolbar to overwrite the previously saved file.
2. Click File on the Ribbon to open the Backstage view and then click the Print tab in the Backstage view to display the Print gallery.
3. Verify the printer name that appears on the Printer Status button will print a hard copy of the document. If necessary, click the Printer Status button to display a list of available printer options and then click the desired printer to change the currently selected printer.
4. Click the Print button in the Print gallery to print the research paper on the currently selected printer (shown in Figure D–1 on page APP 14).
5. If you have one Word document open, click the Close button on the right side of the title bar to close the document and quit Word; or if you have multiple Word documents open, click File on the Ribbon to open the Backstage view and then click Exit in the Backstage view to close all open documents and quit Word.
6. If a Microsoft Word dialog box appears, click the Save button to save any changes made to the document since the last save.

Appendix Summary

In this appendix, you have learned how to create the same research paper as the one shown in Chapter 2, except you used the APA documentation style instead of the MLA documentation style. This appendix presented only the steps required to create this research paper.

Learn It Online

Test your knowledge of chapter content and key terms.

Instructions: To complete the Learn It Online exercises, start your browser, click the Address bar, and then enter the Web address **scsite.com/wd2010/learn**. When the Word 2010 Learn It Online page is displayed, click the link for the exercise you want to complete and then read the instructions.

Chapter Reinforcement TF, MC, and SA

A series of true/false, multiple choice, and short answer questions that test your knowledge of the chapter content.

Flash Cards

An interactive learning environment where you identify chapter key terms associated with displayed definitions.

Practice Test

A series of multiple choice questions that test your knowledge of chapter content and key terms.

Who Wants To Be a Computer Genius?

An interactive game that challenges your knowledge of chapter content in the style of a television quiz show.

Wheel of Terms

An interactive game that challenges your knowledge of chapter key terms in the style of the television show *Wheel of Fortune.*

Crossword Puzzle Challenge

A crossword puzzle that challenges your knowledge of key terms presented in the chapter.

STUDENT ASSIGNMENTS

Apply Your Knowledge

Reinforce the skills and apply the concepts you learned in Chapter 2.

Revising Text and Paragraphs in a Document

Note: This exercise covers tasks presented in Chapter 2 and assumes you completed the Chapter 2 project. To complete this assignment, you will be required to use the Data Files for Students. See the inside back cover of this book for instructions on downloading the Data Files for Students, or contact your instructor for information about accessing the required files.

Instructions: Start Word. Open the document, Apply D-1 Space Paragraph Draft, from the Data Files for Students. The document you open contains a paragraph of text. You are to revise the document as follows: move a word, move another word and change the format of the moved word, change paragraph indentation, change line spacing, find all occurrences of a word, replace all occurrences of a word with another word, locate a synonym, and edit the header.

Perform the following tasks:

1. Copy the word, exploration, from the first sentence and paste it in the last sentence after the word, space, so that it is the eighth word in the sentence.
2. Select the underlined word, safe, in the paragraph. Use drag-and-drop editing to move the selected word, safe, so that it is before the word, mission, in the same sentence. Click the Paste Options button that displays to the right of the moved word, safe. Remove the underline format from the moved sentence by clicking the Keep Text Only button on the Paste Options menu.
3. Display the ruler, if necessary. Use the ruler to indent the first line of the paragraph one-half inch.
4. Change the line spacing of the paragraph to double.
5. Use the Navigation Pane to find all occurrences of the word, sensors. How many are there?
6. Use the Find and Replace dialog box to replace all occurrences of the word, issues, with the word, problems. How many replacements were made?
7. Use Word to find the word, height. Use Word's thesaurus to change the word, height, to the word, altitude.
8. Switch to the header so that you can edit it. In the first line of the header, change the word, Draft, to the word, Modified, so that it reads: Space Paragraph Modified.
9. In the second line of the header, insert the page number (with no formatting) one space after the word, Page.
10. Change the alignment of both lines of text in the header from left-aligned to right-aligned. Switch back to the document text.
11. Change the document properties, as specified by your instructor.
12. Click File on the Ribbon and then click Save As. Save the document using the file name, Apply D-1 Space Paragraph Modified.
13. Print the document properties and then print the revised document, shown in Figure D–42.
14. Use the Research task pane to look up the definition of the word, NASA, in the paragraph. Handwrite the definition of the word on your printout.
15. Change the Search for box to All Research Sites. Print an article from one of the sites.
16. Display the Research Options dialog box and, on your printout, handwrite the currently active Reference Books, Research Sites, and Business and Financial Sites. If your instructor approves, activate one of the services.

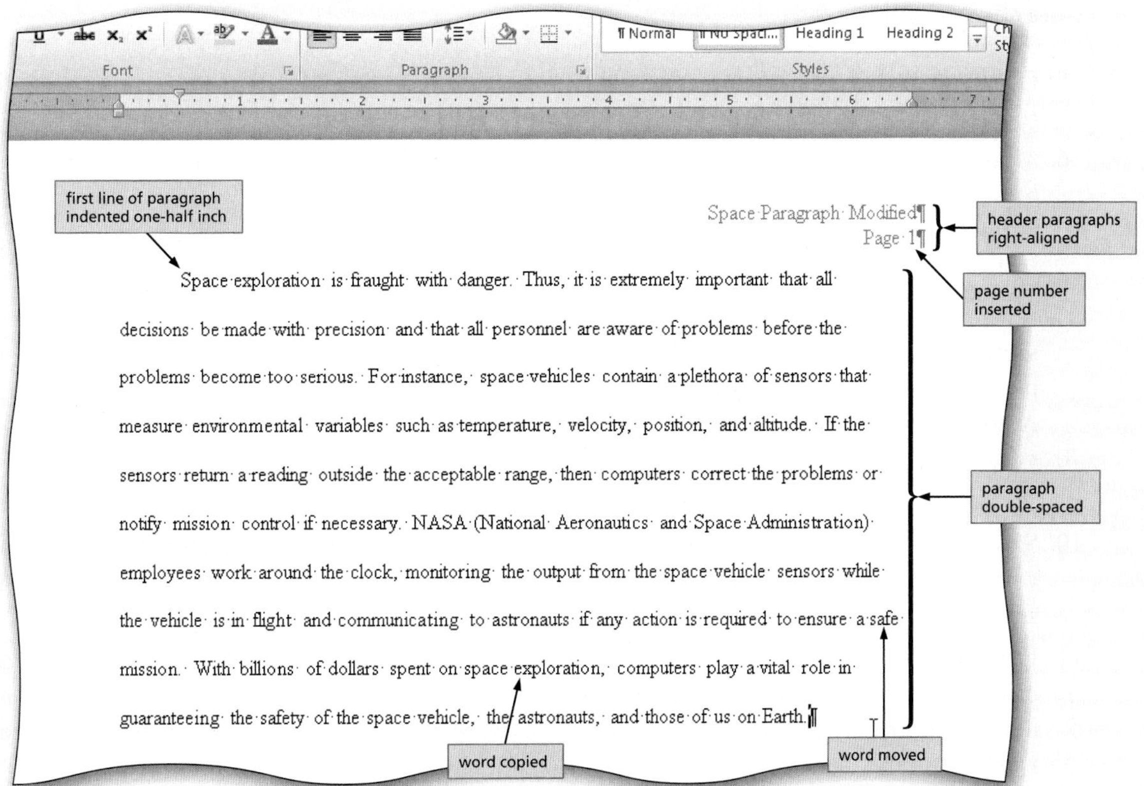

Figure D–42

Extend Your Knowledge

Extend the skills you learned in Chapter 2 and Appendix D, and experiment with new skills. You may need to use Help to complete the assignment.

Working with References and Proofing Tools

Note: To complete this assignment, you will be required to use the Data Files for Students. See the inside back cover of this book for instructions on downloading the Data Files for Students, or contact your instructor for information about accessing the required files.

Instructions: Start Word. Open the document, Extend D-1 Digital Camera Paper Draft, from the Data Files for Students. You will add a footnote, convert the footnote to an endnote, modify the Endnote Text style, use the thesaurus, and translate the document to another language.

Perform the following tasks:

1. Use Help to learn more about footers, footnotes and endnotes, bibliography styles, AutoCorrect, and the Mini Translator.
2. Delete the footer from the document.
3. Determine the APA guidelines for footnotes. Insert the following footnote at an appropriate place in the research paper: For instance, Cass states that digital cameras can last well beyond five years if maintained properly, so consider this a longer-term investment that will create memories lasting you a lifetime.
4. Insert this second footnote at an appropriate place in the research paper: For instance, Adams states that you may be able to crop photos, change the brightness, or remove red eye effects.

Continued >

STUDENT ASSIGNMENTS

Extend Your Knowledge *continued*

5. Convert the footnotes to endnotes, so that the footnotes are on a separate numbered page after the references. Place the title, Footnotes, at the top of the page.
6. Modify the Endnote Text style to 12-point Times New Roman font, double-spaced text with a hanging indent.
7. Use the Find and Replace dialog box to find the word, small, in the document and then replace it with a word of your choice.
8. Add an AutoCorrect entry that replaces the word, camora, with the word, camera. Add this sentence, A field camora usually is more than sufficient for most users., to the end of the second paragraph, misspelling the word camera as written to test the AutoCorrect entry. Delete the AutoCorrect entry just added that replaces camora with the word, camera.
9. Display readability statistics. What are the Flesch-Kincaid Grade Level, the Flesch Reading Ease score, and the percent of passive sentences?
10. Save the document with a new file name and then print it. On the printout, write the number of words, characters without spaces, characters with spaces, paragraphs, and lines in the document. Be sure to include footnote text in the statistics.
11. If you have an Internet connection, translate the research paper into a language of your choice using the Translate button (Review tab | Language group). Figure D–43 shows a sample translated document. Print the translated document. Use the Mini Translator to hear how to pronounce three words in your paper.

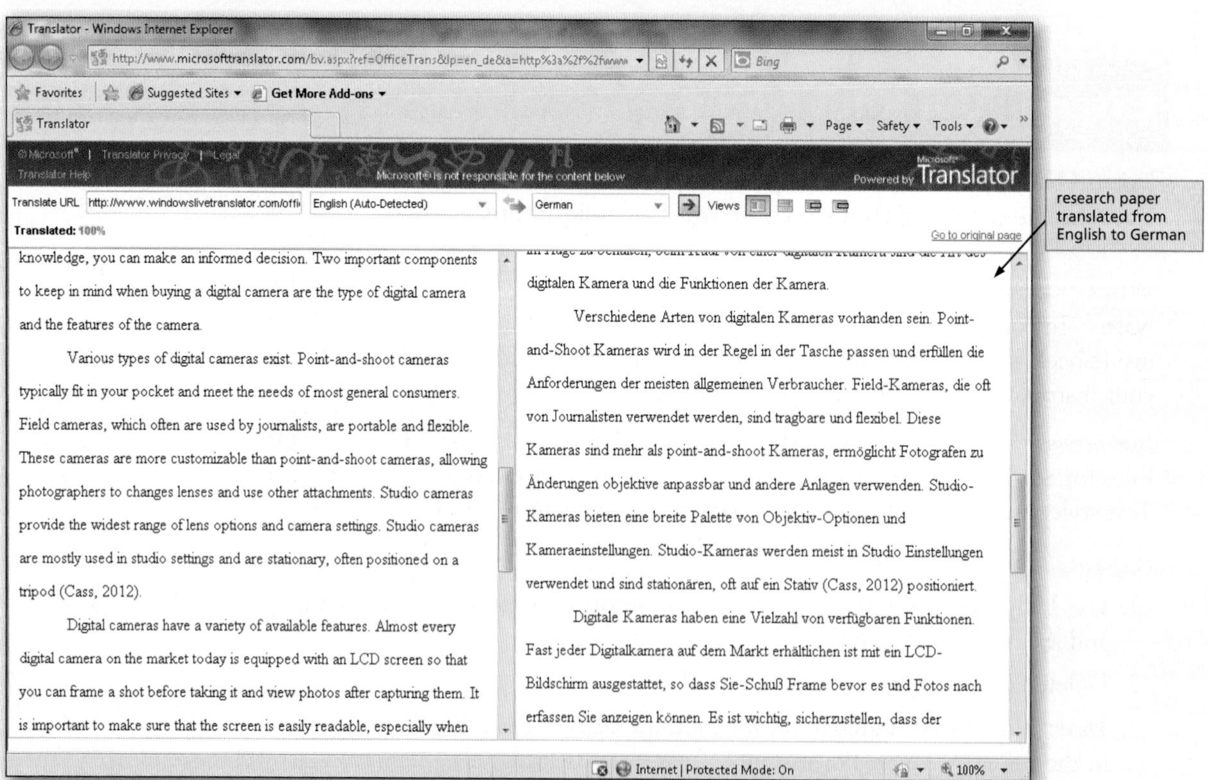

Figure D–43

Make It Right

Analyze a document and correct all errors and/or improve the design.

Inserting Missing Elements in an APA-Styled Research Paper

Note: To complete this assignment, you will be required to use the Data Files for Students. See the inside back cover of this book for instructions on downloading the Data Files for Students, or contact your instructor for information about accessing the required files.

Instructions: Start Word. Open the document, Make It Right D-1 Biometrics Paper Draft, from the Data Files for Students. The document is a research paper that is missing several elements. You are to insert these missing elements, all formatted according to the APA documentation style: title page, header with a running head and page number, manual page breaks, paper title, citations, and source information for the citations.

Perform the following tasks:

1. Insert a header with a running head (Running head: BIOMETRIC TECHNOLOGY) and a page number, formatted according to the APA documentation style.
2. Insert a title page that contains the header, along with the complete paper title (Biometric Technology: No Two the Same), author name (use your name), and school affiliation (use your school). If necessary, insert a manual page break after the end of the title page.
3. On the Abstract page, center the title and then remove the first-line indent from the paragraph below the title.
4. On the first page of the body of the paper, type and center the research paper title above the first paragraph.
5. The Jenkins placeholder (tag name) is missing its source information (Figure D–44). Use the following source information to edit the source: magazine article titled "Fingerprint Readers" written by A. D. Jenkins and M. K. Weavers, magazine name is *Security Today*, publication date is February 2012, article is on pages 55 – 60. The citation should display the author name and publication year.
6. Modify the source of the book authored by Carolina Doe, so that the publisher city is Chicago instead of Dallas.
7. Use the Navigation Pane to display page 5. Use Word to insert the bibliographical list (bibliography). Convert the works cited to regular text. Remove the pp. notation from the magazine entry.
8. Change the document properties, as specified by your instructor. Save the revised document with the file name, Make It Right D-1 Biometrics Paper Modified, and then submit it in the format specified by your instructor.

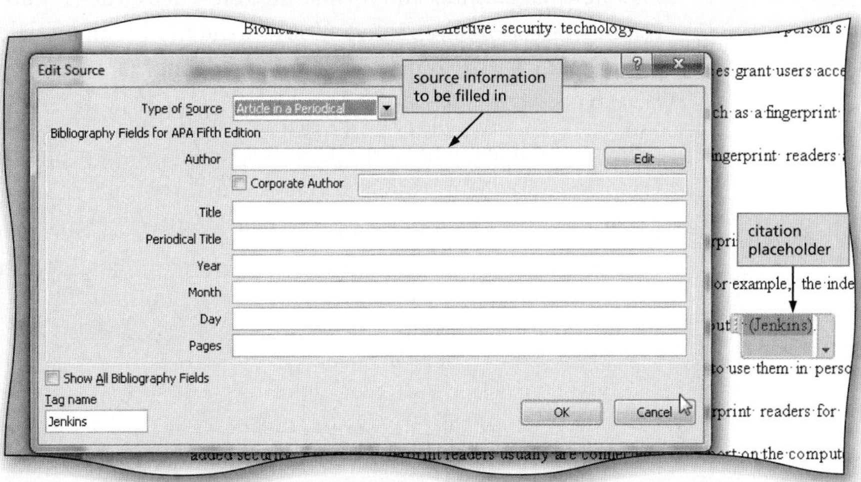

Figure D–44

In the Lab

Design and/or create a document using the guidelines, concepts, and skills presented in this appendix. Labs are listed in order of increasing difficulty.

Lab 1: Preparing a Short Research Paper

Problem: You are a college student currently enrolled in an introductory business class. Your assignment is to prepare a short research paper (275 – 300 words) about video or computer games. The requirements are that the paper be presented according to the APA documentation style and have three references. One of the three references must be from the Web. You prepare the paper shown in Figure D–45 on pages APP 45 – APP 47, which discusses game controllers.

Instructions: Perform the following tasks:

1. Start Word. If necessary, display formatting marks on the screen.
2. Modify the Normal style to 12-point Times New Roman font.
3. Adjust line spacing to double.
4. Remove space below (after) paragraphs.
5. Update the Normal style to reflect the adjusted line and paragraph spacing.
6. Create a header that includes the running head (Running head: GAME CONTROLLERS) at the left margin and the page number at the right margin.
7. Insert the title page as shown in Figure D–45a, ensuring it includes a header, along with the complete paper title (Game Controllers: Enriching the Gaming Experience), author name, and school affiliation. Insert a manual page break after the last line on the title page.
8. Type the Abstract as shown in Figure D–45b. Insert a manual page break after the last line of the abstract.
9. Set a first-line indent to one-half inch for paragraphs in the body of the research paper.
10. Type the research paper as shown in Figure D–45c on page APP 46. Change the bibliography style to APA. As you insert citations, enter their source information (shown in Figure D–45d on page APP 47). If necessary, edit the citations so that they appear as shown in Figure D–45c.
11. At the end of the research paper text, insert a manual page break so that the References page begins on a new page. Enter and format the references title (Figure D–45d). Use Word to insert the references list (bibliography). Convert the bibliography field to text. Remove the pp. notation from the page numbers in the magazine article entry (shown in Figure D–45d).
12. Check the spelling and grammar of the paper at once.
13. Change the document properties, as specified by your instructor. Save the document using Lab D-1 Game Controllers Paper as the file name.
14. Print the research paper. Handwrite the number of words, paragraphs, and characters in the research paper above the title of your printed research paper.

Running head: GAME CONTROLLERS 1

Game Controllers: Enriching the Gaming Experience

Harley Kimble

Longherst University

Figure D–45 (a) Page 1

Running head: GAME CONTROLLERS 2

Abstract

Video games and computer games use a game controller as the input device that directs movements and actions of on-screen objects. Two commonly used game controllers are gamepads and motion-sensing game controllers. A gamepad is held by the player with both hands, allowing the player to control the movement or actions of the objects in the video or computer games. Motion-sensing game controllers allow the user to guide on-screen elements or trigger events by moving a handheld input device in predetermined directions through the air. Game controllers not only enrich the gaming experience but also aid in the movements and actions of players.

Figure D–45 (b) Page 2

Continued >

In the Lab *continued*

Running head: GAME CONTROLLERS 3

Game Controllers: Enriching the Gaming Experience

Video games and computer games use a game controller as the input device that directs movements and actions of on-screen objects. Two commonly used game controllers are gamepads and motion-sensing game controllers (Joyce, 2012). Game controllers not only enrich the gaming experience but also aid in the movements and actions of players.

A gamepad is held by the player with both hands, allowing the player to control the movement or actions of the objects in the video or computer games. Players press buttons on the gamepad, often with their thumbs, to carry out actions. Some gamepads have swiveling sticks that also can trigger events during game play (Cortez & Matthews, 2012). Some gamepads include wireless capabilities; others connect via a cable directly to the game console or a personal computer.

Motion-sensing game controllers allow the user to guide on-screen elements or trigger events by moving a handheld input device in predetermined directions through the air. These controllers communicate with a game console or personal computer via wired or wireless technology. A variety of games, from sports to simulations, use motion-sensing game controllers. Some of these controllers, such as baseball bats and golf clubs, are designed for only one specific kind of game; others are general purpose. A popular general-purpose, motion-sensing game controller is Nintendo's Wii Remote. Shaped like a television remote control and operated with one hand, the Wii Remote uses Bluetooth wireless technology to communicate with the Wii game console (Bloom, 2012).

Game controllers are used primarily to direct movement and actions of on-screen objects. Two popular types are gamepads and motion-sensing game controllers. Games become more enjoyable every day with the use of new and exciting game controllers. What will be next?

Figure D–45 (c) Page 3

References

Bloom, J. (2012). *The gaming experience.* New York: Buffalo Works Press.

Cortez, D., & Matthews, M. (2012, January). Today's game controllers. *Gaming, Gaming, Gaming*, 12-34.

Joyce, A. (2012, February 15). *What gamers want.* Retrieved from http://www.scsite.com

Figure D–45 (d) Page 4

STUDENT ASSIGNMENTS

In the Lab

Lab 2: Preparing a Research Paper

Problem: You are a college student enrolled in an introductory English class. Your assignment is to prepare a short research paper in any area of interest to you. The requirements are that the paper be presented according to the APA documentation style and have three references. One of the three references must be from the Internet. You prepare a paper about trends in agriculture. The abstract and body of the research paper, the second and third pages, are shown in Figure D–46.

Running head: COMPUTERS IN AGRICULTURE 2

Abstract

Although people have worked in agriculture for more than 10,000 years, advances in technology assist with maintaining and protecting land, crops, and animals. The demand to keep food prices affordable encourages those working in the agriculture industry to operate as efficiently as possible. Many farmers use technology on a daily basis to regulate soil moisture and to keep their crops pest free. In addition to keeping the soil moist and reducing maintenance costs, computers also can utilize sensors to analyze the condition of crops in the field and determine whether pests or diseases are affecting the crops. With technology, farming can be much more convenient and efficient.

Figure D–46 (a) Abstract

Instructions: Perform the following tasks:

1. Start Word. Modify the Normal style to 12-point Times New Roman font. Adjust line spacing to double and remove space below (after) paragraphs. Update the Normal style to include the adjusted line and paragraph spacing. Create a header that includes the running head (Running head: COMPUTERS IN AGRICULTURE) at the left margin and the page number at the right margin. Create an appropriate title page (page 1). Create the abstract (page 2) as shown in Figure D–46a. Center and type the title. Set a first-line indent for paragraphs in the body of the research paper.
2. Type the research paper (page 3) as shown in Figure D–46b. Change the bibliography style to APA. As you insert citations, use the source information on page APP 50, making certain you enter them properly formatted according to the APA guidelines.

Computers in Agriculture: Farming on a New Level

Although people have worked in agriculture for more than 10,000 years, advances in technology assist with maintaining and protecting land, crops, and animals. The demand to keep food prices affordable encourages those working in the agriculture industry to operate as efficiently as possible (Newman & Ruiz, 2012).

Almost all people and companies in this industry have many acres of land they must maintain, and it is not always feasible for farmers to take frequent trips around the property to perform basic tasks such as watering soil in the absence of rain. The number of people-hours required to water soil manually on several thousand acres of land might result in businesses spending thousands of dollars in labor and utility costs. If the irrigation process is automated, sensors detect how much rain has fallen recently, as well as whether the soil is in need of watering. According to Barton (2012), the sensors then send this data to a computer that processes it and decides when and how much to water. Brewster (2012) also points out that many automated home irrigation systems are programmable and use rain sensors.

In addition to keeping the soil moist and reducing maintenance costs, computers also can utilize sensors to analyze the condition of crops in the field and determine whether pests or diseases are affecting the crops. If sensors detect pests and/or diseases, computers send a notification to the appropriate individual to take corrective action. In some cases, according to Brewster (2012), the discovery of pests might trigger a pesticide to discharge in the affected area automatically.

Many farmers use technology on a daily basis to regulate soil moisture and to keep their crops pest free. With technology, farming can be much more convenient and efficient.

Figure D–46 (b) Body of Research Paper

Continued >

In the Lab *continued*

a. Type of Source: Article in a Periodical
   Author: B. Barton
   Title: Computers in Agriculture
   Periodical Title: Agriculture Today and Tomorrow
   Year: 2012
   Month: Feb.
   Pages: 53 – 86
b. Type of Source: Book
   Authors: A. Newman and C. Ruiz
   Title: The Agricultural Industry Today
   Year: 2012
   City: New York
   Publisher: Alabama Press
c. Type of Source: Web site
   Author: L. Brewster
   Name of Web page: Agriculture: Expanding and Growing
   Year: 2012
   Month: January
   Day: 3
   Web site: http://www.scsite.com

3. At the end of the research paper text, press the ENTER key once and insert a manual page break so that the References page begins on a new page (page 4). Enter and format the references title. Use Word to insert the bibliographical list. Convert the bibliography field to text. Remove the pp. notation from the page numbers in the magazine article entry.
4. Check the spelling and grammar of the paper.
5. Save the document using Lab D-2 Agriculture Paper as the file name.
6. Print the research paper. Handwrite the number of words in the research paper above the title of your printed research paper.

In the Lab

Lab 3: Composing a Research Paper from Notes

Problem: You have drafted the notes shown in Figure D–47. Your assignment is to prepare a short research paper from these notes.

Instructions: Perform the following tasks:

1. Start Word. Review the notes in Figure D–47 and then rearrange and reword them. Embellish the paper as you deem necessary. Present the paper according to the APA documentation style. Create an AutoCorrect entry that automatically corrects the spelling of the misspelled word, digtal, to the correct spelling, digital. Be sure to add a title page and abstract page. Enter citations and their sources as shown, ensuring they are formatted according to the APA documentation style. Create the references page (bibliography) from the listed sources. Convert the bibliography field to text. Remove the pp. notation from the page numbers in the magazine article entry.

2. If necessary, set the default dictionary. Add the word, Flickr, to the dictionary. Check the spelling and grammar of the paper.
3. Use the Research task pane to look up a definition of a word in the paper. Copy and insert the definition into the document. Be sure to quote the definition and cite the source.
4. Save the document using Lab D-3 Cloud Storage Paper as the file name. Print the research paper. Handwrite the number of words, including the footnotes, in the research paper above the title of the printed research paper.

Cloud Storage:

- When storing data using cloud storage, the user must locate the appropriate Web site. Some sites support only certain file types. Other sites provide more than just storage.
- Cloud storage is one of the many different features available on the Internet.
- Cloud storage allows users to store files on Web sites.
- Computer users may use this type of storage if they do not want to store their data locally on a hard disk or other type of media.

Different Web sites provide different types of cloud storage. Three are Google's Gmail, YouTube, and Windows Live SkyDrive (source: "Cloud Storage and the Internet," an article on pages 23-37 in March 2012 issue of *Internet Usage and Trends* by Leona Carter).

- Google's e-mail program, Gmail, is cloud storage that stores e-mail messages.
- YouTube is different from Gmail, however, because it stores only digital videos (source: pages 22-24 in a book called *Working with the Internet: Cloud Storage* by Robert M. Gaff, published at Jane Lewis Press in New York in 2012).
- Windows Live SkyDrive is a cloud storage provider that accepts any type of file. This type of Web site is used mainly for backup or additional storage space.

Some cloud storage Web sites also provide other services (source: a Web site titled *The Internet: Cloud Storage* by Rebecca A. Ford and Harry I. Garland of Course Technology dated January 2, 2012, viewed on March 7, 2012).

- Flickr provides cloud storage for digital photos and also enables users to manage their photos and share them with others.
- Facebook provides cloud storage for a number of different file types including digital photos, digital videos, messages, and personal information. Facebook also provides a means of social networking.
- Google Docs not only stores documents, spreadsheets, and presentations in its cloud, it also enables its users to create these documents.

Figure D–47

Cases and Places

Apply your creative thinking and problem solving skills to design and implement a solution.

Note: To complete these assignments, you may be required to use the Data Files for Students. See the inside back cover of this book for instructions on downloading the Data Files for Students, or contact your instructor for information about accessing the required files.

1: Create a Research Paper about Preparing for a Career in the Computer Industry

Academic

As a student in an introductory computer class, your instructor has assigned a research paper that discusses educational options available for students pursuing a career in the computer industry. The source for the text in your research paper is in a file called Preparing for a Career in the Computer Industry, which is located on the Data Files for Students. In addition to this source, if your instructor requests, use the Research task pane to obtain information from another source. Add an AutoCorrect entry to correct a word you commonly mistype.

Using the concepts and techniques presented in Chapter 2 and this appendix, along with the text in the file on the Data Files for Students, create and format this research paper according to the APA documentation style. Be sure to check spelling and grammar of the finished paper. Submit your assignment in the format specified by your instructor.

2: Create a Research Paper about Computer Viruses

Personal

The computer you recently purchased included an antivirus program. Because you need practice writing research papers and you want to learn more about computer viruses, you decide to write a paper about computer viruses. The source for the text in your research paper is in a file called Computer Viruses, which is located on the Data Files for Students. In addition to this source, if your instructor requests, use the Research task pane to obtain information from another source. Add an AutoCorrect entry to correct a word you commonly mistype.

Using the concepts and techniques presented in Chapter 2 and this appendix, along with the text in the file on the Data Files for Students, create and format this research paper according to the APA documentation style. Be sure to check spelling and grammar of the finished paper. Submit your assignment in the format specified by your instructor.

3: Create a Research Paper about a Disaster Recovery Plan

Professional

Your boss has asked you to research the components of a disaster recovery plan. Because you learned in college how to write research papers, you decide to present your findings in a research paper. The source for the text in your research paper is in a file called Disaster Recovery Plan, which is located on the Data Files for Students. In addition to this source, if your instructor requests, use the Research task pane to obtain information from another source. Add an AutoCorrect entry to correct a word you commonly mistype.

Using the concepts and techniques presented in Chapter 2 and this appendix, along with the text in the file on the Data Files for Students, create and format this research paper according to the APA documentation style. Be sure to check spelling and grammar of the finished paper. Submit your assignment in the format specified by your instructor.

Index

D

E

T

Quick Reference Summary

Microsoft Word 2010 Quick Reference Summary					
Task	**Page Number**	**Mouse**	**Ribbon**	**Shortcut Menu**	**Keyboard Shortcut**
All Caps	WD 81		Change Case button (Home tab | Font group), UPPERCASE		CTRL+SHIFT+A
AutoCorrect Entry, Create	WD 86		Options (File tab), Proofing (Word Options dialog box)		
AutoCorrect Options button, Use	WD 85	Point to AutoCorrect Options button in flagged word			
Bibliographical List, Create	WD 108		Bibliography button (References tab | Citations & Bibliography group)		
Bibliography Style, Change	WD 89		Bibliography Style box arrow (References tab | Citations & Bibliography group)		
Bold	WD 28	Bold button on Mini toolbar	Bold button (Home tab | Font group)	Font, Font tab (Font dialog box)	CTRL+B
Border Paragraph	WD 160		Border button arrow (Home tab | Paragraph group)		
Building Block, Create	WD 171		Quick Parts button (Insert tab | Text group)		ALT+F3
Building Block, Insert	WD 174		Quick Parts button (Insert tab | Text group		F3
Building Block, Modify	WD 173		Quick Parts button (Insert tab | Text group), right-click building block, Edit Properties		
Bullets, Apply	WD 22		Bullets button (Home tab | Paragraph group)	Bullets	* (ASTERISK), SPACEBAR
Center	WD 14	Center button on Mini toolbar	Center button (Home tab | Paragraph group)	Paragraph, Indents and Spacing tab (Paragraph dialog box)	CTRL+E
Change Case	WD 18		Change Case button (Home tab | Font group)	Font, Font tab (Font dialog box)	SHIFT+F3
Change Spacing before or after Paragraph	WD 43		Spacing Before or Spacing After box arrow (Page Layout tab | Paragraph group)	Paragraph, Indents and Spacing tab (Paragraph dialog box)	

Microsoft Word 2010 Quick Reference Summary *(continued)*

Task	Page Number	Mouse	Ribbon	Shortcut Menu	Keyboard Shortcut
Citation Placeholder, Insert	WD 94		Insert Citation button (References tab | Citations & Bibliography group), Add New Placeholder		
Citation, Edit	WD 91	Click citation, Citations Options box arrow, Edit Citation			
Citation, Insert	WD 90		Insert Citation button (References tab | Citations & Bibliography group), Add New Source		
Clear Formatting	WD 161		Clear Formatting button (Home tab | Font group)		CTRL+SPACEBAR, CTRL+Q
Click and Type	WD 80	Position mouse pointer until desired icon appears, then double-click			
Clip Art, Insert	WD 148		Clip Art button (Insert tab | Illustrations group)		
Color Text	WD 25	Font Color button on Mini toolbar	Font Color button arrow (Home tab | Font group)		
Copy	WD 113		Copy button (Home tab | Clipboard group)	Copy	CTRL+C
Count Words	WD 101	Word Count indicator on status bar	Word Count button (Review tab | Proofing group)		CTRL+SHIFT+G
Custom Dictionary, Set Default, View or Modify Entries	WD 120		Options (File tab), Proofing (Word Options dialog box), Custom Dictionaries button		
Date, Insert Current	WD 170		Insert Date and Time button (Insert tab | Text group)		
Document Properties, Change	WD 49		Properties button (File tab | Info tab)		
Document Properties, Print	WD 123		File tab | Print tab, first button in Settings area		
Double-Space	WD 73		Line and Paragraph Spacing button (Home tab | Paragraph group)	Paragraph, Indents and Spacing tab (Paragraph dialog box)	CTRL+2
Double-Underline	WD 81		Underline button arrow (Home tab | Font group)	Font, Font tab (Font dialog box)	CTRL+SHIFT+D
Envelope, Address and Print	WD 189		Create Envelopes button (Mailings tab | Create group), Envelopes tab (Envelopes and Labels dialog box)		
Field, Convert to Regular text	WD 110				Click field, CTRL+SHIFT+F9
Find Text	WD 115	Select Browse Object button on vertical scroll bar, Find button	Find button (Home tab | Editing group)		CTRL+F
Font Size, Change	WD 16	Font Size box arrow on Mini toolbar	Font Size box arrow (Home tab | Font group)	Font, Font tab (Font dialog box)	CTRL+D
Font Size, Decrease	WD 81	Shrink Font button on Mini toolbar	Shrink Font button (Home tab | Font group)		CTRL+SHIFT+<

Microsoft Word 2010 Quick Reference Summary *(continued)*

Task	Page Number	Mouse	Ribbon	Shortcut Menu	Keyboard Shortcut
Font Size, Decrease 1 point	WD 81				CTRL+[
Font Size, Increase	WD 146	Grow Font button on Mini toolbar	Grow Font button (Home tab | Font group)		CTRL+SHIFT+>
Font Size, Increase 1 point	WD 81				CTRL+]
Font, Change	WD 17	Font box arrow on Mini toolbar	Font box arrow (Home tab | Font group)	Font, Font tab (Font dialog box)	CTRL+D
Footnote, Insert	WD 93		Insert Footnote button (References tab | Footnotes group)		
Formatting Marks	WD 7		Show/Hide ¶ button (Home tab | Paragraph group)		CTRL+SHIFT+*
Go to a Page	WD 117	'Browse the pages in your document' tab in Navigation Pane	Find button arrow (Home tab | Editing group)		CTRL+G
Graphic, Adjust Brightness and Contrast	WD 153		Corrections button (Picture Tools Format tab | Adjust group)	Format Picture, Picture Corrections button (Format Picture dialog box)	
Graphic, Change Border Color	WD 154		Picture Border button (Picture Tools Format tab | Picture Styles group)		
Graphic, Change Color	WD 151		Color button (Picture Tools Format tab | Adjust group)	Format Picture, Picture Color button (Format Picture dialog box)	
Graphic, Flip	WD 157		Rotate button (Picture Tools Format tab | Arrange group)		
Graphic, Move	WD 155	Drag graphic			
Graphic, Resize	WD 34	Drag sizing handle	Shape Height and Shape Width text boxes (Picture Tools Format tab | Size group)	Size and Position, Size tab (Layout dialog box)	
Graphic, Set Transparent Color	WD 152		Color button (Picture Tools Format tab | Adjust group)		
Hanging Indent, Create	WD 81	Drag Hanging Indent marker on ruler	Paragraph Dialog Box Launcher (Home tab or Page Layout tab | Paragraph group), Indents and Spacing tab (Paragraph dialog box)	Paragraph, Indents and Spacing tab (Paragraph dialog box)	CTRL+T
Hanging Indent, Remove	WD 81	Drag Hanging Indent marker on ruler	Paragraph Dialog Box Launcher (Home tab or Page Layout tab | Paragraph group), Indents and Spacing tab (Paragraph dialog box)	Paragraph, Indents and Spacing tab (Paragraph dialog box)	CTRL+SHIFT+T
Header and Footer, Close	WD 78	Double-click dimmed document text	Close Header and Footer button (Header & Footer Tools Design tab | Close group)		
Header, Switch to	WD 75	Double-click dimmed header	Header button (Insert tab | Header & Footer group)		
Hyperlink, Convert to Regular Text	WD 163	Undo Hyperlink (AutoCorrect Options menu)	Hyperlink button (Insert tab | Links group)	Remove Hyperlink	
Indent, Decrease	WD 81	Drag First Line Indent marker on ruler	Decrease Indent button (Home tab | Paragraph group)	Paragraph, Indents and Spacing tab (Paragraph dialog box)	CTRL+SHIFT+M

Microsoft Word 2010 Quick Reference Summary *(continued)*

Task	Page Number	Mouse	Ribbon	Shortcut Menu	Keyboard Shortcut
Indent, First-Line	WD 83	Drag First Line Indent marker on ruler	Paragraph Dialog Box Launcher (Home tab or Page Layout tab | Paragraph group)	Paragraph, Indents and Spacing tab (Paragraph dialog box)	TAB
Indent, Increase	WD 81		Increase Indent button (Home tab | Paragraph group)		CTRL+M
Insertion Point, Move Down/Up One Line	WD 11				DOWN ARROW/ UP ARROW
Insertion Point, Move Down/Up One Paragraph	WD 11				CTRL+DOWN ARROW/ CTRL+UP ARROW
Insertion Point, Move Down/Up One Screen	WD 11				PAGE DOWN/ PAGE UP
Insertion Point, Move Left/ Right One Character	WD 11				LEFT ARROW/ RIGHT ARROW
Insertion Point, Move Left/ Right One Word	WD 11				CTRL+LEFT ARROW/ CTRL+RIGHT ARROW
Insertion Point, Move to Beginning/End of Document	WD 11				CTRL+HOME/ CTRL+END
Insertion Point, Move to Beginning/End of Line	WD 11				HOME/ END
Insertion Point, Move to Bottom of Document Window	WD 11				ALT+CTRL+PAGE DOWN/ ALT+CTRL+PAGE UP
Italicize	WD 24	Italic button on Mini toolbar	Italic button (Home tab | Font group)	Font, Font tab (Font dialog box)	CTRL+I
Justify Paragraph	WD 81		Justify button (Home tab | Paragraph group)	Paragraph, Indents and Spacing tab (Paragraph dialog box)	CTRL+J
Left-Align Paragraph	WD 81		Align Text Left button (Home tab | Paragraph group)	Paragraph, Indents and Spacing tab (Paragraph dialog box)	CTRL+L
Line Spacing, Change	WD 73		Line and Paragraph Spacing button (Home tab | Paragraph group)	Paragraph, Indents and Spacing tab (Paragraph dialog box)	CTRL+[number of desired line spacing, i.e., 2 for double-spacing]
Mailing Label, Print	WD 190		Create Labels button (Mailings tab | Create group)		
Margin Settings, Change	WD 141	Drag margin boundary on ruler	Margins button (Page Layout tab | Page Setup group)		
Move Text	WD 47	Drag and drop selected text	Cut button (Home tab | Clipboard group); Paste button (Home tab | Clipboard group)	Cut; Paste	CTRL+X; CTRL+V
New File, Create from Existing	WD 165		'New from existing' button (File tab | New tab)		

Microsoft Word 2010 Quick Reference Summary *(continued)*

Task	Page Number	Mouse	Ribbon	Shortcut Menu	Keyboard Shortcut
Nonbreaking Space, Insert	WD 175		Symbol button (Insert tab | Symbols group), More Symbols, Special Characters tab (Symbol dialog box)		CTRL+SHIFT+ SPACEBAR
Normal Style, Apply	WD 106		Normal in Quick Style gallery (Home tab | Styles group)		CTRL+SHIFT+S
Normal Style, Modify	WD 71		Styles Dialog Box Launcher (Home tab | Styles group), style box arrow, Modify	Right-click style (Home tab | Styles group), Modify	
Open a Document	WD 45		Open (File tab)		CTRL+O
Page Border, Add	WD 41		Page Borders button (Page Layout tab | Page Background group)		
Page Break, Insert	WD 106		Page Break button (Insert tab | Pages group)		CTRL+ENTER
Page Number, Insert	WD 77		Insert Page Number button (Header & Footer Tools Design tab | Header & Footer group)		
Paste	WD 113		Paste button (Home tab | Clipboard group)	Paste	CTRL+V
Paste Options	WD 156		Paste button arrow (Home tab | Clipboard group)		
Paste Options Menu, Display	WD 114	Paste Options button by moved/copied text			
Picture Style, Apply	WD 37		More button in Picture Styles gallery (Picture Tools Format tab | Picture Styles group)		
Picture Effects, Apply	WD 38		Picture Effects button (Picture Tools Format tab | Picture Styles group)	Format Picture	
Picture, Insert	WD 31		Insert Picture from File button (Insert tab | Illustrations group)		
Preview a Document	WD 124		File tab | Print tab, Next Page and Previous Page buttons		CTRL+P, ENTER
Print Document	WD 51		Print button (File tab | Print tab)		CTRL+P
Quick Style, Apply	WD 166		[style name] in Quick Style gallery (Home tab | Styles group)		CTRL+SHIFT+S, Style Name box arrow
Quit Word	WD 44	Close button on title bar	Exit (File tab)		ALT+F4
Redo	WD 23	Redo button on Quick Access Toolbar			CTRL+Y
Remove Character Formatting	WD 81				CTRL+SPACEBAR
Remove Paragraph Formatting	WD 81				CTRL+Q
Remove Space after Paragraph	WD 74		Line and Paragraph Spacing button (Home tab | Paragraph group)	Paragraph, Indents and Spacing tab (Paragraph dialog box)	CTRL+0 (zero)

Microsoft Word 2010 Quick Reference Summary *(continued)*

Task	Page Number	Mouse	Ribbon	Shortcut Menu	Keyboard Shortcut
Replace Text	WD 116	Select Browse Object button on vertical scroll bar, Find button, Replace tab (Find and Replace dialog box)	Replace button (Home tab | Editing group)		CTRL+H
Research Task Pane, Look Up Information	WD 120	ALT+click desired word	Research button (Review tab | Proofing group)		
Right-Align	WD 76		Align Text Right button (Home tab | Paragraph group)	Paragraph, Indents and Spacing tab (Paragraph dialog box)	CTRL+R
Rulers, Display	WD 82	View Ruler button on vertical scroll bar	View Ruler check box (View tab | Show group)		
Save New Document	WD 12	Save button on Quick Access Toolbar	Save or Save As (File tab)		F12
Save Document, Same File Name	WD 30	Save button on Quick Access toolbar	Save (File tab)		CTRL+S
Scroll, Page by Page	WD 112	Previous Page/Next Page button on vertical scroll bar			CTRL+PAGE UP or CTRL+PAGE DOWN
Scroll, Up/Down One Line	WD 11	Click scroll arrow at top/ bottom of vertical scroll bar			
Scroll, Up/Down One Screen	WD 11	Click above/below scroll box on vertical scroll bar			
Select Block of Text	WD 30	Click beginning, SHIFT-click end			
Select Character(s)	WD 30	Drag through characters			SHIFT+RIGHT ARROW or SHIFT+LEFT ARROW
Select Entire Document	WD 30	In left margin, triple-click	Select button arrow (Home tab | Editing group)		CTRL+A
Select Graphic	WD 30	Click graphic			
Select Group of Words	WD 27	Drag mouse pointer through words			CTRL+SHIFT+RIGHT ARROW
Select Line	WD 15	Click in left margin			SHIFT+DOWN ARROW
Select Multiple Lines	WD 21	Drag mouse pointer in left margin			SHIFT+DOWN ARROW
Select Nonadjacent Items	WD 15	Select first item, hold down CTRL key while selecting item(s)			
Select Paragraph	WD 30	Triple-click paragraph			CTRL+SHIFT+DOWN ARROW or CTRL+ SHIFT+UP ARROW
Select Sentence	WD 30	CTRL-click			
Select Word	WD 30	Double-click word			CTRL+SHIFT+RIGHT ARROW or CTRL+ SHIFT+LEFT ARROW
Shade Paragraph	WD 20		Shading button arrow (Home tab | Paragraph group)		
Shape, Add Text	WD 145			Add Text	

Microsoft Word 2010 Quick Reference Summary *(continued)*

Task	Page Number	Mouse	Ribbon	Shortcut Menu	Keyboard Shortcut
Shape, Apply Style	WD 144		More button in Shape Styles gallery (Drawing Tools Format tab | Shape Styles group)	Format Shape, Color button in left pane (Format Shape dialog box)	
Shape, Insert	WD 142		Shapes button (Insert tab | Illustrations group)		
Single-Space Lines	WD 81		Line and Paragraph Spacing button (Home tab | Paragraph group)	Paragraph, Indents and Spacing tab (Paragraph dialog box)	CTRL+1
Small Caps	WD 81		Font Dialog Box Launcher (Home Tab | Font group), Font tab (Font dialog box)		CTRL+SHIFT+K
Source, Edit	WD 97		Click citation, Citation Options box arrow, Edit Source		
Source, Modify	WD 109		Manage Sources button (References tab | Citations & Bibliography group), Edit button		
Spelling and Grammar, Check at Once	WD 118	Spelling and Grammar check icon on status bar, Spelling	Spelling & Grammar button (Review tab | Proofing group)	Spelling	F7
Spelling, Check as You Type	WD 9	Click word, Spelling and Grammar Check icon on status bar		Right-click error, click correct word on shortcut menu	
Style, Update to Match Selection	WD 74		Right-click style in Quick Style gallery (Home tab | Styles group)	Styles	
Subscript	WD 81		Subscript button (Home tab | Font group)	Font, Font tab (Font dialog box)	CTRL+EQUAL SIGN
Superscript	WD 81		Superscript button (Home tab | Font group)	Font, Font tab (Font dialog box)	CTRL+SHIFT+PLUS SIGN
Symbol, Insert	WD 158		Insert Symbol button (Insert tab | Symbols group)		
Synonym, Find and Insert	WD 118		Thesaurus (Review tab | Proofing group)	Right-click word, click desired synonym on Synonym submenu	SHIFT+F7
Tab Stops, Set Custom	WD 169	Click desired tab stop on ruler	Paragraph Dialog Box Launcher (Home tab or Page Layout tab | Paragraph group), Tabs button (Paragraph dialog box)		
Table Columns, Resize to Fit Table Contents	WD 180	Double-click column boundary	AutoFit button (Table Tools Layout tab | Cell Size group)	AutoFit	
Table, Align Data in Cells	WD 182		Align [location] button (Table Tools Layout tab | Alignment group)		
Table, Apply Style	WD 179		More button in Table Styles gallery (Table Tools Design tab | Table Styles group)		
Table, Center	WD 183	Select table, Center button on Mini toolbar	Select table, Center button (Home tab | Font group)		
Table, Delete Cell Contents	WD 185		Cut button (Home tab | Clipboard group)		Select cell contents, DELETE or CTRL+X

Microsoft Word 2010 Quick Reference Summary *(continued)*

Task	Page Number	Mouse	Ribbon	Shortcut Menu	Keyboard Shortcut
Table, Delete Entire	WD 185		Delete button (Table Tools Layout tab | Rows & Columns group)		
Table, Delete Row or Column	WD 185		Delete button (Table Tools Layout tab | Rows & Columns group)	Select row/column, Delete Rows or Delete Columns	
Table, Insert	WD 176		Table button (Insert tab | Tables group)		
Table, Insert Column	WD 185		Insert Columns to the Left/Right button (Table Tools Layout tab | Rows & Columns group)	Insert	
Table, Insert Row	WD 184		Insert Rows Above/Below button (Table Tools Layout Tab | Rows & Columns group)	Insert	
Table, Merge Cells	WD 185		Merge Cells button (Table Tools Layout tab | Merge group)	Merge Cells	
Table, Select Cell	WD 181	Click left edge of cell	Select button (Table Tools Layout tab | Table group)		
Table, Select Column	WD 181	Click top border of column	Select button (Table Tools Layout tab | Table group)		
Table, Select Entire	WD 181	Click table move handle	Select button (Table Tools Layout tab | Table group)		
Table, Select Multiple Cells, Rows, or Columns, Adjacent	WD 181	Drag through cells, rows, or columns			
Table, Select Next Cell	WD 181				TAB
Table, Select Previous Cell	WD 181				SHIFT+TAB
Table, Select Row	WD 181	Click to left of row	Select button (Table Tools Layout tab | Table Group)		
Table, Split Cells	WD 186		Split Cells button (Table Tools Layout tab | Merge group)	Split Cells	
Text Effect, Apply	WD 19		Text Effects button (Home tab | Font group)		
Text Wrapping, Change	WD 148		Wrap Text button (Drawing Tools format tab | Arrange group)	Wrap Text	
Theme Colors, Change	WD 28		Change Styles button (Home tab | Styles group)		
Underline	WD 27	Underline button on Mini toolbar	Underline button (Home tab | Font group)	Font, Font tab (Font dialog box)	CTRL+U
Underline Words, Not Spaces	WD 81		Font Dialog Box Launcher (Home tab | Font group), Font tab (Font dialog box), Underline style box arrow		CTRL+SHIFT+W
Undo	WD 23	Undo button on Quick Access Toolbar			CTRL+Z
Zoom Document	WD 33	Zoom Out or Zoom In button on status bar	Zoom button (View tab | Zoom group)		
Zoom One Page	WD 41		One Page button (View tab | Zoom group)		